ADIRONDACK BIBLIOGRAPHY

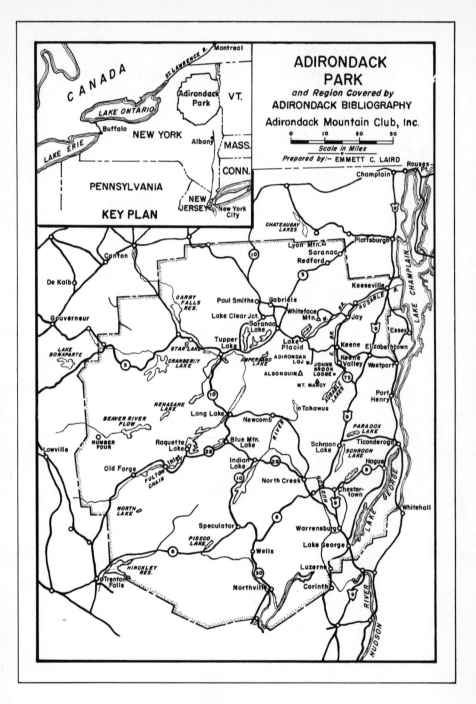

Region Covered by the Adirondack Bibliography

ADIRONDACK
BIBLIOGRAPHY

A List of Books, Pamphlets and
Periodical Articles Published Through the Year 1955

Compiled by the Bibliography Committee of the
ADIRONDACK MOUNTAIN CLUB

Dorothy A. Plum, *Chairman*
Lynette L. Scribner, *Vice-Chairman*

ADIRONDACK MOUNTAIN CLUB, INC.
Gabriels, N. Y.
1958

Distributed by New York University Press,
Washington Square, New York

Manufactured in the United States of America

PREFACE

The compilers of this list have often felt that there were no truer words than those of Ecclesiastes: "Of making many books there is no end." What started some eight years ago as an attempt to "bring Donaldson up to date" has turned into the making of a regional bibliography covering one-fifth of the state of New York. The term "Adirondack" has various meanings. In this bibliography it indicates the region included in the Adirondack State Park and the western Champlain valley; in a few cases areas just outside the Park line, such as Trenton Falls, have been included. Material relating to the French settlements is also listed. The literature of the Adirondacks knows no exact geographical boundary.

In general the items contained in the *Adirondack Bibliography* are printed. But since much important material has appeared in doctoral and master's dissertations, many of which are in typescript, an exception has been made in their case. A few local histories published in mimeograph have also been included. The members of the Bibliography Committee have tried to find as many as possible of the vast number of books, pamphlets and periodical articles relating to the North Country that have been issued through the year 1955. No attempt has been made to list newspaper articles—we leave that to another committee—though several newspaper columns relating to the Adirondacks are included as an addendum to the list of periodicals about the region.

For convenience of use a long bibliography should be broken down into various categories and fully indexed. The special classification devised for this volume is complemented by a detailed index. It should be noted that some topics appear in several divisions. Articles about deer, for instance, may be found under "conservation," under "zoology," and under "hunting," depending on the content of the article. An examination of the table of contents will furnish the clue to the order of subjects. Arrangement by date rather than by alphabetical order is indicated by a note at the beginning of the section. The index should be used to bring together related topics and scattered references.

It has been difficult, in some cases, to decide what should be omitted. John Brown, the liberator, is the subject of many volumes, but do they all belong in an Adirondack bibliography? After examining a long list of references the Committee felt that only material relating to his life at North Elba, and a standard biography, should be included. Reviews appearing in periodicals relating to the Adirondacks have been listed; no search has been made for other reviews.

One of the pleasures of preparing this bibliography has been the opportunity to examine special Adirondack libraries. The Committee is grateful to the following persons who allowed us free access to their collections: Russell M. L.

Carson, Harry W. Hicks, Grace L. Hudowalski, George Marshall, Orra A. Phelps, Marjorie L. Porter, Paul Schaefer and Donald Van Brakle. Book dealers, too, have been generous with advice. We are particularly indebted to James Howgate, Harmon Lockrow and John Skinner.

Probably the largest library collection on the Adirondacks is in the Saranac Lake Free Library. The nucleus of the collection is the personal library of Alfred L. Donaldson, listed in the second volume of his *History of the Adirondacks*. In addition to the large number of printed items, noted here, the library contains important manuscripts and letters. A smaller group of Adirondackana, about fifty books and pamphlets, several of them unique, came from the library of Kenneth Goldthwaite and were presented to the Saranac Lake Free Library by his son, Eaton Goldthwaite. An extensive collection, gathered by Mr. and Mrs. William Munson, was acquired through the efforts of the late William Chapman White, who raised funds for its purchase. The Munson Collection includes more than five hundred books and pamphlets, a large number of photographs, maps and scrapbooks of clippings. An important addition was made to the map collection with the purchase of forty-five rare early eighteenth-century maps. The Library's Adirondack collection is growing steadily. Several hundred additional books, pamphlets and periodicals have been purchased through memorial funds or added by gift. The most recent acquisition in this field is the fine Robert Louis Stevenson Collection of the late Dr. Lawrason Brown, presented by friends in memory of Mr. William Morris.

At Keene Valley the Historical Society maintains a center for local history. Its book collection, the Loomis Collection, contains over four hundred volumes and is housed in the Keene Valley Public Library. The books are supplemented by scrapbooks of clippings, picture files, typescripts of family histories and reminiscences, church and cemetery records and other valuable source material for the history of the Valley. Contributions are made by summer and winter residents.

At Port Henry the Sherman Free Library has important collections on the area. In 1950 it received, through the will of Warner McLaughlin, its Adirondack Book Collection, consisting of over fifteen hundred books and pamphlets on the Adirondacks and northern Vermont. Many rare guidebooks are included. The Library also has part of the McLaughlin stamp collection with numerous stampless covers and postmarks of northern New York. In addition, Port Henry has the Frank S. Witherbee Collection, established in 1910, an outgrowth of Mr. Witherbee's interest and activities in connection with the Champlain Tercentenary. This collection contains one hundred and thirty-three items and is especially strong on the history of the mining industry.

An Adirondack center in the making is the newly established Adirondack Museum at Blue Mountain Lake. Several large collections have been purchased to start its library, as yet not organized. No list of library resources would be complete without mention of the New York State Historical Association's Headquarters House library at Ticonderoga and the special historical collection in the Crandall Library at Glens Falls.

The Committee is particularly grateful to Mr. Frederick T. Kelsey, who made possible the examination of the important source material in the files of the Association for the Protection of the Adirondacks. The following members of the faculty of Vassar College helped with the classification: Gladys E. Baker, John L. George, Madelene Pierce and Scott Warthin. Librarians in charge of special collections have all been interested and helpful. Their cooperation has been a big factor in the making of the Bibliography. Thanks are also due to the following: the Audubon Society Library; the Engineering Societies Library; the New York Public Library; the New York State Library; the State University College of Forestry Library; Vassar College Library; Yale University Library.

We know that this compilation is incomplete. Just today a fellow enthusiast sent a note of the following advertisement from the *Essex County Times & Westport Herald* of March 22, 1843: "Bishop's Trial together with his Life and Confession, as dictated by himself, for sale at this office. Priced 12½ cents. Peddlars supplied at a dollar per dozen." C. Eleanor Hall, who sent the note, says that Bishop was a murderer who was hanged at Elizabethtown in 1843. She has never seen a copy of the pamphlet.

We hope this compilation is reasonably free from error. It is our plan to issue yearly supplements to the Bibliography in the Club periodical, *The Ad-i-ron-dac*, with a cumulation at some future date. Corrections and addenda will be welcome and will be included in the yearly supplements.

This work could not have been compiled without the members of the Bibliography Committee. It could not have been published without the generous support of Club members, under the able chairmanship of Borden H. Mills, Sr., who headed the Bibliography Fund drive.

April 9, 1957   Dorothy A. Plum, *Editor*

MEMBERS OF THE COMMITTEE ON THE *Adirondack Bibliography*

Frances Cregan	Albany Chapter	1949–50
Grace Curtis	New York Chapter	1949–50
Ernest Cushing	Member at large	1949–50
Margaret MacCormack	Keene Valley Chapter	1949
P. Schuyler Miller	Bouquet River Lodge Chapter	1949–date
Dorothy A. Plum	Mid-Hudson Chapter	1949–date
George Roach	Mid-Hudson Chapter	1949
Dorothy J. Sickels	Hurricane Chapter	1949
Frances Denniston	Keene Valley Chapter	1949–51
Dorothy Candlyn	New York Chapter	1949–50
Marion Hemstreet	Albany Chapter	1949–date
Helen James	Albany Chapter	1949–50
Lynette Scribner	New York Chapter	1949–date
Marian Wilkinson	Mid-Hudson Chapter	1949–date
Russell M. L. Carson	Adirondak Loj Chapter	1950–date
Hortense Richardson	Member at large	1950
Laura Greene	Albany Chapter	1951–date
George Marshall	Member at large	1951–date
Erica Schinn	Member at large	1951
Dorothy Johnson	New York Chapter	1953–date
Arthur Newkirk	Bouquet River Lodge Chapter	1953–date
Ruth Worthington	Saranac Lake Chapter	1953–date

CONTENTS

ILLUSTRATIONS

Map of the region covered by the *Adirondack Bibliography*

Frontispiece

Mount Haystack, from Upper Ausable Inlet, reproduced from the Seventh Report of the Adirondack Survey, by Verplanck Colvin

End Papers

INTRODUCTION

To say that in any field of interest understanding is essential to appreciation, and that the broader our knowledge the greater our appreciation, may seem a roundabout approach to the subject of an Adirondack bibliography. But these thoughts are the theme of this introduction.

We may admire the sight of the MacIntyre Mountains rising majestically from the North Elba plateau. We possess a broader vision if, with the act of seeing, there flashes into our consciousness the story of the pioneer iron industry that began so many years ago in the recesses of those great hills. We may be awed by the gloomy cliffs that rise on either side of the Chapel Pond road, and entranced by the tremendous panorama of the High Peaks that lies on the left as we travel from Keene to Lake Placid. These scenes take on more meaning for us if we have some knowledge of what these roads were like a hundred years ago, in the days of horse-drawn stages and wayside inns. The lovely view of Keene Valley from the rock slabs of Baxter is even more intriguing when we know what the village looked like in the time of our grandfathers. If we know the story of the old Adirondack Lodge and its unhappy owner, the Heart Lake region takes on a new poignancy.

One could go on: almost every Adirondack name has its special meaning. This special meaning comes alive for us if we can bring to our beloved mountains the three dimensions of sight, historical perspective and imagination. This is true whether our Adirondack interest is that of a mountaineer delighting in wooded trails and high ascents, or that of a naturalist watching in the spring for the coming of the flowers and birds, or that of an artist reproducing on his canvas the charm of unspoiled wilderness and lofty peaks. These hills can enrich our lives to the degree that we can experience and know them.

How may we experience and know them? Perception, imagination, knowledge and inspiration—these are within ourselves. We are all different and no one can tell us how to develop these qualities. But historical perspective is quite another thing, for the literature of the Adirondacks is a Pierian spring from which all may drink.

Familiarity with Adirondack literature is an important step in acquiring well-rounded experience. The easy way to a good background of Adirondack reading is to take advantage of books or articles that are the result of laborious research by Adirondack historians, scientists and writers. Volumes such as *A History of the Adirondacks*, by Alfred L. Donaldson; *Fifty Years of Conservation in New York State*, by Gurth Whipple; *Historical Sketches of Northern New York and the Adirondack Wilderness*, by Nathaniel B. Sylvester; *The Story of Adirondac*, by Arthur H. Masten; *Peaks and People of the Adirondacks*, by R. M. C. Carson;

Plants and Animals of Mount Marcy, by Charles C. Adams and others; *A History of the Lumber Industry in the State of New York*, by William F. Fox; "The Rocks of the Adirondacks," by Professor E. S. C. Smith of Union College (in *High Spots*, December 1930); and more recently *Township 34*, by Harold K. Hochschild; and *Adirondack Country*, by William C. White, represent the gleanings of many years and cover almost the whole field of Adirondack interest: general, local and natural history, fiction, biography, science and industry; the information is available to us in easy-to-read form without our stirring from our armchairs.

That is a good way of gaining experience, but not the best. To attain the utmost satisfaction and pleasure you must put some source books on your shelves too. Some of these, such as the Reverend Joel T. Headley's *The Adirondack, or Life in the Woods*, which went through several editions, are not hard to find and not expensive. Others, such as *Long Lake*, by John Todd, are rare and precious and not only command a fancy price but challenge the skill and patience of the most adroit and experienced collectors. How many today know where or how a copy may be obtained of *Six Summits*, by Newell Martin? Or the letters, presumably by William C. Redfield, about the Adirondacks in the *Journal of Commerce* during August 1837?

The fun of collecting Adirondackana in itself is an incentive to a fascinating hobby and a game well worth the candle. It can arouse a whole gamut of thrills from the simple pleasure of finding, after a short search, a nice Headley, to the excitement of acquiring a copy of *Recollections of John Howard Redfield* (William C. Redfield's son and biographer) printed for private circulation in 1900. This book has only one Adirondack chapter, but that chapter contains a few facts about the first Mount Marcy expedition that, to the best of our knowledge, are not recorded elsewhere. A copy of the book was lent to me in 1938 by Professor Alfred C. Redfield of Harvard, but sixteen years passed before I was able to find a copy I could put on my shelves. Among other fine and important books that have been printed in limited editions for private circulation are two already mentioned: Hochschild's *Township 34* and Masten's *Story of Adirondac*. Of the latter only 125 copies were published. By their very nature these were already rare items as they came off the press.

The new collector who begins with a definite objective will find later that discrimination contributes to a sustained and permanent interest. Collecting without a fixed goal can soon lose its attraction, because it lacks purpose. A curiosity about mountain names inspired me in 1922 to begin gathering a library of Adirondack books, pamphlets, articles, maps and pictures, which in turn gave me the wonderful opportunity in 1927 of writing *Peaks and People of the Adirondacks*. Although the scope of my collection has spread widely, nomenclature and the historical have remained the controlling considerations. I have collected slowly and carefully, according to my own plan, and after thirty-five years my library, and my interest in its being used to good purpose, are still growing.

Probably the most comprehensive and complete collection of Adirondackana is in the Saranac Lake Free Library. It includes the Alfred L. Donaldson Collection and the Munson Collection. The former was gathered for use in writing *A History of the Adirondacks*. The author-collector was an invalid who came to the mountains for his health, and his *History* and his Collection came into existence against tremendous physical odds. They were possible only because of the even greater spirit and determination of the man. He had plans for a third volume of the *History*, but died before it was begun. During the last two years of his life Donaldson was the frailest human being I have ever known, but his strong personality immediately made one forget the pitiful weakness. His bright and cheery letters in those final years gave not a hint of his losing battle; he lived richly and constructively to the end.

A splendid bibliography is included in the second volume of Donaldson's *History*. The list is divided into two parts: first, the Donaldson Collection; and, second, a long compilation by James A. McMillen supplementing an earlier and slighter bibliography by Miss C. A. Sherrill published in the *Forest, Fish and Game Commission Report* for 1898. It is over thirty years since the Donaldson bibliographies appeared; the Adirondack Mountain Club now carries on the work with its *Adirondack Bibliography*, which expands and brings up to date the previous lists. Since such a massive work will be used mainly for reference, this introduction highlights important items by calling attention to a selective list compiled in 1934 for the Club's *Guide to Adirondack Trails*. This list was intended as a recommendation for a neat little collection for any but advanced collectors. The search for these writings can be a fine sleuthing adventure. There are only a few titles that need to be added to the original list, and I would not take any away. Stars indicate books that are not wholly of Adirondack concern. Since all these volumes are listed in the *Adirondack Bibliography*, publishing details are omitted. Each group is arranged chronologically.

The earliest information concerning the region relates to Indian possession; the following books are recommended:

Indian History:

> *The League of the Iroquois*, by Lewis H. Morgan
> *Aboriginal Occupation of New York*, by William M. Beauchamp
> *The Iroquois*, by S. C. Kimm
> *A History of the New York Iroquois*, by William M. Beauchamp
> *Aboriginal Place Names of New York*, by William M. Beauchamp
> *The Archaeological History of New York*, by Arthur C. Parker

Indian Legends:

> *Vigil of Faith*, by Charles Fenno Hoffman
> *Summer Gleanings*, by John Todd

Indian Myths:

> *Myths and Legends of Our Own Land*, by Charles M. Skinner

The following is a selected list of local and general historical value. The *Documentary History* is recommended to the serious student.

> *Documentary History of the State of New York*, arranged by E. B. O'Callaghan
> *History of St. Lawrence and Franklin Counties*, by Franklin B. Hough
> *The Opening of the Adirondacks* (published anonymously)
> *The History of Lake Champlain*, by Peter S. Palmer
> *Military and Civil History of the County of Essex*, by Winslow C. Watson

Historical Sketches of Northern New York and the Adirondack Wilderness, by Nathaniel B. Sylvester
*Historic Handbook of the Northern Tour, by Francis Parkman
History of Warren County, by H. P. Smith
Pleasant Valley, by George Levi Brown
The Story of Saranac, by Henry W. Raymond
The Adirondack Region, by Richard Coughlin
A History of the Adirondacks, by Alfred L. Donaldson
*The Papers of Sir William Johnson, edited by James Sullivan
*Annals of Tryon County, by William W. Campbell
*Jesuit Relations, selected and edited by Edna Kenton
Peaks and People of the Adirondacks, by Russell M. L. Carson

Here is a list of the old and recent guides to the Adirondacks. The Conservation Department's "Recreation Circulars" and O'Kane's book are valuable for current use. The old Stoddard and Wallace guides are now of great interest for their historical value.

Guidebooks and Circulars:

Descriptive Guide to the Adirondacks, by E. R. Wallace
The Adirondacks, by S. R. Stoddard
Lake George, by Arthur S. Hopkins (Recreation Circular 6)
Adirondack Canoe Routes, by William G. Howard (Recreation Circular 7)
The Trails to Marcy, by Arthur S. Hopkins (Recreation Circular 8)
Lake Placid Trails, by W. D. Mulholland (Recreation Circular 10)
The Lake Placid Country, by T. Morris Longstreth
Trails and Summits of the Adirondacks, by Walter Collins O'Kane

Here are some of the most fascinating books of Adirondack literature.

Travel, Exploration and Adventure:

Wild Scenes in the Forest, by Charles Fenno Hoffman
Letters from the Backwoods and Adirondac, by Joel T. Headley
The Adirondack, or Life in the Woods, by Joel T. Headley
*Letters from the United States, Cuba and Canada, by Lady Amelia Murray
Woods and Waters, or the Saranac and the Racket, by Alfred B. Street
The Hudson, from the Wilderness to the Sea, by Benson J. Lossing
The Indian Pass, by Alfred B. Street
Adventures in the Wilderness, or Camp-Life in the Adirondacks, by William H. H. Murray
Narrative of a Bear Hunt in the Adirondacks, by Verplanck Colvin
Ascent and Barometrical Measurement of Mount Seward, by Verplanck Colvin
Letters from the Woods, by Edward B. Osborne (Often cited by cover title: *Forest, Lake and Random Rhymes*)
Through the Adirondacks in Eighteen Days, by Martin Van B. Ives
The Adirondacks, by T. Morris Longstreth
High Peaks of the Adirondacks, by Robert Marshall
Friendly Adirondack Peaks, by Robert S. Wickham
Township 34, by Harold K. Hochschild
Adirondack Country, by William Chapman White

Belles-Lettres:

In the Wilderness, by Charles Dudley Warner
*Wake Robin, by John Burroughs
*Autobiography of a Journalist, by William J. Stillman
*Little Rivers, by Henry Van Dyke

Biographies:

Personal Reminiscences, by L. E. Chittenden
Biographical Sketch of Verplanck Colvin, from Allen's *History . . . of the Alling-Allens*
Adirondack Murray, by Harry V. Radford
*John Brown, 1800–1859, by Oswald Garrison Villard
Life and Adventures of Nat Foster, by A. L. Byron-Curtiss
*Life and Adventures of "Ned Buntline," by Fred E. Pond
*Letters of William James, edited by Henry James
*Johnson of the Mohawks, by Arthur Pound

Magazine Articles of Miscellaneous Interest:

"Some Account of Two Visits to the Mountains of Essex County, N.Y. in the Years 1836 and 1837 with a Sketch of the Northern Sources of the Hudson," by William C. Redfield. *American Journal of Science and Arts*, April 1838. First recorded ascent of Mount Marcy

"A Forest Story. The Adirondack Woods and Waters," by T. Addison Richards. *Harper's New Monthly Magazine*, September 1859

"The Adirondac Wilderness," by "W." *The Williams Quarterly*, July 1863. The author is Edward P. Wells

"The Racquette Club." *Harper's New Monthly Magazine*, August 1870. Written by Charles Hallock

"Camp Lou," by Marc Cook. *Harper's New Monthly Magazine*, May 1881

"Adirondack Days," by Henry Vane. *Harper's New Monthly Magazine*, October 1881

"Ampersand," by Henry Van Dyke. *Harper's New Monthly Magazine*, July 1885

"Winter in the Adirondacks," by Hamilton Wright Mabie. *Scribner's Magazine*, December 1888

"A Winter Ascent of Tahawus," by C. Grant LaFarge. *Outing*, April 1900

"Alfred Lee Donaldson, Historian of the Adirondacks," by J. F. O'Neill. *Journal of the Outdoor Life*, November 1924

"Saranac Lake Special Number," *Journal of the Outdoor Life*, May 1931

State and Scientific Reports:

*Geology of New York, by Ebenezer Emmons
Topographical Survey of the Adirondack Wilderness: First, Second and Third Reports, by Verplanck Colvin
New York State Fisheries, Game and Forest Commission Annual Reports
The Mammals of the Adirondack Region, by Clinton Hart Merriam
Plants of North Elba, N.Y., by Charles H. Peck, State Botanist
New York State Forest, Fish and Game Commission Annual Reports
New York State Conservation Commission Annual Reports. (Name changed in 1926 to Conservation Department)

Shortly after the organization of the Adirondack Mountain Club in 1922, the first Club publication was issued: *High Peaks of the Adirondacks*, by Robert Marshall, an ardent champion of wilderness protection and a charter member. The author little knew that the Club's pioneer booklet describing the ascent of and view from all the major Adirondack peaks would ultimately become the inspiration of a famous group of mountaineers, the Adirondack Forty-Sixers. Publication of the Marshall brochure was one of the outstanding accomplishments of the Club's first year.

In November 1922 the Club inaugurated a quarterly magazine called *High Spots;* this began as a four-page leaflet and continued until December 1937, when the twenty-four-page final issue commemorated the one hundredth anniversary of the first ascent of Marcy. The next to the last issue (July 1937)

was a forty-eight-page "Mount Marcy Anthology." The current Club periodical, *The Ad-i-ron-dac*, carries on the tradition of *High Spots*.

The Adirondack Mountain Club's aims, published for the first time in the April 1923 issue of *High Spots*, included the following statement: "particular attention to be given to collecting data concerning scenery, history, botany, geology, forestry, fish and game of the Adirondacks." One of the original committees appointed in the first year was a Committee on Information and Publications. The second issue of *High Spots* acknowledged receipt of eight Adirondack books contributed to the Club's budding library, and articles in succeeding issues indicated a continuing interest and growth. The Club has had from its beginning a live and vital interest not only in existing Adirondackana but in making its own contribution thereto. The culmination of this one of its several activities is the *Adirondack Bibliography*. The Club and all historically minded Adirondack enthusiasts are deeply indebted to the hard-working Bibliography Committee for the happy fruition of their long and arduous work. Their unselfish volunteer efforts will result in saving from oblivion much of what has been published about the Adirondacks over the last one hundred and twenty-five years.

Russell M. L. Carson

ADIRONDACK BIBLIOGRAPHY

HISTORY OF THE ADIRONDACK REGION

BIBLIOGRAPHY

Carson, Russell Mack Little. Suggestions for starting an Adirondack library. *In* Adirondack mountain club, inc. Guide to Adirondack trails. Northeastern section and Northville-Placid trail; 4th ed. Albany, 1947. p.108–15. Editions 1–3 of the *Guide* also contain this bibliography. See Carson's article entitled "Finding the Utmost" (collecting Adirondackana) in *High Spots*, July 1933, 10:no.3: 3–4. **1**

Donaldson, Alfred Lee. Bibliography. *In* his History of the Adirondacks. N.Y. Century, 1921. v.2, p.299–314. A list of the author's extensive Adirondack collection, now in the Saranac Lake Free Library. Descriptive and critical annotations. "An Alphabetical Index to the Bibliography in Donaldson's History of the Adirondacks," compiled by the Bibliography Committee of the Adirondack Mountain Club, Poughkeepsie, N.Y. was issued in 1949. 24p. Multilithed. **2**

McMillen, James A. Bibliography. *In* Donaldson, A.L. History of the Adirondacks.

N.Y. Century, 1921. v.2, p.315–63. This bibliography supplements the one compiled by Cecelia A. Sherrill (see no.5 below). With Donaldson's list, noted above, this comprises the most extensive list of Adirondackana to date. **3**

Plum, Dorothy Alice. Adirondack bibliography. *Ad-i-ron-dac*, Jan.–Feb. 1949. 13:no.1: 18. Describes the beginning of the *Adirondack Bibliography*. For other articles on this subject and on the collecting of Adirondackana, see *The Ad-i-ron-dac* for Jan.–Feb., May–June, Nov.–Dec. 1950; Mar.–Apr., May–June 1951; Mar.–Apr., July–Aug. 1953; July–Aug. 1955; 14:15, 57, 132; 15:34, 55; 17:27, 79; 19:76, 79. **4**

Sherrill, Cecelia Adelaide. Bibliography of the Adirondacks. *In* New York (state). Fisheries, game and forest commission. Annual report, 1898. p.423–41. Descriptive note by D.A. Plum in *The Ad-i-ron-dac*, May–June 1950, 14:57. **5**

GENERAL HISTORY

Callan, Estella Folts. Some phases of northern and western New York. An address delivered before the Herkimer county historical society. Nov. 18, 1922. *Herk Co Hist Soc*, 5:160–65. **6**

Carson, Russell Mack Little. Adirondack guides. *High Spots Yrbk*, 1944. p.5–6. illus. "This list of guides includes the names of authors, explorers, scientists, mountain climbers and conservationists." **7**

Carson, Russell Mack Little. Peaks and people of the Adirondacks. Garden City, N.Y. Doubleday, Page & co. 1927. 269p. incl. plates, front. port. maps on end papers. "Published under the auspices of the Adirondack Mountain Club, Inc." Reviewed in *Motordom*, Aug. 1927, 21:no.3:10; in *Mountain Magazine*, Jan. 1928, 6:53–54, "How the Peaks Were Named," by Baron Hasenclever (i.e. Raymond Torrey); in *The Cloud Splitter*,

Oct. 1943, 6:no.7:7, 12. Extracts in *High Spots*, July 1937, 14:no.3:15–17, 31–34, 37–38, 46–47. **8**

Coughlin, Richard. The Adirondack region: history and adventures of early times. Watertown, N.Y. Santway photo-craft co. inc. c1921. 77p. **9**

Crouse, Nellis Maynard. Discoveries of the Jesuits in New York state. *NY State Hist Assn Q*, Jan. 1924. 5:48–68. map. **10**

Cunningham, John Lovell. Three years with the Adirondack regiment, 118th New York volunteers infantry, from the diaries and other memoranda. . . Norwood, Mass. Plimpton press, 1920. 286p. front. plates, ports. Civil War diary. **11**

Dayne, Marie A. Ticonderogue — Fort Carillon. *Am Mo Mag (NY)* Oct. 1896. 9:319–27.

Connecticut soldiers in various campaigns. 12

De Costa, Benjamin Franklin. A narrative of events at Lake George from the early colonial times to the close of the Revolution. N.Y. 1868. 74p. front. folded maps.   13

De Costa, Benjamin Franklin. Notes on the history of Fort George during the colonial and revolutionary periods, with contemporaneous documents and an appendix. N.Y. J. Sabin & sons, 1871. 78p. front. illus. plan, map. "Orderly Book of James McGee at Fort George, July & August 1776 . . . from original manuscript . . . in the New York State Library," p.65–70. Published originally in *The American Bibliopolist*, Apr.–Sept. 1871, 3:109–24, 173–88, 221–52, 325–34. Additions in the issue for Apr. 1877, 9:36–40.   14

Documentary history of the State of New York; arranged . . . by E.B. O'Callaghan . . . Albany, Weed, Parsons & co. 1850–51. 4v. front. plates (partly folded) ports. (2 folded) folded maps, plans (partly folded). Quarto edition. Also issued in octavo edition, 1849–51.   15

Documents relative to the colonial history of the State of New-York . . . Albany, Weed, Parsons & co. 1853–87. 15v. fronts. port. facsim. folded plans, folded maps. Edited by E.B. O'Callaghan and Berthold Fernow.   16

Donaldson, Alfred Lee. A history of the Adirondacks. N.Y. Century, 1921. 2v. front. plates, ports. folded charts, folded maps. Bibliography, v.2, p.229–363. The first comprehensive history of the Adirondacks, not yet superseded. Extracts in *High Spots*, July 1937, 14:no.3:42–43. Mr. Donald Van Brakle of Saranac Lake has furnished the following information: Variant bindings. The original binding is dark-green cloth with gilt lettering. Sometime after publication a number of unbound sets were discovered in the publishing house. These were bound in a lighter, smoother green cloth and remaindered to Mr. E.L.Gray, a bookseller, of Saranac Lake. Mr. Van Brakle has a copy bound in three-quarter black morocco with marbled boards and marbled end papers. It was dedicated to Henry S. Harper with a rhymed inscription by Donaldson, who referred to it as the "Author's special edition de looks" because of a photograph of the author following the preface. The inscription is dated May 25, 1921, and this edition may have been published for presentation purposes. Donaldson inscribed a set in original binding to his wife on May 2, 1921, a possible indication that the de luxe edition was issued subsequently.   17

Dornburgh, Henry. Why the wilderness is called Adirondack. Glens Falls, N.Y. Job dept. Daily times, 1885. 14p. Also in the

Glens Falls *Daily Times*, 1855. Reprinted in *The Tahawus Cloudsplitter*, Mar. 1950–Mar. 1951. This scarce pamphlet includes a detailed history of the Adirondack Iron Works. See Donaldson. v.1, p.139ff.   18

Gillespie, E.T. The warpath. *NY State Hist Assn Proc*, 1910. 10:139–55.   19

Grady, Joseph F. The Adirondacks: Fulton chain — Big Moose region; the story of a wilderness. Little Falls, N.Y. Press of the Journal & Courier co. c1933. 320p. plates, ports. facsim. map on lining paper.   20

Greene, Nelson, ed. History of the Mohawk valley, gateway to the west, 1614–1925; covering six counties of Schenectady, Schoharie, Montgomery, Fulton, Herkimer, Oneida. Chicago, S.J. Clarke publishing co. 1925. 4v. ports. facsims. maps. Includes chapters on Isaac Jogues, the Battle of Lake George, Ticonderoga.   21

Higgins, Ruth Loving. Expansion in New York, with especial reference to the eighteenth century. Columbus, O. Ohio state university, 1931. 209p. (Contributions in History and Political Science, no.14.) Northern New York after 1783, p.138–49.   22

Hogan, William. Considerations on the improvement of northern New-York; addressed to his old neighbours, friends, constituents and fellow citizens of the northern counties. N.Y. H. Anstice, 1842. 20p. Northern New-York Improvement Association plan to promote settlement of waste lands. Copy in the William L. Clements Library, University of Michigan.   23

Jesuits. Letters from missions (North America). The Jesuit relations and allied documents; travel and explorations of the Jesuit missionaries in North America (1610–1791) with an introduction by Reuben Gold Thwaites; selected and edited by Edna Kenton. N.Y. A. & C. Boni, 1925. 527p. front. plates, ports. maps (1 folded).   24

Johnson, Sir William, bart. The papers of Sir William Johnson; prepared for publication by the Division of archives and history. James Sullivan, director. Albany, University of the State of New York, 1921–date. v. 1–.   25

Landon, Harry Fay. The north country, a history, embracing Jefferson, St. Lawrence, Oswego, Lewis and Franklin counties, New York. Indianapolis, Historical publishing co. 1932. 3v.   26

Longstreth, Thomas Morris. The Adirondacks; illustrated with photographs and maps. N.Y. Century, 1917. 370p. front. plates, folded map. 2d edition published in

1920. Reviewed in *The Cloud Splitter*, Dec. 1943, 6:no.9:6–7, 9.   27

Macauley, James. Natural, statistical and civil history of the State of New York. N.Y. 1829. 3v.   28

Macomb landmarks. *Am Scenic & Hist Pres Soc*, 1918. 23:134–46. Short discussion of Macomb's Purchase.   29

Mather, Fred. Adirondack history. *For & Stream*, May 8, 1897. 48:363.   30

Mather, Joseph H. A geographical history of the State of New York: embracing its history, government, physical features, climate, geology, mineralogy, botany, zoology, education, internal improvements, etc. with a separate history of each county. The whole forming a complete history of the state. Utica, N.Y. H.H. Hawley & co. 1848. 432p. front. illus. maps.   31

New York (state). State planning board. State planning for New York. Summary report of progress . . . January 14, 1935. Albany, 1935. 84p. figs. maps. Population, land use, forests, waters, public domain, minerals, highways, public works, recreation, housing, planning.   32

New York (state). World's fair commission. Adirondack division. Region five. Adirondack region. N.Y. Peter J. Carey & sons, inc. 1939. unpaged. illus. maps.   33

New York state historical association. History of the State of New York. . . N.Y. Columbia university press, 1933–37. 10v. fronts. ports. illus. facsims. maps (1 folded). Edited by Alexander C. Flick.   34

Opening of the Adirondacks. With a map and illustrations. N.Y. Hurd & Houghton, 1865. 82p. front. folded map. Munson credits authorship to C.H. Burt.   35

Parker, Wilmond W. The migration from Vermont to northern New York. *NY Hist*, Oct. 1934. 15:398–406. Routes of travel in 1785.   36

Parkman, Francis. Jesuits in North America in the 17th century. Boston, Little, Brown, 1899. 586p. plates. Isaac Jogues, p.305–34, 394–403.   37

Parkman, Francis. Montcalm and Wolfe. Boston, Little, Brown, 1898. 2v. plates, ports. Many references to Lake George, Lake Champlain and Ticonderoga.   38

Peattie, Roderick, ed. The friendly mountains, Green, White, and Adirondacks. N.Y. Vanguard press, 1942. 341p. incl. front. illus. plates, tables, diagrs. (American Mountain Series, ed. by Roderick Peattie, v.2.)   39

Redfield, William Charles. Some account of two visits to the mountains in Essex county, New York, in the years 1836 and 1837; with a sketch of the northern sources of the Hudson. *Am J Sci*, Apr. 1838. ser.1:33:301–23. Separate edition printed in New Haven, by Hamlen, 1838? 23p. Reprinted in *The Family Magazine*, 1838, 5:345–54. Extract printed in *High Spots*, July 1937, 14:no.3:8–9, with title "Imperfect State of Geographical Knowledge." See also his "Geographical Discoveries in New York" in the *Journal of Commerce* for Aug. 18, 1837.   40

Reeves, George W. The story of the north country. *NY State Hist Assn Q*, Apr. 1929. 10:105–18. port. illus.   41

Reid, William Maxwell. Lake George and Lake Champlain, the war trail of the Mohawk and the battleground of France and England in their contest for the control of North America; with 84 illustrations from photographs by John Arthur Maney and two maps. N.Y. Putnam, 1910. 381p. front. plates, plans, folded maps.   42

Seelye, Mrs. Elizabeth (Eggleston). Lake George in history . . . together with a historical map of the Lake George region and a guide to the battlefields and other points of interest in the eastern part of the Adirondack mountains. . . Lake George, N.Y. Author, c1896. 106p. illus. map.   43

Seelye, Mrs. Elizabeth (Eggleston). Saratoga and Lake Champlain in history. 1st ed. Lake George, N.Y. Author, c1898. 111p. plate, maps.   44

Shea, John Dawson Gilmary. Perils of the ocean and wilderness; or, Narratives of shipwreck and Indian captivity. Gleaned from early missionary annals. Boston, P. Donahoe, 1857. 206p. Goupil and Jogues, p.16–103.   45

Simms, Jeptha Root. Frontiersmen of New York, showing customs of the Indians, vicissitudes of the pioneer white settlers, and border strife in two wars. . . Albany, G.C. Riggs, 1882–83. 2v. port. illus.   46

Smith, Clarence C. History of the Adirondacks. *Up-Stater*, May 1929. 1:no.3:3–4, 6–7. illus.   47

Smith, Dorothy. Historic war vessels in Lake Champlain and Lake George. . . Albany, University of the State of New York, 1937. p.123–36. Reprinted from New York State Museum Bulletin 313.   48

Smith, Gerrit. An address to the three thousand colored citizens of New-York who are the owners of one hundred and twenty thousand acres of land, in the State of New-York, given to them by Gerrit Smith. N.Y. 1846. 20p.   49

Smith, Gerrit. Gerrit Smith's land auction. Peterboro, N.Y. 1846. 45p. Half title.   50

Snyder, Charles E. John Brown's tract. *Herk Co Hist Soc*, 1896. 1:94–108. Manuscript copy in Donaldson Collection, Saranac Lake Free Library.   51

Sylvester, Nathaniel Bartlett. The historic muse on Mount MacGregor. Troy, N.Y. 1885. 27p. front. plates, illus. Another edition published in 1887, 35p.   52

Sylvester, Nathaniel Bartlett. Historical sketches of northern New York and the Adirondack wilderness: including traditions of the Indians, early explorers, pioneer settlers, hermit hunters, etc. Troy, N.Y. Wm. H. Young, 1877. 316p. plates, ports. illus. Extracts in *North Country Life*, Spring 1947, Fall 1952–Spring 1953, Spring 1954; 1:no.3:55–56; 6:no.4:39–41, 62; 7:no.1:44–46; 7:no.2:29–31; 8:no.2:52–54.   53

U.S. Works progress administration. New York state. WPA in the Adirondacks. n.p. 1939. Unpaged folder.   54

Van Rensselaer, Cortlandt, 1808–60. Miscellaneous sermons, essays and addresses, edited by his son C. Van Rensselaer. Philadelphia, J.B. Lippincott, 1861. 37–569p. front. (port.). "Historical discourse at the centennial celebration of the Battle of Lake George," p.217–69; "Capture of Ticonderoga," p.506–69.   55

Wakeman, Abram. The great highway, a world's war path; synopsis of essential events occurring chiefly en route between Albany, Lake George, and Lake Champlain. N.Y. c1927. 36p. illus. map.   56

Webster, George O. My story of the Adirondacks. *High Spots*, Jan. 1936, 13:no.1:17–19; July 1936, 13:no.2:15–18; Jan. 1937, 14:no.1:28–31; Apr. 1937, 14:no.2:24–27.   57

White, William Chapman. Adirondack country. N.Y. & Boston, Duell, Sloan & Pearce; Little, Brown, c1954. 315p. map on end papers. Reviewed by Henry Germond in *The Cloud Splitter*, July–Aug. 1954, 17:no.4:8–10; by Michael Nadel in *The Living Wilderness*, Spring–Summer 1955, no. 52:18–19; by Edward D. Hurley in *Appalachia*, Dec. 15, 1955, 30:624; by Nina B. Colman in *North Country Life*, Fall 1954, 8:no.4:53–54.   58

Wynne, John J. The Mohawk martyr missionaries. *NY Hist*, Jan. 1932. 13:59–74.   59

FRENCH SETTLEMENTS, ETC.

Alpina. Neuchâtel? H. Wolfrath, 1848. 3p. Caption title. Colony at Alpina.   60

Appleton, William, ed. "Journal de Castorland." *Mass Hist Soc Proc*, Feb. 1854. 7:326–38.   61

Burnand, Eugene. Notice sur des terres à vendre dans les comtés de Jefferson et de Lewis, état de New-York. Lausanne, Imprimerie d'EMM Vincent fils, 1848? 1 leaf. Colony at Alpina.   62

Chassanis, Pierre. Association pour la possession & exploitation de six cent mille acres de terre concédées par l'état de New York, & situées . . . sur le Lac Ontario. Paris, 1792? 8p. Castorland. Sabin 12220. The New York State Library has a copy with manuscript legal documents appended. English translation in F.B. Hough's "History of Jefferson County," p.46–49.   63

Chassanis, Pierre. Réponse au Mémoire de Mr. Tillier. n.p. n.pub. c.1800. 3p. English translation in F.B. Hough's "History of Lewis County," p.65–67. About Castorland. Tillier's Memorial, to which this is an answer, was published in 1800.   64

Clarke, Thomas Wood. Emigrés of the wilderness. N.Y. Macmillan, 1941. 247p. front. illus. Includes Castorland and Joseph Bonaparte.   65

Compagnie de New-York. Constitution. Paris, Froullé, 1793. 32p. "Fait et passé à Paris, en la demeure susdite de Pierre Chassanis; l'an 1793, ledit jour 28 juin." Translation in F.B. Hough's "History of Lewis County," p.40–50. Castorland.   66

Compagnie de New-York. Description topographique de six cents mille acres de terres dans l'Amérique septentrionale, mises en vente par actions, suivant le plan d'association ci-joint. Prospectus. . . Paris, Froullé, 1792. 14, 8p. Castorland.   67

Compagnie de New-York. Faits et calculus sur la population et le territoire des États-Unis d'Amérique. Traduit de l'anglois. Paris, 1796? 12p. Probably by Peter Chassanis. Issued for promotion of Castorland tract. See Vail, R.W.G. "The Voice of the Old Frontier."   68

Crèvecoeur, Michel Guillaume St. Jean, called Saint Jean de Crèvecoeur. Voyage dans la haute Pensylvanie, et dans l'état de New-York. . . Paris, 1801. 3v. Appendix contains an unsigned letter dated Sept. 4, 1800 about Castorland. A translation of the complete text is given in F.B. Hough's "History of Jefferson County," p.52–55. Extract in his "History of Lewis County," p.105–7.   69

Landon, Harry Fay. French refugees in northern New York. *Up-Stater*, Jan. 1930. 2:no.1:3–4, 23–24. illus. ports.   70

Moore, William A. Some French influences in the early settlement of the Black river valley. *NY State Hist Assn Proc*, 1914. 14:122–31. Includes Castorland.   71

Notice sur Alpina. Terres situées dans les comtés de Jefferson et Lewis, état de New

York. Neuchâtel, Henri Wolfrath, 1847. 64p. plate, map. Settlement near Lake Bonaparte. 72

Papers relating to the French seigniories on Lake Champlain. *In* Documentary history of the State of New York; arranged . . . by E.B. O'Callaghan. Albany, 1850–51. v.1, p.345–76. folded maps. 73

Ralph, Alta M. The Chassanis or Castorland settlement. *NY State Hist Assn Q*, Oct. 1929. 10:333–45. 74

Rosengarten, Joseph George. French colonists and exiles in the United States. Philadelphia, Lippincott, 1907. 234p. French land companies in the United States, p.106–20. 75

Stephens, W. Hudson, ed. Notes of the voyage in '93 towards "Castorland," and operations therein, in Lewis co. N.Y. 1794–'95. Lowville, N.Y. W.H. Stephens, 1868. 8p. Summaries from the *Lewis County Democrat* of addresses by Franklin B. Hough. 76

Sylvester, Nathaniel Bartlett. Castorland, dream city of the French nobility. . . *No Country Life*, Fall 1952–Spring 1953. 6:no.4: 39–41, 62; 7:no.1:44–46; 7:no.2:29–31. Reprinted from his "Historical Sketches of Northern New York." 77

Sylvester, Nathaniel Bartlett. Sistersfield. *No Country Life*, Spring 1954. 8:no.2:52–54. Reprinted from his "Historical Sketches." Castorland. 78

Tillier, Rodolphe. Mémoire pour Rodolphe Tillier, Commissaire-gérant de la Compagnie de New-York. N.Y. J.C. Parisot, 1800. 18p. Copy in the John Carter Brown Library. Caption title. For English translation, see following entry. 79

Tillier, Rodolphe. Translation of a memorial of Rodolphe Tillier's justification of the administration of Castorland, county of Oneida, State of New-York. Rome, N.Y. Printed by Thomas Walker, 1800. 16p. Copy at the New York State Library. Quoted in F.B. Hough's "History of Lewis County," p.57–65. 80

Wyer, James Ingersoll. Later French settlements in New York state, 1783–1800. *NY State Hist Assn Proc*, 1915. 15:176–89. Bibliographic note, p.188–89. Includes short discussions of Castorland and Peter Sailly. 81

FRENCH AND INDIAN WARS

Account of the expedition on Lake Champlain. *Lond Mag*, Dec. 1759. 28:661–63. Reprinted from the *London Gazette*. 82

Amherst, Jeffrey Amherst, 1st baron. Commissary Wilson's orderly book. Expedition of the British and provincial army under Maj. Gen. Jeffrey Amherst against Ticonderoga and Crown Point, 1759. Albany, J. Munsell, 1857. 220p. front. (folded map). (Munsell's Historical Series, no.1.) Edited by J. Watts de Peyster. 83

Bartman, George. The siege of Fort William Henry: letters of George Bartman. *Hunt Lib Q*, Aug. 1949. 12:415–25. Edited by John A. Schutz. Letters written during the siege (1757) by the aide de camp for the area commander, Daniel Welch. 84

Bean, M.D. Storming of Ticonderoga under Major General Sir James Abercrombie, July 8, 1758. *Knick Mag*, July 1850. 36:1–25. 85

Blake, Henry Taylor. The battle of Lake George (September 8, 1755) and the men who won it. N.Y.? 1910? p.109–31. "Read December 20, 1909." Copy in Yale University Library. 86

Blodget, Samuel. A prospective-plan of the battle near Lake George, on the 8th day of September, 1755. With an explanation thereof; containing a full tho' short history of that important affair. Boston, printed by R. Draper, 1755. 5p. plan. 87

Bradley, A.G. Ticonderoga. *Nat Rev*, Feb. 1929. 92:914–21. Battle of Ticonderoga, 1758. 88

Brady, Cyrus Townsend. Colonial fights and fighters. N.Y. McClure & Phillips, 1901. 341p. "Fighting Around Ticonderoga," p.263–86. 89

Brown, Thomas. A plain narrative of the uncommon sufferings and remarkable deliverance of Thomas Brown of Charleston in New England; who returned to his father's house the beginning of Jan., 1760, after being absent 3 years and about 8 months: containing an account of the engagement between a party of English commanded by Maj. Rogers and a party of French and Indians, in Jan., 1757. . . Boston, Fowle & Draper, 1760. 27p. Photostat copy at the New York Public Library. 2d edition published in New York by W. Abbott in 1908 as Extra no.4, pt.1 of *The Magazine of History with Notes and Queries*. 90

Chapais, Thomas. Les Irlandais et la bataille de Carillon. *Rev Can*, Dec. 1910. n.s.4:481–99. 91

Chauncy, Charles. A second letter to a friend; giving a more particular narrative of the defeat of the French army at Lake George, by the New England troops. . . Boston, Edes & Gill, 1755. 16p. 92

Chaussegros de Léry, Joseph Gaspard. Carillon, May 8th to July 2d, 1756. Diary kept at the fort. . . *Ft Ti Mus Bul*, July 1942. 6:128–44. ports. Translation of documents in the Montreal archives. De Léry was military engineer. 93

Cook, Joseph. Extracts from Sketches of Ticonderoga: Burial of Lord Howe, by Edward J. Owen. Ticonderoga, N.Y. Press of the Sentinel, 1899? 3–97p. plates, front. ports. folded map. Cover title: "Historical Ticonderoga." "Reburial of the remains of Lord Viscount Howe. . . " p.81–97.   94

Davies, William Gilbert. Ticonderoga and Crown Point. In his Papers and addresses. N.Y. Cooke, 1907. p.93–108.   95

Death of Lord Howe. NY Hist, Apr. 1936. 18:206–7.   96

Green, Samuel Abbott. Blodget's plan of the battle on the shores of Lake George, 8 Sept., 1755; remarks made before the Massachusetts historical society Mar. 13, 1890. Cambridge, Mass. J. Wilson & son, 1890. 6p. plan (facsim.).   97

Hawks, John. Orderly book and journal of Major John Hawks on the Ticonderoga-Crown Point campaign, under General Jeffrey Amherst, 1759–60. . . N.Y. Society of colonial wars in the State of New York, 1911. 92p.   98

Holden, James Austin. New historical light on the real burial place of George Augustus Lord Viscount Howe, 1758. NY State Hist Assn Proc, 1910. 10:259–366. facsims. port. map. Reprinted in 1911 with title "The Campaign of 1758: New Historical Light . . ."   99

Hurlbut, J. Journal of a colonial soldier during Amherst's expedition against Ticonderoga, 1759. Mag Am Hist, Apr. 1893. 29:395–96.   100

Johnson, Sir William, bart. Camp at Lake George, Sept. 9, 1775. Lond Mag, Nov. 1775. 24:544–46. Defeat of French near Lake George.   101

Johnson, Sir William, bart. Relaçaõ de huma batalha, succedida no campo de Lake Giorge na America Septemtrional, entre as tropas inglezas commandadas pelo coronel Guilhelmo, e as francezas das quaes era commandante o general baraõ Dieskau, aos 30. junho. . .1757(!). . . Lisboa, Rodrigues, 1757. 7p. Abridged translation of the author's letter dated Camp at Lake George, September 9, 1755. Copy in the Library of Congress.   102

Johnson, Sir William, bart. To the governors of the several colonies who raised troops on the present expedition. Camp at Lake George, Sept. 9, 1755. London, E. Owen, 1755. 2p. (London Gazette extra-ordinary. Thursday, October 30, 1755.) Photostat in Yale University Library.   103

Journal de l'affaire du Canada passée le juillet 1758 entre les troupes du roi, commandées par M. le Marquis de Montcalm et celles d'Angleterre, qui au nombre de vingt mille hommes, ont été mises en fuite par trois mille deux cent cinquante François. Rouen, France, 1758. 4p. Copy at the New York Public Library. Battle of Ticonderoga, 1758.   104

Journals of Sir William Johnson's scouts, 1755, 1756. In Documentary history of the State of New York; arranged . . . by E.B. O'Callaghan. Albany, 1850–51. v.4, p.167–85. folded plate. Battle of Lake George, 1755.   105

Knox, Capt. John, d. 1778. An historical journal of the campaigns in North America for the years 1757, 1758, 1759 and 1760 . . . ed. with an introduction, appendix and index by Arthur G. Doughty. . . Toronto, Champlain society, 1914–16. 3v. plates, ports. maps (part folded) facsims. (Publications of the Champlain Society, VIII–X.) Includes journals of Jeffrey Amherst and William Amherst, 1758–60, 3:1–95.   106

Livingston, William. A review of military operations in North America; from the commencement of French hostilities on the frontiers of Virginia in 1753, to the surrender of Oswego, on the 14th of Aug. 1756. Dublin, P. Wilson & J. Exshaw, 1757. 276p. Also published in London by R. & J. Dodsley, 1757 & 1758; in New York by A. & J. Robertson, 1770. Military operations near Ticonderoga and Lake George during the French and Indian War.   107

Long, J.C. Amherst in 1759. NY Hist, Jan. 1934. 15:50–58. British campaign against Ticonderoga and Port Henry.   108

Macdonald, Archibald de Léry. Michael Chartier de Lotbiniere, the engineer of Carillon. NY Hist, Jan. 1934. 15:31–38.   109

Mante, Thomas, fl. 1772. The history of the late war in North-America. . . London, Printed for W. Strahan & T. Cadell, 1772. 542p. folded plans and maps.   110

Montcalm-Gozon, Louis Joseph de, marquis de Saint Véran, 1712–59. Marquis de Montcalm to his wife, July 14th, 1758. Ft Ti Mus Bul, Summer 1949. 8:129–31. facsim. map. Battle of Ticonderoga.   111

Nicolay, John G. The battle of Ticonderoga. Chaut, May 1892. 15:143–45.   112

O'Callaghan, E.B. The repulse at Ticonderoga, in 1758. Col Un Ser Mag, Feb. 1887. 117:128–31.   113

Owen, Edward J. The burial of Lord Viscount Howe; a paper read before the Albany institute. . . Albany, 1893. 45p. plate, map. This address, read January 3, 1893, is reprinted with additions in Joseph Cook's "Extracts from Sketches of Ticonderoga," p.33–80 (see no.94). Reprinted, N.Y. Abbott,

1908, with added title page *The Magazine of History with Notes and Queries*, Extra no.4, pt.2. Another edition with slightly different title published by Brandow, Albany, 1893. 114

Parkman, Francis. The battle of Lake George, 1755. *Atlan*, Oct. 1884. 54:444–56. 115

Pouchot, Pierre. Memoir upon the late war in North America between the French and English, 1755–60. . .translated and edited by Franklin B. Hough with additional notes and illustrations. Roxbury, Mass. Printed for W. Elliot Woodward, 1866. 2v. front. illus. plates (1 folded) port. plans (part folded) folded maps. 116

Putnam, Rufus. Journal of Gen. Rufus Putnam kept in northern New York during four campaigns of the old French and Indian war, 1757–1760. . . Albany, Joel Munsell's sons, 1886. 115p. port. 117

Rea, Caleb. The journal of Dr. Caleb Rea, written during the expedition against Ticonderoga in 1758. Edited by his great-grandson F.M. Roy. Salem, Mass. 1881. 71p. Reprinted from Essex Institute Historical Collections, v.18. 118

Relation de la défense des retranchements sur la hauteur de Carillon, à environ six cents toises du fort, le 8 juillet 1758. (Supposé avoir été redigée par les soins du marquis de Montcalm.) Quebec, Aug. Côte et compagnie, 1844. 7p. Signed: Historicus. Caption title. Copy in Yale University Library. 119

Relation de la prise du Fort Georges, ou Guillaume-Henry, situé sur le lac Saint-Sacrement, & de ce qui s'est passé cette année en Canada. Paris? 1757? 12p. Caption title. 120

Remington, Frederic. Joshua Goodenough's old letter. *Harper*, Nov. 1897. 95:878–89. The author of the letter was one of Rogers' Rangers. 121

Rogers, Mary Cochrane. A battle fought on snow shoes. Derry, N.H. Author, 1917. 66p. ports. plate. On Robert Rogers, 1758. Written by his great-great-granddaughter. For further information on Rogers and his Rangers see *Bulletin of the Fort Ticonderoga Museum*, Jan. 1941, v.6, no.1. 122

Rogers, Robert, 1731–95. Journals of Major Robert Rogers. . .1755–60; with an introduction and notes. . .by Franklin B. Hough. Albany, Joel Munsell's sons, 1883. 297p. front. (folded map). 123

Rogers, Robert, 1731–95. Reminiscences of the French war; containing Rogers' expeditions with the New-England rangers under his command, as published in London in 1765; with notes and illustrations. To which is added an account of the life and military

service of Maj. Gen. John Stark; with notices and anecdotes of other officers distinguished in the French and revolutionary wars. Concord, N.H. Luther Roby, 1831. 275p. port. 124

Sautai, Maurice Théodore. Montcalm at the battle of Carillon (Ticonderoga), (July 8, 1758). Translated from the French by John S. Watts. Ticonderoga, N.Y. Ft. Ticonderoga museum, 1921? 91p. ports. illus. maps. Battle of Ticonderoga, 1758. 125

Searing, James. The battle of Ticonderoga, 1758. *NY Hist Soc Proc*, 1847. 5:112–17. Communicated by Benjamin F. Thompson. 126

Society of colonial wars. New York (state). Account of the battle of Lake George, Sept. 8th, 1755; compiled by the Committee on historical documents and Lake George memorial committee. . . N.Y. H.K. Brewer & co. 1897. 15p. plates, plans. Written by Morris P. Ferris. Republished in 1903 by the Lake George Celebration Committee. 127

Society of colonial wars. New York (state). Daniel Claus' narrative of his relations with Sir William Johnson and experiences in the Lake George fight. Lake George celebration executive committee report. Native troops in our colonial possessions. Major Louis L. Seaman. N.Y. 1904. 40p. (Society of Colonial Wars. Publication 9–11.) 128

Van Rensselaer, Cortlandt, 1808–60. An historical discourse on the occasion of the centennial celebration of the battle of Lake George, 1755. Delivered at Caldwell, N.Y., Sept. 8, 1855. Philadelphia, C. Sherman & son, 1856. 80p. folded map. 129

Wells, Parrish. Dangerous journeys, 1757. Burlington, Vt. Free press printing co. [c]1940. 95p. Based upon contemporary letters and journals of the French and Indian War. 130

Wickes, Frank B. Lord Howe. *NY State Hist Assn Proc*, 1910. 10:238–57. 131

Williams, Thomas. Campaigns against Crown Point in 1755 and 1756. Correspondence of a surgeon in the army. . . *Hist Mag*, Apr. 1870. ser.2:7:209–16. 132

Winslow, John. General John Winslow's letter to the Earl of Halifax, relative to his conduct, and that of the troops under his command, on the Ticonderoga expedition in 1756. *Mass Hist Soc Coll*, 1799. 6:34–39. Dated: Boston, Dec. 30, 1756. 133

THE REVOLUTION

Allen, Ethan. Narrative of the capture of Ticonderoga and of his captivity and treatment by the British. Written by himself. 5th ed. with notes. Burlington, Vt. C. Goodrich

& S.B. Nichols, 1849, ᶜ1838. 50p. 1st edition, Philadelphia, 1779.   134

Bascom, Robert O. Ethan Allen at Fort Ticonderoga. . . Ticonderoga, N.Y. Ticonderoga historical society, 1908. 12p.   135

Bascom, Robert O. Men with Ethan Allen at Ticonderoga. *Ver Ant*, Mar. 1905. 3:142–43. Reprinted from the *Burlington Free Press*. List of men who served under Allen.   136

Bascom, Robert O. Ticonderoga expedition of 1775; list of men with Ethan Allen. . . Anecdotes and data about Allen. . . n.p. 1910. 87p. Copy in the Cleveland Public Library.   137

Becker, John P. 1765–1837. The sexagenary; or, Reminiscences of the American revolution. Albany, J. Munsell, 1866. 234p. ports. incl. front. (Munsell's Series of Local American History, v.5.) Edited by S. DeWitt Bloodgood. Another edition published by Little & Steele in 1883. Based on manuscript of DeWitt Clinton and Gen. Van Schaick.   138

Beman, N. Jr. Nathan Beman's part in leading Ethan Allen to the capture of the fort in 1775: letters. *NY Hist*, Apr. 1947. 28:197–98.   139

Campbell, William W. Annals of Tryon county; or, The border warfare of New York, during the Revolution. N.Y. J. & J. Harper, 1831. 191, 78p. front. (folded map) folded facsims. 2d edition published with title "The Border Warfare of New York. . ." N.Y. Baker & Scribner, 1849. 3d edition (Annals) Cherry Valley, N.Y. Cherry Valley Gazette, 1880. 4th edition (Annals) N.Y. Dodd, Mead, 1924. "Tryon county comprised all of the province west of the tier of counties on the west bank of the Hudson."   140

Chittenden, Lucius Eugene. The capture of Ticonderoga. Annual address before the Vermont historical society, delivered at Montpelier, Vt. Oct. 8, 1872. Rutland, Tuttle co. 1872. 5–127p. From *Vermont Historical Society Proceedings*, 1872.   141

Connecticut infantry. Mott's regiment, 1776. Orderly book of Capt. Icabod Norton of Col. Mott's regiment of Connecticut troops destined for the northern campaign in 1776 at Skenesborough (now Whitehall), Fort Ann and Ticonderoga, N.Y. . . Together with a facsimile of Captain Norton's map of Ticonderoga and Mount Independence. With an introduction by Robert O. Bascom of Fort Edward, N.Y. Fort Edward, N.Y. Press of Keating & Barnard, 1898. 64p. map (facsim.).   142

De Costa, Benjamin Franklin. The fight at Diamond island. N.Y. J. Sabin & sons, 1872. 11p.   143

De Costa, Benjamin Franklin. Who took Ticonderoga? *Galaxy*, Dec. 1868. 6:831–35. Engagement of May 10, 1775.   144

De Fonblanque, Edward Barrington, 1821–95. Political and military episodes in the latter half of the eighteenth century. Derived from the life and correspondence of the Right Hon. John Burgoyne. . . London, Macmillan, 1872. 500p. front. (port.) plates, plans, facsims.   145

de Peyster, John Watts. Major General Philip Schuyler, and the Burgoyne campaign in the summer of 1777. . . N.Y. Holt, 1877. 26p.   146

Digby, William, fl. 1776. The British invasion from the north. The campaigns of Generals Carleton and Burgoyne, from Canada, 1776–1777, with the journal of Lieut. William Digby. . .illustrated with historical notes by James Phinney Baxter. Albany, Joel Munsell's sons, 1887. 412p. front. plates, port. (Munsell's Historical Series, no.16.)   147

Elmer, Ebenezer. Journal kept during an expedition to Canada in 1776. . . *In* New Jersey historical society. Proceedings, 1847–48, ser.1:2:95–146, 150–94; 3:21–56, 90–102. Includes Ticonderoga.   148

Fiske, John. Ticonderoga, Bennington and Oriskany. *Atlan*, Mar. 1889. 63:398–418. 149

Flick, Alexander Clarence. General Knox's Ticonderoga expedition. *NY State Hist Assn Q*, Apr. 1928. 9:119–35.   150

Folsom, William R. Battle of Valcour island. *Ver Quar*, July 1951. 19:133–46.   151

French, Allen. The taking of Ticonderoga in 1775; the British story; a study of captors and captives. . .based upon material hitherto unpublished. Cambridge, Mass. Harvard university press, 1928. 89p. front.   152

Hadden, James Murray. Hadden's journal and orderly books. A journal kept in Canada and upon Burgoyne's campaign in 1776 and 1777. . . Albany, Joel Munsell's sons, 1884. 581p. front. (facsim.) maps (facsim.). (Munsell's Historical Series, no.12.)   153

Hagglund, Lorenzo Frederick. A page from the past: the story of the continental gundelo Philadelphia on Lake Champlain — 1776–1949. Lake George, N.Y. Adirondack resorts press, ᶜ1949. 32p. illus. tables, map. 2d edition; first published in Whitehall, N.Y. ᶜ1936.   154

Hall, Henry. The evacuation of Ticonderoga, in 1777. *Hist Mag*, Dec. 1862. 6:363–68. Read before the Vermont Historical Society at Brattleboro, July 17, 1862.   155

Hall, Hiland. The capture of Ticonderoga in 1775. A paper read before the Vermont historical society, Oct. 19, 1869. *Ver Hist Soc Proc*, Oct. 1869. p.1–32.   156

Johnston, Henry Phelps. An address on "Ticonderoga; or, The defeat of the old world in the new." *In* Sons of the Revolution, New York society. Constitution. . .and the by-laws. . . N.Y. 1892. p.49–63. Battle of 1775.   157

Knox, Henry. Knox's diary during his Ticonderoga expedition. *New Eng Hist & Gen Reg*, July 1876. 30:321–26.   158

Lampee, Thomas C. The Missisquoi loyalists. *Ver Hist Soc Proc*, June 1938. n.s.6:81–139. Includes discussion of the loyalists in the Champlain valley.   159

Mahan, Alfred Thayer. The naval campaign of 1776 on Lake Champlain. *Scrib M*, Feb. 1898. 23:147–60. illus.   160

Murray, Eleanor S. The invasion of northern New York, 1780. *Ft Ti Mus Bul*, July 1946. 7:3–12. port. illus.   161

Nelson, Peter. The battle of Diamond island. *NY State Hist Assn Q*, Jan. 1922. 3:36–53. map.   162

Papers relating to the expedition to Ticonderoga, April and May, 1775. *Conn Hist Soc Coll*, 1860. 1:163–88. Includes a journal of Capt. Edward Mott with various letters and documents.   163

Pausch, Georg. Journal of Captain Pausch, chief of the Hanau artillery during the Burgoyne campaign; tr. and annotated by William L. Stone. . . Albany, Joel Munsell's sons, 1886. 185p. incl. plates, map, front. (port.). (Munsell's Historical Series, no.14.)   164

Pennsylvania infantry. 5th regiment, 1776–1783. Orderly book of the northern army, at Ticonderoga and Mt. Independence, from October 17th, 1776, to January 8th, 1777, with biographical and explanatory notes, and an appendix. Albany, J. Munsell, 1859. 224p. folded map.   165

Reynolds, Grindall. From Ticonderoga to Saratoga. *Unit Rev*, Nov. 1877. 8:505–26. Taking of Ticonderoga in 1775.   166

Root, William L. The capture of Fort Ticonderoga. *Berk Hist & Sci Soc*, 1913. 3:376–92.   167

St. Clair, Arthur, defendant. Proceedings of a general court martial, held at White Plains, in the State of New-York, by order of his excellency General Washington. . .for the trial of Major General St. Clair, August 25, 1778. Major General Lincoln, president. Philadelphia, Hall & Sellars, 1778. 52p. folded map. Court-martial held for the abandonment of Ticonderoga and Fort Independence.   168

Schuyler, Philip, defendant. Proceedings of a general court martial, held at Major General Lincoln's quarters, near Quaker-Hill, in the State of New-York, by order of his excellency General Washington. . .for the trial of Major General Schuyler, October 1, 1778. Major General Lincoln, president. Philadelphia, Hall & Sellars, 1778. 62p. Court-martial held for the abandonment of Ticonderoga and Fort Independence.   169

Stevens, John Austin. The Burgoyne campaign: an address delivered on the battlefield on the one hundredth celebration of the battle of Bemis Heights, September 19, 1877. N.Y. Anson, D.F. Randolph & co. 1877. 43p.   170

Stone, William Leete, 1835–1908. Campaign of Lieut. Gen. John Burgoyne and the expedition of Lieut. Col. Barry St. Leger. . . Albany, J. Munsell, 1877. 461p. front. illus. ports. folded map, facsim. The fight at Diamond Island, p.346–52; Sergeant Lamb's account of his journey through the woods from Fort Miller to Ticonderoga, p.406–12; Description of Ticonderoga and the forts south of it at the time of their occupation by the Americans in the year 1777, p.434–37.   171

Stone, William Leete, 1835–1908, tr. Letters of Brunswick and Hessian officers during the American revolution. . . Albany, Joel Munsell's sons, 1891. 258p. front. (Munsell's Historical Series, no.18.)   172

The Ticonderoga expedition of 1775. *NY State Hist Assn Proc*, 1910. 11:303–89.   173

Trumbull, James Hammond. The origin of the expedition against Ticonderoga, in 1775. A paper read before the Connecticut historical society, Jan. 5, 1869. Hartford, Conn. 1869. 15p. Reviewed in *Historical Magazine*, Feb. 1869. ser.2:no.6:146.   174

Two letters: I. Anthony Wayne and Lake George; letter from General Anthony Wayne to General Schuyler, Ticonderoga, March 23, 1777. II. Washington's announcement of Arnold's treason. St. Louis, Privately printed by W.K. Bixby, 1922. 7 leaves. Facsimile reprint.   175

U.S. War dept. Adjutant-General's office. Continental army. Orderly book of the northern army at Ticonderoga and Mt. Independence from Oct. 17, 1776 to Jan. 8, 1777, with notes and appendix by J. Munsell. Albany, J. Munsell, 1859. 224p. port. map. Sabin 57496 (under title).   176

Wallace, Willard Mosher, ed. The British occupation of Fort Ticonderoga, 1777. *Ft Ti Mus Bul*, 1951. 8:301–20. port. illus. map.

Transcription of manuscript military orders in the Olin Library, Wesleyan University.   177

Watson, Winslow Cossoul. The Adirondacks a century ago. *Am Hist Rec*, Jan. 1873. 2:29–32. Discussion of possible routes of Sir John Johnson's flight through the "Adirondack Desert" in 1776.   178

Who took Ticonderoga? *Ft Ti Mus Bul*, Jan. 1937. 4:55–87. port. illus. Documents relating to the claims of Ethan Allen and others.   179

THE WAR OF 1812

Akeley, Nettie Pomeroy. The battle of Plattsburg. *Vermonter*, 1926. 31:no.1:6–8.   180

Alden, F. Arlington. Vergennes and the battle of Plattsburg. *Vermonter*, Sept. 1914. 19:136–41. illus. Centennial celebration history.   181

Bixby, George F. The first battle of Lake Champlain. Has current history correctly located its site? *Alb Inst Tr*, 1893. 12:122–36. plates, plan, port. maps. Also printed as a separate, Albany, A. J. Parker, 1893.   182

Brown, Gilbert Patten. The victory on Lake Champlain. *Mas Rev*, Apr. 1932. 23:no.6:13–17. illus. port.   183

Burns, James C. Battle of Plattsburgh. Significance of a great victory. . .September 11, 1814. Macomb, Ill. Journal printing co. n.d. 15p. illus. ports.   184

Clark, Byron N. Accounts of the battle of Plattsburgh, 11 September, 1814. *Gen Q Mag*, Jan. 1903. ser.3:3:234–52. Taken from contemporary sources. Also published in *Vermont Antiquarian*, Mar. 1903, 1:75–93.   185

Clark, Byron N. ed. A list of the pensioners of the War of 1812. With an appendix, containing names of volunteers for the defence of Plattsburgh from Vermont towns, a description of the battle. . . Burlington, Vt. Research publishing co. 1904. 171p. plate.   186

Cooper, James Fenimore. The battle of Plattsburgh bay. *Putnam*, Jan. 1869. n.s.3:49–59. Lecture to be delivered before the New York Historical Society.   187

Headley, Joel Tyler. The battle of the lakes. *Harper*, July 1853. 7:208–13. MacDonough's victory on Lake Champlain. Extracted from Headley's "Second War with England."   188

Lossing, Benson John. Scenes of the War of 1812. X. Lake Champlain and the New England coast. *Harper*, July 1864. 29:147–62.   189

McCarthy, Charles Hallan. Battle of Lake Champlain. *Cath World*, Sept. 1914. 99:721–36.   190

Mahan, Alfred Thayer. Commodore Mac-Donough at Plattsburg. *No Am*, Aug. 1914. 200:203–21. Also issued as a separate.   191

Maine troops on Lake Champlain and the loss of the Eagle and the Growler, May–July, 1813. *Moors Ant*, May 1938. 2:34–42.   192

Marshall, Mrs. Helen Mariette (Lawrence). An echo of the battle of Plattsburgh. . . printed in the Plattsburgh Daily republican and reprinted for the Saranac chapter, D.A.R. Champlain, N.Y. Moorsfield press, 1929. 14p. incl. plate, front. (port.). An incident at West Chazy. Set down by Mrs. Charles H. Signor and George Stephenson Bixby.   193

Moore, Amasa C. An address on the battle of Plattsburgh, delivered at the celebration of the anniversary, Sept. 11th, 1843. Plattsburgh, N.Y. J.W. Tuttle, 1844. 12p. Copy in the Henry E. Huntington Library, San Marino, Cal.   194

Moore, Charles H. The battles of Lake Champlain and Plattsburgh, Sept. 11th, 1814. An oration delivered Sept. 11th, 1886, at Saranac, N.Y. . . Plattsburgh, N.Y. J.W. Tuttle, 1886. 20p.   195

New York (state). Plattsburg centenary commission. The battle of Plattsburgh. What historians say about it. Albany, J.B. Lyon, 1914. 70p. plate, plan.   196

New York (state). Plattsburg centenary commission. The battle of Plattsburgh. Why its centennial is to be celebrated. Albany, J.B. Lyon, 1914. 11p.   197

New York (state). Plattsburg centenary commission. Plattsburgh centennial celebration. Official program. . . Albany, J.B. Lyon, 1914. 80p. ports. illus. map. Contains the Book of words of the pageant of the Champlain valley, by Margaret Maclaren Eager. Historical notes by Mrs. George Fuller Tuttle.   198

New York (state). Plattsburg centenary commission. . . .Report. . .to the Legislature April 11, 1917. Albany, J.B. Lyon, 1917. 11p. front. Senate document 60, 1917.   199

New York (state). University. Archives and history division. The centenary of the battle of Plattsburg, 1814. . .at Plattsburg, N.Y., September 6 to 11, 1914. Published under the auspices of the State historian. Albany, 1914. 97p. plates, facsims. front. illus. (incl. maps, ports.). Contains reading list on the battle.   200

Noble, Henry Harmon. The battle of Boquet river. *Am Scenic & Hist Pres Soc*, 1915. 20:587–98. Also issued as a reprint.   201

O'Toole, Edward Jr. The battle of Platts-burg. *NY State Hist Assn Proc*, 1915. 14:423–29. plate. 202

Riddell, William Renwick. A Canadian's view of the battle of Plattsburgh. . . N.Y. 1915. 42p. 203

Robinson, C.W. The expedition to Platts-burg, upon Lake Champlain, Canada, 1814. With an account of it from the Journal of the late General Sir Frederick Philipse Robinson. *Roy Unit Ser Inst J*, Aug. 1916. 61:499–522. folded map. 204

Rochester, John Cornelius. The battle of Plattsburg, edited by Gladys G. Nelson. *Univ Roch Lib Bul*, Winter 1948. 3:30–34. Letters, describing the war in northern New York, written in 1814. 205

Skinner, St. John B.L. The battle of Platts-burgh, an address, delivered before the Lyceum, February 18, 1835. Plattsburgh, N.Y. 1835. 32p. 206

Stahl, John Meloy. The battle of Plattsburg; a study in and of the War of 1812. Argos, Ind. Van Tromp co. 1918. 166p. 207

Taché, Sir Étienne Pascal. Guerre de 1812 à 1815. Bataille navale du Lac Champlain. Par un témoin oculaire. *Soc Hist Mont*, 1860. 3:145–55. 208

Tuttle, John Ellery, ed. The battle of Lake Champlain; the story of an eye-witness. *Outlook*, Nov. 2, 1901. 69:573–78. port. Story of Benjah Phelps retold. 209

Washburn, H.C. The battle of Lake Cham-plain. *US N Inst Proc*, Sept.–Oct. 1914. 49: 1365–86. 210

ARCHAEOLOGY

Auringer, Obadiah Cyrus. Aboriginal stone implements of Queensbury. *NY State Hist Assn Proc*, 1907. 8:103–18. 211

Carson, Russell Mack Little. Traces of Indian occupation of the Adirondacks. *High Spots*, Apr. 1931. 8:no.2:26–28. 212

Champlain valley archaeological society. Bulletin. Dec. 1937–June 1940. v.1, no.1–3. Fort Ticonderoga, N.Y. 1937–40. 3v. plates. 213

Kellogg, David Sherwood. Aboriginal dwell-ing-sites in the Champlain valley. *Am Assn Adv Sci Proc*, 1888. 36:308–10. 214

Kellogg, David Sherwood. A day off. *For Leaves*, Spring 1904. 1:no.2:4–7. illus. Look-ing for Indian artifacts at Chateaugay Lake. 215

Kellogg, Orson. Indian antiquities. *Am Assn Adv Sci Proc*, 1849. 1:138–42. Report of the Committee of the Association of American Geologists and Naturalists examining phe-nomena at Keeseville, Essex County. 216

Miller, Philip Schuyler. A nice warm cave for the night. *High Spots Yrbk*, 1944. p.13–14, 18. illus. 217

Parker, Arthur C. Archaeological history of New York. Albany, University of the State of New York, 1922. 2v. plates, illus. maps. (New York State Museum Bulletins 235–38.)

Includes "Prehistoric Iroquois sites in North-ern New York" by M. Raymond Harrington. 218

Perkins, George Henry. Archaeological re-searches in the Champlain valley. *In* Inter-national congress of anthropology. Memoirs. 1894. p.84–91. 219

Perkins, George Henry. Archaeology of the Champlain valley. *Am Nat*, Dec. 1879. 13: 731–47. illus. 220

Perkins, George Henry. Notes on the archae-ology of the Champlain valley. *Am Assn Adv Sci Proc*, 1879. 28:528–39. 221

Skinner, Alanson Buck. Notes on Iroquois archaeology. N.Y. Museum of the American Indian, 1921. 216p. plates, maps. (Indian Notes and Monographs. Miscellaneous no.18.) 222

Squier, Ephraim George. Aboriginal monu-ments of the State of New York. Washington, Smithsonian Institution, 1850. 188p. plates, illus. maps. (Smithsonian Institution Publi-cation, no.15.) Published also under title "Antiquities of the State of New York," Buffalo, 1851. 223

Vickers, Stan. Delving into the dark ages. *No Country Life*, Summer 1949. 3:no.3:13–14. Archaeological find in a cave near Ticon-deroga. 224

ABORIGINES

Adams, Spencer Lionel. The long house of the Iroquois. Why the Five nations, possessing a rectangular type of lodge like the shape of their ancient realm in up-state New York, called themselves "Ho-De-No-Sau-Nee" (People of the long house). Skeneateles, N.Y. Fairview farm, 1944. 175p. plates, front.   225

Beauchamp, William Martin. Aboriginal occupation of New York. Albany, University of the State of New York, 1900. 199p. plates, folded maps in pocket. (New York State Museum Bulletin 32.) Arranged by county.   226

Beauchamp, William Martin. A history of the New York Iroquois now commonly called the Six nations. Albany, University of the State of New York, 1905. 125–46p. plates, ports. maps. (New York State Museum Bulletin 78.)   227

Beauchamp, William Martin. Indian names in New York, with a selection from other states, and some Onondaga names of plants, etc. Fayetteville, N.Y. Printed by H.C. Beauchamp, 1893. 148p.   228

Beauchamp, William Martin. The Iroquois trail; or, Foot-prints of the Six nations. Fayetteville, N.Y. Author, 1892. 154p.   229

Burger, William H. The first Adirondackers. *No Country Life*, Spring 1953. 7:no.2:19–20.   230

Carson, Russell Mack Little. The unknown guide. *High Spots*, Apr. 1934. 11:no.2:26–28. (Great Adirondack Guides, no.6.) The Indian.   231

Champlain's battle with the Iroquois. *St No Mo*, Sept. 1906. 1:no.5:12–15. illus.   232

Eno, Joel Nelson. A sketch of the relations of New York with the Five nations. *Americana*, July 1924. 18:278–312.   233

Finigan, Elizabeth Moran. The New York state Indians. *US Cath Hist Soc*, Mar. 1921. 15:104–11. "Indians living today on the reservations of New York state and some of their early history."   234

Jackson, Eric P. Mountains and the aborigines of the Champlain lowlands. *Appalachia*, Dec. 1930. 18:121–36.   235

Juvenal, pseud. Real life in the woods. *For & Stream*, Mar. 4, 1899. 52:164. Indian family living in the Adirondacks.   236

Kimm, Silas Conrad. The Iroquois: a history of the Six nations of New York. . . Middleburgh, N.Y. Press of P.W. Danforth, 1900. 122p. incl. front. (port.).   237

Miller, Philip Schuyler. People looking down. *Cloud Splitter*, Feb. 1942. 5:no.2:2–3. Early inhabitants of Adirondacks.   238

Miller, Philip Schuyler. Return to the mountains. *Cloud Splitter*, Sept.–Oct. 1947. 10:no.5: 5–7. Aborigines.   239

Miller, Philip Schuyler. Who came first? *Ad-i-ron-dac*, Sept.–Oct. 1951. 15:94–95, 98. See letter from W.H. Burger and Miller's reply in issue for Jan.–Feb. 1952, 16:16–17.   240

Morgan, Lewis Henry. League of the Ho-dé-no-sau-nee; new ed. with additional matter. Ed. and annotated by Herbert M. Lloyd. . . N.Y. Dodd, Mead, 1904. 2v. in 1. "The first edition (1851) was in two printings, one of which carried in a few cases colored plates of the illustrations made for Morgan's reports to the New York State Board of Regents. In 1901 a two volume annotated edition was issued; thirty copies were printed with colored plates and bound in parchment. Reprinted in 1954 as a Behavior Science Reprint." W.N. Fenton, in *American Anthropologist*, Feb. 1957.   241

Parker, Arthur C. Champlain's assault on the fortified town of the Oneidas, 1615. . . Albany, University of the State of New York, 1919. p.167–73, plate. "Printed in advance of the 14th report of the Director of the New York State Museum, 1917."   242

Root, Elihu. . . .The Iroquois and the struggle for America. Address by Honorable Elihu Root. . .in the Tercentenary celebration of the discovery of Lake Champlain, Plattsburgh, July 7, 1909. Albany, J.B. Lyon, 1909. 11 folios. Press release. Caption title.   243

Smith, H. Perry. Champlain's two expeditions; the American Indian's first experience with gun powder. *Four Tr News*, Apr. 1904. 6:260–61. illus. port.   244

Williams, Dr. Sherman. Champlain's battle with the Iroquois. An address. . . Ticonderoga, N.Y. Ticonderoga historical society, 1908. 10p.   245

INDIAN LEGENDS

Beauchamp, William Martin. Iroquois folk lore, gathered from the Six nations of New York. Selected and arranged for the Onondaga historical association, 1922. Syracuse, N.Y. Dehler press, 1922. 247p.   246

Brewer, Kate. Fanciful tales from legends of the Adirondack Indians. N. Y. & Washington, Neale publishing co. 1905. 59p. plates.   247

Brewer, Kate. When love found out a way. *For Leaves*, Autumn 1908. 5:no.3:3–7. illus. Legend of Saranac.   248

Carson, Russell Mack Little. Adirondack myths and legends. *High Spots*, Oct. 1931. 8:no.4:22–23.   249

Carson, Russell Mack Little. The Indian legend of Head island. *High Spots*, Jan. 1932. 9:no.1:27–28.   250

Carson, Russell Mack Little. Tomo, and the Wild lakes. *High Spots*, Apr. 1932. 9:no.2:24–25, 30. Abridged and rearranged from John Todd's "Summer Gleanings."   251

Dailey, William Nelson Potter. Fireside legends of the Adirondacks. *No Country Life*, Summer 1951. 5:no.3:28–30. As told at Adirondack Lodge by Henry Van Hoevenberg.   252

Donaldson, Alfred Lee. Round the bend. *Outdoor Life*, Jan. 1905. 1:149–51. Legend of Saranac.   253

Forkey, Del. Legends of the land where the partridge drums. *No Country Life*, Fall 1952. 6:no.4:17–18. Indian tale from the Saranac region.   254

Hoffman, Charles Fenno. The flying head, a legend of Sacondaga lake. *In* Griswold, R.W. Prose writers in America. 4th ed. Philadelphia, A. Hart, 1852. p.460–62. From his "Wild Scenes in the Forest and Prairie." Also in *American Monthly Magazine*, Jan. 1836.   255

Hudowalski, Mrs. Grace (Leech). Adota of Tahawi. *Cloud Splitter*, June 1939. 2:no.4:7–8. Ausable Lake.   256

Hudowalski, Mrs. Grace (Leech). Birth of the arbutus. *Cloud Splitter*, May 1942. 5:no.5:7–8.   257

Hudowalski, Mrs. Grace (Leech). Birth of the water lily. *Cloud Splitter*, Apr. 1940. 3:no.3:4–5. Saranac Indians.   258

Hudowalski, Mrs. Grace (Leech). Chemanito creates. *Cloud Splitter*, May 1941. 4:no.5:8–9.   259

Hudowalski, Mrs. Grace (Leech). Devil's pulpit. *Cloud Splitter*, Nov. 1941. 4:no.8:11.   260

Hudowalski, Mrs. Grace (Leech). Diamond rock. *Cloud Splitter*, Oct. 1942. 5:no.7:11. 261

Hudowalski, Mrs. Grace (Leech). Eagle nest trail. *Cloud Splitter*, Jan. 1942. 5:no.1:8.   262

Hudowalski, Mrs. Grace (Leech). Great white stag. *Cloud Splitter*, Dec. 1940. 3:no.8:4.   263

Hudowalski, Mrs. Grace (Leech). Hatchet island. *Cloud Splitter*, Oct. 1941. 4:no.7:11.   264

Hudowalski, Mrs. Grace (Leech). How winter came. *Cloud Splitter*, Jan. 1943. 6:no.1:3.   265

Hudowalski, Mrs. Grace (Leech). Indian park romance. *Cloud Splitter*, Feb. 1941. 4:no.2:6.   266

Hudowalski, Mrs. Grace (Leech). Indian plume. *Cloud Splitter*, Nov. 1940. 3:no.7:7–8. The Saranacs.   267

Hudowalski, Mrs. Grace (Leech). Monawing & Mamatwa. *Cloud Splitter*, Apr. 1941. 4:no.4:6–7.   268

Hudowalski, Mrs. Grace (Leech). Phantom falls. *Cloud Splitter*, Feb. 1940. 3:no.1:3, 5. Buttermilk Falls, Raquette River.   269

Hudowalski, Mrs. Grace (Leech). The Saranacs. *Cloud Splitter*, Mar. 1940. 3:no.2:5–6. Saranac Indians.   270

Hudowalski, Mrs. Grace (Leech). "This little tree." *Cloud Splitter*, Nov.–Dec. 1944. 7:no.6:2. Legend of pine tree.   271

Hudowalski, Mrs. Grace (Leech). A tribe is born. *Cloud Splitter*, May 1940. 3:no.4:4–5.   272

Hudowalski, Mrs. Grace (Leech). Wallface. *Cloud Splitter*, May 1939. 2:no.3:5.   273

Hudowalski, Mrs. Grace (Leech). Where is my home? *Cloud Splitter*, Apr. 1942. 5:no.4:14. Grief of Indians on being forced to leave Adirondacks.   274

Logan, John. The legend of Joe Indian lake. *No Country Life*, Summer 1951. 5:no.3:47–53. Reprinted from an unidentified newspaper clipping.   275

Rice, Charles LeRett. The Indian maiden of Saint Sacrament, a story. Also a brief study of Indian origin, religion and habits. n.p. n.pub. 1926. 52 leaves. Mimeographed. 276

Shorey, Archibald Thompson. The To-gesho. *Cloud Splitter*, June 1939. 2:no.4:14. Legendary Adirondack beast finally wiped out by Indians.   277

Sylvester, Nathaniel Bartlett. Indian legends of Saratoga and of the upper Hudson valley. Troy, N.Y. N.B. Sylvester & co. 1884. 47p. front. illus.   278

LOCAL HISTORY

Butler, Benjamin Clapp. Lake George and Lake Champlain from their first discovery to 1759. Albany, Weed, Parsons & co. 1868. 240p. 2d edition published in New York by Putnam, 1869.   279

Carpenter, Warwick Stevens. The summer paradise in history. Albany, Delaware & Hudson co. 1914. 128p. plates, fig. maps. "A compilation of fact and tradition covering Lake George, Lake Champlain, the Adirondack Mountains, and other sections reached by the rail and steamer lines of the Delaware and Hudson Company." A development of the "Literary and Historic Note Book" by Henry P. Phelps, 1907.   280

Chittenden, A.K. Report on Township 7, Adirondack league club preserve. Baltimore, Md. Chittenden & Patterson. n.d. 139p. map. Dated June 7, 1907.   281

Cleo's researches in local history. *For Leaves*, Autumn 1907. 4:no.3:4–19. illus. ports. William Constable, James Duane, etc.   282

Fouquet, L.M. comp. Lake Champlain, Lake George! the Adirondacs, Lake Memphremagog and Mount Mansfield. Burlington, Vt. R.S. Styles, 1867. 60p. maps. "The Adirondack material is taken from Street's 'Woods and Waters' " (Skinner).   283

Fynmore, Jim. The central Adirondacks. A picture story. Prospect, N.Y. Prospect books, 1955. unpaged. illus. Photographs with brief text. Preface by Howard Thomas. Reviewed by G.G. Cole in *North Country Life*, Summer 1955, 9:no.3:77–78. White Lake and Tupper Lake.   284

Hochschild, Harold K. Township 34: a history, with digressions, of an Adirondack township in Hamilton county in the State of New York. N.Y. Privately printed, 1952. 614p. illus. ports. maps (part folded). Reviewed by A.T. Shorey in *The Cloud Splitter*, Mar.–Apr. 1953, 16:no.2:9–10; by D.A. Plum in *The Ad-i-ron-dac*, Mar.–Apr. 1953, 17:40. In 1953 Mr. Hochschild issued a supplement: "Addendum to Chapter 13, p. 170A–170X." This contains Henry J. Raymond's letters on the Adirondacks, which first appeared in the *New York Times* in 1855.   285

Holden, Austin Wells. A history of the town of Queensbury in the State of New York, with biographical sketches of many of its distinguished men, and some account of the aborigines of northern New York. Albany, J. Munsell, 1874. 519p. front. plates, ports. illus. History of Lake Champlain in colonial times, p.269–508. Louis Fiske Hyde's "His-

tory of Glens Falls," privately printed, 1936, is based on Holden's History.   286

Lake Horicon (Lake George), Lake Champlain, Montreal and Quebec with a map and table of distances. Burlington, Vt. C. Goodrich & co. 1858. 48p. folded map.   287

Lamb, Wallace Emerson. Lake Champlain and Lake George valley. N.Y. American historical co. c1940. 3v. front. ports. illus. maps.   288

Lane, David F. Number 4. *Ad-i-ron-dac*, July–Aug. 1947. 11:no.4:8–10. illus. Brown's Tract.   289

Lane, David F. The Oswegatchie country. *Ad-i-ron-dac*, July–Aug. 1949. 13:76–81, 84. illus.   290

Morehouse union. Report of a committee appointed to examine the lands of A.K. Morehouse, esq. in Herkimer and Hamilton counties, State of New-York; together with the constitution, by-laws, etc. of the Morehouse union. N.Y. 1843? 24p. Piseco Lake area.   291

New York (state). Surveyor general. Report in relation to land owned by the state in the counties of Hamilton, Essex, Clinton, Franklin and St. Lawrence. Albany, 1839. 9p. Assembly document 382, 1839. By O.L. Holley.   292

New York (state). Surveyor general. Report relative to the proposed road from Salisbury-Centre to Racket Lake, and the sale and settlement of state land. Albany, 1840. 7p. Assembly document 153, 1840. Report by O.L. Holley on the value of state lands in Herkimer, Hamilton and Essex counties. 293

Parkman, Francis. Historic handbook of the northern tour; lakes George and Champlain; Niagara; Montreal; Quebec. Boston, Little, Brown, 1885. 180p. front. plates, ports. map. Reprinted in 1899.   294

Reed, William. Life on the border sixty years ago. Fall River, Mass. R. Adams, 1882. 120p. Lively account of life in the Macomb Purchase, No. 1 Tract, 1822–35. Hamilton County.   295

Ryan, Ernest E. comp. . . .Tales of the north country with pictures. . . Rouses Point, N.Y. Northern publishing co. 1942? unpaged. ports. illus.   296

Stephens, W. Hudson. Historical note of the settlement on No. 4, Brown's tract, in Watson, Lewis county, N.Y. With notes of the early settlers. . . Utica, N.Y. Roberts, 1864. 27p. front. (mounted port.). Reprinted in Donaldson's "History of the Adirondacks," v.2, p.260–71.   297

Van de Water, Frederic Franklyn. Lake Champlain and Lake George. . . Indianapolis & N.Y. Bobbs-Merrill co. 1946. 381p. plates, ports. facsims. (American Lakes Series, ed. by M.M. Quaife.) "Bibliographical note," p.358–62. 298

Walworth, Mrs. Ellen (Hardin). The edges of the Adirondacks. *For Leaves,* Winter 1909. 5:no.4:3–10. illus. Luzerne, Mt. McGregor, Saratoga. 299

THE CHAMPLAIN VALLEY

Allen, Joseph Dana. A journal of an excursion made by the corps of cadets of the A.L.S. & M. academy, Norwich, Vt. under the command of Capt. A. Partridge, June 1824. Windsor, Vt. S. Ide, 1824. 48p. Trip around Lake Champlain. 300

Along Champlain shores; a scenic route. *Motordom,* June 1933. p.11–12. 301

Anderson, George Pomeroy. Attractive Lake Champlain. *Land & Wat,* July 1898. n.s.3: 41–42. 302

Armstrong, L.O. Indian pageants on Lake Champlain. *Travel,* July 1909. 14:474–76. illus. 303

Auld, Joseph. Picturesque Burlington, a handbook of Burlington, Vermont and Lake Champlain. . . Burlington, Vt. Free press association, 1893. 190p. front. plates, illus. map. Champlain valley, p.1–34. 304

Bailey, Horace Ward. Historical booklet of the discovery of Lake Champlain. Montpelier, Vt. Lake Champlain tercentenary commission of Vermont, 1909. 30p. illus. maps. Also published in Newbury, Vt. 1909. Crown Point and Ticonderoga, p.16–20. 305

Beck, Raymond. An auto trip to Lake Champlain. *Travel,* July 1909. 14:481–82. illus. map. 306

Bedard, Joseph Armand. Was the Lake Champlain region entirely lost to the French with the downfall of French dominion in America? *NY State Hist Assn Proc,* 1910. 10: 79–94. 307

Bryce, Viscount James Bryce. University and historical addresses delivered during a residence in the United States as ambassador of Great Britain. N.Y. Macmillan, 1913. 433p. "The Tercentenary of the Discovery of Lake Champlain. Address delivered at Burlington, Vt. July 8, 1909," p.265–79. 308

Buckham, John Wright. Lake Champlain, historical and picturesque. *New Eng M,* July 1899. n.s.20:582–603. illus. map. 309

Bush, Robert. Champlain. *NYS Con,* Nov. 1947. 2:no.2:18–20. illus. map. 310

Campbell, Thomas Joseph. The first missionaries on Lake Champlain. *NY State Hist Assn Proc,* 1910. 10:127–38. port. 311

Champlain, Samuel de. Champlain's expeditions to northern and western New York, 1609–1615. *In* Documentary history of the State of New York. Albany, 1850. v.3, p.1–15. folded plate. 312

Champlain, Samuel de. Voyages of Samuel de Champlain, 1604–1618. Edited by W.L. Grant. N.Y. Scribner, 1907. 377p. plates, map. (Original Narratives of Early American History.) Discovery of Lake Champlain, p.161–66. 313

Champlain — greatest of inland lakes, wonderful motor ride along the shore of this historic lake, an inviting vacation center. *Motordom,* June 1929. 23:no.1:16–17. illus. 314

Champlain memorial lighthouse. *No Country Life,* Spring 1952. 6:no.2:31. illus. 315

Charlevoix, Pierre François Xavier de. History and general description of New France. Translated from the original edition and edited with notes, by Dr. John Gilmary Shea. . . N.Y. F.P. Harper, 1900. 6v. plates, fronts. ports. maps. Champlain's discovery of Lake Champlain and Lake George, including a reproduction of the Carte de la Rivière de Richelieu et du Lac Champlain, 1744, v.2, p.15–19. 316

Clarke, Grace M. Historic Lake Champlain. *Vermonter,* May 1908. 13:137–40. illus. map. 317

Clarke, John Mason. The setting of Lake Champlain history. *NY State Hist Assn Proc,* 1910. 10:56–66. Geologic history. 318

Cone, Gertrude E. Early life in the Champlain valley. *No Country Life,* Spring 1949. 3:no.2:35–37, 60–62. From her thesis (no.4392). 319

Coolidge, Guy Omeron. The French occupation of the Champlain valley from 1609 to 1750. *Ver Hist Soc Proc,* Sept. 1938. n.s.6:143–313. A forty-page biographical index follows the article. 320

Copeland, Fred O. Lake Champlain has a spell. *Vermonter,* Oct. 1939. 44:209–11. Historical notes. 321

Crockett, Walter Hill. The French in the Champlain valley. *New Eng M,* May 1901. n.s.24:322–29. 322

Crockett, Walter Hill. A history of Lake Champlain; a record of more than three centuries, 1609–1936. Burlington, Vt. McAuliffe co. 1937. 320p. plates, ports. double map. An earlier edition was published in Burlington by H.J. Shanley & Co. in 1909. 323

Cutting, Elisabeth. Samuel de Champlain and his lake. *NY Hist*, Apr. 1934. 15:175–83.   324

D'Arusmont, Mme. Frances (Wright). Views of society and manners in America... N.Y. E. Bliss & E. White, 1821. 387p. Plattsburgh and Lake Champlain, p.209–19.   325

Davies, William Gilbert. Ticonderoga and Crown Point. *In* Society of colonial wars, N.Y. Addresses delivered...and yearbook, 1906–07. New Haven, 1908? p.38–49. Also published in his "Papers and Addresses," N.Y. R.G. Cooke, Inc. 1907, p.95–108.   326

Duncan, John M. Travels through part of the United States and Canada in 1818 and 1819. Glasgow, University press, 1823. 2v. Lake Champlain, v.2, p.228–34.   327

Dwight, Timothy, 1752–1817. Travels in New-England and New-York. London, Baynes & son, 1823. 4v. port. folded maps. Journeys to Lake George and Crown Point, v.3, p.337ff.   328

Favreau, J. Arthur. La grande semaine; fêtes du troisième centenaire de la découverte du Lac Champlain... Worcester, Mass. Compagnie de publication Belisle, 1909. 194p. ports. illus. maps.   329

First conference of Lake Champlain historians, July 1, 1939. *Ver Hist Soc Proc*, Sept. 1939. n.s.7:185–204. For second conference see issue for Sept. 1940, n.s.8:282–301.   330

Ganley, Albert Charles. Land grants and settlement in the Champlain valley of New York, 1664–1800. 104 leaves. maps. Master's thesis, Cornell University, 1940. Typescript.   331

Gosselin, Auguste Honoré. Champlain et Hudson — la découverte du Lac Champlain, et celle de la Rivière Hudson. A l'occasion du Tricentenaire de ces deux événements, 1609–1909. *Roy Soc Canada Mem*, 1910. 3 ser.3: sect.1:87–110. Also issued as a separate. 332

Hall, Hiland. The New York Dellius patent. *Hist Mag*, Feb. 1868. ser.2:3:74–76. The grant, extending twenty miles north of Crown Point, included the tract bounded by Wood Creek and the Hudson River on the east.   333

Hanotaux, Gabriel. A speech delivered by his excellency...at a banquet given by the Lake Champlain association and the Tercentenary committee, May 1, 1912. N.Y.? 1912. 12p.   334

Hill, Henry Wayland. Lake Champlain. *Travel*, July 1909. 14:469–70. illus.   335

Historic points along Lake Champlain. *Motordom*. June 1932. p.30.   336

Holden, James Austin. The Half-way brook in history. *NY State Hist Assn Proc*, 1905. 6:169–89. plates. Town of Queensbury.   337

Keith, E.F. The Indian runner: a story of the early Adirondacks. *Fur-Fish-Game*, Sept. 1925. 42:no.3:89–90. Early settlers on Lake Champlain.   338

Kellogg, David Sherwood. Early mention of events and places in the valley of Lake Champlain. *Ver Hist Soc Proc*, 1901–2. p.51–64. Also in *Magazine of History*, Feb. 1905, 1:77–84.   339

Kellogg, Henry Theodore. Paper read at Split rock lighthouse, July 12, 1932. n.p. n.d. 11p. Copy in the Sherman Free Library, Port Henry.   340

Lake Champlain. *Fam Mag*, 1843. 8:306–7. illus. Interesting early description including a little material on the Adirondacks.   341

Lake Champlain. Extracted from the *Home Journal*. Montreal, 1857. 2 leaves.   342

Lake Champlain, longest of inland lakes, marvelous panoramas rim its shore, as history unrolls legends every American should know. *Motordom*, June 1930. 24:no.1:14–15. illus.
343

Lake Champlain — the glorious, noted for its scenic panoramas, with mountains on either shore, this 136-mile long lake is a vacationists' mecca. *Motordom*, June 1931. 24: no.12:17. illus.   344

Lake Champlain association. Yearbook. N.Y. 1910–26? Copies located for 1909/10–1913/14, 1916/17, 1920/21–1926/27.   345

Lape, Mrs. Jane (McCaughin). Champlain valley—the warpath of the nations. *NY State Hist Assn Bul*, Nov. 1945. 13:14–16. illus. 346

Lonergan, Carroll Vincent. The northern gateway, a history of Lake Champlain and guide to interesting places in the great valley. n.p. n.pub. c1939. 40p. front. ports. illus. maps. 2d printing, 1941. Revised and reprinted, 1950.   347

Mabie, Hamilton Wright. Story of Lake Champlain. *Outlook*, July 10, 1909. 92:593–605.   348

MacDonald, Archibald de Lery. The seigneurie of Alainville on Lake Champlain. Baltimore, 1929. 36p. (Order of Colonial Lords of Manors in America, New York. Publication no.20.)   349

Mather, Frederic Gregory. Summer days along Champlain. *Outing*, Aug. 1885. 6:524–30. As seen from a boat.   350

Moore, Pliny. Lake Champlain Location no. one; Journal of the preliminary survey, 1785. Champlain, New York. *Moors Ant*, Aug. 1938. 2:113–20. Lake Champlain Location no.1 was tract of 11,600 acres known as the Moorsfield Grant and patented to Pliny Moore. The *Journal* was kept during the survey. 351

Murray, William Henry Harrison. Lake Champlain and its shores. Boston, De Wolfe, Fiske & co. c1890. 261p. front.   352

New York (state). Commerce, Dept. of. Lake Champlain. *No Country Life*, Summer 1950. 4:no.3:33–34. illus.   353

New York (state). Lake Champlain tercentenary commission. The Champlain tercentenary. Final report. . .prepared by Henry Wayland Hill. . . Albany, J.B. Lyon, 1913. 325p. front. plates, port. Contents differ from those of the 1911 report (no.355).   354

New York (state). Lake Champlain tercentenary commission. The Champlain tercentenary. Report. . .prepared by Henry Wayland Hill. Albany, J.B. Lyon, 1911. 534p. plates, facsims. plans, ports. folded maps. Appendix includes "Geology of the Champlain Valley," by John M. Clarke; "Episodes in the History of the Champlain Valley," by F.H. Severance. The 2d edition of this report, noted above, contains the appendix and an analytical index by C.A. Nelson.   355

New York (state). Lake Champlain tercentenary commission. Report transmitted to the Legislature Mar. 23, 1908. Albany, J.B. Lyon, 1908. 22p. Senate document 28, 1908.   356

New York (state). University. . . . Lake Champlain tercentenary. . . Albany, 1909. 32p. illus. map. For descriptions of the Tercentenary see the following articles: Brilliant Commemoration, *Outlook*, June 12, 1909, 92: 351–52; Celebrating at Lake Champlain, *Current Literature*, Aug. 1909, 47:115–20; Crockett, Walter Hill. The Lake Champlain Tercentenary, *Vermonter*, Aug. 1908, 13:229– 30; In Memory of a Great Explorer, *Harper's Weekly*, July 3, 1909, 53:16; Spectator, pseud. Champlain Celebration, *Outlook*, July 31, 1909, 92:784–86; 1609–1909. The Lake Champlain Tercentenary. . . *Travel*, July 1909, 14:483–86.   357

Newton, Hilah Foote. Horses and steamboats on Champlain. *NY Folk Q*, Feb. 1945. 1:33– 45.   358

Nye, Mary Greene. Tories in the Champlain valley. *Ver Hist Soc Proc*, Sept. 1941. n.s.9: 197–203.   359

O'Brien, Edward C. Lake Champlain historical pageant review — 1923. *In* New York state waterways association. 13th Annual convention. 1922. p.86–89.   360

O'Brien, Michael J. Early Irish settlers in the Champlain valley. *Recorder*, Sept. 1927. 4:1–4.   361

The one hundred and fiftieth anniversary of the American revolution in the Crown Point area. . . Crown Point state park, July 4,

1927. . . Albany, Fort Orange press, 1927. 40p. illus.   362

Owen, Robert Emmet. Sketches of Fort Ticonderoga and vicinity. Baltimore, Printed for Fort Ticonderoga museum by Williams & Wilkins, 1924? 48p. illus. Another edition, undated, published by the Troy Times Art Press. Drawings with brief text.   363

Paine, Silas H. Soldiers of the Champlain valley. *NY State Hist Assn Proc*, 1919. 17:301– 428.   364

Palmer, Peter Sailly. History of Lake Champlain, from its first exploration by the French in 1609, to the close of the year 1814. Plattsburgh, N.Y. J.W. Tuttle, 1853. 223p. maps. 2d edition, Albany, J. Munsell, 1866. Issued also on large paper, in an edition of fifty copies. 3d edition, N.Y. Lovell, n.d.   365

Parkman, Francis. A half-century of conflict. Boston, Little, Brown, 1899. 2v. plates, ports. Many references to Lake George, Lake Champlain and Ticonderoga.   366

Pomeroy, S.G. The historical significance of the Champlain tercentenary. *New Eng M*, July 1909. n.s.40:560–69.   367

Pyle, Howard. Through inland waters. *Harper*, May–June 1896. 92:828–39; 93:63–75. illus. Trip up the Hudson and through Lake Champlain.   368

Richards, Frederick Bascom. Historic Champlain valley, beauty of scenery is not all Lake Champlain has to offer the tourist. *Up-Stater*, Nov. 1929. 1:no.6:10, 23, 30. illus.   369

Royce, Mrs. Caroline Halstead (Barton). The first century of Lake Champlain. N.Y. Miller press, 1909. 14 leaves. plates.   370

Rutland railroad co. Across the islands of Lake Champlain. N.Y. Chasmar-Winchell, 190— 81p.   371

Saunders, A.M. Important review of pioneer incidents (Lake Champlain). *Vermonter*, June– July 1933. 38:148–51. Includes historical notes.   372

Schott, Charles Anthony. Fluctuations in the level of Lake Champlain and average height of its surface above the sea. *In* U.S. Coast and geodetic survey. Report, June 1887. p.165– 72. charts, tables.   373

Shattuck, Louis Edgar. The coming Lake Champlain tercentenary celebration. *Travel*, June 1909. 14:396–98. illus.   374

Smith, John Talbot. Lake Champlain, its associations and its beauties. *Travel*, July 1909. 14:471–73. illus.   375

Spargo, John. Behold, the splendor of Champlain! An address. . .June 14, 1938. Burlington, Vt. Lane press, inc. 1938. 13p.   376

Steele, David McConnell. Vacationing in the Lake Champlain country. *Travel*, June 1918. 31:no.2:31–33, 42. illus.   377

Stevens, Franklin G. A family legend of Lake Champlain. *No Country Life*, Fall 1949. 3:no.4: 48–50.   378

Stoddard, Seneca Ray. Historic Lake Champlain. *St No Mo*, July 1906. 1:no.3:9–16. illus.   379

Stuart, James. Three years in North America. . . Edinburgh, Robert Cadell, 1833. 2v. front. (folded map). Lake George and Lake Champlain, v.1, p.164–88.   380

Talbot, Francis Xavier. The blood stained trail of Isaac Jogues. *America*, Sept. 17, 1932. 47:565–67. Visit to Lake Champlain and Lake George.   381

Ter-centenary of Lake Champlain, 1609–1909. n.p. n.pub. n.d. 34p. illus.   382

Thomas, John M. The worth to a nation of a sense for its past. *NY State Hist Assn Proc*, 1910. 10:71–78. Sites of Fort Frederick and Fort Amherst as a state park.   383

Torrey, Joseph. The discovery and occupation of Lake Champlain. A paper read before the Vermont historical society. . .Oct. 16, 1860. *Ver Hist Soc Proc*, 1860. 21:13–27.   384

Tuckerman, Henry Theodore. Lake Champlain. *Atlan*, Sept. 1866. 18:365–66.   385

Tuttle, Maria Jeannette Brookings. Three centuries in Champlain valley; a collection of historical facts and incidents. Tercentenary edition. Plattsburgh, N.Y. Saranac chapter, D.A.R. 1909. 485p. front. illus. ports.   386

Van de Water, Frederic Franklyn. Glimpses of Champlain history. *Am Heritage*, Sept. 1949. n.s.1:20–23. illus. port. map.   387

Vermont. Lake Champlain tercentenary commission. The tercentenary celebration of the discovery of Lake Champlain and Vermont. A report to the General assembly of the State of Vermont. Montpelier, Vt. Capital city press, 1910. 167p. plates, port. map.   388

Vermont. Lake Champlain tercentenary commission. The tercentenary celebration of the discovery of Lake Champlain and Vermont, final report of the Vermont commission: French delegation visit America, presentation of Rodin bust "La France," dedication of Champlain memorial. n.p. 1914. 24p. front. plates. Cover title: Champlain, 1609–1909, Final Report.   389

Vidal de la Blache, Paul. Une journée aux bords du Lac Champlain. Paris, Firmin, 1912. 15p.   390

Walsh, James Joseph. Catholic pioneers along Lake Champlain. *For Leaves*, Autumn 1909. 6:no.3:22–29. illus. port.   391

Walworth, Hiram. A legend of the Saranac. *Am Hist Register*, Oct. 1894. 1:159–66. illus. Story of Charles de Fredenberg.   392

Watson, Winslow Cossoul. The occupation of the Champlain valley. *Am Hist Rec*, May 1872. 1:200–4. map.   393

Watson, Winslow Cossoul. Pioneer history of the Champlain valley; being an account of the settlement of the town of Willsborough by William Gilliland, together with his journal and other papers. . . Albany, J. Munsell, 1863. 231p. (Munsell's Local American History, 1.)   394

Weld, Isaac Jr. Travels through the states of North America. . .during the years 1795, 1796 and 1797; 4th ed. . . London, Stockdale, 1807. 2v. Journey from Albany to St. Johns, v.1, p.274–304. Descriptions of Skenesborough, Lake Champlain, etc.   395

Wilkins, F.H. General items about Lake Champlain. *Vermonter*, Oct. 1915. 20:217–18. Notes of historical interest.   396

THE HUDSON

Bayle, Francis L. History of the Tahawus region. *High Spots*, July 1932. 9:no.3:11–15. Includes extract from Masten's "Story of Adirondac."   397

Beach, Nelson John. 101 years ago. *Cloud Splitter*, June 1942. 5:no.6:5–6. Letter written by Beach in 1841 from the Adirondack Iron Works. For brief sketch of Beach, see p.BB.   398

Bowen, Croswell. Great river of the mountains: the Hudson. N.Y. Hastings house, c1941. 94p. illus. The first 21 pages of pictures are on the Adirondack area.   399

Bruce, Wallace. The Hudson: three centuries of history, romance and invention. N.Y. Bryant union, c1907. 224p. illus. plates, front. folded maps. Centennial edition.   400

Bruce, Wallace. The Hudson river by daylight. N.Y. G. Watson, c1873. 165p. illus. plates, folded map. Adirondacks, p.109–16. Another edition published in 1882, 182p., contains "From Saratoga to the Adirondacks," p.138–53.   401

Carmer, Carl Lamson. The Hudson. *Holiday*, Sept. 1949. 6:no.3:34–41, 82–83. illus. (part. col.). Includes portrait of "Yankee John" Galusha.   402

Carter, Robert. The source of the Hudson. *Appleton*, Mar. 12, 1870. 3:281–82. illus. 403

Greene, Nelson, ed. History of the valley of the Hudson, river of destiny, 1609–1930. Chicago, S.J. Clarke publishing co. 1931. 5v. plates, ports.   404

Hoffman, Charles Fenno. Scenes at the sources of the Hudson. *NY Mirror*, Oct. 7–28,

Dec. 16, 1837. 15:118–19, 124–25, 132, 140–41, 193–94. Signed: C.F.H. Contents: 1. Lake Henderson. A Primitive Forest. A Staunch Woodsman. A Hunter's Camp. The Indian Pass. 2. Village of McIntyre. Earthquakes. Forest Scenes. Hunters' Stories. 3. Mt. Marcy. A Wolf Fight. The Wounded Huntsman. A Generous Hound. 4. Crusting Moose. Withing a Buck. 5. The Dead-clearing.   405

Johnson, Clifton. The picturesque Hudson ... N.Y. Macmillan, 1909. 227p. incl. col. front. plates. (Picturesque River Series.) From Saratoga to source, p.199–227.   406

Lossing, Benson John. The Hudson, from the wilderness to the sea... N.Y. Virtue & Yorston, 1866. 464p. front. illus. Also published in Troy, by H.B. Nims & Co. 1866. 3d edition, 1872. Originally published in *The Art Journal* (London) 1860–61. n.s. v.6–7. Adirondacks, p.1–58.   407

Longstreth, Thomas Morris. The sources of picturesque rivers. I. The Hudson. *Country Life,* June 1922. 42:no.2:60–61. illus.   408

Milbert, Jacques Gerard. Itinéraire pittoresque du Fleuve Hudson et des parties latérales de l'Amérique du Nord, d'après les dessins originaux pris sur les lieux... Paris, Henri Gaugain et cie. 1828–29. 2v. Section 5: "Excursion dans les montagnes aux sources de l'Hudson." The author visited Lake George, Lake Champlain, Schroon Lake.   409

Nelson's Illustrated guide to the Hudson and its tributaries... N.Y. T. Nelson & sons, 1860. 202p. col. front. col. plates (part folded).   410

The river Hudson, together with descriptions and illustrations of the city of New York, Catskill mountains, Lake George, Lake Champlain, Saratoga. N.Y. Ross & Tousey, 1859. 63p. illus. map.   411

Stoddard, Seneca Ray. The headwaters of the Hudson. *Outing,* Oct. 1885. 7:58–63.   412

Van Vorst, Marie. The Hudson river. *Harper,* Mar. 1905. 110:543–54. illus. Includes the headwaters.   413

Van Vorst, Marie. The Indian trail. *Harper Baz,* July–Aug. 1908. 42:653–58, 744–48. illus. Trip along the Indian trail between Lake Placid and Lake Henderson; by a woman reporter assigned to write on the source of the Hudson River.   414

A visit to the States. A reprint of letters from the special correspondent of the Times. 1st–2d ser. London, G.E. Wright, 1887–88. 2v. The Hudson River, v.2, p.83–87. Source of the Hudson.   415

LAKES AND STREAMS

Adirondack Jim's partner. *For & Stream,* Oct. 4, 1883. 21:186. Reprinted from *The Sun.* Winter at Long Lake.   416

Allen, J.C. Romance of two ponds: Potter pond and Sargent pond. *For & Stream,* Nov. 24, 1894. 43:448.   417

Amateur, pseud. Saranac route. *For & Stream,* June 24, Sept. 30, 1875. 4:307; 5:114. Description of trips made in 1860 and 1868.
                                          418

Appleton, Thomas Gold. Life and letters of Thomas Gold Appleton. Prepared by Susan Hale. N.Y. Appleton, 1885. 348p. front. (port.). Trip to Upper Saranac Lake in 1859, p.312–15.   419

Beetle, David Harold. West Canada creek. Utica, N.Y. Observer-Dispatch, 1946. 158p. plates, front. port. Reviewed in *The Cloud Splitter,* Mar.–Apr. 1947. 10:no.2:6.   420

Benedict, Darwin. Postman takes a boat! *Cloud Splitter,* July–Aug. 1948. 11:no.4:3–4. Floating post office on the Fulton Chain. 421

Boyd. Blue mountain lake, Adirondacks. *For & Stream,* July 2, 1874. 2:323.   422

Brown-Serman, W. A mountain-lake idyl; Raquette lake — St. Hubert's isle. The Adirondacks. *Four Tr News,* July 1905. 9:20–23. illus.   423

Bruce, Dwight Hall. The Cranberry lake country. *For & Stream,* Aug. 27, 1891. 37:103. Signed: D.H.B. Discussion of changes in the area.   424

Bryan, Charles W. Jr. The Raquette — river of the forest. *No Country Life,* Fall 1950–Spring 1951. 4:no.4:4–9; 5:no.1:24–29; 5:no.2:20–25. illus. map.   425

Bulger, John D. Big Tupper. *NYS Con,* Apr.–May 1951. 5:no.5:18–19. illus.   426

Bulger, John D. Raquette lake. *NYS Con,* Oct.–Nov. 1950. 5:no.2:14–15. illus.   427

Bush, Robert. Sacandaga; man-made home for record fish. *NYS Con,* Aug.–Sept. 1947. 2:no.1:16–17. illus. map. Reprinted in *North Country Life,* Summer 1948, 2:no.3:30–31, 45. Author listed as Rush.   428

C., A. A red letter day. *For Leaves,* Summer 1904. 1:no.3:38–41. illus. port. Visit to Third and Fourth lakes of the Fulton Chain.   429

Charming lakes in western Adirondacks; Star, Cranberry and Bonaparte lakes, pretty camping spots. *Motordom,* June 1929. 23:no.1:36. illus.   430

Collins, John O. The spirit of the woods. *Four Tr News,* Dec. 1902. 3:249–50. illus. Fulton Chain.   **431**

Cranberry lake motor boat club. Cranberry lake, New York and the western Adirondack region, by James Foster Wilcox. Cranberry Lake, N.Y. 1915. 64p. illus. map.   432

Crary, John C. Tunney developing wallop at Lake Pleasant, Gene's training there helped to win him pugilistic crown — now training for the Tom Heeney fight. *Motordom*, June 1928. 22:no.1:6–7. illus. ports.   433

Curtiss, Arthur Leslie Byron-. The roaring harmony of nature. *No Country Life*, Winter 1954. 8:no.1:11–13. Black River experiences.   434

Davison, J.L. In the Adirondacks in 1858. *For & Stream*, Apr. 22, 1911. 76:613–14. Along the Raquette River.   435

A day at Long lake. *Knick Mag*, June 1860. 55:578–82.   436

Denslow, Van Buren. The Raquette in '55. *Am Mag*, May 1887. 6:3–17. illus. Trip to Raquette River area.   437

Deuel, Charles L. Upper Saranac lake. *NYS Con*, Aug.–Sept. 1950. 5:no.1:26–27. illus.   438

Fish, Mrs. Gretchen (Houghton). History of Indian lake, by Gretchen M. Houghton. *NY State Hist Assn Proc*, 1916. 16:268–75. Prize essay, by student from Indian Lake High School. Also in "Indian Lake High School — 1914," p.5–10.   439

Fish, Mrs. Gretchen (Houghton). Indian lake. *NYS Con*, Apr.–May 1948. 2:no.5:20. map. Reprinted in *North Country Life*, Winter 1952, 6:no.1:55–59.   440

Fitch, Morton Cross. History of Ragged lake in Franklin county, New York. Providence, R.I. 1934. 214p. Mimeographed. Personalities, anecdotes. History of the Owl's Head area. 45 copies issued. Copy in New York State Library.   441

Fosburgh, Peter W. Lake Placid. *NYS Con*, Dec. 1948–Jan. 1949. 3:no.3:22–23. illus.   442

From Gravesend bay to Lake Champlain by way of river and canal. *For & Stream*, Jan. 18, 1902. 58:54.   443

Fuller, A.R. Winter in the Adirondacks. *For & Stream*, Jan. 4, 1883. 19:444. Meacham Lake in winter.   444

The Fulton chain of lakes. *NYS Con*, Oct.–Nov. 1954. 9:no.2:22–23. Map with brief text.   445

Gaither, Harry N. The rock of life. *Conservationist*, Sept. 1920. 3:138–39. illus. Reprinted in *State Service*, Jan. 1921, 5:60–61. Visit to Paradox Lake.   446

Galligan, J.P. Canada lake. *NYS Con*, June–July 1954. 8:no.6:6. Map with brief text.   447

Gavin, Joseph W. Love murder at Big Moose lake. *Mast Detect Mag*, Nov.–Dec. 1929, Jan. 1930. 1:no.3:22–26, 79–80; 1:no.4:20–22, 79–82; 1:no.5:39–41, 70–73. illus. ports.   448

H., Ed M. Schroon lake. *For & Stream*, May 29, 1884. 22:349. Schroon Lake as a resort.   449

Harmes, Edward A. Moose river country. *Ad Mt Club Bul*, July–Aug. 1944. 8:no.4:4, 10.   450

Have you visited these lovely lakes? *Motordom*, June 1932. p.28. Limekiln, Otter, Thirteenth and Seventh lakes.   451

Hoppin, G.M. The Adirondac lakes. *Broad Mag*, Mar. 1869. ser.2:2:263–69.   452

Hungerford, Edward. Black river, its praises are least sung. *No Country Life*, Summer 1947. 1:no.3:19–20. Reprinted from *The Yorker*.   453

Hunter, pseud. The Oswegatchie country. *For & Stream*, Sept. 2, 1875. 5:50. Description of various lakes, etc. How to reach it. 454

Hurley, Donal and Hurley, Richard. A trip through the Fulton chain, plenty of variety in trip by auto up past White and Otter lakes, then by boat from First to Fourth lakes. *Motordom*, Apr. 1927. 20:no.11:2–3. illus. 455

In the Saranac country; world famous resorts lure the traveler to delights of lake and mountain. *Motordom*, June 1930. 24:no.1:26. illus.   456

Juvenal, pseud. The Adirondacks. *For & Stream*, July 15, 1905. 65:46. News from Blue Mountain Lake.   457

Juvenal, pseud. Appreciation of nature. *For & Stream*, Oct. 19, 1907. 69:612. Prof. J.M. Taylor of Colgate University raising fund to build observation tower on top of Blue Mountain.   458

Juvenal, pseud. The tower on Blue mountain. *For & Stream*, Nov. 28, 1909. 71:850. illus. Description of tower built from public subscription.   459

K., F.D. The old days in the woods. *For Leaves*, Dec. 1903. 1:18–20. illus. Reminiscences of the Upper Saranac in the 1860's.   460

Kerst, Dwinal G. Schroon lake. *NYS Con*, Apr.–May 1950. 4:no.5:22–23. illus.   461

Knox, John. Piseco lake. *NYS Con*, June–July 1949. 3:no.6:16–17. Reprinted in *North Country Life*, Summer 1951, 5:no.3:34–35.   462

The lakes of the wilderness. *Gr Rep Mo*, Apr. 1859. 1:335–50. illus.   463

Lane, David F. Cranberry lake — nature's paradise. *Ad-i-ron-dac*, Sept.–Oct. 1947. 11: no.5:8–11. illus.   464

The Lime kiln nature lovers. *Ang & Hunt*, Sept. 1910. 2:484, 486. illus. Limekiln Lake. 465

Long lake. *For & Stream*, Mar. 29, 1883. 20: 173. Long Lake area as a sports center. 466

Lyman, Alexander Steele. On Lake Placid. *NYC Lines Mag*, Sept. 1924. 5:no.6:30. 467

Malcolm, James. Sacandaga dam creates another Lake George in the Adirondacks. *Motordom*, Mar. 1929. 22:no.10:12–13. illus. 468

Marshall, Robert. History of the Cranberry lake region. *Camp Log*, Dec. 1922. p.61–64. illus. 469

Mather, Fred. Wilmurt lake. *For & Stream*, Dec. 11, 1884. 23:389–90. 470

Merritt, Edwin Atkins. Maps of the Racket river and its headwaters, with descriptions of the several routes to the principal bodies of water. Albany, Weed, Parsons & co. 1860. 12p. folded map. 471

Miller, Roland B. Blue mountain lake. *NYS Con*, Oct.–Nov. 1949. 4:no.2:12–13. illus. Reprinted in *North Country Life*, Spring 1955, 9:no.2:36–39, 54. 472

Miller, Roland B. Long lake. *NYS Con*, Oct.– Nov. 1948. 3:no.2:22–23. illus. map. Reprinted in *North Country Life*, Winter 1954, 8:no.1:26–29. 473

Moore, Mrs. N. Hudson. On the Fulton chain. *Four Tr News*, June 1904. 6:363–65. illus. 474

Moose river — do you know it? *Ad-i-ron-dac*, Nov. 1945. 9:no.5:3. Area threatened by Higley and Panther Mountain reservoirs. 475

Morrell, T.S. Sunday in the north woods. *Am Angler*, Nov. 4, 1882. 2:291–93. Signed: Old Izaak. Reprinted from *Chicago Field*. Sunday spent on Long Lake. 476

Mulholland, William D. Cranberry lake. *NYS Con*, Aug. 1946. 1:no.1:10–11. illus. map. 477

Northern scenes and summer skies. View book of the lower Ausable valley. Keeseville, N.Y. Essex county publishing co. n.d. 60p. illus. Copy in the Munson Collection, Saranac Lake Free Library. 478

O'Donnell, Thomas Clay. Birth of a river: an informal history of the headwaters of the Black river. Boonville, N.Y. Black river books, 1952. 158p. illus. Reviewed by Barbara K. Bird in *North Country Life*, Fall 1952, 6:no.4: 53–54, 57. 479

Pearce, W.A. Big Moose lake *NYS Con*, Aug.– Sept. 1955. 10:no.1:9. map. 480

Pearce, W.A. Fourth lake in the Fulton chain. *NYS Con*, Feb.–Mar. 1953. 7:no.4:11. Map with information about fishing etc. 481

Peightal, J.M. Saranac locks. *NYS Con*, Feb.– Mar. 1952. 6:no.4:18. illus. Correction by Fred Derby in Apr.–May issue, p.39. 482

Persons, Joseph. Brant lake; scenic, historic and a sportsman's paradise. *Top o' the World*, Feb. 1939. 3:no.1:6. 483

Pfeiffer, Martin. Paradox lake. *NYS Con*, Feb.–Mar. 1954. 8:no.4:12. Map with descriptive notes. 484

Portsa, pseud. Honnedaga (Jock's) lake. *For & Stream*, Apr. 9, 1891. 36:231. Adirondack League Club's tract. 485

The president's retreat. *Harper W*, June 11, 1887. 31:419, 424. illus. Cleveland's summer retreat on Saranac Lake. 486

R., S.C. Upper Chateaugay lake. *For & Stream*, Sept. 24, 1885. 25:163. 487

The Saranac country; scenic loveliness in the circle of the mountains; three lakes share the fame of this section, Saranac Lake village noted health resort. *Motordom*, June 1929. 23:no.1:26–28. illus. 488

The Saranac country — where great trails meet — hub of the fine highways circling the Adirondacks; this region combines unusual mountain vistas, with lake and forest delights a goal of the motorist, mountain climber, sportsman and rest seeker. *Motordom*, June 1931. 24:no.12:20, 34. illus. 489

Saranac Guide, pseud. Seymour's island. *For & Stream*, Sept. 15, 1881. 17:124. Notes from Blue Mountain Lake. 490

Schaefer, Paul A. Beyond Moose river plains. *Ad-i-ron-dac*, Mar.–Apr. 1946. 10:no.2:8–9. 491

Schaefer, Paul A. A last citadel of the wilderness. *Bul Schools*, Mar. 1948. 34:213–16. illus. Moose River plains. 492

Schaefer, Paul A. Siamese ponds region. *Ad Mt Club Bul*, July–Aug. 1944. 8:no.4:5, 10. Indian Lake, Nut Creek, Wells and Speculator rectangle. 493

Schaefer, Paul A. Wings over Moose river. *Cloud Splitter*, Nov.–Dec. 1945. 8:no.6:3–4. Moose River country seen from the air. 494

Scribner, Frank Kimball and Mayo, Earl W. In the land of the loon. London & N.Y. F.T. Neely, c1889. 238p. front. plates. Cranberry Lake country. 495

Seagears, Clayton B. New York's sporting spots — the Oswegatchie. *NYS Con*, Aug.– Sept. 1955. 10:no.1:48–49. col. illus. 496

Shorey, Archibald Thompson. We trek to Moose river plains. *Cloud Splitter*, Nov.–Dec. 1946. 9:no.6:2–3. 497

Shorey, Archibald Thompson. West Canada lake revisited. *Cloud Splitter*, July–Aug. 1946. 9:no.4:18–19.   498

Smith, Clarence C. The central Adirondacks. *Up-Stater*, July 1930. 2:no.4:5, 14. illus. Fulton Chain.   499

Spears, Eldridge A. A visit to West Canada lakes. *For & Stream*, Aug. 3, 1907. 69:175.   500

Splendid entrances to this scenic region. *Motordom*, June 1932. p.17–18. illus. map. Blue Mountain Lake and Long Lake area.   501

Stoddard, Seneca Ray. Into the western wilds. *St No Mo*, Aug. 1908. 4:122–35. illus. Trip to Fulton Chain and Raquette Lake.   502

Thomas, Howard. Jock's lake. *Up Mo*, Nov. 1941. 2:no.8:22. illus. History of Honnedaga Lake.   503

Tidying up the Adirondacks for the president. *Lit Digest*, June 19, 1926. 89:no.12:32, 37–40. illus. Description of White Pine Camp, near Saranac Lake, President Coolidge's summer home.   504

Tupper lake, a wildwood gem. *Motordom*, June 1934. p.21. illus.   505

Tupper lake — in the forest primeval. *Motordom*, June 1932. p.19. illus.   506

Tupper lake, site of Veteran's mountain camp. *Motordom*, June 1930. 24:no.1:40. 507

Tupper lake in the forest heart, famed hunting and fishing region, surrounding one of the largest Adirondack lakes. *Motordom*, June 1931. 24:no.12:21. illus.   508

Webb, William L. and Patric, Earl F. Rich lake. *NYS Con*, Aug.–Sept. 1955. 10:no.1:41. map.   509

Wing, Ralph K. Hard lines in the Adirondacks. *For & Stream*, July 28, 1887. 29:6. Trip by boat on Raquette River.   510

Zilliox, Robert G. Meacham lake. *NYS Con*, Oct.–Nov. 1955. 10:no.2:19. map.   511

Ausable Chasm

Ausable chasm. *Amat Nat*, July 1907. 4:76–77. Reprinted from *Good Housekeeping*.   512

Ausable chasm. N.Y. F.W. Robinson co. 193—? 12 leaves. illus. Cover title. Copy in Yale University Library.   513

Ausable chasm, a great wonderland. *Motordom*, June 1931. 24:no.12:23. illus.   514

Ausable chasm, a great wonderland; majestic gorge, most noted in the east, gives motorists scenic adventures. *Motordom*, June 1930. 24:no.1:28. illus.   515

Ausable chasm; the Grand Canyon of the east. *Motordom*, June 1929. 23:no.1:30–32. illus.   516

Bonsall, J. Glen of the Adirondacks: AuSable chasm. *Potter Am Mo*, June 1878. 10:401–8.   517

Bryant, Fitch C. Through Ausable chasm. *Travel*, Aug. 1909. 14:525–27. illus.   518

Creegan, L.J. Ausable chasm, the Adirondacks, New York. *Photo-Era*, Apr. 1924. 52:201–3. illus.   519

Guide to Ausable chasm. N.Y. Terwilliger & Peck, 1880? 12p. map.   520

Have you seen Ausable chasm? *Motordom*, June 1932. p.20. illus.   521

MacCalla, Clifford Paynter. Au Sable chasm. "The gate of the Adirondacks." *Scrib Mo*, June 1874. 8:192–98. illus.   522

A new span for Ausable chasm; modern engineering has accomplished the feat of bridging the world famous gorge. *Motordom*, Dec. 1933. p.5. illus.   523

New York (state). Forest, fish and game commission. The Ausable chasm. Special report. . .December 26, 1902. Transmitted to the Legislature March 4, 1903. Albany, Argus co. 1903. 12p. folded table. Assembly document 26, 1903. Survey to be made; possibility of the state's acquiring the land.   524

Porter, Mrs. Marjorie (Lansing). AuSable chasm in story and legend. Elizabethtown, N.Y. Denton press, 1954. 28p. illus. Reviewed by D.A. Plum in *The Ad-i-ron-dac*, Jan.–Feb. 1955, 19:20.   525

Resser, Charles Elmer. Evolution of Ausable chasm. *Sci Mo*, Jan. 1942. 54:29–42. illus. map.   526

Rooney, John Jerome. Ausable chasm. *For Leaves*, Spring 1907. 4:no.1:10–12. illus.   527

Stoddard, Seneca Ray. Au Sable chasm. *St No Mo*, Aug. 1907. 2:243–49. illus.   528

Taylor, Frank Hamilton. "Away down east"; or, My unexpected vacation. N.Y. Leve & Alden, 18—? 47p. illus. "A Side Trip to Au Sable Chasm," p.34–37.   529

Trumbull, Mrs. E.E. A visit to Ausable chasm. *Guide to Nature*, May 1911. 4:28–30. illus.   530

Lake George

Addresses at the presentation of an Indian statue. *NY State Hist Assn Q*, Jan. 1922. 3:30–35. Addresses by George D. Pratt and Dixon Ryan Fox.   531

Benjamin, Samuel Greene Wheeler. Lake George. *Harper*, Aug. 1879. 59:321–39. illus.   532

Budlong, Percy E. Two days on Lake George. *For & Stream*, Apr. 6, 1907. 68:531. Two-day cruise around the lake. 533

Collier, Edward A. Lake George from a rowboat. *Outing*, July 1882. 1:1–3. illus. 534

Curtis, George William. Lotus eating: a summer book. Illustrated by Kensett. . . N.Y. Harper, 1852. 206p. illus. Lake George, p.127–42. 535

Dwight, Timothy. Approach of evening on Lake George. *In* Griswold, R.W. Prose writers of America. 4th ed. Philadelphia, A. Hart, 1852. p.82. 536

Farnham, Charles Haight. Parkman at Lake George. *Scrib M*, July 1901. 30:22–30. Pages from Parkman's diary, 1842. 537

Fort William Henry hotel, Lake George, N.Y. Lake George, descriptive and historical sketches. Lake George, N.Y. T. Roessle & son, 1885. 26p. illus. 538

Hall, Eugene J. The gem of America. *Four Tr News*, Aug. 1902. 3:49–53. illus. 539

Harris, Capt. E.S. Lake George. All about it. By the veteran ex-captain of the steamers that run from the head to the foot. The lake, its shores, bays, mountains and islands. Described in his own style and manner. Edited and published by J.W. Adams of Glens Falls. Glens Falls, N.Y. Glens Falls Republican, 1903. 29p. Copy in the Henry E. Huntington Library, San Marino, Cal. 540

Hopkins, Arthur S. Lake George. Albany, N.Y. state conservation dept. 1955. 23p. illus. folded map. (Recreation Circular, no.6.) Earlier editions published in 1920, 1932, 1935, 1937, 1949. 541

Hopkins, Arthur S. Lake George land of beauty and joy; what the state has done to make a famous pleasure resort more accessible to the people; historical spots abound and add to the lore. *State Service*, Aug.–Sept. 1921. 5:357–63. illus. 542

James, H. Jr. Lake George. *Nation*, Aug. 25, 1870. 11:119–20. Unsigned. 543

Kemp, James Furman. Physiography of Lake George. *NY Acad Sci Ann*, Oct. 21, 1901. 14: 141–42. Abstract in *Science*, Nov. 15, 1901, 14:774. 544

King, Charles Clifford. Andia-ta-roc-te, "Where the mountains close in." Hudson Falls, N.Y. Swigert press, 1935. 67p. illus. port. plans. 545

Lake George. *Putnam*, Aug. 1857. 10:145–61. illus. 546

Lake George. A descriptive and historical sketch. Lake George, N.Y. T.E. Roessle, 1887. 17p. plate, map. 547

Lake George — center of rarest beauties. Here motor trails meet at the door of the mountains with famous points all about. *Motordom*, June 1930. 24:no.1:10–11. illus. 548

Lake George — queen of American lakes. *Motordom*, Aug. 1928. 22:no.3:4–6. illus. 549

Lake George, queen of American lakes, one of the gayest and most diverting of summer places. *Motordom*, June 1929. 23:no.1:12–13. illus. 550

Lake George — the enchanted, called the American Como; this beautiful resort offers the widest diversions, scenic and historic, with gay summer colonies around its borders. *Motordom*, June 1931. 24:no.12:16. illus. 551

Lake George charms the eye. *Motordom*, June 1934. p.8–9. illus. 552

Lake George island camps. *For & Stream*, July 4, 1889. 32:487. 553

Lamb, Wallace Emerson. Historic Lake George; Father Jogues edition. Glens Falls, N.Y. Glens Falls Post co. 1946. 76p. plates, maps. 554

Lamb, Wallace Emerson. Lake George. Facts and anecdotes. Glens Falls, N.Y. Glens Falls Post co. c1934. 52p. front. illus. map. 2d edition published in 1938. 555

Letter from Caldwell, Lake George. *Presbyterian*, Sept. 5, 1863. 33:141. Signed: Z. 556

Levitt, Saul. Lake George. *Holiday*, Sept. 1950. 8:no.3:98–101. illus. 557

Martineau, Harriet. Retrospect of western travel. London, Saunders & Otley, 1838. 3v. Lake George, v.3, p.263–71. 558

Marvin, Henry. A complete history of Lake George, embracing a great variety of information and compiled with an especial reference to meet the wants of the travelling community; intended as a descriptive guide; together with a complete history and present appearance of Ticonderoga. N.Y. Sibells & Maigne, 1853. 102p. folded maps. Reprinted in 1855. 559

Moran, Peter. Lake Sacrament. *Commonweal*, Oct. 19, 1934. 20:582–83. 560

Morris, Frederick K. A Lake George primer. *IOCA Bul*, 1949. 2:no.2:52–56. map. 561

Morse, M.B. Lake George. *Cath World*, Nov. 1880. 32:272. Read at dedication of the Church of the Sacred Heart, Lake George, N.Y. Aug. 8, 1880. 562

Possons, Charles H. The attractions of Lake George and vicinity. . . 3d ed. n.p. 1884. 49p. illus. folded map. 563

Prest, Charles S. Protecting health of Lake George; new law consolidates local boards,

the result of which will be improved sanitary conditions in that beautiful scenic region. *State Service*, July 1918. 2:no.7:68–72. illus.
564

Report of the Society for preservation of scenic and historic places and objects on the battlefield of Lake George. *Am Scenic & Hist Pres Soc*, 1900. 5:49–68.   565

Richards, Frederick Bascom. Historic spots near Lake George. *NY State Hist Assn Q*, Jan. 1922. 3:21–29.   566

Richards, Thomas Addison. Lake George. *Harper*, July 1853. 7:161–70. illus.   567

Samson, William Holland. Mohican point on Lake George, the summer home of Mr. and Mrs. W.K. Bixby, of St. Louis, Mo. With a brief glance at the history of the lake. N.Y. Privately printed, 1913. 65p. plates, map. Edition of 200 copies. Copy at the New York Public Library.   568

Simpson, William. A driving trip to Lake George and vicinity. *For & Stream*, Aug. 2, 1913. 81:133–34, 155. illus.   569

Spafford, Horatio Gates. Lake George. *Amer Mag*, June 1815. 1:42. plate. Signed: Ed. 570

Stoddard, Seneca Ray. Lake George. *St No Mo*, July 1906. 1:no.3:1–8. illus. See also his article with same title in the July 1907 issue, 2:193–207.   571

Streever, Fred L. Lake George. *NYS Con*, Apr.–May 1947. 1:no.5:5–6. illus. Reprinted in *North Country Life*, Spring 1948, 2:no.2:20–23.   572

Sweet, Guy V. A new crown for the queen. *No Country Life*, Spring 1947. 1:no.3:41–42. illus.   573

Torrey, Raymond Hezekiah. Diamond island in Lake George, charming little island, scene of battle in the American revolution, bequeathed to the Scenic society by Mrs. Katrina Trask Peabody. *Scen & Hist Am*, Dec. 1930. 2:72–74. illus.   574

Vacationists like Lake George. *Motordom*, June 1932. p.7. illus.   575

Walsh, Henry Collins. Lake George and its associations. *Travel*, Aug. 1909. 14:522–24. illus.   576

A week at Lake George. *Cath World*, Oct. 1871. 14:78–90.   577

Whiteman, J.A. Lake George camp and canoe chats; gossip on canoes, camps, religion, social manners, medicine and law, gastronomy, politics and marriage. N.Y. Privately printed, 1887? 134p. plates. Part dialogue and part descriptive. Interesting because Adam H. Newcomb brought suit for libel. See Hill, "Brief History," p.116. Whiteman claimed to be printer, not author.   578

Wilson, J. Arbuthnot. The Lake George tour. *Belgravia*, Oct. 1883. 51:413–23. Trip taken by an Englishman.   579

MOUNTAINS AND PASSES

Mount Marcy

Association for the protection of the Adirondacks. Victory mountain park. N.Y. 1919. 44p. front. illus. map. Extract in *High Spots*, July 1937, 14:no.3:43–46. "To acquire by popular subscription, for the public benefit, the summit and adjacent territory of Mt. Marcy." Memorial for World War I.   580

Bulletin of the University of the State of New York. *High Spots*, Dec. 1937. 14:no.4:22–24. Plans for the 100th anniversary celebration of the first recorded ascent of Mt. Marcy. Historical background.   581

Carson, Russell Mack Little. The first ascent of Mount Marcy. *High Spots*, July 1937. 14:no.3:9–12. Reprinted from "The Foot Path," Jan. 7, 14 & 22, 1929.   582

Celebration of the 100th anniversary of the first Mount Marcy ascent. *NYS For Assn NL*, Aug. 1937. p.9–11.   583

Finley, John Huston. The glory of the State of New York, whose highest peak will be part of Victory mountain park in memory of the great victory won in the World war. *State Service*, Aug. 1919. 3:no.8:3–9. illus. Also published separately, Albany, 1919, 7p. illus.   584

Hall, Edward Hagaman. Victory mountain park. *Conservationist*, Apr. 1919. 2:51–55. illus. See no.580 above.   585

House, Homer Doliver. The ascent of Mount Marcy by scientists, August 5, 1837. *NYS Mus Bul*, 1940. 322:17–26.   586

Hudowalski, Mrs. Grace (Leech). Marcy kaleidoscope. *Ad-i-ron-dac*, Mar.–Apr. 1953. 17:30–33. illus. Reprinted in *North Country Life*, Spring 1954, 8:no.2:23–28.   587

Longstreth, Thomas Morris. The great memorial. *Conservationist*, Apr. 1920. 3:55–57. Reprinted in *High Spots*, July 1937, 14:no.3:47–48, with title "Mount Marcy's Great Gift." Proposed purchase of Mt. Marcy.   588

Longstreth, Thomas Morris. Mount Marcy gives a party. *High Spots*, Dec. 1937. 14:no.4:5–6. From the *New York Times*, Aug. 1, 1937. 100th anniversary of the first recorded ascent.   589

MacDonald, Pirie. MacDonald hospice on Mount Marcy. *Cloud Splitter*, Mar. 1942. 5:no.3:2–3. Reprinted in *High Spots Yearbook*, 1944, p.28.   590

Moore, Terris. Winter night on Marcy. *Mt Mag*, Oct.–Nov. 1929. 8:18–20. illus.   591

Mount Marcy. *Am Scenic & Hist Pres Soc,* 1920. 25:308–18.   592

Mount Marcy a memorial of victory. New York state's highest peak a war monument. *Am Scenic & Hist Pres Soc,* 1923. 28:129–33.   593

Nephew, C.L. Mount Marcy in winter. *Mt Mag,* Sept. 1930. 8:11–12. illus.   594

New York acquires Mt. Marcy. *For & Stream,* Mar. 28, 1908. 70:487. Editorial on the purchase of Mt. Marcy from the Raquette Lake Land Company.   595

New York purchases Mount Marcy, *For & Irrig,* Apr. 1908. 15:194.   596

Osborne, Lithgow. Speech. . .from the top of Mt. Marcy in the Adirondacks at the Marcy centenary celebration. *High Spots,* Dec. 1937. 14:no.4:9–11. illus.   597

Pangborn, Georgia Wood. From an Adirondack note-book. *Outlook,* Sept. 2, 1911. 99:28–31. Mt. Marcy experiences.   598

Phelps, Orra A. 1937 ascent of Mt. Marcy via Emmon's route in 1837. *High Spots,* Dec. 1937. 14:no.4:13–14.   599

Stoddard, Seneca Ray. In the beginning: the oldest mountain on earth. *St No Mo,* May 1906. 1:no.1:1–6. illus. col. plate. See also his article "The Oldest Mountain on Earth" in *Forest Leaves,* Summer 1906, 3:no.2:3–7.   600

Stone, Peter. Mountain sunrise. *Ad-i-ron-dac,* Mar.–Apr. 1955. 19:28–29. illus.   601

Storm shelter on Mount Marcy. *Mt Mag,* Oct. 1928. 7:47. illus.   602

Trail to reach top of Mount Marcy; Conservation commissioner tells how tourists may climb the highest peak in the state 5,344 feet above sea level; system of markers explained. *State Service,* May–June 1922. 6,i.e.8:185–95. illus.   603

Victory mountain park committee. . . .Minutes of the organization meeting held in New York city on June 26th, 1919. 16 leaves. Copy in the Minute Book of Association for the Protection of the Adirondacks.   604

Victory mountain park committee. A report of what has been done and a statement of what it is proposed to do. N.Y. 1920? 31p. First report of the committee. Treasurer's report appended.   605

Wessels, William L. 1837 — Mt. Marcy — 1937. *Ad Mt Club Bul,* June 1937. p.3, 8. Author's initials given incorrectly as B.W. Plans for centenary celebration, including brief account of Emmons' ascent.   606

Other Mountains and Passes

Brandreth, Paulina. A mountain lookout. *For & Stream,* Oct. 10, 1914. 83:482–87.

Signed: Paul Brandreth. The summit of Owl's Head.   607

C., C. Mt. Vanderwacker. *For & Stream,* May 11, 1876. 6:221. Winter trip in 1860–61 giving location of this mountain.   608

Carmer, Carl Lamson. Rattlesnake hunter. *In* his Listen for a lonesome drum. . . N.Y, Farrar & Rinehart inc. 1936. p.314–21. Tongue Mountain.   609

Ely, William Watson. Ampersand mountain; a birdseye view of the Adirondacks. *For & Stream,* Sept. 18, 1873. 1:84.   610

Fresn, Mrs. Marion (Strack). The lion couchant of the Champlain valley. *Ad-i-ron-dac,* Nov.–Dec. 1953. 17:116–19, 127. illus. Reprinted in *North Country Life,* Winter 1954, 8:no.1:14–19. Lyon Mountain.   611

Greig, Kathleen L. Mountain mystery. *Four Tr News,* Jan. 1906. 10:133–35. Whiteface.   612

Hoover, M.H. Top o' Whiteface, Wa-Ho-Par-Ten-Ie, grand old sentinel. . . *Motordom.* Dec. 1927. 21:no.7:4–7. illus.   613

Johannsen, Alice E. and Marble, John P. Noonmark, its flora and fauna, by Alice E. Johannsen; and its rock formation, by John P. Marble. St. Huberts, N.Y. Adirondack trail improvement society, 1936. 16p. Revised edition, 1954.   614

. . .Journey to the skies. *No Country Life,* Summer 1955. 9:no.3:50–53. illus. Whiteface Memorial Highway.   615

Knight, M.H. A visit to Mount McGregor. *Four Tr News,* Sept. 1903. 5:169–70. illus.   616

Longstreth, Thomas Morris. Mount Donaldson. *J Outd Life,* Nov. 1924. 21:672. illus.   617

Look at 'em come! *Ad-i-ron-dac,* Nov.–Dec. 1949. 13:130–31. illus. Brief account of the Haystack centennial, Aug. 20, 1949. See also article by Dorothy O. Haeusser "Mt. Haystack Centennial Climb," in *The Cloud Splitter,* Sept.–Oct. 1949, 12:no.5:10–11.   618

Marshall, George. Snowy mountain. *Cloud Splitter,* Nov. 1942. 5:no.8:2–3. History.   619

Marshall, George. Some reflections on Ampersand mountain. *High Spots,* July 1934. 11:no.3:3–5.   620

Miller, William John. Wilmington notch. *Conservationist,* July 1921. 4:99–101. illus. Reprinted in *State Service,* Jan.–Feb. 1922, 6,i.e.8:62–64.   621

North Pole, N.Y. *No Country Life,* Fall 1949. 3:no.4:23–25. illus. The home of Santa Claus on Whiteface Mountain.   622

Pach, Gotthelf. Nippletop mountain, the source of the Hudson. *Recreation,* Nov. 1896. 5:238. illus.   623

Ryder, Letha. Whiteface — then and now. *Cloud Splitter*, Nov. 1943. 6:no.8:3–4. Trips in 1911 and 1935.   624

Schofield, Peter F. A trip through Indian pass. *Ad-i-ron-dac*, Nov.–Dec. 1955. 19:114–15, 117. Based on excerpts from a letter in the Saranac Lake Free Library. Historical note by George Marshall.   625

Shorey, Archibald Thompson. Pharaoh's little ponds. *Ad-i-ron-dac*, Jan.–Feb. 1945. 9:no.1:7.   626

Street, Alfred Billings. The Indian pass. N.Y. Hurd & Houghton, 1869. 201p. Excerpts in *The Cloud Splitter*, Mar.–Apr. 1949, 12:no.2: 7–9. Reviewed in *The Cloud Splitter*, June 1943, 6:no.6:4–5.   627

Van Dyke, Henry. Ampersand. *Harper*, July 1885. 71:217–27. illus. Reprinted in his "Little Rivers," N.Y. Scribner, 1895, p.59–80.   628

A visit to Indian pass. *Knick Mag*, Oct. 1860. 56:335–42.   629

Ward, Peter A. In the shadow of Whiteface. *Cloud Splitter*, May–June 1947. 10:no.3:6–7. Essay on living near Whiteface.   630

Ward, Peter A. Indian pass. *Ad Mt Club Bul*, Mar. 1944. 8:no.2:5–6.   631

Wilmington notch. *Motordom*, June 1932. p.11.   632

COUNTIES

Anderson, George Baker, comp. Our county and its people; a descriptive and biographical record of Saratoga county, New York. Prepared and published under the auspices of the Saratogian. Boston, Boston history co. 1899. 584, 203p. ports.   633

Benton, Nathaniel Soley. A history of Herkimer county; including the upper Mohawk valley, from the earliest period to the present time. . .also biographical notices of the most prominent public men of the county. Albany, J. Munsell, 1856. 497p. front. illus. plates, port. maps (part folded).   634

Christie, Mrs. Elizabeth and Christie, Robert Jr. Hamilton county. *NYS Con*, Oct.–Nov. 1950. 5:no.2:12–13. One page of text accompanied by map showing fire towers, lean-tos, etc.   635

Clio. Stray leaves from the story of Franklin county. . . *For Leaves*, Spring & Summer 1904. 1:no.2:8–13; 1:no.3:31–34. port. illus. See note about the series in Dec. 1901 issue, 1:no.1:4–6.   636

Cole, G. Glyndon. The making of a county: an outline history of St. Lawrence county. *No Country Life*, Spring 1952–Spring 1953. 6:no.2:14–18; 6:no.3:21–26; 7:no.1:40–43; 7:no.2:44–46. illus. maps, chart.   637

Cook, Alice B. Historical sketch of Fulton county centennial celebration, 1839–1939. Gloversville, N.Y. Leader-Republican-Herald, 1940. 52p. front. illus.   638

Curtis, Gates, ed. Our county and its people: a memorial record of St. Lawrence county, New York. . . Syracuse, N.Y. D. Mason & co. 1894. 720, 66, 372p. ports. maps.   639

Diebolt, Alfred L. Economic and social practices in Clinton county as related to the problems of the State normal school in Plattsburgh, New York. n.p. 1938? Reproduced from typewritten copy. Author was head of the Social Studies Department.   640

Drahos, Nicholas. Essex county. *NYS Con*, June–July 1949. 3:no.6:26–29. map. Reprinted in *North Country Life*, Spring 1953, 7:no.2:2–5.   641

Durant, Samuel W. . . .History of St. Lawrence co. New York. With illustrations and biographical sketches of some of its prominent men and pioneers. Philadelphia, L.H. Everts & co. 1878. 521p. plates, port. illus. facsims. map.   642

Essex county, N.Y. Duplicate enrollment books of the enrollment of voters of the county of Essex. . . Elizabethtown, N.Y. 1914. 91 leaves.   643

Everett, Fred. Clinton county. *NYS Con*, Apr.–May 1952. 6:no.5:24–25. Map with brief text; shows fire towers, state-stocked streams, public campsites and state-owned land.   644

Everett, Fred. Saratoga county. *NYS Con*, June–July 1952. 6:no.6:22. Map with brief text; shows fire towers, etc.   645

Everett, Fred. Washington county. *NYS Con*, Dec. 1952–Jan. 1953. 7:no.3:25. Map with brief text; shows fire towers, etc.   646

Fitch, Asa. A historical, topographical & agricultural survey of the county of Washington taken under the direction of the New York state agricultural society. *In* Transactions of the New York state agricultural society, 1848, 1849. 8:875–975; 9:753–944. illus. maps (part folded).   647

Fitch, Asa. Patents and patentees of Washington county, N.Y. *NY Gen & Biog Rec*, Apr. 1943. 74:47–51. "Extracted from 'Notes for a history of Washington county.' " Area around Lake George.   648

Fitch, Asa. Washington county, N.Y. Miscellany. *NY Gen & Biog Rec*, July 1943. 74: 102–5. Extracts from "Notes for a history of Washington county."   649

Franklin county. *NYS Con*, Feb.–Mar. 1951. 5:no.4:12–13. Map showing fire towers, public campsites, trails, etc. Brief text.   650

Frothingham, Washington. History of Fulton county. Syracuse, N.Y. D. Mason & co. 1892. 636, 177p. ports. 651

Frothingham, Washington. History of Montgomery county. Syracuse, N.Y. D. Mason & co. 1892. 456, 349p. ports. Montgomery County originally included most of the area in the present county of Hamilton; also part of Herkimer. 652

Fulton county, N.Y. Election board. Enrollement of voters of the county of Fulton, N.Y. Board of elections... 1915/16. Johnstown, N.Y. 1916. 289 leaves. Mimeographed. 653

Fulton county, N.Y. Election board. Enrollement of voters of the county of Fulton, N.Y. Board of elections. 1931/32. Johnstown, N.Y. 1932. 562 leaves. Mimeographed. 654

Gresham publishing co. History and biography of Washington county and the town of Queensbury, New York, with historical notes on the various towns. Richmond, Ind. 1894. 436p. incl. front. plates, ports. 655

Hardin, George Anson and Willard, Frank Hallett, ed. History of Herkimer county, New York... Syracuse, N.Y. D. Mason & co. 1893. 550, 276p. plates, port. maps. 656

Havens, P.E. Division of Essex county. Argument of Hon. P.E. Havens, of Essex, before the select committee of nine, against the bill setting off the towns of Schroon and Minerva from the county of Essex to the county of Warren. In Assembly, March 25, 1862. n.p. n.pub. 1862? 7p. Copy at the New York State Library. Impassioned plea for Essex County. 657

Haviland, Mrs. Frank, comp. Essex and Warren county cemetery records... Albany? 1925? 114p. "Some of the information was derived from sources other than the cemetery records." 658

Herkimer county, New York. Home defense committee. Herkimer county in the World war, 1916 to 1918; comp. by the Hon. Franklin W. Cristman. Little Falls, N.Y. Journal & Courier co. 1927. 222p. plates, ports. 659

Hill, William Henry, comp. History of Washington county, New York. The Gibson papers, the history of Washington academy, the bench and bar of Washington county for a century. Fort Edward, N.Y. Honeywood press, 1932. 298p. 125 copies privately printed. 660

History of Montgomery and Fulton counties, New York. N.Y. F.W. Beers & co. 1878. 252p. plates. 661

Holden, James Austin. Address in connection with the Warren county centennial celebration. Glens Falls, N.Y. 1913. 3 folios (broad-side). Press release. Copy at the New York State Library. 662

Hough, Franklin Benjamin. A history of Lewis county in the State of New York, from the beginning of its settlement to the present time... Albany, Munsell & Rowland, 1860. 319p. front. illus. plates, ports. 663

Hough, Franklin Benjamin. History of Lewis county, New York, with illustrations and biographical sketches of some of its prominent men and pioneers. Syracuse, N.Y. D. Mason & co. 1883. 606p. plates, ports. tables. Historical part only by Dr. Hough. (Bibliography of...Hough, p.343.) 664

Hough, Franklin Benjamin. A history of St. Lawrence and Franklin counties, New York, from the earliest period to the present time. Albany, Little & co. 1853. 719p. plates, illus. ports. maps. 665

Hurd, Duane Hamilton. History of Clinton and Franklin counties, New York. With illustrations and biographical sketches of its prominent men and pioneers. Philadelphia, J.W. Lewis & co. 1880. 508p. plates, ports. maps. The Adirondacks, by George F. Bixby, p.497–508, illustrated. 666

Johnson, Crisfield. History of Washington county, New York, with illustrations and biographical sketches of some of its prominent men and pioneers. Philadelphia, Everts & Ensign, 1878. 504, 131p. ports. map. 667

King, A.H. North 1 degree west. *Conservationist*, Feb. 1919. 2:26–29. Surveying the boundary line between Hamilton and Warren counties. 668

Lewis county. *NYS Con*, Feb.–Mar. 1952. 6:no.4:22–23. Map with brief text; shows fire towers, state-owned land, public fishing streams, etc. 669

New York (state). Laws, statutes, etc. Laws relating to county boundaries from A.D. 1683 to 1799. *In* New York (state). State land survey. Report for 1895, p.333–401. 670

One hundredth anniversary of formation of Warren county, State of New York, 1813–1913. Sunday August 3, to Saturday August 9, inclusive. Glens Falls, N.Y. Press of the Post-Star, 1912? 47p. History of Warren County with suggestions for celebration. 671

Rider, Edward C. Historical sketches. Written for the Franklin county board of supervisors. n.p. n.pub. n.d. 99p. Cover title: Franklin County in the World War... Copy in the Hicks Collection, Lake Placid Club. 672

Seaver, Frederick J. Historical sketches of Franklin county and its several towns, with many short biographies. Albany, J.B. Lyon, 1918. 819p. 673

Seneca, G.A. Northern Franklin county in the 1800's; stories handed down by Joseph Plumb and his descendants. *No Country Life,* Summer 1951. 5:no.3:36–37.   674

1791. History of Herkimer county, N.Y. with illustrations. . . N.Y. F.W. Beers & co. 1879. 289p. plates, port.   675

Shorey, Archibald Thompson. More about Washington county. *Ad-i-ron-dac,* Nov.–Dec. 1952. 16:113, 115. Historical background etc. for article by Walter Baker (16:86–89).   676

Smith, H. Perry, ed. History of Essex county, with illustrations and biographical sketches of some of its prominent men and pioneers. Syracuse, N.Y. D. Mason & co. 1885. 754p. plates, ports. illus.   677

Smith, H. Perry. History of Warren county, with illustrations and biographical sketches of some of its prominent men and pioneers. Syracuse, N.Y. D. Mason & co. 1885. 702p. plates, ports. illus.   678

Stone, William Leete, 1835–1908, ed. Washington county, New York. Its history to the close of the nineteenth century. N.Y. N.Y. historical co. 1901. 570, 318p. ports.   679

Sylvester, Nathaniel Bartlett. History of Saratoga county, New York, with biographical sketches of some of its prominent men and pioneers. Philadelphia, Everts & Ensign, 1878. 514p. plates, ports. map. 2d edition, published in Richmond, Ind. Gresham Publishing Co. 1893, 636p.   680

U.S. Census office. 2d Census. Census of 1800, Montgomery county, State of New York. Names of residents in the county taken down in 1800, the second census of the United States. St. Johnsville, N.Y. Enterprise & news, 1934. 39p. This census was taken while parts of Herkimer and Hamilton were in Montgomery County. Published originally with title "Mohawk Valley Householders in 1800, contributed by L.D. Sisco" in *New York Genealogical and Biographical Record,* Jan. 1918–Oct. 1919; v.49, p.51, 107–16, 280–91, 330–43; v.50, p.26–33, 274–84, 307–16.   681

Warren county, N.Y. Abstracts of deeds of Warren county, N.Y. from 1813 to 1825. . . Copied from the original records at the Court house at Lake George, N.Y. Copied and compiled by Gertrude A. Barber. N.Y. 1941. 89 folios. Typescript in the New York Public Library.   682

Warren county, N.Y. Courts: Surrogate's court. Abstracts of wills of Warren county, N.Y. Copied from original records at the Surrogate's office, Glens Falls, Warren county, N.Y. Liber A 1813–1850. Copied and compiled by Gertrude A. Barber, July, 1937. N.Y. 1937. 56 folios. Typescript in the New York Public Library.   683

Warren county. *NYS Con,* Oct.–Nov. 1951. 6:no.2:16–17. Map with brief text; shows fire towers, trails, etc.   684

Watson, Winslow Cossoul. Military and civil history of the county of Essex, New York; and a general survey of its physical geography, its mines and minerals, and industrial pursuits, embracing an account of the northern wilderness; and also the military annals of the fortresses of Crown Point and Ticonderoga. Albany, J. Munsell, 1869. 504p. front. plates, ports.   685

Wells, Robert A. County of St. Lawrence. *NYS Con,* Feb.–Mar. 1950. 4:no.4:12–13. 686

Witte, Carl P. The Essex county park commission; its history and development. *Emp For,* 1921. 7:13–14. illus.   687

Writers' program, New York. Warren county, a history and guide. . . N.Y. 1942. 275p. incl. plates, tables, folding maps. Bibliography, p.257–58.   688

CITIES AND VILLAGES

Lake Placid

The Adirondack festival. *New Mus Rev,* Dec. 1926. 26:19. Second festival held at Lake Placid.   689

Boathouse converted into an ideal summer home: Albert Rose residence, Lake Placid. *Arch Rec,* Oct. 1949. 106:96–103. illus. plan.
                    690

Burton, Harold B. Lake Placid. . . *Holiday,* Feb. 1948. 3:no.2:56–61, 127. illus. (part col.).   691

Carroll, George. Healthful sports at Lake Placid. *Health Digest,* Mar. 1937. p.30–31.
                    692

Hayes, Arthur Warring. Lake Placid, its early history and developments, from the time of the Civil war to the present time, as told by Arthur W. Hayes, a citizen, guide and building contractor of the Adirondack mountains. Lake George, N.Y. Adirondack resorts press, c1946. 52p. incl. illus. plates.
                    693

Johnson, Clifton. Highways and byways from the St. Lawrence to Virginia. N.Y. Macmillan, 1913. 340p. plates. (American Highways and Byways.) The Adirondack Winter, p.1–25, describes a stay at Lake Placid. Includes material on John Brown.   694

Lake Placid board of trade. Lake Placid in the Adirondacks. Lake Placid, N.Y. n.d. unpaged. illus.   695

Lake Placid; gem of the Adirondacks; the natural motor center of the Adirondack playgrounds, Placid is now an "all year" resort. *Motordom,* June 1929. 23:no.1:20–21. illus.
                    696

Lake Placid — glamorous heart of the mountains bordered by loftiest mountains, and overlooking two beautiful lakes, this famous center offers rarest diversions. *Motordom*, June 1931. 24:no.12:14–15. illus.   697

Lake Placid, queen of Adirondack beauties set amid the tallest mountains, this is a world famous center. *Motordom*, June 1930. 24:no. 1:22. illus.   698

Lake Placid of peerless charm lies amid the peaks. *Motordom*, June 1933. p.8–9. illus.   699

Lake Placid of world renown. *Motordom*, June 1934. p.9–10. illus.   700

Lake Placid reached through mountain passes. *Motordom*, June 1932. p.9. illus.   701

Lake Placid's building program. *Lake Pl Life*, Mar. 1931. p.27, 35.   702

Lattimer, George M. Sports enthusiasts will view the great Olympic facilities at Lake Placid. *Motordom*, June 1931. 24:no.12:32, 34. illus.   703

Shore owners association of Lake Placid. Constitution, officers, members, etc. . . Hartford, Conn. Plimpton manufacturing co. 1898. 15p. folded maps.   704

Story of Lake Placid. *Lake Pl Life*, Jan. 1931. p.19.   705

Taylor, H.W. Sewage treatment plant remodeled at low cost. *Am City*, Dec. 1932. 47:53–55. diagrs. illus. plan.   706

Thornton, C.A. Lake Placid athletic club. *In* United States eastern amateur ski association. Year book, 1930. p.79–80.   707

Plattsburgh

Adirondack bureau, Plattsburgh, N.Y. Plattsburgh and vicinity. . . Plattsburgh, N.Y. 1924. 32p. "Issued by a group of bankers, business and professional men to set out matters of interest and points of advantage respecting the city of Plattsburgh and vicinity."   708

American legion. New York. Plattsburgh post, no.20. Independence day celebration, given by the American legion, Plattsburgh post. no.20, Monday July 4th, 1921. Plattsburgh, N.Y. Clinton press inc. 1921. 96p. illus. ports.   709

Clinton county military association. The battle of Plattsburgh, 11th September, 1814. An account of the celebration of the anniversary . . .by the citizens of Plattsburgh and the Clinton county military association, September 11, 1843. Plattsburgh, N.Y. R.G. Stone, 1843. 12p. *Plattsburgh Republican* extra.   710

Fifth company records committee. The war record of the Fifth company, New England regiment, second Plattsburg training camp. Cambridge, Mass. Harvard university press, 1922. 65p.   711

Fitzpatrick, Simon E. Plattsburg once upon a time. n.p. n.pub. 1924. 23p. Informal paper read at Plattsburgh Chamber of Commerce luncheon.   712

Fitzpatrick, Simon E. Spots, delivered before Plattsburg rotary club, February 14, 1934. Plattsburgh, N.Y. Tuttle, n.d. 24p. 2d printing, 1944. Historical spots in Clinton County, especially Plattsburgh.   713

French, Allen. At Plattsburg. N.Y. Scribner, [c]1917. 310p. Military training camp at Plattsburgh. See "The Plattsburger," N.Y. [c]1917 for a record of the second camp.   714

Historical sketch of Plattsburgh, New-York, from its first settlement to Jan. 1, 1893. Plattsburgh, N.Y. 1893. 102p. Reprint of an article by Peter S. Palmer in the *Plattsburgh Republican*, supplemented by a sketch bringing Palmer's article up to date.   715

Lansing, W. & son. Souvenir. Industrial edition. The Press. Plattsburgh, N.Y. 1897. 124p. ports. illus. *Plattsburgh Daily Press*.   716

Macdonough memorial. *No Country Life*, Summer 1951. 5:no.3:33. illus.   717

New York (state). Plattsburg centenary commission. Dedication of the Thomas MacDonough memorial. Plattsburgh centenary commission, August eighteenth, nineteen twenty-six, Plattsburgh, New York. Albany, J.B. Lyon, 1926. 79p. incl. front. plate, facsim. folded maps.   718

Palmer, Peter Sailly. History of Plattsburgh, N.Y. from its first settlement to Jan. 1, 1876. Plattsburgh, N.Y. 1877. 83p. Reprinted from the *Plattsburgh Republican*. "In the year 1871 a series of articles were prepared by Peter S. Palmer and published in the Plattsburgh *Republican* under the name of 'Northern New York Historical Society papers.' Paper 'one' of this series, which referred principally to the village of Plattsburgh, is reproduced in the following pages." Griffin. Bibliography of American historical societies, p.733.   719

The past and present of Plattsburgh. Romantic history of a prosperous village. . . The gateway to the Adirondacks. Troy, N.Y. Troy Times print house, 1891. 20p. plates. Reprinted from *Troy Daily Times*, Nov. 28, 1891.   720

Plattsburgh, N.Y. Home for the friendless of northern New York. Charter, constitution, and. . .annual report. . . Plattsburgh, N.Y. J.W. Tuttle, 1877–83. 3v. Copies of reports no.3, 5 and 9 at the New York Public Library.   721

Plattsburgh chamber of commerce. Plattsburgh on Lake Champlain. August 1918.
Plattsburgh, N.Y. 1918? 34p. folded maps.
                                                          722

Porter, Mrs. Marjorie (Lansing). Old Plattsburgh. . . Plattsburgh, N.Y. Clinton press,
1944. 63p. illus. map.   723

Porter, Mrs. Marjorie (Lansing). The pride
of the Saranac. *Ver Hist Soc Proc*, Sept. 1941.
n.s.9:207–16.   724

Possons, Charles H. The attractions of Plattsburgh, N.Y., and vicinity. Its drives, rambles,
views, hotels, places of interest, business
houses, etc. by a visitor. Glens Falls, N.Y.
C.H. Possons, 1885. 30p. illus. See also his
"Sights in Plattsburgh," 1887.   725

Reminiscences of girlhood in Plattsburgh,
N.Y., 1840–ca.1865. *Hobbies*, May 1949. 54:
no.3:158–59. Extracted from an anonymous
memoir apparently written by Charlotte
Moore.   726

U.S. War department. Letter from the Secretary of war enclosing a letter from Smith
M. Weed, offering to donate to the government land for a parade and practice ground
near the military post at Plattsburg, N.Y.
December 11, 1889. Washington, 1889. 2p.
51st Congress, 1st Session, House of Representatives document 37.   727

Weed, Smith Mead. 1776. 1876. Centennial
oration at Plattsburgh, Clinton county, New
York, July 4th 1876, n.p. n.d. 8p. Compares
Plattsburgh in 1776 with 1876. Gives
statistics.   728

Saranac Lake

American legion. New York. Saranac Lake
chapter, no.18. Jubilee book in commemoration of the hospitalization at Saranac Lake
of disabled veterans of the World war, issued
under the auspices of the Jackson A. Mat-
thews post no.614, American legion and
Saranac Lake chapter no.18, Disabled veterans of the World war. Saranac Lake, N.Y.
1925. 100p. illus. ports. Dr. E.L. Trudeau
and Paul Smith, p.35–39.   729

Chalmers, Stephen. Sanitary Saranac Lake.
World's Work, Sept. 1912. 24:581–85.   730

Greenslet, Ferris. The life of Thomas Bailey
Aldrich. Boston, Houghton, 1908. 303p.
plate, ports. Days at Saranac Lake, p.216–27.
                                                          731

Meet the town. Saranac Lake, N.Y. Saranac
Lake, N.Y. Sheridan advertising service,
1927. 48p. illus. maps. Published annually.
                                                          732

Raymond, Henry Warren. The story of Saranac. A chapter in Adirondack history. N.Y.
Grafton press, 1909. 78p. front. illus. port.
                                                          733

Rice, Fred. Fifty years in a health resort.
Saranac Lake, N.Y. ᶜ1937. 51p. Unpaged
supplement (8p.) laid in.   734

Saranac, the metropolis. *Motordom*, June 1932.
p.20. illus.   735

Saranac Lake, N.Y. Board of trade. Saranac
Lake: a town in the Adirondacks. Saranac
Lake, N.Y. Adirondack enterprise press, n.d.
16p. illus. Probably published about 1910.
                                                          736

Saranac Lake, N.Y. Board of trade. Year
book. . .7th year. Saranac Lake, N.Y. Adirondack enterprise press, 1911. Issue for
1911–12 is in the Saranac Lake Free Library.
                                                          737

Saranac Lake, N.Y. Board of trade. Advertising committee. Advertising — entertaining. The question of inviting people the country over to Saranac Lake and providing for
their comfort and amusement. n.p. 1912? 8p.
Unpaged leaflet.   738

Saranac Lake, N.Y. Board of trustees. In and
around Saranac Lake. Saranac Lake, N.Y.
1932. 48p. illus.   739

Saranac Lake, N.Y. Citizens committee. An
opportunity. Available — for suitable use. . .
Saranac Lake, N.Y. 1955. unpaged. illus.
map. Oblong loose-leaf folder.   740

Saranac Lake, N.Y. Consolidated board of
health. Saranac Lake, New York in the Adirondacks. Pioneer health resort. Saranac
Lake, N.Y. Currier press, 1935. 12p. illus.
Unpaged leaflet.   741

Saranac Lake federal savings and loan asso-
ciation. The first fifty years. . .1899–1949.
A report by the president. Saranac Lake,
N.Y. 1949. 12p. illus.   742

Saranac Lake, Adirondack metropolis, fa-
vored by noted Americans. *Motordom*, June
1934. p.20. illus.   743

Saranac Lake and the earthquake. *Pine Log*,
Mar. 1925. 2:no.2:16.   744

Saranac Lake in the Adirondacks. The gateway to the Olympics. Saranac Lake, N.Y.
Currier press, 1932. 36p. illus.   745

Saranac Lake in the Adirondacks. The north
woods city of health & opportunity. Mid-
winter carnival, nineteen hundred & nine.
Saranac Lake, N.Y. J.J. Connors & R.D.
McCartie, 1909? 20p. plates, illus.   746

Saranac Lake industrial settlement. *J Outd
Life*, July 1907. 4:228.   747

Saranac Lake, N.Y. The winter health resort.
Facts about Saranac Lake, hitherto unpublished, for the information of the medical pro-
fession and suffers [sic] from throat and lung
trouble. n.p. n.d. 48p. illus.   748

Saranac Lake, sesame of winter sport, rimmed by mountains and with rinks, slides and trails into the fastnesses, this village draws merrymakers from all points, flapjacks in the open make a royal feast. *Motordom*, Dec. 1931. 25:no.7:10–11. illus. 749

Scott, William Earl Dodge. The garden of the Saranac Lake industrial settlement. *Char*, Dec. 7, 1907. 19:1175–82. illus. 750

Tatlock, William. Plan modified social settlement for Saranac Lake. *J Outd Life*, Dec. 1905. 2:292–93. 751

Trudeau, Francis B. Jr. Saranac Lake and tuberculosis; a dissertation presented to the faculty of the Department of history, Yale university. . .by Frank Trudeau. 132 leaves. illus. Typescript. B.A. thesis, 1942. Appendix contains "Adirondack Guides," a letter from Seaver Miller. 752

White, William Chapman. Living in Saranac Lake in the Adirondacks. Saranac Lake, N.Y. Currier press, c1955. 24p. incl. cover. illus. unpaged. The first edition was prepared at the request of the Trudeau Foundation. The edition cited above is sold for the benefit of the Saranac Lake Free Library. 753

White, William Chapman. . . . Saranac Lake, N.Y. *Sat Eve Post*, Aug. 25, 1951. 224: no.8:34–35, 53–54, 56–60. col. illus. 754

Ticonderoga

Bailey, John H. A rock shelter at Fort Ticonderoga. Fort Ticonderoga, N.Y. 1937. 16p. illus. (Champlain Valley Archaeological Society. v.1.) 755

Bascom, Frederick G. Joseph Cook and Ticonderoga. *NY Hist*, Jan. 1934. 15:43–49. 756

Bascom, Frederick G. Ticonderoga in history. *NY State Hist Assn Proc*, 1911. 11:247–61. Prize essay by student from Glens Falls High School. 757

Bascom, Robert O. Legend of Duncan Campbell. *NY State Hist Assn Proc*, 1901. 2:32–38. 758

Bliss, Alex. A visit to Fort Ticonderoga in 1825. *Ft Ti Mus Bul*, Summer 1949. 8:160–62. illus. 759

Bossom, Alfred Charles. Honor to all brave men who fell at "old Ti." *NY Times Mag*, May 10, 1925. p.10. illus. 760

Bossom, Alfred Charles. The reconstruction of Fort Ticonderoga. *Travel*, Aug. 1909. 14: 530–31. illus. 761

Bossom, Alfred Charles. The restoration of Fort Ticonderoga. *Am Scenic & Hist Pres Soc*, 1913. 18:610–18. 762

Bossom, Alfred Charles. The restoration of Fort Ticonderoga. *Arch*, Aug. 1925. 53:275–79. illus. Brief note by the architect, with many illustrations. 763

Carr, Arthur A. The Indian harvest festival at Ticonderoga. *NY Hist*, Apr. 1948. 29:151–56. 764

Cook, Joseph. Historical address. . .delivered at the first centennial anniversary of the settlement of Ticonderoga, July 25, 1864. Ticonderoga, N.Y. Ticonderoga historical society, c1909. 109p. col. front. plates, ports. illus. Largely taken from his "Home Sketches." 765

Cook, Joseph. Home sketches of Essex county. First number. Ticonderoga. 1. What it is; 2. What it does; 3. What it enjoys; 4. What it needs. By Flavius J. Cook. Keeseville, N.Y. W. Lansing & son, 1858. 139p. 766

Cummings, William A.E. Fort Ticonderoga and its history. *Travel*, July 1909. 14:457–63. illus. map. 767

Daughters of the American revolution. Vermont. Hand's Cove chapter, Shoreham. Historic Mount Independence. Shoreham, Vt. Hand's Cove chapter Vermont DAR, n.d. 28p. front. port. Address by Hon. Robert O. Bascom, p.9–28. 768

Delano, Clayton H. Unveiling of Ticonderoga tablet. *NY State Hist Assn Proc*, 1911. 10: 43–52. 769

Dowling, R.L. Fort Ticonderoga. *Antiques*, July 1946. 50:26–28. illus. A short account of the restoration of the fort. 770

The elm of Ticonderoga. *For & Stream*, May 1916. 86:951. Cutting down of huge elm near Fort Ticonderoga. 771

Fort Ticonderoga. *Four Tr News*, Nov. 1902. 3:195. illus. 772

Fort Ticonderoga (Fort Carillon). Ticonderoga, N.Y.? 1912? 18p. illus. 773

Fort Ticonderoga — key to a continent. *No Country Life*, Summer 1955. 9:no.3:42–49. illus. 774

Fox, Dixon Ryan. The spell of great names. *NY Hist*, Jan. 1934. 15:39–42. 775

Gilchrist, Helen Ives. Fort Ticonderoga in history. Ticonderoga, N.Y. Ft. Ticonderoga museum, 192—? 101p. front. ports. illus. facsims. map. 776

Gilchrist, Helen Ives. The history of Fort Ticonderoga. *NY State Hist Assn Q*, July 1922. 3:147–54. plate, map. 777

Hawthorne, Nathaniel. A visit to Ticonderoga 100 years ago. *Ft Ti Mus Bul*, Jan. 1936. 4:12–17. Hawthorne visited the fort in the summer of 1835. The description reprinted here was published anonymously in the *American Monthly Magazine*, Feb. 1836, with the title "Old Ticonderoga, a Picture of the Past." He later included it in his "The Snow Image."   778

Historic Ticonderoga. *Yorker*, Nov.–Dec. 1949, Jan.–Feb. 1950. 8:28–30, 40–43. port. illus. facsim. maps.   779

Lape, Mrs. Jane (McCaughin). Ticonderoga's Indian festival. *NY Folk Q*, Aug. 1945. 1:167–74.   780

Liberty monument. Unveiling — August 16, 1924. Ticonderoga, N.Y. Ticonderoga, N.Y.? n.d. illus. 12p. Unpaged leaflet. Contains two-page address by Frederick B. Richards.   781

Lord, Clifford L. and Lape, Mrs. Jane (McCaughin). The headquarter hosts of the New York state historical association, Ticonderoga, N.Y. Ticonderoga, N.Y. 1942. 23p. plate.   782

Mayernik, Vincent I. Fort Ticonderoga, military asset or liability. 53 leaves. maps. Master's thesis, Columbia University, 1951. Typescript.   783

Memorial to the Black watch. *NY State Hist Assn Q*, July 1925. 6:246–50.   784

Milholland, John Henry Elmer. The preservation of Fort Ticonderoga by town ownership; an address delivered at Fort Ticonderoga, Sept. 2, 1908. Ticonderoga, N.Y. Ticonderoga historical society, 1908. 4 leaves.   785

Newton, Earle. Ticonderoga, guardian of the northern gateway. *Am Heritage*, Sept. 1949. n.s.1:24–35. illus. ports. maps.   786

Old Ticonderoga. *Am Mo Mag (NY)* Feb. 1836. n.s.1:138–42.   787

Olsen, Godfrey J. Archaeology of Ticonderoga. *NY Hist*, Oct. 1934. 15:407–11. 788

Owen, R. Emmett. Sketches of Fort Ticonderoga. *Harper*, Apr. 1924. 148:633–40. illus.   789

Paltsits, Victor Hugo. Plea for the nationalization of the site of Fort Ticonderoga. An address. . .delivered. . .Sept. 2, 1908. Ticonderoga, N.Y. Ticonderoga historical society, 1908. 5 leaves.   790

Paltsits, Victor Hugo. Ticonderoga in history. *In* Lake Champlain association. Year book, 1912–13. p.40–51.   791

Pell, Howland. The Germain redoubt at Fort Ticonderoga. *Am Scenic & Hist Pres Soc*, 1913. 18:619–25.   792

Pell, John. Ticonderoga; its ruin and restoration. *Country Life*, Aug. 1935. 68:no.4:24–26. illus.   793

Pell, Stephen Hyatt Pelham. Fort Ticonderoga. *Roy Unit Ser Inst J*, Mar. 1914. 58: 386–88. map.   794

Pell, Stephen Hyatt Pelham. Fort Ticonderoga. *Soc Army Hist Res J*, Apr. 1928. 7: 124–25. col. plates, map.   795

Pell, Stephen Hyatt Pelham. Fort Ticonderoga; a short history compiled from contemporary sources. Glens Falls, N.Y. 1935. 100p. illus. maps. An edition printed for the Fort Ticonderoga Museum in 1948 is in Yale University Library.   796

Pell, Stephen Hyatt Pelham. Restoration at Fort Ticonderoga. *Ver Hist Soc Proc*, Dec. 1930. n.s.1:167–68.   797

Pell, Stephen Hyatt Pelham. Restoration of Fort Ticonderoga. *Travel*, July 1909. 14: 464–68. illus.   798

Perry, George W. Ticonderoga. *New Eng M*, Apr. 1901. n.s.24:119–27. illus. map.   799

Pyrke, Berne A. The story of Ticonderoga. *NY Hist*, Jan. 1946. 27:14–37.   800

Radcliff, Clara Adrianna. Ticonderoga in history. *NY State Hist Assn Proc*, 1911. 11: 234–47. Prize essay written by student from Yonkers High School.   801

Richards, Frederick Bascom. The Black watch at Ticonderoga. *NY State Hist Assn Proc*, 1910. 10:367–463. plates.   802

Smith, Justin Harvey. Our struggle for the fourteenth colony. N.Y. Putnam, 1907. 2v. front. plates, illus. ports. facsims. map. Ticonderoga, v.1, p.107–65.   803

Spring, George H. The annual Indian pageant at Ticonderoga. *No Country Life*, Summer 1948. 2:no.3:32–39. illus.   804

Stanley, A.P. Inverawe and Ticonderoga. *Frasers M*, Oct. 1880. n.s.22:501–10.   805

Stanley, Kate E. The stone's story; or, Fort Ticonderoga and its immediate vicinity. Ticonderoga, N.Y. R.R. Stevenson, 1885. 22p.   806

Stoddard, Seneca Ray. Ticonderoga; past and present. . . Albany, Weed, Parsons & co. 1873. 68p. illus.   807

Sullivan, Olive Greene. Fort Ticonderoga; an historical sketch. Hillacre, Privately printed, 1912. 8 leaves. plates. front.   808

Thibault, Donald. Mt. Hope fort — one man's hobby. *No Country Life*, Spring 1951. 5:no.2:37–40, 43. illus. Restoration of the fort by Carroll V. Lonergan.   809

Ticonderoga. *Fam Mag*, 1840. 7:342–43. Description of the fort, taken from the *Boston Times*.   810

Ticonderoga. *Macmil;* Feb. 1896. 73:281–90. Reprinted in *Littell's Living Age,* Mar. 7, 1896, 208:611–20. 811

Ticonderoga, heroic village of America; restored fort where Ethan Allen pounded on the gate now a mecca at the meeting of the trails. *Motordom,* June 1929. 23:no.1:22–23. illus. 812

Ticonderoga and Crown Point. *Motordom,* June 1932. p.11. 813

Ticonderoga and Crown Point — America's most famous forts; where 300 years of war began, motorists now find rarest adventures. *Motordom,* June 1930. 24:no.1:18–19. illus. 814

Ticonderoga chamber of commerce. Historic Ticonderoga. n.p. n.pub. n.d. 31p. illus. map. 815

Ticonderoga historical society. Fort Ticonderoga. n.p. n.d. 10p. plates. Unpaged oblong octavo. 816

Ticonderoga historical society. A memorial tablet at Ticonderoga, a corporation's gift to history. Reprinted by the Ticonderoga pulp and paper co. by permission of the Ticonderoga historical society. Cambridge, Mass. University press, ᶜ1911. 29p. front. illus. 817

Tower, Elizabeth. . . .The John Hancock house, Ticonderoga, N.Y. Ticonderoga, N.Y.? 1926? 16p. 818

Van Rensselaer, Cortlandt, 1808–60. An historical discourse in centennial commemoration of the capture of Ticonderoga, 1759 . . . Philadelphia, Joseph M. Wilson, 1859. 32p. map. 819

Watrous, Elizabeth. Fort Ticonderoga restored. *NY State Hist Assn Proc,* 1902. 5:128–31. 820

Whitman, Roger B. Fort Ticonderoga, a lesson in Americanization. *World's Work,* Oct. 1924. 48:651–57. 821

Wickes, Frank B. Fort Ticonderoga. *NY State Hist Assn Proc,* 1901. 3:12–15. 822

Winter, Marietta A. Ticonderoga in history. *NY State Hist Assn Proc,* 1912. 11:261–67. 823

Other Cities and Villages

Aldridge, George Washington Jr. Crown Point once key to America; New York state now preserving it as a public park, first a French and later a British fortress a century and a half ago. *State Service,* Aug. 1918. 2: no.8:50–59. illus. 824

Arnold, Seward, comp. Reminiscences and early history of old Peru. n.p. 1913. 58p. 825

Baker, Mary E. The old Crown Point road. Its place in history. *Mag Hist,* Nov. 1909, Jan.–Feb. 1910. 10:269–74; 11:22–26, 99–104. Though about a Vermont road, the article includes many incidents about Crown Point. 826

Barker, Elmer Eugene. Celebrating Memorial day (at Crown Point, N.Y.). *Hist Teach Mag,* Mar. 1918. 9:134–37. 827

Barker, Elmer Eugene, ed. Letters of Charles Franklin Hammond to his son John, 1849–1850. *NY Hist,* Jan.–Apr. 1951. 32:61–69, 172–83. Includes data on the blast furnaces at Crown Point. 828

Barker, Elmer Eugene. Monuments to their horses. *NY Hist,* Jan. 1949. 30:43–52. Monuments at Crown Point erected by veterans of the Civil War in memory of their horses. 829

Becker, Howard I. ed. Tahawus — Newcomb and Long Lake, by George and Robert Shaw of Long Lake, 1842–1900. Also, the Rev. John Todd's own story of his visits to Long Lake, 1841–44 written in 1845. n.p. n.pub. 1955. 168, 24, 2, 3 leaves. ports. illus. maps. Mimeographed. 17 copies for private distribution. Manuscript and copy in the Adirondack Museum, Blue Mountain Lake. 830

Benedict, G.G. Manuscript map of Crown Point, over 135 years old. *Ver Ant,* Dec. 1902. 1:37–39. map. 831

Brown, George Levi. Pleasant Valley; a history of Elizabethtown, Essex county, New York. Elizabethtown, N.Y. Post & Gazette print, 1905. 474p. plates, ports. maps. 832

Butler, Benjamin Clapp. . . .From homespun to calico. A centennial address delivered at Luzerne, July 4, 1876. Albany, Weed, Parsons & co. 1877. 52p. At head of title: 1776–1876. "A Peep at Luzerne," p.31–52. 833

Chateaugay; oldest town in Franklin county. *No Country Life,* Summer 1949. 3:no.3:11–13. 834

Chestertown: in 1905 it was a village of two log houses. *Top o' the World,* Feb. 1939. 3: no.1:4. 835

Coke, Edward Thomas. A subaltern's furlough; descriptive of scenes in various parts of the United States, Upper and Lower Canada, New-Brunswick and Nova Scotia. N.Y. J. & J. Harper, 1833. 2v. Trenton Falls, v.1, p.210–15. 836

Cross roads of the north; Rouse's Point (N.Y.) first served by Champlain & Ogdensburg R.R. now part of the Rutland system. *Trains,* Feb. 1941. 1:no.4:37. illus. 837

Crown Point once key to America. *Motordom,* Jan. 1929. 22:no.8:16–17. illus. 838

Dean, Amos. An attempt to present the claims of Long Lake to the consideration of all those who are in search after good land at a low price. Albany, J. Munsell, 1846. 35p. folded map. See Donaldson, Chapter 34.
839

Essex, N.Y. Chamber of commerce. Essex on Lake Champlain. . . n.p. n.pub. 1920. 12p.   840

Fisher, Clarence L. History of the Lyons falls. Boonville, N.Y. Willard press, 1918. 30p. illus. ports.   841

Fountain, Lucy. Keene delights. *Putnam*, Dec. 1869. 14:669–74. A pleasing description of Keene Valley with emphasis on scenery.   842

Gill, William Hanson. Old Fort "Blunder." *Mil Eng*, Mar. 1942. 34:151–52. map. Reprinted as American Map and Geographic Research Service. Historic Structure Series, no.1. Washington, D.C. 1944. Fort Montgomery, near Rouses Point.   843

Hand, Mrs. Susan (Train). Letters of the Hand family, 1796–1912; collected and arranged, with a biographical sketch. . . Printed for private circulation. N.Y. Edwin S. Gorham, 1923. 328p. front. plates, port. illus. Copy in the Loomis Collection, Keene Valley Public Library. Includes many letters written from Elizabethtown.   844

Highlights of a half-century of progress in a friendly town. 1902. Tupper Lake. 1952. n.p. n.pub. 1952? 33p. ports. illus. Foreword by Louis J. Simmons, Village Historian. Advertisements on 39 unnumbered pages and inner covers.   845

Historic Crown Point. *Four Tr News*, Aug. 1903. 5:92. illus.   846

Hough, Marjorie G. Tannery days at Jordan Falls and a tanner's daughter's recollections of life and customs in that now-vanished village. *No Country Life*, Winter 1952. 6:no. 1:41–47.   847

Hudowalski, Mrs. Grace (Leech). Ghost village. *Cloud Splitter*, Mar. 1939. 2:no.1:12. History of Henderson's mining village, Adirondac.   848

Hughes, Charles Evans. A symbol of old world disappointment, Crown Point. *No Country Life*, Summer 1951. 5:no.3:39–40. Speech at the Champlain Tercentenary. 849

In memoriam. President Garfield. Obsequies at Elizabethtown, New York, September 26th, 1881. Elizabethtown, N.Y. Post & Gazette, 1881. unpaged.   850

In memoriam, President McKinley. Obsequies at Elizabethtown, New York, September 19th, 1901. Elizabethtown, N.Y. Post & Gazette print, 1901. 19p.   851

James, William. Letters of William James. Boston, Atlantic Monthly press, 1920. 2v. The Adirondack range, v.1, p.194–95. Keene Valley, v.1, p.194–96; v.2, p.75–79, 90–91, 95. Extract entitled "William James' Mis-adventure Climbing Marcy" in *High Spots*, July 1937, 14:no.3:38–39.   852

Keene Valley, N.Y. Board of trade. Keene Valley, crowning glory of the Adirondacks. n.p. Kamargo press, n.d. Unpaged folder. illus. map. Copy in the Saranac Lake Free Library. An attractive piece of advertising with good illustrations and many quotations from Adirondack authors.   853

Keene Valley in the Adirondacks. *Am For*, Apr. 1910. 16:207. illus.   854

Kellogg, Lewis. A sketch of the history of Whitehall, civil and religious. A discourse delivered on the 27th of June, 1847. Whitehall, N.Y. S.B. Fairman, 1847. 16p.   855

Lape, Mrs. Jane (McCaughin). The McIntyre-MacMartin-Henderson papers at Headquarters house. *NY Hist*, Jan. 1948. 29:118–22. Describes collection of letters relating to Tahawus (Adirondac).   856

Lawrence, Dana. Comments on life and folks. . . Keene Valley, N.Y. Keene Valley memorial association, c1954. 91p. front. (port.). Cover title: A Villager. Reviewed by W.H. Burger in *North Country Life*, Winter 1955, 9:no.1:50, and by D.A. Plum in *The Ad-i-ron-dac*, Jan.–Feb. 1955, 19:20.   857

Lincoln, Frederic F. A concrete industrial village; Mineville, N.Y. in the heart of the Adirondack forest, is being rebuilt in concrete. Wooden buildings fast disappearing. *Cement Age*, Sept. 1909. 9:158–65. illus. 858

Live shell turns up — after 200 years! *Pop Mech*, May 1955. 103:no.5:124–25. Found in restoration of Fort William Henry, Lake George.   859

Lonergan, Carroll Vincent. Historic Crown Point: the story of the forts and the villages. Burlington, Vt. Free press printing co. c1942. 79p. front. illus. ports.   860

Lonergan, Thomas Francis. Historic Crown Point, Fort St. Frederic, Fort Amherst. . . Troy, N.Y. Regal art press, 1936. 29p. front. illus. ports. map.   861

Lowrie, Sarah. Neighborliness and a country community. *Survey*, Apr. 5, 1915. 30:28–33. illus. Neighborhood House, Keene Valley.
862

McClellan, Katherine Elizabeth. Keene Valley. Saranac Lake, N.Y. Author, 1898. 26p. illus. plates, ports. maps.   863

Masten, Arthur Haynsworth. The story of Adirondac. N.Y. Privately printed, 1923.

199p. front. plates, ports. facsims. 125 copies printed. See article by D.A. Plum entitled "Adirondack Rarities" in *The Ad-i-ron-dac*, Sept.–Oct. 1950, 14:110. 864

Maxwell, Archibald Montgomery. A run through the United States, during the autumn of 1840. London, Henry Colburn, 1841. 2v. fronts. (ports.). Trenton Falls, v.1, p.216–27. 865

Miller, Philip Schuyler. Dave Henderson's dream. *Ad-i-ron-dac*, Sept.–Oct. 1945. 9:no. 4:5–6, 8. Adirondac. 866

The Neighborhood house association. Handbook. . . Keene Valley, N.Y. Press Loughead & co. 1911. 39p. illus. 867

The new Baedeker, casual notes of an irresponsible traveller. VII. Trenton Falls, N.Y. *Bookm*, Mar. 1909. 29:32–41. ports. illus. 868

Noble, Henry Harmon. A sketch of the history of the town of Essex, New York, with some account of the mother town, Willsboro. Champlain, N.Y. Moorsfield press, 1940. 19p. 142 copies privately printed. 869

Old Chazy. Reminiscences of Old Chazy given by descendents of the early settlers at a literary and musical entertainment. . . Aug. 23, 1898. Plattsburgh, N.Y. Clinton county farmer, 1898. 44p. 870

Old Keeseville tales. Port Henry, N.Y. Essex county publishing co. 1900. 99p. plate. 871

A peep at Luzerne. Albany, Weed, Parsons & co. 1877. 22p. At head of title: A souvenir. Also printed as p.31–52 of Benjamin Clapp Butler's "From Homespun to Calico, 1877." 872

Pitcher, Charlotte A. The golden era of Trenton Falls. . . Utica, N.Y. Fierstine printing house, 1915. 10–103p. front. plates. Also published in *New York State Historical Association Proceedings*, 1915, p.231–94. 873

Plum, Dorothy Alice. Paean to East Hill. *Ad-i-ron-dac*, May–June 1954. 18:50–51. Keene. 874

Porter, Mrs. Marjorie (Lansing). The fifteenth of Redford. *NY Folk Q*, Aug. 1946. 2:205–8. Annual picnic. 875

Post, Asa. Notes of the settlement of the Boquet valley in Elizabethtown, N.Y. written by Asa Post in 1804. *NY Gen & Biog Rec*, Oct. 1900. 3:193–97. 876

Power, Tyrone. Impressions of America, during the years 1833, 1834 and 1835. London, Richard Bentley, 1836. 2v. fronts. Trenton Falls, v.1, p.369–77. 877

Ranney, Anna (Pennington), Mrs. S.P. Keene Valley in 1864. *High Spots*, July 1934. 11:no.3: 8–11. illus. 878

Roberts, Millard Fillmore. A narrative history of Remsen, New York, including parts of adjoining townships of Steuben and Trenton, 1789–1898. Syracuse, N.Y. Author, 1914. 398p. front. 879

Rock inscriptions at the ruins of old Fort Frederick at Crown Point. *NY State Hist Assn Proc*, 1910. 10:108–13. plate. Letters by Victor Hugo Paltsits and W. Max Reid. 880

Royce, Mrs. Caroline Halstead (Barton). Bessboro; a history of Westport, Essex co. N.Y. n.p. ᶜ1902. 611p. incl. maps. 881

Schroon Lake, summer colony center. *Motordom*, July 1934. p. 22. 882

Seaman, Mrs. Frances (Boone). Mountain moods. *No Country Life*, Winter 1953. 7:no.1: 35–37. Long Lake. 883

Seaman, Mrs. Frances (Boone). One century ago. *Cloud Splitter*, Sept.–Oct. 1952. 15:no.6: 3–6. Based on a manuscript account by Livonia L. Emerson of life at Long Lake. 884

Sherman, John. A description of Trenton Falls, Oneida county, New York. Utica, N.Y. W. Williams, 1830. 18p. 885

Skenesborough; birthplace of the American navy. *No Country Life*, Summer 1954. 8:no.3: 31, 40–41. 886

Spaulding, Samuel S. Spaulding's History of Crown Point, New York from 1800 to 1874. Port Henry, N.Y. Herald printers, 1874. 42p. 887

Spencer, George W. The Adirondack springs, Westport, New York. Port Henry, N.Y. Republican book print, 1888. 19p. Testimonials. 888

Stanley, Frank. The iron industry of Crown Point in the eighteenth and nineteenth century. *Yorker*, Dec. 1943. 2:no.4:6–9. illus. 889

Stanton, Lenthel. "Fort Blunder," the work of an absent-minded nation. *Four Tr News*, Nov. 1905. 9:385. illus. Fort Montgomery, near Rouses Point. 890

Stoddard, Seneca Ray. Keene Valley. *St No Mo*, June 1906. 1:no.2:1–7. illus. 891

Stoddard, Seneca Ray. The Pottersville fair. *St No Mo*, Oct. 1906. 1:no.6:1–5. illus. 892

Taylor, Daniel T. Historical oration delivered at Champlain, N.Y. on the fourth of July 1877. . . Boston, Repository press, 1880. 81p. Also published by the Moorsfield Press, Champlain, N.Y. in 1931; edited, with the addition of notes, by Hugh McLellan. 893

This is Tupper Lake. *No Country Life*, Fall 1955. 9:no.4:28–37. illus. 894

Thomas, Howard. Fort Blunder. *Up Mo*, Feb. 1942. 2:no.11:19. Fort Montgomery. 895

Thomas, Howard. Trenton Falls. *Up Mo,* June 1941. 2:no.3:20. illus.   896

Thomas, Howard. Trenton Falls, yesterday & today. Prospect, N.Y. Prospect books, 1951. 177p. illus. map.   897

Thomas, Marion P. My first trip to Ohio City. *Up Mo,* Dec. 1941. 2:no.9:20–21. illus. Reminiscences of area near Wilmurt.   898

Tierney, Jack. Ghost town of the Adirondacks. *Up Mo,* Feb. 1941. 1:no.11:12–13. Adirondac. History of McIntyre mines.   899

Todd, John. Long Lake; edited by J. Brace, Jr. Pittsfield, Mass. E.P. Little, 1845. 100p.   900

Todd, John. Simple sketches, edited by J. Brace, Jr. Volume second. Pittsfield, Mass. E.P. Little, 1845. 288p. Long Lake, p.73–149.   901

Torrance, Fred. Jay's 150 years. *No Country Life,* Fall 1948. 2:no.4:37–42. illus.   902

Trenton Falls. *Internat Mag,* June 1, 1851. 3:292–95. illus. Excerpts from various publications of N.P. Willis describing the falls.   903

Trenton Falls. *Nat Mag,* Aug. 1852. 1:102–7. illus.   904

Trenton Falls. *Rural NY,* Mar. 10, 1860. 11:81. illus. Brief text.   905

Trost, Alfred H. ed. A history celebrating the 150th anniversary of the town of Essex, New York, 1805–1955... Edited by Alfred H. Trost and Robert C. DeLong. Malone, N.Y. Industrial press, 1955. 62p. illus.   905.1

Tupper Lake national bank. The Tupper Lake national bank: its silver birthday anniversary and an historical souvenir published in observance of the occasion, on June 18, 1931. Tupper Lake, N.Y. 1931. 28p. front.   906

Twichell, Joseph Hopkins. Dr. Bushnell in the woods. *Outlook,* June 2, 1900. 65:261–65 ports. Residence in Keene Valley.   907

Twichell, Joseph Hopkins. In the Adirondacks. *In* Noah Porter, a memorial by friends, ed. by George S. Merriam... N.Y. Scribner, 1893. p.157–65. Keene Valley.   908

Walker, Harry G. Fort Blunder. *No Country Life,* Spring 1948. 2:no.2:12. Story of old Fort Montgomery. Reprinted from the *Ottawa Journal.*   909

Warner, Charles Bond. History of Port Henry, N.Y. by Dr. Charles B. Warner, C. Eleanor Hall collaborating. Rutland, Vt. Tuttle co. 1931. 182p. front. (port.) illus.   910

Warrensburg, N.Y. War committee. Report of the Warrensburgh war committee, 1861–65. Warrensburgh, N.Y. The News press, 1913. 45p. Civil War history.   911

Warrensburgh and Chestertown. Business interests and institutions illustrated and described. Warrensburgh, N.Y. Warrensburgh news, 1898. 24p. illus. Supplement to the *Warrensburgh News.*   912

Webb's Keeseville directory. N.Y. W.S. Webb & co. 1875–77. Includes historical sketch of Keeseville. In collection of Mrs. Marjorie L. Porter.   913

Westport, a noted center of the Champlain region. *Motordom,* June 1932. p.15. illus.   914

William Gilliland's settlement — extract from a letter from a gentleman at Lake Champlain to his friend in New York, dated Willsborough, January 20, 1773. *Mag Am Hist,* Dec. 1881. 7:456–57. Account of recent social events.   915

Willis, Nathaniel Parker, ed. Trenton Falls, picturesque and descriptive. N.Y. Putnam, 1851. 90p. front. plates, illus. Also published in 1865 and 1868 by N. Orr & Co., N.Y., 96p. and in 1862 by J.G. Gregory, N.Y., 96p.   916

Wilson, David. Life in Whitehall: a tale of the ship fever times. Written by a citizen. Whitehall, N.Y. Wm. S. Southmayd & H.W. Buel, publishers, 1849. 57p. "The following work appeared in detached chapters, in '*The Whitehaller.*'" Another edition published by Ingles & Tefft, Whitehall, N.Y., 1900, 76p. ports. plates. Title: "Life in Whitehall During the Ship Fever Times."   917

GEOGRAPHY

GENERAL

Balsey, James Robinson Jr. Techniques and results of aeromagnetic surveying. *In* International geodetic and geophysical union. Association of terrestrial magnetism and electricity. Bulletin 13, 1950. p.413–18. folded map. Used in Oswegatchie quadrangle. 918

Benedict, Farrand Northrop. Barometrical measurements in Essex county. *In* Natural history of New York. Division 4, Geology. Albany, 1842. 2:195–212. 919

Gannett, Henry. A dictionary of altitudes in the United States; 3d ed. Washington, G.P.O. 1899. 775p. (U.S. Geological Survey Bulletin no.160.) 920

Harshberger, John William. Alpine fell-fields of eastern North America. *Geog R*, Apr. 1919. 7:233–55. illus. maps. Includes fell-field on Mt. Marcy. 921

Henry, Joseph. Topographical sketch of the State of New-York, designed chiefly to show the general elevations and depressions of its surface. *Alb Inst Tr*, 1830. 1:87–112. folded plate. 922

Johnson, E.F. Mountains in New York. *Am J Sci*, July 1839. 37:84–89. Discussion of altitudes of Mt. Marcy and Whiteface. 923

Keith, E.F. Mountains and streams of the Adirondacks. *Fur-Fish-Game*, July 1926. 44: no.1:26. Location of various mountains and streams. 924

Kemp, James Furman. Physiography of the Adirondacks. *Pop Sci*, Mar. 1906. 68:195–210. illus. Read Apr. 13, 1905. Abstract in *New York Academy of Science Annals*, 1907, 17:589–91. A discussion of this article by W.M. Davis followed by an answer by Kemp in *Science*, Apr. 20, 1906. n.s.20:630–32. 925

Marshall, Robert Bradford. Results of spirit leveling in New York, 1906 to 1911, inclusive. Washington, G.P.O. 1912. 139p. table. (U.S. Geological Survey Bulletin no.514.) 926

Marshall, Robert Bradford. Spirit leveling in New York, 1895–1905 and 1912–1916. Washington, G.P.O. 1918. 214p. (U.S. Geological Survey Bulletin no.671.) 927

Ruedemann, Rudolf. The tangential master-streams of the Adirondack drainage. *Am J Sci*, Nov. 1931. ser.5:22:431–40. figs. 928

Seymour, Horatio. Topography and history of the State of New-York. *Am Geog Soc Bul*, 1856. 2:128–57. Reprinted with title "A Lecture on the Topography and History of New-York." Utica, N.Y. D.C. Grove, 1856, 41p. Another edition with different introduction published with title "History and Topography of New York. . . " Utica, N.Y. Grove & Bailey, 1870. 32p. Includes discussion of Lake George-Lake Champlain area. 929

Tarr, Ralph Stockman. The physical geography of New York state; with a chapter on climate by E.F. Turner. N.Y. Macmillan, 1902. 397p. illus. maps. Adirondack province, p.13–14; Adirondacks, p.41–52. Mainly reprints of articles in the *Bulletin* of the American Geographical Society. 930

U.S. Geological survey. Water supply papers. Washington, 1896–. The reports of the Division of Hydrography, especially *Operations at River Stations* contained in this series, have miscellaneous data on Adirondack rivers. For description of the *Water Supply Papers* see Boyd, A.M. and Rips, R.E. United States government publications, 1949, p.242–43. 931

EXPLORATION, DESCRIPTION AND TRAVEL

Adirondack, pseud. An Adirondack table-land. *For & Stream*, Sept. 8, 1892. 39:204. North of the high peak area. 932

Adirondack motor routes of adventure; beauty rims the highways of the Adirondacks, en route to mountain, lake and forest resorts, filled with ever-changing scenes. *Motordom*, June 1931. 24:no.12:10–11. illus. 933

The Adirondack mountains. *Harper W*, Aug. 31, 1867. 11:548. illus. Describes a photographers' trip from Malone to Meacham Lake, St. Regis and the Saranacs, North Elba and Harrietstown.   934

Adirondack mountains formed on the bottom of the sea. *NYC Lines Mag*, Nov. 1920. 1:no.8: 27–28. illus.   935

Adirondack scenery. *Appleton*, Sept. 24, 1870. 4:362–66. illus.   936

Adirondack wilderness comprising Lake Champlain, Ausable chasm, Upper and Lower St. Regis, Cascades, John Brown's farm and grave, Lake Placid, Saranac village and Upper and Lower Saranac lakes. Grand Rapids, Mich. James Bayne co. n.d. unpaged. illus. Cover title: "Among the Adirondacks." Two pages of text and forty-seven illustrations.   937

The Adirondacks; land of summer sport. *Motordom*, June 1929. 23:no.1:18–19. illus.   938

The Adirondacks — New York state's 2,000,-000 acre play-ground. *Motordom*, July 1928. 22:no.2:4–7. illus. maps.   939

The Adirondacks an island. *For Leaves*, Autumn 1904. 1:no.4:37.   940

The Adirondacks in autumn glory. *Life*, Oct. 20, 1952. 33:no.16:68–73. illus. Brief text with five illustrations in color by Andreas Feininger.   941

The Adirondacks in 1854. *Ad-i-ron-dac*, Sept.–Oct. 1952. 16:81. Column by William Chapman White reprinted from the *New York Times* "Topics of the Times" of Oct. 17, 1951. Contains extracts from articles by Henry J. Raymond published in the *Times* in 1855.   942

The Adirondacks in 1870. *For & Stream*, June 1, 1901. 56:427.   943

Adirondacks offer camp life solitude, sports or society to summer travelers. *NYC Lines Mag*, July 1927. 8:no.4:28, 102. illus.   944

Adirondacks. The majestic mountain playground; it's yours to enjoy with its lofty peaks, 2000 lakes and famous places for recreation. *Motordom*, June 1930. 24:no.1:7. illus.   945

The Adirondacs. *Harvard Mag*, June 1860. 6:289–96. Trip into the Adirondacks in 1858.   946

Agar, Herbert. The Adirondacks. *New Statesm*, May 30, 1931. 1:501. An Englishman pays brief tribute to the Adirondacks.   947

Among the balsams. *Harper W*, Aug. 11, 1888. 32:591, 597. illus. Journey from North Creek to Blue Mountain Lake, Raquette, etc.   948

Anburey, Thomas. Journal d'un voyage fait dans l'intérieur de l'Amérique septentrionale.

Ouvrage dans lequel on donne des détails précieux sur l'insurrection des Anglo-Américains, et sur la chute désastreuse de leur papier-monnoie. Traduit de l'anglois et enrichi de notes par M. Noël. . . Paris, Chez La Villette, 1793. 2v. plates, folded plan, folded map.   949

Anburey, Thomas. Travels through the interior parts of North America. In a series of letters by an officer. London, William Lane, 1789. 2v. plates, map. Letters written by a lieutenant in Burgoyne's army, 1776–77. Local description, Lake Champlain, Ticonderoga, Saratoga.   950

Appleton, Thomas Gold. Windfalls. Boston, Roberts bros. 1878. 364p. A month in the Adirondacks, p.34–81.   951

Barnaby, H.C.G. Touring the Adirondack lakes. *For & Stream*, July 8, 1905. 65:24–25.   952

Beardslee, Lester A. Adirondack itinerary, by Piseco, pseud. *For & Stream*, July 27. 1876. 6:406–7. Route from New York to Piseco Lake.   953

Beardslee, Lester A. Circumnavigating the Adirondacks, by Piseco, pseud. *For & Stream*, Aug. 27, 1891. 37:104–5.   954

Beauties of the Adirondacks. *State Service*, Oct. 1917. 1:no.3:63–65. illus.   955

Benedict, Farrand Northrop. The wilds of northern New York. *Putnam*, Sept. 1854. 4: 263–70. Donaldson attributes this to F.N. Benedict, Sherrill to M.H. Merwin. See Waddell's "Northern New York," p.12–13.   956

Beetle, David Harold. Up Old Forge way, a central Adirondack story. Utica, N.Y. Utica Observer-Dispatch, 1948. 183p. illus. ports. map. "Reprinted from the Utica *Observer-Dispatch*, Utica, N.Y."   957

Bigelow, Albert. Adirondacks of 1858 and 1859. *For & Stream*, Oct. 5, 1912. 79:423–24. illus. Trip from Raquette Lake through the Marion River to Blue Mountain Lake.   958

Bishop, Nathaniel Holmes. Voyage of the paper canoe; a geographical journey of 2500 miles, from Quebec to the Gulf of Mexico during the years 1874–5. Boston, Lee & Shepard, 1878. 351p. front. illus. maps. Chapters 3 and 4 refer to the Adirondacks. Quotes Colvin reports.   959

Boscq de Beaumont, Gaston du. Aux lacs français des Adirondacks (États-Unis d' Amérique). *Tour du Monde*, June 29, 1901. n.s.7: 301–12. illus. Trip made in 1899, interesting because it gives the impressions of a French traveler. The illustrations are from photographs by Seneca Ray Stoddard.   960

Bowditch, Vincent Yardley. Life and correspondence of Henry Ingersoll Bowditch. Boston, Houghton, 1902. 2v. front. plates, ports. facsim. Trips to the Adirondacks and Reminiscences of John Brown, v.2, p.58–102.   961

Brandreth, Paulina. Spring in the Adirondacks. *For & Stream*, July 22, 1905. 65:62–63.   962

Bridgman, Mrs. Helen (Bartlett). Conquering the world. N.Y. Cloister publishing co. c1925. 264p. Adirondacks, p.169–222.   963

Bromfield, Edward T. ed. Picturesque journeys in America of the Junior united tourist club. N.Y. R. Worthington, 1883. 200p. front. illus. 1884 edition in the Loomis Collection, Keene Valley Public Library. Includes Lake George and the Adirondacks.   964

Brown, Levant Frederick. Autumn in the north woods. *Four Tr News*, Sept. 1904. 7:173–75. illus.   965

Bruce, Dwight Hall. The Adirondacks — recollections and sketches of the great forest. *For & Stream*, Jan. 28, Feb. 11, 1892. 38:74–76, 122–23.   966

Bruce, Wallace. The Adirondacks. *Outing*, June 1883. 2:33–35.   967

Bryant, William Cullen, ed. Picturesque America; or, The land we live in; a delineation by pen and pencil. N.Y. Appleton, 1874. 2v. plates, illus. "The Adirondack Region," by Robert Carter, v.2, p.414–35.   968

Bryant, William Cullen, ed. Picturesque America; or, The land we live in. . .with illustrations on steel and wood by eminent American artists. Rev. ed. N.Y. Appleton, c1894. 720p. front. plates, illus. "The Adirondack Region, with Illustrations by Harry Fenn," p.346–66.   969

Carroll, Charles. Journal of Charles Carroll of Carrollton during his visit to Canada in 1776. . .with a memoir and note by Brantz Mayer. Baltimore, John Murphy for the Maryland historical society, 1876. 110p. ports. Contains descriptions of Lake George, Ticonderoga and Lake Champlain.   970

Carter, Robert. Adirondack scenery. *Appleton*, Sept. 24, 1870. 4:362–66. illus.   971

The changed Adirondacks; our northern lakes and mountains. *For & Stream*, Nov. 26, 1898. 51:431. Reprinted from *Town Topics*, Sept. 15, 1898, 40:no.11:14–15: "Our Northern Lakes and Mountains, by Wanderer, pseud."   972

Cheney, Albert Nelson. Some boyhood memories; VII. A first visit to the Adirondacks. *For & Stream*, Apr. 20, 1901. 56:304.   973

Coffin, Nathaniel Wheeler. Forest Arcadia of northern New York. Embracing a view of its mineral, agricultural and timber resources. Boston, T.O.H.P. Burnham, 1864. 224p. Published anonymously. The author is identified in the New York State Forest Commission Report, 1893, v.1, p.329.   974

Cook, Joel. America, picturesque and descriptive. Philadelphia, H.T. Coates & co. 1900. 3v. fronts. plates. The Adirondacks and their attendant lakes, v.2:271–326.   975

Cornish, Albert. Unfrequented regions of the Adirondacks. *For & Stream*, Mar. 11, 1880. 14:103–4. St. Regis Lake, Moira, Blue Mountain Lake.   976

Covert, William Chalmers. Wild woods and waterways. Philadelphia, Westminster press, 1914. 245p. plates. Ch.4: The Ausable River; Ch.5: Springtime on the Ausable; Ch.7: The Adirondack Woods.   977

Crary, John C. Glorious forest, mountain and lake country opened by new roads in Adirondacks. *Motordom*, Jan. 1929. 22:no.8:10–11. illus.   978

Cruikshank, James A. Looping the Adirondacks. *Field & S*, July 1902. 7:237–41. illus.   979

Curtiss, Arthur Leslie Byron-. The story of a pass in the Adirondacks. Boston, Gorham press, 1917. 224p. front. plates. "This book is a sort of compound of the author's personal experiences and observations, together with stories and yarns picked up by the way."   980

D. My trip to the Adirondack. *Wilkes Spirit*, Sept. 17, 1859. 1:19. Trip to Fenton's.   981

Dailey, Elric J. The Adirondacks. *Fur News*, June 1921. 33:no.6:6–7, 27, 29. illus.   982

Dailey, Elric J. The Adirondacks of to-day. *Fur-Fish-Game*, Sept. 1926. 44:no.3:17–19. illus.   983

Davis, Theodore R. Sketches in the Adirondack region. *Harper W*, Nov. 1868. 12:742, 748. Brief text, full page of illustrations (signed by Davis), chiefly of the section around Adirondac.   984

Davison, J.L. The Adirondacks of 1858 and 1888. *For & Stream*, Mar. 8, 1913. 80:300–1. In 1858 a trip to the Raquette River. In 1888 a 150-mile tramp from Northville to Theresa.   985

Dewey, Melvil. The tonic of the winter woods. *Ind*, Feb. 8, 1915. 81:201–4. illus. Adirondacks in winter.   986

Ellis, Samuel W. Early days in northern New York. *Fur-Fish-Game*, Nov. 1926. 44:no.5:21, 24. Region around Lake Clear.   987

Ely, William Watson. The New York wilderness. 15p. introduction to his Map of the New

York wilderness. N.Y. Colton, 1867. Also in the 1868 edition of the map.   988

Ely, William Watson. A trip to the wilderness. *Rural NY*, Aug. 11, Aug. 25, Sept. 8, 1860. 12:257, 273, 289. maps. Three letters describing a trip from Boonville through Brown's Tract, out by the Saranacs to Port Kent.   989

Emery, Stewart M. Mighty Adirondacks call to the cities. *NY Times Mag*, Aug. 29, 1926. p.7, 21. illus.   990

Entering the wilds, scenic route from Chestertown through the Schroon valley to Schroon Lake and Elizabethtown. *Motordom*, June 1929. 23:no.1:14–15. illus.   991

Faris, John Thomson. Roaming the eastern mountains. N.Y. Farrar & Rinehart, c1932. 327p. plates, maps on end papers. Introduction to the Adirondacks, Ch.5. A week of Adirondack glory, Ch.6.   992

Ferris, George Titus. Our native land; or, Glances at American scenery and places, with sketches of life and adventure. . . N.Y. Appleton, c1882. 615p. illus. incl. map. Adirondacks, p.342.   993

Flint, Peter. The famous land of Leatherstocking. *For & Stream*, Oct. 18, 1913. 81: 510–11. Notes from Paradox, Pyramid lakes, etc.   994

Fosburgh, Peter W. Summertime, Adirondacks. *NYS Con*, June–July 1955. 9:no.6:20–21. illus. Brief text with illustrations in color.   995

Fowler, Barnett. Miami river swamp. *Ad Mt Club Bul*, Sept.–Oct. 1944. 8:no.5:4. Near Speculator and Indian Lake.   996

Glens Falls rotary club. Let's attend. . .Adirondack mountain climbing contest. . .Nov. 2, 1922 to Aug. 16, 1923. . . Glens Falls, N.Y. Bullard press, 1922. 4p. illus. Unique program initiated by Russell Carson. Each weekly club letter contained brief historical sketch of one of the forty-two major peaks in Marshall's "High Peaks." Sketches later used in Carson's "Peaks and People."   997

Glorious are the Adirondack peaks ranging from 1,000 to 5,000 feet and more; famous mountains fill the vacation region. *Motordom*, June 1930. 24:no.1:30. illus.   998

Greenleaf, Elizabeth. How we drove to Gale's. *Outing*, May 1888. 12:131–37. Western Adirondacks.   999

Hallock, Charles. Adirondack memories. *For & Stream*, Aug. 27, 1891. 37:103.   1000

Harte, W. Blackburn. By stage-coach in the Adirondacks. *New Eng M*, Nov. 1890. n.s.3: 362–65.   1001

Hays, Harry P. On Adirondack trails. Reprinted from Altoona Tribune. Dedicated to Henry W. Shoemaker. Altoona, Pa. Times tribune co. 1923. 21p. incl. plates, ports.   1002

Headley, Joel Tyler. The Adirondack; or, Life in the woods. N.Y. Baker & Scribner, 1849. 288p. front. plates. English edition published in London, by Clarke, Beeton & Co. 1852. 1st edition reprinted in 1853 and 1861 by Baker & Scribner. 2d edition, N.Y. Baker & Scribner, 1864. 3d edition, new and enl., N.Y. C. Scribner, 1869. 4th edition, N.Y. Scribner & Armstrong, 1875. Reprinted 1882. A spurious edition, entitled "Letters from the Backwoods and the Adirondac" (105p.), was published in New York by John S. Taylor in 1850. Dublin edition published in 1850 by J.M. M'Glashan with title "Life in the Woods; or, The Adirondack." Reviewed in *Hoog's Instructor*, 1850. n.s.4:382–83.   1003

Henigston, J.W. Up the Hudson, Albany, Troy, Buffalo, Erie and Ontario, Toronto — down the St. Lawrence, Montreal, Quebec — back by Lake Champlain and Bellows Falls towards Boston. *New Mo Mag*, Apr. 1853. 97:499–516.   1004

Hoffman, Charles Fenno. Wild scenes in the forest and prairie. London, Richard Bentley, 1839. 2v. The first 122 pages describe a trip to "the sources of the Hudson." John Cheney and Harvey Holt are the guides. An American edition of this book in one volume appeared in 1843, published in New York by Colyer. Extracts in *High Spots*, July 1937, 14:no.3: 13–15.   1005

Hoffman, Charles Fenno. Wilde scenen im wald und prairie, mit skizzen amerikanischen lebens, aus dem Englischen des Amerikaners C.F. Hoffman von Fr. Gerstacker. Dresden, In der Aruddischen buchhandlung, 1845. 2v. Copy in the British Museum.   1006

Holder, Charles Frederick. The great north woods. *World's Work*, Aug. 1902. 4:2390–94.   1007

Hornaday, John T. In the heart of an autumn forest; beside a silvery lake. *Four Tr News*, Sept. 1905. 9:163–65. illus.   1008

Hubbard, Leonidas Jr. Afoot in nature's game preserve, the Adirondack park region. *Outing*, Nov. 1900. 37:196–201. illus. Trip through the heart of the Adirondack country; short history of the establishment of the Adirondack Park. Reprinted in *Woods and Waters*, Winter 1902–3, 5:no,4:9–11, with title "The Adirondack Park."   1009

Hudowalski, Mrs. Grace (Leech). I've watched a day begin. *Cloud Splitter*, Oct. 1939. 2:no.5:5–6. Description of sunrise in the Adirondacks.   1010

Hungerford, Edward. Pathway of empire. N.Y. McBride, ᶜ1935. 325p. illus. Chapters on the Adirondacks entitled North Country and Lady of the Snows.   1011

Hurley, Donal and Hurley, Richard. A bit o' the Adirondacks. *Motordom*, Oct. 1927. 21: no.5:1–2. illus. Motor trip.   1012

Hurley, Donal and Hurley, Richard. Tourist trails in the Adirondacks; trips to the tops and around scores of mountain peaks in New York's summer playground. *Motordom*, Apr. 1928. 21:no.11:5–6. illus.   1013

In the Adirondacks. *Harper W*, July 12, 1902. 46:892–94. illus.   1014

James, George Wharton. Six weeks in the Adirondacks; life in the "north country" as seen by a Californian. *Four Tr News*, June 1901. 2:363–67. illus.   1015

James, H. Jr. From Lake George to Burlington. *Nation*, Sept. 1, 1870. 11:135–36. Trip by boat and stage.   1016

Jeffers, LeRoy. Glimpses of our northern mountains. *Lincoln*, June 1925. p.18–19. illus. map.   1017

Juvenal, pseud. The Adirondacks in 1898. *For & Stream*, Oct. 1, 1898. 51:262–63. 1018

K., H.H. The heart of the wilderness. *For & Stream*, Sept. 14, 1882. 19:126. Region around Newcomb.   1019

Keith, E.F. The Adirondack mountains. The garden spot for the nature lover. *Fur News*, Aug. 1920. 32:no.2:36.   1020

Kent, Rockwell. An appreciation. *High Spots Yrbk*, 1942. p.9. illus.   1021

Kimball, Francis P. The Adirondacks, America's summer playground. *Motordom*, June 1929. 23:no.1:6–9. illus.   1022

Kimball, Francis P. Fresh enchantment rides the Adirondack trail. *Motordom*, June 1934. p.6–7, 22. illus.   1023

Kimball, Francis P. Hudson-Champlain trail makes its debut; new route to Montreal follows the upper Hudson and beautiful Lake Champlain — saves forty miles, Albany to Canada. *Motordom*, July 1929. 23:no.2:16–17. illus. map.   1024

Kitchin, William Copeman. Wonderland of the east, comprising the lake and mountain region of New England and eastern New York. Boston, Page co. 1920. 331p. col. front. plates (part col.) folded maps. (See America First Series.) Adirondacks and the Lake Champlain country, p.110–44.   1025

Lake, Thomas Peters, The best autumn color tours in America. *Bet Hom & Gard*, Oct. 1955. 33:no.10:69, 123, 125, 127, 129, 172, 287. col. illus. maps. Adirondacks, p.123.   1026

Lanman, Charles. Adventures in the wilds of North America; ed. by Charles Richard Weld. London, Longman, Brown, Green & Longman, 1854. 300p. Adirondacks, p.88–121.   1027

Lanman, Charles. Adventures in the wilds of the United States and British American provinces. . .with an appendix by Lieut. Campbell Hardy. . . Philadelphia, J.W. Moore, 1856. 2v. front. plates. Includes his "Tour to the River Saguenay."   1028

Lewis, Leroy. Following the gasoline trail into the Adirondacks. *Outing*, May 1921. 78:63–64. illus.   1029

Low, A. Augustus. The central Adirondacks — an ideal vacation land. *Motordom*, June 1932. p.26. port. illus.   1030

Mabie, Hamilton Wright. Winter in the Adirondacks. *Scrib M*, Dec. 1888. 4:641–56. illus.   1031

McNulta, John. Fifty years with a fly. *Field & S*, Apr. 1900. 5:210–12. Journey from Albany to Boonville in 1848.   1032

MacQueen, Peter and Smith, J. Hyatt. Life in the Adirondacks. *Munsey*, Feb. 1893. 8: 479–93. illus.   1033

Many wonders fill Adirondack trails; strange and quaint places which the motorist may look for. *Motordom*, June 1930. 24:no.1:23. illus.   1034

Mather, Frederic Gregory. The Adirondacks as they are. *Fr Leslies Pop Mo*, Sept. 1890. 30:354–68. illus.   1035

Mathiasen, Metthea K. Sommer i Adirondack bjergene. Odense, Milóske boghandels forlag, 1911. 135p. plates. Written in Danish.   1036

Mayo, Amory Dwight. Adirondacks in August. *Old & New*, Sept. 1870. 2:343–52. 1037

Mayo, Amory Dwight. A journey to the Adirondacks. *Unit Rev*, Nov. 1875. 4:511–18.   1038

The mighty Adirondacks; a wonderful playground of mountains and lakes. *Motordom*, June 1933. p.6. illus. map.   1039

Mighty Adirondacks, greatest playground in America, two million acres of mountain lakes and forest extend new joys to vacationists. *Motordom*, May 1930. 23:no.12:12–13. illus.   1040

Mr. Dooley on the Adirondacks as reported by T.C.J. in the Elizabethtown Post. *St No Mo*, Aug. 1907. 2:280–83.   1041

Moore, E.A. Little journeys. *Up Mo*, July 1940, July–Aug. 1941. 1:no.4:3; 2:no.4:3; 2:no.5:3. maps. Short trips from Utica through the Adirondacks.   1042

Murray, Hon. Amelia Matilda. Letters from the United States, Cuba and Canada. Two volumes complete in one. N.Y. Putnam, 1856. 410p. Letters 17, 19 and 29 refer to the Adirondacks. Quoted in *Forest Leaves*, Spring 1905, 2:no.2:34–35. Reviewed by Preston Souther in *The Southern Literary Messenger*, June 1856, 22:455–61.   1043

Nichols, William B. Life in the Adirondacks, including the legend of Sabaal, by one of the Q.C. N.Y. C.A. Coffin, 1876. 23p. Published anonymously. Autographed copy at the New York Historical Society basis for author entry.   1044

The north woods thirty-six years ago. *Gard & For*, Dec. 24, 1890. 3:618. Unsigned editorial. Quotes Hammond.   1045

On the great trail of conquest; two centuries of warfare raged along Lake George and Lake Champlain, with gallant Valcour Island, Crown Point, Ticonderoga and Saratoga forming thrilling scenes. *Motordom*, June 1931. 24:no.12:12–13. illus.   1046

Osborne, Edward B. Letters from the woods. [Editorial correspondence.] Random rhymes, from 20 to 70. Annual addresses written for press carriers. Poughkeepsie, N.Y. 1893. 182p. plates, port. Cover title: Forest, Lake and Random Rhymes, and Letters from the Woods. Letters about the Adirondacks written in 1856–71, p.7–44.   1047

Patten, Edmund. A glimpse at the United States and the northern states of America, with the Canadas... London, Effingham Wilson, 1853. 109p. plates. Lake George, Ticonderoga and Plattsburg, p.61–73.   1048

Pauncefote, Maud. The Adirondacks, United States. *Lady's Realm*, Sept. 1902. 12:656–59. illus. Abstracted in *Review of Reviews* (Eng.) v.26, p.298. Chiefly description of section around the Fulton Chain, with general remarks on the way of life in the Adirondacks.   1049

Peachy, Hattie R. A day in the Adirondacks. *For Leaves*, Spring 1909. 6:no.1:46–47.   1050

Plaisted, E.R. Pastures old and new. *Vermonter*, Apr. 1923. 28:no.4:45–49. A letter describing a trip to Lake George and western New York.   1051

Plaisted, E.R. Time and tide. *Vermonter*, Aug. 1923. 28:no.8:107–11. Letter describing a trip through the Adirondacks.   1052

Priest, Irvin. A short history of the caverns and Natural bridge, N.Y. Souvenir. Adirondack mountains. n.p. n.d. 8p. illus. Cover title.   1053

Prime, Samuel Irenæus. Under the trees. N.Y. Harper, 1874. 313p. Adirondacks, p.92–137.   1054

Pychowska, Lucia D. The Adirondacs. *Contin Mo*, Nov. 1864. 6:544–52. (Sketches of American Life and Scenery, V.) Vacation headquarters in Elizabethtown with excursions to Ausable Chasm, etc.   1055

Pychowska, Lucia D. To Saranac and back. *Contin Mo*, Dec. 1864. 6:664–75. (Sketches of American Life and Scenery, VI.) Includes climbing Mt. Marcy from Ausable Lakes.   1056

Radford, Harry V. The lost lake of the Adirondacks. *Woods & Wat*, Winter 1902–3. 5:no.4:12–13. illus. Cold River country. 1057

Raymond, Henry J. A week in the wilderness: notes of a tour of observations through the wilderness of northern New York. *Tahawus Cloudsplitter*, Feb.–May 1953. 4:no.2:9–12; no.3:9–11; no.4:8–11; no.5:8–11. illus. Raymond's articles were published in the *New York Times* June 19, June 26, July 7 and July 14, 1855. They are also reprinted as Addendum to Chapter 13 of Hochschild's "Township 34."   1058

Rice, Walter C. Alone yet not lonely. *Conservationist*, Nov. 1919. 2:163–67. illus. By the fire warden on Ampersand Mountain.   1059

Richards, Thomas Addison. A forest story: 1. The hunting-grounds of the Saranac; 2. The Adirondack woods and waters. *Harper*, Aug.–Sept. 1859. 19:310–23, 454–63.   1060

Roosevelt, Theodore. Diaries, pt.2. *Personality*, May 1928. 2:no.1:69–82. Daily record of a trip through the Adirondacks and White Mountains in August 1871.   1061

Rosecrans, L. A glimpse of the Adirondacks. *Cath World*, Nov. 1876. 24:261–69. Letter describing a trip from Lake George to Lake Champlain by boat, then by stage to Keene Flats.   1062

Scenic trails of the Ausable valley. *Motordom*, June 1932. p.10–11. illus. Motor trails.   1063

Seeger, Frederique. The scenic panorama of New York state. *Fr Leslies Pop Mo*, Nov. 1895. 40:617–30. illus. Adirondacks, p.617–21.   1064

Shorey, Archibald Thompson. The mts. bless them. *Cloud Splitter*, Oct. 1943. 6:no.7:5–6. Account of a measuring job among the high peaks.   1065

Shorey, Archibald Thompson. West of Tupper. *Cloud Splitter*, June 1939. 2:no.4:12. 1066

Sights and sounds of the forest park; high peaks of the Adirondacks hold secrets of beauty open to the vacationist with chasms, gorges and majestic summit views — Ausable chasm one of the outstanding sights every motorist should view. *Motordom*, June 1931. 24:no.12:22–23. illus.   1067

Smith, H. Perry. The modern babes in the wood; or, Summerings in the wilderness. By H. Perry Smith. To which is added a reliable and descriptive guide to the Adirondacks. By E.R. Wallace. Hartford, Conn. Syracuse, N.Y. Columbian book co. W. Gill, 1872. 444p. front. plates, illus. double map. Published by subscription only.   1068

Smith, Ralph H. This was the forest primeval; as revealed by pollen analysis and writings of early travellers and surveyors. *Bul Schools*, Feb. 1954. 40:138–43. illus. Includes the Adirondacks.   1069

Some wild Adirondacks left. *For & Stream*, Aug. 4, 1906. 67:181. Reprinted from Whitehall *Chronicle*. Southeastern Adirondacks.   1070

Southern Adirondacks opens wilderness trails from Speculator to Long lake, primitive grandeur of Adirondacks lures the motorist. *Motordom*, June 1930. 24:no.1:34. illus. 1071

Spears, Eldridge A. The first touch of autumn. *For & Stream*, Sept. 19, 1908. 71:452.   1072

Spears, Eldridge A. Spring in the Adirondacks. *For & Stream*, Apr. 11, 1903. 60:285–86.   1073

Spears, Eldridge A. Spring in the Adirondacks. *For & Stream*, Apr. 10, 1909. 72:572.   1074

Spears, John Randolph. When the snow falls in the Adirondacks. *Scrib M*, Dec. 1901. 30:737–49. illus.   1075

Spears, Raymond Smiley. The new Adirondacks. *Outlook*, May 24, 1916. 113:191–200. illus. Effect of the automobile on the wilderness.   1076

Steele, David McConnell. Vacation journeys east and west... N.Y. Putnam, 1918. 240p. plates, maps. In the Adirondack wilderness, p.89–113.   1077

Stillman, William James. The Adirondacks to-day. *Nation*, Aug. 14, 1884. 39:130–31.   1078

Stillman, William James. The old Rome and new, and other studies... London, Grant Richards, 1897. 296p. The Philosophers' Camp, p.265–96. The preceding chapter, The Subjective of It, p.232–64, has Adirondack background.   1079

Stoddard, Seneca Ray, illus. Adirondacks. *NYS Con*, Feb.–Mar. 1950. 4:no.4:20–23. port. illus. Illustrations also on inside front cover. Reproduction of Stoddard photographs, brief text.   1080

Stoddard, Seneca Ray. The Adirondacks. *St No Mo*, Aug. 1906. 1:no.4:17–27. illus. maps.   1081

Stoddard, Seneca Ray. Old times in the Adirondacks, being a narrative of a trip into the wilderness in 1873. *St No Mo*, Oct. 1906–May 1907, Aug. 1907–Jan. 1908. 1:no.6:9–12; 1:no.7:11–15; 1:no.8:15–16; 1:no.9:13–16; 1:no.10:12–16; 1:no.11:14–16; 1:no.12: 13–16; 2:53–63, 284–93, 345–59, 419–31, 506–12, 562–67; 3:31–42.   1082

Street, Alfred Billings. Woods and waters; or, The Saranac and Racket... N.Y. M. Doolady, 1860. 345p. incl. front. (map) plates, illus. Reviewed in *The Knickerbocker*, Oct. 1860, 56:413–15.   1083

Street, Alfred Billings. Woods and waters; or, Summer in the Saranacs, with two illustrations designed by William Hart and engraved by Avery. N.Y. Hurd & Houghton, 1865. 345p. front. plates. Earlier edition has title "Woods and waters; or, The Saranac and Racket."   1084

Sunday Rock Association, Potsdam, New York. Sunday Rock, an Adirondack landmark. Potsdam, N.Y. Herald-Recorder press, 1929. 55p. Munson ascribes authorship to Charles H. Leete.   1085

Taylor, Benjamin F. Summer-savory gleaned from rural nooks in pleasant weather. Chicago, Griggs, 1879. 212p. The north woods, p.66–77.   1086

Taylor, Frank Hamilton. The Adirondack mountains. N.Y. Giles co. 1892. 31p.   1087

Taylor, Frank Hamilton. Birch bark from the Adirondacks; or, From city to trail... N.Y. Adirondack railway co. C1886. 70p. front. (folded map) illus. 2d edition, 1887, 100p. 3d edition, rev. and improved, 1888, 76p.   1088

Teall, Gardner Callahan. Adirondack country. *Travel*, Aug. 1910. 15:481–84. illus. 1089

That Adirondack lure. *Motordom*, Sept. 1931. p.8.   1090

This summer see northern New York. *No Country Life*, Summer 1947. 1:no.4:11–16. illus.   1091

Thorpe, Thomas B. A visit to "John Brown's tract." *Harper*, July 1859. 19:160–78. illus. map.   1092

The thrilling trail of American victory; entering the Adirondacks over the route of the Burgoyne invasion, a new adventure. *Motordom*, June 1930. 24:no.1:36–38. illus.   1093

Through the Adirondacks by the "Natural highway." Ogdensburg, N.Y. W.S. McKean, 1882. 40p. illus. map.   1094

Todd, John. Summer gleanings; or sketches and incidents of a pastor's vacation. Northampton, Mass. Hopkins, Bridgman, 1852. 281p. front. Tomo, and the Wild Lakes, p.159–78; Old Sabael, p.261–66.   1095

The trail through the mountain heart, scenic beauties and summer colonies lend enchantment to the road from Schroon Lake to Elizabethtown. *Motordom*, June 1930. 24: no.1:12–13. illus.   1096

Vane, Henry. Adirondack days. *Harper*, Oct. 1881. 63:678–93. illus.   1097

Variety of lakes and mountains in the central Adirondacks. *Motordom*, June 1934. p.20. illus.   1098

Vast throngs carried to mountain and seaside resorts; 390 extra cars in week. *NYC Lines Mag*, July 1919. 1:no.6:27. illus.   1099

A voice from the 'North woods.' *Knick Mag*, Sept. 1858. 52:300–2. Black River country.
                                                     1100

Vosburgh, Frederick G. New York state's air-conditioned roof. *Nat Geog M*, June 1938. 73:715–48. illus. (part col.) map.   1101

Waddell, William Coventry Henry. A paper read before the American geographical and statistical society, November 2, 1854. N.Y. Putnam, 1855. 48p. map. Largely based on the report of A.F. Edwards for the Sacket's Harbor and Saratoga Railroad Company. The title of the paper is "Northern New York." It was accompanied by "A Map of the Northern Part of the State of New York, compiled by G. Schroeter, 1854."   1102

Warner, Charles Dudley. In the wilderness. *In* his Complete writings. . . Hartford, American publishing co. 1904. v.6, p.1–136. (Backlog Edition.)   1103

Watson, Elkanah. Men and times of the Revolution; or, Memoirs. . . edited by his son Winslow C. Watson; 2d ed. . . N.Y. Dana & co. 1856. 557p. port. illus. Trip to Vermont by way of Glens Falls, Lake George, Ticonderoga and Crown Point, p.402ff.   1104

Wells, Edward Phineas. The Adirondac wilderness. *Wms Q*, July–Aug. 1863. 10:244–56; 11:1–10. Author's name supplied by Williams College Library.   1105

Western Adirondacks a scenic wilderness; Tupper, Long, Blue Mountain, Racquette and Fulton chain welcomes the motorist. *Motordom*, June 1929. 23:no.1:38. illus. 1106

Whitaker, E.S. Adirondack tours. *For & Stream*, Dec. 7, 1901. 57:452–53.   1107

Whitaker, E.S. Adirondack tours. Parts 1–3. *For & Stream*, July 6–20, 1907. 69:8–9, 48–49, 88–89.   1108

Whitaker, E.S. A memorable trip from the heart of the Adirondacks through the Hudson river, lakes George and Champlain and the St. Lawrence river to Lake Ontario and return. *For & Stream*, Oct. 18, 1907. 69:608–11, 639. illus.   1109

White, William Chapman. Adirondack magic. *Colliers*, Oct. 11, 1952. 130:no.15: 44–45. illus. Brief text with five color pictures.
                                                     1110

Wild charm in western Adirondacks, Tupper lake, Star lake, Cranberry lake in forest heart, thrill the vacationist. *Motordom*, June 1930. 24:no.1:32. illus.   1111

Wildwood trail of the central Adirondacks. *Motordom*, June 1932. p.16–17. illus.   1112

Williams, J. David, ed. America illustrated . . . N.Y. Thomas O'Kane, 1876. 121p. illus. Trenton Falls, p.17–19; Lake George, p.27–29; Sabbath-Day Point, Lake George, p.85–86; In the Adirondacks, p.93–97.   1113

Willis, Charles W. Following the tow-path and through the Adirondacks awheel, by Allan Eric and the "Junior Partner," pseuds. Boston, N.E.R.G. publishing co. 1898. 95p. plates, front.   1114

Wise, David. Summer days on the Hudson: the story of a pleasure tour from Sandy Hook to the Saranac lakes. . . N.Y. Nelson & Phillips, 1875. 288p. illus. Adirondacks, p.246–88.   1115

Wurts, George. Journal of a tour to Niagara Falls, Montreal, Lake Champlain &c. *In* New Jersey historical society. Proceedings, Oct. 1951. 69:342–62. Tour taken in 1851. Includes Lake George and Lake Champlain.
                                                     1116

THE ADIRONDACK AND STATE LAND SURVEYS

Arranged by date

Colvin, Verplanck. Ascent and barometrical measurement of Mount Seward. Albany, Argus co. 1872. 12p. illus. "From the 24th annual report of the New York state museum of natural history for the year 1870. Printed in advance of the report." Also in New York State Museum. 24th Annual Report, 1870, p.171–80.   1117

New York (state). Adirondack survey. Report on a topographical survey of the Adirondack wilderness of New York, by Verplanck Colvin. Albany, Argus co. 1873. 43p. plates, tables, folded maps. Senate document 53, 1873. Reviewed in *American Sportsman*, Mar. 21, 1874 under title "The Adirondack Wilderness."   1118

Report on the topographical survey of the Adirondack wilderness of New York, for the year 1873. . . Albany, Weed, Parsons & co. 1874. 306p. plates, tables, folded maps. Senate document 98, 1874.   1119

7th annual report on the progress of the topographical survey of the Adirondack region of New York, to the year 1879. . . Containing the condensed reports for the years 1874–75–76–77 and '78. . . by Verplanck Colvin. Albany, Weed, Parsons & co. 1880. 536p. plates (part in color and folded) port. tables, folded plan, diagrs. and maps. Assembly document 87, 1879. Contains the following papers: Colvin, Verplanck. Winter Fauna of Mount Marcy, p.363–74; Lintner, J.A. Lepidoptera of the Adirondack Region Collected by W.W. Hill, in 1875–1878, p.375–400; Peck, C.H. Plants of the Summit of Mount Marcy, p.401–12; Chahoon, George. Report on Iron Deposits in the North Eastern Division. (With Industrial Memoranda.) p.413–28.   1120

Annual report of the superintendent of the Adirondack survey. March 7, 1879. Albany, Weed, Parsons & co. 1879. 64p. Assembly document 87, 1879. This is the same report as the first section of the combined report listed above (no.1120).   1121

Annual report of the superintendent of the Adirondack survey. March 5, 1880. Albany, Weed, Parsons & co. 1880. 8p. Assembly document 77, 1880.   1122

Annual report on the progress of the topographical survey of the Adirondack region of New York for the year 1880 (with map of triangulation) by Verplanck Colvin. Transmitted to the Legislature March 1, 1881. Albany, Weed, Parsons & co. 1881. 25p. Assembly document 61, 1881.   1123

Annual report on the progress of the topographical survey of the Adirondack region. . . March 1, 1882. Albany, 1882. 5p. Assembly document 57, 1882.   1124

Annual report on the progress of the topographical survey of the Adirondack region. . . February 28, 1883. Albany, 1883. 29p. Assembly document 177, 1883.   1125

The Adirondack survey. *For & Stream*, Jan. 28, 1875. 3:392–93. Editorial.   1126

Essex county, N.Y. Board of supervisors. Journal of proceedings. Elizabethtown, N.Y. Livingston, 1878. 114p. Letter from Verplanck Colvin asking to have three members appointed to confer with him on the Adirondack Survey, p.64–65.   1127

New York (state). Governor (Alonzo B. Cornell). The Adirondack survey; the Northern wilderness. *In* his Public papers, 1882. Albany, 1882. p.42–44. Lincoln 7:720–22.   1128

Mather, Fred. Adirondack survey notes. *For & Stream*, July 6, 20, Aug. 3–Sept. 28, Nov. 16, 30, Dec. 14, 28, 1882; Mar. 8, May 10, 1883. 18:444, 484; 19:2, 22, 42, 62, 82, 102, 122, 142, 162, 302, 342, 383, 421–22; 20:102, 282.   1129

New York (state). Governor (Grover Cleveland). Message re Assembly bill no.165. *In* his Public papers, 1883. Albany, 1883. p.69–72. Includes comments on the Adirondack survey. Lincoln 7:874–77.   1130

New York (state). Governor (Grover Cleveland). The Adirondack wilderness; the Adirondack survey. *In* his Public papers, 1884. Albany, 1884. p.48–52. State Land Survey, p.52–54. Lincoln 7:983–87, 987–89.   1131

New York (state). State land survey. Report on the Adirondack and state land surveys to the year 1884, with a description of the location of the boundaries of the great land patents and an account of the variation of the magnetic needle in northern New York, between the years 1766 and 1883, with rainfall and temperature tables, and a list of the state lands, by Verplanck Colvin. Albany, Weed, Parsons & co. 1884. 343p. plates, folded maps. Assembly document 126, 1884.   1132

Annual report of the superintendent of the Adirondack state land surveys. . . Albany, 1885. 8p. Assembly document 79, 1885. Submitted Feb. 20, 1885.   1133

Report on the progress of the Adirondack state land survey to the year 1886. With an historical sketch of the work. . .by Verplanck Colvin. . . Albany, Weed, Parsons & co. 1886. 100p. folded maps. Assembly document 80, 1886. Also issued with the Report. . .to the year 1884 appended.   1134

Annual report of the superintendent of the Adirondack state land survey. Assembly document 74, 1887. This one-page document lists the title with the note: Directed not to be printed.   1135

Report on the progress of the state land survey. . . Transmitted to the Legislature February 28, 1888. Albany, Troy press co. 1888. 8p. Assembly document 58, 1888.   1136

Report on the progress of the state land survey. . . Transmitted to the Legislature February 27, 1889. Albany, Troy press co. 1889. 18p. Assembly document 65, 1889.   1137

Report on the progress of the state land survey. . . Transmitted to the Legislature March 3, 1890. Albany, J.B. Lyon, 1890. 32p. plates. Assembly document 95, 1890.   1138

Report on the progress of the state land survey. . . Transmitted to the Legislature February 27, 1891. Albany, J.B. Lyon, 1891. 306p. plates, folded map in pocket. Senate document 48, 1891. Includes the following papers: Colvin, Verplanck. Address Before the New York Farmers, Dec. 11, 1890. . . p.36–54; Mather, Fred. Memoranda Relating to Adirondack Fishes. . . p.113–73. Reprinted from the 1879 Report of the Adirondack Survey: Colvin, Winter Fauna of Mount Marcy, p.221–35; Chahoon, Report on Iron Deposits, p.95–111; Lintner, Lepidoptera of the Adirondack Region, p.189–220; Peck, Plants of the Summit of Mount Marcy, p.175–87. Records of Survey of Boundary Line Between the Counties of Herkimer and Oneida, p.237–63. List of maps in reports, p.285–91.   1139

Report on the progress of the state land survey. . . Transmitted to the Legislature February 29, 1892. Albany, J.B. Lyon, 1892. 17p. Senate document 35, 1892.   1140

Report on the progress of the state land survey. . . Transmitted to the Legislature February 28, 1893. Albany, J.B. Lyon, 1893. 14p. Senate document 32, 1893.   1141

Report on the progress of the state land survey. . . Transmitted to the Legislature February 28, 1894. Albany, J.B. Lyon, 1894. 406p. plates, folded map in pocket. Senate document 84, 1894. The special reports from the 1891 report, as well as the four reports from the 1879 Adirondack survey report, are reprinted in the appendix. Table of Altitudes in the Adirondack Region, p.305–23. Magnetic Observations at and near Albany, N.Y. Between the Years 1688 and 1894, p.369–99.
                                        1142

Report on the progress of the state land survey. . . Transmitted to the Legislature March 1, 1895. Albany, J.B. Lyon, 1895. 7p. Senate document 65, 1895.   1143

Report of the superintendent of the state land survey. . . Transmitted to the Legislature March 2, 1896. Albany, Wynkoop Hallenbeck Crawford co. 1896. 405p. plates, maps Senate document 42, 1896. Laws Relating to County Boundaries from A.D. 1683 to 1799, p.333–401.   1144

Report of the superintendent of the state land survey. . . Transmitted to the Legislature March 9, 1897. Albany, Wynkoop Hallenbeck Crawford co. 1897. 617p. plates, maps, partly folded. With 14 folded maps in separate case. Senate document 42, 1897. Report on the Character of the Forests and Soil of Certain Tracts of State Lands in the Adirondack Region, by Charles H. Peck, p.517–53. Last printed report. Survey abolished in 1900.
                                        1145

Adirondack survey. *Eng & Min J*, Apr. 18, 1885. 39:257–58. Editorial commending work done on the Adirondack State Land Survey.
                                        1146

New York (state). Legislature. Assembly. Report of the special committee to investigate matters connected with the state sur-

veys. Albany, 1885. 10p. Assembly document 137, 1885.   1147

New York (state). State engineer and surveyor. Reply. . .to resolutions relating to maps, etc. filed by the superintendent of the Adirondack survey. Albany, 1885. 2p. Assembly document 73, 1885. See also Assembly document 74, 1885, 1p. for Reply of Comptroller to request to report on maps filed by Colvin.   1148

Colvin, Verplanck. Adirondack and state land surveys. 1887. The Legislature and the Governor. Albany, 1887. 4p. A résumé of the points of disagreement between Colvin and the Governor, with emphasis on vetoes by the Governor of measures relating to the survey, approved by the Legislature.   1149

Colvin, Verplanck. The variation of the needle and the location of the isogonic lines in northern New York. *Alb Inst Tr*, 1887. 11: 181–204. tables.   1150

New York (state). Governor (Roswell P. Flower). Veto, Assembly bill no.1001, making appropriation for the state land survey. *In* his Public papers, 1894. Albany, 1895. p.188–91. Lincoln 9:423–24.   1151

Colvin, Verplanck. Measuring Marcy's height. *High Spots*, July 1937. 14:no.3:27–30. Extract from the *Topographical Survey*. . .3–7th Reports, 1874–79.   1152

Plum, Dorothy Alice. The Colvin reports. *Ad-i-ron-dac*, Mar.–Apr. 1955. 19:34–35, 37. Annotated check list.   1153

OTHER SURVEYS

Arranged by date

New York (state). Canal board. Report. . . relating to the survey of the several branches of the Hudson river, transmitting the report and estimates of the engineer, with a communication. . .from the Surveyor-general. Albany, 1840. 35p. tables. Senate document 61, 1840. Holley was Surveyor-General. 1154

New York (state). Canal board. Report. . . relating to the continuation of the survey of the northern branches of the Hudson river, in obedience to a resolution of the Assembly, of March 24th, 1840. Albany, 1840. 3p. Assembly document 275, 1840.   1155

Guyot, Arnold Henry. Prof. Guyot's report on the various meteorological stations established under the direction of the university. *In* New York (state). University. 64th annual report of the regents, 1851. p.229–41. Reprinted in *American Journal of Science*, Mar. 1852, ser.2:13:272–76, with title "Remarks on the Topography of the State of New York."
                                        1156

New York (state). Governor (Washington Hunt). Communication transmitting the memorial of a committee of the American association for the advancement of science, on a geographical survey of the state. Albany, 1852. 24p. Senate document 41, 1852.   1157

Pickhardt, Wilhelm. Field notes of the surveys of Brant lake tract, Ellice tract, Hague tract, Harris' location of the line dividing Essex and Warren counties, Paradox tract, Schroon tract and tract west of Road patent. N.Y. Author, 1884. 509p.   1158

Topographic survey of the upper Hudson river valley. *In* New York (state). State engineer and surveyor. Annual report, 1895, p.29–50. Assembly document 62, 1896. The survey was made jointly with the U.S. Geological Survey.   1159

New York (state). State engineer and surveyor. Certified copies of ancient field notes and maps, 1772–1796–1797–1798. Albany, J.B. Lyon, 1903. 83p. Extract from the Annual Report for 1903. Totten and Crossfield's Purchase, Macomb's Purchase, Old Military Tract.   1160

T., R.S. Northern Adirondacks—Champlain and Hudson. *Am Geog Soc Bul*, 1906. 38:39–40. Part of column, Geographical Record. Brief account of New York State Geological Survey of the Adirondacks. 1161

Ivory, Edward P. Old-line surveying in the Adirondacks. *Emp For*, 1916. 2:71–74. Resurvey of Township 15 in 1919.   1162

Merrill, George Perkins. Contributions to a history of American state geological and natural history surveys. Washington, G.P.O. 1920. 549p. ports. Geological surveys under Hall, Emmons and others, p.327–62.   1163

The state as a taxpayer. *NYS Con*, Dec. 1950– Jan. 1951. 5:no.3:22–23. illus. Description of the forest survey being conducted by the State University of New York College of Forestry at the request of the State Board of Equalization and Assessment; includes tax figures for 1949.   1164

Adirondacks, Catskills survey enters final six months. *J For*, Nov. 1951. 49:850. Outdoor research on character and quality of privately and publicly owned forest trees.   1165

Davis, James E. Surveying the six million acres. *Northeast Log*, July 1952. 1:no.1:14–15. illus. Adirondack and Catskill park and forest survey completed by the State College of Forestry.   1166

New York (state). Legislature. Joint legislative committee on natural resources. Report ...1952. Albany, Williams press, 1952. 116p. tables, map. Legislative document 77, 1952. First Milmoe Committee report.   1167

New York (state). Legislature. Joint legislative committee on natural resources. Report ...1953. Albany, Williams press, 1953. 146p. illus. tables, folded map. Legislative document 69, 1953. Forest Preserve Survey, p.34–66.   1168

King, A.H. North 1 degree west. *NYS Con*, Oct.–Nov. 1954. 9:no.2:18–19. illus. 1796 survey of Herkimer and Washington county line by Medad Miller. See letter from Warder H. Cadbury in issue for Apr.–May 1955, 9: no.5:40.   1169

Comments on Joint legislative committee report, Document 72, 1954 "New York state's natural resources." Schenectady, N.Y. 1954. 7p. Issued by the Oneida County Forest Preserve Council, the Forest Preserve Association of New York State, Inc. and the Bouquet River Lodge Chapter, Adirondack Mountain Club.   1170

New York (state). Legislature. Joint legislative committee on natural resources. Report ...1954. Albany, Williams press, 1954. 221p. illus. tables, maps (1 folded). Legislative document 72, 1954. Cover title: New York State's Natural Resources. New York State Forest Preserve Survey, p.57–124.   1171

National wildlife federation. NENYIAC comes to New York. Washington, 1955. 14p. Multilithed. John D. Bulger's analysis of the unpublished reports of the New England-New York Interagency Committee. Inventory of watershed resources and presentation of plan for resources development.   1172

New York (state). Legislature. Joint legislative committee on natural resources. Report ...1955. Albany, Williams press, 1955. 285p. illus. tables, maps (1 folded). Legislative document 76, 1955. Cover title: Our Lands, Forests, Waters and Air. Studies of the Forest Preserve, p.228–29.   1173

New York (state). Conservation department, Biological survey, *see* nos.2918–23.
New York (state). Geological survey, *see* nos.2985–87, 2989–91, 3289.
New York (state). Natural history of New York, *see* nos.2990–92, 2994, 3288, 3497, 3520, 4336.

GUIDEBOOKS

Arranged by date

Davison, Gideon Miner. The fashionable tour, in 1825. An excursion to the Springs, Niagara, Quebec and Boston. Saratoga Springs, N.Y. Author, 1825. 169p. map. First published in 1822. Later editions, revised and enlarged, issued with title "The Traveler's Guide Through the Middle and Northern States. . ."   1174

Dwight, Theodore, 1796–1866. The northern traveller; containing the routes to Niagara, Quebec and the Springs. . .with descriptions of the principal scenes, and useful hints to strangers. . . N.Y. Wilder & Campbell, 1825. 213p. front. plates, map. 2d edition, improved and extended, N.Y. A.T. Goodrich, 1826, 382p. (subtitle varies). 3d edition combined with A Northern Tour, by H.D. Gilpin, N.Y. Carvill, 1828, 403p. 4th edition, N.Y. J. & J. Harper, 1830, 444p. 5th edition, N.Y. Goodrich & Wiley, 1834, 432p. 6th edition, N.Y. J.P. Haven, 1841, 250p. Contains description of an excursion to Lake George.   1175

Gilpin, Henry Dilworth. A northern tour; being a guide to Saratoga Springs, Lake George, Niagara, Canada. . .embracing an account of the canals, colleges, public institutions, natural curiosities, &c. Philadelphia, H.D. Carey & I. Lea, 1825. 279p. map. 1176

North American tourist. N.Y. A.T. Goodrich, 1839. 506p. plates, front. folded maps. Lakes George and Champlain, Ticonderoga, p.138–52.   1177

Disturnell, John. New-York state guide containing an alphabetical list of counties, towns, cities. . .with other useful information. . . Albany, J. Disturnell, 1842. 72p. folding map. Map of the State of New York. . .by J. Calvin Smith. Quite a bit of detail on the Adirondacks.   1178

The New York state tourist, descriptive of the scenery of the Hudson, Mohawk and St. Lawrence rivers. Falls, lakes, mountains, springs, railroads and canals. . . N.Y. A.T. Goodrich, 1842. 234p. plates, front. map. Adirondacks, p.200–18.   1179

Disturnell, John. The northern traveller; containing the Hudson river guide and tour to the Springs, Lake George and Canada, passing through Lake Champlain. With a description of all the places on the route mostworthy of notice. N.Y. J. Disturnell, 1844. 84p. 1180

Holley, Orville Luther. The picturesque tourist; being a guide through the northern and eastern states and Canada. . . N.Y. J. Disturnell, 1844. 336p. front. plates, illus. maps. Also published with copyright date 1858. 1181

Tanner, H.S. Travellers' hand book for the State of New-York, the province of Canada . . . 3d ed. N.Y. Geographical establishment, 1845. 166p. maps. Albany to Montreal, p.84–87. From Utica to Sackett's Harbor, p.100–1. Route from Utica to Ogdensburg, by stage, p.102. General information, p.1–11.   1182

Thompson, Zadock. Guide to Lake George, Lake Champlain, Montreal and Quebec, with maps and tables of routes and distances from Albany, Burlington and Montreal. Burlington, Vt. C. Goodrich, 1845. 48p. map. 2d edition, 1851.   1183

Ontario & St. Lawrence steamboat company. The great northern route. American lines. The Ontario and St. Lawrence steamboat company's hand-book for travelers to Niagara Falls, Montreal and Quebec and through Lake Champlain to Saratoga Springs . . . Buffalo, N.Y. Jewett, Thomas & co. 1852. 158p. front. plate, illus. folded map. Also published in 1853 (174p.) and 1854 (175p.).   1184

Thompson, Zadock. Northern guide. Lake George, Lake Champlain, Montreal and Quebec, Green and White mountains and Willoughby lake with maps and a table of distances. Pub. by S.B. Nichols. Burlington, Vt. Stacy & Jameson, 1854. 56p. front. illus. Published in 1845 and 1851 under title "Guide to Lake George. . ."   1185

Disturnell, John. Springs, water-falls, sea-bathing resorts, and mountain scenery of the United States and Canada. . . N.Y. 1855. 227p. front. plates, maps (part folded). Includes Hadley Falls, Luzerne, Lake George, Trenton Falls, etc.   1186

Appleton's Illustrated hand-book of American travel. . . By T. Addison Richards. . . N.Y. Appleton, 1857. 420p. folded front. illus. maps, folded plans. Another edition issued 1857–60. Afterward issued with title "Appleton's Companion Hand-book of Travel." Adirondacks, p.168–70.   1187

Disturnell, John. A trip through the lakes of North America; embracing a full description of the St. Lawrence river, together with all the principal places on its banks, from its source to its mouth; commerce of the lakes etc. forming altogether a complete guide for the pleasure traveler and emigrant. N.Y. 1857. 386p. plates, map. Adirondacks, p.289–98.   1188

Our summer retreats, a handbook to the chief waterfalls, springs, mountain and sea side resorts. . .in the United States. . . N.Y. T. Nelson & sons, 1858. 64p. col. front. col. plates. Lake George and Lake Champlain, p.13–19.   1189

The picturesque tourist; being a guide through the State of New York and upper and lower Canada including a Hudson river guide. . . N.Y. J. Disturnell, 1858. 298p. illus. Includes Lake George and Lake Champlain. 1190

Presbrey, Frank. A summer paradise. Albany, J.W. Burdick, 1859? 24 leaves. illus. On cover: Delaware & Hudson Railroad Co. 1191

Nelson's Illustrated guide to the Hudson and its tributaries. . .N.Y. T. Nelson & sons, 1860. 202p. col. front. col. plates (part folded). Lake George and the Adirondacks, p.166–74. 1192

Nelson's Guide to Lake George and Lake Champlain, with oil-colour views drawn from photographs taken expressly for this work. . . London, N.Y. etc. T. Nelson & sons, 1866. 48p. col. front. 10 col. plates (1 folded) folded map. Reprinted in 1868 and 1869. See also volume with similar title in Nelson's View Books for Tourists series (1860?) and 32p.-undated edition issued in N.Y. Published in London in 1858 and 1859 in series entitled Nelson's Views of American Scenery. Bindings, height and number of advertising pages vary. 1193

Appleton's Hand-book of American travel. The northern tour. . . By Edward H. Hall. 9th annual ed. N.Y. Appleton, 1867. 456p. folded maps, incl. front. folded plans. Adirondacks, p.64–67. Also published in 1870, 1872–74, 1876. 1194

De Costa, Benjamin Franklin. Lake George; its scenes and characteristics, with glimpses of the olden times. To which is added some account of Ticonderoga with a description of the route to Schroon Lake and the Adirondacks. With. . .notes on Lake Champlain. . . N.Y. A.D.F. Randolph, 1868. 181p. front. plates, illus. double map. 2d edition, 1869; 3d edition, 1871?; 4th edition, c1868. 1195

New York central railroad company. Summer routes to Lake Champlain and the Adirondacks. Plattsburgh, N.Y. J.W. Tuttle, c1868. 36p. illus. map. Issued by the Hudson River Railroad Company, later incorporated into the New York Central system. 1196

Taintor, Charles Newhall. The Hudson river route. New York to Albany, Saratoga Springs, Lake George, Lake Champlain, Adirondack mountains, and Montreal. . . N.Y. Taintor brothers, 1869. 121p. plates, illus. folded map. Also issued without map. Later editions published in 1880 (234p.) and 1887 (234p.). 1197

Colt, Mrs. S.S. ed. Tourists' guide through the Empire state. Embracing all cities, towns and watering places, by Hudson River and New York Central route. . . Albany, 1871. 239p. front. plates, illus. Chapters IX, X, Adirondacks; Chapter XIV, Climbing up the Mountain, by S.S. Colt (poem). 1872 edition issued with title "New York State Illustrated." Reprinted in 1876. 1198

De Costa, Benjamin Franklin. Lake Luzerne, Schroon Lake and Adirondacks; 3d ed. N.Y. A.D.F. Randolph, 1871. 186p. plates. 1199

Stoddard, Seneca Ray. Lake George, illustrated; a book of today. Albany, Glens Falls, etc. Weed, Parsons, Author, etc. 1871–1915. illus. maps. Title varies: Lake George and Lake Champlain; Saratoga, Lake George and Lake Champlain (1902). From 1881 to 1902, Saratoga (separately paged) is bound in back. Issued annually. Copies not located for 1872, 1893, 1899, 1904, 1914. Published in variant bindings, with and without maps. 1200

Watson, Winslow Cossoul. A descriptive and historical guide to the valley of Lake Champlain and the Adirondacks. Burlington, Vt. R.S. Styles steam printing house, 1871. 144p. front. plates, folded map. Published anonymously; copyright by Andrew Williams. Author identified in Wallace's Descriptive Guide. 1201

Wallace, Edwin R. Descriptive guide to the Adirondacks. In Smith, H.P. The modern babes in the wood. Hartford, Conn. Columbian book co. 1872. p.239–444. 1202

Butler, Benjamin Clapp. From New York to Montreal. N.Y. American news co. 1873. 155p. Adirondack region, p.117–20. 1203

Faxon's Illustrated hand-book of travel by the Fitchburg, Rutland and Saratoga railway line to Saratoga, lakes George and Champlain, the Adirondacks. . . Boston, Charles A. Faxon, 1873. 193p. illus. folded maps. Revised edition published in 1874. 1204

Without a guide, by a Boston correspondent. For & Stream, July 30, 1874. 2:394. Use Ely's map and Wallace's Guide. 1205

Stoddard, Seneca Ray. The Adirondacks, illustrated. Albany, Glens Falls, etc. Weed, Parsons, Author, etc. 1874–1913. illus. maps. Issued annually; edition note varies. Extracts from 1888 and 1903 issues reprinted in High Spots, July 1932, 9:no.3:25–27, 30. Copy for 1909 not located. 1206

Faxon's Illustrated hand-book of summer travel. . .by Edward S. Sears. . .new and revised edition. Boston, Charles A. Faxon, 1875. 285p. illus. folded maps. 1207

Wallace, Edwin R. Descriptive guide to the Adirondacks; revised and corrected. N.Y. etc. American news co. etc. 1875–99. front. illus. map in pocket. Map is by W.W. Ely.

Place and publisher vary. Probably issued annually. Copies for 1875–76, 1879, 1880–82, 1886–89, 1894–99 have been located.
1208

Appleton's Hand-book of American travel; northern and eastern tour... N.Y. 1876, c1873. 298p. illus. folded maps. Also published in 1872. Previously issued under title "Appleton's Illustrated Hand-book," 1857, and "Appleton's Companion Hand-book." Trips to the Adirondack region, p.58–62.
1209

Appleton's Illustrated hand-book of American summer resorts, including tours and excursions. N.Y. Appleton, 1876–98. illus. maps. Issued annually. Each issue contains a section on Lake George, Lake Champlain and the Adirondacks. Copies located for 1876–77, 1881, 1886, 1890, 1895, 1897–98.
1210

Sweetser, Moses Foster, ed. The middle states: handbook for travellers; guide to the chief cities and popular resorts... Boston, J.R. Osgood co. 1876. 475p. map, plans. Centennial edition. First published in 1874. Adirondack mountains, p.133–58.
1211

Appleton's General guide to the United States and Canada... N.Y. Appleton, 1879–1901. 21v. plates, illus. tables, maps (part folded) folded plans. Also published in two-volume edition. None published 1880–81. Annual 1882–1901. "Revised each year to date of issue." Sections on Adirondacks, Lake George, etc.
1212

Bonsall, J. The northern tourist... Philadelphia, John E. Potter & co. c1879. 160p. illus. The American Catalogue lists this as "The Northern Tourist's Book of Summer Travel."
1213

Butler, Benjamin Clapp. The summer tourist, descriptive of the Delaware & Hudson canal co.'s railroads and their summer resorts...season of 1879... Boston, Franklin press, 1879. 173p. illus. folded map. Also issued for the season of 1880. Includes Lake George and the Adirondacks.
1214

Delaware & Hudson railroad corporation. A souvenir descriptive of the Adirondack mountains, Lake George, Lake Champlain, Saratoga and other points of interest... Albany, 1881. 117p. illus. maps. Also issued in 1891.
1215

Our American resorts. Where to go and how to get there...ed. by Louis M. Babcock... Washington, National news bureau, 1883. 150p. illus. Adirondacks, p.84–88.
1216

Possons, Charles H. publisher. Lake George and Lake Champlain... Glens Falls, N.Y. 1883?–95. illus. folded maps. Published

annually. Title varies: Possons' Guide to Lake George, Lake Champlain and the Adirondacks. Copies located for 1887–93, 1895.
1217

Michigan central railroad company. From city to surf... "The Niagara Falls route." Chicago, Rand, McNally & co. 1888. 104p. front. (folded map) illus. Adirondacks, p.85–89.
1218

Maine central railroad co. The White mountains of New Hampshire, and the woods of Maine. With glimpses of lakes Champlain and George, the Adirondacks and some points in Canada. Boston, Rand Avery supply co. 1891. 108p. plate, map.
1219

New York central railroad company. The Adirondack mountains. Buffalo, N.Y. Matthews-Northrup co. c1893. 32p. illus. map. (Four-track Series, no.6.)
1220

Delaware & Hudson railroad corporation. A summer paradise: information about Lake George, Lake Champlain and the Adirondacks, and other summer resorts and tours on the rail and steamer lines of the Delaware and Hudson company. Albany, 1895–1942, 1948–date. illus. map. Subtitle varies: An illustrated, descriptive guide to the delightful and healthful resorts reached by the Delaware and Hudson company, etc. Issued annually except for 1903, 1919, 1920 and 1943–47.
1221

New York central railroad company. ...In the Adirondack mountains... Buffalo, N.Y. Matthews-Northrup co. 1895. 64p. illus. folded map. (Four-track Series, no.6.)
1222

Rome, Watertown and Ogdensburg railroad co. Routes and rates for summer tours... N.Y. Press of the American bank note co. c1895. 236p. front. illus. folded maps. Contains "The Sportsman's Paradise; the Avenues to the Wilderness." Earlier editions published in 1886, 1888, 1889, 1890, 1891.
1223

Central Vermont railroad. Adirondack by-ways. A varied realm of perfect rest. n.p. n.pub. 1896? 24p. illus. maps. The New York Public Library ascribes authorship to Julian Ralph.
1224

New York central railroad company. Health and pleasure on "America's greatest railroad." Descriptive of summer resorts and excursion routes... N.Y. 1896. 532p. front. illus. maps. (Four-track Series, no.5.) Earlier editions copyrighted in 1894 and 1895. Adirondacks, p.162–82.
1225

Possons, Charles H. Gems of scenery. Adirondack mountains. Lake George. Lake Champlain. Glens Falls, N.Y. c1896. plates. Unpaged oblong octavo.
1226

New York central railroad company. The Adirondack mountains and how to reach them. N.Y. c1898. illus. map. (Four-track Series, no.20.) 1227

Stoddard, Seneca Ray. Bits of Adirondack life. Albany, Albany engraving co. 1898. 13 plates. Illustrated title page and cover. Plates accompanied by guard sheets with descriptive letterpress. 1228

The Hudson river route. New York to West Point, Catskill mountains, Albany, Saratoga Springs, Lake George, Lake Champlain, Adirondack mountains. N.Y. American guide book & directory co. c1902. 386p. illus. map. Cover title: Hudson River and the Adirondacks. Adirondacks, p.209–368. 1229

Goldthwaite, Kenneth W. Guide to the Adirondack mountains; issued by the New York American's system of information bureaus. . . N.Y. c1903. 62p. ports. illus. Photographs by the author. Detailed guide with many descriptions of camps and preserves. Copy in the Saranac Lake Free Library. 1230

Delaware & Hudson railroad corporation. The Adirondacks. Albany, 1904. illus. maps. unpaged. 1231

New York central railroad company. The summer boarder. N.Y. c1904. 96p. illus. (Four-track Series, no.17.) Lake George, Adirondack Mountains, p.24–37. 1232

Delaware & Hudson railroad corporation. A literary and historic note-book for use along the railroad lines of the Delaware & Hudson co. Compiled for the Passenger department by Henry P. Phelps. N.Y. 1907? 77p. illus. Short historical notes arranged in alphabetical order. 1233

Hardie, George Robert. Where to go in the Adirondacks and on Lake George and Lake Champlain. Canton, N.Y. Author, 1909. 96p. illus. maps. 1234

Delaware & Hudson railroad corporation. The gate of the country. Lake Champlain. Lake George. The Adirondack mountains. Albany, c1912. 48p. illus. maps (1 folded). Written by Warwick S. Carpenter. Photographs by the author. 1235

Little travels: a series of practical vacation journeys, from a fortnight to twelve weeks in length. . .accurate itineraries are given. . . *Ind*, June 1, 1914. 78:371–80. illus. Lake George and the Adirondacks, p.373; an itinerary, New York to the Adirondacks and return, covering 15 days. Descriptive information on the points of interest. 1236

MacNair, Henry. The scenic motorway; a motor tour de luxe, featuring New York to Montreal, P.Q. the Berkshires and Adirondacks, the Green and White mountains, the

New England coast. N.Y. c1914. 80p. illus. maps. Reprinted, 1916. 1237

Delaware & Hudson railroad corporation. The Adirondacks, Lake George, Lake Champlain. The summer paradise; a region of romance and beauty on the lines of the Delaware & Hudson company. N.Y. Kendrick-Odell press, 1915? unpaged. illus. Sixteen-page pamphlet, not counting covers. List of publications in back. 1238

Stoddard, Seneca Ray. Picturesque trips through the Adirondacks in an automobile. n.p. c1915. 30p. illus. maps. 1239

Adirondack guide company. Tourist guide of Lake George, Lake Champlain and the Adirondacks. n.p. c1919. 94p. illus. Copyrighted by A.E. Knight. 1240

Adirondack guide; vacationland in picture, story and history. Lake George, N.Y. Adirondack resorts press, etc. 1920–30, 1945–date. illus. (part col.). Edited by Arthur S. Knight. Issued annually. Title varies: The Adirondacks, Guide and History; Guide to the Adirondacks, Vacationland in Picture, Story and History. 1241

Adirondack mountains, Lake Champlain, Lake George. . .covering every part of the Adirondacks and adjacent regions. The tourist paradise of America. . . Automobile road map and guide to the Adirondacks. Watertown, N.Y. Santway photo-craft co. inc. c1921. 62p. incl. illus. maps. 1242

Adirondack bureau, Plattsburgh, N.Y. The Adirondacks. An autumn leaflet. . . Plattsburgh, N.Y. 1923. 24p. 1243

Adirondack chamber of commerce. Vacationing in the Adirondacks. Auburn, N.Y. Fenton press, 1926. 57p. illus. map. Another edition, undated, with paging 56 + 6, issued by the Bullard Press. 1244

Utica daily press. Summer resort guide. Utica, N.Y. 1926. 48p. port. illus. map. Summer resort service started in 1893. Includes many Adirondack resorts. 1245

New York (state). Commerce, Dept. of. Guide to northern New York. Albany, 1944. 22p. Also published in 1945 (70p.) and in 1946 (82p.). 1246

Writers program. New York. New York. A guide to the Empire state. . . N.Y. Oxford university press, 1947. 782p. plates, illus. maps (3 on folded leaf in pocket). (American Guide Series.) First published in 1940. Sponsored by the New York State Historical Association. 1247

Delaware & Hudson railroad corporation. The eastern slope of the Adirondacks, its mountains, lakes and springs. Albany, n.d. unpaged. illus. 1248

Delaware & Hudson railroad corporation. Vacation joys in the summer paradise. . .on the rail and steamer lines of the Delaware & Hudson co. Albany, D & H, n.d. 16p. illus.   1249

New York central railroad company. Adirondacks, Thousand islands, Saratoga Springs. N.Y. n.d. 46p. maps.   1250

The north country. Tourists' hand book of northern New York. . . Watertown, N.Y.

Santway photo-craft co. inc. n.d. 80p. illus. folded map.   1251

U.S. Railroad administration. Adirondacks and the Thousand islands. N.Y. Rand McNally, n.d. 60p. illus.   1252

Van Noy interstate co. Souvenir and guide thru Lake George and Lake Champlain. n.p. n.d. 29p. illus. Cover title: Lake George and Lake Champlain.   1253

GAZETTEERS

Arranged by date

Goodenow, Sterling. A brief topographical & statistical manual of the State of New-York . . . Albany, J. Frary, 1811. 36p. 2d edition (enl. and improved) published in New York by E. Bliss & A. White, 1822.   1254

Spafford, Horatio Gates. A gazetteer of the State of New-York, carefully written from original and authentic materials, arranged on a new plan in three parts. . . Albany, Southwick, 1813. 334p. front. folded map. See New York Historical Society *Collections*, 1821, 3:328–40, for "Remarks on Spafford's Gazetteer. . ." by Samuel Jones, and American Antiquarian Society *Proceedings*, Oct. 15, 1941, 51:278–350, for Julian Boyd's "Horatio Gates Spafford."   1255

Spafford, Horatio Gates. A gazetteer of the State of New-York: embracing an ample survey and description of its counties, towns, cities, villages, canals, mountains, lakes, creeks, and natural topography, arranged in one series, alphabetically. . .with an appendix. Albany, Troy, N.Y. B.D. Packard, Author, 1824. 620p. front. (folded map). 1256

Gordon, Thomas Francis. A gazetteer of the State of New York: comprehending its colonial history; general geography, geology and internal improvements; its political state, a minute description of its several counties, towns and villages. . . Philadelphia, T.G. & B.G. Collins, 1836. 102, 801p. front. illus. maps.   1257

Disturnell, John, comp. A gazetteer of the State of New York, comprising its topography, geology, mineralogical resources, civil divisions, canals, railroads and public institutions, together with general statistics. . . Albany, 1842. 475p. front. folded map. Another edition, 1842, with preface dated Mar. 1842. 2d edition, 1843, 479p. Attributed to O.H. Holley by Sabin and Cushing. 2d edi-

tion, 1843, has compiler's name on title page.   1258

Corey, Allen. Gazetteer of the county of Washington, N.Y. comprising a correct statistical and miscellaneous history of the county and several towns. . . Schuylerville, N.Y. Author, 1850. 200, 227p. incl. maps.   1259

French, John Homer, ed. Gazetteer of the State of New York, embracing a comprehensive view of the geography, geology and general history of the State of New York, and a complete history and description of every county, city, town, village and locality. . . accompanied by a new map of the state. Syracuse, N.Y. R.P. Smith, 1860. 739p. front. plates, illus. maps. 10th edition published in 1861. "Edited and written mostly by Dr. F.B. Hough who collected a large part of the material." Bibliography of Franklin Benjamin Hough, p.330.   1260

The Advance almanac and St. Lawrence county directory for 1862. . . Ogdensburgh, N.Y. J.W. Hopkins, 1862. 108p. folded plate.   1261

Northern New York business directory, containing a business directory of all places on the line of the Rome, Watertown and Ogdensburgh railroad (and its branches), Ogdensburgh and Lake Champlain railroad and the Utica and Black river railroad including all principal places in northern New York, 1867–68. Watertown, N.Y. Lyttle, Hanford & co. 1868. 260p. Compiled by Waite Brothers, Inc. Includes advertising matter.   1262

Child, Hamilton. Gazetteer and business directory of Herkimer county, New York for 1869–70. Syracuse, N.Y. Journal office, 1869. 234p. map.   1263

Child, Hamilton. Gazetteer and business directory of Montgomery and Fulton counties, New York for 1869–70. Syracuse, N.Y.

Journal office, 1870. 315p. incl. front. folded map. **1264**

Farmers' and country merchants' almanac and ready reference book. 1870. Containing historical sketches of the counties of Albany, Rensselaer, Washington, Warren, Schenectady, Saratoga, Rutland and Bennington: together with farmers' names, postal and internal revenue matters, valuable receipts, maxims and information useful to everybody. Albany, C. Van Benthuysen, 1870. 207p. **1265**

Child, Hamilton. Gazetteer and business directory of Saratoga county, N.Y. and Queensbury, Warren county. Syracuse, N.Y. Journal office, 1871. 305p. illus. **1266**

Child, Hamilton. Gazetteer and business directory of Washington county, New York for 1871. Syracuse, N.Y. Journal office, 1871. 261p. **1267**

Child, Hamilton. Gazetteer and business directory of Lewis county, New York for 1872–3. Syracuse, N.Y. Journal office, 1872. 310p. front. map. **1268**

Hough, Franklin Benjamin, ed. Gazetteer of the State of New York, embracing a comprehensive account of the history and statistics of the state with geographical and topographical descriptions of each county, city, town and village in the state. Albany, A. Boyd, 1872. 745 i.e. 752p. front. plate, folded map. **1269**

Child, Hamilton. Gazetteer and business directory of St. Lawrence county, New York for 1873–4. Syracuse, N.Y. Journal office, 1873. various paging. map. **1270**

Lant, J.H. & son. Directory of Warren and Washington counties 1881–2. . .containing names and P.O. addresses of the farmers of the counties. . . Hudson, N.Y. Wm. Bryan, 1881. 354p. illus. **1271**

Kollock, Henry. State of New York, embracing historical, descriptive, and statistical notices of cities, towns, villages, industries and summer resorts in the various parts of the state, together with a complete list of the post offices, counties, towns, lakes, rivers, and railroads, etc. Illustrated with nearly 200 choice engravings. N.Y. 1883. 304p. plates, illus. maps. Adirondacks, p.226, 260–77. Another edition, c1882, 339p. **1272**

Cram, George F. Cram's township and shipper's guide of New York. Accompanied by a complete and original ready reference index, accurately locating all county seats, cities, towns, post-offices, railroad stations, villages, etc. N.Y. 1904? 138p. map. Cover title: Cram's Pocket Map and Hotel Guide of New York. **1273**

Directory of Saranac Lake, Lake Placid and Bloomingdale. Year 1906. Compiled and published by McDonald & Fay, Saranac Lake, N.Y. Saranac Lake, N.Y. 1906? 156p. plates (some folded) illus. Cover title: Adirondack Directory. Also published for 1908, 1910–11. **1274**

Douglas, Edward Morehouse, comp. Gazetteer of the lakes, ponds and reservoirs of the State of New York. Washington, Board of surveys & maps, 1926. 44 leaves. Reproduced from typewritten copy. Revised edition issued in 1931. **1275**

Douglas, Edward Morehouse, comp. Gazetteer of the mountains of the State of New York. Washington, U.S. Map information office, 1927. 36 leaves. Reproduced from typewritten copy. **1276**

ATLASES

Arranged by date

Burr, David H. Atlas of the State of New York. . .drawn. . .under the direction of Simeon DeWitt. . .pursuant to an act of the Legislature, and also the physical geography. N.Y. D.H. Burr, 1829. 29, 50 leaves. 51 maps. Also published in 1839 by Stone & Clark, Ithaca, N.Y. **1277**

Beers, S.N. and Beers, Daniel G. New topographical atlas of St. Lawrence co. New York. From actual surveys by S.N. and D.G. Beers and assistants. Philadelphia, Stone & Stewart, 1865. 94p. incl. illus. 41 col. maps. **1278**

Beers, S.N. and Beers, Daniel G. New topographical atlas of Saratoga co. New York. From actual surveys by S.N. and D.G. Beers and assistants. Philadelphia, Stone & Stewart, 1866. 77p. incl. illus. 33 col. maps. **1279**

Stone and Stewart. New topographical atlas of Washington county, New York. From actual surveys especially for this atlas. Philadelphia, Stone & Stewart, 1866. 73p. incl. illus. 30 col. maps. **1280**

Nichols, Beach. Atlas of Herkimer county, New York. . . N.Y. J.J. Stranahan & B. Nichols, 1868. 32f. illus. maps. **1281**

Nichols, Beach. Atlas of Montgomery and Fulton counties, New York. From actual surveys by and under the direction of B.

Nichols. . . N.Y. J.J. Stranahan & B. Nichols, 1868. 2p. leaf. 28 col. maps.   1282

Beers, Frederick W. Atlas of Clinton co. New York, from actual surveys by and under the direction of F.W. Beers, assisted by George P. Sanford & others. N.Y. F.W. Beers, 1869. 1p. leaf. illus. 20 col. maps.   1283

Asher & Adams. New topographical atlas and gazetteer of New York. . . N.Y. c1871. 80p. incl. maps.   1284

Beers, Daniel G. Atlas of Lewis co. New York. . . Philadelphia, Pomeroy, Whitman & co. 1875. 2, 80, 4p. maps.   1285

Beers, Daniel G. & co. Atlas of Franklin county, New York. From actual surveys and official records. Philadelphia, D.G. Beers & co. 1876. 65p. incl. 21 col. maps.   1286

Beers, Frederick W. County atlas of Warren, New York. From recent and actual surveys and records under the superintendence of F.W. Beers. N.Y. F.W. Beers & co. 1876. 2p. leaf, 2 leaves. illus. 24 col. maps.   1287

Gray, O.W. & son. New topographical atlas of Essex county, New York. . . With a supplement comprising a map of the State of New York. Philadelphia, 1876. 79, 37p. incl. 32 col. maps, illus. plans.   1288

Butler, Benjamin Clapp and Cooper, J.A. comp. The New York wilderness. Hamilton county and adjoining territory. Albany, Weed, Parsons & co. 1879. unpaged. maps.   1289

Koetteritz, J.B. comp. Catalogue of maps, field-notes, surveys, and landpapers of patents, grants and tracts situate within the counties embracing the Forest preserve of the State of New York. *In* New York (state). Forest commission. Annual report for. . . 1890. p.165–317. A revised and enlarged edition of this list was published in the Annual Report for 1892, p.303–501.   1290

Notes on the maps of the White and Adirondack mountains, with maps. *Around the W,* July–Aug. 1894. 1:151–55. Adirondacks, p.151–53.   1291

Century map company, Philadelphia. New Century atlas of Montgomery and Fulton counties, New York. . . Philadelphia, 1905. 144p. incl. 64 col. maps.   1292

Century map company, Philadelphia. New Century atlas of Herkimer county, New York . . . Philadelphia, 1906. 115p. incl. col. maps, partly double.   1293

Beers, J.L. and Bord, C.J. New atlas of the city of Plattsburgh, New York. Field notes by J.L. Beers and C.J. Bord. N.Y. J.L. Beers, 1916. 1p. leaf. 13 col. maps, folded.   1294

Hevenor, Charles D. co. inc. The Hevenor hand book of loose leaf county maps. New York. For executives, district managers, salesmen, associations, tourists, etc. Buffalo, N.Y. 1921. 15, 114p. incl. maps. Added title page : Index for New York State. . .Containing Alphabetical List of Counties, Numerical List of Counties, Alphabetical List of Towns.   1295

United States survey company, inc. Nufold road guides. Rochester, N.Y. 1925. 9v. Includes "Northern New York, the Adirondacks and 1000 Islands."   1296

Miller, Philip Schuyler. Looking down on Marcy. *Ad-i-ron-dac*, Mar.–Apr. 1949. 13: 30–32. Aerial mapping.   1297

PLACE NAMES

Ames, C.H. Poke-o-Moonshine. *For & Stream,* June 29, 1901. 56:503.   1298

Barker, Elmer Eugene. That name — Marcy. *Cloud Splitter,* Nov.–Dec. 1948. 11:no.6:10.   1299

Beauchamp, William Martin. Aboriginal place names of New York. Albany, 1907. 336p. (New York State Museum. Bulletin 108.)   1300

Haas, Dorothy M. Place names of northern New York. *No Country Life,* Fall 1955. 9:no. 4:42–44.   1301

Hale, Edward Everett. Dialectical evidence in the place names of eastern New York. *Am Speech,* Dec. 1929. 5:154–67. Refers to Adirondack names.   1302

Hauptman, Herbert C. Adirondack place names. *High Spots,* Jan. 1932. 9:no.1:16–17.   1303

Hauptman, Herbert C. By their names — *High Spots Yrbk,* 1939. p.72–76.   1304

How Old Forge (N.Y.) was named. *For & Stream,* June 5, 1909. 72:892. Short note on the forge used by John Brown (1734–1803).   1305

Hudowalski, Mrs. Grace (Leech). Hitch-up Matilda. *Cloud Splitter,* June 1941. 4:no.6:12.   1306

Hull, Raymona E. Names on the land in St. Lawrence county. *No Country Life,* Winter 1952. 6:no.1:32–35.   1307

Leete, Charles Henry. A study in geographic names. Reprint from the *Herald-Recorder*, Potsdam, N.Y. Mar. 1927. 12p. Copy in the Saranac Lake Free Library.   1308

Miller, Philip Schuyler. By guess and by gosh. *Ad-i-ron-dac*, Mar.–Apr. 1946. 10:no. 2:6–7.   1309

Miller, Philip Schuyler. Those poetic red men. *Cloud Splitter*, Mar. 1942. 5:no.3:4–5.
                                                                     1310

Miller, Philip Schuyler. Why the Bouquet? *Ad-i-ron-dac*, Jan.–Feb. 1947. 11:no.1:4–5.
                                                                     1311

Mills, Borden H. Sr. Charles Fenno Hoffman's Indian place names. *Ad-i-ron-dac*, July–Aug. 1948. 12:no.4:4–7.   1312

Mills, Borden H. Sr. Who was John? *Ad-i-ron-dac*, Sept.–Oct. 1951. 15:97–98, 100. Johns Brook was probably named for John Gibbs.
                                                                     1313

Mills, Borden H. Sr. Who was John? *Cloud Splitter*, Jan.–Feb. 1948. 11:no.1:4–6. Johns Brook.   1314

Prince, John Dyneley. Some forgotten Indian place-names in the Adirondacks. *J Am Folk-Lore*, Apr.–June 1900. 13:123–28. Quotations in *Forest Leaves*, Autumn 1906, 3:no.3: 24–25, with title "Indian Place-names in the Adirondacks." Abenaki names obtained from Mitchel Sabattis.   1315

Ruttenber, Edward Manning. Footprints of the red man. Indian geographical names in the valley of Hudson's river. . .their location and the probable meaning of some of them. Newburgh, N.Y. Journal print, c1906. 241p. Adirondack names, p.70–72, 184–89. Published under the auspices of the New York State Historical Association.   1316

Scribner, Mrs. Lynette (Langer). North country place names. *Ad-i-ron-dac*, Mar.–Apr. 1955. 19:32–33.   1317

Scribner, Mrs. Lynette (Langer). Some Lake Champlain place names. *Ad-i-ron-dac*, May–June 1955. 19:50.   1318

Spears, Raymond Smiley. Adirondack place names. *For & Stream*, May 25, 1901. 56:403.
                                                                     1319

Spears, Raymond Smiley. Poke-o-Moonshine. *For & Stream*, June 22, 1901. 56:484.   1320

Thompson, H.H. Adirondack nomenclature. *Field & S*, July 1905. 10:286–87.   1321

Thompson, H.H. "What's in a name?" — "Millions in it." *Am Angler*, Sept. 29, 1883. 4:199–200. Signed: H.H.T.   1322

ADIRONDACK PRESERVE,
THE ADIRONDACK PARK, CONSERVATION

GENERAL AND HISTORICAL

American scenic and historic preservation society. Annual reports, 1–30. 1895–1924. Albany, 1896–1925. 30v. plates, maps. Continued in 1929 by *Scenic and Historic America*. Contains material on the Adirondack Park, the Forest Preserve and sites in the Adirondack area. 1323

Benedict, Darwin. The New York Forest preserve: formative years, 1872–1895. 212 leaves. Master's thesis, Syracuse University, Maxwell Graduate School of Citizenship, Albany program, 1953. Typescript. Reviewed by D.A. Plum in *The Cloud Splitter*, Mar.–Apr. 1954, 17:no.2:6–7. Copies in New York State Library and Saranac Lake Free Library. 1324

Byrne, Wayne H. New York's forests — a public trust. *Ad-i-ron-dac*, July–Aug. 1953–Jan.–Feb. 1954. 17:76–77, 88–91, 104, 114–15; 18:12–15. 1325

Carson, Russell Mack Little. The Adirondack forest. *Bul Schools*, Apr. 1, 1936. 22:142–46. illus. Forest Preserve. 1326

Carson, Russell Mack Little. The Adirondack Forest preserve. *High Spots*, Oct. 1934–Oct. 1935. 11:no.4:3–11; 12:no.1:18–20; 12: no.2:16–17; 12:no.3:19–23; 12:no.4:31–33. illus. 1327

Carson, Russell Mack Little. The Adirondack mountain club. *High Spots*, Dec. 1937. 14:no.4:17–20. History of the Forest Preserve. 1328

Duryea, Perry B. Our Forest preserve. *NYS Ranger Sch*, 1951. p.7–8. Reprinted with editorial comment from the *New York State Conservationist* of Dec. 1951–Jan. 1952. 1329

The forests of the state. *In* New York (state). University. Arbor day annual, 1911. p.11–18. illus. History of the Forest Preserve and the Adirondack Park with a summary of the state's program in forestry. 1330

Higley, Warren. New York. *Am Forestry Assn Proc*, 1896. 11:99–103. History of the Forest Preserve. 1331

Hopkins, Arthur S. Land Acquisition for Forest preserve purposes in New York state,

1916–1944. *NY Forester*, Dec. 1944. 1:no.5: 2–6. 1332

Hopkins, Arthur S. Within and without the blue line. *NYS Con*, Apr.–May 1951. 5:no. 5:10–11. illus. Correction in June–July issue, p.31. Brief explanation of the term "blue line" and summary of the history of the Preserve. 1333

Howard, William Gibbs. Recreational use of state forests. *For Worker*, Jan. 1932. 8:no. 1:1–3. Short history of Forest Preserve and development of recreational use. 1334

Illick, Joseph S. and Hopkins, Arthur S. comps. Chronological recording of important legislative and administrative developments relating to the state Forest preserve. . . 1665–1952. *In* New York (state). Legislature. Joint legislative committee on natural resources. Report, 1953. Albany, 1953. p.121–31. Appendix A. 1335

Kennedy, John S. The forest parks of New York. *Am For*, Dec. 1910. 16:695–98. illus. Historical sketch of Adirondack, Catskill and Palisade parks. 1336

Kimball, Francis P. The state completes its skyland park. The new Adirondack playground. . . *NY Times Mag*, May 20, 1928. p.12–13. illus. 1337

Lincoln, Charles Zebina. The constitutional history of New York from the beginning of the colonial period to the year' 1905. . . Rochester, Lawyers co-operative publishing co. 1906. 5v. The Forest Preserve, v.3, p.391–454. 1338

Mills, Borden H. Sr. This is the state Forest preserve: how it came to be, what it is and where it is. *Bul Schools*, Mar. 1952. 38:167–71. illus. map. 1339

New York (state). Forest commission. Tracts and patents of northern New York in which the lands of the Forest preserve are situated. *In* its Annual report for the year 1893. 1:73–149. plates. Compiled by William F. Fox. The illustrations are by S.R. Stoddard. 1340

New York (state). Governor. State of New York. Messages from the governors, com-

prising executive communications to the Legislature and other papers relative to legislation, from the organization of the first colonial assembly in 1683 to and including the year 1906, with notes. Ed. by Charles Z. Lincoln. Albany, J.B. Lyon, 1909. 11v. ports.
1341

New York (state). Laws, statutes, etc. Compendium of laws relative to the Adirondack wilderness from 1774 to 1894. Albany, J.B. Lyon, 1894. 468p. New York State Forest Commission. Annual Report, 1893. v.2. 1342

New York (state). Laws, statutes, etc. Previous legislation pertaining to trees, forests and public lands. *In* New York (state). Forest commission. Annual report, 1885. 1:131–60.
1343

Ostrander, George N. A discussion of article VII, section 7 of the state constitution. (Historical sketch and recommendations.) *NY Forestry*, Oct. 1914. 1:no.2:11–14. Notes

changed attitude toward practice of forestry on state lands. 1344

Ostrander, George N. History of the New York Forest preserve. *J For*, Apr. 1942. 40: 301–4. 1345

Shorey, Mrs. Anna (Snow). Gleanings from Donaldson. *Cloud Splitter*, Mar.–Apr. 1952. 15:no.2:10–11. Background for history of the Forest Preserve. 1346

Shorey, Archibald Thompson. New York's Forest preserve. *Bul Schools*, Apr. 1935. 21: 147–48. illus. 1347

Welch, Fay. The Adirondacks. *Ad-i-ron-dac*, Mar.–Apr. 1955. 19:36–37. From a speech at the annual meeting of the Adirondack Mountain Club, 1954. 1348

Welch, Fay. Our New York state Forest preserve: a priceless natural resource. . .let's not lose it. Utica, N.Y. Horrocks-Ibbotson co. 1953. 4p. Unpaged leaflet. 1349

1872–1884

This section and the four that follow are arranged by date.

New York (state). Commissioners of state parks. Annual report, 1872. Albany, Argus printing co. 1873. 23p. Senate document 102, 1873. Hasse states that only one report was issued (in three different editions). This is the first report for the Adirondack preserve, submitted by Verplanck Colvin. 1350

A grand sporting park. *Am Sportsman*, Aug. 1873. 2:169. Editorial on setting aside the Adirondack range as a game preserve and park. 1351

The Adirondack park. *For & Stream*, Sept. 11, 1873. 1:73. 1352

The people's hunting ground. *For & Stream*, Sept. 25, 1873. 1:101. Reprinted from the *New York Times*. Hunting, fishing and the need for a park. 1353

The state park. *For & Stream*, Oct. 9, 1873. 1:136. Editorial on desirability of forming an Adirondack park. 1354

French, J. Clement. The Adirondack park. *For & Stream*, Nov. 27, 1873. 1:244. Letter to editor approving establishment of park.
1355

Adirondack state park. *Harper*, Nov. 1873. 47:936–37. Editorial in favor of a state park.
1356

The state park. *For & Stream*, Jan. 15, 1874. 1:358. Need for an Adirondack park. 1357

Adirondack park and the preservation of our forests. *For & Stream*, Mar. 19, 1874. 2:88.
1358

McC., J.H. Destruction of the Adirondack region. *For & Stream*, May 7, 1874. 2:196.
1359

T., O.A. Adirondack woods and worries. *For & Stream*, Oct. 1, 1874. 3:117. On trespass. 1360

Agan, Patrick H. Views on the proposed Adirondack state park. *In* Wallace, E.R. Descriptive guide to the Adirondacks. . .5th edition. 1876. p.233–37. Letter to Wallace from a member of the State Park Commission (1872). 1361

Man, Albon. How to make a park of the Adirondack region, at small cost. Copy of a letter to the Hon. J. F. . . . S. . . . n.p. n.pub. 1880? 12p. Dated Nov. 22, 1880. Copy in the Saranac Lake Free Library. 1362

Despoiling the Adirondacks. *For & Stream*, Aug. 31, 1882. 19:83. Plea for the establishment of a park. 1363

Dawson, George. Winter talks on summer pastimes. The Adirondack state park. *For & Stream*, Feb. 8, 1883. 20:22–23. Signed: G.D. On final passage of an act creating the Adirondack Park. 1364

R., J. Jr. Save the woods. *For & Stream*, Aug. 9, 1883. 21:27. Need to stop lumbering in the Moose River area. 1365

Morrell, T.S. A riverie. *Am Angler*, Oct. 20, 1883. 4:244–46. Short history and description of the Adirondacks expressing hope of saving them from complete spoilation.   1366

Save the Adirondacks. *For & Stream*, Dec. 13, 1883. 21:381. Editorial on the need to stop lumbering.   1367

Leeds, Albert Ripley. Facts gathered from eight years of personal inspection as to the alleged destruction of the Adirondack forests. *NY Acad Sci Tr*, Dec. 17, 1883. 3:35–37.   1368

Save the Adirondacks. *For & Stream*, Dec. 20, 1883. 21:402. Editorial on petition of the Chamber of Commerce for protection of the Adirondack watershed.   1369

New York (state). Legislature. Assembly. Report presented by Mr. Rogers, of Seneca, to the Committee on agriculture, and adopted . . .as a reply to a resolution. . .passed February 1, 1883, in regard to the preservation of the forests of the state. Albany, 1883. 7p. Assembly document 130, 1883. Recommends passage of Senate bill authorizing the appointment of a commission to study the forests of the state and to report with recommendations.   1370

New York. Chamber of commerce of the State of New York. Save the Adirondack forests and the waterways of the State of New-York. Opinions of the press. N.Y. 1883. 26p. Copies in the Sherman Free Library, Port Henry, American Museum of Natural History and Yale School of Forestry.   1371

Smith, George W. Speech. . .on the bill to prohibit sales of state lands in certain counties in the Adirondacks. n.p. n.pub. 1883? 23p. The speech, p.1–6, is followed by other speeches and reprints of articles about Assemblyman Smith.   1372

The Adirondack forests. *For & Stream*, Jan. 3, 1884. 21:449. On investigation of forest lands by the Senate Committee.   1373

M., S.R. Save the Adirondacks. *For & Stream*, Jan. 3, 1884. 21:450–51. Need for action.   1374

The crime against the Adirondacks. *Harper W*, Jan. 5, 1884. 28:2. Editorial.   1375

Sylvester, Nathaniel Bartlett. The mountains, forests and waters of the Adirondack wilderness. *Am Angler*, Jan. 5, 1884. 5:2–4. Geographical description of the area that should be made a park.   1376

The Adirondacks. *For & Stream*, Jan. 17, 1884. 21:489. An editorial on Senator Lansing's bill to establish a state park.   1377

Preserving the Adirondack wilderness. *Am Angler*, Jan. 19, 1884. 5:34–36. Reprint of the official report on lands that should be acquired for a park. By Senators Koch, Lansing and Lynde.   1378

An Adirondack bill. *For & Stream*, Jan. 31, 1884. 22:1. Editorial on Chamber of Commerce's bill for an appropriation of $500,000 for acquisition of more state land.   1379

The Adirondack woods still in peril. *Harper W*, Mar. 8, 1884. 28:150. Editorial on the conservation battle.   1380

The Adirondack bill. *For & Stream*, May 22, 1884. 22:325. Text of bill passed by the Legislature.   1381

The Adirondack forests. *For & Stream*, June 19, 1884. 22:401. Editorial on the Sargent group's investigation of the forest situation. Expedition financed by Morris K. Jesup. 1382

Adirondack preservation. *For & Stream*, Aug. 21, 1884. 23:67. Desirable for state to control private holdings in whole area.   1383

The Adirondacks. *Harper W*, Dec. 6, 1884. 28:795, 802–3, 805. illus. On wanton destruction in the Adirondacks and the difficulty of getting legislative action.   1384

New York (state). Legislature. Senate. Report of the special committee on state lands, in the Adirondack region. Albany, 1884. 35p. Senate document 23, 1884. The appendix to this report is: Report of the Superintendent of the Adirondack Survey on the public lands in the Adirondacks.   1385

Seeger, Ferdinand. The Adirondack forests. Necessity of their preservation. An address. N.Y. 1884. 10p.   1386

Thomson, Lemon. An address before the Albany institute on the Adirondack wilderness. . .March 18, 1884. Albany, Weed, Parsons & co. 1884. 22p. Against the Adirondack park. Favors Benedict's proposal for reservoirs.   1387

1885–1894

Sargent, Charles Sprague. Forest destruction. *Harper W*, Jan. 24, 1885. 29:58. Two illustrations on p.56.   1388

The Adirondack forests. *For & Stream*, Jan. 29, 1885. 24:2. Editorial on the Forest Commission.   1389

The Adirondack forests. *Harper W*, Feb. 7, 1885. 29:82–83. Comments on report of the Commission to investigate the Adirondack forests. 1390

The Adirondack forestry bill. *For & Stream*, Apr. 16, 1885. 24:221. Editorial on Senator Law's Forestry Commission bill permitting forest management. 1391

Adirondack Forest commission. *For & Stream*, May 21, 1885. 24:325. Editorial objecting to appointment of Mr. Basselin, a lumberman, to the Commission. 1392

Are the Adirondack forests safe? *Harper W*, May 30, 1885. 29:338. Criticism of appointments to the Forestry Commission. 1393

Ballou, William Hosea. An Adirondack national park. *Am Nat*, June 1885. 19:578–82. Suggestion that the federal government take over the Adirondack area as a national park. 1394

The Adirondack question. *Harper W*, Nov. 28, 1885. 29:770. "A wise settlement of the question requires general familiarity with the facts, and a decided expression of intelligent opinion to the Legislature." 1395

Brooklyn constitution club. The forests of the Adirondacks. A serious question for the people of the State of New York. Report adopted April 1st, 1885. N.Y. George F. Nesbitt & co. 1885. 11p. 1396

Colvin, Verplanck. Speech delivered. . .at the annual banquet of the New York Board of trade and transportation. . .1885. N.Y. George F. Nesbitt & co. 1885. 8p. Cover title: The Adirondacks. 1397

Harrison, Jonathan Baxter. The Adirondack forests, and the problem of the great natural water-ways of the State of New York. Franklin, N.H. 1885. 4 leaves. Folio broadsides. Reprinted from the New York *Tribune*. A series of letters designed to bring public action to stop destruction of the forests. 1398

New York (state). Forest commission. List of lands belonging to the State of New York which form the Forest preserve. *In* its Annual report, 1885. 1:205–356. 1399

New York (state). Forestry commission. Report. . .transmitted to the Legislature, January 23, 1885. Albany, Weed, Parsons & co. 1885. 57p. plates, map. Sargent Committee report. Also published as Assembly document 36, 1885, without plates and map. 1400

New York (state). Governor (David B. Hill). Forest preservation. *In* his Public papers, 1885. Albany, 1885. p.25–26. Lincoln 8:22–23. 1401

New York (state). Legislature. Senate. Committee on agriculture. Report. . .relating to the subject of the forests. Albany, 1885. 46p. Senate document 40, 1885. Includes bill submitted by F.B. Hough and his paper entitled "The Duty of the Legislature with Reference to Its Woodlands." 1402

New York. Board of trade and transportation. The preservation of the Adirondack forests and their relation to the commerce of the state. . . Report adopted. . .April 8th, 1885. n.p. n.pub. 1885. 7p. 1403

Paul sees a great light. *For & Stream*, June 10, 1886. 26:385. Editorial on timber thieves in the Adirondacks. 1404

A dangerous measure. *Gard & For*, Apr. 11, 1888. 1:73–74. Editorial against proposal to lease sections of the Forest Preserve. 1405

Dangers threaten the Adirondack forest from every direction. *Gard & For*, Apr. 18, 1888. 1:86. Editorial on the Durant bill. 1406

New York (state). Forest commission. List of state lands in the Forest preserve; except those known as prison lands. . . *In* its Annual report, 1888. p.123–405. 1407

New York (state). Forest commission. Special report. . .embodying suggestions respecting further legislation. Albany, 1888. 14p. Assembly document 39, 1888. 1408

State forest-lands of New York. *Gard & For*, Feb. 27, 1889. 2:97. Editorial against the Forest Commission's plan to lease state land. 1409

Railroads in the Adirondack reservation. *Gard & For*, Apr. 3, 1889. 2:158–59. Editorial favoring legislation preventing the building of railroads in the preserve. Further comment in the issues for Apr. 17 and July 10, 1889, 2:181–82, 325. 1410

Harrison, Jonathan Baxter. Forests and civilization. II–V, VII. *Gard & For*, July 17, 24, Aug. 7, 21, Sept. 11, 1889. 2:345–46, 358–59, 382, 406–7, 441–42. A series of letters on the destruction of the Adirondack forests, the buying up of large tracts by capitalists and clubs, dangers of fire etc. Advocates an exhibition of the Adirondacks at the World's Fair (1892) pointing out the denudation of the forests. For editorial comment see the Aug. 7 issue, 2:373. 1411

The Adirondack reservation. *Gard & For*, Oct. 16, 1889. 2:493. Editorial comment on a series of letters in the *New York Times* giving a depressing picture of depredations in the Adirondacks. 1412

Legislation for the Adirondacks. *Gard & For*, Jan. 29, 1890. 3:49. Editorial on bills. See also issues for Mar. 12, Apr. 30 and June 11, 1890, 3:121, 209, 282. 1413

Forestry in New York. *NY Lumber*, Feb. 15, 1890. 8:no.88:3. Meeting of New York Forestry Association. Preservation of forest conditions on mountain lands in proposed Adirondack park. 1414

Snap shots. *For & Stream*, Mar. 13, 1890. 34: 141. Editorial comment on passage of bill authorizing Forest Commission to buy land in the Adirondacks. 1415

Harrison, Jonathan Baxter. The Adirondack park project. *For & Stream*, Mar. 20, 1890. 34:166. Approval of bill authorizing purchase of land by the Forest Commission. 1416

New Adirondack legislation. *NY Lumber*, Apr. 1, 1890. 8:no.91:3–4. Editorial approving recommendation of Governor Hill for commission of five to fix boundaries of Adirondack Park. 1417

The Adirondacks. *NY Lumber*, Apr. 15, 1890. 8:no.92:3–4. Reprinted in *Forest and Stream*, Apr. 24, 1890, 34:270. Editorial on great benefits to be derived from an Adirondack park. 1418

Railroads in the Adirondacks. *NY Lumber*, May 15, 1890. 8:no.94:3. Regrets failure of bill that would have prevented grants to railroad companies of public land in Adirondack area. 1419

Harrison, Jonathan Baxter. Forest interests and discussion. *For & Stream*, June 5, 1890. 34:386–87. New York State Forestry Association in favor of preservation of New York's mountain forests. 1420

W., R.D. Forest destruction. *Gard & For*, Oct. 15, 1890. 3:506–7. 1421

The proposed state forest-park. *Gard & For*, Oct. 22, 1890. 3:510. 1422

Adirondack league club. Preserve the forests. N.Y. 1890. 12p. 1423

New York (state). Governor (David B. Hill). Communication. . .relative to that portion of northern New York known as the "Adirondacks" for use by persons seeking health and recreation. Albany, 1890. 3p. Assembly document 85, 1890. Suggests appointing committee to investigate whole subject. Also in his Public papers, 1890, p.50–52. Lincoln 8:936–38. 1424

New York (state). Governor (David B. Hill). Communication. . .relative to the use of state lands in the "Adirondacks" for park purposes. Albany, 1890. 2p. Senate document 29, 1890. Lincoln 8:936–38. 1425

New York (state). Governor (David B. Hill). Memorandum filed with Senate bill no.91, for purchase of lands within the Forest preserve. Approved. *In* his Public papers, 1890. Albany, 1891. p.68–69. 1426

New York (state). Legislature. Senate. Report of the Committee on finance, relative to establishing a state park in the Adirondack wilderness. Albany, 1890. 7p. Senate document 35, 1890. 1427

Protection of the Adirondack forests. n.p. n.pub. c.1890. 26p. One-page petition, followed by long list of names. Addressed to the Legislature by citizens of New York. 1428

The Adirondack reservation. *Gard & For*, Feb. 4, 1891. 4:49. Editorial on the demand for the Adirondack Park. 1429

Destruction of the Adirondacks. *Harper W*, May 30, 1891. 35:399. Against railroad corporation attempts to invade the Adirondacks. 1430

Railroads in the Adirondacks. *Gard & For*, June 10, 1891. 4:265–66. Danger to the Adirondack area. 1431

Means, David MacGregor. The proposed Adirondack park. *Nation*, Sept. 3, 1891. 53: 175–76. Unsigned editorial on special report of the Forest Commission. 1432

Report of the New York Forest commission. *Gard & For*, Oct. 14, 1891. 4:481–82. Favorable editorial. 1433

Cleveland, Grover. Speech at a meeting to demand new legislation concerning the Adirondack park, New York, January 24, 1891. *In* his Writings and speeches. N.Y. Cassell, c1892. p.233–37. 1434

Colvin, Verplanck. Address before the New York farmers, Dec. 11, 1890. Followed by extracts from Essex county Republican of Dec. 12, 1889. *In* New York (state). State land survey. Report on the progress. . .1891, p.36–54. Reprinted in State land survey. Report on the progress. . .1894, p.101–21. 1435

New York (state). Forest commission. The Adirondack park. *In* its Annual report, 1891. p.106–204. plates. Lake George Islands, p.195–204. Description of famous places in the Adirondacks. Illustrations by S.R. Stoddard. 1436

New York (state). Forest commission. Forest and park. *In* its Annual report, 1891. p.96–105. List of Adirondack trees, p.103–5. Reprinted with additions in the Report for 1893, v.1, p.229–46. 1437

New York (state). Forest commission. Special report. Shall a park be established in the Adirondack wilderness? Albany, 1891. 47p. tables, folded map. Senate document 19, 1891. 1438

New York (state). Legislature. Assembly. Committee on public lands and forestry. In the matter of the inquiry concerning the administration of the laws in relation to the Forest preserve by the Forest commission, etc. Report adopted by the Assembly, April 23, 1891. Albany, 1891. 7p.   1439

New York (state). Legislature. Assembly. Committee on public lands and forestry. Reports of the majority and minority. . . relative to the administration of the laws in relation to the Forest preserve by the Forest commission. Albany, 1891. 12p. Assembly document 81, 1891. Followed by a 615p. transcript of testimony.   1440

New York (state). Legislature. Senate. Communication from the Adirondack park association, accompanied by a bill entitled "An act creating a state forest park in the Adirondack region." Albany, 1891. 11p. Senate document 39, 1891.   1441

Smith, George W. The Adirondack question. A memorial to the Legislature of the State of New York. Herkimer, N.Y. 1891. 4p. Dated March 1891.   1442

New York (state). Governor (Roswell P. Flower). Memorandum filed with Assembly bill no.1422, to establish the Adirondack park. Approved. In his Public papers, 1892. Albany, 1892. p.189–91. Lincoln 9:145–47.   1443

Smith, George W. An Adirondack programme. For & Stream, Mar. 2, 1893. 40:185. Resolution to the Legislature; for preservation of the Adirondacks.   1444

The Adirondack park. For & Stream, Mar. 30, 1893. 40:269. Proposed law for the protection of the Adirondacks.   1445

The Adirondack park. Gard & For, Apr. 19, 1893. 6:171. Comments on Act of 1893.   1446

Canada. Royal commission on forest reservation and national park. Papers and reports upon forestry, forest schools, forest administration and management in Europe, America, and the British possessions, and upon forests as public parks and sanitary resorts. Collected by Mr. A. Kirkwood. . .to accompany the Report of the Royal commission. . . Toronto, Warwick & sons, 1893. 278p. tables. Bound with the Report. Adirondacks, p.220–48.   1447

Canada Royal commission on forest reservation and national park. Report upon forestry, forest schools, etc. . . Toronto, Warwick & sons, 1893. 40p. folded map. Adirondacks, p.22–23, 34–38.   1448

New York (state). Forest commission. Forest and park. In its Annual report, 1893. 1:225–366. plates. The 1891 report of the N.Y.S. Forest Commission, reprinted with additional material and different illustrations. Stoddard plates.   1449

New York (state). Governor (Roswell P. Flower). The Adirondack park. In his Public papers, 1893. Albany, 1894. p.35–39. Excerpt in Forest and Stream, Jan 5, 1893, 40:8. Lincoln 9:184–87.   1450

New York (state). Governor (Roswell P. Flower). Communication. . .relative to the preservation of the state's Forest preserve. Albany, 1893. 3p. Assembly document 79, 1893. Cancellation of tax sales of Adirondack lands. Also in his Public papers, 1893, p.90–93. Lincoln 9:218–21.   1451

New York. Board of trade and transportation. Joint letter to Governor Flower protesting against the approval of bill to amend the law of 1885. N.Y. 1893. 2p.   1452

New York. Board of trade and transportation. Opposition to "Forest preserve bill." N.Y. 1893. 1 leaf. Broadside. Urging letters to Governor Flower opposing Senate bill no.626.   1453

Lumberman and forester. Gard & For, Mar. 21, 1894. 7:111. Comments on Pinchot's speech at Forestry Congress in Albany. Quotes extract on suitability of Adirondacks for forest management.   1454

Lumbering on state lands. Gard & For, Apr. 18, 1894. 7:151.   1455

Forestry in the constitution of the State of New York. Gard & For, Sept. 12, 1894. 7:361–62. Editorial urging use of the north woods for forest management. Further comment on p.372 of issue for Sept. 19, 1894.   1456

The Adirondack forests. For & Stream, Oct. 20, 1894. 43:331. An editorial on Article VII, Section 7, of the Constitution.   1457

Colvin, Verplanck. The Adirondack forest. Am Forestry Assn Proc, Dec. 1894 & Jan. 1896. 11:142–47.   1458

New York (state). Forest commission. Special report. n.p. n.d. 22p. Assembly document 22, 1894. Purchase of additional land in Forest Preserve. See editorial in Garden and Forest, May 7, 1894, 7:91.   1459

New York (state). Governor (Roswell P. Flower). Communication from the Governor calling the attention of the Legislature to Senate bill no.846, relating to the maintenance of the Adirondack park, April 11, 1894. Albany, 1894. 3p. Assembly document 62, 1894. Also in his Public papers, 1894, p.125–27. Lincoln 9:377–79.   1460

New York (state). Governor (Roswell P. Flower). Forest preservation. In his Public papers, 1894. Albany, 1895. p.5–8. Summary of year's activities. Lincoln 9:298–300.   1461

New York (state). Governor (Roswell P. Flower). Forest preservation: address of welcome to the American forestry association. . . March 16, 1894. *In* his Public papers, 1894. Albany, 1895. p.504–13.   1462

New York (state). Governor (Roswell P. Flower). Veto, Senate bill no.861, to amend the penal code, relating to tax sales of Adirondack lands. *In* his Public papers, 1894. Albany, 1895. p.369–71. Lincoln 9:530–31.   1463

New York. Board of trade and transportation. Legislation, how it may and should be methodized. Report of the special committee. . . with proposed amendments. . .by Simon Sterne and others. N.Y. 1894. 18p.   1464

1895–1914

Schenck, M. Adirondack lands. *For & Stream*, Dec. 14, 1895. 45:515. State Fish, Game and Forest Commission approves purchase from W. Seward Webb of 75,000 acres in Herkimer and Hamilton counties.   1465

New York (state). Forest commission. Communication. . .recommending that the Legislature make appropriation for the purchase of land within the boundaries of the proposed forest preserve. Albany, 1895. 2p. Senate document 30, 1895.   1466

New York (state). Legislature. Assembly. Committee on public lands and forestry. Report. . .relative to Adirondack lands and tax sales. Albany, 1895. 189p. Assembly document 38, 1895.   1467

The plunder of the Adirondack reservation. *Gard & For*, Mar. 11, 1896. 9:101–2. Editorial on report of the investigating committee.   1468

The Adirondack land grab bill. *For & Stream*, Apr. 25, 1896. 46:333.   1469

The Forestry amendment. *For & Stream*, Oct. 31, 1896. 47:341.   1470

The Adirondack blue line. *For & Stream*, Nov. 7, 1896. 47:361.   1471

Forestry and the New York constitution. *Gard & For*, Nov. 11, 1896. 9:451. Editorial on the Constitutional Convention of 1894.   1472

New York (state). Governor (Levi P. Morton). State forest and game preserves; State land survey. *In* his Public papers, 1896. Albany, 1896. p.34–36. Extract entitled "Adirondack Deer" appeared in *Forest and Stream*, Jan. 11, 1896, 46:30. Lincoln 9:668–70.   1473

New York (state). Legislature. Assembly. Report and testimony of the special committee appointed to investigate the depredations of timber in the Adirondack preserve, 1895. Albany, 1896. 922p. Assembly document 67, 1896.   1474

New York (state). Legislature. Assembly. Report of the special committee appointed to investigate the depredations of timber in the Forest preserve, 1895. Albany, 1896. 31p. Assembly document 60, 1896. Without testimony.   1475

The north woods. *Gard & For*, Jan. 20, 1897. 10:21–22. Comment, with quotations, on Governor Black's message.   1476

Suggestions in reference to forest management in New York. *Forester*, Apr. 1, 1897. 3: 53–54. Recommends scientific forestry. 1477

Carter, Ernest. Reclaiming the Adirondacks. *Outlook*, Sept. 25, 1897. 57:230–31.   1478

New York (state). Forest, fish and game commission. List of lands belonging to the Forest preserve, 1897. N.Y. & Albany, Wynkoop Hallenbeck Crawford co. n.d. 282p.   1479

New York (state). Legislature. Assembly. Report of the special committee appointed to conduct an investigation as to what land should be acquired within the Forest preserve in order to protect the watershed. Albany, 1897. 187p. Assembly document 46, 1897.   1480

Peck, Charles Horton. Report on the character of the forests and soil of certain tracts of state lands in the Adirondack region. *In* New York (state). State land survey. Report. . . 1897, p.517–53. Report for 1896.   1481

Burnham, John Bird. Errors in the official Adirondack map. *For & Stream*, Oct. 22, 1898. 51:323. The 1893 State Forest Commission map.   1482

Reynolds, Cuyler. Forest preservation in the State of New York. *New Eng M*, Oct. 1898. n.s.19:203–16. illus. New York's efforts to preserve the Adirondacks; importance of region to the state and the lumber industry of the north woods.   1483

New York (state). Forest preserve board. . . .Annual report, 1897–1900. Albany, 1898–1901. 4v. For document numbers see Hasse. Abolished; with the Fisheries, Game and Forest Commission merged into the Forest,

Fish and Game Commission. (Laws of 1901.)
1484

New York (state). Governor (Frank S. Black). Forests. *In* his Public papers, 1897–98. Albany, 1898. p.12–21, 227–32. Lincoln 9:750–52, 834–37. 1485

New York (state). Assembly. Report of the special committee appointed to continue the investigation as to what lands should be acquired within the Forest preserve in order to protect the watersheds therein. Albany, 1898. 39p. Assembly document 55, 1898. Report dated Mar. 31, 1898. 1486

Fox, William Freeman. Dispelling an illusion. *Forester*, Nov. 1899. 5:264–65. Letter to citizens of Minnesota assuring them that creation of a large park does not interfere with material prosperity of region. Adirondacks and Catskills given as examples. 1487

Ives, Martin Van Buren. Through the Adirondacks in eighteen days. N.Y. & Albany, Wynkoop Hallenbeck Crawford co. 1899. 119p. plates, ports. "Originally intended for a legislative report...but on account of its voluminousness it was thought best to transmit a synopsis of the same to that body, and to submit the original to the general public." It was included as an appendix to the official report. Reviewed in *The Cloud Splitter*, Mar. 1943, 6:no.3:8. 1488

New York (state). Governor (Theodore Roosevelt). The forests of the state. *In* his Public papers, 1899. Albany, 1899. p.25. 1489

New York (state). Legislature. Assembly. Report of the special committee appointed to investigate as to what additional lands shall be acquired within the Forest preserve in order to protect the water sheds and for the agricultural experiment station. Albany, 1899. 16p. Assembly document 43, 1899. The appendix to this document is Martin Van Buren Ives' "Historical Narrative. Through the Adirondacks in Eighteen Days." For separately published edition see his "Through the Adirondacks in Eighteen Days" (no. 1488). 1490

Forest management in New York. *Forester*, Mar. 1900. 6:60–61. List of amendments for added protection of Forest Preserve. 1491

Pinchot, Gifford. Working plans for the New York Forest preserve. *Outing*, Apr. 1900. 36:89–90. 1492

The Adirondack forest. *For & Stream*, July 21, 1900. 55:41. 1493

Forestry for the New York preserve. *Forester*, July 1900. 6:164–65. Work of Division of Forestry of U.S. Dept. of Agriculture in co-operation with state government to bring about repeal of Article 7, Section 7. 1494

New York (state). Legislature. Assembly. Report of the special committee appointed to investigate as to certain matters pertaining to the state park and Forest preserve. Albany, 1900. 14p. Assembly document 63, 1900. Dated Feb. 28, 1900. 1495

New York. Board of trade and transportation. Letter to the Legislature and for general distribution, urging the creation of a single headed forestry commission in place of the Fisheries, game and forestry commission. N.Y. 1900. 2 leaves. 1496

The New York commission. *For & Stream*, Jan. 12, 1901. 56:21. Editorial on Governor Odell's proposal to combine the Forestry, Fish and Game commission with the Forest Preserve Board. 1497

The New York fish commission. *For & Stream*, Jan. 12, 1901. 56:30. Proposal to combine the Forestry, Fish and Game Commission with the Forest Preserve Board, from Governor Odell's message. 1498

The New York commission. *For & Stream*, Jan. 19, 1901. 56:41. Editorial on the measure introduced by Assemblyman Allds following the recommendation of Governor Odell to combine the Forestry, Fish and Game Commission with the Forest Preserve Board. 1499

Wadsworth, W.A. New York forest, fish and game interest. *For & Stream*, Mar. 9, 1901. 56:185. Discussion of pending legislation on abolishing the Forest, Fish and Game Commission. 1500

New York (state). Forest, fish and game commission. List of lands in the Forest preserve, 1901. Albany, J.B. Lyon, 1901. 367p. Supplement to the 6th Annual Report. 1501

New York (state). Governor (Benjamin B. Odell Jr.). Forest preserve board and Forestry, fish and game commission. *In* his Public papers, 1901. Albany, 1907. p.22–23. Lincoln 10:192–93. 1502

Wolcott, W.E. The Adirondack forest. *For & Stream*, Jan. 25, 1902. 58:65. Opposes any change in the state Constitution. 1503

The Adirondack forests. *For & Stream*, Feb. 8, 1902. 58:101. Editorial on Davis bill to permit cutting of timber. 1504

Carl, David. The Adirondack park. *For & Stream*, Feb. 8, 1902. 58:104. Wants no change in N.Y.S. Constitution. 1505

Jordan, D.A. Concerning the Adirondack forests. *For & Stream*, Feb. 8, 1902. 58:104. Against scientific forestry. 1506

The Adirondack forests. *For & Stream*, Feb. 22, 1902. 58:141. Editorial opposing scientific cutting in the Forest Preserve.   1507

Hoffman, F. von. Scientific forestry. *For & Stream*, Feb. 22, 1902. 58:145. In favor of selective cutting on the Forest Preserve. 1508

Spears, John Randolph. The destruction of the Adirondack forests. *For & Stream*, Feb. 22, 1902. 58:144–45. Against amendments to raid the Adirondacks.   1509

Hoffman, F. von. The Adirondack forests. *For & Stream*, Mar. 8, 1902. 58:189.   1510

Schenck, M. The Adirondack forests. *For & Stream*, Mar. 15, 1902. 58:205. In answer to F. von Hoffman's article "Scientific Forestry" in the issue for Feb. 22, 1902, 58:145.
1511

The Adirondack forest. *For & Stream*, Mar. 22, 1902. 58:221. Editorial on the New York Board of Trade and Transportation's "Memorial to the Legislature" opposing the Davis bill.   1512

New York. Board of trade and transportation. Forestry committee. Memorial addressed to Legislature of the State of New York setting forth the convincing reasons for the rejection of the measures to open the state Forest preserve to the lumberman. *For & Stream*, Mar. 22, 1902. 58:224–25.   1513

Hoffman, F. von. Proper management of the Adirondack forests. *Field & S*, Mar.–Apr. 1902. 7:48–50.   1514

Another bad Adirondack bill. *For & Stream*, Apr. 5, 1902. 58:261. Editorial opposing Senator Brown's bill.   1515

DeWitt, William G. Adirondack streams menaced. *For & Stream*, Apr. 5, 1902. 58:270. Opposing the Brown bill.   1516

Murray, William Henry Harrison. The ownership of the Adirondacks. *Field & S*, July 1902. 7:195–96. port.   1517

Association for the protection of the Adirondacks. The Adirondack forests. *For & Stream*, Aug. 30, 1902. 59:163. Summary of measures concerning the Adirondacks defeated in the Legislature.   1518

Association for the protection of the Adirondacks. A few reasons why the Adirondacks should be preserved. N.Y. 1902. 4p. Dated Aug. 21, 1902. Reprinted in *Field & Stream*, Oct.–Nov. 1902. 7:456–58.   1519

New York (state). Governor (Benjamin B. Odell Jr.). The Forest preserve. *In* his Public papers, 1902. Albany, 1907. p.14–16. Lincoln 10:338–39.   1520

New York (state). Assembly. Report of the special committee appointed to investigate as to certain matters pertaining to the Forest preserve. Albany, 1902. 14p. Assembly document 50, 1902. Dated Mar. 1, 1902.   1521

New York. Board of trade and transportation. Forest preservation. Should pending amendments to article VII, section 7 of the state constitution relating to the state Forest preserve be passed? N.Y. 1902. 13 numbered leaves. Argument against the adoption of the proposed amendment.   1522

"Adirondack," pseud. Extending state ownership in the Adirondack park. *Woods & Wat*, Spring 1903. 6:no.1:14–15. illus.   1523

Paige, Charles L. Preserves and wild lands. *For & Stream*, July 25, 1903. 61:64–65. On right of individuals and clubs to own land in the Forest Preserve. Answer to letters in the July 4 issue (Didymus and Spears).   1524

Wolcott, W.E. Camps on state lands. *For & Stream*, Sept. 19, 1903. 61:223. Policy of state toward those who have erected camps on state land in the Adirondacks.   1525

State ownership of lands within the Adirondacks demanded by the people. *Woods & Wat*, Autumn 1903. 6:no.3:17–19.   1526

Association for the protection of the Adirondacks. The Adirondack park: a sketch of the origin, romantic charms and the practical uses of the Adirondack park, and some reasons for the acquisition of land and reforestation by the State of New York. N.Y. 1903. 32p. illus. (Association for the Protection of the Adirondacks. Publication no.4.) Donaldson lists E.H. Hall as author. Reprinted in *Amateur Sportsman*, Sept.–Dec. 1903, 29:no. 5:14, 29; 29:no.6:14–15; 30:no.1:13, 30; 30: no.2:8–9.   1527

Association for the protection of the Adirondacks. Letter to the New York Legislature relating to the Lewis water storage commission bill, Apr. 16, 1903. N.Y. n.d. 1p. 1528

Association for the protection of the Adirondacks. A plea for the Adirondack and Catskill parks. N.Y. 1903. 30p. (Association for the Protection of the Adirondacks. Publication no.3.)   1529

New York (state). Legislature. Assembly. Adirondack committee. Report. . .April 16, 1903. Albany, 1903. 19p. Assembly document 46, 1903.   1530

New York. Board of trade and transportation. Circular letter. Protest against the Lewis water storage commission bill and urging the adoption of the Stevens substitute bill prepared by the Board of trade and transportation. N.Y. 1903. 2 leaves.   1531

New York. Board of trade and transportation. To the editor of the N.Y. Times. N.Y. 1903. 3p. Opposing the Water Storage Commission bill.   1532

New York. Board of trade and transportation. The water storage humbug: the amended Lewis bill a bad measure; the Stevens bill, Assembly 1766, commended. N.Y. 1903. 6p. Copy in the New York Public Library. 1533

Adirondack forests. *For & Stream*, Jan. 16, 1904. 62:41. Editorial on hearing of Legislative Committee on Adirondack Forests. 1534

Stanton, Sanford E. Preserve Adirondack forests. *Recreation*, Feb. 1904. 20:152–53. 1535

Remodeling New York's forest policy. Situation at Albany and extracts from the report of the special committee of the Senate on the future policy of the state in relation to the Adirondacks and forest preservation. *For & Irrig*, Mar. 1904. 10:119–23. 1536

Prospective legislation at Albany. *For & Irrig*, Apr. 1904. 10:147. Includes measures affecting the Forest Preserve. 1537

"Adirondack," pseud. New York's great forest and mountain park for the people. *Woods & Wat*, Spring 1904. 7:no.1:10–11. 1538

Forest legislation in New York; important amendments to the fire law, boundaries of the Adirondack and Catskill park defined, proposed amendment of constitution. *For & Irrig*, June 1904. 10:273–78. 1539

"Adirondack," pseud. State land purchases in the Adirondack park. *Woods & Wat*, Summer 1904. 7:no.2:15–16. 1540

"Adirondack," pseud. Protection of the Adirondacks — great state policy. *Woods & Wat*, Autumn 1904. 7:no.3:21–22. 1541

New York (state). Governor (Benjamin B. Odell Jr.). Cornell school of forestry; Forest preserve. *In* his Public papers, 1904. Albany, 1907. p.15–18. Reprinted in *Forest and Stream*, Jan. 16, 1904, 62:47. Lincoln 10:605–8. 1542

New York (state). Legislature. Assembly. Special committee of the Assembly on the Adirondacks. Report. . .April 13, 1904. Albany, 1904. 11p. Assembly document 60, 1904. 1543

New York (state). Legislature. Senate. Report of the special committee. . .on the future policy of the state in relation to the Adirondacks and forest preservation. Transmitted to the Legislature February 24, 1904. Albany, 1904. 14p. folded map. Senate document 28, 1904. 1544

Danger to Adirondack forest reserve. *Sport Rev*, Mar. 4, 1905. 27:229. Editorial on resolution before the Legislature to permit removal of dead timber. 1545

Association for the protection of the Adirondacks. Adirondack timber thieving. *For & Stream*, Mar. 25, 1905. 64:234. Letters to

Governor Frank W. Higgins on selling timber from state lands. 1546

Adirondack timber thieves. *For & Stream*, Mar. 25, 1905. 64:229. Editorial on charges of the Association for the Protection of the Adirondacks, implicating Commissioner Middleton and Chief Protector Pond. 1547

Spears, Raymond Smiley. The Adirondack park. *For & Stream*, Apr. 22, 1905. 64:315. Boundaries of the park. 1548

The Adirondack timber investigation. *For & Stream*, May 6, 1905. 64:349. Editorial on selling timber from Adirondack state lands. 1549

Adirondack timber stealing. *For & Stream*, May 6, 1905. 64:358. Selling timber on forest land in the Preserve. 1550

A betrayal of trust. *For & Stream*, Sept. 2, 1905. 65:185. Editorial on charges of Raymond S. Spears that state lands near Ampersand Pond have been sold. 1551

Spears, Raymond Smiley. Selling Adirondack state lands. *For & Stream*, Sept. 2, 1905. 65:187–88. Illegal sale of state lands. See also no.1558. 1552

Adirondack state land sales. *For & Stream*, Sept. 16, 1905. 65:237. See no.1552. 1553

The Adirondack lands. *For & Stream*, Sept. 23, 1905. 65:245. Editorial on investigation of Adirondack state land sales. See no.1552. 1554

Adirondack state lands. *For & Stream*, Sept. 23, 1905. 65:248. Series of three articles on Commissioner Whipple's investigation of land sale irregularities. 1555

Spears, Raymond Smiley. Adirondack state lands. *For & Stream*, Oct. 14, 1905. 65:308–9. For additional statement about illegal state land sales see no.1552. 1556

Adirondack land sales. *For & Stream*, Nov. 11, 1905. 65:385. Editorial on Commissioner Whipple's investigation; see also no.1552. 1557

Whipple, James Spencer. Adirondack state land sales. *For & Stream*, Nov. 11, 1905. 65:388–89. Commissioner Whipple's answer to Raymond S. Spears (no.1552). 1558

The Deckhand, pseud. Raymond S. Spears and Adirondack lands. *For & Stream*, Nov. 18, 1905. 65:419. Comments on controversy between R.S. Spears and Commissioner Whipple. 1559

Juvenal, pseud. Adirondack conditions. *For & Stream*, Nov. 18, 1905. 65:406. State lands problem and general conditions. 1560

Spears, Raymond Smiley. Adirondack state lands. *For & Stream*, Nov. 18, 1905. 65:408–9.

Reply to Commissioner Whipple (no.1558). 1561

Cristaboro, Charles. Strenuous game wardenship. *For & Stream*, Dec. 9, 1905. 65:473. Burnham's razing of camps located illegally on state lands. 1562

Save the Adirondacks. *Outlook*, Dec. 30, 1905. 81:1053–54. Editorial calling attention to spoilation of the Adirondack forests by lumbering operations. 1563

New York (state). Forest, fish and game commission. List of lands in the Forest preserve, 1905. Albany, 1905. 394p. Supplement to the 10th Annual Report. 1564

New York (state). Governor (Frank Higgins). Message to the Legislature concerning the state's Forest preserve. *In* his Public papers, 1905. Albany, 1906. p.47–52. Lincoln 10: 753–57. 1565

New York (state). Legislature. Assembly. Adirondack committee. Report. . .April 11, 1905. Albany, 1905. 20p. Assembly document 31, 1905. Extract in *Forest and Stream*, May 6, 1905, 64:355, with title "The Adirondacks and Lake George." 1566

New York. Board of trade and transportation. Increased water supply for greater New York. . . A state water commission and a New York city water supply commission advocated. N.Y. 1905. 8p. 1567

New York. Board of trade and transportation. "Lumber thieves in the people's forests." N.Y. 1905. 1 leaf. Signed: Edmund Philo Martin. Approving recommendation of Governor Higgins and urging him to relieve from office officials through whose neglect lumber was cut or removed from state lands, and urging passage of amendment to the law to compel prosecution of trespasses and theft. 1568

Adirondack cottage sites. *For & Stream*, Feb. 17, 1906. 66:266. Report of Camp-Fire Club meeting reprinted from the *Jamestown (N.Y.) Morning Post*. Includes résumé of J.S. Whipple's speech recommending that the state lease camp sites. 1569

Squatters to be fired. *Field & S*, Feb. 1906. 10:1059. Buildings on state lands near Raquette Lake to be torn down. 1570

Protection of Adirondack forests. *Sh & Fish*, Apr. 12, 1906. 40:5. Editorial approving bill for purchase of forest lands. 1571

Carl, David. The Adirondack forest again. *For & Stream*, Aug. 4, 1906. 67:170–71. Against the storage project. 1572

Adirondack preservation. *For & Stream*, Oct. 6, 1906. 67:533. Part of Democratic party platform. 1573

Stoddard, Seneca Ray. Adirondack storage reservoirs. "In answer to criticism." *St No Mo*, Nov. 1906. 1:no.7:5–9. illus. 1574

Association for the protection of the Adirondacks. The Adirondack appropriation bill of 1906. Reasons why the state should make liberal provision for extending the Forest preserve within the Adirondack. . .and Catskill parks. . . N.Y. 1906. 19p. (Association for the Protection of the Adirondacks. Publication no.6.) 1575

Association for the protection of the Adirondacks. Letter Apr. 21, 1906 on concurrent resolution proposing amendment to section 7 of article VII. N.Y. 1906. 2p. 1576

New York (state). Legislature. Assembly. Adirondack committee. Report. . .April 3, 1906. Albany, 1906. 13p. Assembly document 57, 1906. 1577

To flood Adirondack lands. *For & Stream*, Jan. 19, 1907. 68:87. Editorial showing the dangers of the water storage project. 1578

Stoddard, Seneca Ray. To his excellency the Governor. *St No Mo*, Jan. 1907. 1:no.9:5–12. Editorial on the need of a law to prevent cutting. 1579

Fighting to preserve Adirondack forests. *Sport Rev*, Feb. 9, 1907. 31:149. Short editorial on Merritt resolution to flood Adirondack lands. 1580

Storage reservoirs in the Adirondacks. *Outlook*, Feb. 9, 1907. 85:292–93. Editorial opposing proposed amendment to N.Y.S. Constitution permitting Adirondack state lands to be used as a storage reservoir. 1581

Stoddard, Seneca Ray. The rape of the mountains. *St No Mo*, Feb. 1907. 1:no.10:5–9. In favor of storage reservoirs. 1582

The Adirondack forest reserve in danger. *Outlook*, Mar. 16, 1907. 85:589–90. Against the water storage bill. 1583

Fernow, Bernhard Eduard. The Adirondacks. *Outlook*, Mar. 16, 1907. 85:624–25. Letter to the editor giving argument for exploiting valuable features of the Adirondacks; article on p.867, "Water Storage Grab," and letter by Samuel F. Adam, p.625–26. See also nos. 1581 and 1583. 1584

The Adirondack water grab. *Field & S*, Mar. 1907. 11:1042. 1585

The Merritt resolution. *For & Irrig*, Mar. 1907. 13:117–18. Various opinions on dams for storage of water in the Adirondacks. 1586

The protection of the Adirondacks. *For & Stream*, Apr. 20, 1907. 68:615. Includes a letter opposing the flooding of state lands signed by E.H. Hall, Secretary of the Association for the Protection of the Adirondacks, and a report of the 6th annual meeting of the Association.   1587

Bills that should be passed. *For & Stream*, May 18, 1907. 68:767. Editorial on bills affecting the Adirondacks.   1588

The Fuller-O'Brian water power bill. *St No Mo*, May 1907. 2:8–12. map.   1589

Parker, Clarence L. Who's who in the water storage deal? *St No Mo*, June 1907. 2:121–27.   1590

Parker, Clarence L. Legislative results. *For & Stream*, July 6, 1907. 69:15. Includes the defeat of Merritt-O'Neil resolution commonly called "water storage grab."   1591

Parker, Clarence L. The water question. *St No Mo*, Aug. 1907. 2:275–79.   1592

Another Adirondack forest grab. *For & Irrig*, Sept. 1907. 13:462–63. Plan to have county supervisors lay out roads through the Adirondacks stopped by Attorney-General Jackson.   1593

Schwartz, G. Frederick. The Adirondacks are a park, not a timber reserve... *For & Irrig*, Nov. 1907. 13:601. Letter in answer to article in Sept. issue on efforts to overcome the law against cutting in the Forest Preserve. In favor of wild lands.   1594

Agar, John Giraud. Paper read at the convention called by the Albany chamber of commerce...March 14, 1907, to consider the pending constitutional amendment relating to the construction of dams and the storage of waters on the Forest preserve for public purposes. N.Y. 1907. 32p. (Association for the Protection of the Adirondacks. Publication no.12.)   1595

Association for the protection of the Adirondacks. A brief review of the depredations upon the Adirondack forests accomplished or attempted during the past few years, with reference to the proposed amendment to section 7 of article VII of the constitution. Together with a statement by Governor Hughes of his attitude, letters from prominent citizens, and the action of the People's institute of New York. N.Y. 1907. 20p. illus. (Association for the Protection of the Adirondacks. Publication no.9.)   1596

Association for the protection of the Adirondacks. The conservation of the waters and woods of the State of New York. An address ...in favor of a comprehensive plan of water storage, and appropriations for extending the Forest preserve and replanting. N.Y. 1907. 15p. (Association for the Protection of the Adirondacks. Publication no.15.)   1597

Association for the protection of the Adirondacks. The Legislature of the State of New York for 1907. N.Y. 1907. 7p. (Association for the Protection of the Adirondacks. Publication no.10.)   1598

Association for the protection of the Adirondacks. A letter to the members of the Legislature of the State of New York for 1907 concerning the proposed amendment to section 7 of article VII of the constitution relating to the Forest preserve. N.Y. 1907. 16p. (Association for the Protection of the Adirondacks. Publication no.8.) Includes reprint of letter from the New York *Evening Post*, by R.S.S. (probably Raymond Smiley Spears) entitled "Peril of the Adirondacks." Water storage bill.   1599

Association for the protection of the Adirondacks. Tinkering with the constitution. Some reasons why the proposed amendment... should not be adopted; together with letters from Charles Sprague Smith of the People's institute of New York and Dr. Walter B. James on the subject. N.Y. 1907. 12p. (Association for the Protection of the Adirondacks. Publication no.11.)   1600

Graves, Henry Solon. Address...at the American museum of natural history...April 25, 1907, giving reasons why the constitution of the State of New York should not be amended so as to permit water storage in the Adirondack park. N.Y. 1907. 10p. (Association for the Protection of the Adirondacks. Publication no.14.)   1601

New York. Board of trade and transportation. A bill for water power development introduced by Senator Fuller and Assemblyman John Lord O'Brian. An act authorizing the state Water power commission to devise plans for progressive development under state management and control and making an appropriation therefor. N.Y. 1907. 4p.   1602

New York. Board of trade and transportation. The water storage schemes to enrich the schemer. N.Y. 1907. 7p.   1603

New York. Board of trade and transportation. Committee on forests. The pending constitutional amendment relating to the state Forest preserve. Argument against proposed amendment to article seven, section VII of the state constitution introduced by Assemblyman Merritt. N.Y. 1907. 8p. Addressed to the Legislature. Signed by Edmund P. Martin.   1604

Whipple, James Spencer. Value of the woods. *Amat Sportsman*, Mar. 1908. 38:no.5:12–13. An address before the N.Y.S. Legislature on need for more land in Adirondacks and Catskills.   1605

Railways and forest fires. *For & Stream*, Oct. 17, 1908. 71:607. Editorial on suggestion of the Fish and Game Commission that railroads use a fuel other than coal in Adirondacks.   1606

New York (state). Governor (Charles E. Hughes). Forest preserves and game laws. *In* his Public papers, 1908. Albany, 1909. p.31–33.   1607

Necessity of protecting Adirondacks and Catskills. *Sport Rev*, Aug. 14, 1909. 36:159. Discussion at meeting of Northeastern State Foresters and directors of American Forestry Association.   1608

New York (state). Conservation commission. List of lands in the Forest preserve, 1909. Albany, 1909. 440p. Supplement to the Commission's 14th Annual Report.   1609

New York (state). Legislature. Senate. Report of the special committee on the policy of the state in relation to the Adirondacks for forest preservation, and the shellfish industry. Albany, 1909. 9p. Senate document 37, 1909.
                                              1610

New York. Board of trade and transportation. Water storage in the N.Y. state Forest preserve. A proposed constitutional amendment that would make it practicable and safe. N.Y. 1909. 4p.   1611

Whipple, James Spencer. Commissioner Whipple's report. *For & Stream*, Jan. 22, 1910. 74:136–37.   1612

Water conservation in New York state. *Sci Am*, Feb. 12, 1910. 102:138. Editorial on the water storage project.   1613

Carl, David. Flooding the Adirondack park. *For & Stream*, Mar. 19, 1910. 74:456. Against the storage project.   1614

Carl, David. Exploiting the Forest preserve. *For & Stream*, Mar. 26, 1910. 74:493–94. Opposing the leasing of camp sites.   1615

Commercializing the Adirondacks. *For & Stream*, Apr. 16, 1910. 74:618. Opposing water storage project.   1616

Public parks for private use. *For & Stream*, Apr. 16, 1910. 74:607. Short editorial opposing private camp sites and new dam construction.   1617

Governor Hughes' policy of water conservation. *McClure*, Apr. 1910. 34:703–4. Storage reservoirs.   1618

The Merritt bill. *Ang & Hunt*, Apr. 1910. 2:207–8. For development of electrical power in the Adirondacks.   1619

Carl, David. The poor man's woods and the rich man's dams. *For & Stream*, May 7, 1910. 74:733–34. Opposing the building of dams in the Adirondacks.   1620

New York. *Am For*, May 1910. 16:311. News from the states; Robert W. Higbie urges purchase of 1,000,000 acres of Adirondack land.
                                              1621

The state land scandal. *Ang & Hunt*, Sept. 1910. 2:504. Reprint of editorials from several papers.   1622

Hendrickson, John H. Abolish the Forest, fish and game commission. *Ang & Hunt*, Oct. 1910. 2:509–10.   1623

New York (state). Forest, fish and game commission. List of lands in the Forest preserve purchased 1866–1909. Albany, 1910? 263p.   1624

New York (state). Governor (Charles E. Hughes). The Forest preserve. *In* his Public papers, 1910. Albany, 1910. p.19–22.   1625

New York. Board of trade and transportation. The water storage bills. N.Y. 1910. 4p. Report on bills introduced by Senator Cobb and Assemblyman Fowler developing a plan for water storage within and outside the Forest Preserve.   1626

Parker, Clarence L. Letting dogs into the woods. *For & Stream*, Mar. 25, 1911. 76:98. Opposes two bills that would permit use of dogs in the Adirondacks.   1627

Pinchot to inspect the Adirondacks. *Field & S*, Sept. 1911. 16:455.   1628

Hands off the Adirondacks. *For & Stream*, Dec. 9, 1911. 77:844. Editorial opposing Pinchot's proposals for scientific forestry (no.1632).   1629

Spears, Eldridge A. The Adirondacks. *For & Stream*, Dec. 16, 1911. 77:873. Comments unfavorably on article by Gifford Pinchot in *Forest and Stream*, Dec. 9, 1911 (no.1632).
                                              1630

Spears, Raymond Smiley. The Adirondacks. *For & Stream*, Dec. 23, 1911. 77:903. Comments on Pinchot's article in *Forest and Stream*, Dec. 9, 1911 (no.1632) and approves editorial "Hands Off" (no.1629) in the same issue.   1631

Pinchot, Gifford. Forest conservation in the Adirondacks. N.Y. 1911. 10p. Caption title. Unsigned. Report prepared on behalf of the National Conservation Association for the Camp-Fire Club, of America. Also in *Forest and Stream*, Dec. 9, 1911, 77:837–39, 856, with title "Pinchot on the Adirondack Problem"; in *Field and Stream*, Jan. 1912, 16:949–55, with title "The Adirondack Forest Problem"; and in *American Forestry*, Jan. 1912, 18:51–59, with title "The Adirondack Problem."   1632

Snyder, O.L. The importance of the preservation of the Adirondack forests. *In* New York state waterways association. 2d annual convention, 1911. p.39–41.   1633

Pinchot, Gifford. Public or private interests? *Outlook*, Mar. 30, 1912. 100:729–31. A plea for forest conservation in the Adirondacks. **1634**

Pettis, Clifford Robert. Possible advantage to the State of New York by opening the Forest preserves. *Soc Am For Proc*, July 1913. 8:197–201. Reviews legislation concerning the Forest Preserve. Correct construction of the Constitution not the best treatment of the Preserve. **1635**

The forestry amendment. *For & Stream*, Nov. 1, 1913. 81:560. Editorial opposing amendment that would permit the building of dams and reservoirs in the Forest Preserve. **1636**

The Adirondack Forest preserve. *Am Scenic & Hist Pres Soc*, 1913. 18:224–43. Includes life of Paul Smith. **1637**

Baldwin, Arthur J. The right of eminent domain and its relation to water storage. *In* New York state waterways association. 4th annual convention, 1913. p.36–40. Approval of Burd amendment. **1638**

Hornaday, William Temple. Our vanishing wild life; its extermination and preservation. N.Y. Scribner, 1913. 411p. illus. maps. The Adirondack State Park, p.347–48. **1639**

Pettis, Clifford Robert. Benefits to be derived if use of Forest preserve were permitted. *Emp St For Prod Assn Proc*, 1913. 8:60–66. **1640**

Smith, Edward North. The interest of northern New York in water storage. *In* New York state waterways association. 4th annual convention, 1913. p.108–13. Approval of Burd amendment. **1641**

Gaylord, Frederick Alan. The forestry situation in New York. *Field & S*, Aug. 1914. 19:426. Discussion of suggested reforms for Adirondacks and Catskills. **1642**

Gaylord, Frederick Alan. A reply to certain statements relative to the state Forest preserve. *NYS For Assn Bul*, Oct. 1914, 1:no.2:31–39. Forester's reply to an article in the March 1913 *Board of Trade Journal*. **1643**

Goldthwaite, Kenneth W. Constitutional amendment affecting the Adirondacks. *NYS For Assn Bul*, Oct. 1914. 1:no.2:40–41. Reprinted from the *Adirondack Enterprise*. **1644**

Ordway, Samuel Hanson. The forestry provisions of the New York state constitution. *NYS For Assn Bul*, Oct. 1914. 1:no.2:18–20. Lists changes that should be made. **1645**

Toumey, James William. State forest administration with particular reference to the State of New York. *NYS For Assn Bul*, Oct. 1914. 1:no.2:5–10. illus. Plan for state forest service. On proposed amendment permitting cutting in the Forest Preserve. **1646**

Smith, Thomas M. Keep the Adirondacks intact. *Field & S*, Nov. 1914. 19:759–60. Opposing amendments to the Constitution. **1647**

Agar, John Giraud. Revision of the state constitution. State policy of forest and water power conservation. An address. . .at the annual meeting of the Academy of political science. . .November 20, 1914. N.Y. 1914. 23p. (Association for the Protection of the Adirondacks. Publication no.24.) **1648**

New York (state). Conservation commission. List of lands in the Forest preserve, January 1, 1914. Albany, 1914. 503p. Appendix to the 3d Annual Report. **1649**

1915–1937

Chapman, Herman Haupt. The crisis in New York. *Am For*, Mar. 1915. 21:168–71. Plan to reorganize the Conservation Commission and give it control of the Forest Preserve. **1650**

Graves, Henry Solon. The Adirondacks. *Field & S*, Mar. 1915. 19:1154–56. Address before the American Forestry Association. **1651**

Protect the Adirondack wilderness. *Field & S*, July 1915. 20:301. Work of the Camp-Fire Club of America. Reprinted from the New York *Evening World*. **1652**

Rhees, Rush. Sale of lands outside the Adirondack and Catskill parks. *NYS For Assn J*, Oct. 1915. 2:no.4:28–29. Land outside the Park but within the Preserve. **1653**

Whipple, James Spencer. The best use of the Forest preserve by the whole people. *NYS For Assn J*, Oct. 1915. 2:no.4:14–16. **1654**

New York. Board of trade and transportation. Hon. Elihu Root, president, Constitutional convention, Albany, N.Y. N.Y. 1915. 2 leaves. Dated August 17, 1915. Signed: P.F. Schofield. Protest against proposal to establish a conservation commission of nine members. **1655**

Pettis, Clifford Robert. Resources of the Forest preserve. Albany, J.B. Lyon, 1915.

41p. diagrs. (New York State Conservation Commission. Division of Land and Forests. Bulletin 12.) 1656

Pettis, Clifford Robert. Forest provisions of New York state constitution. *For Quar*, Mar. 1916. 14:50–60. 1657

Van Norden, Ottomar H. Shall we commercialize our parks? *NYS For Assn J*, Oct. 1916. 3:no.2–4:15–18. 1658

W., J.D. A wide-open preserve. *For & Stream*, Oct. 1916. 86:1215. Permits for open camps. 1659

For New York forest lands. *Am For*, Nov. 1916. 22:674. 1660

New York to buy forests. *Am For*, Dec. 1916. 22:723. 1661

Association for the protection of the Adirondacks. . . .To members. . . n.p. n.d. 1p. Letter dated Oct. 16, 1916, on "Proposition no. one." 1662

Association for the protection of the Adirondacks. Bond issue for Forest preserve extension. N.Y. 1916. 1p. Press release dated May 29, 1916. 1663

Hugo, Francis M. On Forest preserve. *Emp St For Prod Assn Proc*, 1916. 11:57–68. 1664

New York state Forest preserve. *Am Scenic & Hist Pres Soc*, 1916. 21:282–93. See also 22d Annual Report, 1917, p.311–23. 1665

Hopkins, Arthur S. New lands in the Forest preserve. *Conservationist*, July 1917. 1:99–102. illus. Buying lands from individuals. 1666

Pratt, George DuPont. Saving the forests and wild life; fascination of the primeval woods and how New York is conserving them for the benefit of all the people—immense area of Forest preserve. *State Service*, Aug. 1917. 1:no.1:32–37. illus. port. 1667

Sweet, Thaddeus C. Constitution causes loss of trees, Speaker Sweet pleads for change in organic law in the interest of the Forest preserve. Public losing use of immense tracts of timber. *State Service*, Sept. 1917. 1:no.2:70–72. port. tables. 1668

Agar, John Giraud. State policy of land purchase for the Forest preserve. *Emp St For Prod Assn Proc*, 1917. 12:105–18. 1669

Association for the protection of the Adirondacks. . . .Land purchase for the Forest preserve. Suggestion for a state policy. The Lake Placid situation. N.Y. 1917. 16p. (Association for the Protection of the Adirondacks. Publication no.28.) 1670

Pratt, George DuPont. Adding to the state Forest preserve; enormous tract in Adirondacks and Catskills being acquired; area includes vast wilderness of forest, lake and mountain. *State Service*, Oct. 1918. 2:no.10: 47–50. 1671

Additions to the Forest preserve. *Conservationist*, Nov. 1918. 1:170. Report on progress in buying additional lands with funds made available through the bond issue of 1917. 1672

Increasing the Forest preserve by private gift. *Conservationist*, Dec. 1918. 1:189. Donation of the Shore Owners' Association of Lake Placid to buy the slopes of Mackenzie and Saddleback. 1673

Pratt, George DuPont. Forest conservation in New York; the Forest preserve is owned collectively by all the people of the state. *Nat Hist*, Jan. 1919. 19:84–103. illus. map. 1674

Pettis, Clifford Robert. Public use of the Forest preserve. *Conservationist*, May 1919. 2:67–71. Rules. 1675

Results of the bond issue. *Conservationist*, Sept. 1919. 2:140–41. Report on lands bought through the bond issue. 1676

New York. *Am For*, Nov. 1919. 25:1495–96. News from the states. Purchase of Santa Clara Lumber Company tract in Township 27, Franklin County. 1677

New York (state). Conservation commission. Registration of guides in the Forest preserve counties of New York state. Rules and regulations. Albany, 1919. 15p. 1678

Carlisle, John Nelson. Wants lumbering in Forest preserve; former state official would repeal prohibitory provisions in constitution and permit cutting of mature timber regulated by a special board. *State Service*, Mar. 1920. 4:231–34. illus. 1679

Whipple, James Spencer. Opposes lumbering in Forest preserve; great wooded tracts in the Adirondacks and Catskills should be maintained in their natural state undisturbed by the lumberman. *State Service*, Apr. 1920. 4: 346–50. illus. 1680

Getman, Anson. Title to forest lands. *Conservationist*, Nov. 1920. 3:166–68. Problems that arise in searching titles. 1681

New York (state). Conservation commission. List of lands in the Forest preserve. Mar. 20, 1920. Albany, 1920. 320p. Legislative document 84, 1920. Appendix to the 1919 Annual Report. 1682

State Forest preserve. *Am Scenic & Hist Pres Soc*, 1920. 25:301–8. 1683

Hall, Edward Hagaman. Ill-considered water power bills. *NYS Assn St Bul*, Apr. 1, 1921. 1:no.7:6. 1684

Addition to the state forest. *State Service*, Oct.–Nov. 1921. 5:631. illus. Gore around Lake Colden. 1685

Conservation in New York. *Survey*, Nov. 12, 1921. 47:236–37. Editorial on curtailment of service of the Conservation Commission, especially for fire protection. Includes tribute to George D. Pratt. 1686

An important acquisition. *Conservationist*, Nov. 1921. 3:169. Lake Colden gore purchased from the McIntyre Iron Company. 1687

New York (state). Commission to investigate the title to lands in counties containing parts of the Forest preserve. Report. Albany, 1921. 20p. Legislative document 37, 1921. 1688

State regulation of private forests. *Emp St For Prod Assn Bul*, May 1922. 14:7–8. Discussion of bill controlling forests on private lands in the Adirondacks. Text of the bill and further discussion in issue for Mar. 1923, 16:1–4. 1689

Carpenter, Warwick Stevens. Mountain slope protection and recreational development in the Adirondacks. Albany, Argus co. 1922. 24p. plate, map. Contains memorial to the Adirondack Mountain Club urging the Club to endorse the program outlined in this publication. For action of the Club see *High Spots*, Dec. 1922, "Committee Majority Rejects Carpenter Memorial-Motion." 1690

New York (state). Conservation commission. Registered guides in the New York state Forest preserve and St. Lawrence reservation. Albany, 1922. 14p. front. Also issued in 1920. 1691

New York state association. Committee on the state park plan. A state park plan for New York, with a proposal for the new park bond issue. N.Y. Brown printing & binding co. 1922. 83p. illus. maps. 1692

The state park bond issue bill is introduced. *NYS Assn St Bul*, Jan. 22, 1923. 3:no.2:6. Suggests $5,000,000 to purchase additional land for the Forest Preserve. 1693

Unified park plan for New York state, more land asked for Adirondacks, Catskills and Finger lakes, Alleghany park and other pleasure grounds need more money for development. *State Service*, Jan.–Feb. 1923. 7:24–28. illus. 1694

What the press says about the state park bond issue bill, some editorial comments. *NYS Assn St Bul*, Feb. 19, 1923. 3:no.4:3–11. (Supp.) 1695

Hearing on park and conservation bill. *NYS Assn St Bul*, Mar. 21, 1923. 3:no.6:3. 1696

Parks and conservation. *NYS Assn St Bul*, Apr. 3, 1923. 3:no.7:3. Discussion of bill before the Legislature. 1697

A forum on the proposed waterpower amendment. *NY Forestry*, July 1923. 9:78–90. 1698

Preserve the Forest preserve. *Outlook*, Oct. 17, 1923. 135:258–59. Opposition to constitutional amendment allowing the building of hydroelectric plants in the Forest Preserve. 1699

Forest reserves in the State of New York. *Science*, Nov. 2, 1923. n.s.58:344. Resolution of the Executive Board of the American Engineering Council of the Federated American Engineering Societies approving use of timber in the Adirondack and Catskill preserves. For letter opposing see Van Name, W.G. "New York State Forest," in issue for Nov. 30, 1923, n.s.58:444. 1700

Waugh, Frank A. Conservation ad absurdum. *Sci Mo*, Nov. 1923. 17:498–505. illus. Professional forester's views on Section 7, Article VII, of New York state Constitution. Excerpts appeared in *Empire State Forest Products Association Bulletin*, Jan. 1924, 18:10–11. 1701

Committee to prevent the exploitation of the Adirondacks. The Adirondack raid: an address to the voters of the State of New York. N.Y. 1923? 15p. illus. 1702

Committee to prevent the exploitation of the Adirondacks. Governor Smith opposes the Adirondack raid. N.Y. 1923. 4p. Unpaged leaflet. Letter to John G. Agar. 1703

New York (state). Governor (Alfred E. Smith). Message recommending the adoption of program for the development of state parks, April 18, 1923. *In* his Public papers, 1923. Albany, 1924. p.181–88. Includes mention of bill to extend the "blue line" and Lake George Park. 1704

Recknagel, Arthur Bernard. The forests of New York state. N.Y. Macmillan, 1923. 107p. front. plates, tables. The Forest Preserve from the forester's point of view. 1705

State regulation of private forests in the Adirondack park. Albany, New York state association, 1923. 8p. Supplement to the State Bulletin, v.3, no.5, Mar. 5, 1923. 1706

Hosmer, Ralph Sheldon. A forest policy of New York. *Am For*, June 1924. 30:349–50. 1707

New York (state). Governor (Alfred E. Smith). Message on development of state parks, January 22, 1924. *In* his Public papers, 1924. Albany, 1926. p.189–93. Includes acquisition of land at Lake George. 1708

New York (state). State council of parks. State park bond issue—what the state park bond issue, to be voted on at the November election, will do for you. n.p. 1924. 8p. 1709

New York. State park committee for western & central N.Y. Vote Yes for bond issue for state parks. . .November 4, 1924. Buffalo, N.Y. 1924. 4p. Unpaged leaflet. 1710

New York state association. Committee on the state park plan. The state park plan for New York revised to show progress to date with the proposal for the new park bond issue; 2d ed. Jan. 1924. n.p. 1924. 96p. illus. maps (partly folded).   1711

State park bond issue. . . n.p. n.pub. 1924? 8p. Vote for the state park bond issue.   1712

Vote for proposition no.1 as printed on the official ballot on November 4th, 1924. Playgrounds for the use of all the people. n.p. n.pub. n.d. 20p. illus. Issued by the New York State Council of Parks, Commissioners of the Palisades Interstate Park, Westchester County Park Commission and Long Island State Park Commission. State park bond issue.   1713

New York acquires Tongue mountain peninsula. Am For, Nov. 1925. 31:697.   1714

Hosmer, Ralph Sheldon. Steps toward a comprehensive forest policy of the State of New York. NY Forestry, 1925. p.32–34. illus.
1715

New York (state). State council of parks. Annual report, 1925. N.Y. 1925. 78p. illus. maps. The only report issued. Transferred to the Conservation Department. Forest Preserve region, p.51–53.   1716

Recknagel, Arthur Bernard. Forest regulation without representation; the timberland owner must have a voice in the decisions which affect his forest management. A viewpoint. NY Forestry, 1925. p.40–41. Opposes Strauss bill regulating cutting on private timberland in the Adirondacks.   1717

Knox, Earle B. Forest preserves—the people's playground. Field & S, June 1927. 32:no.2: 50–56. illus. Description of the Forest Preserve and its administration.   1718

Association for the protection of the Adirondacks. Rescue the forests; a call for legislation to save the vanishing private forests of New York state. N.Y. 1927. 15p.   1719

New York (state). Governor (Alfred E. Smith). Forest preserve. Lake George. In his Public papers, 1928. Albany, 1928. p.84.   1720

New York (state). Governor (Alfred E. Smith). Annual message, 1928. In his Public papers, 1928. Albany, 1928. p.82. Includes paragraph on development of the Forest Preserve region.
1721

Hopkins, Arthur S. Bond issues for state forests. J For, Feb. 1929. 27:132–37. Reviews New York state policy.   1722

Lawyer, George A. Adirondack forestry conditions. Up-Stater, Mar. 1929. 1:no.2:14–15. illus. Approves cutting of timber on state lands.   1723

Lawyer, George A. The Forest preserve and the Adirondack park. Up-Stater, May 1929. 1:no.3:10–11. map.   1724

Lawyer, George A. The Adirondacks, parks and forest. Up-Stater, Sept. 1929. 1:no.5:11. Editorial advocating proper utilization of forest resources, flood prevention and river regulation.   1725

Forest preserve safeguard upheld; section 7, article VII, of New York state constitution successfully invoked to prevent bob-sleigh run on state land. Scen & Hist Am, Mar. 1930. 2:35–36.   1726

The value of the wilderness. Scen & Hist Am, Mar. 1930. 2:42.   1727

Lawyer, George A. Is the Forest preserve a luxury? Up-Stater, May 1930. 2:no.3:6–8, 26–32.   1728

Recknagel, Arthur Bernard. Forest taxation, the Forest preserve and their relation to economic welfare. Up-Stater, May 1930. 2: no.3:19.   1729

Our Forest preserve. Up-Stater, July 1930. 2:no.4:20–21. Reprint of an editorial from the New York Evening Post, June 20, 1930.
1730

Carlisle, Floyd Leslie. Mr. Carlisle at Saranac lake. Up-Stater, Sept. 1930. 2:no.5:34, 36. Reprint of editorial on water storage from the Watertown Times, Aug. 27, 1930.   1731

Lawyer, George A. The Forest preserve. Up-Stater, Sept. 1930. 2:no.5:15.   1732

Sane conservation proposals, opposing interests establish a basis of agreement for use of the New York state Forest preserve. Up-Stater, Sept. 1930. 2:no.5:8–9. illus. Includes text of speeches from New York State Economic Congress conference at Lake Placid, July 21, 1930.   1733

New York state development association, inc. The Saranac Lake meeting. The summer meeting. . .at Saranac Lake, August 26, 1930, results in amendment of by-laws regarding the Forest preserve and open discussion by Floyd L. Carlisle of many matters of great interest. Up-Stater, Sept. 1930. 2:no.5:11–12, 17.   1734

Mulholland, William D. The reforestation amendment. NYS Ranger Sch, 1930. p.23–24. The Hewitt amendment.   1735

Some aspects of the proposed change in state policy in the Adirondack and Catskill parks. NYS Ranger Sch, 1930. p.34–36. In favor of forestry practice.   1736

Stanton, E. MacD. and others. Analysis of the tree cutting amendment improperly called the reforestation amendment (Senate no.2330) 1930. n.p. Forest preserve association, n.d.

4p. chart. Signed: E. MacD. Stanton, Richard D. Moot, J.S. Apperson, Irving Langmuir. Earlier edition, undated, 3p. Against the amendment.   1737

Lawyer, George A. The penalty. *Up-Stater*, Jan. 1931. 3:no.1:9. Editorial criticizing Article VII, Section 7.   1738

Great projects open the Adirondacks; New York state's forest park, largest in the nation, gains noted highway this year, Blue mountain and Tongue mountain routes spur the traveler. *Motordom*, Apr. 1931. 24:no.10:10–11. illus.   1739

Largest park. *Survey*, May 15, 1931. 66:227. map. Adirondack Park.   1740

Adirondack largest public park. *Am For*, May 1931. 37:309.   1741

The biggest park in America; Adirondacks now passes the Yellowstone in size, 4,604,000 acres of recreation in one of the finest motoring regions in the world. *Motordom*, June 1931. 24:no.12:9. map.   1742

Howard, William Gibbs. The Hewitt amendment. *NYS For Assn NL*, June 1931. p.3. 1743

New York extends application of Forest tax law and enlarges Adirondack park. *For Worker*, July 1931. 7:no.4:1. Brief notes on 1930–31 legislation.   1744

Brown, Nelson C. New York at the crossways: the people of New York state will vote on a $20,000,000 reforestation plan in November. *Am For*, Nov. 1931. 37:682–83. Hewitt reforestation plan.   1745

Billboards to be removed from Adirondack park. *Am For*, Dec. 1931. 37:762.   1746

Apperson, John S. and others. Comments on the questions and answers appearing in pamphlet distributed by the direction of the New York state reforestation commission on amendment no.3 to be voted on November 3rd, 1931. Schenectady, N.Y. 1931. 4p. Signed: J.S. Apperson, Irving Langmuir, Richard D. Moot, E. MacD. Stanton. Dated October 9, 1931. Against the tree cutting amendment.   1747

Association for the protection of the Adirondacks. Defeat the "recreational amendment": protect the natural beauty of our wild forest lands. N.Y. 1931? 4p. Unpaged leaflet. Against Porter-Brereton amendment for the construction of "recreational facilities" in the Forest Preserve.   1748

Dapping, W.O., Rogers, C.S. and Rabenold, Elwood M. Before the people of the State of New York. In the matter of the Hewitt reforestation amendment. N.Y. New York state fish, game and forest league, 1931. 27p. A memorandum opposing the Hewitt reforestation amendment.   1749

Mohawk valley hiking club. Think—and act. Schenectady, N.Y. 1931? 4p. (Bulletin 2, Educational Series.) Against the Porter-Brereton recreation amendment.   1750

New York (state). Governor (Franklin D. Roosevelt). Statement by the Governor upon signing bill extending area of Adirondack park by including all forest lands desirable for forest and park purposes and insuring preservation. *In* his Public papers, 1931. Albany, 1937. p.599–600.   1751

New York state reforestation commission. Vote Yes on proposed amendment no.3, November 3, 1931. Reforestation... Albany, n.d. 12p.   1752

Schenectady county conservation council, inc. Commercialization of our state parks. Schenectady, N.Y. 1931? 4p. Unpaged leaflet. (Bulletin no.3.) Against the recreation amendment. Statement dated Dec. 1931. Signed: J.S. Apperson, Irving Langmuir, E. MacD. Stanton and Richard D. Moot.
                                        1753

Schenectady county conservation council and Mohawk valley towns association conservation committee. Tree cutting with your money... Schenectady, N.Y. 1931. 4p. Signed: Dr. R.C. Hill. Against the amendment.   1754

Howard, William Gibbs. Forests and parks of the Empire state. *Am For*, Mar. 1932. 38:165–68. illus.   1755

Recreation amendment meets opposition. *NYS For Assn NL*, Apr. 1932. p.5–6. Porter-Brereton resolution.   1756

New York adds 24,000 acres to Forest preserve. *For Worker*, July 1932. 8:no.4:1. Brief announcement of a large addition in the Beaver River area.   1757

Adirondack preserve policy threatened. *Am For*, Sept. 1932. 38:515. Opposition to the Porter-Brereton recreation amendment. 1758

Important issues. *Nature M*, Oct. 1932. 20:186. Proposed amendment to New York state Constitution to permit commercial exploitation of the Forest Preserve.   1759

Marshall, Robert. The perilous plight of the Adirondack wilderness. *High Spots*, Oct. 1932. 9:no.4:3. Recreation amendment.   1760

Two proposals for voters. *NYS For Assn NL*, Oct. 1932. p.1. Editorial against the Porter-Brereton amendment.   1761

Save the wilderness. *Nature M*, Nov. 1932. 20:203. Voters in New York asked to throw their Adirondacks and Catskills open to exploitation.   1762

Schaefer, Paul A. Defend the wilderness. *Nature M*, Nov. 1932. 20:234, 246–47. illus.
1763

Adirondack mountain club, inc. Conservation committee. Commercialization of the Forest preserve. n.p. 1932. 4p. Unpaged leaflet. Should attempt to acquaint people with the dangers attending the passage of the Porter-Brereton recreation amendment. 1764

Camp fire club of America. Committee on conservation and wild life. An Adirondack park plan. . . N.Y. 1932. 3 unnumbered leaves. Copy in Yale University Library.
1765

Carson, Russell Mack Little. Sabbath is for man, not man for the Sabbath. *High Spots*, Oct. 1933. 10:no.4:3–5. On the preservation of the wilderness. Balance between use and protection. Comments in *High Spots*, Jan. 1934, 11:no.1:10–14, by Paul A. Schaefer, Arnold W. Knauth, Samuel N. Spring, Howard Carlson, Godfrey Dewey, Clarence L. Fisher and Robert Marshall. 1766

Rabenold, Elwood M. Tinkering with constitution decried. *NYS For Assn NL*, Nov. 1933. p.5–6. Summary of speech by president of the Fish, Game and Forest League. 1767

Van Derveer, James D. Camp no.20, C.C.C. *NYS Ranger Sch*, 1933. p.35–37. illus. Located at Wanakena. 1768

Graves, Henry Solon. A national plan for American forestry. *Geog R*, Jan. 1934. 24:129–33. New York's Forest Preserve a pioneer in state forest policy, p.131. 1769

Howard, William Gibbs. The Civilian conservation corps and the forests. *Bul Schools*, Apr. 2, 1934. 20:164–67. plates. Results of first half year of C.C.C. work in forestry, conservation work and trails. 1770

Van Derveer, James D. Camp S-84, CCC, on the Ranger school forest. *NYS Ranger Sch*, 1934. p.35–37. illus. 1771

Marshall, Robert. Fallacies in Osborne's position: an open letter to the Conservation commissioner of New York. *Liv Wild*, Sept. 1935. no.1:4–5. Truck trails in the Adirondacks. 1772

Torrey, Raymond Hezekiah. Truck trails in the Adirondacks. *Liv Wild*, Sept. 1935. no.1:3, 5. On problems brought up by the unauthorized use of truck trails. 1773

Houghton, Augustus H. Why the Adirondack park? *High Spots*, Oct. 1935. 12:no.4:19–23.
1774

Howard, William Gibbs. C.C.C. work on the New York state Forest preserve. *High Spots*, Oct. 1935. 12:no.4:9–13. 1775

Torrey, Raymond Hezekiah. "Truck trails" in the Forest preserve. *High Spots*, Oct. 1935. 12:no.4:17–18. 1776

Yard, Robert Sterling. Statement to the Trails conference of the Adirondack mountain club at Albany, October 4, 1935. *High Spots*, Oct. 1935. 12:no.4:15–17. 1777

Wild lands. *J For*, Nov. 1935. 23:893–95. Editorial on New York state's policy with a short history of the Forest Preserve. 1778

Osborne, Lithgow. Truck trails in the Adirondack Forest preserve, by Lithgow Osborne. Comments on Commission's truck trail policy, by Robert Marshall. *Am For*, Jan. 1936. 42:3–6. illus. Also published separately, 1936, 8p. 1779

Committee reports on Adirondack truck trails. *Am For*, Mar. 1936. 42:130. 1780

Torrey, Raymond Hezekiah. Adirondack truck trails stopped. *Liv Wild*, Nov. 1936. no.2:15. 1781

Association for the protection of the Adirondacks. To the members of the Association—four documents of importance in connection with current developments in relation to the Association objectives in protecting the wilderness character of the New York Forest preserve. N.Y. 1936. 17 folios. 1782

Foote, James A. Position of the Wilderness society on proposed ski trails in the Adirondack park. n.p. Ski committee of New York state trails conference, inc. 1936. 4p. Address advocating a plan that "will prove a happy medium between the needs of the winter skier and the demands of the summer hiker" and that can be carried out without amending the state Constitution. 1783

Illick, Joseph S. Significant forestry trends in New York state. *J For*, May 1937. 35:452–59. Short history of Forest Preserve showing connection between forestry and parks. 1784

Howard, William Gibbs. New York state's Forest preserve policy. *J For*, Aug. 1937. 35:762–68. 1785

Gibbs, John T. Speech. . .from Adirondack loj at the Mt. Marcy centenary celebration. . . *High Spots*, Dec. 1937. 14:no.4:20–22. Brief remarks on the Forest Preserve. 1786

Apperson, John S. Minority report on fire truck trails. Schenectady, N.Y. Forest preserve association of New York state, inc. 1937. 4p. Letter to Lithgow Osborne, Conservation Commissioner; report of Governor Lehman's committee inspecting fire truck trails. Fire truck trails not needed if principal cause of forest fires is removed. 1787

Schenectady county conservation council, inc. Wild charm of the Adirondacks being destroyed. Schenectady, N.Y. 1937. 6p. Exchange of letters between Secretary of the Council and the Conservation Department.

On construction of new ranger's cabin at Lake Colden.   1788

1938–1955

Foote, James A. The Adirondacks—keep them wild. *Nat Parks,* June 1938. no.65:13–14.
                                                     1789

Burnham, John Bird. The future of the Adirondack state park. *Nat Parks,* Dec. 1938. no.66:26.   1790

New York (state). Committee on conservation of the natural resources of the state. Public hearing, June 23, 1938 (on Adirondack forests). Albany, 1938. 143p. Mimeographed.   1791

Osborne, Lithgow. The Adirondack park and the New York state Forest preserve. *Nat Parks,* Nov. 1939. no.67:6–9.   1792

Forest preserve association of New York state, inc. George Foster Peabody memorial committee. Report. n.p. n.pub. 1939. 4p. illus. Unpaged leaflet. Gift of French Point (on Lake George) to the state as memorial to G.F. Peabody.   1793

Osborne, Lithgow. New York state parks. *Bul Schools,* Mar. 1940. 26:231–33. illus. Includes the Forest Preserve.   1794

The collection of a daily fee proposed for use of improved and supervised recreational areas in the Adirondack and Catskill parks. *NYS For Assn NL,* Apr. 1940. p.5–6.   1795

Hudowalski, Mrs. Grace (Leech). Adirondacks—a national park? *Cloud Splitter,* June 1940. 3:no.5:1. Editorial on Senator Mead's bill to establish an Adirondack national park.
                                                     1796

Burton, Harold B. "Pro" Whiteface. *Cloud Splitter,* Feb. 1941. 4:no.2:10. Whiteface ski amendment.   1797

Hudowalski, Edward C. "Con" Whiteface. *Cloud Splitter,* Feb. 1941. 4:no.2:11. Whiteface ski amendment.   1798

Neisel, W.J. Adirondacks and the national wilderness. *Liv Wild,* July 1941. no.6:4. Against the resolution to permit the state to build ski trails on Whiteface.   1799

The Whiteface ski trail amendment. *Ad Mt Club Bul,* Oct. 1941. 5:no.6:5–11. Arguments pro and con.   1800

Elkins, Frank. Amendment number four. *Ski Bul,* Nov. 1941. 12:no.2:7–8. Ski trail on Whiteface.   1801

New Yorkers, guard your wilderness. *Nat Parks,* July–Sept. 1944. no.78:23.   1802

Loope, P. Fay. Violation of the Forest preserve—Lake Sanford mines. *High Spots Yrbk,* 1944. p.9–11. illus.   1803

Welch, Fay. The Adirondacks: today & tomorrow. *High Spots Yrbk,* 1944. p.25. illus. Wise use of the Adirondacks.   1804

New Yorkers, guard your Adirondacks. *Nat Parks,* Apr.–June 1945. no.81:19.   1805

Schaefer, Paul A. Impending tragedy in the Adirondacks. *Nature M,* Dec. 1945. 38:537. Panther Mountain and Higley Mountain reservoirs.   1806

Adirondack mountain club, inc. Shall the Forest preserve be lumbered? Albany, 1945. 12p. illus. A brief prepared by Paul Schaefer and Paul Lauffer, representing the Club's Conservation Committee, stating why the Adirondack Mountain Club opposes lumbering on state lands in the Forest Preserve. 1807

Benedict, Mrs. Martha (Nord). Moose river. *Cloud Splitter,* Jan.–Feb. 1946. 9:no.1:6–7.
                                                     1808

Schaefer, Paul A. The Adirondacks: pattern of a battle of woods and waters. *Liv Wild,* Mar. 1946. no.16:13–22. illus. A summary of the struggle by conservationists to preserve the wilderness.   1809

Benedict, Mrs. Martha (Nord). Forest preserve in the Legislature. *Cloud Splitter,* Mar.–Apr. 1946. 9:no.2:12–13.   1810

Benedict, Mrs. Martha (Nord). What "gives" on Capitol Hill. *Ad-i-ron-dac,* Mar.–Apr. 1946. 10:no.2:3. Review of 1946 legislation. 1811

Schaefer, Paul A. Land of the deer (the Adirondack dam threat). *Nat Parks,* Apr.–June 1946. no. 85:20–25. illus.   1812

The Association opposes Adirondack structures. *Nat Parks,* Apr.–June 1946. no.85:25. Opposes Young-Reoux resolution.   1813

Miller, Philip Schuyler. Blue lines and red patches. *Cloud Splitter,* May–June 1946. 9:no.3:7–8. Adirondack Park-Forest Preserve.
                                                     1814

Review of the Forum on recreation in New York state's Forest preserve. *Ad-i-ron-dac,* July–Aug. 1946. 10:no.4:10–11.   1815

Benedict, Mrs. Martha (Nord). Conservation: Commissioner Duryea states his position on pending threats to the Forest preserve. *Ad-i-ron-dac*, Nov.–Dec. 1946. 10:no.6:3. 1816

Adirondack Moose river committee. Impending tragedy of the Moose river region. March 1, 1946. 3d reprint. Albany, 1946. 4p. Unpaged leaflet.   1817

Adirondack Moose river committee. An urgent note to all who want to protect New York's wildlife and natural forests. n.p. n.pub. 1946? 4p. illus. map. Unpaged leaflet. Against Panther Mountain dam.   1818

Apperson, John S. Forest preserve in danger. n.p. Forest preserve association of New York state, inc. 1946. 4p. Against the mining, recreation and ski trail amendments.   1819

Forest preserve association of New York state, inc. From report of the President read and approved at the annual meeting, June 7, 1946. . . n.p. 1946. 4p. Against the mining, recreation, ski trail and flooding amendments.   1820

New York (state). Governor (Thomas E. Dewey). Conservation. *In* his Public papers, 1946. Albany, 1947. p.25. Recommends new conservation headquarters in the heart of the Adirondacks and additional public campsites in the Forest Preserve.   1821

Your Forest preserve — a time for decision. *NYS Con*, Dec. 1946–Jan. 1947. 1:no.3:2–3, 27. Advocates recreational development.
1822

Hudowalski, Mrs. Grace (Leech). Threats to New York state's Forest preserve. *Cloud Splitter*, Jan.–Feb. 1947. 10:no.1:17. Excerpts from speech to the New York State Conservation Council.   1823

Brewer, George. Our heritage is threatened. *An King*, Feb. 1947. 50:11–15. illus. On the two amendments to open the forest reserve for permanent buildings for recreational purposes and to permit mining operations. 1824

Sachs, Edna D. A forest preserve without a forest? *NYS Bus Prof W*, Feb. 1947. 13:21–22. Also issued as a reprint. Against three proposals to amend the state Constitution (Graves, Wicks and Young-Reoux amendments). 1825

Duryea, Perry B. Moose river menace! *NYS Con*, Feb.–Mar. 1947. 1:no.4:18–19. illus. Threat to wilderness area.   1826

Benedict, Mrs. Martha (Nord). Conservation hearing. *Ad-i-ron-dac*, Mar.–Apr. 1947. 11: no.2:10–11.   1827

Beetle, David Harold. Kilroy was not here. *No Country Life*, Spring 1947. 1:no.3:16–18, 60. Site of Higley and Panther Mountain dams.   1828

Hosmer, Ralph Sheldon. Our Forest preserve; a rich heritage. *No Country Life*, Spring 1947. 1:no.3:39–40, 62–63. Condensed from the *Bulletin to the Schools*.   1829

Governor orders full-scale survey of Adirondack power proposals. *NYS Con*, Apr.–May 1947. 1:no.5:23.   1830

Bill to prevent Adirondack dams killed. *Nat Parks*, Apr.–June 1947. no.89:22.   1831

Schaefer, Paul A. Victory in defeat. *Cloud Splitter*, May–June 1947. 10:no.3:2–5. Moose River issue.   1832

The Forest preserve, no.1– Jan. 1947– edited by Paul Schaefer. Schenectady, N.Y. Friends of the Forest preserve, 1947–date. Published irregularly. Covers Adirondack and Catskill preserves. Includes summaries of legislation and source material.   1833

Adirondack mountain club, inc. The proposed mining and recreation amendments, a danger to the Forest preserve. . . Albany, 1947? 4p. Unpaged leaflet.   1834

Schaefer, Paul A. Moose river: frontier of decision. *Ad-i-ron-dac*, Mar.–Apr. 1948. 12: no.2:3, 7.   1835

Chapman, Herman Haupt. Recreational interests as affecting professional forestry activities. *J For*, Apr. 1948. 46:290–93. Includes discussion of the New York State Forest Preserve.   1836

Adirondacks Panther mountain dam. *Nat Parks*, Apr.–June 1948. no.93:33–36.   1837

State board approves Panther mountain dam. *Lumber Camp News*, May 1948. 10:no.1:14.
1838

Howard, William Gibbs. New York's Forest preserve. *J For*, Aug. 1948. 46:612–13.   1839

Continuing Wilderness defense mobilized to defeat the Higley mt. dam; the Adirondack Moose river committee, of New York, has taken leadership in opposing a later proposal of the Black river regulating district. . . *Liv Wild*, Summer 1948. no.25:23–24. map. In News Items of Special Interest. Quotes Howard Zahniser, representing the Wilderness Society.   1840

Adirondack dam project still pending. *Nat Parks*, Oct.–Dec. 1948. no.95:34.   1841

For and against the Panther mountain dam, Black river regulating district board approves plans for controversial project. *Emp Statesman*, Dec. 1948. 5:no.2:7–10, 32–33. For the dam, by Edwin S. Cullings. Against the dam, by Paul Schaefer.   1842

Black river regulating district. The facts about Panther mountain reservoir. A statement by the Board, Dec. 1948. Watertown,

N.Y. 1948. 28p. folded maps. 2d edition, Oct. 1952, 39p. 3d edition, Jan. 1953, 38p. illus. folded maps.   1843

Newkirk, Arthur Edward. Panther mt. reservoir opposed. *Ad-i-ron-dac*, Jan.–Feb. 1949. 13:11.   1844

Panther mountain dam must be stopped. *Nat Parks*, Jan.–Mar. 1949. no.96:25–26.   1845

Forster, Herman. Commercialization of the Forest preserve. *NYS Con Council*, Feb. 23, 1949. no.89:1–3. map.   1846

King, A.H. Chains and links; surveying the boundaries of state Forest preserve. *NYS Con*, Apr.–May 1949. 3:no.5:10–11. illus.   1847

Miller, Philip Schuyler. "A mixed record of defeat. . ." *Liv Wild*, Spring 1949. no.28:25. In News Items of Special Interest. Quotes from *The Ad-i-ron-dac*, May–June 1949.   1848

Adirondack mountain club, inc. The Williamson-Reoux "recreation" amendment: a new threat to the Adirondack and Catskill parks. . . Albany, 1949. 4p. Unpaged leaflet. Against an amendment that would authorize the state to construct permanent enclosed buildings etc. in the Forest Preserve.   1849

The Forest preserve; supplemental bulletins. 1949– Schenectady, N.Y. Friends of the Forest preserve, 1949–date. Published irregularly. Contain valuable source material. 1850

New York (state). Conservation department. Specifications for the construction & maintenance of trails in the Forest preserve, June 1949. Albany? 1949? 9p. Mimeographed. Latest edition of pamphlet first prepared by William G. Howard and distributed by the Adirondack Mountain Club in 1923.   1851

Miller, Philip Schuyler. The River regulation committee. *Ad-i-ron-dac*, Mar.–Apr. 1950. 14:42–44.   1852

Benedict, Mrs. Martha (Nord). Conservation notes. *Cloud Splitter*, May–June 1950. 13:no.3: 14–15. Panther Mountain dam.   1853

Benedict, Mrs. Martha (Nord). Five years of Moose river. *Ad-i-ron-dac*, July–Aug. 1950. 14:86–87.   1854

Foss, William M. Signboards in the Adirondack park. *NYS Con*, Aug.–Sept. 1950. 5: no.1:8–9. illus.   1855

"On July 11, 1950, the Court of appeals of the State of New York rendered its decision on the so-called Panther mountain dam case. . ." *Liv Wild*, Summer 1950. no.33:21. Quotes report of Milo R. Kniffen. In News Items of Special Interest.   1856

Threats to lumber the state's wilderness. . . *Liv Wild*, Summer 1950. no.33:22. Brief note in News Items of Special Interest. Quotes from article "Shall the Forest Preserve Be Lumbered?" in *The Forest Preserve*.   1857

Miller, Philip Schuyler. Moose river opinion. *Ad-i-ron-dac*, Sept.–Oct. 1950. 14:104.   1858

Seven proposals for better protection of the Adirondack and Catskill preserves. . . *Liv Wild*, Autumn 1950. no.34:34–35. Brief note in News Items of Special Interest. Lists points adopted by the New York State Conservation Council.   1859

Panther mountain dam threat ended. *Nat Parks*, Oct.–Dec. 1950. no.103:147.   1860

Adirondack Moose river committee. Panther dam must be stopped—but it is even more important to stop the Black river board. Fort Plains, N.Y. 1950. 4p. ports. Large unpaged leaflet.   1861

Cullings, Edwin Sanford. Panther mountain reservoir. *NYS Ranger Sch*, 1950. p.9–12. illus. In favor of the reservoir.   1862

Getting at the sources. *Ad-i-ron-dac*, Nov.–Dec. 1951. 15:105, 113. Summary of Ostrander Committee hearing including four-part program to prevent inroads into the Forest Preserve.   1863

Miller, Philip Schuyler. Breaking open the Preserve. *Ad-i-ron-dac*, Nov.–Dec. 1951. 15: 110–11.   1864

Our Forest preserve. *NYS Con*, Dec. 1951–Jan. 1952. 6:no.3:2–7. illus. maps. A series of articles by officials of the Conservation Department stating "what we know about the Forest Preserve, and also what our experience and training lead us to believe might be done to improve it." See "Forever Wild" (2) on p.1. Articles are by Perry B. Duryea, P.W. Fosburgh, E.W. Littlefield, Robert W. Darrow, Arthur W. Holweg, Clayton B. Seagears, William D. Mulholland and J. Victor Skiff. Map on inner cover.   1865

Hopkins, Arthur S. State lands do pay taxes. *NYS Con*, Dec. 1951–Jan. 1952. 6:no.3:35. illus.   1866

"The attack on the Adirondack Forest preserve has begun again. . ." *Liv Wild*, Winter 1951–52. no.39:35–36. Reprint of *New York Times* editorial, Nov. 23, 1951.   1867

Moore, Frank C. Assuring a conservation audience. . . *Liv Wild*, Winter 1951–52. no.39: 34–35. Extract from address at the annual meeting of the New York State Conservation Council. Also in *The Forest Preserve*, Jan. 1952, p.9–11.   1868

Mills, Borden H. Sr. The attitude of the Conservation department as to the Forest preserve. *Cloud Splitter*, Jan.–Feb. 1952. 15: no.1:8–9.   1869

Conservationists examine state park cutting policies. A summary of discussions. *Lumber Camp News*, Feb. 1952. 13:no.10:17, 19, 21.
1870

Our Forest preserve. *NYS Con*, Feb.–Mar. 1952. 6:no.4:2–7. Discussion, begun in the previous issue, is continued by leaders outside the Conservation Department, with brief editorial comment. Contributors are Gustav A. Swanson, Paul Schaefer, John E. Hammett, Frederick T. Kelsey, William Pearson Tolley and Gerald Kenwell. Illustration on inside front cover.
1871

No longer wild? *Ad-i-ron-dac*, Mar.–Apr. 1952. 16:23–25, 37. Discussion of Conservation Department statements in the Dec. 1951–Jan. 1952 *New York State Conservationist*. See letter from Paul G. Lauffer and reply by P. Schuyler Miller, p.33–34; also article "To Get the Facts," p.36–37. Another letter from Lauffer is in the May–June issue, 16:54. Comment by George E. Goldthwaite in column "The President Says," July–Aug. 16: 63, 75.
1872

Our Forest preserve. *NYS Con*, Apr.–May 1952. 6:no.5:2–9. Final series. Contributions by Nathaniel L. Goldstein, W.B. Greeley, Ira N. Gabrielson, H.H. Chapman, Harold C. Ostertag, Lithgow Osborne, O. Byron Brewster, Donald M. Tobey, Perry B. Duryea and Wheeler Milmoe.
1873

Our Forest preserve. Press comment. *NYS Con*, Apr.–May 1952. 6:no.5:26–28. illus.
1874

Apperson, John S. Withhold or use? Conflict in the Adirondacks. *Land*, Spring 1952. 9:62–63. From a talk given to the Glens Falls chapter of the Adirondack Mountain Club.
1875

Continuing an "examination of our policy with regard to the Forest preserve". . . *Liv Wild*, Spring 1952. no.40:34–37. Extract and summary of articles in the *New York State Conservationist*, Dec. 1951–Jan. 1952 through Apr.–May 1952.
1876

Miller, Philip Schuyler. Policy by fiat. *Ad-i-ron-dac*, May–June 1952. 16:44–46. Implications of "service charge" for campsites in the Forest Preserve. See also Miller's article "License—Not Lease" in issue for July–Aug. 16:70, 74, giving Conservation Department's position.
1877

Hardy, Ruth Gillette. Conservation in New York state. *Appalachia*, June 15, 1952. mag. no.114:118. Brief summary of the issues raised in the *New York State Conservationist* and the action taken by various groups.
1878

The Forest preserve. *NYS Con*, June–July 1952. 6:no.6:35. Brief note on Advisory Committee appointed by Assemblyman Milmoe, with names of members.
1879

Forest preserve mail. *NYS Con*, June–July 1952. 6:no.6:28–29. illus.
1880

Hopkins, Arthur S. Some thoughts on zoning the Forest preserve. *NYS Con*, June–July 1952. 6:no.6:6–8. illus.
1881

Miller, Philip Schuyler. The Milmoe advisory board. *Ad-i-ron-dac*, July–Aug. 1952. 16:65. For letters by Paul Lauffer and Edgar B. Nixon on Adirondack Mountain Club cooperation with the Committee see Sept.–Oct. issue, 16:82–83.
1882

McCarthy, Keith R. Forever wild? *Am For*, Aug. 1952. 58:no.8:6–9, 43. illus. maps.
1883

Ketledge, Edwin H. Forest preserve. *NYS Con*, Aug.–Sept. 1952. 7:no.1:37. Letter to editor asking position of the Conservation Department.
1884

Marshall, George. "The Forest preserve itself is a major use zone". . . *Liv Wild*, Summer 1952. no.41:36. Comment on questions raised in recent issues of the *New York State Conservationist;* partially reprinted in *The Ad-i-ron-dac*, Nov.–Dec. 1952, 16:103, with title "What Is Zoning?"
1885

Black river regulating district. The facts about Panther mountain reservoir; 2d ed. Oct. 1952. n.p. 1952. 39p.
1886

Forest preserve. *NYS Con*, Oct.–Nov. 1952. 7:no.2:37. More letters.
1887

Forest preserve association of New York state, inc. Re-zoning N.Y. state Forest preserve. n.p. 1952. 3p. Issued July 1952, reprinted in September. Comment with criticism on Hopkins' proposal.
1888

Forest with phony front. 1p. Reprint of editorial from the Utica *Observer-Dispatch*, July 16, 1952; against Hopkins' rezoning article in the *New York State Conservationist*.
1889

Friends of the Forest preserve, inc. Legislative, legal & field report. . .January 1953. Schenectady, N.Y. 1952. 4p. Unpaged leaflet; signed: Paul Schaefer. (Supplemental Bulletin to *The Forest Preserve*.)
1890

Milmoe, Wheeler. Our study of the Forest preserve. *NYS Con*, Dec. 1952–Jan. 1953. 7:no.3:8–9. Progress report by the chairman of the Joint Legislative Committee on Natural Resources.
1891

The fact that the New York state Forest preserve exists. . . *Liv Wild*, Winter 1952–53. no.43:29. Brief comment on Adirondack Mountain Club Conservation Committee report of Nov. 8, 1952.
1892

Littlefield, Edward Winchester. The future of the Forest preserve act. Where do we go from here? *NYS Con*, Feb.–Mar. 1953. 7:no.4: 17.   1893

Ham, Philip W. Panther mountain reservoir. *Ad-i-ron-dac*, Mar.–Apr. 1953. 17:37, 40. Brief trip into Moose River country.   1894

Littlefield, Edward Winchester. The Forest preserve controversy. *Gard J*, Mar.–Apr. 1953. 3:38–39, 59. illus.   1895

Marshall, George. Imperishable freshness! *Ad-i-ron-dac*, Mar.–Apr. 1953. 17:28–29, 34. Dangers to the Forest Preserve. Also issued as a reprint. Quoted in the *Living Wilderness*, Spring 1953, no.44:22–23.   1896

Zahniser, Howard. New York's Forest preserve. *Liv Wild*, Spring 1953. no.44:18–21. illus.   1897

Welch, Fay. Our New York state Forest preserve. *Ad-i-ron-dac*, May–June 1953. 17:56–59. Address before the Oneida County Forest Preserve Council, Jan. 29, 1953. Includes comments by Walter Biesemeyer and reply by Welch. The address was also issued as a separate, Utica, 1953, 4p. leaflet.   1898

Milmoe, Wheeler. Conserving New York state's natural resources. *NY Forester*, Nov. 1953. 10:no.4:7–9. Extract from address before the New York State Conservation Council, Oct. 1953. Complete text in New York State Joint Legislative Committee on Natural Resources Report, 1954, p.44–56.   1899

Black river regulating district. The facts about Panther mountain reservoir; 3d ed. Watertown, N.Y. 1953. 38p. illus. folded maps.   1900

What about Black river floods? n.p. n.d. 1p. Broadside reprint of editorial from the Utica *Observer-Dispatch*, Mar. 28, 1953. Distributed Apr. 1953 by Friends of the Forest Preserve, Inc.   1901

Milmoe, Wheeler. Letter to the editor. *NYS Con*, Feb.–Mar. 1954. 8:no.4:36. On Milmoe Committee research (Joint Legislative Committee on Natural Resources).   1902

Newkirk, Arthur Edward. The Forest preserve—precious, always in danger. *Ad-i-ron-dac*, Mar.–Apr. 1954. 18:40. Discusses four proposed amendments affecting the Forest Preserve.   1903

Club states Forest preserve policy. *Ad-i-ron-dac*, May–June 1954. 18:59. Statement made by the Conservation Committee of the Adirondack Mountain Club.   1904

Welch, Fay, ed. Foresters speak for article XIV, sec. 1. *Ad-i-ron-dac*, May–June 1954. 18:54–55. Excerpts from letters.   1905

Views on the Forest preserve. *NYS Con*, June–July 1954. 8:no.6:2–6. illus. Views of the Conservation Department. See Oct.–Nov.

issue, p.36–37, for letters from Charles W. Cole and John Coggeshall on this subject.
                                                      1906

Forest preserve. *Argonaut*, July 1954. 3:no.6: 3–4.   1907

Conservation committee visits Moose river. *Ad-i-ron-dac*, July–Aug. 1954. 18:70–71. Reports by Paul Lauffer, Herbert C. Allen and George Marshall.   1908

Detached areas of the Forest preserve. *NYS Con*, Aug.–Sept. 1954. 9:no.1:28. Milmoe Committee's resolutions.   1909

Newkirk, Arthur Edward. The future of the Forest preserve. *Ad-i-ron-dac*, Sept.–Oct.—Nov.–Dec. 1954. 18:88–89. Statement made at the Conservation Forum held by the Adirondack Mountain Club.   1910

Forest preserve association of New York state, inc. Two kinds of forest management in conflict. Schenectady, N.Y. 1954. 4p. Signed: J.S. Apperson, President.   1911

Foss, William M. Detached areas of the state Forest preserve. *In* New York (state). Legislature. Joint legislative committee on natural resources. Report, 1954. p.78–81.   1912

Foss, William M. Some suggested policy changes in connection with recreation in the Forest preserve. *In* New York (state). Legislature. Joint legislative committee on natural resources. Report, 1954. p.86–89.   1913

Illick, Joseph S. General review of state preserve studies and problems. *In* New York (state). Legislature. Joint legislative committee on natural resources. Report, 1954. p.62–75.   1914

Schaefer, Paul. A land acquisition program for the Adirondacks and Catskills. *In* New York (state). Legislature. Joint legislative committee on natural resources. Report, 1954. p.117–20.   1915

Marshall, George. Adirondack Forest preserve. A letter to the editor. *Argonaut*, Jan. 14, 1955. p.1–2.   1916

Lehman, Donald J. Battle of Panther mountain: the Black river valley, badly in need of flood control, faces big odds in its battle for Panther mountain dam. . . *Rural NY*, Feb. 19, Mar. 5, 1955. 105:132–33, 173–75. illus. In favor of opening the Forest Preserve.   1917

1955 Forest preserve legislation: proposed amendments to article XIV, section 1 of the constitution. *Ad-i-ron-dac*, Mar.–Apr. 1955. 19:38.   1918

Mills, Borden H. Sr. Panther dam. *Ad-i-ron-dac*, May–June 1955. 19:55. Letter reprinted from the New York *Herald Tribune*.   1919

The proposed highway amendment. *Ad-i-ron-dac*, May–June 1955. 19:52–53.   1920

New York Forest preserve. *Liv Wild*, Spring–Summer 1955. no.52:19. Against Panther Mountain dam.   1921

Panther mountain dam. *Cloud Splitter*, July–Aug.—Sept.–Oct. 1955. 18:no.4:2–3; 18:no.5:1–2.   1922

Panther dam—final decision Nov. 8, 1955. *Ad-i-ron-dac*, Sept.–Oct. 1955. 19:98–99. Also issued as a one-page reprint.   1923

For the Forest preserve. *NYS Con*, Oct.–Nov. 1955. 10:no.2:30. Finch, Pruyn and Company offer land to the state.   1924

Price, Fraser P. The Forest preserve lands outside the blue line. I—Financial aspects. *Ad-i-ron-dac*, Nov.–Dec. 1955. 19:116, 119.   1925

Attorney general forbids drilling for oil or gas in the Forest preserve. *In* New York (state). Legislature. Joint legislative committee on natural resources. Report, 1955. p.104–7. Opinion of Dec. 23, 1954, Nathaniel L. Goldstein.   1926

Citizens for water conservation. The Panther mountain story...vote for amendment 7. Watertown, N.Y. 1955. 14p. illus.   1927

Citizens for water conservation. Labor division. Why the New York state working man and woman will vote yes! on amendment 7... Watertown, N.Y. Watertown publishers, inc. 1955. 4p. illus. Unpaged leaflet. In favor of Panther Mountain dam.   1928

Foss, William M. State highway improvements as related to the Forest preserve. *In* New York (state). Legislature. Joint legislative committee on natural resources. Report, 1955. p.75–78. Highway map, Appendix R, in back of volume.   1929

Friends of the Forest preserve, inc. Be sure to register in October so that you can vote NO on amendment #7... Schenectady, N.Y. 1955. 4p. chart. Unpaged leaflet.   1930

Friends of the Forest preserve, inc. This year we can write the last chapter to the sordid story of Panther dam. Schenectady, N.Y. 1955? 1p. Folded broadside. Against the Wise amendment.   1931

Illick, Joseph S. Statement on detached areas of state Forest preserve in New York. *In* New York (state). Legislature. Joint legislative committee on natural resources. Report, 1955. p.47–66. tables.   1932

League of women voters, Watertown, N.Y. An analysis of amendment seven to the state constitution with pros and cons. n.p. n.pub. 1955. 4p. Unpaged leaflet.   1933

Pettis, Clifford Robert. Public use of the Forest preserve. Albany, New York state conservation department, 1955. 16p. illus. diagrs. (Recreation Circular 2.) Other editions published in 1919, 1925, 1932, 1935–37, 1949.
                                        1934

CONSTITUTIONAL CONVENTIONS AND AMENDMENTS AFFECTING THE FOREST PRESERVE

Arranged by date

Note: Other references to proposed amendments are included in the preceding section.

New York. Board of trade and transportation. Proposed amendment to the constitution of the State of New York to preserve its forests, with reasons why. June 1894. n.p. n.pub. n.d. 29p. Preface signed Darwin R. James.   1935

McClure, David. Speeches on the proposed forest preserve amendment. *In* New York (state). Constitutional convention, 1894. Revised record. Albany, 1900. 4:124–47. Extracts printed under title "Our Forest Preserves," in *Forest Leaves*, Spring 1904, 1:no.2:37–41. See article by Borden H. Mills Sr. entitled "David McClure and the Forest Preserve," *The Ad-i-ron-dac*, Nov.–Dec. 1949, 13:116–19.   1936

New York (state). Constitutional convention, 1894. Revised record... Albany, Argus co.

1900. 5v. Report of the special committee on state forests, v.2, p.1201.   1937

The New York constitution. *Am For*, Sept. 1915. 21:941–42. Editorial on the new constitution opposing the "forever wild" provision.   1938

Spears, Raymond Smiley. People of New York must fight to save Adirondacks. The proposals now pending before the constitutional convention, if adopted, mean that the last of the state's great playground is doomed forever. *For & Stream*, Aug. 1915. 84:461–62. illus.   1939

Association for the protection of the Adirondacks. Answers to objections to the conservation article of the proposed constitution. N.Y. 1915. 11p.   1940

Lamon, Francis H. Conservation as provided by the proposed constitutional amendment. *In* New York state waterways association.

Proceedings, 1915. 6:76–79. Discussion of Article VII of the proposed constitution of New York state.   1941

New York (state). Constitutional convention, 1915. Committee on conservation of natural resources. Report. . .relative to the several proposed amendments, July 30, 1915. 20p. *In* New York (state). Constitutional convention, 1915. Documents. Albany, J.B. Lyon, 1915. (Document no.28.)   1942

New York. Board of trade and transportation. What every voter should know. A momentous question. Vote for constitutional amendment number four. N.Y. 1915. 16p.   1943

Schofield, Peter F. and Gardner, Frank S. Conservation of the state's natural resources. The Adirondacks. The source of water for municipal supply. . . Reprinted from The Paper mill wood and pulp news. N.Y. 1915? 8p. Cover title: Analysis of Propositions Pending in the Constitutional Convention Relating to the State Forest Preserve.   1944

Oppose Ferris amendment; strong effort to prevent construction of power houses and lines in New York Forest preserve. *Elec W*, Sept. 22, 1923. 82:622.   1945

Adirondack Forest preserve threatened. *Sci Am*, Nov. 1923. 129:311. Editorial opposing Ferris amendment.   1946

Adirondack raid amendment overwhelmed. Carried in only one county. *NYS Assn St Bul*, Dec. 1, 1923. 3:no.12:4. Includes the vote by counties.   1947

Long Lake tax-payers association. Vote No on the proposed amendment to section 7 of article 7 of the constitution in relation to the Forest preserve. Herkimer, N.Y. C. Rasbach, 1923. 1 leaf. Broadside.   1948

Myrick, Herbert. Continental super power trust aims to grab Adirondack preserve unless people defeat amendment no.3. N.Y. 1923. 1 leaf. Press release dated Oct. 29, 1923.   1949

Saranac Lake. Chamber of commerce. Save the Adirondacks from the spoiler. Saranac Lake, N.Y. Currier press, 1923. 20p. illus.   1950

Saranac Lake. Chamber of commerce. Save the Adirondacks from spoilers by defeating amendment no.3. Saranac Lake, N.Y. 1923. 10p. illus.   1951

New York. Board of trade and transportation. Docket. . .January 12, 1927. . . N.Y. 1927. 20p. Includes report from the Committee on Forests entitled "Protect Whiteface Mountain in Adirondacks from Defacement" (against amendment to authorize highway).   1952

New York. Board of trade and transportation. Eternal vigilance is the price of the Adi-

rondacks! Save Whiteface in the Adirondacks! N.Y. 1927. 1 leaf.   1953

Nibbling. *Sat Eve Post*, Jan. 7, 1928. 200:no.1: 32. Editorial opposing Whiteface Memorial Highway.   1954

The constitutional convention. *NYS For Assn NL*, May 1938. p.5–8. Discusses new section of Article VII.   1955

Hudowalski, Mrs. Grace (Leech). "Article VII, section 7" is vigorously upheld at constitution convention committee hearing. . . *Ad Mt Club Bul*, June–July 1938. 2:no.4:2, 10.   1956

Ostrander, George N. The proposed forestry amendment. *NYS For Assn NL*, Nov. 1938. p.2.   1957

Forest preserve association of New York state, inc. Comments on proposal no.39 submitted to the constitutional convention April 18 and proposal 350 submitted May 19, 1938, to amend article VII of the constitution. Schenectady, N.Y. 1938. 4p. Urges retaining present wording of Article VII, Section 7. Includes list of 54 organizations approving proposal to keep wording.   1958

Forest preserve association of New York state, inc. Comments on proposal no.80 submitted to the constitutional convention, April 25, 1938, to amend section 16 of article VII. Schenectady, N.Y. 1938. 4p. Advocates removing Section 16 from the Constitution and incorporating its good features in statute law. Includes list of 53 organizations in favor of retaining present wording of Article VII, Section 7.   1959

Forest preserve association of New York state, inc. Comments on proposal no.82, submitted to the constitutional convention, April 25, 1938. Schenectady, N.Y. 1938. 4p. Against Proposal no.82. Includes list of 53 organizations urging that present wording of Article VII, Section 7, be retained. Another edition dated May 3, 1938.   1960

Forest preserve association of New York state, inc. Comments on proposal no.114, submitted to the New York state constitutional convention, April 26, 1938. Schenectady, N.Y. 1938. 2p. Opposes the proposal. Includes names of 54 organizations advocating that present wording of Article VII, Section 7, be retained.   1961

Forest preserve association of New York state, inc. Comments on proposals before the constitutional convention, introduction numbers 412, 441, 444, 629 and 630 dated May 24 and 26-1938, pertaining to the New York state Forest preserve. Schenectady, N.Y. 1938. 4p. Urging that wording of Article VII, Section 7, of state Constitution be kept. Includes list of 55 organizations supporting the proposal.   1962

Schenectady county conservation council, inc. Comments on proposal introductory no.538, print no.566, to amend article VII, section 7 of the New York state constitution, and submitted to the constitutional convention on May 26, 1938. n.p. 1938. 2p. Opposes the proposal on the ground that it nullifies, though it restates, Article VII, Section 7. Includes list of 56 organizations in favor of keeping present wording.   1963

Marshall, George. New York protects its wilderness. *Liv Wild*, Mar. 1939. no.4:14. Brief statement on victory won by retaining wilderness provision in the state Constitution.   1964

Forest preserve association of New York state, inc. Article XIV, sections 1–2–3–4 New York state constitution adopted 1938. Schenectady, N.Y. 1939. 4p. Comments on New York State Constitutional Convention, by J.S. Apperson.   1965

Legislative and legal report, April 1952. Ostrander reservoir amendment approved by overwhelming majority; Supreme court sustains Stokes act banning Panther mt. dam. Schenectady, N.Y. 1952. 4p. (Supplemental Bulletin to *The Forest Preserve*, Apr. 1952.) Extract in *Living Wilderness*, Spring 1952, no.40:33.   1966

The people of New York have won an important victory. . . *Liv Wild*, Spring 1953. no.44: 21–22. Comments by Paul Schaefer on the

passage of the Cooke-Ostrander amendment.   1967

Benedict, Mrs. Martha (Nord). The Ostrander amendment. *Cloud Splitter*, May–June 1953. 16:no.3:2–3.   1968

New York Forest preserve. *Liv Wild*, Autumn 1953. no.46:40–41. Editorial on approval of Amendment no.9.   1969

Mills, Borden H. Sr. The conservation army wins another battle. *Ad-i-ron-dac*, Nov.–Dec. 1953. 17:108, 125. On approval of the Ostrander-Cooke amendment.   1970

Adirondack Moose river committee. This is WHY powerful self-serving private interests must NOT be permitted to block the Ostrander constitutional amendment in the 1953 N.Y. state Legislature. Schenectady, N.Y. 1953. 4p. illus. Folio leaflet.   1971

Council of conservationists for amendment no.9. 6 reasons why you should vote YES on amendment #9. . . N.Y. 1953. 8p. Unpaged folder.   1972

Friends of the Forest preserve, inc. Legislative report. Let's finish the job. Schenectady, N.Y. 1953. 4p. Unpaged leaflet analyzing the vote on the Cooke-Ostrander amendment.   1973

Richard, Edmond H. The moves leading to the introduction of the Ostrander amendment as summarized by the Mohawk-Hudson federation of conservation councils. . . Fort Plain, N.Y. 1953? Unpaged folder.   1974

LITIGATION

Arranged by Date

New York (state). Attorney general. Jurisdiction over the Lake George islands—opinion of the Attorney general. *In* New York (state). Forest commission. Annual report, 1886. p.149–54.   1975

Beaver river reservoir. Before the Forest commission and the commissioners of the Land office. In the matter of the purchase of the lands of William Seward Webb, to quiet claims for damages affected by the statement of claim and brief abstract of evidence. Herkimer, N.Y. 1895. 122p. See Annual Report of the Forest, Fish and Game Commission for 1907–1908–1909, p.387–89; and New York Reports, v.190, p.468–81.   1976

New York (state). Court of appeals. The people of the State of New York, respondent, v. Benton Turner, appellant. *In* New York reports, v.145, p.451–62. Argued Mar. 13, 1895; decided Apr. 9, 1895. See also v.117, p.227ff. On the state's title to land in the

Forest Preserve. For a discussion of this case see article by E.H. Leggett (no.1978).   1977

Leggett, Edward H. The state's title to lands in the Forest preserve. *In* New York (state). Fisheries, game and forest commission. Annual report, 1897. p.438–54. illus. Review of legal action.   1978

New York (state). Court of appeals. People of the State of New York ex rel. The Forest commission, appellant, v. Frank Campbell, Comptroller of the State of New York, respondent. *In* New York reports, v.152, p.51–59. Argued Feb. 1, 1897; decided Mar. 2, 1897. Upholds power of the Forest Commission. For a description of this case see Annual Report of the Fisheries, Game and Forest Commission, 1896, p.461–68.   1979

U.S. Supreme court. Turner v. New York. Error to the Court of appeals of the State of New York. . . Argued April 19, 20, 1897.– Decided October 18, 1897. *In* U.S. Reports, v.168, p.90–95. Judgment affirmed.   1980

New York (state). Supreme court. Appellate division, 3d department. Adirondack railway company, respondent, v. Indian river company and others, appellants. March term 1898. *In* Reports of cases, v.27, p.326–35. 1981

New York (state). Court of appeals. The people of the State of New York, appellant, v. the Adirondack railway company, respondent, impleaded with the Indian river company et al. *In* New York reports, v.160, p.225–48. Argued June 19, 1899; decided Oct. 3, 1899. Upholding the right of the state to condemn land needed for the Adirondack Park. Reverses the decision of the Appellate Division, which ruled that, by filing a map and serving notice on the occupants, the Adirondack Railway Company had acquired a lien on the disputed land. 1982

Title to land in the Forest preserve. *Forester*, May 1900. 6:118–19. Case of Ferris J. Meigs. 1983

New York (state). Court of appeals. Nehasane park association, respondent, v. Aaron Lloyd, appellant. *In* New York reports, v.167, p.431–40. Affirming judgment of Appellate Division on tax case, 1901. 1984

Adirondack lands. *For & Stream*, May 21, 1904. 62:413. Editorial on decision by Arthur L. Andrews, referee, in action for ejectment of occupants on lands claimed by state. 1985

Suit against Cornell. *For & Irrig*, July 1905. 11:295. A review of the case. Attorney-General Mayer bringing action to deprive Cornell of land. 1986

Spears, Raymond Smiley. Some legal aspects of the case of Rockefeller vs. La Mora. *For & Stream*, Oct. 21, 1905. 65:335–36. Lawsuit concerning the ejection of occupants of tract bought by Rockefeller in the Santa Clara township. 1987

New York (state). Attorney general. Opinions rendered by the Governor. State forest preserve—trespass thereon. *In* his Annual report, 1905, p.247–62. 1988

New York (state). Supreme court. Appellate division, 3d department. George Pashley, respondent, v. Charles Bennett, appellant. October 1905. *In* Reports of cases, v.108, p.102–3. Illegal sale of lumber cut on Forest Preserve. 1989

New York (state). Supreme court. Appellate division, 4th department. The people of the State of New York, respondent, v. the Brooklyn cooperage co., appellant, impleaded with Cornell university, defendant. *In* Reports of cases, v.114, p.723–33. July 12, 1906. 1990

New York (state). Court of appeals. People of the State of New York, respondent, v. the Brooklyn cooperage company, appellant, impleaded with another. *In* New York reports, v.187, p.142–60. Argued Dec. 19, 1906; decided Jan. 8, 1907. Cornell University case. Appellate Division decision affirmed. 1991

New York (state). Supreme court. Appellate division, 3d department. Saranac land and timber co., plaintiff-respondent, against James A. Roberts, as Comptroller of the State of New York, defendant-opponent. Case and exceptions on appeal. Albany, J.B. Lyon, 1907. 487p. maps. State's title to land in the Forest Preserve. This case is discussed in article by E.H. Leggett in New York State Fisheries, Game and Forest Commission Annual Report, 1897, p.440. Judge Coxe's opinion, p.446–47. See also 125 Reports of Cases 333 and New York Reports, v.195, p.303–24. Judgment affirmed. 1992

New York (state). Court of appeals. People of the State of New York, respondent, v. Mary L. Fisher et al., appellants. *In* New York reports, v.190, p.468–81. Argued Dec. 4, 1907; decided Jan. 14, 1908. Chase opinion. Appeal from a judgment in the Appellate Division, Jan. 21, 1907. 1993

Adirondack timber stealing. *For & Stream*, Feb. 8, 1908. 70:219. Conviction of Charles Klock and Harvey Gaylord. 1994

Spears, Raymond Smiley. Adirondack timber thefts. *For & Stream*, Apr. 4, 1908. 70:538. Comment on conviction of Charles Klock and Harvey Gaylord. 1995

Association for the protection of the Adirondacks. Drowned lands on the Saranac river. A statement of the facts involved in the suit... against the Paul Smith's electric light and power and railroad company for a permanent injunction restraining the defendant from taking lands belonging to the Forest preserve and destroying the timber thereon. N.Y. 1908. 22p. plates. (Association for the Protection of the Adirondacks Publication no.17.) Extracts with title "Adirondack Drowned State Lands" in *Forest and Stream*, Aug. 1, 1908. 71:176. 1996

New York (state). Supreme court, Warren county. Albert Newcombe, plaintiff, v. George N. Ostrander and George F. Underwood, as executors, and Helen E. Foulds, as executrix of and trustees under the last will and testament of George R. Finch, deceased, defendants. *In* Miscellaneous reports, v.66, p.103–10. Jan. 1910 term. Definition of wild forest land. 1997

New York (state). Supreme court. Appellate division, 3d department. The people of the State of New York, respondent, v. the Brooklyn cooperage company, appellant, impleaded with Cornell university, defendant. *In* Reports of cases, v.147, p.267–81. Nov. 15, 1911. Cornell University appeal.   1998

An Angler, pseud. The Eagle lake dam case. *For & Stream*, Aug. 15, 1914. 83:211. Report of hearing on lowering the level of Eagle Lake.   1999

New York (state). Court of appeals. Marian Low, individually, and as sole executrix of the last will and testament of A. Augustus Low, deceased, plaintiff-respondent vs New York central & Hudson river railroad company, defendant-appellant. Appeal book. Saratoga Springs, N.Y. Saratogian book & job print, 1914. 488p. Fire damage to plaintiff's estate near Childwold in 1908. Copy in Yale University Library.   2000

New York (state). Court of appeals. The people of the State of New York, plaintiff-appellant, against Santa Clara lumber company, defendant-respondent. Actions 1 and 2. The people of the State of New York, plaintiff-appellant, against George N. Ostrander, defendant-respondent. The people of the State of New York, plaintiff-appellant, against Santa Clara lumber company, George N. Ostrander and George N. Ostrander, Helen E. Foulds and George F. Underwood as executors of the last will and testament of George R. Finch, deceased, defendants-respondents. Action no.3. Exhibit book, volume 1... Albany, J.B. Lyon, 1914. 508p. folded maps. Cutting and removal of timber in Township 47, Totten and Crossfield purchase. Includes important source material on the history of the Totten and Crossfield purchase. For decision see New York Reports, v.213, p.61–67 and p.226–32.   2001

New York (state). Court of appeals. People of the State of New York, respondent, v. the New York central and Hudson river railroad company, appellant. *In* New York reports, v.213, p.136–40. Argued Oct. 12, 1914, decided Nov. 24, 1914. Judgment of Appellate Division reversed. Case grew out of damage to the Forest Preserve by fire. Method of ascertaining cost of damage.   2002

New York (state). Supreme court. Appellate division, 3d department. The people of the State of New York, respondent, v. the New York central and Hudson river railroad company, appellant. (Action no.2) Mar. 13, 1914. *In* Reports of cases, v.161, p.322–29. Action by state for damages by fire to Forest Preserve.   2003

New York (state). Public service commission. In the matter of the application of the New York central and Hudson river railroad company for permission to substitute coal burning locomotives for service on its Adirondack division between Remsen and Malone Junc-

tion, instead of oil burning locomotives. Brief of the Conservation commission and the Association for the protection of the Adirondacks. Albany, J.B. Lyon, 1914. 41p. Copy in Yale University Library.   2004

New York (state). Public service commission. ...In the matter of oil-burning locomotives on the Adirondack division of the New York central railroad company, and on the Carthage & Adirondack branch of the Saint Lawrence division of said railroad. Brief of the Conservation commission... Albany, 1918. 21p. Copy in Yale University Library.   2005

New York (state). Supreme court. 4th district. New York state versus Spencer G. Prime, John F. O'Brien and Stevens hotel co., inc. Memorandum in support of motion. n.p. n.pub. 192—? 43p.   2006

New York (state). Supreme court. 4th district. New York state versus Spencer G. Prime, John F. O'Brien and Stevens hotel co., inc. Plaintiff's reply brief. n.p. n.pub. 192—? 32p.   2007

New York (state). Supreme court. Appellate division, 3d department. The people of the State of New York, appellant, v. Walter C. Witherbee and others, respondents. *In* Reports of cases, v.199, p.272–78. Dec. 8, 1921. Spencer G. Prime case.   2008

New York (state). Supreme court. Appellate division, 3d department. The people of the State of New York, appellant, v. Spencer G. Prime and others, respondents. *In* Reports of cases, v.208, p.445–49. Mar. 5, 1924. 2009

New York (state). Court of appeals. In the Court of appeals of the State of New York. The Association for the protection of the Adirondacks and John G. Agar respondents against Alexander MacDonald...and William G. Howard... Brief submitted in support of the constitutionality of chapter 417 of the Laws of 1929, by Lewis, Garvin & Kelsey, as *amicus curiae*, representing the public park and playgrounds district of North Elba, Essex county, New York... N.Y. Appeal printing co. 1930. 89p. Brief argued by Walter T. Stock. On the constitutionality of the "bob-sled run" bill. Includes history and interpretation of Article VII, Section 7. See also New York Reports, v.253, p.234–42. 2010

New York (state). Supreme court. Appellate division, 3d department. The Association for the protection of the Adirondacks and another, plaintiffs, v. Alexander MacDonald, Conservation commissioner of the State of New York, and another, defendants. Jan. 15, 1930. *In* Reports of cases, v.228, p.73–82. Bob-sled case.   2011

New York (state). Court of appeals. Wellington Kenwell, appellant, v. Clarence F. Lee, as supervisor of the Town of Inlet, et al., respondents. *In* New York reports, v.261, p.113–17. Case involving the use of Bug Lake, in the Forest Preserve, as a town water supply, 1932–33. 2012

Parks = billboards, people v. Sterling. *Am City*, Sept. 1944. 59:127. Editorial comment on legality of advertising signs on private property in the Forest Preserve. 2013

U.S. Circuit court (2d circuit). For the Second circuit. Civil no.1145. United States of America, petitioner vs. certain easement rights in 228.15 acres of land in Essex and Hamilton counties, State of New York, David McElwee et al. defendants and State of New York, defendants-appellants. Supplemental brief on behalf of the Association for the protection of the Adirondacks as *amicus curiae*, in support of the appeal taken by the State of New York. N.Y. Pandick press, 1945. 6p. Presented by Marshall McLean, counsel. Taking land for railroad to Sanford mines. 2014

U.S. Circuit court (2d circuit). . . .United States of America, petitioner, vs. certain easement rights in 228.15 acres of land in Essex and Hamilton counties, State of New York, David McElwee, et al. defendants and State of New York, defendants-appellants. Brief on behalf of the Association for the protection of the Adirondacks as amicus curiae, in support of the appeal taken by the State of New York. . . N.Y. Pandick press, 1945? 24p. Brief signed Marshall McLean. For report of this case see Federal Reporter, 2d ser. v.160, p.479–82. 2015

New York (state). Supreme court. 4th district. . . .Brief on behalf of defendant, System properties, inc. N.Y. 1946. 182p. Water level of Lake George. 2016

New York (state). Supreme court. 4th district. People of the State of New York et al., plaintiff against System properties, inc. et al., defendants. . . Brief for the Lake George association, intervenor. N.Y. Bar press, 1946. 29p. Brief submitted by Charles H. Tuttle, June 28, 1946. Against artificial regulation of water level in Lake George. 2017

New York (state). Supreme court. 4th district. . . . .Reply brief for the defendant, System properties, inc. N.Y. 1946. 75p. LeBoeuf & Lamb, attorneys. Lake George water level. 2018

Forest preserve association of New York state, inc. Analysis of Judge Andrew J. Ryan's opinion rendered Sept. 4, 1947. . . Schenectady, N.Y. 1948. 2p. Supplement to 2d edition of the Forest Preserve Association's "Lake George Water Level History," pointing out an error in Judge Ryan's opinion in the Lake George water level case. The opinion is in Miscellaneous Reports, v.189, p.993–1005. 2019

New York (state). Supreme court. Appellate division, 4th department. In the matter of the application of the Adirondack league club, petitioner, against the Board of the Black river regulating district and William R. Adams, president. . .respondents. Proceeding no.1. . . Proceeding no.2. . . N.Y. Reporter co. inc. 1949. 4v. 2020

New York (state). Supreme court. Appellate division, 4th department. In the matter of the application of the Adirondack league club, petitioner, against the Board of the Black river regulating district and William R. Adams, president. . .respondents. Proceeding no.2. Record in procedure to review a determination. . .pursuant to article 78 of the Civil practice act. N.Y. Reporter co. inc. 1949. 2v. 2021

New York (state). Court of appeals. In the matter of Adirondack league club, appellant, against Board of Black river regulating district et al., respondents. In the matter of Adirondack Moose river committee, inc., et al., appellants, against Board of Black river regulating district et al., respondents. *In* New York reports, v.301, p.219–23. Argued May 26, 1950; decided July 11, 1950. Reversed the decision of the Appellate Division and remitted proceeding to Special Term. See also v.300, p.624–25. Panther Mountain reservoir. 2022

Miller, Philip Schuyler. Who watches the watchmen? *Ad-i-ron-dac*, Sept.–Oct. 1951. 15: 86, 90. The Black River Regulating District challenges the Stokes Act. 2023

New York (state). Supreme court. Jefferson county. Black river regulating district. . . plaintiffs vs Adirondack league club, defendant. . . Brief on behalf of the Adirondack Moose river committee, inc. the Friends of the Forest preserve, inc. . . amicus curiae. Walton, N.Y. Reporter co. 1951. 72,viiip. 2024

New York (state). Supreme court. Appellate division, 4th department. Black river regulating district and William R. Adams, Henry E. Smith and Alfred H. Stiles, Jr. . .plaintiffs-appellants, vs. Adirondack league club, defendant-respondent. Brief for the appellants. n.p. n.pub. 1952. 8p. 2025

New York (state). Supreme court. Appellate division, 4th department. Black river regulating district and William R. Adams, Henry E. Smith and Alfred H. Stiles Jr. . .plaintiffs-appellants, vs. Adirondack league club, defendant-respondent. Papers on appeal from judgment and order. . . Walton, N.Y. Reporter co. inc. 1952. 75p.   2026

New York (state). Court of appeals. Black river regulating district and William R. Adams, Henry E. Smith and Alfred H. Stiles, Jr. . .plaintiffs-respondents against Adirondack league club, defendant-appellant. Brief for defendant-appellant. N.Y. Bar press, inc. 1953? 83p. Argued by Charles H. Tuttle.
2027

New York (state). Court of appeals. Black river regulating district and William R. Adams, Henry E. Smith and Alfred H. Stiles, Jr. . .plaintiffs-respondents against Adirondack league club, defendant-appellant. Brief on behalf of Adirondack Moose river committee, inc. the Friends of the Forest preserve, inc. American planning and civic association, the Wild life management institute, the National parks association, the Wilderness society and the Association for the protection of the Adirondacks, *amici curiae*. Walton, N.Y. Reporter co. inc. 1953. 38p. Brief by Milo R. Kniffen.   2028

New York (state). Court of appeals. Black river regulating district and William R. Adams, Henry E. Smith and Alfred H. Stiles, Jr. . .plaintiffs-respondents against Adirondack league club, defendant-appellant. Brief on behalf of the Attorney general. . . n.p. n.pub. 1953. 37p. Argued by Edward L. Ryan.   2029

New York (state). Court of appeals. Black river regulating district and William R. Adams, Henry E. Smith and Alfred H. Stiles, Jr. . .plaintiffs-respondents against Adirondack league club, defendant-appellant. Record on appeal. N.Y. Reporter co. inc. 1953. 107p.   2030

New York (state). Supreme court. Appellate division, 4th department. Black river regulating district and William R. Adams, Henry E. Smith and Alfred H. Stiles, Jr. . .plaintiffs-appellants, vs Adirondack league club, defendant-respondent. Brief for defendant-respondent. N.Y. Bar press, inc. 1953. 59p. Argued by Charles H. Tuttle.   2031

New York (state). Supreme court. Appellate division, 4th department. Black river regulating district and William R. Adams, Henry E. Smith and Alfred H. Stiles, Jr. . .plaintiffs-appellants, vs. Adirondack league club, defendant-respondent. Brief on behalf of Adirondack Moose river committee, inc. the Friends of the forest preserve, inc. American planning and civic association, the Wild life management institute and the Wilderness society, *amici curiae*. n.p. n.pub. 1953. 42p.
2032

New York (state). Supreme court. Appellate division, 4th department. Black river regulating district and William R. Adams, Henry E. Smith and Alfred H. Stiles Jr. . .plaintiffs-appellants, vs. Adirondack league club, defendant-respondent. Brief on behalf of the Attorney general. . . Batavia, N.Y. Batavia times, law printers, 1953. 28p. Supporting the constitutionality of the Stokes Act. Argued by Edward L. Ryan, Assistant Attorney-General.   2033

New York (state). Supreme court. Appellate division, 4th department. Black river regulating district et al., appellants, v. Adirondack league club, respondent. May 27, 1953. *In* Reports of cases, v.282, p.161–73. See also p.829.   2034

New York (state). Supreme court. Appellate division, 4th department. In the matter of the application of the Adirondack league club, petitioner against the Board of the Black river regulating district et al., respondent. Proceeding no.1. . .Reply brief for all petitioners in proceeding no.2. . . n.p. 1953. 14p.   2035

New York (state). Court of appeals. Black river regulating district and William R. Adams, Henry E. Smith and Alfred H. Stiles, Jr. . .plaintiffs-respondents against Adirondack league club, defendant-appellant. Brief for respondents. n.p. n.pub. 1954. 76p.   2036

New York (state). Court of appeals. Black river regulating district and William R. Adams, Henry E. Smith and Alfred H. Stiles, Jr. . .plaintiffs-respondents against Adirondack league club, defendant-appellant. Reply brief for appellant. N.Y. Bar press, inc. 1954? 38p. Argued by Charles H. Tuttle.   2037

New York (state). Court of appeals. Black river regulating district and William R. Adams, Henry E. Smith and Alfred H. Stiles, Jr. . .plaintiffs-respondents against Adirondack league club, defendant-appellant. Reply brief on behalf of Adirondack Moose river committee, inc. the Friends of the Forest preserve, inc. American planning and civic association, the Wild life management institute, the National parks association, the Wilderness society and the Association for the protection of the Adirondacks, *amici curiae*. n.p. n.pub. 1954. 12p. Argued by Milo R. Kniffen.
2038

New York (state). Court of appeals. Board of the Black river regulating district, appellant, v. Adirondack league club, respondent. *In* New York reports, v.309, p.798–99. Argued Oct. 3, 1955; decided Oct. 13, 1955. Motion to dismiss appeal granted.   2039

CONSERVATION

Arranged by date

New York (state). Forest commission. Annual report, 1885–1894. Albany, Argus printing co. 1886–95. 11v. plates, tables, folded maps in pocket. Succeeded by the Fisheries, Game and Forest Commission (later the Forest, Fish and Game Commission).   2040

New York (state). Fisheries, game and forest commission. Annual report, 1895–1899. Albany & N.Y. 1896–1900. 5v. plates (part col.) tables, maps. The Commission also issued a series of three so-called preliminary reports (2, 3 and 5), 1897–1900.   2041

Juvenal, pseud. Adirondack deer and woods. *For & Stream*, Oct. 6, 1900. 55:267. Opposing the deer law and commenting on devastation of forests by lumber companies; see comment by J.A. Learned, "The Adirondack Deer," 55:289.   2042

New York (state). Forest, fish and game commission. Annual report of the Superintendent of the state forests, 1900–1910. Albany & N.Y. 1901–11. 6v. plates (part col.) tables, maps. Preliminary reports were also issued for 1900 and 1901. Report for 1901 included portfolio of 100 plates.   2043

Forest, fish and game commission. *For & Stream*, Mar. 9, 1901. 56:181. Editorial on abolishment of the Commission.   2044

Fernow, Bernhard Eduard. The Forest, fish and game commission. *Recreation*, July 1902. 17:62–63. Criticism of the 1900 Report.   2045

Association for the protection of the Adirondacks. Letter to Gov. Frank W. Higgins protesting reappointment of Commissioner Middleton and Chief game protector Pond, Mar. 20, 1905. N.Y. 1905. 7p.   2046

Whipple, James Spencer. Forests, fish and game. *For & Stream*, June 23, 1906. 66:989–91. Need to conserve New York state's forests, fish and game.   2047

Parkinson, Edward K. Adirondack interests —forests and game on the increase. *For & Stream*, Feb. 9, 1907. 68:216–17. illus.   2048

Whipple, James Spencer. The protection of forests, fish and game. *For Leaves*, Summer 1907. 4:no.2:3–7. illus.   2049

Juvenal, pseud. Commissioner Whipple's work. *For & Stream*, Sept. 14, 1907. 69:417. Touring the Adirondacks in interest of forest preservation.   2050

Hughes, Charles Evans. Conservation of natural resources in the State of New York. *In* Conference of governors. Proceedings, 1908. Washington, 1909. p.314–26. Mainly on the Adirondacks.   2051

Dix, John Alden. Statement on the conservation bill. n.p. n.d. Broadside. Press release dated July 13, 1911.   2052

New York (state). Conservation commission. Conservation committee report. *For & Stream*, Jan. 20, 1912. 78:79, 96–97. Summary of the Commission's first Annual Report.   2053

Dix, John Alden. The Governor's message. . . Conservation, p.14–18. n.p. n.d. unpaged. Press release, Jan. 3, 1912.   2054

New York (state). Conservation department. Annual report, 1911–date. Albany, 1912–date. plates, fold. maps, fold. profiles, tables (part fold.) diagrs. (part fold.). 1911–14 issued in two parts, Division of Lands and Forests, and Division of Inland Waters. Issued by the Conservation Commission, 1911–26; by the Conservation Department, 1927–date.   2055

New York (state). Laws, statutes, etc. Conservation law as amended to the close of the regular session of 1916. Albany, J.B. Lyon, 1916. 409p. Also issued in 1928 (680p.). 2056

Goldthwaite, Kenneth W. The plan of conservation and its execution. *Conservationist*, Mar. 1917. 1:35–38. illus.   2057

New York (state). Conservation commission. Violations of the conservation law disposed of during the month of. . . no.1–34. Mar. 1917–Dec. 1919. Albany, 1917–19. 34 nos. Monthly. Discontinued with Dec. 1919. 2058

Pratt, George DuPont. Conservation in the Adirondacks: an address given at Lake Placid. *NY Forestry*, Jan. 1918. 4:no.4:5–13.   2059

Pettis, Clifford Robert. Conservation in New York state. *NY State Hist Assn Q*, Apr. 1922. 3:77–82.   2060

Committee majority rejects Carpenter memorial-motion. *High Spots*, Dec. 1922. 1:no. 2:3–4. The memorial referred to is printed in Warwick S. Carpenter's "Mountain Slope Protection and Recreational Development in the Adirondacks" (no.1690).   2061

Committee outlines policy on conservation issues. *High Spots*, Dec. 1922. 1:no.2:1, 4. Report of the Conservation Committee, Henry S. Graves, chairman. The first definite statement of conservation policy by the Adirondack Mountain Club.   2062

Brandreth, Paulina. Commercialism or conservation? An illuminating article on what is happening in the Beaver river country, by Paul Brandreth, pseud. *For & Stream*, Sept. 1925. 95:582–83, 639–40. illus.   2063

Adams, Charles Christopher. Importance of preserving wilderness conditions. *NYS Mus Bul*, 1929. 279:37–46. plates. Also published as a separate.   2064

Howard, William Gibbs. Fifty years of conservation in New York state. *Bul Schools*, Apr. 1935. 21:138–43, 145–46. illus. Reprinted in New York State Ranger School *Alumni News*, 1935, p.3–10.   2065

Hosmer, Ralph Sheldon. The fifty years of conservation program takes final form. *NYS For Assn NL*, May 1935. p.1–3.   2066

Gorrie, R. Maclagan. Forests as public playgrounds in America. *Scot Geog Mag*, Nov. 1935. 51:363–65. On the work of the New York State Conservation Department in the Adirondacks and the Catskills.   2067

Whipple, Gurth Adelbert. A history of half a century of the management of the natural resources of the Empire state, 1885–1935. Albany, J.B. Lyon, c1935. 199p. illus. tables. Cover title: Fifty Years of Conservation in New York State, 1885–1935.   2068

Conservation department acquires property on Lake George. *NYS For Assn NL*, Nov. 1936. p.6. Seven hundred acres for development as a public campsite.   2069

Apperson, John S. Land utilization through preservation and land utilization for consumption. n.p. 1936. 4p.   2070

Apperson, John S. Man-made erosion in the Adirondacks and utilization through preservation. n.p. 1936. 6p. Unpaged folder. Two addresses, one on the results of unwise logging, the other pointing out the bad results from present state land purchase procedure.   2071

Burnham, John. The progress of conservation in New York state. *NYS Sport*, Aug.–Oct. 1937. 3:no.3:3, 8; 3:no.4:5, 10. illus.   2072

New York (state). Conservation department. The conservation fund. What is it? How is it raised? How is it spent? Why is there an unexpended balance? Should it be spent and how? By Lithgow Osborne. . . Albany, J.B. Lyon, 1939. 12p. See Whipple, Gurth. "Fifty Years of Conservation," p.114–15 (no.2068).   2073

Benedict, Darwin. Sidelights on the Tahawus railroad. *Ad Mt Club Bul*, May–June 1944. 8:no.3:5, 8. Conservation problems brought up by mining development.   2074

Benedict, Mrs. Martha (Nord). Conservation legislation. *Ad-i-ron-dac*, Mar.–Apr. 1945. 9:no.2:4.   2075

Conservation forum resume. *Ad-i-ron-dac*, Dec. 1945. 9:no.6:6–10. Conservationists meet to discuss postwar plans involving "woods, streams and hills, the wildlife that lives therein," and pledge support to a positive program.   2076

Schaefer, Paul A. Sunlight and shadow on the Moose river. *Cloud Splitter*, Mar.–Apr. 1948. 11:no.2:2–4.   2077

Barker, Elmer Eugene. Conservation issues. *Cloud Splitter*, July–Aug., Sept.–Oct. 1948. 11:no.4:14–15, 19; 11:no.5:16–17.   2078

Barker, Elmer Eugene. Conservation notes. *Cloud Splitter*, Jan.–Feb., May–June, Nov.–Dec. 1949; Jan.–Feb., Mar.–Apr. 1950. 12:no.1:14; 12:no.2:15–16; 12:no.3:13–14; 12:no.6:10–11; 13:no.1:10–13; 13:no.2:8–11.   2079

Miller, Philip Schuyler. Conservation in the 1949 Legislature. *Ad-i-ron-dac*, May–June 1949. 13:55.   2080

Fosburgh, Peter W. Weather and conservation. *NYS Con*, Feb.–Mar. 1950. 4:no.4:16–17.   2081

Miller, Philip Schuyler. ADK and conservation: 1950. *Ad-i-ron-dac*, May–June 1950. 14:51.   2082

Miller, Philip Schuyler. Conservation prospect: 1951. *Ad-i-ron-dac*, Jan.–Feb. 1951. 15:8–9. Statement by the chairman of the Conservation Committee, Adirondack Mountain Club.   2083

Apperson, John S. Conservation in the Adirondacks: past, present, and future. n.p. n. pub. 1951? Broadside. Talk before the Glens Falls Chapter, Adirondack Mountain Club, January 16, 1951. Reprinted in *The Ad-i-ron-dac*, May–June 1951, 15:49, 55.   2084

Miller, Philip Schuyler. Report of the Conservation committee: 1952. *Ad-i-ron-dac*, Jan.–Feb. 1953. 17:12–13, 19. See also letter from Brockenbrough Evans in issue for May–June, 17:47.   2085

Dome island. *Ad-i-ron-dac*, Sept.–Oct.—Nov.–Dec. 1954. 18:98. Plan to preserve Lake George island. See also brief note in *Living Wilderness*, Winter 1954–55, no.51:38.   2086

Hardy, Ruth Gillette. Conservation in New York. *Appalachia*, Dec. 15, 1954. mag.no.119:296–97. Brief summary. See also summary in issue for June 15, 1954, p.114–15.   2087

FORESTRY AND FIRE PROTECTION

Arranged by date

Hough, Franklin Benjamin. State forestry; source of pleasure and profit in the Adirondacks. Albany, n.d. 3p. Title from the New York State Library List of Additions, v.3, p.769.   2088

Schofield, Peter F. Forests and rainfall. *Pop Sci*, Nov. 1875. 8:111–12. Observation on absorption of rain by New York forests. 2089

Hough, Franklin Benjamin. . . .Report upon forestry. From the committee appointed to memorialize Congress and the state Legislature, regarding the cultivation of timber and the preservation of forests. Salem, Me. Salem press, 1878. 14p. From the Proceedings of the American Association for the Advancement of Science, St. Louis, Aug. 1878. 2090

U.S. Agriculture, Department of. . . .Report upon forestry, prepared under the direction of the Commissioner of agriculture. . .Washington, G.P.O. 1878–84. 4v. Volumes 1–3 prepared by Franklin B. Hough. Adirondacks, v.1, p.436–41. 2091

Sargent, Charles Sprague. The Adirondack forests. *Nation*, Dec. 6, 1883. 37:464. A plea for the conservation of Adirondack forests. For answers see Sage, D. Decay of spruce in the Adirondacks (in the issue for Dec. 20), and Packard, A.S. Jr. Decay of spruce in the Adirondacks and northern New England (issue for Dec. 27, 1883). 2092

Hough, Franklin Benjamin. Address. . .on state forest management, before the Committee on the preservation of the Adirondack forests of the Chamber of commerce of the State of New-York. January 14, 1884. N.Y. Press of the Chamber of commerce, 1884. 13p. 2093

Pringle, Cyrus Guernsey. "Extracts from Report upon the forests of northern New York." *In* U.S. Census. 10th census. 1880. Washington, 1884. v.9, p.501–6. 2094

Forest fires. *For & Stream*, Feb. 5, 1885. 24: 21. Editorial on prevention of fires in the Adirondacks. 2095

The Adirondack forests: a symposium. *Outing*, Apr. 1885. 6:77–83. By Charles Sprague Sargent and others. 2096

Forest commission report. *For & Stream*, Jan. 7, 1886. 25:462–63. 2097

New York (state). Legislature. Senate. Finance committee. Report. . .on the alleged misconduct of the Forest commission. Albany, 1887. 48p. Senate document 73, 1887. 2098

The Adirondack forests in danger. *Gard & For*, Mar. 28, 1888. 1:49. Editorial on the faults of the Forest Commission. 2099

Adirondack custodians. *For & Stream*, July 26, 1888. 31:1. Editorial on the Forest Commission. 2100

The Adirondack forests. *Gard & For*, Mar. 6, 1889. 2:109. Editorial expressing adverse criticism of the Forest Commission. 2101

The Adirondack forests. *For & Stream*, Oct. 31, 1889. 33:281. Forest Commission taking strong stand against devastation. 2102

Higley, Warren. The condition and needs of forestry legislation in the State of New York, an abstract. *NY Acad Sci Tr*, Dec. 9, 1889. 9:62–69. 2103

New York (state). Forest commission. Protect the forests: duties of supervisors, laws and rules. Albany, 1890. 22p. 2104

Fox, William Freeman. Forestry matters in New York. *Am Forestry Assn Proc*, 1891, 1892 & 1893. 10:62–71. Discussion of Catskills and Adirondacks. Read at World's Fair Congress, Oct. 1893. 2105

Fox, William Freeman. A forestry experiment station. *In* New York (state). Fisheries, game and forest commission. Annual report, 1896. p.328–33. Recommends purchase of a special tract of land for experiments. 2106

Proposed change in forestry practice in New York. *Gard & For*, Feb. 10, 1897. 10:52. Editorial on report of the Fisheries, Game and Forest Commission. 2107

Adirondack forest interest. *For & Stream*, Mar. 13, 1897. 48:201. Editorial on the Wagstaff Committee's recommendation for preservation of the watersheds of the Mohawk and Hudson rivers. 2108

Fernow, Bernhard Eduard. Adirondack forestry problems. *In* New York (state). Fisheries, game and forest commission. Annual report, 1898. p.354–66. plates, illus. Reprinted with slight revision in *The Forester*, Oct. 1900, 6:229–34. Also published as Bulletin no.5 of the New York State College of Forestry, Cornell University, 1902, 5p. 2109

Price, Overton Westfeldt. Working plans in the state preserve. *In* New York (state). Fisheries, game and forest commission. Annual report, 1898. p.418–22. plates, illus. Lumbering. 2110

Spears, Raymond Smiley. Adirondack ruin. *For & Stream*, June 17, 1899. 52:464. Forest fires. 2111

Fires in Nehasane park. *Forester*, Oct. 1899. 5:238. Forest protection from fire and methods of fire fighting. . 2112

Price, Overton Westfeldt. Studying the Adirondack forest. *Forester*, Jan. 1900. 6:19–20. Working plan for the St. Regis Paper Company tract, Franklin County. 2113

Cleveland, Treadwell Jr. The forest laws of New York. *Forester*, Apr. 1901. 7:81–85. Historical summary. 2114

Fernow, Bernhard Eduard. Progress of forest management in the Adirondacks; third annual report of the Director of the New York state college of forestry. Ithaca, N.Y. 1901. 40p. (New York State College of Forestry. Bulletin 3, Mar. 1901.) Describes the work at Axton, N.Y.   2115

Hosmer, Ralph Sheldon and Bruce, Eugene Sewell. . . .A forest working plan for Township 40, Totten and Crossfield purchase, Hamilton county, New York state Forest preserve, preceded by A discussion of conservative lumbering and the water supply, by Frederick H. Newell. Washington, G.P.O. 1901. 64p. charts, folded map. (U.S. Department of Agriculture Bulletin 30.) First published in the New York State Forest, Fish and Game Commission Annual Report for 1900, p.157–236. For comment see editorial entitled "The Adirondack Forests," *Forest and Stream*, July 27, 1901. 57:61. Reviewed in *The Forester*, Oct. 1901, 7:258–60. illus.   2116

The New York Forest preserve. *For & Stream*, Jan. 11, 1902. 58:30. Change in law needed to permit private owners to cut trees down to 10 inches instead of 12.   2117

Fernow, Bernhard Eduard. Forestry in New York state. *Science*, Jan. 17, 1902. n.s.15:91–96.   2118

Fernow, Bernhard Eduard. Forestry in New York. *Recreation*, Apr. 1902. 16:312–13. What foresters are trying to do in the Adirondacks.   2119

Williams, Asa S. The Adirondack park. *For & Irrig*, Apr. 1902. 8:141–42. Examination of Adirondack woodlands, work done by Asa S. Williams and R.C. Bryant.   2120

Fernow, Bernhard Eduard. Forestry and the New York state constitution. *Recreation*, Aug. 1902. 17:145–47.   2121

Hosmer, Ralph Sheldon and Bruce, Eugene Sewell. A forest working plan for Townships 5, 6 and 41, Totten and Crossfield purchase, Hamilton county, New York state Forest preserve. *In* New York (state). Forest, fish and game commission. Annual report, 1902–3. p.373–456. plates, folded map.   2122

Pettis, Clifford Robert. Special report on the gathering of spruce seed. *In* New York (state). Forest, fish and game commission. Annual report, 1902–3. p.66–73. plates.   2123

The Adirondacks. *For & Stream*, Feb. 28, 1903. 60:170. Extract from report of the Superintendent of State Forests.   2124

Spears, Raymond Smiley. Adirondack ruin. *For & Stream*, June 13, 1903. 60:465. Forest fires.   2125

Juvenal, pseud. Adirondack notes. *For & Stream*, June 20, 1903. 60:483. Forest fires.   2126

Pettis, Clifford Robert. The New York forest fire law. *For Quar*, July 1903. 1:134–39.   2127

Knechtel, A. Forest fires in the Adirondacks. *For Quar*, Nov. 1903. 2:2–13.   2128

New York. Board of trade and transportation. The state forests. Forest fires, their danger to life and property, system of protection in use in other countries and states, water power should be conserved, a water storage law recommended, waste lands should be reforested, official licensed guides should be created, repeal for the Forest preserve condemnation law. Report of the Committee on forests. N.Y. 1903. 16p.   2129

Locomotive sparks and forest fires. *For & Stream*, Feb. 13, 1904. 62:121. Editorial on hearing before Senate Forestry Commission.   2130

The crisis at Albany. *For & Irrig*, Mar. 1904. 10:99. Editorial on the need for help from the railroads to prevent forest fires.   2131

Adirondack forest fires. *For & Stream*, May 7, 1904. 62:369.   2132

Fire fighting in the Adirondacks. *Chaut*, Nov. 1904. 40:276–77.   2133

Forest fires of 1903 in New York state. *Ind*, Dec. 8, 1904. 57:1345.   2134

Fox, William Freeman. How forest fires may be prevented. *Woods & Wat*, Winter 1904–5. 7:no.4:15–18. illus.   2135

Fox, William Freeman. Fire! fire! fire! An appeal to the citizens of the Adirondack and Catskill regions. Albany, Evening union co. 1904. 16p. Issued by the Forest, Fish and Game Commission.   2136

Fox, William Freeman. Forest fires of 1903. Albany, Oliver A. Quayle, 1904. 55p. plates, tables. (Unnumbered bulletin of the Forest, Fish and Game Commission.)   2137

Suter, Herman Milton. . . .Forest fires in Adirondacks in 1903. Washington, G.P.O. 1904. 15p. front. (folded map). (U.S. Forestry Bureau Circular no.26.) Also published by the Association for the Protection of the Adirondacks as its Publication no.5.   2138

Fires in the Adirondacks. *Field & S*, June 1905. 10:182.   2139

Ruin wrought by forest fires. *J Outd Life*, June 1905. 2:99–101.   2140

Bruce, Eugene Sewell. Practical forestry in New York. *For & Irrig*, July 1905. 11:331–34.   2141

Reforestry in the Adirondacks. *Sh & Fish*, Sept. 21, 1905. 38:465. Title supplied. Editorial on work in progress.   2142

New York (state). Attorney-general's office. To the honorable, the Governor of the State of New York. . . n.p. n.pub. 1905. 24p. Report of investigation of unlawful cutting of timber in the Forest Preserve, Apr. 28, 1905. Copy in files of the Association for the Protection of the Adirondacks. 2143

McClintock, J.Y. Forestry in New York state. *For & Irrig*, Apr. 1905. 11:165–67. Includes discussion of Adirondack and Catskill preserves. 2144

Locomotives to fight forest fires. *Sport Rev*, Aug. 11, 1906. 30:145. Editorial on use of special locomotives equipped with pumps on top of boilers. 2145

Parker, Clarence L. Forest protection. *For & Stream*, Feb. 9, 1907. 68:216. 2146

Parker, Clarence L. Adirondack forest protection. *For & Stream*, Mar. 2, 1907. 68:334–35. Reviews recent attempts at Forest Preserve legislation. 2147

Parker, Clarence L. Adirondack forest lands. *St No Mo*, Apr. 1907. 1:no.12:7–12. 2148

Knechtel, A. The forests of New York. *In* New York (state). University. Arbor day annual, 1907. p.16–20. illus. Fire fighting and forest restoration. 2149

Spears, Eldridge A. Forest fires in the Adirondacks. *For & Stream*, July 25, 1908. 71:138. Reviews fires of the season and discusses means of protection. 2150

Adirondack fires out. *For & Stream*, Aug. 1, 1908. 71:174. 2151

Juvenal, pseud. In the Adirondacks. *For & Stream*, Oct. 17, 1908. 71:617. Forest fires. 2152

Brown, George L. Forest fires in Essex county. *For & Stream*, Nov. 21, 1908. 71:817. Costs of fighting forest fires. 2153

Brown, George L. Fire breaks in Essex county. *For & Stream*, Dec. 12, 1908. 71:938. Urges further fire protection for the Adirondack forests. Answered by F.L. Purdy in issue for Jan. 2, 1909. 2154

Donaldson, Alfred Lee. Forest fires and their prevention. *Outlook*, Dec. 19, 1908. 90:876–78. A review of forest fires in the Adirondacks, showing disastrous results; suggestions for prevention. 2155

Case 494. *In* New York (state). Public service commission, 2d district. 2d annual report, 1908. v.1, p.440–41. Ordering a hearing on Forest Preserve fires caused by railway locomotives. 2156

Radford, Harry V. . . .Artificial preservation of timber and History of the Adirondack beaver. Albany, J.B. Lyon, 1908. p.345–418. plates, illus. folded maps. Reprinted from the 10th, 11th and 12th reports of the New York

State Forest, Fish and Game Commission. Bibliography, p.358, 391–94. 2157

Whipple, James Spencer. Address to the Legislature of the State of New York (in joint session). . .Albany, February 3, 1908. Albany, J.B. Lyon, 1908. 19p. On forests and forestry, by the Commissioner of Forests, Fish and Game. 2158

Whipple, James Spencer. Forest preservation and restoration. *In* New York (state). University. Arbor day annual, 1908. p.16–18. illus. Brief historical résumé with statement of need to push the state's reforestation program. 2159

Purdy, Fred Leslie. Adirondack fires and preserves. *For & Stream*, Jan. 2, 1909. 72:14–15. Answer to G.L. Brown's article, "Fire Breaks," Dec. 12, 1908, 71:938. 2160

P., E.K. Conference on forest fires. *For & Stream*, Jan. 9, 1909. 72:58. Meeting of forty representatives with various interests in the Adirondacks. 2161

P., E.K. Commissioner Whipple's report. *For & Stream*, Jan. 16, 1909. 72:96–97. Changes needed to prevent forest fires. 2162

Whipple, James Spencer. Forest fires. *Outing*, Aug. 1909. 54:427–37. illus. Discussion of the Adirondack fires of 1899, 1903, 1908 and methods of fire prevention. 2163

Spears, Eldridge A. Measures to prevent forest fires. *For & Stream*, Sept. 25, 1909. 73:497. Inspection of railroad locomotives on the Malone & Montreal Rail Road. 2164

Preventing Adirondack forest fires. *Conservation*, Dec. 1909. 15:788. Condensed from the Boston *Transcript*. 2165

Forest fires. *For Leaves*, Winter 1909. 5:no.4:54–56. illus. Forest fires in 1908. 2166

Pettis, Clifford Robert. Tree planting in the Adirondacks. *For Leaves*, Winter 1909. 5:no.4:43–44. 2167

Adirondack forest fire investigation. *In* New York (state). Public service commission, 2d district. 3d annual report, 1909. v.1, p.87–95. See also p.562–63. 2168

New York (state). Public service commission, 2d district. In the matter of fire prevention along the lines of the railroads in the Adirondack Forest preserve. Submitted Mar. 22, 1909. Decided Apr. 1, 1909. Albany, 1909. 95p. tables. (Opinions and decisions. no.49.) Binder's title: Electrifying the Mohawk & Malone R.R. 2169

Cary, Austin. Forestry policy of typical states—New York. *Ann Am Acad*, Mar. 1910. 35:248–51. 2170

Spears, Raymond Smiley. State forest fire service. *Ang & Hunt*, Mar. 1910. 2:143–48. illus.   2171

New York (state). Commissioners to investigate the management and affairs of the Forest, fish and game commission. Abstract of report of Commissioners Roger P. Clark and H. Leroy Austin. . . Albany? 1910. 61 leaves. News release. Copy in the New York State Library.   2172

Pettis, Clifford Robert. Reforesting. Albany, J.B. Lyon, 1910. 25p. (New York State Forest, Fish and Game Commission Bulletin 2.)
2173

Gianini, Charles A. A hike with a fire patrolman. *For & Stream*, Oct. 21, 1911. 77:612–13. illus. Trip with Trume Haskell of the Wilmurt district. Includes a description of French Louis of West Canada lakes.   2174

Moon, Frederick Frank. Forest conditions of Warren county. *In* New York (state). Forest, fish and game commission. 16th annual report. p.79–107. plates, maps. Also published as New York State Conservation Commission Bulletin no.6, Albany, J.B. Lyon, 1911, 31p. illus. folded maps (col.).   2175

Wiley, George Martin, comp. Forests of New York. . . Albany, New York state education department, 1911. 53p. illus. (Arbor Day Annual, May 5, 1911.)   2176

Sterling, Ernest Albert. A definite state policy: New York state's progress in reforesting the Adirondacks. *Am Forestry*, July 1912. 18: 421–30. illus.   2177

Gaylord, Frederick Alan. Forestry and forest resources in New York. Albany, 1912. 58p. front. plates. (New York State Conservation Commission. Division of Lands and Forests. Bulletin 1.) Extracts in *American Forestry*, Nov. 1912, 18:685–701, illus. Later editions of Bulletin 1 are by A.S. Hopkins and are entitled "General Forestry." General and statistical material about the Adirondack Forest Preserve.   2178

Miller, Warren Hastings. Dynamite in forest fire fighting. *Am Forestry*, Nov. 1913. 19:769–75. illus. Demonstration at Cat Mountain station on experimental tract of the New York State College of Forestry, Syracuse.   2179

Pettis, Clifford Robert. $60,000 loss in New York state. *Am Forestry*, Nov. 1913. 19:750–52. Forest fires.   2180

New York (state). Conservation commission. . . .Special report. . .on the efficiency of the top-lopping law. Transmitted to the Legislature March 13, 1913 Albany, J.B. Lyon, 1913. 12p. illus. Assembly document 46, 1913. Report signed: C.R. Pettis. Tracts visited include Brandreth Preserve, Whitney Preserve, Santa Clara Lumber Company's holdings.   2181

Canada. Commission of conservation. Committee on forests. Forest protection in Canada, 1912–1914. Toronto, Bryant press, 1913–15. 2v. plates, folded map. Adirondack Forest Preserve—fires and fire prevention, pt.3.
2182

Fernow, Bernhard Eduard. A brief history of forestry, in Europe, the United States and other countries; 3d ed. rev. Toronto, University press, 1913. 506p. First published in 1907; revised and enlarged edition issued in 1911.   2183

Dickerson, Mary Cynthia. Forestry in the State of New York. *Am Mus J*, Oct.–Nov. 1914. 14:221–24. Recommends planned cutting in the Forest Preserve.   2184

Bruce, Eugene Sewell. The forestry problem in the Adirondacks. *NYS For Assn Bul*, Apr. 1915. 2:no.2:30–35.   2185

Howard, William Gibbs. Development of forest fire protection in New York state. *NYS For Assn Bul*, Apr. 1915. 2:no.2:45–46. 2186

Witherbee, Walter C. A timberland owners' fire protective association for the Adirondacks. *NYS For Assn Bul*, Apr. 1915. 2:no. 2:8–9.   2187

Demonstration needed. *Conservationist*, Sept. 1915. 1:140. Reprinted from the *Adirondack Enterprise*. Need better ways to use forest lands.   2188

Blauvelt, George A. Roads and fire trails in the Forest preserve. *NYS For Assn J*, Oct. 1915. 2:no.4:26–27.   2189

Clinton, George. Cutting mature timber in the state forests. *NYS For Assn J*, Oct. 1915. 2:no.4:20–21.   2190

Dow, Charles Mason. The problem of conservation in New York. *NYS For Assn J*, Oct. 1915. 2:no.4:3–5. illus.   2191

Carpenter, Herbert S. Co-operation in forest administration. *NYS For Assn J*, Oct. 1916. 3:no.2–4:26–28.   2192

Pratt, George DuPont. Public policy in relation to forest lands. *Conservationist*, Jan. 1917. 1:3–7. Address before the Empire State Forest Products Association, Dec. 19, 1916. 2193

Howard, William Gibbs. Getting the jump on forest fires. *Conservationist*, Apr. 1917. 1: 56–59. illus. Description of the forest fire protective force in the Adirondacks.   2194

Austin, H. Leroy. No lumbering in state forests, people should not permit commercial interests to cut timber in Adirondacks and Catskills; much of the area already devastated. *State Service*, Oct. 1917. 1:no.3:40–45. illus.   2195

Recknagel, Arthur Bernard. Make state forests productive; scientific lumbering in Adirondacks should be permitted under restrictions, is the argument of a forester who has studied the subject. *State Service*, Oct. 1917. 1:no.3:33–40. illus. 2196

Pratt, George DuPont. Fire department for the forests. *Am City* (Town and country ed.) Oct. 1918. 19:255–58. illus. 2197

Society of American foresters. Sample plot committee. Plan for permanent sample plots in the Adirondacks. *J For*, Dec. 1918. 16: 922–27. 2198

New York (state). Legislature. Senate. Conservation committee. Plant and acquire forests, one of the pressing duties of New York state, by James S. Whipple. Transmitted to the Legislature April 12, 1918. Albany, J.B. Lyon, 1918. 37p. illus. Senate document 50, 1918. Includes legal history of forest preservation in the Adirondacks. 2199

New York (state). Laws, statutes, etc. Conservation law in relation to lands and forests. Albany, J.B. Lyon, 1918?– Copies located for 1918–19, 1923, 1929, 1931–32, 1934, 1937, 1940, 1946, 1948. 2200

Pratt, George DuPont. A state-wide forest policy. *Conservationist*, Dec. 1919. 2:179–82. illus. 2201

Association for the protection of the Adirondacks. Committee on conservation of state waters, lands and forests. Forestry program. N.Y. 1919. 4p. Addressed to the Chamber of Commerce. Copy in files of the Association. 2202

Howard, William Gibbs. Mountain top builders. *Conservationist*, Jan. 1920. 3:11–13. illus. Construction of fire towers in the Adirondack and Catskill preserves. 2203

Pettis, Clifford Robert. Legislative machinery for enforcement of private forestry measures. *J For*, Jan. 1920. 18:6–8. 2204

Pratt, George DuPont. New York's forestry program. *Am Forestry*, Jan. 1920. 26:51–53. 2205

Pettis, Clifford Robert. Driving home the fire lesson. *Conservationist*, June 1920. 3:90–93. Posting signs to remind the public of the fire hazards. 2206

Pratt, George DuPont. Forest conservation in New York state. *Cor For*, June 1920. 1:9–11. 2207

Howard, William Gibbs. The telephone in forest protection. *Conservationist*, Aug. 1920. 3:122–23. Reprinted in *State Service*, Oct.–Nov. 1921, 5,i.e.7:432–33, with title "Telephones Help to Protect Forests. . ." 2208

Recknagel, Arthur Bernard. New York's forests and their future. *Am Forestry*, Sept. 1920. 26:518–21. illus. table. 2209

Baker, Hugh Potter. Forestry and a forest policy for New York. *NY Forestry*, Feb. 1920. 7:no.1:24–31. 2210

Belyea, Harold Cahill. Some observations on empirical forestry in the Adirondacks. *J For*, Feb. 1921. 19:115–28. table. 2211

Cleaves, Howard H. The forest's fire department. *Conservationist*, July 1921. 4:107–9. illus. 2212

Behre, Charles Edward. A study of windfall in the Adirondacks. *J For*, Oct. 1921. 19: 632–37. tables. 2213

Howard, William Gibbs. What the state has accomplished in fire protection. *Emp St For Prod Assn Bul*, Dec. 1921. no.12:8–14. 2214

Howard, William Gibbs. Forest fires. Albany, J.B. Lyon, 1921. 52p. plates, illus. (New York State Conservation Commission Bulletin 10, rev.) Earlier edition, 1914. 2215

Woolsey, Theodore S. Public forestry on private land. Reprinted from the *Journal of Forestry*, Feb. 1922. n.p. 1922? 5p. 2216

Hopkins, Arthur S. The forest fire hazard in the Adirondack and Catskill regions. *J For*, Oct. 1922. 20:629–32. chart. 2217

Five year effort of Association in forest taxation legislation nears final success. Supplement to *The Seed Tree*, Feb. 1923. n.p. 1923. 2p. Summary of forest taxation and proposed law by the Association for the Protection of the Adirondacks. 2218

Simmons, J.R. Replacing a vanished forest. *Bul Schools*, Apr. 1923. 9:149–50. illus. Need for good forest practice and reforestation. The author was Secretary-Forester of the New York State Forestry Association. 2219

Macdonald, Alexander. The press and reforestation. Address. . .before the New York state publishers' association. Syracuse, January 25, 1924. Albany, J.B. Lyon, 1924. 12p. illus. Includes material on the Adirondacks. 2220

Belyea, Harold Cahill and Woolsey, T.S. Jr. A forest policy for New York state. *J For*, Jan. 1925. 23:10–19. "The idea that a pleasure forest or Adirondack park can never be cut must be corrected." 2221

New York suffers from fall fires. *Am For*, Jan. 1925. 31:56. Adirondack and Catskill preserves closed Oct. 31, 1924. 2222

Marshall, Robert. Recreational limitations to silviculture in the Adirondacks. *J For*, Feb. 1925. 23:173–78. 2223

Macdonald, Alexander. Policy for forest land acquisition by New York state. *J For*, May–June 1925. 23:457–59. 2224

Hall, Edward Hagaman. New York state forest policy. *NY Forestry*, 1925. p.35–39. 2225

Lindgren, G.S. Fire-weather in the Adirondacks. *Am Met Soc Bul*, Feb. 1926. 7:30–31. 2226

Sealy, G.A. The Watson school forest. *Bul Schools*, Mar. 1, 1926. 12:166–67. plate. Town of Watson, Lewis County. 2227

Forest depletion in the State of New York with particular reference to the Adirondacks. *Emp St For Prod Assn Bul*, Feb. 1927. 25:1–4. tables. 2228

Prescott, Herbert F. New York state's forests. *Bul Schools*, Apr. 1, 1927. 13:194–97. illus. 2229

Francis, Henry R. Forestry in New York's state parks. *Am For*, June 1927. 33:349–51, 384. 2230

Association for the protection of the Adirondacks. The depletion of the private forests of New York state. N.Y. 1927. 7p. Signed: E.H. Hall. 2231

Carlisle, John Nelson. Reforestation by a public utility; reforestation goal of the Northern New York utilities, inc. is ten million trees planted by 1930. *Gr & NYS Con*, Apr. 1928. 6:no.11:13. Planting on watersheds of the Black, Beaver and Oswegatchie rivers. 2232

Stickel, Paul W. Comparative forest fire hazard in the northeast. *J For*, Apr. 1928. 26:456–63. tables. Elk Lake and Cranberry Lake among the regions investigated. 2233

New York (state). Conservation department. Program of the fifth annual Adirondack forestry tour September 21–24, 1928. Albany, J.B. Lyon, 1928. 46p. illus. folded map. 2234

Prater, P.F. Wallace. The Cranberry lake forest fire weather station. *Emp For*, 1928. 14:48–50. 2235

Schwartz, G. Victor. Five months of forest recreation. *Emp For*, 1928. 14:17–21. illus. Job at state campsite on Lake George. 2236

Faulks, Edward B. The campsite ranger's job. *Emp For*, 1929. 15:37–40. Sacandaga public campsite. 2237

Hopkins, Arthur S. General forestry (revised). Albany, J.B. Lyon, 1930. 31p. illus. (New York State Conservation Department Bulletin no.1.) First published in 1912 (see no. 2178). 2238

New York (state). Reforestation commission. Preliminary report transmitted to the Legislature February 6, 1930. Albany, 1930. 6p. Legislative document 63, 1930. 2239

Brown, Nelson C. New York looks ahead. *J For*, May 1930. 28:728–33. Also issued as a reprint. Review of New York state policy. 2240

Bayle, Francis L. Forest fires. *High Spots*, Sept. 1930. 7:no.3:4–5. illus. 2241

Seligman, Edwin R.A. A forest policy for New York. Address delivered July 21, 1930, at Lake Placid. Watertown, N.Y. Department association, 193— 15p. Reprinted from the September issue of the *Up-Stater*. 2242

Prescott, Herbert F. New York's great reforestation program. *Bul Schools*, Apr. 1, 1931. 17:177–80. plates. History and results of reforestation program. Explanation and promotion of Hewitt amendment. 2243

Recknagel, Arthur Bernard. Review of legislation 1931. *NYS For Assn NL*, June 1931. p.5–6. 2244

Simmons, Frederick C. Jr. Forest policies of New York state. 137 leaves. plates, maps. Master's thesis, Yale School of Forestry, June 1931. Typescript. Written from the forester's point of view. 2245

New York (state). State university. College of forestry, Syracuse. The Hewitt reforestation program for New York. Syracuse, 1931. 13p. 2246

Stickel, Paul W. Measurement and interpretation of forest fire-weather in the western Adirondacks. . .in cooperation with the New York state college of forestry. Syracuse, N.Y. 1931. 115p. illus. diagrs. (New York State University College of Forestry, Syracuse. Technical Bulletin no.34.) Also issued as Bulletin, v.4, no.3a, Dec. 1931. 2247

Empire state forest products association. Special committee on forest fire suppression. Report. *NYS For Assn NL*, Nov. 1933, p.1–3; Nov. 1934, p.16–19. 2248

Stickel, Paul W. Weather and forest fire hazard with special reference to the upper altitudinal spruce-balsam forest region of northern New York. *J For*, Jan. 1934. 32:76–79. chart, table. Statistics from Elk Lake fire-weather station. 2249

Hopkins, Arthur S. New York state's reforestation program. *Bul Schools*, Apr. 1, 1936. 22:154–56. plates. Progress of reforestation program since 1929. 2250

Apperson, John S. Forests upstream and downstream: a series of addresses. Schenectady, N.Y. Forest preserve association of New York state, inc. 1936. 8p. Contents: I. Man-made Erosion in the Adirondacks; II. Utilization Through Preservation; III. Upper Watershed Forests Differ in Purpose from Downstream Forests. State's failure to protect critical slopes at the sources of rivers. 2251

Howard, William Gibbs. Progress in forestry in New York state in 1937. *NYS For Assn NL*, Mar. 1938. p.1–5. 2252

Hosmer, Ralph Sheldon. The state constitution and forestry. *NYS For Assn NL*, Nov. 1938. p.5–7. 2253

Littlefield, Edward Winchester. Spruce and balsam reproduction occurring under a porcupine-damaged Scotch pine plantation in the Adirondacks. Albany, New York state conservation department, 1938. unpaged. (Notes on Forest Investigations, no.9, Apr. 9, 1938.) Mimeographed. 2254

Gibbs, John T. When the woods are closed. *High Spots Yrbk*, 1939. p.77–79. Forest fires. 2255

Diebold, Charles H. Effect of fire and logging upon the depth of the forest floor in the Adirondack region. *Soil Sci Soc Proc*, 1941. 6:409–13. illus. 2256

Fowler, Albert. The fire head. *High Spots Yrbk*, 1942. p.30–32. illus. Fire fighting. 2257

Hopkins, Arthur S. New York state's reforestation program. Albany, New York state conservation department, 1942. 36p. figs. map. (New York State Conservation Department Bulletin 20.) Revised edition issued in 1950. "This bulletin summarizes the history and progress of public and private reforestation in New York state since 1899." 2258

Schaefer, Paul A. Adirondack forests in peril. *Nat Parks*, July–Sept. 1945. no.82:19–23. illus. 2259

Dubuar, James Francis. Does New York need a forest inventory? *J For*, Mar. 1946. 44:176–77. Vast holdings in the Adirondacks and Catskills should be inventoried. Reprinted from *Alumni News*, New York State Ranger School, 1944. 2260

Williams, Kinne F. Putting eyes in the skies. *NYS Con*, Aug. 1946. 1:no.1:16. illus. Building a fire tower on Mt. Adams, Essex County. 2261

Howard, William Gibbs. New York's Forest practice act. *J For*, June 1947. 45:405–7. 2262

Hicks, Harry Wade. Great fires of 1903. *NYS Con*, Aug.–Sept. 1947. 2:no.1:9–10. illus. Excerpt in *North Country Life*, Fall 1948, 2:no. 4:7–8, 51–52. 2263

Littlefield, Edward Winchester. Forest planting in New York. Albany, New York state conservation department, 1947. 31p. figs. (New York State Conservation Department Bulletin 2.) Replaces "Reforesting" by C.R. Pettis. Reprinted in 1950. 2264

Howard, William Gibbs. State of New York forestry policy. *NYS Con*, Aug.–Sept. 1948. 3:no.1:12–13. illus. 2265

Wolf, Robert E. A partial survey of forest legislation in New York state. 353 leaves. Master's thesis, New York State University College of forestry, Syracuse, 1948. Typescript. Omits fish and game legislation; includes very few legislative acts on water and water power. 2266

Amadon, Arthur F. Trees for the people of New York. *Bul Schools*, Mar. 1949. 35:264–67. illus. History and current status of state tree nurseries. 2267

Littlefield, Edward Winchester. This state takes care of its trees. *Bul Schools*, Mar. 1949. 36:200–4. Forest Practice Act. 2268

Lauffer, Paul G. Must we eat our forests? *Ad-i-ron-dac*, Mar.–Apr. 1949. 13:33. First of four articles; others have title: "Our Vanishing Forests." 2269

Lauffer, Paul G. Our vanishing forests—II–IV. *Ad-i-ron-dac*, May–June—Sept.–Oct. 1949. 13:64, 86, 104–5. 2270

Wilkins, John. Life on an Adirondack; or, How to impress the public. *NYS Con*, Dec. 1949–Jan. 1950. 4:no.3:8–9. illus. By fire observer on West Mountain. 2271

Miller, Philip Schuyler. "Perpetual forests." *Ad-i-ron-dac*, Jan.–Feb. 1950. 14:9. 2272

Miller, Philip Schuyler. ADK and forestry legislation: 1950. *Ad-i-ron-dac*, May–June 1950. 14:56–57. 2273

Newkirk, Arthur Edward. Perpetual forests or continuing waste, which way in 1951? *Ad-i-ron-dac*, Nov.–Dec. 1950. 14:119, 124. 2274

Shorey, Archibald Thompson. Conservation in 1897. *Cloud Splitter*, Nov.–Dec. 1950. 13: no.6:6. 2275

Apperson, John S. Perpetual production forests and preservation forests. This statement was presented to the Joint legislative committee of N.Y. state on river regulation... Jan. 20, 1950. n.p. 1950. 8p. 3d edition, revised, March 1950. Issued by the Adirondack Mountain Club and the Oneida County Forest Preserve Council. Five editions were issued. 2276

Miller, Roland B. The big blow of 1950. *NYS Con*, Dec. 1950–Jan. 1951. 5:no.3:18. illus. Minor mention of the Adirondacks. 2277

Timber salvage program planned. Conservation department working on plans. *Lumber Camp News*, Jan. 1951. 12:no.9:1, 14. illus. 2278

Wind damage in the Adirondacks. *J For*, Feb. 1951. 49:151. 2279

The storm of Nov. 25, 1950. *NYS Con*, Feb.–Mar. 1951. 5:no.4:2–7. illus. map on inside front cover. Includes official communications of Commissioner Duryea and Attorney-General Goldstein, summary of action by the Legislature and action by the Conservation Department. See monthly Salvage Reports Apr.–May 1951 through Feb.–Mar. 1952. Reports usually every two months thereafter. 2280

Emergency action taken in Adirondack blow-down area. *J For*, Mar. 1951. 49:228. 2281

State seeks salvage bids in Adirondacks. *Lumber Camp News*, Mar. 1951. 12:no.11:7. 2282

Miller, Philip Schuyler. The blow-down. *Ad-i-ron-dac*, Mar.–Apr. 1951. 15:26–27, 40. Storm of November 1950. See also his "Blow-down Aftermath" in issue for July–Aug. 15: 68–69. 2283

Salvage jobs being let. *Lumber Camp News*, Apr. 1951. 12:no.12:6. 2284

State windfall unlikely to go for news print. *Ed & Pub*, Apr. 21, 1951. 84:no.17:112. Conservation Department contracts with lumber mills for disposal of blowdown trees. See also brief summary in *Business Week*, June 23, 1951, no.1138:118–20. "Storm-felled trees. . ." 2285

Forest area closed to public. *Lumber Camp News*, July 1951. 13:no.3:14. List of areas closed on account of blowdown. 2286

New York foresters inspect timber damage. *Lumber Camp News*, Sept. 1951. 13:no.5:10. Meeting of New York section of the Society of American Foresters. 2287

New York maps fire fighting plan. *Lumber Camp News*, Sept. 1951. 13:no.5:11. 2288

Youngs, George J. "The great windstorm of November 25, 1950." *NYS Ranger Sch*, 1951. p.14–15, 19. illus. 2289

New York (state). Governor (Thomas E. Dewey). Message. . .in relation to hurricane damage in the Adirondack area. Albany, 1951. 3p. Legislative document 30, 1951. Proposes bill to finance salvage work. 2290

Curry, John R. and Church, Thomas W. Jr. Observations on winter drying of conifers in the Adirondacks. *J For*, Feb. 1952. 50:114–16. illus. 2291

Littlefield, Edward Winchester. Why don't we make the lumbermen reforest? *NYS Con*, Feb.–Mar. 1952. 6:no.4:25. illus. 2292

Kingsbury, Corydon D. The state forests of New York. *Bul Schools*, Mar. 1952. 38:172–76. figs. map. History and current status of state production forests, including some in the Adirondacks. 2293

Patterson, William C. Blowdown—what next? *Cloud Splitter*, Mar.–Apr. 1952. 15:no. 2:4–6. 2294

Hopkins, Arthur S. Planning for fire. *Lumber Camp News*, Apr. 1952. 13:no.12:8–9. illus. 2295

Hopkins, Arthur S. Planning for fire. *NYS Con*, Apr.–May 1952. 6:no.5:20–21. illus. map. 2296

Apperson, John S. Better forestry. . . *Liv Wild*, Spring 1952. no.40:37. Reprint of letter to the *New York Times* urging better management of commercial forests and less controversy over the Forest Preserve. 2297

Hurley, W.J. Project E 2. *NYS Con*, Oct.–Nov. 1952. 7:no.2:22–23. Lumber company problems of salvage under state contracts. 2298

Foss, William M. After the storm. *NYS Con*, Dec. 1952–Jan. 1953. 7:no.3:2–3. illus. Summary of Conservation Department's work following the storm of November 1950. 2299

Williams, Kinne F. Closing the woods. *NYS Con*, Dec. 1952–Jan. 1953. 7:no.3:24–25. 2300

Fosburgh, Peter W. Fire in the Cold river blow-down. *NYS Con*, Aug.–Sept. 1953. 8: no.1:2–4. map. 2301

Marshall, George. The renewed menace of "fire truck roads" to the wild forest character of the Forest preserve. A forward to Robert Marshall's "Calkins Creek." *Ad-i-ron-dac*, Sept.–Oct. 1953. 17:100. See letter from A.T. Shorey in Nov.–Dec. issue, 17: 109, and Marshall's reply in Jan.–Feb. 1954 issue, 18:16–17. Also letters from Katherine Flickinger and Howard Zahniser in the Mar.–Apr. 1954 issue, 18:34–36. 2302

Marshall, Robert. Calkins creek. *Ad-i-ron-dac*, Sept.–Oct. 1953. 17:101. Wilderness character destroyed by fire truck road. 2303

Allen, David G. Fire in the Cold river blow-down (2). *NYS Con*, Oct.–Nov. 1953. 8:no. 2:20–23. Pictures with explanatory text. 2304

Foss, William M. The big timber blow-down (as of December 31, 1952). *In* New York (state). Legislature. Joint legislative committee on natural resources. Report, 1953. p.50–51. table. 2305

Seagears, Clayton B. State has top forest-fire-fighting team. *Cloud Splitter*, Jan.–Feb. 1954. 17:no.1:4–5. 2306

Forest fire report. *NYS Con*, Apr.–May 1954. 8:no.5:30–31. 2307

Foss, William M. $750,000 for state forests. *NYS Con*, Apr.–May 1954. 8:no.5:2. Inception of a long-range management program. 2308

Hyde, Solon. New York state forest fire control. *Northeast Log*, May 1954. 2:no.9:8–9, 46. illus. 2309

Tranquille, Dante. A babe in the woods. *Am For*, July 1954. 60:no.7:18–19. illus. Brief text with two-page spread of pictures. Diane Evans, daughter of Forest Ranger on Bald Mountain. 2310

Hyde, Solon. Fire control—then and now. *NYS Con*, Oct.–Nov. 1954. 9:no.2:4–5. illus. 2311

Foss, William M. Salvage operations in the Forest preserve as of December 1, 1953. *In* New York (state). Legislature. Joint legislative committee on natural resources. Report, 1954. p.121. 2312

Littlefield, Edward Winchester and Eliason, Everett J. Seed collection and tree production of Boonville Scotch pine. *NY Forester*, Feb. 1955. 12:no.1:18. 2313

Hiscock, L. Harris. Fire in the north. *Ad-i-ron-dac*, Sept.–Oct. 1955. 19:92–94. 2314

Fohrman, Fred E. Long pond mt. fire. *NYS Con*, Oct.–Nov. 1955. 10:no.2:16, 27. Preceded by note from Solon Hyde. 2315

Foss, William M. Progress report on timber salvage operations. *In* New York (state). Legislature. Joint legislative committee on natural resources. Report, 1955. p.82–88. illus. table. 2316

FISH AND GAME

Arranged by date

New York (state). Laws, statutes, etc. Game laws of the State of New York, as amended to 1872, inclusive. And certified as correct by the Secretary of state. With an appendix of forms and proceedings under the same. Albany, Parker & Herrick, 1872. 60p. 2317

New York (state). Laws, statutes, etc. The game laws of the State of New York. . . Albany, Weed, Parsons & co. 1873. 43p. 2318

N., S.S. The Adirondacks. *For & Stream*, Sept. 2, 1875. 5:54. Letter on disregard of game laws. 2319

Game protection. *For & Stream*, Sept. 16 & 23, 1875. 5:88, 104. On Hoxie, who hired forty trappers to work for him. Prosecution by the Hudson River Sportsmens Association. 2320

New York (state). Laws, statutes, etc. The game laws of the State of New York. Printed for the New York association for the protection of game. September, 1875. n.p. 1875?

14p. Copy at the New York Public Library has amendments of 1876 (2p.) tipped in. 2321

Lawlessness in the Adirondacks. *For & Stream*, June 22, 1876. 6:322. Firing at sportsmen. 2322

French, J. Clement. Are the Adirondacks played out? *For & Stream*, Nov. 9, 1876. 7:218. Depletion of game and fish. 2323

McKean, W.S. Adirondack association. *Am Angler*, Aug. 2, 1884. 6:70. Meeting to form a game protective association in the Adirondack area. 2324

Adirondack game wardens. *For & Stream*, Oct. 2, 1884. 23:181. Editorial on violations of game law and need to appoint woodsmen as wardens. 2325

L. Adirondack game protection. *For & Stream*, Oct. 2, 1884. 23:185. Need to appoint men familiar with the woods for game protection. 2326

Sherman, Richard U. Adirondack game protection. *For & Stream*, Oct. 16, 1884. 23:226–27. Answer to L. (in issue for Oct. 2) defends present protectors and enforcement of law. 2327

L. Adirondack game preservation. *For & Stream*, Oct. 23, 1884. 23:247. Reply to Sherman (Oct. 16, 1884) defending original position. 2328

Merriam, Clinton Hart. Adirondack game protection. *For & Stream*, Oct. 30, 1884. 23:265. In reply to L. (Oct. 2, 1884) notes that the game laws are better observed in some areas than in others. 2329

Northrup, M.S. Adirondack game protection. *For & Stream*, Nov. 6, 1884. 23:287. Notes on game and protection. 2330

Pot hunters in the woods. *For & Stream*, Nov. 26, 1885. 25:341. Editorial on establishing salt licks in Hamilton County. 2331

Portsa, pseud. Adirondack game. *For & Stream*, Nov. 25, 1886. 27:346. Increase in larger animals. 2332

Dr. Ellsworth Elliot, Jr. convicted. *Am Angler*, Aug. 18, 1888. 14:97–98. Editorial on conviction for violation of game laws. 2333

New York (state). Laws, statutes, etc. Fish and game laws of the State of New York, also laws for the preservation of the forests, including amendments thereto, passed in 1888; comp. . .by George Edwin Kent. . . Troy, N.Y. Troy press co. printers, 1888. 135p. 2334

Worden, George H. Not guilty; or, The farce of Adirondack game protection. *Outing*, Apr. 1889. 14:67–70. 2335

New York (state). Laws, statutes, etc. ...
Game laws of the State of New York. An act
for the protection, preservation and propagation of birds, fish and wild animals in the
State of New York and the different counties
thereof. .. Albany, Banks & brothers, 1892.
40p.   2336

New York (state). Laws, statutes, etc. Game
laws of the State of New York so far as they
affect northern counties; compiled by H.
Conkling. Albany, 1892. 52p. Title from
Hasse.   2337

Bruce, Dwight Hall. The Adirondacks. *For
& Stream*, Jan. 26, 1893. 40:73. Report made
to the New York State Association for the
Protection of Fish and Game.   2338

Witherbee, Walter C. Quail in northern New
York. *For & Stream*, Nov. 11, 1893. 41:407.
Releasing West Virginia quail near Port
Henry. A report from Ticonderoga by "S"
appears in the issue for July 21, 1894, 43:
50.   2339

Fish, forests and politics. *For & Stream*, Feb.
2, 1895. 44:81. Editorial on the Senate Committee on Fish and Game.   2340

New York fish commission. *For & Stream*,
Feb. 2, 1895. 44:88-89. Proposed consolidation of the Fish and Forest Commission with
the Senate Committee on Fish and Game.
                                        2341

S. An Adirondack capture. *For & Stream*,
Feb. 23, 1895. 44:151. Capture of French
Louis (Louis Seymour) and an Indian rene-
gade from the St. Regis Reservation for killing deer illegally.   2342

S. Adirondack otters. *For & Stream*, Dec. 14,
1895. 45:517.   2343

Spears, Raymond Smiley. The spell of an
otter's eyes. *For & Stream*, Dec. 28, 1895. 45:
562. Notes on otters at West Canada Creek.
                                        2344

New York (state). Laws, statutes, etc. The
fish and game law of the State of New York,
providing for the protection, preservation
and propagation of birds, fish and wild animals, as revised and enacted by the Legislature of 1895. Albany, Banks & brothers,
1895. 101p.   2345

New York (state). Legislature. Senate. Committee on the fish and game laws. Report. ..
transmitted. ..January 15, 1895. Albany,
J.B. Lyon, 1895. 10p. Senate document 12,
1895.   2346

From the game-fields. Maine and the Adirondacks. *Recreation*, June 1896. 4:304-8.
Includes letters on hunting in the Adirondacks by Jos. A. Cox, Seaver A. Miller and
D.S. Smith.   2347

Simpson, John Boulton. Protector William
H. Burnett. *For & Stream*, Dec. 12, 1896. 47:
472. Defense of Burnett's work.   2348

New York (state). Laws, statutes, etc. Fisheries, game and forest law of the State of New
York, relating to game, fish and wild animals, and to the Forest preserve and Adirondack park. As revised and enacted by the
Legislature of 1895 and amended by the
Legislature of 1896. Albany, W.H. Crawford
co. 1896. 167p.   2349

Cayadutta, pseud. The Adirondack game
law. *For & Stream*, Mar. 20, 1897. 48:226-
27.   2350

Miller, Seaver Asbury. Adirondack game
interests. *For & Stream*, Mar. 27, 1897. 48:
249. Comment on legislation.   2351

McHarg, John B. Jr. Anent the Adirondack
moose, the panther and the wolf. *For &
Stream*, Apr. 24, 1897. 48:325. Notes on extinction.   2352

New York (state). Laws, statutes, etc. Fisheries, game and forest law of the State of New
York. Relating to game, fish and wild animals, and to the Forest preserve and Adirondack park. As revised and enacted by the
Legislature of 1892 and amended by the Leg-
islatures of 1895, 1896, and 1897. Albany,
1897. 144p.   2353

New York (state). Laws, statutes, etc. Fisheries, game and forest law of the State of New
York, relating to game, fish and wild animals and to the Forest preserve and Adirondack park. As revised and enacted by the
Legislature of 1892 and amended by the Leg-
islatures of 1895, 1896, 1897 and 1898. Albany, Pub. by the clerks of the Senate and
Assembly, 1898. 136p.   2354

The Essex county protector. *For & Stream*,
Nov. 11, 1899. 53:387. On Game Protector
Fletcher Beede's enforcement of game laws.
                                        2355

Spears, Raymond Smiley. In the north woods.
For & Stream, Nov. 25, 1899. 53:427. Lack
of enforcement of game laws.   2356

B. Adirondack game. *For & Stream*, Dec. 16,
1899. 53:491-92. Game legislation.   2357

New York (state). Governor (Theodore Roosevelt). Letter to Fisheries, game and forest
commission. *In* his Public papers, 1899. Albany, 1899. p.205-6. Recommends rigid protection of game and fish.   2358

New York (state). Laws, statutes, etc. Fisheries, game and forest law of the State of New
York, relating to game, fish and wild animals,
and to the Forest preserve and Adirondack
park. As revised and enacted by the Legis-
latures of 1895, 1896, 1897, 1898 and 1899.
Albany, 1899. 144p.   2359

Roosevelt, Theodore. New York fish and game interests. From Governor Roosevelt's message. *For & Stream*, Jan. 13, 1900. 54:27. Conservation. 2360

Fish possessed during close season, though taken from waters outside the state. Construction of the act for the protection of birds, fish and wild animals in the State of New York (chap. 488, Laws 1892). *Alb Law J*, Oct. 20, 1900. 62:243–50. Decision of Court of Appeals, Oct. 2, 1900. 2361

New York (state). Laws, statutes, etc. The forest, fish and game law of the State of New York. Relating to the Forest preserve, fish, game and the International park. Albany, J.B. Lyon, 1900. 95p. 2362

New York fish and game. *For & Stream*, Feb. 2, 1901. 56:89. From the Report of the Forest, Fish and Game Commission. 2363

Moose, elk and beaver for the Adirondacks. *Woods & Wat*, Autumn 1901. 4:no.3:13. 2364

New York (state). Laws, statutes, etc. Forest, fish and game law relating to the Forest preserve, fish, game and the Adirondack and International parks. . . . Albany, J.B. Lyon, 1901–4. 4v. Gives amendments each year. 2365

New York game interests. *For & Stream*, Feb. 15, 1902. 58:125–26. Reports on deer, elk and moose. 2366

New York's new protectors. *For & Stream*, June 21, 1902. 58:481. Editorial approving the new law increasing the number of game protectors from thirty-eight to fifty. 2367

Juvenal, pseud. The Adirondack man killings. *For & Stream*, Nov. 1, 1902. 59:350. Relation between new game laws and hunting accidents. 2368

Restoring the moose and elk to the Adirondacks. *Woods & Wat*, Autumn 1902. 5:no.3: 9–10. 2369

80 elk and 20 moose at large in the Adirondacks and *Woods and waters* did it. *Woods & Wat*, Winter 1902-3. 5:no.4:16. 2370

Guides make suggestions for amending game laws. *Amat Sportsman*, Feb. 1903. 28:no.4: 16–17. Editorial on recommendations of the Adirondack Guides Association. 2371

Official report of the State of New York on the moose, elk and bear of the Adirondacks. *Woods & Wat*, Spring 1903. 6:no.1:11–13. illus. Extract from the Annual Report of the Forest, Fish and Game Commission, 1902. 2372

New York state again officially declares for *Woods and waters'* moose, elk, bear and beaver movements. *Woods & Wat*, Winter 1903–4. 6:no.4:10–13. illus. 2373

Juvenal, pseud. Adirondack deer and elk. *For & Stream*, July 2, 1904. 63:8–9. Increase in Blue Mountain Lake area. 2374

Brown, Elon Rouse. The Adirondack forests. *For & Stream*, Oct. 22, 1904. 63:341. Defends Legislature and its fish and game laws. 2375

Brown's tract guides association. Fish, game and forest laws of the State of New York, relating to the game and fish of the Forest preserve and Adirondack park. Boonville, N.Y. Herald, print. 1904. 23p. Includes list of members. 2376

Governor Higgins and game protection. *Sh & Fish*, Jan. 12, 1905. 37:285. Brief note on the Governor's message. 2377

Adirondack game. *Sh & Fish*, Feb. 9, 1905. 37:365. Comment on Commissioner Middleton's report. 2378

Adirondack game losses. *Sh & Fish*, Feb. 9, 1905. 37:369–70. Report from Philo Scott. 2379

Whish, John D. The big game of the Adirondacks. *Woods & Wat*, Spring 1905. 8:no.1: 11–14. illus. From 10th Annual Report of the Forest, Fish and Game Commission. 2380

Elk and moose in the Adirondacks. *Field & S*, Oct. 1905. 10:605. 2381

Drake, John S. Adirondack moose and elk. *For & Stream*, Nov. 11, 1905. 65:396. Report on increased number. 2382

The New York game protector. *For & Stream*, Dec. 2, 1905. 65:445. Editorial on the appointment of John B. Burnham as District Game Protector. 2383

New York (state). Forest, fish and game commission. Adirondack game in 1904. Albany, Brandow printing co. 1905. 34p. Unnumbered bulletin of the Forest, Fish and Game Commission. From 10th Annual Report. 2384

Essex county bears and deer. *Sh & Fish*, Jan. 4, 1906. 39:265. Essex County desires exceptions to state fish and game laws. See letter from Peter Flint entitled "Deer Hounding in the Adirondacks" on p.268–69 of this issue and comment by Harry V. Radford, "Essex County Deer Hounding" in issue for Jan. 11, 1906, 39:291. 2385

What is the answer? *Field & S*, Mar. 1906. 10:1164. Report of an Italian greyhound lost in the Adirondacks for two years. 2386

Adirondack game. *Sh & Fish*, May 3, 1906. 40:65. Brief editorial on the progress of bill for restocking the Adirondacks with moose and beaver. Note on signing of the bill appears in the issue for May 10, 1906, 40:84–85. 2387

To identify Adirondack dogs. *For & Stream*, May 26, 1906. 66:823. Need for licensing dogs.   2388

Brown, George L. Gun licenses. *For & Stream*, Jan. 6, 1907. 68:138. Wants graded hunting licenses.   2389

The fish and game laws of New York. *Arms & Man*, Jan. 10, 1907. 41:270.   2390

The American bison society. *Arms & Man*, Jan. 17, 1907. 41:296–97. Plan to restock the Adirondacks.   2391

For a bison herd in the Adirondacks. *For & Stream*, Mar. 16, 1907. 68:409. Bill proposed by Mr. Hooper of Essex County with backing of the American Bison Society.   2392

Hornaday, William Temple. A buffalo herd for the Adirondacks. *Arms & Man*, May 9, 1907. 42:109–10. Approving bill for purchase of buffalo to be placed in Essex County.   2393

Moose and deer increasing in the Adirondacks. *Am Field*, June 29, 1907. 67:615–16. Increase due to stocking.   2394

A bison herd for the Adirondacks. *Sport Rev*, July 13, 1907. 32:33. Proposal of American Bison Society that Legislature appropriate $20,000 for establishment of herd in the Adirondacks. For comments on Governor Hughes' veto of the appropriation see issue for July 27, 32:92.   2395

Burnham, John Bird. Adirondack animals. *In* New York (state). Forest, fish and game commission. Annual reports, 1907–1908–1909. p.372–79. Part of the Annual Report of the Chief Game Protector. Statistics on deer and other animals taken.   2396

Spears, Raymond Smiley. Adirondack observations. *For & Stream*, Mar. 28, 1908. 70:496. Supply of game.   2397

New game law. *St No Mo*, July 1908. 4:50–53. Editorial criticizing "sportsman's law."   2398

Williams, A.P. The Adirondacks in summer: a game protector's trip through the forests of Herkimer and St. Lawrence counties. *Field & S*, Feb. 1909. 13:877–83. illus.   2399

Spears, Eldridge A. Adirondack game. *For & Stream*, Mar. 20, 1909. 72:456.   2400

In the Adirondacks. *For & Stream*, June 16, 1909. 54:462. Two letters, the first signed D.H.B. concerning Adirondack moose question; the second on general Adirondack conditions, signed by Raymond S. Spears. 2401

New York (state). Laws, statutes, etc. . . .Forest, fish and game law. An act for the protection of the forests, fish and game of the state. Enacted by the Legislature of nineteen

hundred and nine. Albany, J.B. Lyon, 1909. 206p.   2402

New York (state). Laws, statutes, etc. . . .Forest, fish and game law. An act for the protection of the forests, fish and game of the state. Enacted by the Legislature of nineteen hundred and nine and amended by the Legislature of nineteen hundred and ten. Albany, J.B. Lyon, 1910. 234p.   2403

Game in the Adirondacks. *For & Stream*, Jan. 7, 1911. 76:37. Report on various types of game.   2404

The need for more wardens. *For & Stream*, Apr. 8, 1911. 76:536. Letters written by Rawson L. Hayes and A Sympathiser, with editorial comment.   2405

Woodchuck, pseud. Conditions in the Adirondacks. *For & Stream*, Apr. 29, 1911. 76: 658, 677–78. Types of violations of hunting laws. Answer to Sympathiser, pseud. (no. 2405).   2406

New York (state). Laws, statutes, etc. . . .Forest, fish and game law; an act for the protection of the forests, fish and game of the state. Enacted by the Legislature of 1909 and as amended by the Legislature of 1911. Albany, J.B. Lyon, 1911. 295p.   2407

New York (state). Laws, statutes, etc. . . .Conservation law in relation to fish and game. Albany, J.B. Lyon, 1912–37. Copies located for 1912–14, 1916–26, 1928, 1930–31, 1933, 1937.   2408

Whish, John D. Closed territory increasing. *For & Stream*, Sept. 7, 1912. 79:303. Increase in posted land in Essex County.   2409

Rice, Arthur F. Practical game conservation: I. The Adirondacks. *Field & S*, Nov. 1912. 17:741–44. illus.   2410

Flint, Peter. Some game law suggestions. *For & Stream*, Mar. 7, 1914. 82:306–7. illus. Notes on deer, black bear and pheasant near Ticonderoga.   2411

Pratt, George DuPont. Checking up New York's game resources. *Am Game Prot Assn Bul*, Oct. 1918. 7:11–14. Paper read before the International Association of Fish, Game and Conservation Commissioners.   2412

New York (state). Conservation department. Syllabus of the laws relating to fish and game. Albany, 1918–37? Issued for 1918, 1921, 1922, 1923, 1937.   2413

Wild animals in the Adirondacks, on both public and private preserves, game is declared to be plentiful this year; new deer law may result in extermination of that animal. *State Service*, Sept. 1919. 3:no.9:68–71. illus.   2414

Randall, Willet. Wild turkeys in the Adirondacks. *Conservationist*, Nov. 1921. 4:170–73. illus. 2415

New York (state). Planning division. Report of Advisory committee on mosquito control and wild life conservation submitted to New York state planning council. Albany, 1936. 11p. Mimeographed. 2416

Schaefer, Paul A. Adirondack fauna. *Cloud Splitter*, May–June 1946. 9:no.3:5–6, 14. Decline of wildlife in Adirondacks. 2417

Randall, Willet. The coyote is coming! *Rural NY*, Dec. 2, 1950. 100:819. illus. Growing menace and spread of the coyote in the Adirondacks. 2418

Barick, Frank B. The edge effect of the lesser vegetation of certain Adirondack forest types with particular reference to deer and grouse. Syracuse, N.Y. 1950. 146p. illus. (Roosevelt Wildlife Bulletin, v.9, no.1; Bulletin of State College of Forestry, v.23, no.4.) 2419

Chase, Greenleaf T. DeBar mountain wildlife refuge. *Bul Schools*, Mar. 1953. 9:199–203. illus. 2420

Fish

Lamberton, A.B. A trip to the John Brown tract with young salmon in midwinter. *For & Stream*, Mar. 23, 1876. 6:100. Stocking streams. 2421

Nets in Lake Champlain. *For & Stream*, Feb. 10, 1881. 16:32. Law controlling use. 2422

Sears, George Washington. The exodus of the trout. *Am Angler*, Nov. 19, 1881. 1:19. Signed: Nessmuk. Need for restocking in the Adirondacks. 2423

Graves, Calvin. Does "restocking" pay? *Am Angler*, Mar. 11, 1882. 1:163. Worth-while in the Fulton Chain. 2424

The pending fish laws of New York. *Am Angler*, May 13, 1882. 1:313–14. Extracts from Newman bill introduced May 13, 1882. 2425

Mather, Fred. Adirondack fishes. *For & Stream*, Dec. 14, 1882. 19:390. Proposal to note distribution of fish on Stoddard map. Requests cooperation from sportsmen. 2426

Merriam, Clinton Hart. Illegal fishing in Lake Champlain. *For & Stream*, Feb. 22, 1883. 20:71–72. 2427

Lakin, C.H. A protest from a guide. *Am Angler*, May 5, 1883. 3:276. Guide from Blue Mountain Lake protests that sportsmen are fishing out of season. 2428

Matteson, O.B. Fish culture and protection in the Adirondacks. *Am Angler*, Jan. 26, 1884. 5:53. 2429

Sherman, Richard U. The Adirondack hatchery. *For & Stream*, Dec. 11, 1884. 23:391–92. 2430

Sherman, Richard U. The Adirondack state hatchery. *Am Angler*, Dec. 20–27, 1884. 6:385–87, 406–8. 2431

Lawlessness in the Adirondacks. *For & Stream*, Dec. 3, 1885. 25:369. Interference with the fish hatchery on Little Clear Pond. 2432

Portsa, pseud. The Adirondack hatchery. *For & Stream*, Feb. 4, 1886. 26:31. 2433

Green, Seth. Location of the new hatchery. *Am Angler*, Aug. 20, 1887. 12:120–21. On Mill Creek near Lake Pleasant. 2434

Green, Seth. Forest protection and the trout. *Am Angler*, Mar. 3, 1888. 13:139. Relationship between forest cover and the number of trout. 2435

Green, Seth. Fish hatchery at Blue Mountain lake. *Am Angler*, May 26, 1888. 13:334 Site selected for William W. Durant. 2436

Green, Seth. Work at the Fulton fish hatchery. *Am Angler*, June 16, 1888. 13:382. Report on fish distribution. 2437

Green, Seth. The Fulton chain hatchery. *Am Angler*, Aug. 4, 1888. 14:75. 2438

Shall the Adirondacks be stocked with bass? *For & Stream*, Oct. 15, 1891. 37:245. 2439

Northrup, M.S. Bass in the Adirondacks. *For & Stream*, Oct. 22, 1891. 37:273. Interested in stocking East Canada Lake with bass. 2440

Cheney, Albert Nelson. Black bass in Lake George. *For & Stream*, Mar. 19, 1898. 50:231. On legislative hearing for changing dates of bass season. 2441

Hallock, Charles. The black bass of Lake George. *For & Stream*, Apr. 9, 1898. 50:291. 2442

Mather, Fred. Modern fish culture in fresh and salt water... N.Y. Forest & stream publishing co. 1900. 333p. front. illus. Adirondack frost fish, p.208–10. 2443

Stone, Livingston. Sturgeon hatching in the Lake Champlain basin. *For & Stream*, Oct. 19, 1901. 57:308–9. 2444

Wolcott, W.E. The Adirondack fish mortality. *For & Stream*, July 4, 1903. 61:10. Forest fires are the chief reason for the destruction of fish in Adirondack streams. 2445

Cobb, John Nathan. The commercial fisheries of the interior lakes and rivers of New York and Vermont. *In* U.S. Commission of fish and fisheries. Annual report, 1903. 29:225–48. tables. Summary appeared in *Forest and Stream*, Apr. 15, 1905, 64:298–99. In-

cludes Lake George and Lake Champlain.
2446

Nets in Lake Champlain. *For & Stream*, Feb. 11, 1905. 64:104.   2447

Bishop, Bainbridge. Unwise fish protection on Lake Champlain. *For & Stream*, Mar. 11, 1905. 64:196–97.   2448

Water pollution and fish. *For & Stream*, Mar. 11, 1905. 64:189.   2449

New York (state). Lake Champlain fishing committee. Report of committee appointed to investigate interstate and international questions relative to fishing in Lake Champlain April 18, 1905. Albany, 1905. 6p. Assembly document 53, 1905.   2450

New York (state). Legislature. Joint committee on uniform legislation for the protection of fish in Lake Champlain. Report. . . April 2, 1908. Albany, 1908. 7p. Senate document 35, 1908.   2451

Wolcott, W.E. Adirondack trout season. *For & Stream*, Sept. 11, 1909. 73:421. Suggestions for improving fishing.   2452

Whish, John D. Black bass season in Lake George. *For & Stream*, May 25, 1912. 78:661–62. Change of the bass season due to the opposition of the Lake George Association.
2453

Whish, John D. Landlocked salmon in Lake George. *For & Stream*, July 20, 1912. 79:78. port.   2454

Flint, Peter. Are game fish increasing in the Adirondacks, and where?—A serious question confronting the Conservation commission. *For & Stream*, Jan. 3, 1914. 82:9–10, 28.
2455

Flint, Peter. Fishing conditions on Eagle lake; removal of an old and established dam causes trouble. *For & Stream*, Jan. 17, 1914. 82:82, 93. Made water level drop four feet. Answered by John D. Moore, *Forest and Stream*, Feb. 21, 1914, 82:246.   2456

Fish experts confer on Lake Champlain. *For & Stream*, Dec. 1929. 99:906–7. Editorial on Champlain region watershed survey.   2457

Dubuar, James Francis. The fisherman's problem. *NYS Ranger Sch*, 1938. p.12–15.
2458

Greeley, John R. Keys to landlocks. *NYS Con*, Feb.–Mar. 1947. 1:no.4:16–17. illus. Salmon project in several Adirondack lakes.
2459

Greeley, John R. The latest on landlocks. *NYS Con*, Dec. 1947–Jan. 1948. 2:no.3:9. Salmon in some Adirondack lakes.   2460

Greeley, John R. Four years of landlocked salmon study. Albany, New York state conservation department, 1948. 16p. illus. (Fish and Wildlife Information Bulletin no.2.) Includes investigation of Adirondack lakes and streams.   2461

Lawrence, W.M. Cranberry lake fishing threatened. *NYS Con*, Aug.–Sept. 1949. 4: no.1:34.   2462

Zilliox, Robert G. Trout restoration in the Adirondacks. *NYS Con*, Apr.–May 1951. 5: no.5:14–16. illus. Conservation Department's program.   2463

Lawrence, W.M. Cranberry lake—a new management policy. *NYS Con*, Dec. 1951–Jan. 1952. 6:no.3:30. Restocking program.
2464

Haskell, David C. A comparison of the growth of lake trout fingerlings from eggs taken in Seneca, Saranac, and Raquette lakes. *Prog Fish Cul*, Jan. 1952. 14:15–18.
2465

Haskell, David C. and others. Survival and growth of stocked lake trout yearlings from Seneca and Raquette lake breeders. *Prog Fish Cul*, Apr. 1952. 14:71–73.   2466

Lawrence, W.M. and Zilliox, Robert G. Trout restoration in the Adirondacks: progress report. *NYS Con*, June–July 1952. 6:no.6: 11. illus.   2467

Zilliox, Robert G. Trout restoration program. *NYS Con*, Apr.–May 1954. 8:no.5: 22–23. illus.   2468

Webster, Dwight A. A survival experiment and an example of selective sampling of brook trout (*Salvelinus fontinalis*) by angling and rotenone in an Adirondack pond. *NY Fish & Game J*, July 1954. 1:214–19. Pond on Brandreth Preserve.   2469

Fosburgh, Peter W. Trout from heaven. *NYS Con*, Feb.–Mar. 1955. 9:no.4:8–10. illus. chart. Stocking by plane.   2470

Adirondack league club. Fishery survey of certain waters of the Adirondack league club preserve, IV: Mountain pond, Taylor pond, Combs lake, Canachagala lake, Horn lake, Third and Fourth Bisby lakes with notes on waters previously surveyed, 1953. n.p. 1954. 52 leaves. tables. Reproduced from typewritten copy. Signed: Dwight A. Webster.
2471

Adirondack league club. Fishery management report for 1954. n.p. 1955. 26, 7 leaves. tables. Reproduced from typewritten copy. Signed: Dwight A. Webster. Appendix I, Control of whitefish and frostfish in Little Moose Lake as a possible means for increasing the food supply for landlocked salmon, by Paul C. Neth.   2472

Bear

Sportsmen and naturalists enthusiastically endorse *Woods and waters'* new black bear campaign. *Woods & Wat*, Spring 1902. 5: no.1:16–17. 2473

How shall we save the black bear? *Woods & Wat*, Summer–Autumn 1902. 5:no.2:16–17; 5:no.3:17. 2474

And now the black bear shall be saved. *Woods and waters'* bill is ready for the Legislature. *Woods & Wat*, Winter 1902–3. 5:no. 4:20–21. 2475

Woods and waters black bear preservation bill has passed the N.Y. Senate. *Woods & Wat*, Spring 1903. 6:no.1:19–20. 2476

At the last moment of the Legislature the enemies of game protection defeat the black bear preservation bill. *Woods & Wat*, Summer 1903. 6:no.2:20–21. 2477

Woods and waters will resume the black bear preservation fight in the coming Legislature. *Woods & Wat*, Autumn 1903. 6:no.3:20–21. 2478

Woods and waters' black bear preservation bill again in the N.Y. Legislature. *Woods & Wat*, Winter 1903–4. 6:no.4:22. 2479

Ransacker, pseud. The wild and woolly Adirondacks. *For & Stream*, Feb. 20, 1904. 62: 146–47. Long-distance humorous shots made by a man from California at New Yorkers, and the Adirondack bear question. 2480

Brown, George L. The Adirondack bears. *For & Stream*, Feb. 27, 1904. 62:168. Against protection of the bear in Essex County. 2481

Brown, George L. The folly of bear protection. *For & Stream*, Mar. 12, 1904. 62:211. 2482

Spears, John Randolph. The Adirondack bears. *For & Stream*, Mar. 26, 1904. 62:251–52. A plea for protection of bears in the Adirondacks. 2483

Sweeping legislative victory. *Woods and waters'* black bear preservation bill becomes a law... *Woods & Wat*, Spring 1904. 7:no.1:22. 2484

Radford, Harry V. Is the bear a game animal? *Sh & Fish*, Oct. 12, 1905. 39:9–10. 2485

Bears in the Adirondacks. *For & Stream*, June 9, 1906. 66:903. Editorial opposing the bear protection law. 2486

Chase, Greenleaf T. Bear facts (2). *NYS Con*, Oct.–Nov. 1954. 9:no.2:2. 2487

Beaver

Rice, Arthur F. Adirondack beaver. *For & Stream*, Dec. 5, 1896. 47:445. Increase of beaver in St. Regis area. 2488

Spears, Eldridge A. Adirondack beaver. *For & Stream*, June 13, 1903. 60:464–65. Report of beaver along the Indian River. 2489

Beavers for the Adirondacks. *Sh & Fish*, Dec. 15, 1904. 37:207. See also editorials in issues for Aug. 17 and Sept. 21, 1905, 38:365, 445. 2490

Beaver's restoration already begun. *Woods & Wat*, Winter 1904–5. 7:no.4:12. illus. 2491

Adirondack beaver. *Sh & Fish*, Jan. 4, 1905. 39:265. Report on beaver liberated near Big Moose Lake. 2492

Beaver for the Adirondacks. *Sport Rev*, May 13, 1905. 27:511. Release of more beaver by Harry V. Radford on John Brown's Tract. 2493

Beaver signs at Big Moose lake. *Sh & Fish*, Oct. 19, 1905. 39:29. Reported by J.H. Higby. 2494

Adirondack beaver signs. *Sh & Fish*, Apr. 26, 1906. 40:46. 2495

Radford, Harry V. Bringing back the beaver: its successful reintroduction to the Adirondack region. *Four Tr News*, Apr. 1906. 10: 274–76. Reprinted in *Forest Leaves*, Spring 1907, 4:no.1:36–41. 2496

Adirondack beaver. *For & Stream*, Apr. 28, 1906. 66:671. illus. Letters signed G. Frank Gray and D.F. Sperry on beaver stocking. Includes a short history of the program. 2497

Radford, Harry V. Return of the beaver. *St No Mo*, July 1906. 1:no.3:81–82. illus. 2498

The Adirondack beaver. *For & Stream*, Oct. 12, 1907. 69:567. Editorial on the restocking program. 2499

Hofer, T.E. Catching beaver for the Adirondacks. *For & Stream*, Oct. 12, 1907. 69:571–73. illus. Capture in Montana and distribution in New York lakes and streams. 2500

Willoughby, Charles H. Beavers and the Adirondacks. *Conservationist*, May 1920. 3:67–70. illus. 2501

Peck, Robert B. The renaissance of the beaver from an interesting experiment in 1905; the restocking of these industrious animals has become a vexatious problem in the Adirondacks today. *For & Stream*, Apr. 1921. 91: 152–54, 182–87. illus. 2502

Yo, pseud. Beaver for Adirondacks. *For & Stream*, Aug. 1921. 91:358. Letter to editor in answer to Peck (2502). 2503

Wilson, H.G. The beavers of the Adirondack country. *Fur News*, Aug. 1922. 36:no.2:47. History of restocking. 2504

New York (state). Conservation department. Black gold: the story of the beaver in New York state, by Gardiner Bump and Arthur H.

Cook... Albany, 1941. 16p. illus. map. (Management Bulletin no.2.)   2505

Patric, Earl F. A beaver management program for the Huntington forest. 117 leaves. mounted photographs, tables, charts, diagr. map. Master's thesis, State University of New York, College of Forestry, Syracuse, 1952. Typescript. Abstract in Graduate Theses, p.57.   2506

Deer

Deer slaughter in the Adirondacks. *For & Stream*, Nov. 26, 1874. 3:249. Editorial on guides killing deer near Keeseville.   2507

Fenton, Charles. Adirondack slaughter. *For & Stream*, Mar. 18, 1875. 4:91.   2508

Butchering deer in the Adirondacks. *For & Stream*, June 7, 1877. 8:287. Series of letters on hunting out of season.   2509

Shurter, Joseph W. The Adirondacks — "floating." *For & Stream*, May 26, 1881. 16: 328–29. Deer hounding on Cedar River, Hamilton County.   2510

Ondack, Adrion, pseud. Hounding vs still-hunting. *For & Stream*, June 2, 1881. 16:349. Deer slaughter and the need of game protection.   2511

Hardy. The Adirondack doe slaughter. *For & Stream*, July 20, 1882. 18:490.   2512

Fuller, A.R. Adirondack deer complications. *For & Stream*, July 10, 1884. 22:467. Need for enforcement of game laws.   2513

Adirondack deer hounding. *For & Stream*, Dec. 11, 1884. 23:386. Letters on deer hounding signed AuSable and Cap Lock.   2514

G., B.A. Deer in the Adirondacks. *For & Stream*, Dec. 18, 1884. 23:406. Wants deer hounding prohibited.   2515

Adirondack deer hounting. *For & Stream*, Jan. 8, 1885. 23:465–67. Letters by Seymour Van Santvoord, "Fair Play" and C.L. Parker discussing deer hunting and hounding.   2516

Deer in the Adirondacks. *For & Stream*, Jan. 15, 1885. 23:485. Letters signed "Cap Lock" and C.W. Puffer.   2517

F.; M.L. Deer in the Adirondacks. *For & Stream*, Jan. 22, 1885. 23:506. Objection to deer hounding.   2518

Adirondack deer hounding. *For & Stream*, Jan. 29, 1885. 24:8–9. Communications signed "A Trustee of the St. Lawrence Game Club," I.H.W., and M.S. Northrup. In favor of abolishing hounding. See also editorial in Jan. 15, 1885 issue, p.481, "Adirondack Deer Hounding."   2519

St. Lawrence game club, a trustee. *For & Stream*, Jan. 29, 1885. 24:2. Adirondack deer hounding.   2520

Leonard, Peter A. Deer in the Adirondacks. *For & Stream*, Feb. 12, 1885. 24:47. From a report made to commissioner Richard U. Sherman. Opposes deer hounding.   2521

L. Deer in the Adirondacks. *For & Stream*, Feb. 19, 1885. 24:66. Guides start hunting before season opens.   2522

Adirondack deer law. *For & Stream*, Mar. 5, 1885. 24:101. Editorial on Curtis bill forbidding hounding.   2523

The deer hounding bill passed. *For & Stream*, Apr. 30, 1885. 24:265. Editorial on passage of non-hounding bill.   2524

The deer hounding law. *For & Stream*, June 18, 1885. 24:405. Editorial asking for observation of new non-hounding law.   2525

Adirondack deer. *For & Stream*, June 25, July 16, 1885; Jan. 21, Jan. 28, Feb. 18, 1886; Dec. 29, 1887; Mar. 22, 1888; Oct. 16, 1890. 24:425, 485; 25:501, 506; 26:1, 69; 29:441; 30:165; 35:249. Editorials and letters on deer hounding.   2526

A word to some northwoods guides. *For & Stream*, July 2, 1885. 24:445. Editorial on enforcement of deer hounding law.   2527

W., W.C. The Adirondack deer. *For & Stream*, Aug. 20, 1885. 25:66. For abolishment of deer jacking.   2528

Guide, pseud. Deer in the Adirondacks. *For & Stream*, Aug. 27, 1885. 25:87. Stop night hunting.   2529

P., J.L. Adirondack deer. *For & Stream*, Sept. 3, 1885. 25:104. Favors abolishing deer jacking.   2530

Panthers and deer. *For & Stream*, Sept. 10, 1885. 25:121. Editorial on the increase of panthers in the Adirondacks.   2531

Deer in the Adirondacks. *For & Stream*, Sept. 17, 1885. 25:147. Reprinted from the New York *Herald*. Sportsmen do not obey law.   2532

Fenton, Charles. The Adirondack deer. *For & Stream*, Oct. 15, 1885. 25:227. Lack of enforcement of the deer hounding law.   2533

Musset, pseud. Adirondack deer and hounds. *For & Stream*, Oct. 22, 1885. 25:247. Approval of non-hounding law. Need for enforcement in Beaver River area.   2534

Deer and panthers. *For & Stream*, Oct. 22, 1885. 25:241. Editorial on the inadequacy of the bounty on panthers.   2535

Ampersand, pseud. Deer in the Adirondacks. *For & Stream*, Nov. 19, 1885. 25:327. Wants to know effect of non-hounding law.   2536

Ned, pseud. Deer near Lake George. *For & Stream*, Dec. 3, 1885. 25:367. Approving the deer hounding law.   2537

Cap Lock, pseud. The Adirondack deer. *For & Stream*, Dec. 10, 1885. 25:385. Lack of enforcement of deer law in Moose River country. 2538

Musset, pseud. The Adirondack deer. *For & Stream*, Dec. 17, 1885. 25:405. More efficient force needed for enforcement of the law. 2539

The Adirondack deer law. *For & Stream*, Dec. 31, 1885. 25:441. Editorial on results of deer hounding law. 2540

Deer in the Adirondacks. *For & Stream*, Dec. 31, 1885. 25:449–50. Many points of view on non-hounding law. 2541

Nitram, pseud. Save the Adirondack deer. *For & Stream*, Feb. 11, 1886. 26:48–49. Approval of floating. 2542

The deer hounding bill. *For & Stream*, Feb. 25, Mar. 4, Mar. 18, 1886. 26:81, 105, 147. Editorial, discussion and communications. 2543

The Utica association. *For & Stream*, Feb. 25, 1886. 26:87. Their stand on deer protection in the Adirondacks. 2544

The sentiment against hounding. *For & Stream*, Mar. 11, 1886. 26:127. illus. Series of letters on deer hounding. 2545

Mr. Palmer's shy deer. *For & Stream*, Mar. 18, 1886. 26:141. Editorial on Assemblyman Palmer's speech in favor of hounding. 2546

The anti-hounding law. *For & Stream*, Mar. 25, 1886. 26:165–67. Arguments in favor of the law. 2547

Bishop, Bainbridge. The anti-deer hounding law. *For & Stream*, Apr. 1, 1886. 26:184. 2548

Deer hounding. *For & Stream*, Apr. 8, 1886. 26:205–6. Text of bill before the New York Senate. 2549

The deer hounding bill. *For & Stream*, Apr. 22, 1886. 26:244. Reprints of newspaper articles on Senate hearings on the deer hounding bill. See also editorial in April 8 issue, p.201. 2550

A shy senator. *For & Stream*, May 20, 1886. 26:325. Editorial on Senator Cullen of New York, who opposed the deer hounding bill. 2551

X. June deer floating. *For & Stream*, July 8, 1886. 26:469. Guides trying to catch offenders. See also editorial on p.465. 2552

The boycott in the woods. *For & Stream*, July 29, 1886. 27:1. Editorial suggesting a boycott of landlords who defy deer law. 2553

Amrach, pseud. Adirondack deer. *For & Stream*, Nov. 4, 1886. 27:287. Objection to disregard of law. 2554

Rushton, J.H. Adirondack deer. *For & Stream*, Feb. 24, 1887. 27:86. Deer need more protection. 2555

Mr. Parker's deer. *For & Stream*, July 7, July 14, 1887. 28:509, 529. Editorials on a man who bragged about killing deer out of season. In issue for July 14 (28:533) A.M. Parker claims he was telling a yarn. 2556

P., C.B. Adirondack guides. *For & Stream*, Oct. 27, 1887. 29:267. Complaint about guides using dogs unlawfully. 2557

Portsa, pseud. Adirondack deer. *For & Stream*, Nov. 4, 1887. 29:287. Appreciation of the deer hounding law. 2558

Adirondack deer hounding. *For & Stream*, Dec. 22, 1887. 29:429. Need for a better law. 2559

Roosevelt, Robert Barnwell. Adirondack deer hounding. *For & Stream*, Dec. 29, 1887. 29:448. Thinks abolishment of hounding might discourage sportsmen. 2560

Spears, John Randolph. Adirondack abominations. *For & Stream*, July 19, 1888. 30:513. Approval of editorial with same title in July 12 issue (30:489). 2561

Dr. Bailey and his deer. *For & Stream*, Aug. 9, 1888. 31:46. Arrest and escape of unlawful hunter. 2562

C., H. Hound and deer. *For & Stream*, Aug. 16, 1888. 31:63. Deer hounding in the Adirondacks. Probably by Horace Caruthers. 2563

Caruthers, Horace. Adirondack deer and hounds. *For & Stream*, Sept. 27, 1888. 31:186. 2564

Shall Adirondack does be spared? *For & Stream*, Nov. 8, 1888. 31:301. Editorial on increased sentiment for protecting does. For approval, see article by E.S.W. "Save Adirondack Does," Nov. 29, 31:368. 2565

Musset, pseud. Adirondack deer. *For & Stream*, Dec. 27, 1888. 31:457. Advocating protection of does. 2566

A Veteran, pseud. Adirondack deer. *For & Stream*, Feb. 7, 1889. 32:47. More legislative protection for deer needed. 2567

Cap Lock, pseud. Adirondack deer. *For & Stream*, Feb. 14, 1889. 32:64. Approving a resolution of the Black River Fish and Game Association. 2568

Nitram, pseud. Adirondack deer. *For & Stream*, Mar. 7, 1889. 32:132–33. Note on the decrease in number of deer. 2569

Musset, pseud. Adirondack deer. *For & Stream*, Oct. 17, 1889. 33:245. Opposed to deer hounding. 2570

Holberton, Wakeman. The Adirondack deer law. *For & Stream*, Oct. 31, 1889. 33:287. Approves limiting the bag. See also article by The Law, pseud. "The Adirondack Deer Law," p.287. 2571

Musset, pseud. Adirondack deer. *For & Stream*, Dec. 5, 1889. 33:385. Need for new game laws. 2572

Gordon, William H. The Adirondack deer law. *For & Stream*, Dec. 26, 1889. 33:452. Hunting season too long. 2573

A Veteran, pseud. Adirondack deer. *For & Stream*, Jan. 23, 1890. 34:6. Objection to a resolution by a group of hotelkeepers and guides extending the season for hunting. 2574

Snap shots. *For & Stream*, Mar. 20, 1890. 34:165. Editorial on Adirondack deer hounding. 2575

B., J.W. Adirondack deer hounding. *For & Stream*, Sept. 18, 1890. 35:169. Protest against hounding. 2576

L., D.C. Adirondack deer. *For & Stream*, Oct. 23, 1890. 35:270. Deer hounding. 2577

Musset, pseud. Adirondack deer supply. *For & Stream*, Nov. 6, 1890. 35:311. Answer to L. (Oct. 23, 1890) on hounding in the Beaver River area. 2578

Saint Lawrence, pseud. New York fish and game interests. *For & Stream*, Dec. 11, 1890. 35:414–15. Discussion of hounding and floating. Suggests protective measures. 2579

Cap Lock, pseud. Adirondack deer. *For & Stream*, Jan. 15, 1891. 35:513. Advocates limiting the bag of hunters. 2580

Musset, pseud. Adirondack deer. *For & Stream*, Oct. 22, 1891. 37:271. Opposed to deer hounding. 2581

Wolcott, W.E. Report on Adirondack deer. *For & Stream*, Jan. 19, 1893. 40:54. 2582

Burnham, John Bird. Adirondack deer law. *For & Stream*, July 29, 1893. 41:75. 2583

Wolcott, W.E. Adirondack deer season of 1893. *For & Stream*, Feb. 3, 1894. 42:92–93. Includes estimated number killed in various areas. 2584

Portsa, pseud. Adirondack deer. *For & Stream*, Apr. 21, 1894. 42:335. Report of game checking trip. 2585

F., R.P. Adirondack deer. *For & Stream*, Sept. 29, 1894. 43:267. Persecution of deer. 2586

Lloyd, Herbert M. The Adirondack deer. *For & Stream*, Dec. 29, 1894. 43:559. Need to change hunting laws. 2587

Musset, pseud. The Adirondack deer. *For & Stream*, Jan. 5, 1895. 44:8. Wants better protection for deer. 2588

Morton, Levi Parsons. New York forestry and the deer. *For & Stream*, Jan. 12, 1895. 44:29. From the Governor's message to the Legislature. 2589

Wolcott, W.E. The Adirondack deer. *For & Stream*, Feb. 23, 1895. 44:150. Extracts from Utica *Herald;* annual summary of deer situation in the north woods. 2590

New York deer. *For & Stream*, Mar. 30, 1895. 44:241. Editorial on Niles bill forbidding hounding and killing does with young. 2591

Spears, Raymond Smiley. Slaughtering Adirondack deer. *For & Stream*, June 22, 1895. 44:509. 2592

Spears, Raymond Smiley. Those Adirondack dead deer. *For & Stream*, July 6, 1895. 45:7. 2593

Rawson, Edward Sidney. The Adirondack deer supply. *For & Stream*, July 27, 1895. 45:74. 2594

Spears, Raymond Smiley. Adirondack deer. *For & Stream*, Sept. 14, 1895. 45:227. Wants hounding abolished. 2595

Allen, J.C. Adirondack deer. *For & Stream*, Nov. 9, 1895. 45:402. Objection to deer hounding. 2596

Whitney, Casper W. The passing of the Adirondack deer. *Harper W*, Nov. 23, 1895. 39:1119–20. illus. Signed: C.W.W. Drawing by E.M. Ashe. Against hounding and jacking. 2597

Spears, Raymond Smiley. Adirondack deer hounding. *For & Stream*, Dec. 7, 1895. 45:493. 2598

Fox, William Freeman. Report of superintendent of forests on the Adirondack deer. *In* New York (state). Fisheries, game and forest commission. Annual report, 1895. p.159–204. plates. Sherrill lists under title: "The Adirondack Deer, Their Habits and Characteristics. . ." Followed by "Digest of Reports and Opinions Relating to the Adirondack Deer and to Laws for Their Protection," p.204–40. 2599

Adirondack deer. *For & Stream*, Jan. 4, 1896. 46:11. Letters from J.C. Allen, M. Schenck and Charles Fenton on various phases of deer hunting. 2600

Adirondack deer. *For & Stream*, Jan. 11, 1896. 46:30–31. Letters by F.E. Oliver, J.H.R. and R.S. Spears demanding better protection for deer. 2601

Adirondack deer. *For & Stream*, Jan. 25, 1896. 46:67. Editorial in favor of a bill forbidding the killing of deer in water. 2602

Adirondack deer. *For & Stream*, Jan. 25, 1896. 46:72. Letters by M. Schenck and Musset on deer protection by prohibiting hounding and floating. 2603

The Adirondack deer supply. *For & Stream*, Feb. 8, 1896. 46:116. Letters by William H. Hacker and P.S.R. on the scarcity of deer. 2604

Forbes, John E. Adirondack deer. *For & Stream*, Feb. 15, 1896. 46:135. Wants good hunting law properly enforced. 2605

Graves, James M. Adirondack deer. *For & Stream*, Feb. 15, 1896. 46:135. Sportsmen should keep their representatives informed of need of game preservation. 2606

Adirondack deer and guides. *For & Stream*, Mar. 7, 1896. 46:196. Letters on necessary changes in deer laws, signed S.E. Stanton, P.S.R. and John E. Forbes. 2607

Higby, J.H. Adirondack deer. *For & Stream*, Mar. 21, 1896. 46:236. Opposing hounding. 2608

Parker, Clarence L. Adirondack deer. *For & Stream*, Apr. 4, 1896. 46:273. Need of tightening the deer laws. 2609

Cayadutta, pseud. Adirondack deer. *For & Stream*, May 2, 1896. 46:356. Letter on dogs running deer. 2610

Spears, Raymond Smiley. Adirondack deer. *For & Stream*, May 2, 1896. 46:356. Objects to floating and hounding of deer. 2611

Hunter, Jack. Adirondack deer. *For & Stream*, May 9, 1896. 46:375. Need stricter enforcement, not more stringent laws. 2612

Adirondack deer. *For & Stream*, May 30, 1896. 46:429. Editorial on new legislation shortening the time for hounding and jacking. 2613

Spears, Raymond Smiley. Does deer hounding make deer shy? *For & Stream*, July 25, 1896. 47:66. 2614

Deerslayer, pseud. Defends deer roping. *For & Stream*, Oct. 31, 1896. 47:346. See also a criticism, "Confessions of a Deer Slayer," Nov. 7, p.369; Deerslayer's reply, Nov. 7, p.369, and a group of letters "Water Killing Deer," Nov. 14, p.385. 2615

Deerslayer, pseud. Water killing deer. *For & Stream*, Nov. 21, 1896. 47:406. Answers criticism of Nov. 7, p.369. 2616

Schenck, M. Deer and hounding. *For & Stream*, Dec. 5, 1896. 47:446. Increase of deer in Lake George area due to prohibition of hounding in Washington County. 2617

Fox, William Freeman. Adirondack deer facts and figures. *For & Stream*, Jan. 16, 1897. 47:46–48. From Report of the Superintendent of Forests. 2618

Ran into a deer. *For & Stream*, Mar. 27, 1897. 48:254. Bicycle hit deer near Morehouseville. 2619

A Sportsman, pseud. Adirondack deer killing. *For & Stream*, Aug. 14, 1897. 49:128. Lack of law enforcement at Raquette Lake. 2620

Sanger, William Cary. The Adirondack deer law. *In* Grinnell, G.B. Trail and campfire; the book of the Boone & Crockett club. N.Y. 1897. p.264–78. 2621

Rice, Arthur F. Adirondack deer and the laws. *For & Stream*, Oct. 8, 1898. 51:287. 2622

Spears, Raymond Smiley. Adirondack deer, guides and woodsmen. *For & Stream*, Oct. 15, 1898. 51:305. Increase of game due to new law. 2623

Burnham, John Bird. The Adirondack deer law. *For & Stream*, Nov. 12, 1898. 51:391. Signed: J.B.B. Followed by editorial comment from Boonville *Herald*. 2624

Spears, Raymond Smiley. Adirondack hounding. *For & Stream*, Feb. 11, 1899. 52:109. 2625

B. The Adirondack deer law. *For & Stream*, Mar. 18, 1899. 52:206. 2626

Woodward, J.H. Protection of deer in the Adirondacks. *For & Stream*, Feb. 4, 1899. 52:86. 2627

Higby, J.H. Adirondack deer and hounds. *For & Stream*, Apr. 1, 1899. 52:246. 2628

Adirondack deer and snows. *For & Stream*, Apr. 8, 1899. 52:268. Suffering and death of many deer due to heavy snows. 2629

Adirondack wolves and deer. *For & Stream*, Apr. 15, 1899. 52:290. Quotes from letters of Chief Protector Pond. 2630

An Adirondack hound at large case. *For & Stream*, July 15, 1899. 53:47. Fining Frank C. Ives for allowing dogs to run deer. 2631

An Adirondack deer hounding case. *For & Stream*, Aug. 12, 1899. 53:121. Editorial comment on the Ives case. 2632

Burnham, John Bird. Adirondack deer hounding. *For & Stream*, Oct. 28, 1899. 53:345. 2633

B. The Adirondack deer law. *For & Stream*, Nov. 11, 1899. 53:384–86. 2634

Burnham, John Bird. Adirondack deer hounding. *For & Stream*, Nov. 18, 1899. 53:410–11. 2635

Adirondack deer law violators punished. *For & Stream*, Dec. 2, 1899. 53:444. 2636

Gale, J. Thomson. Hounding deer at Tupper lake. *Recreation*, Jan. 1900. 12:38. Deplores illegal use of dogs. 2637

Learned, John A. The Adirondack deer. *For & Stream*, Oct. 13, 1900. 55:289. Letter to editor on shortening of deer season. Comments on Juvenal's article in Oct. 6 issue, 55:267.　　　　　　　　　　　　2638

Adirondack hounding. *For & Stream*, Nov. 10, 1900. 55:370. On violation of deer law.
　　　　　　　　　　　　　　　　　　2639

Mr. Woodruff's deer. *For & Stream*, Dec. 8, 1900. 55:441. Editorial on the persecution of the Lieutenant-Governor of New York state for killing deer out of season.　　　2640

Shurter, Joseph W. The Adirondack deer. *For & Stream*, Dec. 29, 1900. 55:508. On the length and time of the deer hunting season.
　　　　　　　　　　　　　　　　　　2641

Woodruff, Timothy L. The Adirondack deer. *For & Stream*, Jan. 26, 1901. 56:69–70. Letter from the Lieutenant-Governor read at Brown's Tract Guides Association meeting.
　　　　　　　　　　　　　　　　　　2642

R., J.H. An Adirondack deer snarer convicted. *For & Stream*, Apr. 20, 1901. 56:308. Conviction of Bonno.　　　　　　　2643

West, Rodney. The anti-hounding law. *Recreation*, June 1901. 14:445.　　　　　　2644

Hull, George S. The Adirondack deer. *For & Stream*, July 6, 1901. 57:5. For a later and shorter hunting season.　　　　　　2645

Gale, J. Thomson. The Adirondack deer. *For & Stream*, July 27, 1901. 57:66–67. Need for guides and sportsmen to obey game law.
　　　　　　　　　　　　　　　　　　2646

Juvenal, pseud. Adirondack notes. *For & Stream*, Dec. 7, 1901. 57:446–47. Suggests a new law for hunting Adirondack deer.　2647

Stanton, Sanford E. Adirondack deer. *For & Stream*, Dec. 14, 1901. 57:471. Wants hunting season closed before heavy snows.　　2648

Lg. Adirondack deer. *For & Stream*, Dec. 21, 1901. 57:487–88. Need for additional protection.　　　　　　　　　　　2649

Levenson, Henry Astbury. Adirondack deer. *For & Stream*, Dec. 28, 1901. 57:512. Signed: The Old Shekarry. Deer not dying out.　2650

Wolcott, W.E. The Adirondack deer. *For & Stream*, Nov. 22, 1902. 59:410. Review of the hunting season.　　　　　　　　2651

Graves, James M. The New York deer law. *Recreation*, Nov. 1902. 17:361–62. Answered by Ed. Fay in Jan. 1903 issue, 18:33–34. 2652

Levenson, Henry Astbury. The Adirondack deer. *For & Stream*, Jan. 3, 1903. 60:10. Signed: The Old Shekarry. On shortening the deer season.　　　　　　　2653

The Adirondack deer. *For & Stream*, Feb. 7, 1903. 60:106. Extract from report of the New York Forest, Fish and Game Commission.
　　　　　　　　　　　　　　　　　　2654

Wolcott, W.E. Adirondack deer. *For & Stream*, Aug. 29, 1903. 61:166. Report on the number of deer.　　　　　　　　2655

Wolcott, W.E. Adirondack deer season. *For & Stream*, Nov. 21, 1903. 61:401–2.　　2656

Shurter, Joseph W. Adirondack deer hunting. *For & Stream*, Jan. 9, 1904. 62:28. Followed by statement of Peter Flint from the Elizabethtown *Post and Gazette*. Opposes suggestion to shorten hunting season.　　2657

Cap Lock, pseud. Adirondack deer. *For & Stream*, Jan. 16, 1904. 62:48. Opposes suggestion to shorten hunting season.　　2658

The Adirondack deer. *For & Stream*, Feb. 6, 1904. 62:105–6. Symposium giving views of N.H. Davis, J.H. Rushton, C.L. Parker on changes in the deer law.　　　　　2659

Pond, J. Warren. The Adirondack deer supply. *For & Stream*, Apr. 2, 1904. 62:272–73. Report on number of deer.　　　　2660

Wolcott, W.E. The Adirondack deer season. *For & Stream*, Nov. 26, 1904. 63:449.　2661

Wolcott, W.E. Adirondack deer hunting. *For & Stream*, Dec. 2, 1905. 65:454. A review of the season.　　　　　　　　2662

West, Rodney. Restoring hounding. *For & Stream*, Jan. 6, 1906. 66:18–19.　　2663

Wolcott, W.E. The Adirondack deer situation. *For & Stream*, Sept. 15, 1906. 67:414.
　　　　　　　　　　　　　　　　　　2664

F., C.S. The Adirondack deer season. *For & Stream*, Oct. 13, 1906. 67:577. Opposes change in deer season from September 1 to October 1.
　　　　　　　　　　　　　　　　　　2665

The Adirondack deer law. *For & Stream*, Oct. 27, 1906. 67:647. Editorial.　　　2666

Bradshaw, W.A. The Adirondack deer law. *For & Stream*, Nov. 10, 1906. 67:736.　2667

The lumber camp deer butchers. *For & Stream*, Dec. 1, 1906. 67:855. Killing of deer out of season to feed the lumber camp crews.
　　　　　　　　　　　　　　　　　　2668

Bradshaw, W.A. Save the deer. *For & Stream*, Dec. 15, 1906. 67:944. Deer law.　　2669

Shurter, Joseph W. Adirondack deer. *For & Stream*, Dec. 22, 1906. 67:985. Deer law. 2670

The Adirondack deer. *For & Stream*, Mar. 9, 1907. 68:367. Editorial urging that more care be taken of the deer in winter to prevent great mortality through starvation.　　2671

Timber cutters and the deer. *For & Stream*, Apr. 6, 1907. 68:527. Editorial on shooting deer for lumber camp meat.　　　　2672

The Adirondack deer season. *For & Stream*, July 27, 1907. 69:127. Changes in the deer hunting laws due to passage of Mills Assembly bills. 2673

Wolcott, W.E. New York deer season. *For & Stream*, Sept. 28, 1907. 69:493. Discussion of amended deer hunting law. 2674

Deer hounding. *For & Stream*, Oct. 12, 1907. 69:567. Unlawful in New York state. 2675

Shurter, Joseph W. The Adirondack deer season. *For & Stream*, Dec. 14, 1907. 69:935. Advises changes in law (because of increase of deer). 2676

Gibbs, A.D. How about hounding deer? *Field & S*, Dec. 1907. 12:686. Resolution to allow deer hounding approved by the Essex County Republican convention. 2677

Temple, A.D. Deer hunting with dogs. *Field & S*, Jan. 1908. 12:769–70. In favor of hounding. 2678

Parker, Clarence L. Open season for deer. *For & Stream*, Feb. 15, 1908. 70:256. Need for open season due to great increase in number of deer. 2679

Gibbs, A.D. More about deer hounding. *Field & S*, Feb. 1908. 12:866–67. 2680

Parker, Clarence L. Mistaken for deer shootings. *St No Mo*, Feb. 1908. 3:85–91. Letter on the foolishness of shortening the deer season. Followed by letter by A.M. Church, "An Association View," p.92–93 (against deer hounding), and two editorials "Which Shall It Be?" p.93–101, and "A Safe and Sane Law," p.101–2. 2681

Open season for deer. *St No Mo*, Mar. 1908. 3:163–69. Editorial in favor of longer season. 2682

West, Rodney. A good law for the deer. *Field & S*, Mar. 1908. 12:967. 2683

The deer hounding question. *St No Mo*, Apr. 1908. 3:219–24. Editorial, followed on p.225–26 by endorsement of "Safe and Sane Law." 2684

Parker, Clarence L. Deer protection. *For & Stream*, Jan. 9, 1909. 72:54–55. Suggestions for protecting deer in the Adirondacks. 2685

West, Rodney. How Adirondack deer wintered. *For & Stream*, Mar. 26, 1910. 74:498. Report on deer. 2686

Wolcott, W.E. The deer season. *For & Stream*, Apr. 23, 1910. 74:657. Changes needed in the deer laws. 2687

West, Rodney. Deer hounding again, or not? *For & Stream*, Dec. 17, 31, 1910. 75:975, 1059. In favor of anti-hounding law but opposed to the destruction of permanent camps. 2688

W., J.G. Killing does. *For & Stream*, Nov. 30, 1912. 79:688–89. A few dead does left in woods because of new doe law. 2689

Spears, Raymond Smiley. The New York doe law. *For & Stream*, Feb. 1, 1913. 80:141. Thinks it will make for fewer shooting accidents if hunters have to distinguish between bucks and does. 2690

Flint, Peter. Shall the buck law be changed? Together with a discussion on conservation matters by one who has studied for years conditions in N.Y. state. *For & Stream*, Jan. 24, 1914. 82:103–4. port. 2691

Cleaves, Howard H. A splendid winter for deer. *Conservationist*, Mar. 1919. 2:38–41. illus. 2692

Deer of New York forests in danger, new law permitting killing of does may lead to extermination of state's big game, it also results in the taking of more human life. *State Service*, Nov. 1919. 3:no.11:3–5. illus. 2693

A review of the deer season. *Conservationist*, Dec. 1919. 2:190–91. 2694

New York (state). Conservation commission. Whitetail deer in New York; a study of the operation of the buck law, by Warwick S. Carpenter. Albany, New York state Conservation commission, 1919? 31p. illus. tables. 2695

Adirondack deer herd threatened with extermination. *Lit Digest*, Feb. 21, 1920. 64:no.8:115–19. 2696

Everett, Edward A. Should the one-deer law be repealed? Lively controversy over legislation relating to the shooting of deer in the state Forest preserve—Governor Smith and Conservation commission ask for repeal. *State Service*, Mar. 1920. 4:207–9. port. 2697

Wilcox, Allan H. Save the deer. *Up Mo*, Mar. 1941. 1:no.12:16–17. illus. 2698

Darrow, Robert W. The whitetail in New York. *NYS Con*, Dec. 1947–Jan. 1948. 2:no.3:10–13. Review of legislation affecting deer hunting in New York. 2699

Fowler, Barnett. The Bear pond deer jacking case. *NYS Con*, Feb.–Mar. 1949. 3:no.4:27. ports. A detailed report of case noted briefly in preceding issue. 2700

Kerst, Dwinal G. The Bear pond deer jacking case. *NYS Con*, Feb.–Mar. 1949. 3:no.4:26–27. ports. Capture of Silas Nadeau and Howard Schryer. 2701

Darrow, Robert W. What's happening to our deer range? *NYS Con*, Dec. 1950–Jan. 1951. 5:no.3:6–8. illus. 2702

Adirondack deer problem. *NYS Con*, Feb.–Mar. 1952. 6:no.4:28–29. map. On proposed legislation to establish an open season for antlerless deer. 2703

Tranquille, Dante. Operation reindeer. *No Country Life*, Winter 1952. 6:no.1:36–40.

illus. Adirondack League Club's deer feeding program; seven photographs taken at Honnedaga.   2704

Cheatum, Evelyn Leonard. Adirondack deer. A new proposal for their management in wilderness areas. *NYS Con*, Apr.–May 1953. 7:no.5:5. map.   2705

Notes on the 1953 deer season. *NYS Con*, Feb.–Mar. 1954. 8:no.4:32–33.   2706

Cheatum, Evelyn Leonard. Wilderness deer. *NYS Con*, June–July 1954. 8:no.6:25–27. illus. map. Legislation for controlled harvest of antlerless deer. See also "Antlerless Deer Season in Wilderness Areas," Aug.–Sept. 1954 issue, p.29.   2707

Severinghaus, C.W. The Moose river plains. *NYS Con*, Aug.–Sept. 1954. 9:no.1:8–9. illus. map. With particular reference to deer. 2708

Drahos, Nicholas and Irving, Roy. New York's first 2-deer special season. *NYS Con*, Oct.–Nov. 1954. 9:no.2:26–27. illus. Issuing permits for wilderness deer season. See Letters to the Editor in Dec. 1954–Jan. 1955 issue, p.34–35.   2709

Bromley, A.W. Report on the experimental 2-deer season in the Adirondacks. *NYS Con*, Feb.–Mar. 1955. 9:no.4:25–26. illus. chart.
                                       2710

Bromley, A.W. The 1954 deer kill in New York. *NYS Con*, Apr.–May 1955. 9:no.5:34–35. table.   2711

Bromley, A.W. Spotlight on New York's deer herd. *NYS Con*, Apr.–May 1955. 9:no.5:18. illus.   2712

Darrow, Robert W. Deer hunting—then and now. *NYS Con*, Aug.–Sept. 1955. 10:no.1:19–23. illus. (part col.).   2713

Elk

Elk for the Adirondacks. *For & Stream*, Jan. 5, 1901. 56:5. Thirty elk offered by William C. Whitney.   2714

The Adirondack elk. *For & Stream*, Sept. 19, 1903. 61:213. Editorial urging law against hunting in certain parts of the north woods.
                                       2715

K., E.H. Adirondack elk killed. *For & Stream*, Sept. 30, 1905. 65:272. Wanton killing of elk.   2716

Radford, Harry V. Elk in the Adirondacks. *For & Stream*, Feb. 10, 1906. 66:226. Another offer for restocking.   2717

Radford, Harry V. Who will liberate these elk in the Adirondacks? *Sh & Fish*, Feb. 15, 1906. 39:391. Herd of twenty-five offered.
                                       2718

Elk in the Adirondacks. *Sh & Fish*, Mar. 29, 1906. 39:505. Brief editorial on liberation of

seventeen elk at Newcomb. See also article entitled "Adirondack Game" in issue for Apr. 5, 1906, p.525, on liberation of twenty-three elk in Warren County.   2719

Gothamite, pseud. Elk for the Adirondacks. *Sport Rev*, June 2, 1906. 29:594–95. Elk from New Hampshire shipped to Newcomb for restocking.   2720

Radford, Harry V. Elk in the Adirondacks. *St No Mo*, June 1906. 1:no.2:12–13. illus. port.   2721

Radford, Harry V. Adirondack elk increasing. *Sh & Fish*, Aug. 30, 1906. 40:407.   2722

Elk for Adirondacks. *Arms & Man*, Jan. 24, 1907. 41:325. Brief note on Radford's project.
                                       2723

Elk in the Adirondacks. *Sport Rev*, Feb. 23, 1907. 31:205. Editorial on the release of more elk by Radford.   2724

Adirondack elk. *For & Stream*, Apr. 20, 1907. 68:615. illus. A few elk released at Thirteenth Pond.   2725

Westervelt, V.R. Adirondack elk increasing. *Field & S*, Apr. 1908. 12:1069–70.   2726

Elks, Benevolent and protective order of. Committee on the elk in the Adirondacks. A report on the results of the liberation of a carload of elk in the Adirondacks through cooperation of the Benevolent and protective order of elks in New York state with the New York state conservation commission. n.p. n.pub. 1918? 8p. illus.   2727

Mahoney, Justin T. Mr. Mahoney and the elk. *NYS Con*, Aug.–Sept. 1947. 2:6–7. illus. Shooting of an elk in the Adirondacks; review of the elk stocking program tried in 1916.
                                       2728

Moose

A moose in the Adirondack. *Am Rev*, May 1852. 9:440–43.   2729

S., E.C. Moose in New York state. *For & Stream*, Apr. 2, 1874. 2:116. One shot at Raquette Lake in 1861.   2730

Nitram, pseud. Moose in the Adirondacks. *For & Stream*, Feb. 25, 1886. 26:84. Proposal to restock.   2731

Grant, Madison. The vanishing moose and their extermination in the Adirondacks. *Century*, Jan. 1894. 47:345–56. Partially reprinted in New York (state). Forest, Fish and Game Commission. Annual Report, 1901, p.234–38, with title "Adirondack Moose."
                                       2732

Restore moose to the Adirondacks. *Woods & Wat*, Spring 1900. 3:no.1:8.   2733

Chill, M. The last moose killed in New York state. *For & Stream*, May 12, 1900. 54:367.

Comment by J.H.R. and J.L. Davison in issue for May 26, 1900, 54:405. 2734

The last Adirondack moose. *For & Stream*, June 9, 1900. 54:445. A summary of recent articles. 2735

Ames, C.H. Adirondack moose stocking. *For & Stream*, July 21, 1900. 55:46. Advocates restocking. 2736

That Adirondack moose. *For & Stream*, Nov. 10, 1900. 55:361. Brief editorial on herd of five released from Ne-Ha-Sa-Ne Park. 2737

Spears, Raymond Smiley. That Adirondack moose—one point of view. *For & Stream*, Dec. 1, 1900. 55:425–26. 2738

That Adirondack moose. *For & Stream*, Dec. 8, 1900. 55:450–51. Quotation from the *Adirondack Enterprise* on the case against three guides for shooting and possessing a moose. 2739

Guides from all sections of the Adirondacks say the moose CAN and SHOULD be restored. *Woods & Wat*, Winter 1900. 3:no.4:12–13. illus. 2740

Brown's tract guides association. *For & Stream*, Jan. 26, 1901. 56:70. Copy of a resolution approving stocking the Adirondacks with moose. 2741

Moose in the Adirondacks. *Field & S*, Jan. 1901. 5:757. 2742

King, Thomas G. The moose murderers mulcted. *Recreation*, Feb. 1901. 14:115–16. Capture of guide who shot a moose released by Dr. Webb. 2743

Soon shall the mighty moose roam through the Adirondacks. *Woods & Wat*, Spring 1901. 4:no.1:11–13. 2744

Governor Odell signs *Woods and waters*' moose bill. . . *Woods & Wat*, Summer 1901. 4:no.2:14. 2745

A documentary history of the famous moose bill. *Woods & Wat*, Autumn 1901. 4:no.3:16–17. 2746

New York state officially credits moose bill triumph to *Woods and waters*. *Woods & Wat*, Spring 1902. 5:no.1:8. 2747

"*Woods and waters*" wins its great four-years' moose fight. *Woods & Wat*, Summer 1902. 5:no.2:14. 2748

Pellet, J.B. Tame Adirondack moose. *For & Stream*, Dec. 6, 1902. 59:448. 2749

Famous men who helped *Woods and waters* win the great moose bill triumph. *Woods & Wat*, Winter 1902–3. 5:no.4:18. 2750

Radford, Harry V. Restoration of king moose. *Four Tr News*, June 1903. 4:275–77. illus. Also in *Field and Stream*, July 1903, 8:225–27; and in *Woods and Waters*, Autumn 1903, 6:no.3:9–11. 2751

How moose for the Adirondacks are captured, transported and delivered. *Woods & Wat*, Summer 1904. 7:no.2:12–13. illus. Two pages of pictures with brief text. 2752

More moose for the Adirondacks. *Sh & Fish*, Feb. 16, 1905. 37:392. See also editorials in the Apr. 6 and May 11 issues, 37:525 and 38:85; editorial on Adirondack moose and elk, Oct. 5, 1905, 38:505. 2753

Westover, Myron Fayette. Moose and the Adirondacks. *For & Stream*, Aug. 15, 1908. 71:254. illus. Failure to restore moose. 2754

Webster, George O. Who killed the last moose? *High Spots*, July 1935. 12:no.3:35–36. 2755

SOIL AND WATER CONSERVATION

Markham, Charles C. The waste of Adirondack forests. *For & Stream*, Feb. 19, 1874. 2:21. Objection to dam on the Raquette River. 2756

Chahoon, George. The water supply of rivers. *Pop Sci*, July 1878. 13:288–92. Reprinted in *Stoddard's Northern Monthly*, Apr. 1908, 3:213–17. Spruce duff in Wilmington, Essex County. 2757

Fanning, John Thomas. Report on a water supply for New York and other cities of the Hudson valley. N.Y. 1881. 38p. diagrs. tables, maps. Desirability of Lake George and vicinity as future water supply for New York City. 2758

Fanning, John Thomas. Report no.2 on a water supply for New York and other cities of the Hudson valley. N.Y. 1884. 36p. plate, map. A report on the storage of water and runoff of the Adirondack streams and a general survey of the Adirondack watershed. 2759

Rafter, George W. Report on upper Hudson storage. *In* New York (state). State engineer and surveyor. Annual report, 1895. p.89–195. plates, folded tables, folded maps. 2760

Rafter, George W. Second report on survey of the upper Hudson valley. *In* New York (state). State engineer and surveyor. Annual report, 1896. p.804–58. tables (part folded). 2761

Rafter, George W. Natural and artificial forest reservoirs of the State of New York. *In* New York (state). Fisheries, game and forest commission. Annual report, 1897. p.372–437. plates, tables, folded map. "The Clearing of the Timber Within the Flow Line of the Indian Lake Reservoir" by Robert E. Horton, p.398–401; "The Construction of the Dam" by Wallace Greenalch, p.401–7. 2762

Whitford, David E. Water supply from the Adirondack forest. *In* New York (state). State engineer and surveyor. Annual report, 1898. p.445–566. diagr.   2763

Rafter, George W. and others. The Indian river dam, by George W. Rafter, Wallace Greenalch and Robert E. Horton. *Eng News*, May 18, 1899. 41:310–15. plate, illus. maps. Also published as a 16p. separate.   2764

Rafter, George W. On the application of the principles of forestry and water storage to the mill streams of the State of New York. N.Y. 1899. 17p. Includes a list of the proposed reservoirs of the Hudson River system.
2765

Rafter, George W. . . .Water resources of the State of New York. . . Washington, G.P.O. 1899. 2v. plates, illus. maps. (U.S. Geological Survey. Water-Supply and Irrigation Paper no.24–25.)   2766

Merchants association of New York. An inquiry into the conditions relating to the water-supply of the city of New York. N.Y. I.H. Blanchard co. 1900. 627p. folded plans, diagrs. tables, folded maps. The Adirondack Mountains, p.88–92. Appendix E: "A Water Supply from the Adirondack Mountains for the City of New York" by George W. Rafter, p.309–52.   2767

Newell, Frederick Haynes. Report of progress of stream measurements for the calendar year 1900. *In* U.S. Geological survey. 22d Annual report, 1900–1. pt. 4, p.9–506. illus. maps. New York State Streams, p.81–85. Schroon River, p.104–6.   2768

Rafter, George W. The future water supply of the Adirondack mountain region and its relation to enlarged canals in the State of New York. *In* New York (state). Forest, fish and game commission. Annual report, 1901. p.461–78.   2769

Burnham, John Bird. Lake Champlain pollution refuted. *For & Stream*, Jan. 2, 1904. 62:9. See also Burnham's article in the issue for Jan. 16, 62:49.   2770

Smith, Milford H. Lake Champlain pollution refuted. *For & Stream*, Jan. 2, 1904. 62:9–10.   2771

Hatch, Edward Jr. Lake Champlain pollution. *For & Stream*, Jan. 9, 1904. 62:30.   2772

Clark, D. Crawford. Lake Champlain pollution. *For & Stream*, Jan. 16, 1904. 62:49.   2773

Riley, John B. Lake Champlain waters and fish. *For & Stream*, Jan. 23, 1904. 62:69. Pollution of Lake Champlain.   2774

Dale, Thomas Nelson. Water resources of Fort Ticonderoga quadrangle, Vermont and New York. *In* U.S. Geological survey. Water supply and irrigation papers, no.110. 1904. p.126–29.   2775

Protecting the forest reserves. *For & Stream*, Dec. 30, 1905. 65:525. Editorial on hearings of River Improvement Commission on dams on certain Adirondack rivers.   2776

Before the River improvement commission. In the matter of the construction of storage dams in the Forest preserve pursuant to chapter 734 of the Laws of 1904. Brief in reply on behalf of the Indian river co. 1905. 36p. Copy in files of the Association for the Protection of the Adirondacks.   2777

Before the River improvement commission. In the matter of the Petition for the construction of reservoirs flooding state lands on the Sacondaga and Saranac rivers. Brief on behalf of the Association for the protection of the Adirondacks. 1905. 20p. Copy in Association files.   2778

Leighton, Marshall Ora. Preliminary report on the pollution of Lake Champlain. Washington, G.P.O. 1905. 119p. plate, map. (U.S. Geological Survey. Water-Supply and Irrigation Paper no. 121.)   2779

New York (state). River improvement commission. Report, 1–2. Albany, 1905–6. No.1 is Senate document 5, 1905, 4p. No.2 is Assembly document 35, 1906, 33p. Includes reports of hearings on East and West Canada Creeks, Sacandaga River, Raquette River and Saranac River.   2780

Rafter, George W. Hydrology of the State of New York. Albany, University of the State of New York, 1905. 902p. (New York State Museum Bulletin 85.)   2781

Wilder, Henry J. and Belden, H.L. Soil survey of the Vergennes area, Vermont-New York. *In* U.S. Bureau of soils. Field operations, 1904. Washington, 1905. p.73–94. tables, maps (1 in portfolio). Includes Port Henry and Ticonderoga sheets of the U.S. Geological Survey.   2782

Carl, David. Dams in the Adirondacks. *For & Stream*, Aug. 11, 1906. 67:211.   2783

Stoddard, Seneca Ray. The question of pure water. Shall we safeguard the sources of the Hudson? *St No Mo*, Sept. 1906. 1:no.5:2–9. illus. maps.   2784

New York (state). Water supply commission. First–sixth annual report. . .1906–1910. Albany, J.B. Lyon, 1906–11. 6v. plates, diagrs. atlas, maps (partly folded). Superseded by the Conservation Commission.   2785

Adam, Samuel F. Adirondacks. *Outlook*, Mar. 16, 1907. 85:625–26. Attempt to prove that storage project would be an effective means of preventing forest fires.   2786

Adirondack land flooding. *For & Stream*, Mar. 30, 1907. 68:495. Hearing on dams in the Adirondacks. 2787

New York state water-storage and water-power investigations. *Eng News*, Apr. 30, 1908. 59:490. Includes discussion of Freeman's studies on Sacandaga project (no. 2790). 2788

Our polluted waters. *For & Stream*, July 18, 1908. 71:87. Editorial on pollution of Lake Champlain and Hudson River valley. 2789

New York (state). Water supply commission. Studies of water storage for flood prevention and power development and control. Albany, J.B. Lyon, 1908. 252p. plates, charts, plans, tables, maps. Reprinted from the 3d Annual Report of the State Water Power Commission with revisions. Appendix A: "Report of John R. Freeman on the Sacandaga River near Its Confluence with the Hudson," p.31–217. 2790

New York's conservation of water resources. *R of Rs*, Jan. 1910. 41:77–87. illus. Includes discussion of water storage reservoirs in the Adirondacks. 2791

Spears, Raymond Smiley. The Hudson watershed. *For & Stream*, Jan. 1, 1910. 74:13–14. Low water at Corinth due to overcutting in the headwaters. 2792

Spears, Eldridge A. The passing of Hess' Riffs. *For & Stream*, Mar. 12, 1910. 74:420. Beauty spots destroyed by building of Hinckley reservoir and damming West Canada Creek 2793

Bird, John. The Lake Champlain situation. *For & Stream*, Apr. 8, 1911. 76:541. Regulations agreed upon by the International Fisheries Commission of the U.S. and Canada. 2794

McCulloh, Walter. Water resources of the State of New York. *Assn Eng Soc J*, Oct. 1911. 47:135–54. charts, illus. Includes discussion of Adirondack streams. 2795

New York (state). Water supply commission. Final order for the regulation of the flow of the Hudson river, etc. Albany, J.B. Lyon, 1911. 28p. map. Assembly document 53, 1911. 2796

New York. Board of trade and transportation. Committee on forests. The policy of New York state with reference to the development of water power. N.Y. 1911. 16p. 2797

Stephen, John W. Forest conditions of Oneida county. Albany, New York state conservation commission, 1911. 20p. plates, folded map (col.). (New York State Conservation Commission Bulletin 4.) 2798

Synopsis of the Report of the Joint committee of the Legislature of the State of New

York on the conservation and utilization of water power. n.p. n.pub. n.d. Broadside. Release dated Jan. 29, 1912. Copy in files of the Association for the Protection of the Adirondacks. 2799

Van Kennen, George E. . . .Statement of Hon. George E. Van Kennen, Chairman of the Conservation commission, State of New York, before the Joint judiciary committees of the Senate and Assembly on the water storage bills. Albany, N.Y. Feb. 29, 1912. Albany, J.B. Lyon, 1912. 23p. Cover title. Includes Sacandaga above Northville, Ausable and Indian rivers. 2800

New York (state). Conservation commission. Report. . .to the Legislature on the subject of high and low water in Lake George, under provisions of chapter 255, Laws 1912. Albany, J.B. Lyon, 1913. 6p. folded diagr. 2801

Cullings, Edwin Sanford. Water power possibilities in New York state. *Emp St For Prod Assn Proc*, 1914. 9:84–95. 2802

Maxon, E.T. and Cone, W.R. Soil survey of Clinton county, New York. *In* U.S. Soils bureau. Field operations of the Bureau of soils, 1914. Washington, 1919. p.237–69. tables, map. Also published as Cornell Extension Bulletin, no.3, July 1916. 2803

New York (state). Conservation commission. Power possibilities on the Oswegatchie river. Albany, J.B. Lyon, 1914. 66p. tables, folded map. 2804

New York. Board of trade and transportation. Forest and water storage policy of the State of New York. N.Y. 1914. 14p. Letter to Governor Glynn from Peter F. Schofield. 2805

New York (state). Conservation commission. The power possibilities of the Saranac river. Albany, J.B. Lyon, 1915? 18p. plates, tables, diagrs. folded maps. Detailed investigation giving profile of the Saranac River from Lake Champlain to Saranac Lake village. 2806

New York (state). Conservation commission. Division of waters. Report on the water power and storage possibilities of the Raquette river. *In* New York (state). Conservation commission. Annual report, 1915. p.130–211. 2807

Pratt, George DuPont. Conservation of the state's water resources. *In* New York state waterways association. 6th Annual convention. Proceedings. 1915. p.49–51. Need for control of forestry practices on private lands in the Forest Preserve. 2808

New York (state). Conservation commission. Division of waters. Report on the water power and storage possibilities of the Raquette river.

Albany, J.B. Lyon, 1916. 112p. front. illus. tables, maps.   2809

The good ship art. 7, sec. 7, by the first mate. *Conservationist*, Feb. 1917. 1:19–22. illus. The use of a scow to carry rocks to preserve the islands in Lake George from damage by waves from power boats.   2810

Carlisle, Floyd Leslie. Forest preserve and storage reservoirs. *In* New York state waterways association. 9th Annual convention. Proceedings. 1918. p.70–74.   2811

New York (state). Conservation commission. Division of waters. Report on the water power and storage possibilities of the St. Regis river. Albany, J.B. Lyon, 1918. 39p. illus. tables, folded maps. Reprinted from the Commission's 6th Annual Report. 2812

Ostrander, George N. The state policy for the development of water power...address delivered at the 13th annual convention of the Empire state forest products association. Albany, 1918. 4 leaves. Short history of water power legislation.   2813

Storage reservoirs in the Adirondacks and water conservation in New York. *Sci Mo*, Mar. 1919. 8:287–88.   2814

Cobb, George H. The present status of water storage and regulation. *In* New York state waterways association. 10th Annual convention. Proceedings. 1919. p.34–38. Chiefly on the Adirondack preserve. Includes history of the Black River Regulating District.   2815

New York (state). Conservation commission. Water power resources of the State of New York. Albany, 1919. 45p. tables, folded map. Errata slip tipped in. Although on the state as a whole, contains much on the Adirondacks.   2816

New York (state). Conservation commission. Division of waters. Report on the water power and storage possibilities of the Black river. Albany, J.B. Lyon, 1919. 141p. front. plates, charts, tables, maps.   2817

Cullings, Edwin Sanford. The Machold water storage law. *In* New York state waterways association. 11th Annual convention. Proceedings. 1920. p.84–88. With special reference to the Black River Regulating District.   2818

New York (state). Governor (Nathan L. Miller). Message from the Governor relative to the development of the water powers of the state. Albany, J.B. Lyon, 1920. 7p. Legislative document 58, 1921. Includes recommendation to change the Constitution to include water power development in the Forest Preserve.   2819

Berkey, Charles P. and Sanborn, James F. A geological survey of the principal dam

sites of the upper Hudson watershed and the Oxbow site on the upper Raquette, for the New York water power investigation... N.Y. 1921. 2v. plate, map. Reproduced from typescript. Copy in Columbia University Library. A preliminary inspection of sixteen sites from the source of the Hudson to Luzerne and the lower courses of the Cedar, Indian, Schroon and Sacandaga rivers and Loon Lake.   2820

New York (state). State engineer and surveyor. Report on the water power and storage possibilities of the Hudson river. Albany, J.B. Lyon, 1922. 75p. incl. tables, plates, folded profiles, diagrs. folded chart.   2821

Some views of the Adirondack property owners association on a proposed river regulating district for the Raquette river. *NY Forestry*, Jan. 1923. 9:17–18.   2822

Sargent, E.H. Storage reservoirs on Hudson river, now floods can be prevented and water flow increased during seasons of drought; preliminary plans for the Sacandaga now being prepared. *State Service*, May–Oct. 1923. 7: i.e.9:166–69. illus.   2823

Cullings, Edwin Sanford. How a river control district is building its reservoir. *Eng News R*, May 1, 1924. 92:763–64. map. Organization of Black River Regulating District and details of Stillwater reservoir.   2824

Citizen's committee for the protection of the state's waterpower resources. Keep the Forest preserve, the parks and the water resources...in the hands of the people. N.Y. 1926. 7p. Copy in files of the Association for the Protection of the Adirondacks.   2825

Empire state gas and electric association. Water power in New York state; what its development will mean for the public. N.Y. 1926. 42p. front. illus. Includes a section on inland streams and flood prevention and power.   2826

Empire state gas and electric association. River regulation in New York state. Public benefits derivable from the control of flashy streams in the Adirondacks. N.Y. 1927. 24p. illus. map. Fulton Chain, Lake Flower, Black River, etc.   2827

Machold, H. Edmund. Storage reservoirs; an address at the National republican club, February 5, 1927. n.p. n.pub. 1927? 8p. Copy in the Saranac Lake Free Library. 2828

Cullings, Edwin Sanford. Record runoff from Black river watershed, New York. *Eng News R*, July 19, 1928. 101:98–100. map. Good effect of reservoirs encourages extension of storage system.   2829

Cullings, Edwin Sanford and Hazen, Allen. A report on the control of floods in northern

New York rivers to a committee representing the mayors of the cities and villages of northern New York. Watertown, N.Y. New York development association, inc. 1928. 55p. illus. tables, map.   2830

New York (state). Laws, statutes, etc. Conservation law in relation to water power as amended to the close of the regular session of 1928. Albany, J.B. Lyon, 1928. 64p.   2831

Lawyer, George A. River regulation by storage reservoirs; reservoirs create beautiful lakes and campsites, improve fishing, prevent floods and aid industrial development. *Up-Stater*, July 1929. 1:no.4:3–5, 22. illus.
                                                        2832

Cullings, Edwin Sanford. Control of floods by storage reservoirs. *Up-Stater*, Sept. 1929. 1: no.5:3–5, 23–24. illus. map. Author's name misspelled in article. Suggestions for control of floods in Adirondack rivers.   2833

Cullings, Edwin Sanford. Storage reservoirs and state land: only about one half of one percent of the state land in the Forest preserve needs to be flooded to build all necessary Adirondack reservoirs. *Up-Stater*, Nov. 1929. 1:no.6:11, 21.   2834

New York (state). Conservation department. Water power and control commission. Water power resources of the State of New York. Albany, J.B. Lyon, 1929. 43p. folded map. Includes a list of lands required for storage in Forest Preserve.   2835

Cullings, Edwin Sanford. Storage reservoirs and state land payment to the state. *Up-Stater*, Jan. 1930. 2:no.1:10, 16, 21.   2836

Johnson, S.A. Damming the Sacandaga river for New York's largest lake. *Exp Eng*, July 1930. 8:257–61. illus. maps. Conklingville dam.   2837

New York development association. A report on control of floods in northern New York rivers. *Up-Stater*, July 1930. 2:11.   2838

Harnessing the upper Hudson. The completion of the new Sacandaga reservoir. . . *Oil Pow*, Nov. 1930. 5:148–54. illus. map.   2839

New York (state). Hudson river regulating district. Sacandaga reservoir. Albany, J.B. Lyon, 1930? 31p. plates, diagrs. History of the reservoir.   2840

Sargent, E.H. Controlling the Hudson. *In* New York state waterways association. 21st Annual convention. Proceedings. 1930. p.30–34. On the Hudson River Regulating District and the Sacandaga reservoir and Conklingville dam.   2841

U.S. War department. Chief of engineers. Ausable river, N.Y. Letter from the Secretary of war transmitting report from the Chief of

engineers on the Ausable river, N.Y. covering navigation, flood control, power development and irrigation. Washington, G.P.O. 1930. 20p. map. U.S. Congress, 71st Congress, 2d Session. House document 488. 2842

U.S. War Department. Chief of engineers. Bouquet river, N.Y. Letter from the Secretary of war transmitting report from the Chief of engineers on the Bouquet river, N.Y. covering navigation, flood control, power development and irrigation. Washington, G.P.O. 1930. 32p. U.S. Congress, 71st Congress, 2d Session. House document 490. 2843

U.S. War department. Chief of engineers. Saranac river, N.Y. Letter from the Secretary of war transmitting report from the Chief of engineers on Saranac river, N.Y. covering navigation, flood control, power development and irrigation. Washington, G.P.O. 1930. 19p. map. U.S. Congress, 71st Congress, 2d Session. House document 492. 2844

Lake George association. Water committee. Report on the cause and effect of abnormally high and low water in Lake George. n.p. n.pub. 1932. 15p. Report prepared by E. MacD. Stanton, dated Aug. 19, 1932.   2845

Forest preserve association of New York state, inc. The tragic truth about erosion. Schenectady, N.Y. 1934. 20p. illus. map. Reprint from *New York Times* of article by Hugh Hammond Bennett, "Soil Loss Through Erosion Threatens Our Basic Asset," with foreword by Forest Preserve Association showing application to Adirondacks.   2846

New York (state). State planning board. The St. Lawrence power development and the Adirondack water powers. A memorandum submitted to the Water resources committee of the New York state planning board, by E.S. Cullings, hydraulic engineer, Watertown. Albany, 1934. 8p. maps. (Bulletin 10, July 27, 1934.) Mimeographed.   2847

Machold, H. Edmund. Hudson river regulating district. The Sacandaga reservoir. *In* Simms, Jeptha Root. Trappers of New York. . . St. Johnsville, N.Y. 1935. p.291–93.
                                                        2848

Need of artificial lakes in Forest preserve. *State Service*, Jan. 1935. p.54.   2849

Forest preserve association of New York state, inc. World famous scenery being destroyed. Schenectady, 1937. 8p. illus. Lake George water level.   2850

New York (state). Executive department. Division of state planning. A preliminary survey of the water resources, by Edwin S. Cullings. Albany, 1937. 20p. maps, charts. (Bulletin no.29.) Mimeographed.   2851

White, O.H. An economic study of land utilization in Clinton county, New York.

Ithaca, N.Y. New York state agricultural experiment station, 1937. 52p. illus. tables, maps, folded map laid in. (Bulletin 689.)   2852

New York (state). Executive department. Division of state planning. A preliminary survey of the water resources of New York. The Black river. Albany, 1938. 49p. charts, maps. (Bulletin no.30.) Mimeographed. 2853

New York (state). Executive department. Division of state planning. A preliminary survey of the water resources of New York. The Hudson river (including Metropolitan district), by Edwin S. Cullings. Albany, 1938. 72p. charts, maps. (Bulletin no.31.) Mimeographed.   2854

New York (state). Executive department. Division of state planning. A preliminary survey of the water resources of New York. Northern Adirondack rivers. St. Lawrence river, by Edwin S. Cullings. Albany, 1939. 89p. charts, maps. (Bulletin no.33.) Mimeographed. Includes the Oswegatchie, Grass, Raquette, St. Regis, Salmon, Chateaugay rivers.   2855

Forest preserve association of New York state, inc. Lake George: a mill pond. Schenectady, N.Y. 1941. 18p. illus. Bound with this is a three-page supplement dated Oct. 7, 1942. Shows the extensive damage caused by flooding for private power purposes.   2856

Lake George association. The President's report on the annual meeting of the Lake George association on August 28, 1942. Particularly with reference to action taken regarding the question of water levels in Lake George. Diamond Point, N.Y. 1942. 3 leaves. Copy in New York Public Library.   2857

Lake George association. Some pertinent facts regarding the question of water levels in Lake George. Diamond Point, N.Y. 1942. 12p.   2858

New York (state). Legislature. Joint committee on Lake George water conditions. Public hearing. Minutes of hearing, August 17–20, 1943. n.p. 1943. 255 leaves. Mimeographed. Copy in New York State Library.   2859

New York (state). Legislature. Joint committee on Lake George water conditions. Public hearing. Minutes of meeting, October 22, 1943. n.p. 1943. 78 leaves. Mimeographed. Copy in New York State Library.   2860

Schaefer, Paul A. Tragedy of the Hudson. *Cloud Splitter*, Sept.–Oct. 1944. 7:no.5:10–11. Pollution of the upper Hudson.   2861

Black river regulating district. River regulation in the Black river regulating district 1920–1945. An accounting to those who have paid the cost. Watertown, N.Y. 1945. 48p. port. illus. folded map.   2862

Lake George protective association, inc. Lake George protective assoc., inc. n.p. n.d. Broadside. Letter on Lake George water level; dated Aug. 23, 1945; addressed to H.A. Reoux and signed by Irving Langmuir, president of the Association.   2863

New York (state). Legislature. Joint committee on Lake George water conditions. Lake George; rev. Mar. 1945. Albany, 1945. 239p. plates, maps (part folded). Legislative document 67, 1945. Important source material.   2864

Tuttle, Charles Henry. Report by Charles H. Tuttle as counsel for the Lake George association and as a member of its water levels committee. Diamond Point, N.Y. 1945. 7p. Copy in New York Public Library.   2865

New York (state). Legislature. Joint committee on interstate cooperation. Progress report of the special committee on pollution abatement, Feb. 15, 1947. Albany, Williams press, 1947. 96p. tables, maps. Summaries of stream pollution, including Adirondack area.   2866

Newkirk, Arthur Edward. ??Ought there to be a law?? *Ad-i-ron-dac*, Mar.–Apr. 1947. 11: no.2:11. Proposed Lake George pollution bill.   2867

Forest preserve association of New York state, inc. Lake George water level history. Schenectady, N.Y. 1948. 11p. An eight-page edition was issued July 1948.   2868

Barker, Elmer Eugene. The Ostertag anti-pollution law. *Ad-i-ron-dac*, July–Aug. 1949. 13:74, 87.   2869

Black river regulating district. Conservation of water resources. Watertown, N.Y. 1949. 49p. illus. folded maps.   2870

Simmons, Louis J. Proposed new dam across Raquette river near Hollywood will create 5-mile lake. *Lumber Camp News*, Dec. 1950. 12:no.8:19.   2871

Lake George protective association, inc. Lake George. n.p. 1950. 2p. Reprint of editorial in *New York Times* urging Attorney-General Goldstein to press for the appeal of Justice Ryan's decision in the Lake George water level case. Extracts from letters of E. MacD. Stanton, Charles H. Tuttle, P. Schuyler Miller, etc.   2872

Arnow, Theodore. The ground-water resources of Fulton county, New York, prepared by the U.S. Geological survey in cooperation with the Water power and control commission. Albany, 1951. 41p. diagrs. maps (part folded in pocket). (New York Water

Power and Control Commission Bulletin GW-24.)   2873

Forest preserve association of New York, inc. Lake George water levels (continued). Schenectady, N.Y. 1951. 7p. Criticism of the position taken by the Lake George Association.
                                                            2874

Lake George protective association, inc. State set to press Lake George issue, by Warren Weaver, Jr.; The battle resumes, by Charles H. Tuttle; Missing islands, by J.S. Apperson. n.p. 1951. 4p. Unpaged leaflet. A series of letters on the Lake George water level, reprinted from various sources.   2875

Dubuar, James Francis. Big and little reservoirs. *NYS Ranger Sch*, 1953. p.19–21. illus. Stillwater reservoir.   2876

Cushman, Robert Vittum. The groundwater resources of Washington county, New York, prepared by the U.S. Geological survey in cooperation with the Water power and control commission. Albany, 1953. 65p. illus. maps (part folded in pocket). (New York State Water Power and Control Commission Bulletin GW-33.)   2877

Feuer, Reeshon, Garman, William L. and Cline, Marlin. Soils of Essex county, New York, 1955. Ithaca, N.Y. Cornell university, 1955. fig. maps (part col.). (Soil Association Leaflet no.4.) Folded broadside; soil association map with six pages of text on verso.
                                                            2878

NATURAL HISTORY

GENERAL

A., P.H. Spring notes from the Adirondacks. *For & Stream*, May 28, 1874. 2:242–43. News and weather notes. 2879

Adams, Charles Christopher and others. Plants and animals of Mount Marcy, New York, by Charles C. Adams, George P. Burns, T.L. Hankinson, Barrington Moore and Norman Taylor. *Ecology*, Apr., Aug., Oct. 1920. 1:71–94, 204–33, 274–88. illus. tables. Also issued as a Contribution of the Roosevelt Wildlife Experiment Station of the New York State College of Forestry, Syracuse, and as Contribution no.24 of the Brooklyn Botanic Garden. 2880

Adirondack weather. *Outdoor Life*, Feb. 1904. 1:4–5. 2881

Adirondack weather in last ten years. *Outdoor Life*, Oct. 1904. 1:104–5. 2882

American association for the advancement of science. Summer, meeting, Section E—geology and geography. *Science*, Sept. 27, 1907. n.s.26:397–404. Meeting held at Plattsburgh, July 3–7, 1907. Contains summaries of.the following papers: Woodworth, J.B. "Abandoned Shorelines"; Fairchild, H.L. "Iroquois Extinction"; Ruedemann, R. "The Lower Siluric Paleography of the Champlain Basin"; Clarke, J.M. "Lake Champlain"; Newland, D.H. "The Iron Ores of the Adirondack Region." 2883

Bainbridge, G.H. Woodland recollections. *Bul Schools*, Mar. 1947. 33:216–18. illus. Experiences with birds and mammals in the Adirondacks and Catskills. 2884

Barick, Frank B. Environmental analysis of forest edges in relation to wildlife. *In* 10th North American wildlife conference, 1945. p.126–36. illus. tables. Also issued as a reprint. Huntington Forest. 2885

Beach, James E. Inventory of the Rich lake marsh, Huntington forest, Newcomb, N.Y. 179 leaves. mounted figs. tables. maps. Master's thesis, State University of New York, College of Forestry, Syracuse, 1949. Typescript. Abstract in Graduate Theses, p.53. 2886

Bennett, Walter James. The sleet storm in northern New York, March 25–27. *Mo Weath Rev*, Mar. 1913. 41:372–73. Severe storm, St. Lawrence County. 2887

Bishop, Ruth. The Mignon Talbot sanctuary. *Ad-i-ron-dac*, Sept.–Oct. 1948. 12:no.5:15. In Essex County. 2888

Brown, George L. Bears, trout, foxes, game. *For & Stream*, Feb. 4, 1905. 64:91. Nature notes. 2889

Brown, Lawrason. Some weather observations in the Adirondacks. *Med News*, Aug. 20, 1904. 85:341–43. charts. 2890

Buckley, John Leo. A comparative ecological study of three hydrophytic areas on the Huntington forest. 112 leaves. plates. tables. charts. maps. Master's thesis, State University of New York, College of Forestry, Syracuse, 1947. Typescript. Abstract in Graduate Theses, p.54. 2891

Burnham, John Bird. Adirondack notes. *For & Stream*, Aug. 16, 1902. 59:128. Notes on bears and a visit to a cave near Black Mountain. 2892

Burnham, John Bird. The eastern Adirondack winter. *For & Stream*, Feb. 16, 1901. 56:130. Signed: J.B.B. Severe winter in Ausable valley. 2893

Burnham, John Bird. Spring in the Adirondacks. *For & Stream*, Apr. 27, 1901. 56:330. Signed: J.B.B. 2894

Byrne, Mrs. Margaret H. (Myers). Algonquin astronomy. *Ad-i-ron-dac*, Mar.–Apr. 1950. 14:33. illus. Observations from Whiteface. 2895

C., A. Adirondack winter notes. *For & Stream*, Dec. 29, 1881. 17:431. Brief nature notes from the Moira. 2896

Carleton, Geoffrey. A back yard in the north woods. *Bul Schools*, Mar. 1932. 18:206–8. Observation of birds and small animals at Elizabethtown. 2897

Carter, L.T. Adirondack notes. *For & Stream*, Jan. 20, 1912. 78:81. Nature notes. 2898

Climate of the State of New-York. *Am Q J Agric & Sci*, Apr. 1845. 1:205–15. Includes discussion of the Adirondack area and the Champlain valley. 2899

Corliss, Albert H. A study of the Adirondack wilderness. *Am Angler*, Nov. 24–Dec. 1, 1883. 4:324–26, 338–40. Description of the woods. 2900

Dorp. Adirondack winter notes. *For & Stream*, Mar. 3, 1906. 66:344. Nature notes. 2901

Early spring in the Adirondacks. *For & Stream*, Apr. 9, 1898. 50:291. Earliest record for ice to go out. 2902

Egler, Frank Edwin. Establishment of a natural area on the Huntington wildlife forest. *Science*, July 4, 1941. 94:16–17. 2903

Fletcher, J.P. Adirondack notes. *Amat Sportsman*, Feb. 1905. 32:no.4:19. Nature notes on wildlife after the hunting season. 2904

Foot, Lyman. Severity of cold at Plattsburgh on Lake Champlain. *Am J Sci*, May 1821. ser.1:3:366–67. 2905

From the wilderness. *Vicks*, Apr. 1883. 6:120. Winter nature note near Whiteface. 2906

Gaither, Harry N. My woodland intimates. *Conservationist*, Feb. 1920. 3:28–29. Winter wildlife at an Adirondack camp. 2907

Gurnee, Russell H. Explorations in Paradox quadrangle: a search for the "Lost Pharaoh" cave. *NSS News*, Aug. 1952. 10:no.8:1, 5. 2908

Hay, John L. Adirondack natural wonders. *Up Mo*, Aug. 1941. 2:no.5:14–15. illus. On caves, balanced rocks, etc. 2909

Henry, Alfred Judson. Variation of precipitation in the Adirondack region. *Mo Weath Rev*, Mar. 1907. 35:118. table. 2910

Hine, Charles. After the storm. *Cloud Splitter*, Nov. 1942. 5:no.8:5–6. Description of storm damage at Avalanche Lake. 2911

Horton, Robert Elmer. Adirondack rainfall summit. *Mo Weath Rev*, Jan. 1907. 35:8–11. chart, map, tables. 2912

Hudowalski, Mrs. Grace (Leech). Meteorological observatory on Whiteface. *High Spots Yrbk*, 1944. p.15–18. illus. 2913

L., D. Adirondack notes. *For & Stream*, Mar. 9, 1876. 6:67. Weather conditions in Saranac and St. Regis regions. 2914

Moore, N. Hudson. Hunting with an operaglass, the birds and flora of the Adirondacks. *Four Tr News*, Aug. 1902. 3:68–96. 2915

Mordoff, Richard Alan. The climate of New York state. Ithaca, N.Y. 1949. 72p. maps, tables. (Cornell Extension Bulletin 764.) Earlier editions published in 1925 and 1934 as Bulletin 444. 2916

Needham, James George. A biological examination of Lake George, N.Y. *Sci Mo*, May 1921. 12:434–38. 2917

New York (state). Conservation commission. A biological survey of Lake George, N.Y. by James G. Needham and others. Albany, J.B. Lyon, 1922. 78p. illus. tables, maps. 2918

New York (state). Conservation department. ...A biological survey of the Champlain watershed. Supplemental to Nineteenth annual report, 1929. Albany, J.B. Lyon, 1930. 321p. illus. tables, form, maps. (Biological Survey IV.) 2919

New York (state). Conservation department. ...A biological survey of the Oswegatchie and Black river systems... Supplemental to Twenty-first annual report, 1931. N.Y. Burland printing co. inc. 1932. 344p. illus. tables, diagrs. forms, maps. (Biological Survey VI.) 2920

New York (state). Conservation department. ...A biological survey of the Raquette watershed. Supplemental to Twenty-third annual report, 1933. Albany, J.B. Lyon, 1934. 301p. illus. facsims. diagrs. forms, tables, maps. (Biological Survey VIII.) 2921

New York (state). Conservation department. ...A biological survey of the St. Lawrence watershed. (Including the Grass, St. Regis, Salmon, Chateaugay systems and the St. Lawrence between Ogdensburg and the international boundary.) Supplemental to Twentieth annual report, 1930. Albany, J.B. Lyon, 1931. 261p. illus. table, diagrs. forms, maps. (Biological Survey V.) 2922

New York (state). Conservation department. ...Biological survey of the upper Hudson watershed. Supplemental to Twenty-second annual report, 1932. Albany, J.B. Lyon, 1933. 341p. illus. tables, diagrs. forms, maps. (Biological Survey VII.) 2923

Perry, Clair Willard. Underground empire: wonders and tales of New York caves, by Clay Perry. N.Y. Stephen Daye, c1948. 221p. illus. Includes Adirondacks. 2924

Perry, Mary. The goodness of bad weather. *Outing*, May 1915. 66:189–90. Storm in Indian Lake region. 2925

Poor, Hustace H. An ecologist looks at the Adirondacks. *Audubon Mag*, May–June 1953. 53:104–8. illus. Elk Lake. 2926

Radford, Harry V. Adirondack notes. *Arms & Man*, July 4, 1907. 42:299. Written from North Creek. 2927

Rice, Arthur F. An Adirondack camp. *Recreation*, Mar. 1897. 6:150–53. illus. Nature observations. 2928

St. M., O. Winter at Indian lake. *For & Stream*, Mar. 29, 1883. 20:166–67. Nature notes. 2929

Seaman, Mrs. Frances (Boone). Spring break-up. *Cloud Splitter*, May–June 1954. 17:no.3:2–4.   2930

Sears, Paul B. What worth wilderness? *Bul Schools*, Mar. 1953. 39:186–89. figs. Values of wild life areas to biologist and forester.   2931

Shaw, Samuel P. The ecology of an artificial Adirondack pond. 128 leaves. mounted photographs, tables, maps (1 in pocket). Master's thesis, State University of New York, College of Forestry, Syracuse, 1947. Abstract in Graduate Theses, p.61.   2932

Skinner, Winslow W. The relative humidity of the Adirondack region. *NY Med J*, June 4, 1892. 55:631–32.   2933

Soper, Edgar Kirke and Osbon, C.C. The occurrence and uses of peat in the United States. Washington, G.P.O. 1922. 207p. illus. maps, tables. (U.S. Geological Survey Bulletin 728.) Adirondack deposits, p.45–47, 125–43.   2934

Spears, Raymond Smiley. Adirondack news and observations. *For & Stream*, Mar. 6, 1909. 72:376–77. Game and nature notes.   2935

Spears, Raymond Smiley. Adirondack observations. *For & Stream*, July 2, 1910. 75:14. Nature notes from the Nat Foster country.
2936

Spears, Raymond Smiley. Adirondack spring notes. *For & Stream*, Apr. 20, 1895. 44:304.
2937

Spears, Raymond Smiley. The drought in the Adirondacks. *For & Stream*, July 25, 1908. 71:141.   2938

Sportsman, pseud. An open winter. *For & Stream*, Feb. 22, 1913. 80:235. Winter notes from Eagle Lake.   2939

Totten, J.G. On the sudden disappearance of the ice of our northern lakes in the spring. *Am J Sci*, Nov. 1859. ser.2:28:359–64. Observations on Lake Champlain at Plattsburgh. Read before the American Association for the Advancement of Science, Aug. 1859.   2940

Tyler, Alanson Ranger. Adirondack weather has charms. *Ad-i-ron-dac*, Nov.–Dec. 1948. 12:no.6:4–5. illus.   2941

Welch, Fay. Where is our snow? *High Spots Yrbk*, 1940. p.11–14. Snow cover.   2942

ENTOMOLOGY

Collins, Donald L. Blackout for blackflies. *NYS Con*, June–July 1955. 9:no.6:30–31, 46. map. Followed by "Paradox Lake Blackfly Control Experiment," by Chester J. Yops.
2943

Comstock, G.F. List of Lepidoptera taken at Keene Valley, N.Y., with additions from State museum records. n.p. n.pub. n.d. p.557–64. Reprinted from the Report of the State Entomologist, 1904. (New York State Museum Bulletin 97.)   2944

Connola, Donald P. Recent research on two important forest insect problems in New York. *NYS Ranger Sch*, 1954. p.25–28, 32. illus. Tent caterpillar and white pine weevil.
2945

Connola, Donald P. and others. Survey and control studies of beetles attacking wind-thrown trees in Adirondacks, by D.P. Connola, C.J. Yops, J.A. Wilcox and D.L. Collins. *J Econ Ent*, Apr. 1953. 46:249–54. 2946

De Foliart, Gene R. The life histories, identification and control of black flies (Diptera: Simuliidae) in the Adirondack mountains. 98 leaves. Doctoral thesis, Cornell University, 1951. Typescript.   2947

Destruction of Adirondack timber by insects. *In* New York (state). Forest commission. Annual report, 1893. v.1, p.367–74.   2948

Dowden, Philip Berry and Carolin, Valentine Mott. Natural control factors affecting spruce budworm in the Adirondacks during 1946–1948. Reprinted from the *Journal of Economic Entomology*, Dec. 1950, 43:774–83.
2949

Drake, Carl John. Contribution toward the life history of Galeatus peckhami Ashmead. *In* New York (state). State university. College of forestry, Syracuse. Papers from the Department of forest entomology. Syracuse, 1922. p.105–10. illus.   2950

Drake, Carl John. Heteroptera in the vicinity of Cranberry lake. *In* New York (state). State university. College of forestry, Syracuse. Papers from the Department of forest entomology. Syracuse, 1922. p.54–86. illus. 2951

Drake, Carl John. The life history of the birch tingitid, Corythucha pallipes Parshley. *In* New York (state). State University. College of forestry, Syracuse. Papers from the Department of forest entomology. Syracuse, 1922. p.111–16. illus.   2952

Drake, Carl John. A new Ambrosia beetle from the Adirondacks; notes on the work of Xyloterinus politus Say. *Ohio J Sci*, Apr. 1921. 21:201–5. illus. fig. 2953

Felt, Ephraim Porter. Aquatic insects of the Saranac region. *In* New York (state). Forest, fish and game commission. 6th annual report, 1900. p.499–531. illus. col. plates. 2954

Felt, Ephraim Porter. Insects affecting forest trees; reprinted from the 7th report, Forest, fish and game commission, State of New York. Albany, J.B. Lyon, 1905. p.479–534. 2955

Foss, William M. Pest control through forest management. *NYS Ranger Sch*, 1947. p.5–6, 31. illus. Spruce budworm. 2956

Glasgow, Robert Douglass. The Adirondack black fly investigation. *High Spots*, June 1930. 7:no.2:14–15. 2957

Harmes, Edward A. Simuliidae. *High Spots Yrbk*, 1944. p.19–20. illus. Humorous article on black flies. 2958

Hatch, Melville Harrison. A preliminary list of the Coleoptera of the Cranberry lake region, New York, exclusive of the Buprestidae, Cerambycidae and Ipidae. *In* New York (state). State university. College of forestry, Syracuse. Technical publication 17, June 1924. p.273–312. 2959

Heil, Fritz. Introducing the forest pond and stream. *High Spots*, July 1932. 9:no.3:19–20. 2960

Jaynes, Harold Andrus and Spears, Charles Frederick. Biological and ecological studies of the spruce budworm. Reprinted from the *Journal of Economic Entomology*, Apr. 1949, 42:221–25. Studies made in northern New York in 1946 and 1947. 2961

Jaynes, Harold Andrus and Drooz, A.T. The importance of parasites in the spruce budworm infestations in New York and Maine. Reprinted from the *Journal of Economic Entomology*, Dec. 1952, 45:1057–61. 2962

Jordan, Karl. On a small collection of Siphonaptera from the Adirondacks, with a list of the species known in the State of New York. Reprinted from *Novitates Zoologicae*, Sept. 1929, 35:168–77. Fleas. 2963

Leonard, Mortimer Demarest. A list of the insects of New York with a list of the spiders and certain other allied groups. Ithaca, N.Y. 1928. 1121p. map. (New York State Agricultural Experiment Station, Ithaca. Memoir 101.) The Adirondack area is one of the faunal districts. 2964

Lintner, Joseph Albert. Entomological contributions. *In* New York (state). Museum. 30th, 42d, 47th and 48th annual reports. Albany, 1876, 1888, 1893, 1894. p.141–54, 281–86, 179–80, 376–77. Collections made in the Adirondacks, including that of W.W. Hill. 2965

Lintner, Joseph Albert. Lepidoptera of the Adirondack region collected by W.W. Hill, in 1875–1878. *In* New York (state). Adirondack survey. 7th annual report. . .to the year 1879. . . p.375–400. Reprinted in New York (state). State land survey. Report on the progress. . .1891, p.189–220, and in State land survey. Report on the progress. . .1894, p.255–87. Also issued as a separate, Albany, Weed, Parsons & co. 1880. "Mainly a reprint of list in the 30th annual report of the New York State Museum of Natural History, 1879, p.141–54, and the advance sheets of Entomological Contributions, no.IV. Revised." 2966

Metcalf, Clell Lee. Black flies, and other biting flies of the Adirondacks. *NYS Mus Bul*, 1932. 289:5–58. illus. 2967

Metcalf, Clell Lee and Sanderson, Wilford Edwin. Black flies, mosquitoes and punkies of the Adirondacks. Albany, University of the State of New York, 1931. 40p. illus. (New York State Museum Circular 5.) 2968

Metcalf, Clell Lee and Sanderson, Wilford Edwin. Control of biting flies in the Adirondacks. *NYS Mus Bul*, 1932. 289:59–78. illus. 2969

Mundinger, Frederick George. A preliminary list of the Buprestidae and Cerambycidae of the Cranberry lake region. *In* New York (state). State university. College of forestry, Syracuse. Technical publication no.17, June 1924. p.313–20. 2970

Murray, William Henry Harrison. The black fly in the Adirondacks. *Golden Rule*, July 11, 1877. 2:no.42:1. 2971

Needham, James George and others. Aquatic insects in New York state; a study conducted . . .under the direction of Ephraim Porter Felt. . .by James G. Needham and others. Albany, New York state museum, 1903. 517p. plates (some col.) figs. (New York State Museum Bulletin 68, Entomology 18.) 2972

Needham, James George and Betton, Cornelius. Aquatic insects in the Adirondacks. *In* New York (state). Museum. 54th annual report, 1900. 4:383–612. illus. plates. Also in New York State Museum Bulletin 47, 1901, p.383–612. 2973

Needham, James George. The summer food of the bullfrog (Rana catesbiana Shaw) at Saranac inn. *In* Felt, E.P. May flies and midges of New York. Third report on aquatic insects. Albany, 1905. p.9–17. table. (New York State Museum Bulletin 86.) 2974

New York (state). State entomologist. 15th–18th annual reports, 1899–1902. Albany, 1900–3. 4v. (New York State Museum Bulletins 31, 36, 53, 64.) These years include E.P. Felt's entomological reports on Clinton, Franklin, St. Lawrence, Warren and Washington counties. 2975

Notman, Howard. Two new staphylinids from Cranberry lake, New York. In New York (state). State university. College of forestry, Syracuse. Technical publication 17, p.270–72. (Bulletin, v.24, no.22, June 1924.) 2976

Old Forge eradicates black flies. Lumber Camp News, June 1949. 11:no.2:23. 2977

Osborn, Herbert. Homoptera in the vicinity of Cranberry lake. In New York (state). State university. College of forestry, Syracuse.

Papers from the Department of forest entomology. Syracuse, 1922. p.24–54. illus. 2978

Osborn, Herbert and Drake, C.J. An ecological study of the Hemiptera of the Cranberry lake region. In New York (state). State university. College of forestry, Syracuse. Technical bulletin 16, p.5–86. 1922. 2979

Osborn, Herbert. Life history notes on Cranberry lake Homoptera. In New York (state). State university. College of forestry, Syracuse. Technical bulletin 16, p.87–104. 1922. 2980

Stone, Alan and Jamnack, Hugo A. The black flies of New York state (Diptera: Simuliidae). Albany, 1955. 144p. illus. (New York State Museum Bulletin 349.) 2981

Wheeler, Arthur Leslie. Adirondack pests. For & Stream, Aug. 21, 1909. 73:300. Black flies and mosquitoes. 2982

GEOLOGY

Arranged by date

Jessup, Augustus E. Geological and mineralogical notice of a portion of the northeastern part of the State of New-York. Acad N Sci Ph J, 1821. 2:pt.1:185–91. 2983

Hubbard, Oliver Payson. Geological and mineralogical notices. Am J Sci, July 1837. ser.1:32:230–35. Includes discussion of formations at Trenton Falls and Brown's Tract. 2984

Emmons, Ebenezer. Annual report of the 2d geological district. In New York (state). Legislature. Assembly documents: 1837, no.161, p.97–153 (ed. 2, p.99–155); 1838, no.200, p.185–252; 1839, no.275, p.201–39; 1840, no.50, p.259–353; 1841, no.150, p.113–36. "First report describes reconnaissance of east and west portions of the Adirondacks; second report chiefly filled with details of St. Lawrence and Essex counties, also many details about iron mines, with an account of his ascent of Mt. Marcy; third report describes Hamilton, Clinton and Warren counties; fourth report takes up the iron ores at length, specially those at Lake Henderson; fifth report describes Hamilton, Essex and Franklin counties, and iron ores of Clinton and Franklin." Ellis. "Visit to the Mountains of Essex," in report for 1837, p.240–50. First use of name "Adirondack." 2985

New York (state). Governor (William L. Marcy). Communication from the Governor, relative to the Geological survey of the state.

Albany, 1837. 212p. Assembly document 161, 1837. Transmitting reports of Torrey, DeKay, Beck, Emmons, etc. 2986

New York (state). Governor (William L. Marcy). Communication from the Governor, relative to the Geological survey of the state. Albany, 1838. 384p. folded plates, charts, maps. Assembly document 200, 1838. Includes reports of DeKay, Beck and Emmons. 2987

Mather, William Williams. Annual report of the first geological district. In New York (state). Legislature. Assembly document 50, 1840. Washington County, p.209–58. 2988

New York (state). Governor (William H. Seward). Communication from the Governor, transmitting several reports relative to the Geological survey of the state. Albany, 1840. 484p. Assembly document 50, 1840. Includes reports from DeKay and Emmons (with a special report by Farrand Benedict). 2989

Emmons, Ebenezer. Geology of New-York, part II. Comprising the survey of the second geological district. Albany, 1842. 437p. illus. plates, maps. (Natural History of New York, Division 4, pt.2.) Second geological district comprises Warren, Essex, Clinton, Franklin, St. Lawrence, Jefferson and Hamilton counties. 2990

Vanuxem, Lardner. Geology of New York; part III. Comprising the survey of the third geological district. Albany, 1842. 306p. (Natural History of New York, Division 4, pt.3.) Includes Fulton, Herkimer and Oneida counties.   2991

Mather, William Williams. Geology of New York, part I. Comprising geology of the first geological district. Albany, 1843. 653p. plates. (Natural History of New York, Division 4, pt.1.) Scattered references to Washington County.   2992

Emmons, Ebenezer. Agricultural geology. *Am Q J Agric & Sci*, July 1845. 2:1–14. plate. Includes description of Adirondack district.   2993

Hall, James. Palaeontology of New York. Albany, 1847–94. 8v. in 14. illus. plates. (Natural History of New York, Division 6.) Additional information may be found in the author's "Contributions to the Palaeontology of New York...1855, '56, '57 & 1858." Albany, 1858, 17p. illus.   2994

Hyatt, Alpheus. On the geology of the Adirondacks. *Essex Inst Proc*, 1868. 6:5–6.   2995

Stevens, R.P. On glacial movements in northern New York. *Am J Sci*, Aug. 1873. ser.3:6: 144–45.   2996

Hall, James. Note upon the geological position of the serpentine limestone of northern New York... *Am J Sci*, Oct. 1876. ser.3: 12:298–300. Abstract of paper read before the American Association for the Advancement of Science.   2997

Leeds, Albert Ripley. Notes upon the lithography of the Adirondacks. *In* New York (state). Museum. 30th annual report, 1876. p.79–109. Also published in *American Chemist*, Mar. 1877, 7:328–39. Abstract with title "Lithography of the Adirondacks" in *American Journal of Science*, Sept. 1877, ser.3:14: 240–41. Reprint published, undated, with author's name listed on cover as Albert B. Leeds. Rocks collected in Essex County, mostly in the town of Keene.   2998

Hall, Charles Edward. Laurentian magnetic iron ore deposits of northern New York accompanied by a geological map of Essex co. *In* New York (state). Museum. 32d annual report, 1878. p.133–40. Also in New York State Geologist, 4th Annual Report, 1884, p.23–34. map. Issued as a reprint. Albany, Van Benthuysen, 1880, with title "Magnetic Iron Ores of the Laurentian System of Northern New York."   2999

Willcox, Joseph. Notes on glacial action in northern New York and Canada. *Acad N Sci Ph Proc*, 1883. 35:257–59. In Lewis and St. Lawrence counties.   3000

Britton, Nathaniel Lord. On the occurrence of a schistose series of crystalline rocks in the Adirondacks. *NY Acad Sci Tr*, Nov. 30,

1885. 5:72. Followed by remarks of A.A. Julien, p.73.   3001

Upham, Warren. Glaciation of mountains in New England and New York. *Appalachia*, May 1889. 5:291–312. Adirondacks, p.306–7.   3002

Pumpelly, Raphael. The relation of secular rock-disintegration to certain transitional crystalline schists. *Geol Soc Am Bul*, Feb. 19, 1891. 2:209–22. figs. Discussion, p.223–24.   3003

Walcott, Charles Doolittle. Correlation papers, Cambrian. Washington, G.P.O. 1891. 447p. folded maps. (U.S. Geological Survey Bulletin 81.) "Adirondack subprovince," p.201–7, 343–47 and scattered references.   3004

Appalachian mountain club. July 4, 1892— Twenty-seventh field meeting. Boston, n.d. p.91–93. Extracted from *Appalachia*, v.7, no. 1. Includes report of Colvin's talk on the study of rocks and mountains.   3005

Kemp, James Furman. A review of the work hitherto done on the geology of the Adirondacks. *NY Acad Sci Tr*, Oct. 24, 1892. 12: 19–24. Abstract. Also issued as a separate.   3006

Upham, Warren. The Champlain submergence. *Geol Soc Am Bul*, Nov. 9, 1892. 3:508–11. Abstract.   3007

Van Hise, Charles Richard. Correlation papers on Archean and Algonkian. Washington, G.P.O. 1892. 549p. Various references to the Adirondacks.   3008

Smyth, Charles Henry Jr. Lake filling in the Adirondack region. *Am Geol*, Feb. 1893. 11: 85–90. Also issued as reprint.   3009

Smyth, Charles Henry Jr. Report on a preliminary examination of the general and economic geology of four townships in St. Lawrence and Jefferson counties, New York. *In* New York (state). Museum. 47th annual report, 1893. p.685–709. Also in New York State Geologist, 13th Annual Report, 1893, p.491–515.   3010

Smyth, Charles Henry Jr. On gabbros in the southwestern Adirondack region. *Am J Sci*, July 1894. ser.3:48:54–65. illus.   3011

Van Hise, Charles Richard. Principles of North American pre-Cambrian geology. *In* U.S. Geological survey. 16th annual report. 1894–95. pt.1, p.571–843. The Adirondack district, p.771–73.   3012

Kemp, James Furman. Crystalline limestones, ophicalcites and associated schists of the eastern Adirondacks. *Geol Soc Am Bul*, Mar. 21, 1895. 6:241–62. map.   3013

Kemp, James Furman. Illustrations of the dynamic metamorphism of anorthosites and related rocks in the Adirondacks. *Geol Soc Am Bul*, Dec. 1895. 7:488–89. Abstract. 3014

Cushing, Henry Platt. On the existence of pre-Cambrian and post-Ordovician trap dikes in the Adirondacks. *NY Acad Sci Tr*, May 18, 1896. 15:248–52. 3015

Kemp, James Furman. The pre-Cambrian topography of the Adirondacks. *NY Acad Sci Tr*, May 18, 1896. 15:189–90. Abstract. 3016

Cushing, Henry Platt. Report on the boundary between the Potsdam and pre-Cambrian rocks north of the Adirondacks. *In* New York (state). Geological survey. 16th annual report. 1896. p.1–27. charts, map. 3017

Kemp, James Furman. Physiography of the eastern Adirondack region in the Cambrian and Ordovician periods. *Geol Soc Am Bul*, Apr. 30, 1897. 8:408–12. plate, map. 3018

Taylor, B.F. Lake Adirondack. *Am Geol*, June 1897. 19:392–96. 3019

Hitchcock, Charles Henry. The eastern lobe of the ice-sheet. *Am Geol*, July 1897. 20:27–33. Includes discussion of glaciation in the Adirondacks. Reviewed in *Independent*, July 15, 1897, 49:905. 3020

Darton, Nelson Horatio. Preliminary description of the faulted region of Herkimer, Fulton, Montgomery and Saratoga counties. *In* New York (state). Museum. 48th annual report, 1897. 2:11–12, 31–53. plates, map. Also in New York State Geologist, 14th Annual Report, 1894, p.11–12, 31–53. 3021

Kemp, James Furman and Newland, D.H. Preliminary report on the geology of Washington, Warren and parts of Essex and Hamilton counties. *In* New York (state). Museum. 51st annual report, 1897. 2:499–553. plates, maps. Also in New York State Geologist, 17th Annual Report, 1897, p.499–553. 3022

Smyth, Charles Henry Jr. Report on crystalline rocks of the western Adirondack regions. *In* New York (state). Museum. 51st annual report, 1897. 2:469–97. plates. Also in New York State Geologist, 17th Annual Report, 1897, p.469–97. 3023

Cushing, Henry Platt. Syenite-porphyry dikes in the northern Adirondacks. *Geol Soc Am Bul*, Feb. 26, 1898. 9:239–56. plate. 3024

Brigham, Albert Perry. Note on trellised drainage in the Adirondacks. *Am Geol*, Apr. 1898. 21:219–22. 3025

Kemp, James Furman, Newland, D.H. and Hill, B.F. Preliminary report on the geology of Hamilton, Warren and Washington counties. *In* New York (state). Museum. 52d annual report, 1898. 2:137–62. maps. Also in New York State Geologist, 18th Annual Report, 1898, p.137–62. Also published in Albany, 1900, as "Contributions from the Geological Department of Columbia University, no.74." 3026

Smyth, Charles Henry Jr. and Newland, D.H. Report on progress made during 1898, in mapping the crystalline rocks of the western Adirondack region. *In* New York (state). Museum. 52d annual report, 1898. 2:129–35. plates. Also in New York State Geologist, 18th Annual Report, 1898, p.129–35. 3027

Smyth, Charles Henry Jr. Geology of the Adirondack region. *Appalachia*, May 1899. 9:44–51. 3028

Kemp, James Furman and Hill, B.F. Preliminary report on the precambrian formations in parts of Warren, Saratoga, Fulton and Montgomery counties. *In* New York (state). Museum. 53d annual report, 1899. 1:r17–35. plates, maps. Also in New York State Geologist, 19th Annual Report, 1899, p.r17–35. 3029

Kemp, James Furman. The titaniferous iron ores of the Adirondacks. *In* U.S. Geological survey. Annual report, 1899. 19:no. 3:377–422. plates (part col.) figs. maps. Abstracts in *Geological Society of America Bulletin*, Aug. 1895, 7:15; *American Geologist*, Oct. 1895, 16:241–42; *Science*, Sept. 6, 1895, n.s.2:281–82; *Ottawa Naturalist*, Oct. 1895, 9:153. 3030

Kemp, James Furman. Pre-Cambrian sediments in the Adirondacks. *Am Assn Adv Sci Proc*, Dec. 1900. 49:157–84. Also in *Science*, July 20, 1900, n.s.12:81–98. Abstract in *Engineering and Mining Journal*, June 30, 1900, 69:769–70. 3031

Cushing, Henry Platt. Recent geologic work in Franklin and St. Lawrence counties. . . *In* New York (state). Museum. 54th annual report, 1900. 1:r23–95. Also in New York State Geologist, 20th Annual Report, 1900, p.r23–95. 3032

Kemp, James Furman. Pre-Cambrian sediments in the Adirondacks. An address. . .before the Section of geology and geography, American association for advancement of science, June, 1900. Easton, Pa. Chemical publishing co. 1900. 28p. (Columbia University Geological Department. Contributions, v.9, no.70.) 3033

Cushing, Henry Platt. Origin and age of an Adirondack augite-syenite. *Geol Soc Am Bul*, Nov. 27, 1901. 12:464. Abstract. 3034

Kemp, James Furman. Recent progress in investigation of the geology of the Adirondack region. *NY Acad Sci Ann*, 1901. 13:506–7. Abstract in *Science*, Dec. 28, 1900, n.s.12:1006. 3035

Ogilvie, Ida Helen. Glacial phenomena in the Adirondacks and Champlain valley. *J Geol*, May–June 1902. 10:397–412. 3036

Dale, Thomas Nelson. Structural details in the Green mountain region and in eastern New York. Washington, G.P.O. 1902. 22p. plates. (U.S. Geological Survey Bulletin 195.) 3037

Kemp, James Furman. Graphite in the eastern Adirondacks. *USGS Bul*, 1904. 225:512–14. Partially reprinted in *Engineering and Mining Journal*, May 26, 1904, 77:844, with title "Graphite in the Adirondacks." Abstract in *Mineral Industry*, 1903, 12:184–85, with title "Graphite—New York." 3038

Fairchild, Herman LeRoy. Ice erosion theory a fallacy. *Geol Soc Am Bul*, Feb. 13, 1905. 16: 13–74. plates, map. Adirondacks given as example. 3039

Cushing, Henry Platt. Geology of the northern Adirondack region. Albany, New York state education department, 1905. 453p. plates, tables, folded maps. (New York State Museum Bulletin 95.) Mainly Clinton and Franklin counties. 3040

Perkins, Llewellyn R. The Adirondacks; our oldest mountains. *J Outd Life*, June 1906. 3: 171–73. illus. 3041

Adams, Frank Dawson and others. Report of a special committee on the correlation of the precambrian rocks of the Adirondack mountains, the "original Laurentian area" of Canada, and eastern Ontario. *J Geol*, Apr.–May 1907. 15:191–217. Special committee of the General International Committee on Geological Nomenclature. 3042

Cushing, Henry Platt. Asymmetric differentiation in a bathylith of Adirondack syenite. *Geol Soc Am Bul*, Dec. 1907. 18:477–92. folded maps. 3043

Newland, David Hale. On the associations and origin of the non-titaniferous magnetites in the Adirondack region. *Econ Geol*, Dec. 1907. 2:763–73. 3044

Mills, Frank S. The economic geology of northern New York; valuable deposits of pyrites, graphite and iron ores abound, but mining is neglected because of various unfavorable conditions. *Eng & Min J*, Feb. 22, 1908. 85:396–98. 3045

Newland, David Hale. Geology of the Adirondack magnetic iron ores. With a report on the Mineville-Port Henry mine group, by James F. Kemp. Albany, University of the State of New York, 1908. 182p. plates, diagrs. folded maps. (New York State Museum Bulletin 119.) 3046

Miller, William John. Ice movement and erosion along the southwestern Adirondacks.

Am J Sci, Apr. 1909. ser.4:27:289–98. illus. map. 3047

Van Hise, Charles Richard and Leith, Charles Kenneth. . . .Pre-Cambrian geology of North America. Washington, G.P.O. 1909. 939p. folded maps. (U.S. Geological Survey Bulletin 360.) Adirondacks, p.597–621. Bibliography of Adirondack Pre-Cambrian geology, p.647–50. 3048

Miller, William John. Pleistocene geology of the southwestern slope of the Adirondacks. *Geol Soc Am Bul*, Feb. 5, 1910. 20:635–37. Abstract. 3049

Miller, William John. Trough faulting in the southern Adirondacks. *Science*, July 15, 1910. n.s.32:95–96. 3050

Bastin, Edson Sunderland. Economic geology of the feldspar deposits of the United States. Washington, G.P.O. 1910. 85p. plate, maps (part folded). (U.S. Geological Survey Bulletin 420.) Adirondacks, p.54–57. 3051

Kemp, James Furman. Pre-Cambrian formations in the State of New York. *In* XIth International geological congress, Stockholm, 1910. Compte rendu, p.699–719. map. Also published as a separate, Stockholm, 1912. 3052

Fairchild, Herman LeRoy. The glacial waters in the Black and Mohawk valleys. Albany, University of the State of New York, 1912. 47p. plate, map. (New York State Museum Bulletin 160.) 3053

Miller, William John. Early Paleozoic physiography of the southern Adirondacks. *In* New York (state). Museum. 66th annual report, 1912. 1:80–94. Also in New York State Museum Bulletin 164, p.80–94. Abstract in *Geological Society of America Bulletin*, Dec. 23, 1913, 24:701. 3054

Miller, William John. Variations of certain Adirondack basic intrusives. *J Geol*, Feb.–Mar. 1913. 21:160–80. illus. table, maps. 3055

Kemp, James Furman. New point in the geology of the Adirondacks. *Geol Soc Am Bul*, Mar. 30, 1914. 25:47. Abstract with brief discussion. 3056

Miller, William John. Magmatic differentiation and assimilation in the Adirondack region. *Geol Soc Am Bul*, June 29, 1914. 25:243–63. 3057

Taylor, William Rivers. Letter on geology of Keene Valley. *Brick Ch Life*, Aug. 1914. 21: 228–29, 238. 3058

Miller, William John. The geological history of New York state. Albany, University of the State of New York, 1914. 130p. plates, illus. maps (part folded). (New York State Mu-

seum Bulletin 168.) Revised edition issued as
Bulletin 255, 1924.   3059

Cushing, Henry Platt. Age of the igneous
rocks of the Adirondack region. *Am J Sci*,
Mar. 1915. ser.4:39:288–94.   3060

Miller, William John. The great rift on
Chimney mountain. *NYS Mus Bul*, 1915.
177:143–46. plates, figs. Hamilton County.
                                            3061

Fairchild, Herman LeRoy. Pleistocene uplift
of New York and adjacent territory. *Geol Soc
Am Bul*, June 1, 1916. 27:235–62. table, maps.
Hudson-Champlain valley.   3062

Miller, William John. Origin of foliation in
the pre-Cambrian rocks of northern New
York. *J Geol*, Sept.–Oct. 1916. 24:587–619.
                                            3063

Alling, Harold Lattimore. The glacial lakes
and other glacial features of the central Adirondacks. *Geol Soc Am Bul*, Nov. 30, 1916. 27:
645–72. plates, figs. maps.   3064

Newland, David Hale. Plastic deformation
of Grenville limestone. *In* New York (state).
Museum. 70th annual report, 1916. 1:145–
47. Port Henry area.   3065

Bowen, Norman Levi. The problem of anorthosites. *J Geol*, Apr.–May 1917. 25:209–43.
Adirondack anorthosite, p.219–27.   3066

Johnson, Douglas Wilson. Date of local glaciation in the White, Adirondack and Catskill
mountains. *Geol Soc Am Bul*, Sept. 21, 1917.
28:543–52. Abstract with discussion by J.W.
Goldthwait in v.28, p.136.   3067

Cushing, Henry Platt and Bowen, N.L.
Structure of the anorthosite body in the Adirondacks. *J Geol*, Sept.–Oct. 1917. 25:501–9.
                                            3068

Bowen, Norman Levi. Adirondack intrusives.
J Geol, Sept.–Oct. 1917. 25:509–12.   3069

Cushing, Henry Platt. Adirondack intrusives.
J Geol, Sept.–Oct. 1917. 25:512–14.   3070

Miller, William John. . . .The Adirondack
mountains. Albany, University of the State
of New York, 1917. 97p. plates, illus. figs.
maps (2 folded). (New York State Museum
Bulletin 193.) Bibliography, p.88–92.   3071

Miller, William John. Adirondack anorthosite. *Geol Soc Am Bul*, Sept. 30, 1918. 29:99–
100. Abstract with discussion by W.S.
Bayley and Frank Fitch Grout, p.399–462.
                                            3072

Miller, William John. Banded structures of
the Adirondack syenite-granite series. *Science*,
Dec. 6, 1918. n.s.48:560–63.   3073

Miller, William John. Pegmatite, silexite and
aplite of northern New York. *J Geol*, Jan.–
Feb. 1919. 27:28–54. Abstract in *Geological
Society of America Bulletin*, Mar. 31, 1919, 30:
93.   3074

Alling, Harold Lattimore. Some problems of
the Adirondack precambrian. *Am J Sci*,
July 1919. ser.4:48:47–68. illus. charts. 3075

Miller, William John. How the Adirondacks
were made. *Conservationist*, Mar. 1920. 3:35–
38. illus. Reprinted in *State Service*, Sept.–Oct.
1920, 4:664–66, with title "Making of Adirondack Mountains."   3076

Hoover, M.H. Wonderful Adirondack region
was among first-born land in the United
States. *NYC Lines Mag*, June 1920. 1:no.3:
29–34. illus.   3077

Miller, William John. Features of a body of
anorthosite-gabbro in northern New York.
J Geol, Jan.–Feb. 1921. 29:29–47.   3078

Miller, William John. Anorthosite gabbro in
northern New York. *Geol Soc Am Bul*, Mar.
31, 1921. 31:140–41. Abstract.   3079

Nason, Frank Lewis. The sedimentary phases
of the Adirondack magnetic iron ores. *Econ
Geol*, Dec. 1922. 17:633–54. table. Discussed
by W.J. Miller in *Economic Geology*, Dec. 1922,
17:709–13; and by D.H. Newland in *Economic Geology*, Apr.–May 1923, 18:291–96.
                                            3080

Ruedemann, Rudolf. Existence and con-
figuration of pre-Cambrian continents. *NYS
Mus Bul*, 1922. 239–40:65–152. maps. Adirondacks considered representative of whole
problem.   3081

Miller, William James. Pre-Cambrian folding in North America. *Geol Soc Am Bul*, Dec.
30, 1923. 34:679–702. Includes discussion.
Northern New York, p.691.   3082

Agar, William Macdonough. Contact metamorphism in the western Adirondacks. . .
Lancaster, Pa. Lancaster press, inc. 1923.
p.95–174. plates, illus. maps. Doctoral thesis,
Princeton University, 1922. Reprinted from
the *Proceedings of the American Philosophical
Society*, Oct. 1923, 62:95–174.   3083

Nason, Frank Lewis. Sedimentary phases of
Adirondack magnetites. *Econ Geol*, Apr.–May
1924. 19:288–97. tables.   3084

Alling, Harold Lattimore. The origin of the
foliation and the naming of syntectic rocks.
Am J Sci, July 1924. ser.5:8:12–32. charts.
Includes the Adirondacks.   3085

Cook, John H. The disappearance of the last
glacial ice sheet from eastern New York.
NYS Mus Bul, 1924. 251:158–76. fig.   3086

Wilson, Morley Evans. The Grenville pre-
Cambrian subprovince. *J Geol*, May–June
1925. 33:389–407. Abstract in British Association for the Advancement of Science. Report of 92d meeting, 1925, p.388–89.   3087

Alling, Harold Lattimore. Genesis of the Adirondack magnetites. *Econ Geol*, June–July 1925. 20:335–63. diagrs. tables.   3088

Miller, William John. Remarkable Adirondack glacial lake. *Geol Soc Am Bul*, Sept. 30, 1925. 36:513–20. map.   3089

Miller, William John. Present status of the pre-Cambrian geology of northern New York. *Geol Soc Am Bul*, Mar. 30, 1926. 37:219–20. Abstract.   3090

Alling, Harold Lattimore. Stratigraphy of the Grenville of the eastern Adirondacks. *Geol Soc Am Bul*, Dec. 30, 1927. 38:795–804.   3091

Gillson, Joseph A. and others. Adirondack studies; the age of certain of the Adirondack gabbros and the origin of the reaction rims and peculiar border phases found in them, by Joseph A. Gillson, W.H. Callahan and W.B. Millar. *J Geol*, Feb. 1928. 36:149–63. illus. diagrs.   3092

Osborne, Freleigh Fitz. Certain magmatic titaniferous iron ores and their origin. *Econ Geol*, Nov.–Dec. 1928. 23:724–61, 895–922. Includes a discussion of Lake Sanford deposits.   3093

Chadwick, George Halcott. Adirondack eskers. *Geol Soc Am Bul*, Dec. 30, 1928. 39:923–29. maps. Abstracts published in *Geological Society of America Bulletin*, Mar. 30, 1928, 39:216; and in *Pan-American Geology*, Mar. 1928, 49:147.   3094

Balk, Robert. Primary structure of the Adirondack anorthosite. *Geol Soc Am Bul*, Mar. 30, 1929. 40:183–84. Abstract. Abstract also in *Pan-American Geologist*, Feb. 1929, 51:67–68.   3095

Miller, William John. Significance of newly found Adirondack anorthosite. *Am J Sci*, Nov. 1929. ser.5:18:383–400. fig.   3096

Alling, Harold Lattimore. Ages of the Adirondack gabbros. *Am J Sci*, Dec. 1929. ser.5: 18:472–76.   3097

Buddington, Arthur Francis. Granite phacoliths and their contact zones in the northwest Adirondacks. *NYS Mus Bul*, 1929. 281: 51–107. plates, folded map. Abstracts in *Geological Society of America Bulletin*, Mar. 30, 1929, 40:100–1, and in *Pan-American Geologist*, Mar. 1929, 51:144.   3098

Balk, Robert. Structural survey of the Adirondack anorthosite. *J Geol*, May–June 1930. 38:289–302. Abstract in *Washington Academy of Science Journal*, June 19, 1930, 20:241–42.   3099

Alling, Harold Lattimore. Feldspars in the Adirondack anorthosite. *Am Min*, July 1930. 15:267–71.   3100

Smith, Edward Staples Cousens. The rocks of the Adirondacks. *High Spots*, Dec. 1930–Jan. 1931. 7:no.4—8:no.1:21–24. Reprinted with title "Mt. Marcy's Geological Background" in Mt. Marcy Anthology, *High Spots*, July 1937, v.14, no.3, p.4–6, illus. 3101

Newland, David Hale. Main features of Adirondack geology; age and origin of the Adirondacks; the oldest region on earth, and the account of how nature concealed her mineral wealth and scattered hundreds of lakes among mountains. *Up-Stater*, Jan. 1931. 3:no.1:5–6. illus.   3102

Newland, David Hale. Structures in Adirondack magnetites. *Geol Soc Am Bul*, Mar. 31, 1931. 42:238. Abstract. Abstract also in *Pan-American Geologist*, May 1931. 55:306–7.   3103

Buddington, Arthur Francis. Adirondack magmatic stem. *J Geol*, Apr.–May 1931. 39: 240–63. tables. Errata, July–Aug. 1932, 40: 466. Abstracts in *Pan-American Geologist*, Feb. 1931, 55:65–66, and in *Geological Society of America Bulletin*, Mar. 31, 1931, 42:189. 3104

Balk, Robert. Structural geology of the Adirondack anorthosite. *Min & Pet Mitt*, 1931. 41:3/6:308–434. plates, illus. diagrs. maps. Also issued as a separate with imprint, Leipzig, Akademische Verlagsgesellschaft M.B.H. 1931. A structural study of the problem of magmatic differentiation.   3105

Alling, Harold Lattimore. Adirondack anorthosite and its problems. *J Geol*, Apr.–May 1932. 40:193–237. illus. tables, diagr. maps.   3106

Buddington, Arthur Francis. Gravity stratification as a criterion in the interpretation of the structure of certain intrusives of the northwestern Adirondacks. *In* 16th International geological congress. Report. 1935. 1:347–52. map. Abstract in *Pan-American Geologist*, Sept. 1933, 60:151–52.   3107

International geological congress, 16th. Guidebook 1, excursion A1. Washington, G.P.O. 1933. 118p. plates, figs. maps. Article on the geology of the Adirondacks, by C.R. Longwell and Robert Balk, p.21–36.   3108

Miller, William John. Mode of emplacement of anorthosite. *Geol Soc Am Proc*, 1934. 47:99. Abstract.   3109

Grout, Frank Fitch and Longley, W.W. Relation of anorthosite to granite. *J Geol*, Feb. 1935. 43:133–41. table.   3110

Buddington, Arthur Francis. Origin of anorthosite in the Adirondacks and in general. *Am Geophys Union Tr*, 1936. 17:255–56. 3111

Buddington, Arthur Francis. Some problems of Adirondack geology of general significance. *Wash Acad Sci J*, Sept. 15, 1938. 28:420–21. Abstract.   3112

Alling, Harold Lattimore. Metasomatic origin of the Adirondack magnetite deposits. *Econ Geol*, Mar.–Apr. 1939. 34:141–72. illus. tables.   3113

Buddington, Arthur Francis. . . .Adirondack igneous rocks and their metamorphism. N.Y. Geological society of America, 1939. 354p. illus. plates, tables (part folded) diagrs. maps (1 folded). (Geological Society of America Memoir 7.)   3114

Wheeler, Robert R. Cambro-Ordovician trilobites of the Adirondack border. *Geol Soc Am Bul*, Dec. 1, 1941. 52:1976–77. Abstract.
                                                    3115

Meyerhoff, Howard Augustus. The Adirondacks past and present. *High Spots Yrbk*, 1942. p.18–19. illus.   3116

The Adirondacks half as old as is the earth itself; new measurements of age. *Sci NL*, Mar. 28, 1942. 41:201. Reprinted with slight additions from *Science*, Mar. 13, 1942, Supplement, p.11.   3117

Alling, Harold Lattimore. The Adirondack magnetite deposits. *In* Ore deposits as related to structural features, ed. by W.H. Newhouse. Princeton, 1942. p.143–46. fig.   3118

Mountain study. *Hobbies*, Aug. 1943. 48:79. Geology of the Adirondacks.   3119

Miller, William John. Emplacement of Adirondack anorthosite. *Am Geophys Union Tr*, Oct. 1943. 24:pt.1:257–65.   3120

Balk, Robert. Comments on some eastern Adirondack problems. *J Geol*, Sept.–Oct. 1944. 52:289–318. illus. diagr. map.   3121

Stephenson, Robert Charles. Linear orientation of tabular plagioclase crystals in anorthosite. *Pa Acad Sci Proc*, 1946. 20:98–101. illus. Lake Sanford, Essex County.   3122

Chadwick. George Halcott. Dying mountains. *Cloud Splitter*, Jan.–Feb. 1947. 10:no.1: 2–3.   3123

Evrard, Pierre. Statistical relation between TiO_2, Fe_2O_3, and FeO in rocks and ores during differentiation of a titaniferous magma. *Geol Soc Am Bul*, Mar. 1947. 58:127–210. 3124

Phelps, Orra A. Glacial footprints. *Cloud Splitter*, Mar.–Apr. 1948. 11:no.2:8–9. Evidence of glaciation in the high peaks.   3125

Buddington, Arthur Francis. Origin of granitic rocks of the northwest Adirondacks. *Geol Soc Am Mem*, Apr. 10, 1948. 28:21–43. llius. map.   3126

Broughton, John Gerard. Adirondack fundamentals. *Ad-i-ron-dac*, Sept.–Oct. 1948. 12: no.5:10–11. illus. Reprinted in *North Country Life*, Spring 1949, 3:no.2:27–28.   3127

Koch, George. Adirondack geology. *IOCA Bul*, Winter 1948. 2:no.1:11–14, 20. illus.
                                                    3128

Evrard, Pierre. The differentiation of titaniferous magmas. *Econ Geol*, May 1949. 44: 210–32.   3129

Engel, Albert Edward John. Studies of cleavage in the metasedimentary rocks of the northwest Adirondack mountains, New York. *Am Geophys Union Tr*, Oct. 1949. 30:767–84. illus. map.   3130

Buddington, Arthur Francis. Composition and genesis of pyroxene and garnet related to Adirondack anorthosite and anorthosite-marble contact zones. *Am Min*, Sept.–Oct. 1950. 35:659–70. illus.   3131

Engel, Albert Edward John and Engel, Celeste G. Stratigraphy and metamorphic reconstitution of parts of the Grenville series in the northwest Adirondacks; a report of progress. *Geol Soc Am Bul*, Dec. 1950. 61:1457. Abstract.   3132

Levin, Samuel Benedict. Origin of hornblende rims on Adirondack garnet. *Geol Soc Am Bul*, Dec. 1950. 61:1482. Abstract.   3133

Crowl, George Henry. Erosion surfaces in the Adirondacks. 48 leaves. plates, maps in pocket. Doctoral thesis, Princeton University, 1950. Typescript. Abstract in *Geological Society of America Bulletin*, Dec. 1950. 61:1565. Erosional history of the Adirondacks compared with that of the Appalachians.   3134

Engel, Albert Edward John and Engel, Celeste G. Stratigraphy and metamorphic reconstitution of parts of the Grenville series in the northwest Adirondacks, a report of progress. *Am Min*, Mar.–Apr. 1951. 36:313–14. Abstract.   3135

Levin, Samuel Benedict. Origin of hornblende rims on Adirondack garnet. *Am Min*, Mar.–Apr. 1951. 36:319. Abstract.   3136

Read, H.H. Note on the development of large garnets in Sutherland magmatites; addendum on Adirondack giant garnets. *Geol Mag*, May 1951. 88:189–91.   3137

Buddington, Arthur Francis. Chemical petrology of some metamorphosed Adirondack gabbroic, syenitic and quartz syenitic rocks. *Am J Sci*, 1952. Bowen volume, p.38–84.
                                                    3138

Engel, Albert Edward John and Engel, Celeste G. Grenville series in the northwest Adirondack mountains, New York. *Geol Soc Am Bul*, Sept. 1953. 64:1013–97. plates. 3139

Buddington, Arthur Francis and Leonard, Benjamin Franklin 3d. Chemical petrology and mineralogy of hornblendes in northwest Adirondack granitic rocks. *Am Min*, Nov.–Dec. 1953. 38:891–902. tables.   3140

Jaffe, Howard William. Amygdular camptonite dikes from Mount Jo, Mount Marcy quadrangle, Essex county, New York. *Am Min*, Nov.–Dec. 1953. 38:1065–77. illus. tables, map.   3141

Buddington, Arthur Francis, Fahey, Joseph John and Vlisidis, Angelina Calomeris. Iron and titanium oxide minerals of Adirondack rocks. *Geol Soc Am Bul*, Dec. 1953. 64:1403. Abstract. Abstract also in *American Mineralogist*, Mar.–Apr. 1954, 39:318–19. See also article by Buddington and James Robinson Balsey Jr. "Iron and Titanium Oxide Minerals of Adirondack Rocks and Their Magnetic Properties," in *Geophysics*, July 1954, 19:635–36 (abstract).   3142

Engel, Albert Edward John and Engel, Celeste G. Compositional evolution of a major marble unit, Grenville series, northwest Adirondack mountains, New York. *Geol Soc Am Bul*, Dec. 1953. 64:1417–18. Abstract.   3143

Walton, Matt Savage Jr. Metamorphism and granitization in the eastern Adirondacks. *Geol Soc Am Bul*, Dec. 1953. 64:1486–87. Abstract.   3144

Walton, Matt Savage Jr. Differential metamorphic mobilization and the Adirondack eruptive sequence. *Am Geophys Union Tr*, 1953. 34:350. Abstract.   3145

King, B.C. . . .Structural geology: the Appalachians. Part I, New England. *Sci Prog*, July 1955. 43:484–501. Adirondacks, p.486–88.   3146

Buddington, Arthur Francis, Fahey, Joseph John and Vlisidis, Angelina Calomeris. Thermometric and petrogenetic significance of titaniferous magnetite. *Am J Sci*, Sept. 1955. 253:497–532. Includes Adirondacks.   3147

Brown, J.S. and Engel, Albert Edward John. Revision of stratigraphy and structural features in the Grenville series, Edwards-Balmat district, northwest Adirondacks, New York. *Geol Soc Am Bul*, Dec. 1955. 66:1536. Abstract.   3148

THE CHAMPLAIN AND HUDSON VALLEYS

Desor, E. Deposits of marine shells in Maine, on Lake Champlain and the St. Lawrence. *Boston Soc Nat Hist Proc*, 1848–51. 3:357–58.   3149

Billings, Elkanah. Fossils of the Chazy limestone, with descriptions of new species. *Can Nat*, Dec. 1859. 4:426–70.   3150

Hunt, Thomas Sterry. The geology of Port Henry, New York. *Can Nat*, Mar. 1883. ser.2:10:420–22. Abstract of an unpublished paper.   3151

Brainerd, Ezra and Seely, Henry M. The original Chazy rocks. *Am Geol*, Nov. 1888. 2:323–30. map.   3152

Whitfield, Robert Parr. Observations on some imperfectly known fossils from the calciferous sand rock of Lake Champlain and descriptions of several new forms. *Am Mus Nat Hist Bul*, Mar. 1889. 2:41–65. plates.   3153

Brainerd, Ezra and Seely, Henry M. The calciferous formation in the Champlain valley. *Am Mus Nat Hist Bul*, June 1890. 3:1–23. plates, maps. Also published in the *Geological Society of America Bulletin*, Apr. 29, 1890, 1:501–11. Abstract in *American Journal of Science*, Jan.–June 1890, ser.3:39:235–38. Ticonderoga.   3154

Brainerd, Ezra. The Chazy formation in the Champlain valley. *Geol Soc Am Bul*, Mar. 17, 1891. 2:293–300. plate.   3155

Kemp, James Furman. Gestreifte magnetit-krystalle aus Mineville, Lake Champlain-gebiet, Staat New York. *Z Kristall*, Apr. 1891. 19:183–87.   3156

Kemp, James Furman and Marsters, Vernon Freeman. The trap dikes of the Lake Champlain region. Washington, G.P.O. 1893. 62p. plates. (U.S. Geological Survey Bulletin 107.) Abstract in *New York Academy of Sciences Transactions*, Oct. 19, 1891, 11:13–23.   3157

Kemp, James Furman. Gabbros on the western shore of Lake Champlain. *Geol Soc Am Bul*, Feb. 23, 1894. 5:213–24. figs.   3158

Baldwin, Samuel Prentiss. Pleistocene history of the Champlain valley. *Am Geol*, Mar. 1894. 13:170–84. plate, fig. Also issued as a separate.   3159

Cushing, Henry Platt. Faults of Chazy township, Clinton county, N.Y. *Geol Soc Am Bul*, Mar. 1895. 6:285–96.   3160

Kemp, James Furman. The iron-ore bodies at Mineville, Essex county, New York. *Science*, June 14, 1895. n.s.1:669–70. Abstract.   3161

Wright, George Frederick. Glacial phenomena between Lake Champlain, Lake George and the Hudson river. *Science*, Nov. 22, 1895. n.s.2:673–78. maps.   3162

Van Ingen, Gilbert and White, Theodore Greely. An account of the summer's work in geology on Lake Champlain. *NY Acad Sci Tr*, Oct. 28, 1896. 15:19–23.   3163

Brainerd, Ezra and Seely, Henry M. The Chazy of Lake Champlain, New York. *Am Mus Nat Hist Bul*, 1896. 8:305–15. figs. Ticonderoga.   3164

Kemp, James Furman. Geology of the magnetites near Port Henry, N.Y. especially those of Mineville. *Am Inst Mining Eng Tr*, Feb. 1897. 27:146–203. illus. diagrs. map.   3165

Suess, Edward. La face de la terre (Das antlitz der erde). Traduit de l'allemand, avec l'autorisation de l'auteur et annotée, sous la direction de Emm. de Margerie. Paris, A. Colin & cie. 1897–1918. 3v. in 6. front. (port.) illus. plates (part folded) maps (part folded). "Champlain Terraces and Marine Deposits," v.2, p.753–62.   3166

Wright, George Frederick. Glacial observations in the Champlain-St. Lawrence valley. *Am Geol*, Nov. 1898. 22:333–34.   3167

Van Ingen, Gilbert. The Potsdam sandstone of the Lake Champlain basin. *NYS Mus Bul*, 1902. 52:529–45. In the report of the State Paleontologist for 1901.   3168

Peet, Charles Emerson. Glacial and postglacial history of the Hudson and Champlain valleys. *J Geol*, July–Aug., Oct.–Nov. 1904. 12:415–69, 617–60.   3169

Raymond, Percy Edward. The trilobites of the Chazy limestone. *Carneg Mus Ann*, Mar. 1905. 3:328–86. illus. Crown Point.   3170

Raymond, Percy Edward. The Chazy formation and its fauna. *Carneg Mus Ann*, July 1905. 3:498–596. plates. Abstract published under title "The Fauna of the Chazy Limestone" in *American Journal of Science*, Nov. 1905, ser.4: 20:353–82. Doctoral thesis, Yale University.   3171

Woodworth, Jay Backus. Ancient water levels of the Champlain and Hudson valleys. Albany, University of the State of New York, 1905. p.65–265. illus. plates, maps (some folded). (New York State Museum Bulletin 84.)   3172

Seely, Henry Martyn. Beekmantown and Chazy formations in the Champlain valley, contributions to their geology and paleontology. *In* Vermont. State geologist. 5th Report on mineral industries and geology, 1905–6. p.174–87. plates.   3173

Seely, Henry Martyn. Cryptozoa of the early Champlain sea. *In* Vermont. State geologist. 5th Report on mineral industries and geology, 1905–6. p.156–73. plates.   3174

Ruedemann, Rudolf. Cephalopoda of the Beekmantown and Chazy formations of the Champlain basin. Albany, University of the State of New York, 1906. 611p. illus. plates (partly folded). (New York State Museum Bulletin 90; Paleontology 14.)   3175

Ruedemann, Rudolf. The lower Siluric paleogeography of the Champlain basin. *Science*, Sept. 27, 1907. n.s.26:399–400. Abstract of speech before the American Association for the Advancement of Science.   3176

Kemp, James Furman. The Mineville-Port Henry mine group. *In* Newland, David H. Geology of the Adirondack magnetic iron ores. Albany, 1908. p.57–88. plates, diagrs. folded map. (New York State Museum Bulletin 119.)   3177

Miller, William John. Pre-glacial course of the upper Hudson river. *Geol Soc Am Bul*, May 22, 1911. 22:177–86. fig.   3178

Barker, Elmer Eugene. Glacial pot-holes at Crown Point, New York. *J Geol*, July–Aug. 1913. 21:459–64. plates.   3179

Fairchild, Herman LeRoy. Pleistocene marine submergence of the Connecticut and Hudson valleys. *Geol Soc Am Bul*, June 29, 1914. 25:219–42. tables, map.   3180

Barker, Elmer Eugene. Ancient water levels of the Crown Point embayment. *NYS Mus Bul*, 1916. 187:165–90. plates, figs. folded maps. Also issued as a separate, Albany, 1916.   3181

Fairchild, Herman LeRoy. Postglacial features of the upper Hudson valley. Albany, University of the State of New York, 1917. 22p. folded map in pocket. (New York State Museum Bulletin 195.)   3182

Hudson, George Henry. The interesting geological features at the Champlain assembly, Cliff Haven, New York. . . Albany, University of the State of New York, 1917. 12p. plates, illus. Also published in the 70th Annual Report of the New York State Museum, 1916, v.1, p.149–60.   3183

Fairchild, Herman LeRoy. Pleistocene marine submergence of the Hudson, Champlain and St. Lawrence valleys. Albany, University of the State of New York, 1919. 76p. plate, map. (New York State Museum Bulletin 209–10.)   3184

Goldring, Winifred. The Champlain sea; evidence of its decreasing salinity southward as shown by the character of the fauna. *In* New York (state). Museum and science department. 17th report of the director, 1920. p.153–94. plates, diagrs. folded map. (New York State Museum Bulletin 239–40.)   3185

Swinnerton, Allyn Coats. Block fault structures near Ticonderoga, New York. *Geol Soc Am Bul*, Mar. 31, 1931. 42:202. Abstract. Abstract also in *Pan-American Geologist*, May 1931, 55:310.   3186

Swinnerton, Allyn Coats. Geology of the vicinity of Ticonderoga. *Ohio J Sci*, July 1931. 31:284. Abstract.   3187

Hudson, George Henry. The dike invasions of Champlain valley, New York. *NYS Mus Bul*, 1931. 286:81–99. plates, folded maps. Followed by Appendix I: The Dikes of

Valcour Island and of the Peru and Platts-burg Coast Line, by G.H. Hudson and H.P. Cushing, p.100–9. Appendix II: Analysis of Grenville Inclusives and Discussion, by H.P. Cushing, p.110–12. 3188

Hudson, George Henry. The faults systems of the northern Champlain valley. *NYS Mus Bul*, 1931. 286:5–80. Figs. 1–20. 3189

Swinnerton, Allyn Coats. Structural geology in the vicinity of Ticonderoga, New York. *J Geol*, July–Aug. 1932. 40:402–16. 3190

Quinn, Alonzo Wallace. Normal faults of the Lake Champlain region. *J Geol*, Feb.–Mar. 1933. 41:112–43. illus. map. Abstracts in *Pan-American Geologist*, Mar. 1930, 53:144, and *Geological Society of America Bulletin*, Mar. 31, 1930, 41:113–14. 3191

Chapman, Donald Harding. Late-glacial and postglacial history of the Champlain valley. *Am J Sci*, Aug. 1937. ser.5:34:89–124. maps. Abstract in Vermont. State geologist. Report on the mineral industries and geology, 1941–42, p.48–52, map. 3192

Rodgers, John. Stratigraphy and structure in the Upper Champlain valley. *Geol Suc Am Bul*, Nov. 1937. 48:1573–88. maps. 3193

Wheeler, Robert R. Late Cambrian Sauki-inae in the Champlain valley. *Geol Soc Am Bul*, Dec. 1, 1941. 52:2036–37. Abstract. 3194

Howell, Benjamin Franklin. Burrows of for-alites from the Cambrian of the Champlain valley. *Geol Soc Am Bul*, Dec. 1, 1943. 54:1831. Abstract. 3195

Oxley, Philip. Chazyan stratigraphy west of the Champlain thrust, New York and Ver-mont. *Geol Soc Am Bul*, Dec. 1950. 61:1492. Abstract. 3196

Oxley, Philip. Chazyan reef facies relation-ships in the northern Champlain valley. *Denison Univ Sci Lab J*, Aug. 1951. 42:art.10: 92–106. illus. 3197

Hagner, A.F. and Collins, L.G. Source and origin of magnetite at Scott mine, Sterling lake, New York. *Science*, Dec. 23, 1955. n.s. 122:1230–31. 3198

OTHER LOCALITIES

Steel, John Honeywood. Report on the geo-logical structure of the county of Saratoga, N.Y... Saratoga Springs, N.Y. Davison, 1822. 56p. Preprint from New York State Board of Agriculture *Memoirs*, 1823, p.44–84. Pages 155–61 contain his "Notes to the geological survey." 3199

DeKay, James Ellsworth. Observations on the structure of trilobites, and descriptions of an apparently new genus. With notes on the geology of Trenton Falls. By Professor James Renwick. *Ly Nat Hist Annals*, Sept. 1823. 1:174–89. 3200

Hough, Franklin Benjamin. Observations on the geology of Lewis county. *Am Q J Agric & Sci*, May–June 1847. 5:267–74, 314–27. 3201

Kellogg, Orson. A remarkable geological development in Elizabethtown, Essex county, N.Y. *Am Assn Adv Sci Proc*, 1849. 1:135–38. 3202

Hall, James. On the geology of the Ausable region. *Alb Inst Proc*, 1878. 2:247–50. 3203

Kemp, James Furman. The great shear-zone near Avalanche lake in the Adirondacks. *Am J Sci*, Aug. 1892. ser.3:44:109–14. illus. 3204

Eakle, Arthur Starr. On some dikes occur-ring near Lyon mt. Clinton co. N.Y. *Am Geol*, July 1893. 12:31–36. plate. 3205

Ries, Heinrich. A Pleistocene lake-bed at Elizabethtown, Essex county, New York. *NY Acad Sci Tr*, Nov. 27, 1893. 13:107–9. 3206

Cushing, Henry Platt. Preliminary report on the geology of Clinton county. *In* New York (state). Museum. 47th annual report, 1893. p.667–83. folded maps. Also in New York State Geologist, 13th Annual Report, 1893, p.473–89. 3207

Kemp, James Furman. Preliminary report on the geology of Essex county. *In* New York (state). Museum. 47th and 49th an-nual reports, 1893 and 1895. p.625–66; pt.2, p.22–23, 575–614. plate, maps. Also in New York State Geologist, 13th and 15th Annual Reports, 1893 and 1895, p.431–72 and p.22–23, 575–614. The section from the 15th Annual Report of the State Geologist was published separately as Contributions from the Geological Department of Colum-bia University, no.55, Albany, 1897. 3208

White, Theodore Greely. The geology of Essex and Willsboro townships, Essex county, N.Y. *NY Acad Sci Tr*, May 21, 1894. 13:214–33. illus. tables. 3209

Kemp, James Furman. Geology of Moriah and Westport townships, Essex county, N.Y. *In* New York (state). Museum. 48th annual report, 1894. v.1, appendix p.323–55. plates, maps. Also in New York State Museum Bulletin 14, p.323–55. 3210

Cushing, Henry Platt. Report on the geol-ogy of Clinton county. *In* New York (state). Museum. 49th annual report, 1895. 2:21–22, 499–573. plates, charts, tables, maps. Also in New York State Geologist, 15th An-nual Report, 1895, p.21–22, 499–573. 3211

White, Theodore Greely. The faunas of the upper Ordovician strata at Trenton Falls, Oneida co. N.Y. *NY Acad Sci Tr*, Dec. 16, 1895. 15:71–96. 3212

White, Theodore Greely. The original Trenton rocks. *Am J Sci*, Dec. 1896. ser.4:2:430–32. Abstract. Trenton Falls.   3213

Reynolds, Cuyler. Indian kettles. *Sci Am*, June 11, 1898. 78:379. illus. Includes pot holes of Lake George area.   3214

Cushing, Henry Platt. Preliminary report on the geology of Franklin county. *In* New York (state). Museum. 52d annual report, 1898. 2:73–128. plates, map. Also in New York State Geologist, 18th Annual Report, 1898, p.73–128.   3215

Kemp, James Furman. Geology of the Lake Placid region. *In* New York (state). Museum. 52d annual report, 1898. 1:47–67. plate, folded map. Also in New York State Museum Bulletin 21, 1898, p.47–67.   3216

Merrill, George Perkins. On the Ophiolite of Thurman, Warren co. N.Y. with remarks on the Eozoon canadense. *Am J Sci*, Mar. 1899. ser.3:37:189–91.   3217

Cushing, Henry Platt. Augite syenite gneiss near Loon lake, New York. *Geol Soc Am Bul*, Apr. 1, 1899. 10:177–92. plate. Abstracts in *American Geologist*, 23:106, and *Science*, Jan. 27, 1899, n.s.9:141.   3218

Cushing, Henry Platt. Geology of Rand Hill and vicinity, Clinton county. *In* New York (state). Museum. 53d annual report, 1899. p.r37–82. maps. Also in New York State Geologist, 19th Annual Report, 1899, p.r37–82.   3219

Merrill, George Perkins. Notes on the serpentinous rocks of Essex county, New York . . . *In* U.S. National museum. Proceedings, 1899. 12:595–98.   3220

Comstock, Frank Nason. An example of wave-formed cusp at Lake George, New York. *Am Geol*, Mar. 1900. 25:192–94. illus.   3221

Finlay, George I. Preliminary report of field work in the town of Minerva, Essex co. *In* New York (state). Museum. 54th annual report, 1900. 1:r96–102. Also in New York State Geologist, 20th Annual Report, 1900, p.r96–102. Accompanied by geologic map.   3222

Kemp, James Furman. The Cambro-Ordovician outlier at Wellstown, Hamilton county, N.Y. *NY Acad Sci Ann*, 1901. 14:113–15. Abstract. Abstract with discussion by A.A. Julien in *Science*, May 3, 1901, n.s.13:710.   3223

Ogilvie, Ida Helen. . . .Geology of the Paradox lake quadrangle, New York. . . Albany, New York state education department, 1905. 508p. plates, geologic map in pocket. (New York State Museum Bulletin 96. Geology 10.)   3224

Cushing, Henry Platt. . . .Geology of the Long lake quadrangle. Albany, New York state education department, 1907. p.451–531. plates, diagrs. geologic map in pocket. (New York State Museum Bulletin 115. Geology 14.)   3225

Miller, William John. . . .Geology of the Remsen quadrangle, including Trenton Falls and vicinity. . . Albany, University of the State of New York, 1909. 51p. illus. plates, folded geologic map in pocket. (New York State Museum Bulletin 126. Education Bulletin 440.)   3226

Kemp, James Furman and Ruedemann, R. Geology of the Elizabethtown and Port Henry quadrangles. Albany, University of the State of New York, 1910. 173p. plates, figs. map. (New York State Museum Bulletin 138.)   3227

Miller, William John. Geology of the Port Leyden quadrangle, Lewis county, New York. Albany, University of the State of New York, 1910. 61p. plates, fig. map. (New York State Museum Bulletin 135.)   3228

Miller, William John. . . .Geology of the Broadalbin quadrangle, Fulton-Saratoga counties, New York. Albany, University of the State of New York, 1911. 65p. illus. plates, folded maps (1 in pocket). (New York State Museum Bulletin 153.)   3229

Miller, William John. Exfoliation domes in Warren county, N.Y. *NYS Mus Bul*, 1911. 149:187–94.   3230

Miller, William John. Contact action of gabbro on granite in Warren county, New York. *Science*, Oct. 1912. n.s.36:490–92.   3231

Cushing, Henry Platt. Geology of Saratoga Springs and vicinity. Albany, University of the State of New York, 1914. 177p. plates, figs. folded maps. (New York State Museum Bulletin 169.)   3232

Miller, William John. . . .Geology of the North Creek quadrangle, Warren county, New York. Albany, University of the State of New York, 1914. 90p. illus. plates, folded map. (New York State Museum Bulletin 170.)   3233

Martin, James Cook. The pre-Cambrian rocks of the Canton, New York, quadrangle. Albany, University of the State of New York, 1916. 112p. illus. plates, folded maps. Reprint of New York State Museum Bulletin 185. Doctoral thesis, Princeton University, 1913.   3234

Miller, William John. Geology of the Lake Pleasant quadrangle, Hamilton county, N.Y.

Albany, University of the State of New York, 1916. 75p. plate, fig. map. (New York State Museum Bulletin 182.) 3235

Stoller, James Hough. Glacial geology of the Saratoga quadrangle. Albany, University of the State of New York, 1916. 50p. plates, figs. map. (New York State Museum Bulletin 183.) 3236

Miller, William John. Geology of the Blue mountain, New York, quadrangle. Albany, University of the State of New York, 1917. 68p. plate, map. (New York State Museum Bulletin 192.) 3237

Buddington, Arthur Francis. Foliation of the gneissoid syenite-granite complex of Lewis county, New York. *NYS Mus Bul*, 1918. 207–8:101–10. plates, diagrs. 3238

Buddington, Arthur Francis and Smyth, C.H. Jr. Lake Bonaparte quadrangle. *NYS Mus Bul*, 1918. 196:30–32. 3239

Alling, Harold Lattimore. Geology of the Lake Clear region. *In* New York (state). Museum. 14th annual report of the director, 1918. p.111–45. plates, diagrs. col. maps (folded). (New York State Museum Bulletin 207–8.) 3240

Miller, William John. Magnetic iron ores of Clinton county, New York. *Econ Geol*, Nov. 1919. 14:509–36. Discussed by David Hale Newland in *Economic Geology*, Mar. 1920, 15:177–80. Answered by Miller in article entitled "Origin of Adirondack Magnetite Deposits" in *Economic Geology*, Apr.–May 1921, 16:227–33. Abstract of original article in *Geological Society of America Bulletin*, Mar. 31, 1919. Abstract of reply in *Geological Society of America Bulletin*, Mar. 31, 1921, 32: 63–64. 3241

Miller, William John. Geology of the Lake Placid quadrangle. . .with a chapter on Pleistocene geology by Harold L. Alling. Albany, University of the State of New York, 1919. 106p. plates, map. (New York State Museum Bulletin 211–12.) Alling, p.71–95. 3242

Miller, William John. Geology of the Schroon lake quadrangle. Albany, University of the State of New York, 1919. 102p. plates, diagrs. map. (New York State Museum Bulletin 213–14.) 3243

Upham, Warren. Drumlins at Lake Placid. *Geol Soc Am Bul*, Mar. 31, 1920. 31:128–30. Abstract. 3244

Chadwick, George Halcott. . . .The Paleozoic rocks of the Canton quadrangle. . . Albany, University of the State of New York, 1920. 60p. plates, illus. folded map. (New York State Museum Bulletin 217–18.) 3245

Alling, Harold Lattimore. Glacial geology. *NYS Mus Bul*, 1921. 229–30:62–84. plates, illus. Mt. Marcy quadrangle. 3246

Kemp, James Furman. Geology of the Mount Marcy quadrangle. . . Albany, University of the State of New York, 1921. 86p. illus. folded map. (New York State Museum Bulletin 229–30.) 3247

Miller, William John. Geology of the Luzerne quadrangle. Albany, University of the State of New York, 1921. 66p. plate, map. (New York State Museum Bulletin 245–46.) 3248

Kemp, James Furman and Alling, Harold Lattimore. Geology of the Ausable quadrangle. Albany, University of the State of New York, 1925. 126p. illus. tables, map. (New York State Museum Bulletin 261.) 3249

Balk, Robert. Report on the field work done for the New York state geological survey in geological mapping of the Newcomb quadrangle, Essex county, N.Y. *In* New York (state). Museum. 21st report, 1926. p.30–33. 3250

Miller, William John. Geology of the Lyon mountain quadrangle. Albany, University of the State of New York, 1926. 101p. plates, diagrs. map. (New York State Museum Bulletin 271.) 3251

Smyth, Charles Henry Jr. and Buddington, Arthur Francis. . . .Geology of the Lake Bonaparte quadrangle. . . Albany, University of the State of New York, 1926. 106p. plates, folded map in pocket. (New York State Museum Bulletin 269.) 3252

Balk, Robert. Geology of the Newcomb quadrangle. Albany, University of the State of New York, 1932. 106p. illus. map. (New York State Museum Bulletin 290.) 3253

Dale, Nelson Clark. . . .Preliminary report of the geology of the Russell quadrangle. Albany, University of the State of New York, 1934. 16p. folded map. (New York State Museum Circular 15.) 3254

Reed, John Calvin. Geology of the Potsdam quadrangle. Albany, University of the State of New York, 1934. 98p. illus. plates, folded maps. (New York State Museum Bulletin 287.) Also published as doctoral thesis, Princeton University. 3255

Dale, Nelson Clark. Geology of the Oswegatchie quadrangle. Albany, University of the State of New York, 1935. 101p. illus. map. (New York State Museum Bulletin 302.) 3256

Buddington, Arthur Francis. Geology of the Santa Clara quadrangle, New York. Albany, University of the State of New York, 1937. 56p. plate, map. (New York State Museum

Bulletin 309.) Reviewed by Robert Balk in *Economic Geology*, Mar.–Apr. 1937, 33:228–29, and by John Rodgers in *The American Journal of Science*, Feb. 1938, ser.5:35:149–51. 3257

Cannon, Ralph Smyser Jr. Geology of the Piseco lake quadrangle. Albany, University of the State of New York, 1937. 107p. illus. map. (New York State Museum Bulletin 312.) Reviewed by Robert Balk in *Economic Geology*, Mar.–Apr. 1937, 33:229–30, and by John Rodgers in *The American Journal of Science*, Feb. 1938, ser.5:35:149–51. 3258

Gallagher, David. Origin of the magnetite deposits at Lyon mountain, N.Y. Albany, University of the State of New York, 1937. 85p. plates, figs. (New York State Museum Bulletin 311.) Reviewed by Robert Balk in *Economic Geology*, Mar.–Apr. 1938, 33:226–27, and by John Rodgers in *The American Journal of Science*, Feb. 1938, ser.5:35:149–51. 3259

Krieger, Mrs. Medora (Hooper). Geology of the Thirteenth lake quadrangle, New York. Albany, University of the State of New York, 1937. 124p. illus. map. (New York State Museum Bulletin 308.) Reviewed by Robert Balk in *Economic Geology*, Mar.–Apr. 1938, 33:227–28, and by John Rodgers in *The American Journal of Science*, Feb. 1938, ser.5:35:149–51. 3260

Whitcomb, Lawrence. Possible landslip scars on the Bouquet river at Willsboro, N.Y. *Science*, June 10, 1938. n.s.87:530–31. June 1937 landslide. 3261

Whitcomb, Lawrence. Paleozoic portion of the Willsboro quadrangle, New York. *Geol Soc Am Bul*, Dec. 1, 1938. 49:1906. Abstract. 3262

Newland, David Hale. The landslide on the Bouquet river near Willsboro, N.Y. Albany, University of the State of New York, 1938. 7p. illus. (New York State Museum Circular 20.) 3263

Miller, William John. Origin of the magnetic iron ores in the Lyon mountain region, N.Y. *Econ Geol*, Dec. 1939. 34:947. Abstract. 3264

Gordon, Clarence Everett. Wasting stagnant ice near Lake Placid, N.Y. *Geol Soc Am Bul*, Dec. 1, 1941. 52:1906. 3265

Buddington, Arthur Francis and Whitcomb, Lawrence. ...Geology of the Willsboro quadrangle, New York. Albany, University of the State of New York, 1941. 137p. illus. plates, tables, maps (folded map in pocket). (New York State Museum Bulletin 325.) 3266

Newland, David Hale and Vaughan, Henry. Guide to the geology of the Lake George region. Albany, University of the State of New York, 1942. 234p. figs. geologic map in color. (New York State Museum Handbook 19.) 3267

Stephenson, Robert Charles. The relations of the anorthosite and gabbro in the Lake Sanford area, New York. *Am Geophys Union Tr*, 1942. 23:345–46. Abstract. 3268

Marble, John Putnam. Possible age of allanite from Whiteface mountain, Essex county, New York, *Am J Sci*, Jan. 1943. 241:32–42. illus. Also issued as a reprint. 3269

Balsley, James Robinson Jr. Vanadium-bearing magnetite-ilmenite deposits near Lake Sanford, Essex county, New York. Washington, G.P.O. 1943. 123p. plate, table, folded maps in pocket. (U.S. Geological Survey Bulletin 940–D.) 3270

Stephenson, Robert Charles. Titaniferous magnetite deposits of the Lake Sanford area, New York. N.Y. American institute of mining and metallurgical engineers, 1945. 25p. illus. tables, maps. (American Institute of Mining and Metallurgical Engineers Technical Publication 1789.) Also called *Mining Technology*, Jan. 1945. Abstracts published in *Economic Geology*, Jan.–Feb. 1945, 40:94, and *American Geophysical Union Transactions*, 1942, pt.2, p.345–46. Doctoral thesis, Johns Hopkins University. 3271

Stephenson, Robert Charles. Titaniferous magnetite deposits of the Lake Sanford area, New York. Albany, University of the State of New York, 1945. 95p. plates, illus. maps (part folded in pocket). (New York State Museum Bulletin 340.) 3272

Jaffe, Howard William. Postanorthosite gabbro near Avalanche lake in Essex county, New York. *J Geol*, Mar.–Apr. 1946. 54:105–16. illus. tables, maps. 3273

Bardill, John Duclos. Magnetic surveys, Dannemora magnetite district, Clinton county, N.Y. College Park, Md. U.S. Bureau of mines, 1947. 7p. plate, map. (U.S. Bureau of Mines Report of Investigations, no.4002.) Processed. 3274

Bardill, John Duclos. Magnetic surveys, Redford-Clayburg magnetite district, Saranac and Black Brook, Clinton co. N.Y. College Park, Md. U.S. Bureau of mines, 1947. 6p. map. (U.S. Bureau of Mines Report of Investigations, no.4003.) Processed. 3275

Bardill, John Duclos. Magnetic surveys, Russian station magnetite district, Clinton county, N.Y. College Park, Md. U.S. Bureau of mines, 1947. 7p. plates. (U.S. Bureau of Mines Report of Investigations, no.4008.) Processed. 3276

Levin, Samuel Benedict. Petrology and genesis of Gore mountain garnet, New York. *Geol Soc Am Bul*, Dec. 1948. 59:1335–36. Abstract.   3277

Jaffe, Howard William. The Avalanche (Colden) dike. *Ad-i-ron-dac*, May–June 1949. 13:52–54, 57. illus.   3278

Shaub, Benjamin Martin. Magnetic anomalies of the Russell, N.Y. quadrangle. Albany? 1949. 9p. illus. (New York State Science Service Report of Investigation, 2, May 1949.) Preliminary report. Processed. His "Magnetic Anomalies of the Santa Clara, N.Y. Quadrangle" was published in July 1954 as Report. . .4; Paradox Lake, Report . . .5, July 1954.   3279

Postel, Albert Williams. Geology of Clinton county magnetite district, New York. Washington, G.P.O. 1952. 88p. illus. tables, charts, maps in pocket. (U.S. Geological Survey Professional Paper 237.)   3280

Buddington, Arthur Francis. Geology of the Saranac quadrangle, New York. Albany, 1953. 100p. plates, tables, maps. (New York State Museum Bulletin 346.)   3281

Burnham, Koert D., Butterfield, H.M. and Hall, A.L. Geology of the Willsboro, N.Y. wollastonite deposits. Preprint of paper delivered before Los Angeles meeting of American institute of mining and metallurgical engineers. February 18, 1953. Boston, Cabot carbon co. 1953. 8p. illus. map.   3282

MINERALOGY

Agar, William Macdonough. The minerals of St. Lawrence, Jefferson and Lewis counties, New York. *Am Min*, Oct.–Nov. 1921. 6:148–53, 158–64. maps   3283

Alling, Harold Lattimore. The Adirondack graphite deposits. Albany, University of the State of New York, 1918. 150p. illus. maps (part folded). (New York State Museum Bulletin 199.)   3284

Amberg, C.R. and McMahon, J.F. comps. Wollastonite, an industrial mineral: a report. Alfred, N.Y. New York state college of ceramics, n.d. 60p. illus. figs. tables. (Ceramic Experiment Station Bulletin no.4.) Results of studies made for the Industrial and Development Division, Office of Technical Studies, U.S. Department of Commerce, 1947–48. Includes contributions by C.R. Amberg, K.D. Burnham, Eugene Wainer, Martin Levitin, Mark Neitlick, Richard Palmer, A.J. Kirsch and J.F. McMahon.   3285

Barth, Thomas Fredrik Weiby. Mineralogy of the Adirondack feldspars. *Am Min*, Apr. 1930. 15:129–43. illus. diagrs.   3286

Bastin, Edson Sunderland. Origin of certain Adirondack graphite deposits. *Econ Geol*, Mar. 1910. 5:134–57. illus. tables, diagrs. Abstract in *Science*, May 13, 1910, n.s.31: 758–59.   3287

Beck, Lewis Caleb. Mineralogy of New York; comprising detailed descriptions of the minerals hitherto found in the State of New York, and notices of their uses in the arts and agriculture. Albany, 1842. 536p. illus. plate. (Natural History of New York, Division 3.)   3288

Beck, Lewis Caleb. Report on Mineralogical and chemical department of survey. *In* New York (state). Legislature. Assembly documents: 1840, no.50, p.37–111; 1841, no.150, p.3–23. Includes Essex, Clinton, Franklin, St. Lawrence, Saratoga, Washington and Warren counties.   3289

Beck, Richard. Nature of ore deposits; tr. and revised by Walter Harvey Weed. . . N.Y. Hill publishing co. 1909. 685p. illus. diagr. map. Titaniferous magnetites of the Adirondacks, p.22–23.   3290

Bernheimer, Alan Weyl. Fluorescence in Herkimer quartz crystals. *Rocks & Min*, May 1936. 11:67.   3291

Blake, William Phipps. Association of apatite with beds of magnetite. *Am Inst Mining Eng Tr*, Feb. 1892. 21:159–60. Lake Sanford ore bed.   3292

Blake, William Phipps. Lanthanite and allanite in Essex county, N.Y. *Am J Sci*, Nov. 1858. ser.2:26:245–46.   3293

Brainerd, A.F. Note on a deposit of fire sand in Clinton county. *Am Inst Mining Eng Tr*, Feb. 1886. 14:757–59. Near Mooer's Forks.   3294

Chahoon, George. Report on iron deposits in the north eastern division (with industrial memoranda). *In* New York (state). Adirondack survey. 7th annual report. . .to year 1879. . . p.413–28. Reprinted in New York (state). State land survey. Report on the progress. . .1891, p.95–111; and State land survey. Report on the progress. . .1894, p.159–76. Also issued as separate, Albany, Weed, Parsons & co. 1880.   3295

Clinton, George W. Notice of the graphite of Ticonderoga. *Alb Inst Tr*, 1830. 1:233–35. Appendix by Henry H. Homes published in *Albany Institute Transactions*, 1887, 11:53–54.   3296

Cox, Charles Francis. Additional notes on recently discovered deposits of diatomaceous earth in the Adirondacks. *NY Acad Sci Tr*, Nov. 20, 1893. 13:98–101.   3297

Cox, Charles Francis. On recently discovered deposits of diatomaceous earth in the Adirondacks. *NY Acad Sci Tr*, May 8, 1893. 12:219–20.   3298

Cross, Roselle Theodore. Anent the "Collector's paradise." *Min Coll*, Apr. 1899. 6:33–34. Observations and corrections of locations in Valiant, W.S. "A Collector's Paradise," *Mineral Collector*, Mar. 1899.   3299

Cross, Roselle Theodore. Hunting for crystals in northern New York. *Min Coll*, Aug. 1903. 10:87–92. St. Lawrence and Herkimer counties.   3300

Crystalline graphite—New York. *Min Ind*, 1908. 17:493–94.   3301

Cumings, W.L. The Mineville magnetites. *Eng & Min J*, July 7, 1906. 82:25–26. diagr. Shape of ore body at the Cheever mine. 3302

Dana, Edward Salisbury. Mineralogical notes. 1. Allanite. *Am J Sci*, Jan.–June 1884. ser.3:27:479. Crystal from Port Henry.   3303

Eckel, Edwin C. Pyrite deposits of the western Adirondacks, New York. *USGS Bul*, 1905. 260:587–88.   3304

Edwards, Arthur Mead. Microscopical examination of two minerals. *Ly Nat Hist Proc*, 1870. p.96–98. Minerals from Thurman Station.   3305

Elwell, Wilbur J. A mineralogical trip through northern New York. *Rocks & Min*, Feb. 1936. 11:20–21. Visited Gouverneur, Port Henry, Lake Placid, etc.   3306

Hall, James. Notice of the plumbago of Ticonderoga. *Am J Sci*, Jan. 1823. 6:178. From Cobble Hill.   3307

Hartnagel, Chris Andrew. A brief account of economic minerals in northern and central New York. *Up-Stater*, Jan. 1930. 2:no.1:12–13, 15.   3308

Jackson, Charles T. On eupyrchroite of Crown Point, New York. *Am J Sci*, Nov. 1851. ser.2:12:73–74.   3309

Julien, Alexis Anastay. On a form of graphite found at Ticonderoga, N.Y. *NY Acad Sci Tr*, May 14, 1883. 2:148–49. Brief abstract of paper read before the society.   3310

Kemp, James Furman. Notes on the minerals occurring near Port Henry, N.Y. *Am J Sci*, July 1890. ser.3:40:62–64.   3311

Kemp, James Furman. The ore deposits of the United States and Canada. . . 5th ed. entirely rewritten and enlarged. N.Y. & London, Scientific publishing co. 1903. 481p. plate, illus. tables, maps.   3312

Ladoo, Raymond Bardeen. Wollastonite, a new industrial mineral. *Eng & Min J*, Nov. 1950. 151:no.11:95–97. illus. Willsboro deposit.   3313

Larsen, Esper Signius and Schaller, W.T. Serendibite from Warren county, New York, and its paragenesis. *Am Min*, Oct. 1932. 17:457–65. diagr. table. Found in large quantities west of Johnsburg.   3314

Leonard, Benjamin Franklin 3d. Magnetite deposits of the St. Lawrence county district, New York. *Geol Soc Am Bul*, Dec. 1950. 61:1481–82. Abstract.   3315

Levin, Samuel Benedict. Garnet evidence in Adirondack petrogeny. *NY Acad Sci Tr*, Mar. 1949. ser.2:11:no.5:156–62.   3316

Levin, Samuel Benedict. Genesis of some Adirondack garnet deposits. *Geol Soc Am Bul*, June 1950. 61:519–65. illus. maps. Reprint published as Columbia University thesis.   3317

Lindgren, Waldemar. Mineral deposits. N.Y. McGraw, 1913. 883p. illus. diagrs. Magnetites of the Adirondacks, p.756–57. 3318

Loomis, Frederick Brewster. Field book of common rocks and minerals, for identifying the rocks and minerals of the United States and interpreting their origins and meanings. N.Y. G.P. Putnam, c1923. 278p. plate. Brief mention of locales in the Adirondacks where various minerals and rocks are found. 3319

McKeown, Francis A. and Klemic, Harry. Reconnaissance for radioactive materials in northeastern United States during 1952. Washington, 1953. 68p. figs. tables. maps. (Trace Elements Investigative Report TEI-317A.) Prepared for the Atomic Energy Commission. Adirondacks, p.12–19. 3320

Maynard, George William. The iron ore of Lake Champlain, United States of America. *Iron & Steel*, May 1874. 1:109–36. Refers to the Adirondack region proper as well as to that immediately bordering on Lake Champlain. Includes discussion. 3321

Merrill, Frederick James Hamilton. . . .Mineral resources of New York state. . . Albany, University of the State of New York, 1895. p.365–595. 2 folded maps incl. front. (New York State Museum Bulletin 15.) Adirondacks, p.532–37.   3322

Millar, Wilton Tisdale. Investigation of magnetite deposits at Star Lake, St. Lawrence county, N.Y. Washington, G.P.O. 1947. 14p.

figs. (U.S. Bureau of Mines. Report of Investigations, no.4127.) 3323

Miller, William John. Genesis of certain Adirondack garnet deposits. *Am Min*, June 1938. 23:399–408. map. Abstracts in Dec. 1937 and Mar. 1938 issues, 22:pt.2:9 and 23:174. 3324

Miller, William John. Origin of pyrite deposits of St. Lawrence county, New York. *Econ Geol*, Jan.–Feb. 1926. 21:65–67. 3325

Miller, William John. Some crystal localities in St. Lawrence county, New York. *Am Min*, Apr. 1921. 6:77–79. 3326

Nason, Frank Lewis. The importance of the iron ores on the Adirondack region. *Am Iron & Steel Inst Yrbk*, 1922. 12:168–207. illus. diagrs. tables, folded maps. 3327

Nason, Frank Lewis. Notes on some of the iron-bearing rocks of the Adirondack mountains. *Am Geol*, July 1893. 12:25–31. 3328

Nason, Frank Lewis. Some New York minerals and their localities. Albany, University of the State of New York, 1888. 19p. plate. (New York State Museum Bulletin 4.) Newcomb tourmalines and pyroxenes from Ticonderoga. 3329

New graphite discovery. *Eng & Min J*, Dec. 9, 1916. 102:1014. Between Lake George and Lake Champlain. 3330

New York state mineral resources, a survey. *NYS Lab Ind Bul*, Feb. 1950. 29:no.2:9–13, 33. 3331

Newland, David Hale. The microstructure of titaniferous magnetites; discussion of paper by J.T. Singewald Jr. *Econ Geol*, Sept. 1913. 8:610–13. 3332

Newland, David Hale. The mineral resources of the State of New York. Albany, University of the State of New York, 1921. 315p. tables, map. (New York State Museum Bulletin 223–24.) 3333

Newland, David Hale. Minerals of Whiteface mountain. *Rocks & Min*, June 1935. 10:81–82. 3334

Newland, David Hale. Pyrite in northern New York. *Eng & Min J*, Dec. 1, 1917. 104:947–48. 3335

Newton, E.H. Catalogue of the minerals of Washington county. *In* New York state agricultural society. Transactions, 1849. 9:857–62. 3336

No platinum in Adirondacks. *Eng & Min J*, Dec. 15, 1917. 104:1053. 3337

Norton, S. The iron ores of New York state. *Iron Age*, Feb. 17, 1910. 85:382–87. illus. Synopsis of address before the Society of Engineers of Eastern New York, Feb. 9, 1910. 3338

Osborne, Freleigh Fitz. Adirondack magnetite deposits. *Econ Geol*, Aug. 1934. 29:500–1. 3339

Postel, Albert Williams. Magnetite deposits of the Clinton county district, New York. *Geol Soc Am Bul*, Dec. 1950. 61:1494. Abstract. 3340

Reed, Donald Frank and Cohen, Charles J. Further investigation of the Redford-Clayburg magnetite district, Clinton county, N.Y. Washington, U.S. Bureau of mines, 1949. 14p. plates. (U.S. Bureau of Mines Report of Investigations, no.4447.) Processed. 3341

Reed, Donald Frank and Cohen, Charles J. Star Lake magnetite deposits, St. Lawrence county, N.Y. (Nov. 1945 to Nov. 1946). College Park, Md. U.S. Bureau of mines, 1947. 34p. maps. (U.S. Bureau of Mines Report of Investigations, no.4131.) Processed. Supplements Millar's work (no.3323). 3342

Ries, Heinrich. Allanite crystals from Mineville, Essex county, New York. *NY Acad Sci Tr*, May 17, 1897. 16:327–29. illus. 3343

Ries, Heinrich. Economic geology, with special reference to the United States; new and rev. ed. N.Y. Macmillan, 1910. 589p. plates, illus. tables, maps. Distribution of magnetites in the United States Adirondack region, p.352–57. 3344

Ries, Heinrich. The monoclinic pyroxenes of New York state. *NY Acad Sci Ann*, Mar. 17, 1895. 9:124–80. Augites: The Adirondack area, p.144–55. Contains many other references to the Adirondack area. 3345

Ries, Heinrich. Notes of recent mineral developments at Mineville. *In* New York (state). Museum. 56th annual report, 1902. 1:r125–26. Also in New York State Geologist, 22d Annual Report, 1902, p.125–26. 3346

Rowley, Elmer B. Brown tourmaline: a new American locality. *Rocks & Min*, Sept.–Oct. 1955. 30:461–63. North shore of Brant Lake. 3347

Rowley, Elmer B. Vesuvianite crystals from Essex county, New York. *Rocks & Min*, Nov.–Dec. 1948. 23:906–7. On Olmstedville-Minerva road. 3348

Sanford, Robert S. and Stone, L.H. Investigation of Broughton and Ring magnetite deposits, Essex co. N.Y. College Park, Md. U.S. Bureau of mines, 1949. 4p. fig. maps. (U.S. Bureau of Mines Report of Investigations, no. 4404.) Processed. 3349

Schmidt, A. Die magnetit-lagerstatten bei Port Henry im Staat New York. *Z Prak Geol*, Sept. 19, 1887. 5:318. 3350

Seybert, Henry. Analysis of the tabular spar, from the vicinity of Willsborough, Lake Champlain, and of the pyroxene and colophonite, which accompany it. *Am J Sci*, Jan.-June 1822. 5:113–18.   3351

Silliman, Benjamin. Notices of minerals and rocks chiefly in Berkshire, Mass. and contiguous to the waters of the upper Hudson and the lakes George and Champlain. *Am J Sci*, Oct. 1821. 4:40–50.   3352

Singewald, Joseph Theophilus. The titaniferous ores in the United States, their composition and economic value. Washington, G.P.O. 1913. 145p. plates, maps, tables. (U.S. Bureau of Mines Bulletin 64.)   3353

Slocum, Horace W. Rambles in a collector's paradise. *Rocks & Min*, June—Nov.-Dec. 1948. 23:497–503, 579–89, 675–80, 771–77, 892–98. illus. maps. Mineral localities in St. Lawrence County.   3354

Smith, Edward Staples Cousens and Kruesi, Oscar. Polycrase in New York state. *Am Min*, Sept.-Oct. 1947. 32:585–87. illus. Correction in Jan.-Feb. 1948 issue, 33:92–93. Day, Saratoga County.   3355

Smock, John Conover. Iron ores of New York; revised by F.J.H. Merrill. *NYS Mus Bul*, 1895. 15:529–43. Brief extract from his First Report on the Iron Mines and Iron-ore Districts in the State of New York. (Museum Bulletin 7, June 1889.)   3356

Smyth, Charles Henry Jr. Crystalline limestones and associated rocks of the northwestern Adirondack region. *Geol Soc Am Bul*, Mar. 22, 1895. 6:263–84. illus.   3357

Smyth, Charles Henry Jr. The genetic relations of certain minerals of northern New York. *NY Acad Sci Tr*, May 18, 1896. 15:26–70. "Northwestern portion of the Adirondack area of crystalline rocks, comprising parts of St. Lawrence, Jefferson and Lewis counties, N.Y."   3358

Smyth, Charles Henry Jr. Metamorphism of a gabbro occurring in St. Lawrence county, N.Y. *Am J Sci*, Apr. 1896. ser.4:1:273–81. Town of Russell.   3359

Smyth, Charles Henry Jr. On the genesis of the pyrite deposits of St. Lawrence county. *NYS Mus Bul*, 1912. 158:143–82. plates. 3360

Smyth, Charles Henry Jr. Report on the crystalline rocks of St. Lawrence county. *In* New York (state). Museum. 49th annual report, 1895. 2:20–21, 477–97. Also in New York State Geologist, 15th Annual Report, 1895, 2:20–21, 477–97.   3361

Some of the mineral resources of New York. *Am Q J Agri & Sci*, July 1846. 4:27–44. Includes discussion of Adirondack deposits of iron and building materials.   3362

Stratton, Everett Franklin and Joyce, James Wallace. A magnetic study of some iron deposits. Washington, G.P.O. 1932. 32p. diagrs. (U.S. Bureau of Mines Technical Paper 528.) Part of the field work was done in the Mineville area.   3363

Troost, G. Description of a new crystalline form of quartz. *Acad Nat Sci Ph J*, June 4, 1822. 2:pt.2:212–14. Quartz crystals from Lake George.   3364

Valiant, W.S. A collector's paradise. *Min Coll*, Mar.-Aug. 1899. 6:1–5, 29–33, 51–56, 67–72, 84–89, 93–98. Mineral localities in the Adirondack area.   3365

Vanuxem, Lardner. Description and analysis of the table spar, from the vicinity of Willsborough, Lake Champlain. *Acad Nat Sci Ph J*, Mar. 5, 1822. 2:pt.1:182–85.   3366

Vogdes, Anthony. Notes on the distribution of iron ores in the United States. Compiled from various geological reports. Fort Monroe, Va. U.S. Artillery school, 1886. 24p. Magnetic Ores of Adirondack, p.8–10.   3367

Watts, Arthur Simeon. The feldspar of the New England and north Appalachian states. Washington, G.P.O. 1916. 181p. plates, illus. tables, map. (U.S. Bureau of Mines Bulletin 92.) Scattered references to the Adirondacks.   3368

Wheeler, Everett P. 2d. Massive leucocoxene in Adirondack titanium deposit. *Econ Geol*, Sept.-Oct. 1950. 45:574–77. Description of mineral association.   3369

Whitlock, Herbert Percy. ...List of New York mineral localities. Albany, University of the State of New York, 1903. 108p. (New York State Museum Bulletin 70, Mineralogy 3.)   3370

Whitlock, Herbert Percy. Minerals from Lyon mountain, Clinton county. *NYS Mus Bul*, 1907. 107:55–96. plates.   3371

Whitney, J.D. On the occurrence of the ores of iron in the Azoic system. *Am Assn Adv Sci Proc*, 1856. 9:209–16. Discussion of the iron ores of northern New York compared to others of the same age. Also published in *American Journal of Science*, Nov. 1856, ser.2: 22:38–44, and in *Mining Magazine*, July-Aug. 1856, 7:67–73.   3372

Zimmer, Paul William. Anhydrite and gypsum in the Lyon mountain magnetite deposit of the northeastern Adirondacks. *Am Min*, Nov.-Dec. 1947. 32:647–53.   3373

Zodac, Peter. The editor goes afield; his experiences on a four day collecting trip. *Rocks & Min*, Jan. 1937. 12:3–14. Collecting trip through northern New York, including Ausable Forks, Mineville and Keene Valley.   3374

PLANT SCIENCE

GENERAL

Baehni, Charles. Esquisses de géographie botanique américaine. *In* Institut national genevois. Bulletin, 1937. 51–A:9–30. plate. Adirondacks, p.12–14. 3375

Baldwin, Henry Ives. Soil temperatures and evaporation in a paper birch—white pine forest, Long Lake, Hamilton county, New York. *Ecology,* Jan. 1933. 14:75. 3376

Bray, William L. The development of the vegetation of New York state. Syracuse, N.Y. Syracuse university, 1915. 186p. plates, map. (New York State College of Forestry, Technical Publication 3.) 2d edition published in 1930 as Technical Publication 29. Vegetation of the Adirondacks is treated in many places, generally and in detail. See also his "Aim and Outcome of Reconnaissance Survey of the Vegetation on New York State" in the *Empire Forester,* 1916, 2:6–8. illus. 3377

Britton, Mrs. Elizabeth Gertrude (Knight). The storing of seeds by squirrels. *Torreya,* Sept. 1901. 1:108–9. White pine seeds at Chilson Lake. 3378

Dobbin, Frank. An August outing. *Am Bot,* Jan. 1907. 11:112–15. Botanical expedition near head of Lake Champlain. 3379

Eggleston, Willard Webster. Peter Kalm's visit to Lake Champlain in July, 1749. *Ver Bot C Bul,* Apr. 1907. 2:32–33. 3380

Gunderson, Alfred. Field trip (Torrey botanical club) to Mount Marcy, Aug. 6–8, 1937. *Torreya,* Feb. 1938. 38:9. 3381

Hagelstein, Robert. An Adirondack myxomycete. *Mycologia,* Jan.–Feb. 1935. 27:86–88. illus. 3382

Harshberger, John William. The plant formation of the Adirondack mountains. *Torreya,* Nov. 1905. 5:187–94. 3383

House, Homer Doliver. Bibliography of the botany of New York state, 1751–1940. Albany, University of the State of New York, 1942. 2v. (New York State Museum Bulletin 328–29.) Section on the Adirondack mountains; also a section on each of the counties in the Adirondack preserve. 3384

Kalm, Peter. Travels into North America. . . translated into English by John Reinhold Forster. Warrington, Eng. 1770. 3v. plates. Observations in Champlain valley, v.2, p.309–17, v.3, p.1–44. 2d edition published in London in 1772. Another edition edited by Adolph B. Benson, New York, Wilson-Erickson Inc. 1937, 2v. 3385

Parsons, Arthur L. Peat: its formation, uses and occurrence in New York. *In* New York (state). Museum. 57th annual report, 1903. pt.1, p.15–88. Includes Adirondacks. 3386

Peck, Charles Horton. Plants of Bonaparte swamp. *In* New York (state). Museum. 53d annual report, 1899. p.858–61. Part of the Annual Report of the State Botanist. Eastern shore of Lake Bonaparte. 3387

Peck, Charles Horton. Whence the seeds? *Bot Gaz,* Mar. 1878. 3:23. Short discussion of plants growing in logged-off area of Essex County. Answer to a question in the Jan. 1878 issue quoting article by O.S. Phelps that appeared originally in the *Plattsburg Republican,* Sept. 1, 1877, and was reprinted with title "Growth of a Tree" (no.3516). 3388

Prentiss, Albert Nelson. Notes on the Adirondacks. *Torrey Bot C Bul,* Apr. 1883. 10:43–45. Botanical trip to Blue Mountain Lake. 3389

Ries, Heinrich. Uses of peat and its occurrence in New York. *In* New York (state). Museum. 55th annual report, 1901. p.r53–90. plates, tables. 3390

Rommell, L.G. and Heiberg, S.O. Types of humus layer in the northeastern United States. *Ecology,* July 1931. 12:567–608. tables. 3391

Schweinfurth, Charles. Botanizing in the Adirondack region. *High Spots,* Apr. 1931. 8: no.2:14–15. Lake George, Keene Valley, Johns Brook, Heart Lake. 3392

Torrey botanical club. Field meeting and botanical symposium at Little Moose lake. *Torreya,* Aug. 1906. 6:176–77. 3393

Walters, Charles S. Adirondack lake shore vegetation. I. Deer island and Big Wolf island permanent quadrants. 81 leaves. mounted photographs, tables, maps. Master's thesis, State University of New York, College of Forestry, Syracuse, 1940. Typescript. 3394

Young, Vernon Alphus. Plant distribution as influenced by soil heterogeneity in the Cranberry lake region of the Adirondack mountains. *Ecology,* Apr. 1934. 15:154–96. 3395

FUNGI

Burnham, Stewart Henry. The admirable Polyporus in the flora of the Lake George region. *Torreya,* June 1916. 16:139–42. 3396

Hunt, Willis Roberts. Collections of rusts made in New York state. *Mycologia,* Sept.–Oct. 1929. 21:288–91. Three-month collection trip along the Moose River. 3397

Kauffman, Calvin Henry. The fungi of North Elba. *NYS Mus Bul*, 1915. 179:80–104. Also issued as reprint. 3398

Krieger, Louis Charles Christopher. A popular guide to the higher fungi (mushrooms) of New York state. Albany, University of the State of New York, 1935. 538p. plates, illus. map. (New York State Museum Handbook 11.) 3399

Mains, Edwin Butterworth. A new species of Cordyceps with notes concerning other species. *Mycologia*, Nov.–Dec. 1937. 29:674–77. fig. Includes discussion of species collected in the Adirondacks. 3400

Murrill, William Alphonso. Collecting fungi in the Adirondacks. *NY Bot Gar J*, Nov. 1912. 13:174–78. 3401

Murrill, William Alphonso. Lake Placid fungi. *Mycologia*, Mar. 1924. 16:96–98. 3402

Murrill, William Alphonso. Melanoleuca pulverulentipes Murrill, sp. nov. *Mycologia*, May 1917. 9:179. 3403

Murrill, William Alphonso. Omphalopsis pallida Murrill, sp. nov. *Mycologia*, Jan. 1917. 9:41. 3404

Murrill, William Alphonso. Preliminary list of Upper St. Regis fungi. *Mycologia*, Nov. 1915. 7:297–306. illus. plates. 3405

Peck, Charles Horton. Report of the second class in the second department—botany. *Alb Inst Tr*, 1876. 8:152–66. Adirondack fungus, p.158–59. 3406

Smith, Alexander Hanchett. A preliminary list of fungi from the Huntington forest. *Roos Wildlife Bul*, Nov. 1940. 7:383–86. 3407

Smith, Clayton Orville. Notes on the species of Agaricus (Psalliota) of the Champlain valley. *Rhodora*, Sept. 1899. 1:161–64. 3408

Snell, Walter Henry. Notes on Boletes. *Mycologia*, May–June 1932, May–June 1933, July–Aug. 1934, Jan.–Feb., Sept.–Oct. 1936. 24:334–41; 25:221–32; 26:348–59; 28:13–23, 463–75. plate, table. 3409

LICHENS AND MOSSES

Burnham, Stewart Henry. Hepaticae of the Lake George flora. *Bryologist*, July 1919. 22:33–37. 3410

Burnham, Stewart Henry. Lichens of the Lake George region. *Bryologist*, Jan., Mar., May, July 1922. 25:1–8, 34–37, 58–59, 72–78. 3411

Burnham, Stewart Henry. The mosses of the Lake George flora. *Bryologist*, Mar., May, July 1920. 23:17–26, 38–45, 54–60. 3412

Burnham, Stewart Henry. Supplementary list of the Bryophytes of the Lake George region. *Bryologist*, Sept. 1929. 32:94–98. 3413

Demarest, Josephine M. Lichens. *High Spots*, Apr. 1934. 11:no.2:18–19. 3414

Demarest, Josephine M. A very few mosses. *High Spots*, Jan. 1932. 9:no.1:22–23. illus. 3415

Harris, Carolyn Wilson. Lichens of the Adirondack league club tract. *Bryologist*, July 1907. 10:64–66. 3416

Harris, Carolyn Wilson. A list of the foliaceous and fruticous lichens collected at Chilson lake, Essex county, New York. *Bryologist*, May 1906. 9:48–52. 3417

Haynes, Caroline Coventry. A list of the hepatics collected in the vicinity of Little Moose lake, Adirondack league club tract, Herkimer county, New York. *Bryologist*, July 1906. 9:62–63. 3418

Haynes, Caroline Coventry. Notes on a colony of hepatics found associated on a dead fungus. *Bryologist*, Mar. 1905. 8:31–32. On Adirondack League Club tract. 3419

Heady, Harold Franklin. Annotated list of the mosses of the Huntington forest. Syracuse, N.Y. 1942. 58p. (Roosevelt Wildlife Bulletin, v.8, no.2.) Also issued as Bulletin of the New York State College of Forestry, v.15, no.2a. 3420

Jackson, Herbert Spencer. The Mycological society of America. Summer foray (at Seventh lake). *Mycologia*, May–June 1935. 27:323–27. Description of trip with list of "Noteworthy Collections." 3421

Levy, Daisy J. Preliminary list of mosses collected in the neighborhood of Huletts Landing, Lake George, N.Y. *Bryologist*, May 1919. 22:23–26. 3422

Lowe, Josiah Lincoln. The genus Lecidea in the Adirondack mountains of New York. *Lloydia*, Dec. 1939. 2:225–310. illus. 3423

Lowe, Josiah Lincoln. A preliminary list of the lichens of the Huntington forest. *Roos Wildlife Bul*, Nov. 1940. 7:371–82. 3424

Mycological society of America. The summer foray. *Mycologia*, May–June 1934. 26:277–78. First announcement of trip to be held at Seventh lake Aug. 21–24, 1934. Signed by B.O. Dodge, F.C. Stewart and H.M. Fitzpatrick as committee members. ·3425

Smith, Mrs. Annie (Morrill). A list of mosses collected on the Adirondack league club tract, Herkimer county, New York. *Bryologist*, July 1906. 9:63–66. 3426

Smith, Mrs. Annie (Morrill). Seligeria doniana on Chilson lake. *Bryologist*, Oct. 1901. 4:63. 3427

Torrey, Raymond Hezekiah. Cladoniae of the north woods. *Torreya*, May–June 1934. 34:57–74. plates. 3428

York, Harlan Harvey. A peridermium new to the northeastern United States. *Science,* Nov. 19, 1926. n.s.64:500–1. Collected at Round Lake, near Woodgate, N.Y. 3429

FERNS

Aspidium fragrans Swartz. *Torrey Bot C Bul,* Sept. 1873. 4:42. Brief note on station at Avalanche Lake. 3430

Benedict, Ralph Curtis. An Adirondack fern list. *Am Fern J,* July–Sept. 1916. 6:81–85. Supplementary list by A.W. Brown in issue for Jan.–Mar. 1917, 7:18–19. 3431

Benedict, Ralph Curtis. Fern miscellany: Pilot Knob, N.Y. *Am Fern J,* Apr.–June 1953. 43:74–83. illus. 3432

Benedict, Ralph Curtis. Pilot Knob supplement. *Am Fern J,* Apr.–June 1954. 44:69–72. 3433

Burnham, Stewart Henry. Braun's holly fern. *Am Fern J,* Jan. 1914. 4:1–5. Includes discussion of locations on Lake George and in the Adirondacks. 3434

Burnham, Stewart Henry. The ferns of the Lake George flora. *Am Fern J,* July–Sept. 1916—Apr.–June 1917. 6:85–90, 97–105; 7: 12–15, 54–63. illus. A partial reprint was issued. Supplementary list of the ferns of the Lake George flora, Oct.–Dec. 1923, 13:109–13. 3435

Burnham, Stewart Henry. Lake George flora stations for Botrychium lanceolatum. *Am Fern J,* Oct.–Dec. 1917. 7:124. Brief note supplementing his "Ferns of the Lake George Flora" (no.3435). 3436

Davenport, George Edward. Notes on Botrychium simplex, Hitchcock. Salem, Mass. Printed by J.H. Choate, 1877. 22p. plates. Supplementary note on location of fern on John Brown's Tract, p.20–21. 3437

Gilbert, Benjamin Davis. Aspidium spinulosum. *Torrey Bot C Bul,* Dec. 1879. 6:366–68. 3438

Gilbert, Benjamin Davis. The fern flora of New York. *Fern Bul,* Oct. 1903. 11:97–105. Adirondack region specifically designated. 3439

Hazen, Tracy Elliot. The habitat of the slender cliff-brake. *Torreya,* Nov. 1902. 2:176. Ausable Chasm location. 3440

House, Homer Doliver. Additions to the fern flora of New York state. *Am Fern J,* Jan.–Mar. 1933. 23:1–7. Adirondack locations. 3441

House, Homer Doliver. Some roadside ferns of Herkimer county, New York. *Fern Bul,* Jan. 1902. 10:14–16. 3442

Killip, Ellsworth Paine. A year's collecting in the northeastern United States. *Am Fern J,* Oct.–Dec. 1918. 8:121–26. "The Adirondack and Green Mountains," p.123–25. 3443

Knauz, Marie B. Ferns and club-mosses at Little Moose lake, Adirondack mountains. *Trillia,* Oct. 1930. 9:41–42. 3444

Lewis, Charles Smith. Ferns of the Marcy region. *Am Fern J,* Jan.–Mar. 1926. 16:10–17. 3445

Lewis, William Fisher. Some Adirondack rarities. *Am Fern J,* Apr.–June 1927. 17:37–43. 3446

MacCammon, Gordon W. Bracken fern: its silvicultural aspects in the northeastern forest. 95 leaves. mounted photographs, table, maps (1 in pocket). Master's thesis, State University of New York, College of Forestry, Syracuse, 1938. Typescript. 3447

Millington, Mrs. Lucy A. (Bishop). Aspidium thelypteris Swartz. *Torrey Bot C Bul,* Sept. 1872. 3:43–44. Collection made at Elizabethtown. 3448

Peck, Charles Horton. Aspidium fragrans Swartz. *Torrey Bot C Bul,* July 1871. 2:28. 3449

Phelps, Mrs. Orra (Parker). Notes on Adirondack ferns. *High Spots,* Oct. 1931. 8:no.4: 27–28. 3450

Shorey, Archibald Thompson. Ferns in the Adirondacks. *Ad-i-ron-dac,* May–June 1948. 12:no.3:4, 13. 3451

Shorey, Archibald Thompson. A hiker notices some ferns. *High Spots,* July 1935. 12:no.3: 25–26. 3452

FLOWERING PLANTS

Bond, Miriam Apthorp. Spring flowers. *High Spots,* Apr. 1933. 10:no.2:22–24. 3453

Brainerd, Ezra. Scirpus validus and allies in the Champlain valley. *Rhodora,* Dec. 1904. 6:231–32. 3454

Britton, Nathaniel Lord. Symphoricarpos racemosus Michx. var. pauciflorus Robbins, in New York state. *Torrey Bot C Bul,* Oct. 1881. 8:114. Short note telling of discovery near Port Henry. 3455

Burnham, Stewart Henry. Additional notes on new forms of Rudbeckia. *Am Bot,* Feb. 1914. 20:22–23. Includes Lake George region. 3456

Burnham, Stewart Henry. Additions to the flora of the Lake George region. *NYS Mus Bul,* 1925. 266:109–10. 3457

Burnham, Stewart Henry. Flora of Buck mountain. *Orn & Bot,* Feb. 1892. 11:809. 3458

Burnham, Stewart Henry. The Naiadales of the flora of the Lake George region. *Torreya*, May 1917. 17:80–84.   3459

Burnham, Stewart Henry. Notes on the flora of the Lake George region. *Torreya*, Feb. 1902. 2:27.   3460

Burnham, Stewart Henry. Quadrilliums. *Am Bot*, May 1918. 24:66–67. Brief note on Trillium grandiflorum at Lake George.   3461

Burnham, Stewart Henry. The sedges of the Lake George flora. *Torreya*, July 1919. 19: 125–36.   3462

Caldwell, Dorothy W. Adirondack wild flowers. *High Spots*, June 1930. 7:no.2:10–11. 3463

Caldwell, Dorothy W. Notes on early June flowers in the Johns Brook region. *High Spots*, Apr. 1932. 9:no.2:26–27.   3464

Dr. Engelmann exhibited specimen of black spruce with mistletoe from Adirondacks. *Acad Sci St L Tr*, 1868. 3:lxxxii.   3465

Fisher, George Clyde. A station for the ram's-head lady's slipper. *Torreya*, July–Aug. 1921. 21:63–64.   3466

Gifford, John Clayton. The dwarf mistletoe, Razoumofskya pusilla. *Plant World*, Aug. 1901. 4:149–50. Discovered at Panther Pond by William Howard.   3467

Gilbert, Benjamin Davis. A few plants of the north woods. *Torrey Bot C Bul*, Nov. 1879. 6:362–63. Beaver Lake near Number Four.3468

Gray, Asa. New parasitic plant of the mistletoe family. *Am Nat*, Mar. 1872. 6:166–67. Arceuthobium in Warren and Essex counties.   3469

Gray, Asa. A notice of some new, rare, or otherwise interesting plants from the northern and western portions of the State of New York. *Ly Nat Hist Proc*, 1834. 3:221–38.   3470

Haberer, Joseph Valentine. Plants of Oneida county, New York, and vicinity. *Rhodora*, May–June 1905. 7:92–97, 106–10.   3471

Heady, Harold Franklin. Annotated list of the ferns and flowering plants of the Huntington wildlife station. *Roos Wildlife Bul*, Nov. 1940. 7:234–369. illus.   3472

Heady, Harold Franklin. Littoral vegetation of the lakes of the Huntington forest. Syracuse, N.Y. 1942. 37p. illus. charts, tables. (Roosevelt Wildlife Bulletin, v.8, no.1, June 1942.) Also published as Bulletin of the New York State College of Forestry, v.15, no.2.   3473

Hollick, Charles Arthur. Hieracium aurantiacum L. *Torrey Bot C Bul*, Jan. 1882. 9:12. Observations at Port Henry.   3474

Hough, Franklin Benjamin. A catalogue of the indigenous, naturalized and filicoid plants, of Lewis county, arranged according to the natural method adopted by Professor Torrey, in the state catalogue. *In* New York (state). University. 59th annual report of the regents, 1846. p.249–83. Also published separately, Albany, Van Benthuysen, 1846, 35p.   3475

Houghton, Frederick. Native cold-hardy plants. *Bul Schools*, Mar. 1948. 34:191–94. illus. Plants of the Adirondacks.   3476

House, Homer Doliver. High spots for wild flowers. *High Spots*, Apr. 1935. 12:no.2:12–13. illus.   3477

House, Homer Doliver. Notes on local floras. *In* New York (state). Museum. Bulletins 176, 179, 188, 197, 219–20, 233–34, 243–44. 1915–23. Essex County: 243–44:21–26. Fulton County: 176:22–28; 179:40; 197:52. Hamilton County: 243–44:27–30. Herkimer County: 176:28–29; 219–20:240–41; 243–44:30. Lewis County: 233–34:9–11. Oneida County: 176: 32–39; 179:44–47; 188:62–63; 233–34:41–47. St. Lawrence County: 188:63–64; 243–44:51. Saratoga County: 243–44:52. Warren County: 188:65; 243–44:53. Washington County: 233–34:15; 243–44:54.   3478

Howe, Marshall Avery. A note on the "flowering" of the lakes in the Adirondacks. *Torreya*, Oct. 1903. 3:150–54.   3479

Knieskern, Peter D. Catalogue of plants found in the county of Oneida.. : *In* New York (state). University. 55th annual report of the regents, 1842. p.273–99.   3480

Knight, Elizabeth G. Albinism. *Torrey Bot C Bul*, Nov. 1881. 8:125. Brief observation on Pontederia cordata and Epilobium angustifolium in vicinity of Indian River.   3481

Knowlton, Clarence Hinckley. Butomus umbellatus at Lake Champlain. *Rhodora*, Feb. 1930. 32:18–19.   3482

Millington, Mrs. Lucy A. (Bishop). Arceuthobium shedding its seed. *Torrey Bot C Bul*, Dec. 1872. 3:55–56. Signed: L.A.M.   3483

Muenscher, Walter Conrad. Butomus umbellatus in the Lake Champlain basin. *Rhodora*, Feb. 1930. 32:19–20.   3484

Muenscher, Walter Conrad and Clausen, R.T. Notes on the flora of northern New York. *Rhodora*, Nov. 1934. 36:405–7.   3485

Muenscher, Walter Conrad. The occurrence of Littorella americana in New York. *Rhodora*, May 1934. 36:194.   3486

Murrill, William Alphonso. Botanical features of Lake Placid. *NY Bot Gar J*, May 1924. 25: 142–45.   3487

Paine, John Alsop. Catalogue of plants found in Oneida county and vicinity. Albany, 1865. 140p. "From the Report of the regents of the University of the State of New York, presented March 22, 1865." Not a county flora, includes locations from other parts of the state. Reviewed by Asa Gray in the *American Journal of Science*, Jan. 1866, 41:130–32, with additions. 3488

Peck, Charles Horton. Plants of North Elba. *In* New York (state). Museum. 53d annual report, 1899. 1:65–266. map. Also in New York State Museum Bulletin 28, 1899, p.65–266. 3489

Peck, Charles Horton. Plants of the summit of Mount Marcy. *In* New York (state). Adirondack survey. 7th annual report. . .to the year 1879. . . p.401–12. Reprinted in New York (state). State land survey. Report on the progress. . .1891, p.175–87; and in State land survey. Report on the progress. . .1894, p.241–54. Also in New York State Museum, 52d Annual Report, 1898, 1:657–73. Issued as a separate. Excerpt in *High Spots*, July 1934, 11:no.3:12–14. 3490

Phelps, Mrs. Orra (Parker). Flowering plants in the Adirondacks. *Ad-i-ron-dac*, May–June 1948. 12:no.3:5, 8. 3491

Smith, Mrs. Annie (Morrill). Botany of the Little Moose region. *In* Adirondack league club. Report, 1896. p.54–58. 3492

Smith, Mrs. Annie (Morrill). Flora of Honnedaga lake. *In* Adirondack league club. Handbook, 1894. p.48–54. 3493

Smith, Mrs. Annie (Morrill). List of plants found on the Adirondack league club tract. *In* Adirondack league club. Yearbook, 1898. p.59–72. Her "Corrected and Enlarged List of Plants. . .Hepatics Contributed by Miss Caroline Coventry Haynes" appeared in the *Yearbook* for 1904, p.43–61. 3494

Stevens, George Thomas. The flora of the Adirondacks. *Alb Inst Tr*, Feb. 1868. 6:67–82. Also issued as a separate, Albany, J. Munsell, 1868. 18p. Observations confined chiefly to the county of Essex. 3495

Taylor, Norman. The flora above timber line of Mount Marcy. *Am Scenic & Hist Pres Soc*, 1920. 25:317–18. 3496

Torrey, John. Flora of the State of New York. Albany, 1843. 2v. illus. plates. (Natural History of New York, Division 2.) 3497

Tweedy, Frank. Utricularia resupinata, Greene. *Torrey Bot C Bul*, Feb. 1880. 7:19. Brief note on collecting at Number Four and along shores of Big Moose Lake. 3498

Wood, Ella A. Wild flowers of northern New York. *Flower Grower*, Apr. 1925. 12:173–74. 3499

TREES AND SHRUBS

Adirondack trees. *J Outd Life*, June 1905. 2:111–12. Check list. 3500

Bullard, Herbert F. Identifying Adirondack evergreen trees. *High Spots*, Jan. 1933. 10:no.1:19–21. 3501

Clark, Judson Freeman. On the form of the bole of the balsam fir. *For Quar*, Jan. 1903. 1:58–60. chart. 3502

Congdon, Joseph Whipple. Rhododendron maximum L (near New Russia). *Torrey Bot C Bul*, Sept. 1875. 6:56. 3503

Destruction of spruce trees. *Torrey Bot C Bul*, Apr. 1873. 4:15–16. Parasite Arceuthobium destroying black spruce in Adirondacks. See also "New Mistletoe" in issue for Nov. 1871, 2:42–43, and "Arceuthobium" in issue for Dec. 1871, 2:47–48. 3504

Eggleston, Willard Webster. The Crataegi of Fort Frederick, Crown Point, New York. *Torreya*, Mar. 1904. 4:38–39. 3505

Egler, Frank Edwin. Trees from Marcy to Manhattan. *Bul Schools*, Mar. 1941. 27:215–18. illus. 3506

Fernow, Bernhard Eduard. A list of trees occurring or likely to occur on the Club preserve. *In* Adirondack league club. Yearbook, 1905. p.34–40. Reprinted in Yearbooks for 1906 to 1909. 3507

Fox, William Freeman. The Adirondack black spruce. *In* New York (state). Forest, fish and game commission. Annual report, 1894. p.119–98. plates, tables. Reprint (82p.) issued by J.B. Lyon, Albany, in 1895. 3508

House, Homer Doliver. Dwarf mistletoe on white pine. *Rhodora*, July 6, 1935. 37:268. 3509

Howard, William Gibbs. Adirondack trees. *Ad-i-ron-dac*, July–Aug. 1948. 12:no.4:12–13. illus. 3510

Littlefield, Edward Winchester. A new station for Calluna. *Rhodora*, July 1931. 33:162–63. 3511

Littlefield, Edward Winchester. An uncommon association of pines in northern New York. *Rhodora*, July 1928. 30:129–31. 3512

Parry, Charles Christopher. Visit to the original locality of the new species of Arceuthobium in Warren county, N.Y. *Am Nat*, July 1872. 6:404–6. For brief note of discovery by Lucy Millington, see p.166 of this journal. 3513

Peck, Charles Horton. The black spruce. *Alb Inst Tr*, 1876. 8:283–301. Also issued as a separate. 3514

Peck, Charles Horton. The spruces of the Adirondacks. Albany, 1897. 13p. Read before the Albany Institute, Nov. 16, 1897. 3515

Phelps, Orson S. The growth of a tree, from its germ or seed. . . n.p. n.pub. n.d. 20p. Text is followed by a poem, "Autumn Leaves." First page of text has subtitle "Written for the *Republican*." Copy in the Loomis Collection, Keene Valley Public Library.   3516

Sargent, Charles Sprague. Notes on Crataegus in the Champlain valley. *Rhodora*, Feb. 1901. 3:19–31.   3517

Sears, John Henry. Notes on the forest trees of Essex, Clinton and Franklin counties, New York. *Essex Inst Bul*, 1881. 13:174–88. Sabin lists reprint under Essex Institute.   3518

Welch, Fay. A preliminary survey of the woody plants of Buck island. *Emp For*, 1921. 7:32–35. illus. An island in Cranberry Lake.   3519

ZOOLOGY

GENERAL

DeKay, James Ellsworth. Zoology of New York; comprising detailed descriptions of all the animals hitherto observed within the State of New York... Albany, 1842–44. 6v. in 5. plates (partly col.). (Natural History of New York, pt.1.)   3520

Eldridge, David C. An economic survey of the wildlife of Lewis county, New York. 83 leaves. charts, tables, forms. Master's thesis, State University of New York, College of Forestry, Syracuse, 1952. Typescript. Abstract in Graduate Theses, p.55–56.   3521

Hough, Franklin Benjamin. Catalogue of reptiles and fishes from St. Lawrence county, N.Y. procured for the state Cabinet of natural history by F.B. Hough. *In* New York (state). Cabinet of natural history. 5th annual report, 1852. p.23–28.   3522

King, Ralph Terence. Forest zoology and its relation to a wildlife program on the Huntington forest. *Roos Wildlife Bul*, Sept. 1941. 7:461–505. tables.   3523

Roithmayr, Charles M. Analysis of wildlife productivity of a logged area on the Huntington wildlife forest. 100 leaves. mounted photographs, tables, charts, map. Master's thesis, State University of New York, College of Forestry, Syracuse, 1954. Typescript. Abstract in Graduate Theses, p.58.   3524

FISH

Bean, Tarleton Hoffman. Catalogue of the fishes of New York. Albany, University of the State of New York, 1903. 784p. (New York State Museum Bulletin 60.)   3525

Bean, Tarleton Hoffman. The food and game fishes of New York: notes on their common names, distribution, habits and mode of capture. Albany, J.B. Lyon, 1903. p.251–460. illus. col. plates. From 7th Report of the Forest, Fish and Game Commission.   3526

Brown, George L. Trout in forest fires. *For & Stream*, June 13, 1903. 60:467. Brief letter on

fire at Elizabethtown. See answer in June 27 issue, 60:506. Trout mortality in the Adirondacks.   3527

Clarke, Robert. Fishes of northern New York...letter to editors. *Sci Am*, Feb. 21, 1852. 7:182. Resuscitation of frozen fish. 3528

DeKay, James Ellsworth. Catalogue of the fishes inhabiting the State of New York as classified and described in pt.4 of the New York fauna, with a list of the fishes inhabiting the state discovered since the publication of the zoology. *In* New York (state). Museum. 8th annual report, 1854. p.49–69.   3529

Dence, Wilford Albert. Life history, ecology and habits of the dwarf sucker, Catostomus commersonnii utawana Mather, at the Huntington wildlife station. *Roos Wildlife Bul*, June 1948. 8:81–150.   3530

Dence, Wilford Albert. The occurrence of "free-living" ligula in Catlin lake, central Adirondacks. *Copeia*, July 28, 1940. p.140. Also issued as a reprint.   3531

Dence, Wilford Albert. Preliminary reconnaissance of the waters of the Archer and Anna Huntington wild life forest station and their fish inhabitants. *Roos Wildlife Bul*, Jan. 1937. 6:610–72. plate, map.   3532

Dence, Wilford Albert. An unusual feeding incident in the great northern pike (Esox lucius). *Copeia*. June 30, 1938. p.96.   3533

Flint, Peter. How about the plain fishes? The first pike perch taken in Lake George described. *For & Stream*, June 6, 1914. 82:761–62.   3534

Food for trout. *Field & S*, Nov. 1907. 12:594–95.   3535

Francis, John M. A mystery fish, what is it? *Amer Ang*, Mar. 1921. 5:555–56. Peculiar fish caught at Round Lake.   3536

Fuller, A.R. Frostfish of the Adirondacks. *For & Stream*, Sept. 27, 1883. 21:168.   3537

Fuller, A.R. Pickerel in the Adirondacks. *In* New York (state). Fisheries commission. 21st annual report, 1891. p.132–34.   3538

Greeley, John R. The effect of size at planting on survival and time of downstream migration of Atlantic salmon in a tributary of Lake George. *NY Fish & Game J*, July 1955. 2:161–72. illus. tables. Huddle Brook. 3539

Greeley, John R. Salmon of Lake George. *NYS Con*, Apr.–May 1953. 7:no.5:30–31. illus. 3540

Greeley, John R. Survivals of planted Atlantic salmon in Lake George. *NY Fish & Game J*, Jan. 1955. 2:1–12. illus. tables. 3541

Kendall, William Converse and Dence, Wilford Albert. The fishes of the Cranberry lake region. *Roos Wildlife Bul*, Feb. 1929. 5:219–308. 3542

Mather, Fred. Adirondack fishes. *For & Stream*, Mar. 11, 1886. 26:129. Quotes with comments letter from A.R. Fuller on habits of Miller's thumb (Uranidea gracilis). 3543

Mather, Fred. Memoranda relating to Adirondack fishes, with descriptions of new species... *In* New York (state). State land survey. Report on the progress...1891, p.113–73. Reprinted in State land survey. Report on the progress...1894, p.177–240. 3544

Mather, Fred. Memoranda relating to Adirondack fishes, with descriptions of new species, from researches made in 1882. Albany, Weed, Parsons & co. 1886. 56p. plates. (State of New York. Adirondack survey.) From the appendix to the 12th report. Printed in advance of the report at Colvin's expense. Reviewed in *Forest and Stream*, Jan. 21, 1886, 25:501. 3545

Mather, Fred. Report on fishes and other aquatic life of Adirondack region. *In* New York (state). Commissioner of fisheries. 14th annual report, 1889. p.124–82. plate. 3546

Mead, Charles W. An Adirondack perch-pike problem. *Copeia*, Jan. 22, 1919. no.65:1–2. An abundance of pike and scarcity of perch. See also *Copeia*, May 7, 1919, no.69:24–25. 3547

Mead, Charles W. Pike-fishing incidents. *Copeia*, Sept. 22, 1915. no.22:35–36. Stony Creek Pond no.1. 3548

Merriam, Clinton Hart. The fish of Lake Champlain. *US Fish Com Bul*, Aug. 12, 1884. 4:287–88. 3549

Sherman, Richard U. The Bisby trout. *Am Ang*, Oct. 13–20, 1883. 4:225–26, 241–42. illus. Game fishes of America. Fresh water series. Trout found in Bisby lakes. 3550

Smallwood, William Morton. Preliminary report on diseases of fish in the Adirondacks, a contribution to the life history of Clinostomum marginatum. Syracuse, N.Y. 1914. 27p.

(New York State University. College of Forestry, Syracuse, Technical Publication, no.1.) 3551

Spears, Eldridge A. The trout in the tank. *For & Stream*, June 14, 1902. 58:470. Trout thriving in a tank in front of Will Light's hotel on West Canada Creek. 3552

Webber, Samuel. "Frostfish" of the Adirondacks. *For & Stream*, Feb. 23, 1882. 18:73. Frostfish of the Fulton Chain are whitefish, not smelts. 3553

AMPHIBIANS AND REPTILES

Bachmann, P.H. William. Salamanders of the Adirondacks. *Ad-i-ron-dac*, Sept.–Oct. 1949. 13:106–7. 3554

Bishop, Sherman Chauncey. The salamanders of New York. Albany, 1941. 365p. plates, illus. maps. (New York State Museum Bulletin 324.) Includes lists of salamanders found in each Adirondack county. 3555

Dunn, Emmet Reid. Clemmys muhlenbergi at Lake George, New York. *Copeia*, Aug. 15, 1919. no.72:68. Brief note on Muhlenberg's turtle. 3556

Evermann, Barton Warren. Notes on some Adirondack reptiles and amphibians. *Copeia*, Apr. 15, 1918. no.56:48–51. Based on observations made at Axton, 1900, 1901 and 1903. 3557

Green, Harold T. Notes on middle states amphibians and reptiles. *Copeia*, Sept. 15, 1923. no.122:99–100. Includes collection made in Essex County. 3558

Weber, Jay Anthony. Herpetological observations in the Adirondack mountains, New York. *Copeia*, Oct. 25, 1928. no.169:106–12. Essex County. 3559

BIRDS

Achilles, Laurence. Nesting of the Arctic three-toed woodpecker in the Adirondacks. *Bird Lore*, Sept.–Oct. 1906. 8:158–60. 3560

Adams, Charles Christopher. Notes on the relation of birds to Adirondack forest vegetation. *Roos Wildlife Bul*, Mar. 1923. 1:487–519. figs. maps. Cranberry Lake. 3561

Ayres, Douglas. Adirondack bird notes. *Cloud Splitter*, May–June 1948. 11:no.3:5–6. 3562

Bagg, Egbert. Birds of Oneida county, New York. *Auk*, Apr. 1894. 11:162–64. Eight new records. 3563

Bagg, Egbert. Breeding of wild ducks in New York. *For & Stream*, Mar. 9, 1901. 56:189. Includes various breeding places in the Adirondacks. 3564

Bagg, Egbert. Lincoln's finch (Melospiza lincolni) breeding in Hamilton county, N.Y.

Nutt Orn C Bul, Oct. 1878. 3:197–98.   3565

Bagg, Egbert. Nesting·of the black-throated blue warbler. *Orn & Ool*, June 1887. 12:90–91.   3566

Barick, Frank B. Evening grosbeaks in the Adirondacks in late June. *Auk*, July 1946. 63:444–45.   3567

Bates, Mrs. Frank. Bohemian waxwings and robin in Lewis county, N.Y. *Bird Lore*, Mar.–Apr. 1923. 25:125.   3568

Bates, Mrs. Frank. Evening grosbeaks in 1921–22. *Bird Lore*, Nov.–Dec. 1922. 24:437.   3569

Belknap, James B. Incursion of Brunnich's murre in northern New York. *Kingbird*, Mar.–Apr. 1951. 1:13–14.   3570

Benton, Allen H. Yellow-billed cuckoo at Lake Placid. *Kingbird*, June–July 1951. 1:59.   3571

Bird study at Cranberry lake. *Camp Log*, 1931. 17:12–13. Includes list of birds observed.   3572

Birds of the Adirondacks. List of permanent residents and visitors, with dates of the earliest recorded observations of the latter. *Outdoor Life*, Oct. 1904. 1:97. Preface signed L.B. (Lawrason Brown). Also issued as a reprint which was advertised in Volume 2 of the *Journal of the Outdoor Life*. Prepared by the Trudeau Bird Club under the direction of Dr. Lawrason Brown.   3573

Bishop, Bainbridge. Wild ducks breeding in New York. *For & Stream*, Mar. 16, 1901. 56:205. Lake Champlain.   3574

Blake, Louise C. Nesting warblers. *Bul Schools*, Mar. 1946. 32:194–95. Observations at Joe Indian Lake.   3575

Brand, Albert Rich. Hunting the loon·call. *High Spots Yrbk*, 1939. p.6–12. illus. Recording the call of the loon; also bird photography.   3576

Bump, Gardiner and others. The ruffed grouse, life history, propagation, management. Albany, New York state conservation department, 1947. 915p. front. illus charts, tables. Various references to the Adirondacks.   3577

Burroughs, John. Wake-robin. Boston, Houghton, Mifflin, 1902. 233p. front. 1st edition published by Hurd & Houghton in 1871. The Adirondacks, p.69–92.   3578

C. Lake Champlain ducks and gulls. *For & Stream*, Jan. 26, 1895. 44:64.   3579

Caldwell, Dorothy W. Notes on fall birds. *High Spots*, Oct. 1935. 12:no.4:34–35.   3580

Caldwell, Dorothy W. Notes on winter birds. *High Spots*, Jan. 1934. 11:no.1:8–10.   3581

Caldwell, Dorothy W. Trail notes on Adirondack birds. *High Spots*, July 1931. 8:no.3:11–12.   3582

Carleton, Geoffrey. Bird notes from Essex county. *Kingbird*, Oct. 1951. 1:86–88.   3583

Carleton, Geoffrey, Poor, Hustace and Scott, Oliver K. Cape May warbler breeding in New York state. *Auk*, Oct. 1948. 65:607. 3584

Chahoon, George. Birds of the Adirondacks. *Pop Sci*, May 1900. 57:40–47.   3585

Chahoon, George. Some notes on Adirondack birds. *Warbler*, 1st quarter, 1905. ser.2: 1:4–14. illus.   3586

Coleman, Robert H. List of Adirondack birds. *In* Donaldson, A.L. A history of the Adirondacks. N.Y. 1921. v.2, p.291–96. 3587

Cook, Fannie S. Bohemian waxwings in northern New York. *Bird Lore*, May–June 1923. 25:188.   3588

Coues, Elliott. The willow grouse in New York. *Nutt Orn C Bul*, Jan. 1878. 3:41.   3589

Darrow, Robert W. Seasonal food preferences of adult and of young grouse in New York state. *In* 4th North American wildlife conference. Proceedings, 1939. p.585–90. tables, charts. Includes Adirondacks.   3590

Dence, Wilford Albert. Tree swallow mortality from exposure during unseasonable weather. *Auk*, July 1946. 63:440.   3591

Eaton, Elon Howard. Birds of New York. . . Albany, University of the State of New York, 1910–14. 2v. illus. part col. plates, diagrs. folded map. (New York State Museum Memoir 12.) Mt. Marcy region, 1:42–50.   3592

Fisher, Albert Kenrick. Another specimen of Siurus motacilla at Lake George, N.Y. *Nutt Orn C Bul*, Oct. 1881. 6:245.   3593

Fisher, Albert Kenrick. The large-billed water thrush at Lake George, N.Y. *Nutt Orn C Bul*, Apr. 1880. 5:117.   3594

Fleisher, Edward. Evening grosbeak in summer in the Adirondack mountains. *Auk*, Jan. 1943. 60:107. At Elk Lake.   3595

Flint, Peter. About owls. *For & Stream*, Sept. 23, 1905. 65:250.   3596

Flint, Peter. The hermit grouse of Fox island. *Sh & Fish*, Dec. 29, 1904. 37:244–45. illus. At Eagle Lake.   3597

Flint, Peter. Horned owls. A true story of owl character. *Sh & Fish*, Oct. 20, 1904. 37:24–25.   3598

Fuller, A.R. Adirondack bird notes. *For Leaves*, Summer 1905. 2:no.3:18–19.   3599

G., C.A. Birds in Hamilton county. *For & Stream*, July 13, 1907. 69:53. Common birds near Morehouseville. Author probably Charles A. Gianini. 3600

George, John Lothar and Mitchell, Robert Thomas. Calculations on the extent of spruce budworm control by insectivorous birds. *J For*, June 1948. 46:454–55. Studies at Lake Clear Junction. Also issued as reprint. 3601

George, John Lothar and Mitchell, Robert Thomas. The effects of feeding DDT-treated insects to nestling birds. *J Econ Ent*, Dec. 1947. 40:782–89. At Lake Clear Junction. Complete report in files of Patuxent Research Refuge, Laurel, Md. Also issued as reprint. 3602

George, John Lothar and Mitchell, Robert Thomas. Notes on two species of Calliphoridae (Diptera) parasitizing nestling birds. *Auk*, Oct. 1948. 65:549–52. Lake Clear Junction. Also issued as reprint. 3603

Gianini, Charles A. Birds in the Adirondacks. *For & Stream*, Feb. 24, 1912. 78:243. illus. 3604

Hall, F.H. Some western Adirondack birds. *Wilson Bul*, Dec. 1906. n.s.13:120–27. 3605

Hoffman, Ralph. A guide to the birds of New England and eastern New York. . . Boston, Houghton, Mifflin, 1904. 357p. front. illus. plates. 3606

Johnson, Charles Eugene. The bay-breasted warbler in the Adirondacks of N.Y. *Auk*, Apr. 1927. 44:255–56. 3607

Johnson, William Schuyler. Bob-white in northwestern New York. *Auk*, July 1897. 14: 316. 3608

Johnson, William Schuyler. The passenger pigeon (Ectopistes migratorius) in Lewis county, New York. *Auk*, Jan. 1897. 14:88. 3609

Kennard, Frederic Hodge. Notes on the breeding of the American crossbill in Hamilton county, New York. *Auk*, July 1895. 12: 304–5. Forked Lake. 3610

Kennard, Frederic Hodge. Two unique nesting-sites in and about camp buildings in Hamilton county, New York. *Auk*, July 1895. 12:314. Forked Lake. 3611

Kittredge, Joseph Jr. Ruby-crowned kinglet in summer in the Adirondack mts. N.Y. *Auk*, Jan. 1925. 42:144. 3612

Lane, Margaret. A few Adirondack birds. *High Spots*, July 1933. 10:no.3:16–17. 3613

Lawrence, Robert. Capture of the great gray owl in the Adirondacks, N.Y. *Nutt Orn C Bul*, Apr. 1880. 5:122. 3614

Lesperance, Thomas A. Storms and unusual visitors in Lake Champlain area. *Kingbird*, Oct. 1953. 3:56. 3615

Lewis, May D. A merganser family. *Bird Lore*, July–Aug. 1916. 18:233–34. illus. 3616

Lewis, Norman. A blue heron incident. *Bird Lore*, Nov.–Dec. 1934. 36:363–64. 3617

Loope, P. Fay. Bird life on the peaks. *High Spots Yrbk*, 1940. p.22–24. 3618

Meade, Gordon Montgomery. Calcium chloride—a death lure for crossbills. *Auk*, July 1942. 59:439. 3619

Meade, Gordon Montgomery. Regional reports. Adirondacks. *Kingbird*, Mar.–Apr. 1951 —May 1955. 1:36–38, 71–72, 103;. 2:16–17, 51, 93–94; 3:15, 75; 4:19–21, 56–57, 82–83, 112–14; 5:23–24. 3620

Merriam, Clinton Hart. Breeding of the pine linnet in northern New York. *For & Stream*, July 18, 1878. 10:463. Black River section of Lewis County. 3621

Merriam, Clinton Hart. Nest and eggs of the Blackburnian warbler. *Auk*, Jan. 1885. 2:103. 3622

Merriam, Clinton Hart. Nesting of the banded three-toed woodpecker (Picoides americanus) in northern New York. *Nutt Orn C Bul*, Oct. 1878. 3:200. 3623

Merriam, Clinton Hart. Preliminary list of birds ascertained to occur in the Adirondack region, northeastern New York. *Nutt Orn C Bul*, Oct. 1881. 6:225–35. Addenda in *Nuttall Ornithological Club Bulletin*, Apr. 1882, 7:128; Oct. 1882, 7:256–57, and in *The Auk*, Jan. 1884, 1:58–59. 3624

Merriam, Clinton Hart. Remarks on some of the birds of Lewis county, northern New York, with remarks by A.J. Dayan. *Nutt Orn C Bul*, Apr.–July 1878, Jan. 1879. 3:52–56, 123–28; 4:1–7. 3625

Miller, James Henry. The great gray owl in Lewis county, N.Y. *Auk*, Apr. 1890. 7:206. In the Town of Watson. 3626

Miller, Waldron de Witt. Richardson's owl and other owls in Franklin county, New York. *Auk*, Nov. 1915. 32:228. 3627

Nesting of the groshawks near Big Moose, New York. *Kingbird*, Dec. 1952. 1:83. 3628

Palmer, Ralph Simon. A bird with a history. *Bul Schools*, Mar. 1950. 36:227–29. plates. Evening grosbeak first reported in New York state at Elizabethtown in 1875. Winter migrations irregular. Not yet found nesting in the Adirondacks. 3629

Parkes, Kenneth C. Notes on some birds of the Adirondacks and Catskill mountains, New York. *Carneg Mus Annals*, 1954. 33:149–78. 3630

Pashley, Samuel. Study of birds. *High Spots*, July 1936. 13:no.2:13–14. 3631

Pennock, Charles John. Nesting of the passenger pigeon (Ectopistes migratorius) in New York. *Auk*, Apr. 1912. 29:238–39.   3632

Phelps, Orra A. Birds of the Adirondacks. *Ad-i-ron-dac*, May–June 1948. 12:no.3:6, 14.   3633

Phelps, Mrs. Orra (Parker). Some 1937 Adirondack observations. *Bul Schools*, Mar. 15, 1938. 24:127. Bird observations at Lake Arnold open shelter and swallow migration near Lake Placid.   3634

Porter, Mrs. Marjorie (Lansing). The passing of the pigeons. *No Country Life*, Fall 1950. 4:no.4:30–33. Early accounts of wild pigeons in northern New York.   3635

Radford, Harry V. Photographing a loon's nest. *Field & S*, July 1901. 6:284–85. illus. Accompanied by note on loons in the Adirondacks.   3636

Ralph, William La Grange and Bagg, Egbert. Annotated list of the birds of Oneida county, N.Y. and its immediate vicinity. *Oneida Hist Soc Proc*, 1886. 3:101–47. Also issued as a separate, Utica, N.Y. Ellis H. Roberts & Co. 1886. See also their "Additional Notes. . ." in *The Auk*, July 1890, 7:229–32.   3637

Roosevelt, Theodore and Minot, Henry Davis. The summer birds of the Adirondacks in Franklin county, N.Y. N.Y. 1877. 4p. for bibliographical description and notes of other issues, see *Bibliographical Society of America. Papers*, v.39, p.22–25. Also in his "Works," National Edition, 1926, v.5, p.402–6. Reprinted in *Roosevelt Wildlife Bulletin*, Mar. 1923 and Sept. 1929.   3638

Saunders, Aretas Andrews. The summer birds of the northern Adirondack mountains. *Roos Wildlife Bul*, Sept. 1929. 5:327–499. plates, illus. map.   3639

Sawyer, Edmund Joseph. Land birds of northern New York. A pocket guide to common land birds of the St. Lawrence valley and the lowlands in general of northern New York. Watertown, N.Y. Watertown bird club, c1916. 85p. col. front. illus.   3640

Severinghaus, C.W. A ruffed grouse, Bonasa umbellus, that did not abandon her nest. *Auk*, July 1950. 67:384.   3641

Shainin, Vincent. American and arctic three-toed woodpeckers in the Adirondacks. *Auk*, Jan. 1939. 56:84–85.   3642

Shattuck, George Cheever. Notes from northern New York. *Auk*, Apr. 1901. 18:199. Brief bird notes from Chateaugay lakes.   3643

Silloway, Perley M. Relation of summer birds to the western Adirondack forest. Syracuse, N.Y. Syracuse university, 1923. 91p. col. plates, figs. (Roosevelt Wildlife Bulletin, v.1,

no.4, Mar. 1923.) Cranberry Lake. Colored plates by Edmund J. Sawyer.   3644

Spears, Raymond Smiley. Causes of bird scarcity. *For & Sream*, Jan. 8, 1910. 74:51–52. Shortage of woodcock in Adirondacks due to professional hunters.   3645

Spears, Raymond Smiley. The ruffed grouse scarcity. *For & Stream*, Dec. 7, 1907. 69:892–93. Decrease due to forest fires etc.   3646

Sterling, Ernest Albert. Adirondack birds in their relation to forestry. *For Quar*, Oct. 1902. 1:18–25.   3647

Sterling, Ernest Albert. Notes on the spring migration of birds in the northern Adirondacks, New York. *Auk*, July 1902. 19:297–300.   3648

Stoner, Dayton. The golden eagle in eastern New York. *Bul Schools*, Mar. 15, 1939. 25:114–17. illus.   3649

Stoner, Dayton. Great gray owl from New York state. *Auk*, Apr. 1938. 55:279–80.   3650

Stoner, Dayton. Noteworthy records for northeastern New York, winter 1939–40. *Auk*, July 1940. 57:406–7.   3651

Stoner, Dayton. Occurrence of Wilson's petrel (Oceanites oceanicus) in Franklin county, N.Y. *Auk*, July 1934. 51:367.   3652

Sypulski, John L. Climate and the birds and a list of birds found in the vicinity of the New York state Ranger school. *NYS Ranger Sch*, 1933. p.44–50.   3653

Terres, John Kenneth. Great horned owls dying in the winter of 1939–40. *Auk*, Oct. 1940. 57:571–72.   3654

Terres, John Kenneth. Short-billed marsh wren in the western Adirondacks. *Auk*, Apr. 1941. 58:263–64.   3655

Turner, Melvin Hart. Vireo philadelphicus in the Adirondack region. *Auk*, July 1884. 1:291.   3656

Van Sant, F.A. An Adirondack lunch counter. *Bird Lore*, Jan.–Feb. 1901. 3:18–19. illus. Bird feeding at Jay, N.Y.   3657

Vogt, William. Orchard oriole in the Adirondacks. *Auk*, Oct. 1931. 48:606.   3658

Weber, Jay Anthony. Bay-breasted warbler breeding in the Adirondacks, N.Y. *Auk*, Jan. 1927. 44:111.   3659

Weyl, Edward Stern. Notes from the Mt. Marcy region, N.Y. *Auk*, Jan. 1927. 44:112–14. Supplements Eaton's "Birds of New York," v.1, p.42 (no.3592).   3660

Whitfield, Robert Parr. Former abundance of the wild pigeon in central and eastern New York. *Auk*, July 1890. 7:284–85.   3661

Wild geese on the Upper Ausable lake. *For & Stream*, Mar. 29, 1902. 58:246.   3662

Willson, Minnie Moore. A tragedy of the Adirondacks; an intimate study of a family of wax-wings which was unexpectedly discovered and cared for at a summer camp. *For & Stream*, Mar. 1920. 90:122. 3663

Wolcott, W.E. New York ruffed grouse. *For & Stream*, Sept. 16, 1899. 53:226–27. Includes the Adirondacks. 3664

Wolfe, Lloyd Raymond. The herring gulls of Lake Champlain. *Auk*, Oct. 1923. 40:621–26. plate. 3665

Wolfe, Lloyd Raymond. Richardson's owl in New York. *Auk*, Oct. 1923. 40:693–94. 3666

Wright, C.F. The opportunity for ornithology at Cranberry lake. *Camp Log*, 1917. 3:18–19. illus. 3667

MAMMALS

General

Adirondack animals. *For & Stream*, Mar. 23, 1907. 68:456–57. From the report of Commissioner Whipple. 3668

Adirondack foxes. *For & Stream*, Mar. 17, 1894. 42:226. 3669

Batchelder, Charles Foster. Some facts in regard to the distribution of certain mammals in New England and northern New York. *Bost Soc Nat Hist Proc*, Oct. 1896. 27:185–93. Smaller mammals living in Adirondacks. 3670

Batchelder, Charles Foster. An undescribed shrew of the genus Sores. *Biol Soc Wash Proc*, Dec. 8, 1896. 10:133–34. Shrew found at Beede's, Essex County. 3671

Brainerd, W.H. New York state's fur-bearing animals. *Field & S*, Dec. 1910. 15:788–89. 3672

Brown, George L. Lynx in Essex county, N.Y. *For & Stream*, Feb. 11, 1899. 52:104. 3673

Burnham, John Bird. Panthers in the Adirondacks. *For & Stream*, Sept. 4, 1909. 73:374. Dates of last bounties paid and authenticated reports. 3674

Chase, Greenleaf T. and Westervelt, Earl. The latest on coyotes. *NYS Con*, Dec. 1950–Jan. 1951. 5:no.3:12–13. illus. 3675

Chase, Greenleaf T. New York's coyote control problem. *NYS Con*, Dec. 1949–Jan. 1950. 4:no.3:14–15. illus. 3676

Colvin, Verplanck. Winter fauna of Mount Marcy. *In* New York (state). Adirondack survey. 7th annual report. . .to the year 1879. . . p.363–74. Reprinted in New York state). State land survey. Report on the progress. . .1891, p.221–35; and State land survey. Report on the progress. . .1894, p.289–303. Also in *Albany Institute Transac-*

tions, 1879, 9:11–26; and in *The Rod and Gun*, Apr. 8, 1876, 8:20–21. Issued as separates, Albany, 1876, 16p. and Albany, 1880, p.361–74. 3677

Dailey, Elric J. Fur-bearers of the Adirondacks. *Conservationist*, Dec. 1921. 4:179–81. illus. Also in *State Service*, Mar.–Apr. 1922, 6:104–6. illus. 3678

Dugmore, Arthur Radclyffe. Wild life and the camera; illus. Philadelphia, Lippincott, 1912. 332p. plates. The story of a porcupine hunt, p.49–60. Photography in the Adirondacks. 3679

Eaton, Theodore Hildreth and Chandler, Robert Flint Jr. The fauna of forest-humus layers in New York. Ithaca, N.Y. Cornell university, 1942. 26p. illus. tables. (New York State Agricultural Experiment Station, Ithaca. Memoir 247.) Includes seven Adirondack sites. 3680

Evicted tenants. *Harper W*, Feb. 28, 1885. 29:136, 139. illus. Brief article on animals no longer found in the Adirondacks. 3681

F., P.D. A black Adirondack hare. *For & Stream*, Mar. 23, 1907. 68:454. Captured near Cedar River Flow. 3682

Fisher, Albert Kenrick. Capture of an opossum in Essex county, N.Y. *For & Stream*, Apr. 2, 1885. 24:184. 3683

Fosburgh, Peter W. Panther. *NYS Con*, June–July 1951. 5:no.6:12–13. illus. 3684

Fraleigh, Lucy B. Camping with chipmunks. *Nature M*, Aug. 1927. 10:123–26. illus. Indian Lake. 3685

Fuller, Raymond Tifft. A naturalist on skis. *Travel*, Jan. 1939. 72:no.3:10–13, 42. illus. Wild animals in Adirondacks in winter. 3686

Goodwin, George G. Big game animals of the northeastern United States. *J Mam*, Feb. 1936. 17:48–50. Notes on wolf and cougar in Adirondacks. 3687

Grant, Madison. Notes on Adirondack mammals with special reference to the fur-bearers. *In* New York (state). Forest, fish and game commission. Annual report, 1902–3, p.319–34. plates. Also issued as a reprint. 3688

Hamilton, W.J. Jr. and Cook, Arthur H. The biology and management of the fisher in New York. *NY Fish & Game J*, Jan. 1955. 2:13–35. tables, map. The fisher is increasing in the Adirondacks. 3689

Harper, Francis. . . .Animal habitats in certain portions of the Adirondacks, by Francis Harper and Jean Sherwood Harper. Notes on mammals of the Adirondacks, by Francis Harper. The habits of mammals at an Adirondack camp, by Lucy B. Fraleigh. Albany, University of the State of New York, 1929.

176p. illus. (New York State Museum Hand-
book 8.)   3690

Hatt, Robert Torrens. The red squirrel: its
life history and habits, with special reference
to the Adirondacks of New York and the
Harvard forest. Syracuse, N.Y. Syracuse university, 1929. 146p. (Roosevelt Wildlife Annals, v.2, no.1, Jan. 1929.) Also issued as
Bulletin of the New York State College of
Forestry at Syracuse, N.Y., v.2, no.1b. 3691

Hatt, Robert Torrens. Relation of the meadow
mouse Microtus P. pennsylvanicus to the
biota of a Lake Champlain island. *Ecology*,
Jan. 1928. 9:88–93.   3692

Hubbard, Gerard Fruin. Woods fear, a fall-
ing tree is the only thing in the woods that
will really hurt you. *Field & S*, Dec. 1927. 32:
no.8:34–35, 75–76. illus. Discussion of animal
life in western Adirondacks.   3693

Is the panther coming back? *For & Stream*,
Jan. 1917. 87:25–26.   3694

Johnson, Charles Eugene. The muskrat in
New York: its natural history and economics.
Roos Wildlife Bul, Mar. 1925. 3:205–320.
illus. figs. maps.   3695

Johnson, Charles Eugene. Porcupine quills
in a fox skull. *J Mam*, Nov. 1934. 15:319.
Fox shot in the Adirondacks.   3696

Johnson, Charles Eugene. Preliminary reconnaissance of the land vertebrates of the Archer
and Anna Huntington wild life forest station.
Roos Wildlife Bul, Jan. 1937. 6:557–608.
plate.   3697

Juvenal, pseud. More about the panther.
For & Stream, Feb. 23, 1901. 56:145.   3698

Juvenal, pseud. Old guides say panthers still
roam Adirondacks. *For & Stream*, Apr. 1917.
87:165.   3699

Merriam, Clinton Hart. The mammals of
the Adirondack region. N.Y. H. Holt & co.
1886. 316p. Reprinted from his "Vertebrates
of the Adirondack Region." Sherrill.   3700

Merriam, Clinton Hart. Mammals of the
Adirondack region, northeastern New York.
With an introductory chapter treating of the
location and boundaries of the region, its
geological history, topography, climate, general features, botany and faunal position. . .
N.Y. Press of L.S. Foster, 1884. 316p. Reprinted from the *Transactions of the Linnaean
Society*, New York, Vols. 1 and 2.   3701

Merriam, Clinton Hart. The pine mouse in
northern New York. *Am Nat*, Sept. 1885. 19:
895.   3702

Merriam, Clinton Hart. Preliminary revision
of the Pumas (Felis concolor group). *Wash
Acad Sci Proc*, Dec. 11, 1901. 3:577–600. Includes discussion of Adirondack species. 3703

Merriam, Clinton Hart. The red squirrel in
the Adirondacks. *Rand Notes*, Aug. 1884.
1:5–6.   3704

Merriam, Clinton Hart. The vertebrates of
the Adirondack region, northeastern New
York. *Linn Soc NY Tr*, 1882, 1884. 1:5–106;
2:5–214. Reprint issued in 1882 includes only
general introduction and part of the section
on mammals.   3705

Miller, Gerrit Smith Jr. Key to the land
mammals of northeastern North America.
Albany, University of the State of New York,
1900. 160p. (New York State Museum Bulletin 38.)   3706

Miller, Gerrit Smith Jr. Preliminary list of
the mammals of New York. Albany, University of the State of New York, 1899. 390p.
(New York State Museum Bulletin 29.) 3707

More talk about coyotes. 1. Hunting the mystery animal, by Fred S. Streever. 2. Trapping
them, by Ed. Maunton. *NYS Con*, Dec. 1952-
Jan. 1953. 7:no.3:16–19. illus.   3708

Muir, George. Adirondack wolves and panthers. *For & Stream*, Sept. 28, 1895. 45:270.
Plentiful in 1873.   3709

Muss-Arnolt, G. That Adirondack deer. *For
& Stream*, Nov. 11, 1893. 41:406. Comments
on Burnham's caribou.   3710

Oddly named beast. *For & Stream*, Jan. 14,
1911. 76:45. Pennant's marten one of the few
Adirondack animals with own names.
                                            3711

Oja, Oscar W. "Friend fox." Does instinct or
reason rule his behavior? *Bul Schools*, Mar.
1953. 9:195–98. illus.   3712

Paulmier, Frederick Clark. The squirrels and
other rodents of the Adirondacks. *In* New
York (state). Forest, fish and game commission. Annual report, 1902–3, p.335–51. col.
plates. Also issued as a reprint.   3713

R. Panthers and deer. *For & Stream*, Nov. 5,
1885. 25:286–87. Thinks few panthers in the
Adirondacks.   3714

Radford, Harry V. Adirondack woodchucks.
Sh & Fish, Sept. 27, 1906. 40:488. Comments
by J.F. Roberts in article entitled "Woodchuck Hunting" in issue for Oct. 4, 1906, 40:
507.   3715

Radford, Harry V. Red squirrels and chipmunks. *For Leaves*, Winter 1904. 2:no.1:19–20.
                                            3716

Radford, Harry V. Tree climbing woodchucks. *Arms & Man*, Aug. 8, 1907. 42:418–
19.   3717

Schoonmaker, W.J. The fisher as a foe of the
porcupine in New York state. *J Mam*, Aug.
1938. 19:373. Indian Lake village and Brant
Lake.   3718

Schoonmaker, W.J. Notes on the home range of the porcupine in New York state. *J Mam*, Aug. 1938. 19:378. Observations in the Adirondacks. 3719

Schoonmaker, W.J. Porcupine eats water lily pads. *J Mam*, Feb. 1930. 11:84. On Little Square Pond, Franklin County. 3720

Schueler, Robert L. A correlation of fox food habits with wild foods available on the Huntington forest. 168 leaves. mounted photographs, charts, maps (part folded). Master's thesis, State University of New York, College of Forestry, Syracuse, 1948. Typescript. Abstract in Graduate Theses, p.59–60. 3721

Schueler, Robert L. Red fox habits in a wilderness area. *J Mam*, Nov. 1951. 32:462–64. Study at the Huntington Wildlife Forest. 3722

Seagears, Clayton B. The coyote, unbidden guest. *NYS Con*, Apr.–May 1949. 3:no.5:40. Coyote in Adirondacks. 3723

Seagears, Clayton B. The lynx is back. *NYS Con*, Dec. 1951–Jan. 1952. 6:no.3:40. illus. Specimen caught in Washington County. 3724

Seaman, Mrs. Frances (Boone). Days our forefathers knew. *Cloud Splitter*, May–June 1951. 14:no.3:8–10. Bobcats, coyotes and moose near Long Lake. 3725

Severinghaus, C.W. and Tanck, John E. Speed and gait of an otter. *J Mam*, Feb. 1948. 29:71. Study at Cedar River Flow, Lake Pleasant township. 3726

Shapiro, Jacob. Life history and ecology of the porcupine (Erethizon dorsatum dorsatum) (Linn.) on the Archer and Anna Huntington wildlife forest experiment station, Newcomb, N.Y. 239 leaves. mounted photographs, tables, diagrs. maps (1folded). Master's thesis, State University of New York, College of Forestry, Syracuse, 1947. Typescript. Abstract in Graduate Theses, p.60. 3727

Shorey, Archibald Thompson. The Adirondack rat mystery. *Ad-i-ron-dac*, Mar.–Apr. 1953. 17:38. 3728

Smiley, James. A few cats. *Fur News*, Jan.–Feb. 1919. 29:no.1:20, 22, 24, 26; 29:no.2:20, 22–23. illus. Description of various members of cat family in the Adirondacks. 3729

Spears, Eldridge A. The waterproof woodchuck. *For & Stream*, Mar. 29, 1902. 58:249. West Canada Creek flooded burrows during hibernation but woodchucks emerged undamaged. 3730

Spears, Raymond Smiley. Carrying skunks by their tails. *For & Stream*, Dec. 14, 1907. 69:932. Notes on skunks in the Adirondacks. 3731

Spears, Raymond Smiley. Reading the snow. *Atlan*, Dec. 1908. 102:791–96. Animal tracks. 3732

Spears, Raymond Smiley. Woodchuck ways. *For & Stream*, July 31, 1909. 73:176. 3733

Stoner, Dayton. Extant New York state specimens of the Adirondack cougar. Albany, University of the State of New York, 1950. 34p. illus. map. (New York State Museum Circular 25.) Description and history of specimens by the former State Zoologist. 3734

Van Etten, Robert C. The ecology and population distribution of the eastern chipmunk (Tamias striatus lysteri) on the Huntington forest. 132 leaves. mounted photographs, tables, charts, diagrs. maps. Master's thesis, State University of New York, College of Forestry, Syracuse, 1951. Typescript. Abstract in Graduate Theses, p.64. 3735

Walsh, John. The tragedy of Brant lake. *For Leaves*, Winter 1904. 2:no.1:9–13. illus. Death of a skunk. 3736

Wilson, Robert M. A preliminary study of the raccoon, Procyon lotor lotor L. on the Huntington forest. 95 leaves. mounted photographs, tables, charts, maps. Master's thesis, State University of New York, College of Forestry, Syracuse, 1953. Typescript. Abstract in Graduate Theses, p.64–65. 3737

Winter fauna of Mt. Marcy. *For & Stream*, May 4, 1876. 6:200. 3738

Bear

Brown, George L. Adirondack bears. *For & Stream*, Sept. 29, 1906. 67:499. 3739

Brown, George L. Adirondack bears not blessings. *For & Stream*, Jan. 30, 1904. 62:85. 3740

Brown, George L. Essex county black bears. *For & Stream*, Dec. 29, 1906. 67:1027. Bears killing sheep at Wilmington. 3741

Chahoon, George. The Adirondack black bear. *In* New York (state). Forest, fish and game commission. Annual report, 1901. p.243–49. illus. plates (1 col.). Reprinted, Albany, J.B. Lyon, 1903. Excerpts in *Forest and Stream*, Dec. 19, 1903, 61:484. 3742

Radford, Harry V. Is the Adirondack black bear passing? *Woods & Wat*, Winter 1901–2. 4:no.4:12. 3743

Schoonmaker, W.J. Notes on the black bear in New York state. *J Mam*, Nov. 1938. 19:501–2. Adirondack observations. 3744

Spears, Raymond Smiley. About Adirondack bears. *For & Stream*, Sept. 7, 1895. 45:204. 3745

Beaver

Beakbane, A.B. The case against the beaver; they have increased to such alarming proportions in the Adirondacks that they are fast destroying the trout streams. *For & Stream*, May 1922. 92:203, 236, 239–40. illus.   3746

Beaver in the Adirondacks. *For & Stream*, Jan. 1915. 84:3. Note concerning the number of beaver.   3747

Beaver on the increase. *Field & S*, Dec. 1910. 15:787–88.   3748

Brandreth, Paulina. Adirondack beaver. *For & Stream*, Sept. 19, 1908. 71:452. Note on beaver in Herkimer County.   3749

Brandreth, Paulina. The Adirondack beaver pest. *For & Stream*, July 1922. 92:308.   3750

Brimmer, F.E. Beaver in the Adirondacks. *Outing*, May 1921. 78:70–71, 88–91. illus.   3751

Brown, Charles P. Notes on Adirondack beaver. *J Mam*, Nov. 1946. 27:394–95.   3752

Buckley, John L. The ecology and economics of the beaver (Castor canadensis Kuhl) with a plan for its management on the Huntington wildlife forest station. 251p. plates, tables, charts. Doctoral thesis, State University of New York, College of Forestry, Syracuse, 1950. Typescript. Abstract in Graduate Theses, p.54–55.   3753

Cole, Charles Woolsey. Beaver vs. trout. *High Spots Yrbk*, 1940. p.15–19. Destruction by beavers in Cranberry Lake region.   3754

Donovan, William. Beaver in the Adirondacks. *Camp Log*, 1919. 5:16–17. illus.   3755

Harlow, William Morehouse. Beavers resume earlier work. *J Mam*, Aug. 1928. 9:252. Cranberry Lake.   3756

Hutton, T. Radcliffe. Trowel-tail makes good. *Field & S*, Aug. 1920. 25:384. illus.   3757

Johnson, Charles Eugene. The beaver in the Adirondacks; its economics and natural history. *Roos Wildlife Bul*, July 1927. 4:501–641. illus. map.   3758

Johnson, Charles Eugene. An investigation of the beaver in Herkimer and Hamilton counties of the Adirondacks. *Roos Wildlife Bul*, Aug. 1922. 1:117–86. illus. map.   3759

Juvenal, pseud. Adirondack beavers. *For & Stream*, July 24, 1909. 73:131. illus. Short note on beaver near Blue Mountain Lake.   3760

Leet, Ernest D. New York's beaver problem. *Am For*, Apr. 1923. 29:199–203, 248. illus.   3761

Lempfert, O.C. Adirondack beaver; interesting facts concerning this marvelous little engineer of the woods. *For & Stream*, Sept. 1926. 96:538–39, 564–66. illus.   3762

Radford, Harry V. History of the Adirondack beaver (Castor canadensis Kuhl.). Its former abundance, practical extermination, and reintroduction. *In* New York (state). Forest, fish and game commission. Annual reports for 1904–1905–1906. p.388–419. plates (some col.) illus. maps. Also issued as a separate, with his "Artificial Preservation of Timber," Albany, 1908.   3763

Randall, Willet. The north woods beaver. . . *Rural NY*, Apr. 2, 1955. 105:236, 247. illus.   3764

Reid, Kenneth A. Effects of beavers on trout waters. *Northeast Log*, Aug.–Sept. 1952. 1: no.2:7, 21. illus. At Whitney Park.   3765

Schoonmaker, W.J. My friend, the beaver. *High Spots Yrbk*, 1940. p.20–21. illus. p.44–45. In defense.   3766

Sterling, Ernest Albert. The return of the beaver to the Adirondacks. *Am For*, May 1913. 19:292–99. illus.   3767

Townsend, Charles Haskins. The beaver in the Adirondacks. *NY Zoo Soc Bul*, Mar. 1919. 22:47–48. illus.   3768

Warren, Edward Royal. The beaver, its work and its ways. Baltimore, Md. Williams & Wilkins, 1927. 177p. front. plates, illus. plans, maps. (Monograph of the American Society of Mammalogists, no.2.)   3769

Webb, William L. Bureau of missing beaver. *NYS Con*, Apr.–May 1954. 8:no.5:12–13. illus. Study of beaver on Huntington Wildlife Forest.   3770

Webb, William L. The first northeastern logger. *Northeast Log*, Apr. 1954. 2:no.8:6–7. illus. On the Huntington Wildlife Forest.   3771

Willoughby, Charles H. Big increase of beaver in state. *State Service*, Sept.–Oct. 1920. 4:627–30.   3772

Deer

Adirondack deer statistics. *For & Stream*, Nov. 23, 1895. 45:449.   3773

The Adirondack whitetail. *NYS Con*, June–July 1952. 6:no.6:20–21. Brief text with photographs by Robert H. Van De Mark.   3774

B., C.H. A spotted Adirondack buck. *For & Stream*, Jan. 21, 1899. 52:45.   3775

Boardman, William Henry. Adirondack league club deer. *For & Stream*, June 29, 1895. 44:530.   3776

Boardman, William Henry. How deer live in winter. *In* Adirondack league club. Yearbook, 1904. p.36–41. illus. Excerpts from a diary on winter feeding of deer.   3777

Brandreth, Paulina. Days with the deer. *For & Stream*, Mar. 18–25, 1905. 64:213–14, 234–

35. Articles usually signed "Paul Brandreth." 3778

Brandreth, Paulina. Deer in winter, each year many deer perish miserably in the deep snow. *For & Stream*, Jan. 1929. 99:26–27, 70. illus. 3779

Brandreth, Paulina. Northern whitetails, concerning the habits and characteristics of an outstanding member of the American deer family. *For & Stream*, Nov. 1927. 97:656–58, 686. illus. 3780

Brandreth, Paulina. The white tailed deer. *Field & S*, Oct. 1911. 16:606–14. illus. 3781

Brandreth, Paulina. Winter killing of Adirondack deer. *For & Stream*, Feb. 1927. 97:121. 3782

Burnham, John Bird. The Adirondack "caribou." *For & Stream*, Oct. 14, 1893. 41:316–17. illus. Red deer in the Adirondacks. Comment by G. Muss-Arnolt, "That Adirondack Deer," in issue for Nov. 11, 1893, 41:406. 3783

Burnham, John Bird. The history of the Adirondack deer. *High Spots*, Jan. 1935. 12:no.1:9–11. 3784

Camperout, pseud. Water killing deer. *For & Stream*, Nov. 28, 1896. 47:425. 3785

Carpenter, Warwick Stevens. Making friends with the wild; the deer of Johnny Geroux. *Conservationist*, Sept. 1918. 1:136–38. illus. 3786

Cayadutta, pseud. Adirondack deer destruction. *For & Stream*, July 13, 1895. 45:27. 3787

Chase, Frank. Adirondack deer and forests. *For & Stream*, July 9, 1904. 63:32. 3788

Chase, Harry. Doc Warren's pets. *For & Stream*, Oct. 5, 1907. 69:528–29. illus. 3789

Chenango, pseud. Adirondack deer prospects. *For & Stream*, Aug. 27, 1898. 51:168. 3790

Flint, Peter. Harold tells how the deer wintered in Paradox and Schroon. *For & Stream*, July 11, 1914. 83:50–51. Information from Harold L. Maguire, an old Adirondack guide. 3791

Howland, George B. The story of Dolly. *Conservationist*, Dec. 1919. 2:185–87. illus. Friendship between a deer and a dog on farm near Piseco. 3792

Johnson, Charles Eugene. On the supposed relation of deer to cedars bordering certain Adirondack lakes. *J Mam*, Aug. 1927. 8:213–21. illus. Refuted by John B. Burnham in article entitled "The Plimsoll Line in White Cedars," *Journal of Mammalogy*, Feb. 1928, 9:43–47. 3793

Maguire, H. F. and Severinghaus, C.W. Wariness as an influence on age composition of whitetailed deer killed by hunters. *NY Fish & Game J*, Jan. 1954. 1:98–109. tables. Many Adirondack observations. 3794

Maynard, Leonard Amby and others. Food preferences and requirements of the whitetailed deer in New York state, by L.A. Maynard, Gardiner Bump, Robert Darrow, J.C. Woodward. Albany, J.B. Lyon, n.d. 35p. illus. tables. Includes summary of a two-year experiment at Willsboro, 1931–33. 3795

Merriam, Clinton Hart. Deer in the Adirondacks. *For & Stream*, Apr. 24–May 15, 1884. 22:243–44, 264–65, 283–84, 302–3. 3796

Morton, Glen H. and Cheatum, Evelyn Leonard. Regional differences in breeding potential of white-tailed deer in New York. *J Wildlife Man*, July 1946. 10:242–48. tables, map. Differences between southern New York state and the Adirondack area. 3797

R., J.H. Adirondack deer. *For & Stream*, Apr. 5, 1888. 30:207. Discussion of number of deer in the Adirondacks. 3798

Reed, Frank A. Deer in the economy of the northeast. *Northeast Log*, June 1954. 2:no.10:17. illus. 3799

Richard, Edmond H. Deer production versus doe reduction in the Adirondacks. n.p. n.pub. 1951. 12p. Copy in the collection of the Friends of the Forest Preserve. 3800

Schoonmaker, W.J. Size and weight of Adirondack deer. *J Mam*, Feb. 1936. 17:67–68. 3801

Severinghaus, C.W. Deer weights as an index of range conditions in the Adirondack region. *NY Fish & Game J*, July 1955. 2:154–60. tables. 3802

Severinghaus, C.W. Fall movements of Adirondack deer. *NYS Con*, Oct.–Nov. 1952. 7:no.2:6–7. illus. 3803

Severinghaus, C.W. Springtime in New York—another angle. What goes on in our Adirondack deer yards. *NYS Con*, Apr.–May 1953. 7:no.5:2–4. illus. 3804

The shooting of the phantom deer. *Ang & Hunt*, Nov. 1910. 2:572. port. Shooting of the first pure albino deer by 'Arve Eastman on the Granshue. 3805

Skiff, J. Victor. The whitetail in New York. *NYS Con*, Oct.–Nov. 1947. 2:no.2:6–7. Discussion of habits and characteristics. 3806

Spiker, Charles Jolley. Some late winter and early spring observations on the white-tailed deer of the Adirondacks. *Roos Wildlife Bul*, Oct. 1933. 6:327–85. illus. folded map. 3807

Townsend, Myron Thomas and Smith, Morden Whitney. The white-tailed deer of the Adirondacks. *Roos Wildlife Bul*, Oct. 1933. 6:161–325. plates, illus. folded maps. 3808

Will, pseud. Deer and panthers. *For &
Stream*, Nov. 26, 1885. 25:343. Description of
panther killing deer at Jock's Lake Outlet.
                                                    3809

Wolves

Brandreth, Paulina. Wolves in the Adirondacks. *For & Stream*, Oct. 27, 1894. 43:356.
As told to her by Reuben Cary.   3810

Cheney, Albert Nelson. Wolves in the Adirondacks. *For & Stream*, Dec. 31, 1891. 37:
468. Questions extinction.   3811

Higby, J.H. Adirondack wolves. *For &
Stream*, Apr. 17, 1897. 48:304–5.   3812

J., H.S. Adirondack wolves. *For & Stream*,
Apr. 3, 1897. 48:265. Question about pres-
ence of wolves, occasioned by a newspaper
account of an encounter with wolves.   3813

Moffett, Thomas F. The "last Adirondack
wolf" is not yet. *For & Stream*, Apr. 1923. 93:

187. illus. Carl Lawrence recently killed a
wolf near Whiteface Mountain, a mile from
Wilmington.   3814

Northrup, M.S. Wolves in the Adirondacks.
For & Stream, Mar. 6, 1890. 34:125. Wolves
cause death of several dogs belonging to
Louis Seymour on West Canada Lake. 3815

Stewart, H. Wolves in the Adirondacks. *For
& Stream*, May 8, 1897. 48:363. Accompanied
by a note signed C.H.D.   3816

The wolf scandal in Franklin county. *No
Country Life*, Spring 1947. 1:no.3:43. 3817

Wolves in the Adirondacks. *For & Stream*,
Oct. 27, 1894. 43:353. Editorial on reports of
wolves.   3818

Wolves in the Adirondacks. *For & Stream*,
Sept. 21, 1895. 45:243. Editorial on wolf
killed near Brandreth Lake.   3819

SOCIAL AND ECONOMIC HISTORY

COMMERCE AND INDUSTRY

GENERAL

An Adirondack board of trade. *St No Mo*, Feb. 1908. 3:110–12. Example set by the Lake Placid Board of Trade. 3820

Adirondack motor club sets fast pace, F.P. Stanley, dynamic president of swift growing organization, takes business efficiency as his creed, Club branches and service now extend throughout the forest region. *Motordom*, June 1931. 24:no.12:30. port. 3821

Amstuz, J.O. New frontiers for pioneers; Committee of industrial preparedness coordinates facilities in 13-county area in northeastern New York state. *Dun's R*, Apr. 1952. 60:no.2288:14–15, 89–95. map. 3822

Arto Monaco's Land of makebelieve. *No Country Life*, Summer 1955. 9:no.3:22–27. illus. Brief text. 3823

Buck, Robert J. Banking resources of northern and central New York. *Up-Stater*, Jan. 1930. 2:no.1:8. 3824

Bulletin. Proposed Adirondack organization. 1924—November—1924. Broadside signed by Herbert S. Carpenter, Chairman. To organize Chambers of Commerce. 3825

Burger, William H. Adirondack Coney island. *Ad-i-ron-dac*, Mar.–Apr. 1954. 18:29. Devices to attract the tourist. 3826

Burnham, John Bird. Maple sugar in the Champlain valley. *For & Stream*, Apr. 19, 1902. 58:304. Report on the excellent season. Signed: J.B.B. 3827

Cleaveland, Dorothy Kendall. The trade and trade routes of northern New York from the beginning of settlement to the coming of the railroads. *NY State Hist Assn Q*, Oct. 1923. 4:205–31. 3828

Dempswolff, Richard Frederic. Frontier lives again in Frontier town. *Pop Mech*, June 1953. 99:no.6:82–85. illus. 3829

Goldthwaite, Kenneth W. A winter vacation that paid for itself. *Country Life*, Feb. 1906. 9:440–41, 458. illus. Gathering spruce gum near source of north branch of Saranac River. 3830

The Gould paper company. *Lumber Camp News*, Sept. 1948. 10:no.5:1, 6. illus. History of Lyons Falls company. 3831

Grinnell, George Bird. Foxes in captivity. *J Mam*, Aug. 1923. 4:184. Silver fox farm near Saranac Lake. 3832

Guides and tourists. *For & Stream*, May 3, 1883. 20:261. 3833

Hamilton, W.J. Jr. The fur-bearers of New York state. *Sci Mo*, Feb. 1935. 40:182–87. Annual harvest of fur; includes Adirondacks. 3834

Hoyle, Raymond J. and Stillinger, John R. Wood-using industries of New York. Syracuse, N.Y. N.Y. State college of forestry, 1949. 133p. figs. map. (Bulletin of the New York State College of Forestry, v.22, no.2. Technical Publication no.27, revised,) A 1946 census including comparisons with surveys of 1912, 1919 and 1926. Includes a directory of manufacturers with addresses. 3835

John Jacob Astor correspondence. Fur trade with lower Canada, 1790–1817, edited by Hugh McLellan. *Moors Ant*, May 1937–Feb. 1938. 1:5–26, 111–24, 191–205, 270–83. 3836

Mineral and agricultural resources of New York. *Am Q J Agric & Sci*, Oct. 1846. 4:169–95. tables. Products by county. 3837

A new use of waste products. *For Quar*, Sept. 1908. 6:237–39. Paper board products company developed a process for utilizing sawmill waste for manufacturing pulpboard. 3838

New York (state). Commerce, Department of. Business facts. Albany, 1952. various p. Supplement, 1954. "Capital District" includes Warren, Saratoga and Washington counties; "Mohawk Valley," Hamilton and Herkimer counties; "Northern Area," Franklin, Clinton and Essex counties. 3839

New York (state). Commerce, Department of. The mineral industries of New York state. Albany, 1950. 108p. tables, maps. Text prepared by Roland B. Peterson. Covers all commercial mineral products, including building materials. Statistical data generally not later than 1946.   3840

New York (state). Commerce, Department of. New York state means business in the northern area. . . Albany, 1946. 24p. illus. tables, diagr. map. Includes Jefferson, Lewis, St. Lawrence, Franklin, Clinton and Essex counties. Warren, Saratoga and Washington counties are covered by similar publication, ". . .In the Capital District"; Herkimer, Hamilton and Fulton by ". . .In the Mohawk Valley."   3841

New York (state). State college of agriculture, Cornell university. Department of agricultural economics. Agricultural economics series. Ithaca, N.Y. 1953. These bulletins contain census data as follows: 877, Hamilton County; 878, Herkimer County; 880, Lewis County; 898, Saratoga County; 909, Warren County; 910, Washington County; 866, Clinton County; 872, Essex County; 873, Franklin County; 897, St. Lawrence County.   3842

Opposes acid plants in Adirondacks. *Field & S*, Feb. 1915. 19:1069. Opposition of the Camp-Fire Club of America.   3843

Peterson, Ronald B. Economic trends in the Forest preserve regions of New York state. *In* New York (state). Legislature. Joint legislative committee on natural resources. Report, 1954. p.110–12.   3844

Plattsburgh, N.Y. Council of community services. Directory of community services in Plattsburgh and Clinton county, 1954–1955. Plattsburgh, N.Y. n.d. 56p.   3845

Porter, Mrs. Marjorie (Lansing). Blueberries; a "Grapes of wrath" industry in early Clinton county. *No Country Life*, Summer 1952. 6:no.3:40–42.   3846

Porter, Mrs. Marjorie (Lansing). Frontier town and frontier life. *No Country Life*, Summer 1953. 7:no.3. The entire issue is devoted to Frontier Town, "America's only historical pioneer log village."   3847

Porter, Mrs. Marjorie (Lansing). R. Prescott & son, incorporated. Over a century at Keeseville on the Au Sable river. Keeseville, N.Y., Burlington, Vt. George Little co. 1954. unpaged. port. illus. maps. The firm manufactures chairs, coffins and TV cabinets.   3848

Pugh, Harold W. Blue fox farming. *Conservationist*, Aug. 1919. 2:124–25. illus. Experimenting with blue fox at U.S. Biological Survey fur farm near Keeseville.   3849

Santa's workshop. *Yorker*, Nov.–Dec. 1950. 9:20–21. illus. North Pole, N.Y.   3850

Santa's workshop. . .is the no.1 tourist attraction in the east. *No Country Life*, Summer 1955. 9:no.3:34–41. illus.   3851

Sisson, George W. The story of the Racquette river paper company, one of the north country's most stable industries. *No Country Life*, Summer 1951. 5:no.3:15–17. Adapted from radio script.   3852

The Upper Hudson and Champlain valley business directory containing the names. . .of businessmen in the cities and villages. . .on the line of the Delaware and Hudson, and Central Vermont railroads, 1895/96. Newburgh, N.Y. L.P. Waite & co. ᶜ1895. 388p.   3853

White, William Chapman. Christmas is their business. *Sat Eve Post*, Dec. 19, 1953. 226:no.25:34–35, 77–79. illus. North Pole, N.Y.   3854

Williams, Frank Martin. New York state's great water power, millions of tons of coal could be saved annually if undeveloped streams of the state were harnessed; pressing need of storage reservoirs. *State Service*, July–Aug. 1922. 6,i.e.8:227–35. illus.   3855

Williamson, Chilton. New York's struggle for Champlain valley trade, 1760–1825. *NY Hist*, Oct. 1941. 22:426–36.   3856

Zimmerman, W.E. and Lutz, E.A. The pulp and paper industries of New York state. An economic analysis. Albany, New York state division of commerce, 1942. 111p. figs. maps.   3857

ARTS AND CRAFTS

"Arto Monaco, toys." *No Country Life*, Fall 1948. 2:no.4:21–23. illus. Toy factory at Upper Jay.   3858

Boire, Harold A. Redford—rare American glass. *Antiques*, Aug. 1955. 68:137–39. illus.   3859

Craftsmen's exhibit at Saranac Lake. *No Country Life*, Summer 1949. 3:no.3:22. illus.   3860

McLaughlin, Warner. Glass making in the Champlain valley and northern New York. *Ver Quar*, Jan. 1946. n.s.14:5–17. Redford glassworks.   3861

McLaughlin, Warner. A history of the Redford crown glassworks at Redford, Clinton county, N.Y. *NY Hist*, July 1945. 26:368–77.   3862

Porter, Mrs. Marjorie (Lansing). Adirondack craftsmen's exhibit. *No Country Life*, Summer 1948. 2:no.3:28–29, 43. illus. At Saranac Lake.   3863

Porter, Mrs. Marjorie (Lansing). Redford glass. *No Country Life*, Spring 1953. 7:no.2:16–18.   3863.1

FORESTRY AND LUMBERING

Abel, G.W. and Recknagel, A.B. Ten-year growth on girdling plots in the Adirondacks. *J For*, Dec. 1942. 40:966. table.   3864

Accelerated growth of spruce after cutting in the Adirondacks. *J For*, Nov. 1917. 15:896–98. Reports by A.B. Recknagel and John Bentley Jr. 3865

An active season in Adirondacks. *NY Lumber*, Jan. 15, 1905. 38:no.446:11. One of the greatest years for logging industry. 3866

"Adirondack," pseud. Destruction of young spruce for rustic architecture. *Woods & Wat*, Winter 1903–4. 6:no.4:14–15. 3867

Adirondack forestry council. *NY Forester*, June 1944. 1:no.2:6–7. Brief account of organization. 3868

Adirondack lumber manufacturers & shippers association. Special report. Utica, N.Y. 1909. 7 unnumbered leaves. List of officers, members and by-laws. Copy in Yale University Library. 3869

Adirondack lumbermen's club organized. *Northeast Log*, Jan. 1953. 1:no.6:31. 3870

Adirondack rivers and lumbermen. *For & Stream*, June 17, 1899. 52:464. Reprint from Albany *Journal*, June 7, 1899. 3871

Allen, Shirley Walters. New forests for northern New York. *Am For*, Mar. 1928. 34:141–42, 181. illus. Reforestation program of the Northern New York Utilities Company. 3872

Armstrong, George R. The forests and economy of Lewis county, New York. Syracuse, N.Y. State University of New York, College of forestry, 1954. 49p. illus. (State University of New York. College of Forestry Bulletin 33.) 3873

B., P.A Wood technology. *Camp Log*, 1927. 13:11–13. illus. Collecting trips to Indian and Cat mountains. 3874

Baker, Hugh Potter. Disadvantage of logging to a fixed diameter limit in the Adirondack forests. *Emp St For Prod Assn Proc*, 1915. p.43–59. Also issued as a reprint. 3875

Baker, Hugh Potter and McCarthy, Edward F. Fundamental silvicultural measures necessary to insure forest lands remaining reasonably productive after logging. *J For*, Jan. 1920. 18:13–22. illus. Adirondacks used as an example. 3876

Balizet, Charles Edward. The management plan for the Pack demonstration forest at Warrensburg, N.Y. for the period 1930 to 1940. 154 leaves. tables, folded maps. Master's thesis, State University of New York, College of Forestry, Syracuse, 1931. Typescript. 3877

Beardslee, Lester A. An Adirondack winter trip, by Piseco, pseud. *For & Stream*, May 19, 1887. 28:366. Visit to logging camps up the Raquette River and on Tupper Lake. 3878

Beeman, Lyman A. Conservation is our business. *NYS Con*, Aug.–Sept. 1952. 7:no.1:18–19. By the president of Finch, Pruyn and Company, Inc. 3879

Beeman, Lyman A. Pulp country. *NYS Con*, Aug.–Sept. 1949. 4:no.1:4–7. illus. Finch, Pruyn cutting program. 3880

Belyea, Harold Cahill. Current annual increment of red spruce and balsam fir in the western Adirondacks. *J For*, Oct. 1922. 20:603–5. table. 3881

Belyea, Harold Cahill. The second crop of pulpwood. *Can For J*, Aug. 1918. 14:1836–40. Brandreth Park. 3882

Belyea, Harold Cahill. Some ratios of form in Adirondack swamp spruce. *J For*, Jan. 1925. 23:43–48. tables. 3883

Belyea, Harold Cahill. A study of mortality and recovery after logging. *J For*, Nov. 1924. 22:768–79. tables. Cranberry Lake. 3884

Belyea, Harold Cahill. A suggestion for forest regions and forest types as a basis of management in New York state. *J For*, Dec. 1922. 20:854–68. 3885

Benedict, Darwin. Yuppee, tiay, timber! *Cloud Splitter*, Jan.–Feb. 1948. 11:no.1:7–8. Brand marks. Lumbering in Adirondacks. 3886

Bird, Mrs. Barbara (Kephart). Calked shoes. Life in Adirondack lumber camps. Photographs by Royal G. Bird. Prospect, N.Y. Prospect books, 1952. 141p. illus. Reviewed by Raymona E. Hull in *North Country Life*, Summer 1952, 6:no.3:53–54. Part published under title "I Married a Forester" in *North Country Life*, Spring 1951–Summer 1952, 5:no.2:48–51; 5:no.3:41–46; 5:no.4:9–14; 6:no.1:24–31, 70; 6:no.2:32–35; 6:no.3:27–30. illus. 3887

Bowman, Isaiah. Forest physiography:physiography of the United States and principles of soils in relation to forestry. N.Y. Wiley, c1911. 759p. illus. maps. Adirondack mountains, p.578–84. Brief summary. 3888

Braun, Emma Lucy. Deciduous forests of eastern North America. Philadelphia, Blakiston, 1950. 596p. maps. An attempt to portray the deciduous forest past and present, to give data on its composition and aspect, and to trace through geologic time the present pattern of forest distribution. 3889

Bray, William L. . . .History of forest development on an undrained sand plain in the Adirondacks. Syracuse, N.Y. Syracuse university, 1921. 47p. plates, folded maps incl. front. (State University of New York. College of Forestry, Syracuse. Technical Publication no.13.) 3890

Briegleb, Philip A. Form-class tables for the Adirondack red spruce. 75 leaves. mounted photograph, tables, charts. Master's thesis, State University of New York, College of Forestry, Syracuse, 1930. Typescript.   3891

Broderick, R.E. Lumber industry conditions in Vermont and the eastern Adirondacks. *Lumber Camp News*, Dec. 1951. 13:no.8:6.
3892

Broderick, R.E. The lumber industry in northern New York, western Pennsylvania. *Northeast Log*, Jan. 1953. 1:no.6:25.   3893

Brown, Nelson C. Cableway logging in the Adirondacks. *Wood*, Jan. 1950. 5:24, 50. illus.
3894

Brown, Nelson C. Chute logging in New York. *J For*, May 1934. 32:575–79. illus. Includes discussion of pulpwood pole chutes operated on steep slopes of the Adirondacks.
3895

Bryant, Ralph Clement. Silviculture at Axton and in the Adirondacks generally *J For*, Nov. 1917. 15:891–95.   3896

Buck, C.J. Lumbering of hardwoods in the Adirondack mountains. New Haven, 1905. 60 leaves. Typescript at the Yale School of Forestry.   3897

Buckley, John L. A comparative ecological study of three hydrophytic areas on the Huntington forest. 112 leaves, tables, charts, maps. Master's thesis, State University of New York, College of Forestry, Syracuse, 1947. Typescript. Abstract in Graduate Theses, p.54.   3898

Burnham, Koert D. White cedar lasts longer. The most durable wood grown in the Adirondacks responds well to forest management. *NYS Con*, Apr.–May 1951. 5:no.5:24–25. illus.   3899

C., S.A. Merchantable timber of the Adirondacks. *For & Stream*, June 1, 1893. 40:471.
3900

Cain, Robert L. Adirondack lake shore vegetation. II. Winter killing of beech on Huntington forest lake shores. 91 leaves. mounted photographs, tables, figs. maps. Master's thesis, State University of New York, College of Forestry, Syracuse, 1942. Typescript. 3901

Camp 5. *NYS Con*, Feb.–Mar. 1949. 3:no.4: 20–22. illus. Photographs taken at Finch, Pruyn and Company camp overlooking Boreas Ponds.   3902

Campbell, R.H. An Adirondack forest experiment. *Can For J*, Nov. 1917. 13:1384–88. illus.   3903

Carmer, Carl Lamson. Road-monkey and whistle-punk. *In* his Listen for a lonesome drum. . . N.Y. Farrar & Rinehart, inc. 1936. p.271–93. Gould Lumber Camp.   3904

Casanova, Frank E. The effect of deer browsing on forest regeneration in the central Adirondacks with special reference to the balsam fir. 111 leaves. illus. charts, tables, folded maps. Master's thesis, State University of New York, College of Forestry, Syracuse, 1940. Typescript.   3905

Chandler, B.A. Results of cutting at Ne-Ha-Sa-Ne park in the Adirondacks. *J For*, Apr. 1919. 17:378–85. charts.   3906

Chandler, Robert Flint Jr. Cation exchange properties of certain forest soils in Adirondack section. Washington, U.S. Department of agriculture, 1939. p.491–505. illus. (Contribution from New York State Agricultural Experiment Station, Ithaca.) Also in *Journal of Agricultural Research*, Oct. 1, 1939, 59:491–505.   3907

Charlton, John W. The Adirondack forest products association. *NY Forester*, Oct. 1945. 2:no.5:7–9.   3908

Churchill, Howard L. Approximate cost of private forestry measures in the Adirondack mountains. *J For*, Jan. 1920. 18:26–30. 3909

Churchill, Howard L. An example of industrial forestry in the Adirondacks. *J For*, Jan. 1929. 27:23–26.   3910

Churchill, Howard L. An example of private forestry in the Adirondacks. *NY Forestry*, July 1919. 6:15–17.   3911

Churchill, Howard L. Practical handling of freehold timberlands. *Pulp & Pa*, Feb. 1927. p.260–61, 264. Finch, Pruyn operations in the Adirondacks.   3912

Cook, David B. and Littlefield, Edward Winchester. Grosbeak damage to Scotch pine. *J For*, Apr. 1945. 43:269–72. illus. Injury may prove sufficiently serious to affect advisability of planting Scotch pine in the Adirondacks.   3913

Cook, David B. Growth study for Finch, Pruyn & company. *Cor For*, May 1924. 4:40. illus.   3914

Cook, David B. Pulpwood. *NYS Con*, Feb.–Mar. 1948. 2:no.4:8–9. illus.   3915

Cooper, William Skinner. The ecological life history of certain species of ribes and its application to the control of the white pine blister rust. *Ecology*, Jan. 1922. 3:7–16. Part of the field work was done in the Adirondacks. 3916

Cope, Joshua Alban. A self liquidating forestry project in Saratoga county, N.Y. *Emp St For Prod Assn Bul*, Jan. 1, 1936. 53:3–5. Experiment with hardwood pulp near Corinth, N.Y.   3917

Cope, Joshua Alban. Winter injury to hardwoods in 1933–34. *J For*, Nov. 1935. 33:939–40.   3918

Coville, Perkins. Silvicultural problems on the management of forests of the Adirondack hardwood type. 72 leaves. tables (partly folded) map. Master's thesis, Cornell University, 1920. Typescript. 3919

Cron, Robert H. A management plan for the Archer and Anna Huntington wildlife forest station of Newcomb, New York for the period 1937–1947... 271 leaves. mounted photographs, tables, maps (1 folded). Master's thesis, State University of New York, College of Forestry, Syracuse, 1937. Typescript. 3920

Cruikshank, Barton. Some evils of lumbering and their remedies. *Woods & Wat*, Autumn 1903. 6:no.3:7–8. 3921

Curry, John R. Early lumbering in the Adirondacks. *Northeast Log*, May 1953. 1:no.9: 13, 22. illus. Abstracted from Hochschild's "Township 34." 3922

Curry, John R. Forest management problems and research in the central Adirondacks. *NY Forester*, May 1953. 10:no.2:7–10. Includes description of research program of Northeastern Forest Experiment Station at Paul Smiths. Followed by comment by Esmond W. Sears, p.10–11. 3923

Curry, John R. and Church, Thomas W. Winter injury of conifers in the Adirondacks. *Northeast Log*, July 1952. 1:no.1:10, 15. illus. Résumé of *Journal of Forestry*, Feb. 1952, 50: 114–16. 3924

Dana, Samuel T. and Greeley, William B. Timber growing and logging practice in the northeast. Washington, G.P.O. 1930. 112p. illus. charts. (U.S. Department of Agriculture Technical Bulletin no.166.) 3925

Davis, James E. Forest land use studies and the Adirondack-Catskill survey. *NYS Ranger Sch*, 1951. p.16–19. 3926

Defebaugh, James Elliot. History of the lumber industry in America. Chicago, American lumberman, 1900–7. 2v. plates, ports. Adirondacks, v.1, p.404–5, v.2, p.387–407. 3927

Donahue, Roy Luther. Forest-site quality studies in the Adirondacks. I. Tree growth as related to soil morphology. Ithaca, N.Y. Cornell university, 1940. 44p. illus. figs. maps. (New York State Agricultural Experiment Station, Ithaca. Memoir 229.) 3928

Dubuar, James Francis. The 1915 red pine plantation. *NYS Ranger Sch*, 1955. p.7–8, 15. illus. tables. Ranger School Forest. 3929

Empire state forest products association. Annual report of the forester and secretary... Nov. 13, 1924. 2p. port. illus. Reprinted from the *Lumber World Review*, Nov. 10, 1924. Report is by A.B. Recknagel. 3930

Empire state forest products association. Let's give forest conservation a hand. Syracuse, N.Y. 1954. 12p. figs. Plea for deferred forest tax constitutional amendment, modified workmen's compensation for logging and lumbering industries and lumbering in the Forest Preserve. 3931

Fernow, Bernhard Eduard. Practical forestry in the Adirondacks. *Sci Am*, Mar. 30, 1901. Supplement. 51:21116–17. 3932

Field day planned at Old Forge. *Lumber Camp News*, June 1948. 10:no.2:22. Woodsmen's field day. See also article "Woodsmen's Field Day a Big Success" in Aug. issue, 10:no.4:3. 3933

Finch Pruyn company operates in Blue mountain area. *Lumber Camp News*, Mar. 1952. 13:no.11:5–7. 3934

Finch Pruyn company uses Wyssen skyline crane. *Lumber Camp News*, Dec. 1949. 11: no.8:10. illus. 3935

Forest planting. *St No Mo*, Feb. 1908. 3:102–4. Editorial in favor of leaving fallen trees etc. 3936

A forest policy for New York state. *In* Empire state forest products association. Annual meeting, 1924. Reprinted from *Lumber World Review*, Nov. 25, 1924, p.2. Summarizes addresses of E. Hagaman Hall (representing the Association for the Protection of the Adirondacks), W.G. Howard (for the Conservation Commission) and others. 3937

Forestry in New York would play lone hand. *Am Lumberman*, Jan. 8, 1921. no.2382:49. Editorial on the speech of George N. Ostrander before the Dec. 2, 1920 meeting of the Empire State Forest Products Association. Reprinted in *Empire State Forest Products Association Bulletin*, May 1921, no.9:9–10. 3938

Forestry leaders meet at Tupper Lake. *Lumber Camp News*, Sept. 1951. 13:no.5:2. 3939

Fosburgh, Peter W. The big boom. *NYS Con*, Apr.–May 1947. 1:no.5:16–17. Reprinted in *North Country Life*, Summer 1947, 1:no.4:52–55. Reminiscences of logging. 3940

Fosburgh, Peter W. Camp 3. *NYS Con*, Oct.–Nov. 1951. 6:no.2:4–6. illus. Problems of a lumber company in the Adirondacks. 3941

Fox, William Freeman. History of the lumber industry in the State of New York. *In* New York (state). Forest, fish and game commission. Annual report, 1900. p.237–82. plates, col. map. Appendix (p.283–305) is "Roll of Pioneer Lumbermen." 3942

Fox, William Freeman. ...A history of the lumber industry in the State of New York. Washington, G.P.O. 1902. 59p. front. plates.

(U.S. Department of Agriculture. Bureau of Forestry Bulletin 34.) Reviewed in *Forestry and Irrigation*, Sept. 1902, 8:381–85 with title "The Lumber Industry in New York." 3943

Gifford, John Clayton. In the Adirondacks. *Recreation*, Aug. 1900. 13:88. illus. Brief note on log driving. 3944

Graves, Henry Solon. . . .Practical forestry in the Adirondacks. . . Washington, G.P.O. 1899. 85p. front. plates, maps (1 folded). (U.S. Department of Agriculture. Division of Forestry Bulletin 26.) Reviewed in *American Geographical Society Bulletin*, 1901, 33:452–53. 3945

Griffiths, Richard E. Frost damage to trees. *NYS Ranger Sch*, 1953. p.39–41. illus. Observations on Ranger School Forest. 3946

Hale, H.M. Lumbering the hardwoods, Adirondacks, New York. New Haven, 1905. 14 leaves. plates. Typescript in the Yale School of Forestry. 3947

Hammarstrom, Carl. A management plan for the Archer and Anna Huntington wildlife forest station at Newcomb, N.Y. 113 leaves. tables, charts, maps (3 in pocket). Master's thesis, State University of New York, College of Forestry, Syracuse, 1936. Typescript. 3948

Harper, V.L. Timber resources of New England and New York with special reference to pulpwood supplies. *Pap Ind*, Dec. 1946. 28:1358–60. Includes discussion of Adirondack area. 3949

Harpp, N.H. White pine depletion—Warren & Essex counties. *NY Forester*, Aug. 1945. 2:no.4:8–9. 3950

Hawley, Ralph Chipman. Forestry at Nehasane park. *J For*, Nov. 1920. 18:681–92. 3951

Heiberg, Svend O. Cutting based upon economic increment. *J For*, Aug. 1942. 40:645–51. tables. Economic increment charts for eastern pine and hemlock in the Pack Demonstration Forest. 3952

Heiberg, Svend O. Does economic cutting pay? *J For*, Feb. 1945. 43:109–12. Application to a stand of white pine on Pack Demonstration Forest. 3953

Heiberg, Svend O. White pine research. *NY Forester*, May 1953. 10:no.2:1–7. Comment by C.H. Foster. 3954

Heimburger, Carl Constantine. Forest-type studies in the Adirondack region. Ithaca, N.Y. 1934. 122p. incl. illus. tables, diagrs. map. (New York Agricultural Experiment Station, Ithaca. Memoir 165.) Doctoral thesis, Cornell University, 1933. Reviewed by B. Moore in *Ecology*, Oct. 1935, 16:648–51. 3955

Hensel, James A. A silvicultural working plan for the second-growth hardwoods on the New York state Ranger school forest. 201 leaves. tables, folded maps in pocket. Master's thesis, State University of New York, College of Forestry, Syracuse, 1955. Typescript. 3956

Hirt, Ray Roland. Canker development by Cronartium ribicola on young Pinus strobus. *Phytopathology*, Dec. 1939. 29:1067–76. illus. chart, table. Investigation carried on at Pack Forest. 3957

Hirt, Ray Roland. The development of blister rust on young planted northern white pine. *J For*, Dec. 1939. 37:967–69. In Pack Forest. 3958

Hirt, Ray Roland. The development of decay in living trees inoculated with Fomes pinicola. *J For*, July 1938. 36:705–9. Experiments carried on in Pack Forest. 3959

Hirt, Ray Roland. Distribution of blister-rust cankers on eastern white pine according to age of needle-bearing wood at time of infection. *J For*, Jan. 1944. 42:9–14. Observations made at Warrensburg. 3960

Hirt, Ray Roland. Evidence of resistance to blister rust by eastern white pine growing in the northeast. *J For*, Dec. 1948. 46:911–13. 3961

Hirt, Ray Roland. The progress of blister rust in planted northern white pine. *J For*, May 1936. 34:506–11. 3962

Hirt, Ray Roland. The relation of certain meteorological factors to the infection of eastern white pine by the blister-rust fungus. Syracuse, N.Y. Syracuse university, 1942. 65p. (State University of New York. College of Forestry, Syracuse. Technical Publication no.59.) Studies made near Warrensburg. 3963

Hirt, Ray Roland. Relation of stomata to infection of Pinus strobus by Cronartium ribicola. *Phytopathology*, Mar. 1938. 28:180–90. illus. tables. Studies made on Pack Forest. 3964

Hirt, Ray Roland. Relative susceptibility to Cronartium ribicola of five-needled pines planted in the east. *J For*, Dec. 1940. 38:932–37. Experiment on eleven species of pines in the Adirondacks and central New York. 3965

Holcomb, Harry W. Damage to merchantable white pine in New York state by blister rust disease. *NYS Ranger Sch*, 1949. p.15, 28. Study made near Tupper Lake. 3966

Holst, M.J. Notes on the Norway spruce–white pine weevil relationship in the Adirondacks. *NYS Ranger Sch*, 1955. p.16–17, 40. 3967

Hosmer, Ralph Sheldon. Studying the American forests. In the Empire state. *Forester*,

Feb. 1900. 6:36. The Division of Forestry of the U.S. Department of Agriculture gathered data for a working plan on land owned by the McIntyre Iron Company. 3968

Hoyle, Raymond J. Timber cut from forests of New York state in 1953. *Northeast Log*, Jan.–Feb. 1955. 3:no.7:6–7, 22–23; 3:no.8: 14–16. illus. tables. Area I includes the Adirondacks. 3969

Hoyt, Gould J. A study of accelerated growth of red spruce on the Huntington forest. 58 leaves. tables, charts. Master's thesis, State University of New York, College of Forestry, Syracuse, 1948. Typescript. Abstract in Graduate Theses, p.71. 3970

Illick, Joseph S. An outstanding decade in the development of forestry in New York state. *In* New York (state). Legislature. Joint legislative committee on natural resources. Report, 1953. p.47–50. History of forestry in New York state, 1885–94. 3971

Improvements about complete at Gould paper mill. *Lumber Camp News*, June 1949. 11:no.2:1, 4. illus. At Lyons Falls. 3972

Isenecker, Elmer S. Grading hardwoods in the Adirondacks. *Emp For*, 1918. 4:52–53. illus. 3973

Jaenicke, R. Walter. A silviculture working plan for the Pack demonstration forest 1940–1950. 195 leaves. tables, maps in pocket. Master's thesis, State University of New York, College of Forestry, Syracuse, 1941. Typescript. 3974

Jenkins, Robert B. Economical log loading. *Northeast Log*, July 1954. 3:no.2:8–9, 38. illus. At Conifer. 3975

Juvenal, pseud. Lumbering in the Adirondacks. *For & Stream*, Dec. 15, 1906. 67:939. illus. 3976

Kellogg, R.S. Cut clean and keep out fire. *Am For*, Nov. 1922. 28:694–95. illus. 3977

Kinney, Chester. Sample plot work. *Emp For*, 1932. 18:49–50. Remeasurement of 19 sample plots in the Adirondacks. 3978

Kittredge, Joseph Jr. and Belyea, H.C. Reproduction with fire protection in the Adirondack mountains. *J For*, Dec. 1923. 21: 784–87. 3979

Kling, Edwin M. McKeever in the "teens," village had active lumbering program. *Lumber Camp News*, Sept. 1949. 11:no.5:1, 4, 7. illus. 3980

Knechtel, A. Natural reproduction in the Adirondack forests. *For Quar*, Jan. 1903. 1: 50–55. Work done in Township 5, Hamilton County. 3981

Larson, Charles C. Some highlights from a study of the Adirondack forest economy. *In* New York (state). Legislature. Joint legislative committee on natural resources. Report, 1954. p.113–17. 3982

Larson, Charles C. Timber resources and the economy of the Saranac Lake–Lake Placid area. Syracuse, N.Y. State university of New York, College of forestry, 1954. 42p. illus. diagrs. tables, maps. (State University of New York College of Forestry Bulletin 32.) 3983

Larson, E.V. Forest research advisory council meets at Paul Smith's, New York. *Lumber Camp News*, July 1950. 12:no.6:6. 3984

Levison, J.J. Report on the lumber industry of the Adirondack mountains. New Haven, 1905. 133 leaves. plates. Typescript in Yale School of Forestry. 3985

Littlefield, Edward Winchester. A plantation of ponderosa pine in northern New York. *J For*, May 1944. 42:364–65. Stand is southwest of Plattsburgh. 3986

Littlefield, Edward Winchester and Fosburgh, Peter W. The Turner tract. *NYS Con*, Oct.–Nov. 1955. 10:no.2:6–7. illus. "Logging does not necessarily destroy the forest." 3987

Log driving program at low ebb. *Lumber Camp News*, May 1950. 12:no.1:1. illus. Finch, Pruyn the only drive. 3988

Logging in the Cold river country. *Lumber Camp News*, Apr. 1952. 13:no.12:5. illus. 3989

The lumbering industry in Tupper Lake. *Lumber Camp News*, Aug. 1949. 11:no.4:1–2. illus. 3990

Lumsden, George Q. Sample working plan for Adirondack hardwoods. *Emp St For Prod Assn Bul*, Oct. 1922. 15:9–16. tables. 3991

Luther, Thomas C. Private forest planting. *Bul Schools*, Apr. 1, 1931. 17:181–82. plate. Private 7,000-acre preserve of which 4,000 acres reforested. Early and rare example of good work on private land in Forest Preserve county. 3992

McCarthy, Edward Florince. Accelerated growth of balsam fir in the Adirondacks. *J For*, Mar. 1918. 16:304–7. 3993

McCarthy, Edward Florince. Diameter growth of tolerant softwood trees in northern forest. *Emp For*, 1918. 4:32–33. diagrs. 3994

McCarthy, Edwin Florince. Forest improvement, a pioneer job. *NYS Ranger Sch*, 1933. p.14–17. table. Problems on Ranger School Forest. 3995

McCarthy, Edward Florince and Hoyle, Raymond J. Knot zones and spiral in Adirondack red spruce. *J For*, Nov. 1918. 16: 777–91. illus. charts, tables.   3996

McCarthy, Edward Florince. Observations on unburned cut-over lands in the Adirondacks. *J For*, Apr. 1919. 17:386–97. charts, tables.   3997

McCarthy, Edward Florince and Hoyle, Raymond J. Production of pulp on balsam lands. *Paper*, Oct. 23, 1918. 23:no.7:14–18. Near Brandreth Lake.   3998

McCarthy, Edward Florince. Variations in northern forest and their influence on management. *J For*, Dec. 1921. 19:867–71. Comparison of Ontario forest with Adirondacks.   3999

McCarthy, Edward Florince and Belyea, Harold Cahill. . . .Yellow birch and its relation to the Adirondack forest. Syracuse, N.Y. Syracuse university, 1920. 50p. incl. front. illus. folded diagrs. (State University of New York. College of Forestry, Syracuse. Technical Publication no.12.)   4000

McIntyre, H.L. Report on forest pest problems in New York. *J For*, Nov. 1939. 37:879–83.   4001

MacTruck, Otto. Destruction of standing timber in the Cranberry lake region by increment borers. *Camp Log*, 1925. 11:37–38.   4002

Maisenhelder, Louis Carl. A study of the growth of spruce and fir in the central Adirondacks. 38 leaves. figs. Master's thesis, Cornell University, 1932. Typescript. Study made at the request of Finch, Pruyn and Company.   4003

Mason, C.W. The coming of the tractor. *Lumber Camp News*, May 1949. 11:no.1:12. First tractor used in the pulpwood business at North Lake operations of the Gould Paper Company.   4004

Mason, C.W. Woodsmen's carnival a great success. *Northeast Log*, Oct. 1952. 1:no.3:9, 30. illus.   4005

Meagher, George S. and Recknagel, Arthur Bernard. The growth of spruce and fir on the Whitney park in the Adirondacks *J For*, May 1935. 33:499–502.   4006

Meissner, Hans A. Logging trends in the white pine region of New York state. *NYS Ranger Sch*, 1944. p.28–29. In the Lake George and Lake Champlain areas.   4007

Mols, Herbert Joseph. Hardwood utilization in the Adirondacks. 31, 13 leaves. mounted photographs, tables, folded map (blueprint). Master's thesis, Cornell University, 1937. Typescript.   4008

Myer, J.E. A summer study of Adirondack birch. *Emp For*, 1920. 6:57–59. illus.   4009

Najer, Alfred. A lumberman's viewpoint. *NY Forester*, May 1926. 2:no.2:3–4. Management plan for privately owned wood lots.   4010

The new Riverside mill rebuilt by the Northern lumber co. *Northeast Log*, Sept. 1955. 4: no.3:8–9. illus. Near North Creek.   4011

New York (state). College of forestry. Progress of forest management in the Adirondacks. Ithaca N.Y. 1901. 40p. (New York State College of Forestry. Cornell University Bulletin 3.) Reviewed in *Science*, Apr. 5, 1901, n.s.13:542–44.   4012

New York (state). State university. College of forestry, Syracuse. Forest acreage and timber volume in the Adirondack and Catskill regions, by Miles J. Ferree and James E. Davis. Syracuse, N.Y. 1954. 19p. tables, map. (Bulletin 35.) Extract in New York State. Joint Legislative Committee on Natural Resources Report, 1954, p.91–99.   4013

New York (state). State university. College of forestry, Syracuse. Tree-volume tables, based on forest site; Adirondack and Catskill regions of New York state. Syracuse, N.Y. 1954. 8p. (Bulletin 29.)   4014

New York foresters meet at Speculator. *Lumber Camp News*, July 1950. 12:no.6:15. Report of the meeting of the New York section of the Society of American Foresters.   4015

Northeastern loggers association holds annual meeting. *Northeast Log*, Oct. 1952. 1: no.3:23. Held at Tupper Lake.   4016

Old logging camp. The Barnes camp in 1915. *Northeast Log*, Dec. 1954. 3:no.6:14–15, 57. illus. Near Boonville.   4017

Operation at Jessup river completed. *Lumber Camp News*, Sept. 1948. 10:no.5:5. Completion of lumbering on one of the last stands of virgin timber in the Adirondacks.   4018

Oskamp, Joseph. Tree behavior on important soil profiles in the Peru, Plattsburg, and Crown Point areas in Clinton and Essex counties. Ithaca, N.Y. Cornell university agricultural experiment station, 1938. 26p. illus. charts, map. (New York State Agricultural Experiment Station, Ithaca. Bulletin 705.)   4019

Packard, A.S. Decay of spruce in the Adirondacks and northern New England. *Nation*, Dec. 27, 1883. 37:525–26.   4020

Paul Bunyan visits the Moose river. *Northeast Log*, Sept. 1954. 3:no.3:5. illus. Brief note of giant pine felled by McHale Brothers.   4021

Pearce, John. The effect of deer browsing on certain western Adirondack forest types. Syracuse, N.Y. Syracuse university, 1937.

61p. illus. tables, map. (Roosevelt Wildlife Bulletin, v.7, no.1.) Also published as New York State University. College of Forestry, Syracuse. Bulletin, v.10, no.2. A revision of his master's thesis "The Influence of Browsing by White-tailed Deer. . .on Western Adirondack Forests." State University of New York, College of Forestry, Syracuse, 1935. 105 leaves. 4022

Pinchot, Gifford. The Adirondack spruce: a study of the forest in Ne-ha-sa-ne park with tables of volume and yield and a working-plan for conservative lumbering. N.Y. Critic co. 1898. 157p. plates, tables. 4023

Pinchot, Gifford. The forests of Ne-Ha-Sa-Ne park in northern New York. *Gard & For*, Apr. 12, 1893. 6:168–69. 4024

Plice, M.J. and Hedden, G.W. Selective girdling of hardwoods to release young growth of conifers. *J For*, Jan. 1931. 29:32–40. tables. Experiment on Finch, Pruyn and Company lands in the Adirondacks. 4025

Potter, Shirley W. Jr. The 1915 red pine plantation. *NYS Ranger Sch*, 1948. p.39–46. tables. 4026

Potter, Shirley W. Jr. Work progress on the Ranger school forest. *NYS Ranger Sch*, 1947. p.20–23. illus. tables. 4027

Pulling, A.V.S. The importance of wild life and recreation in forest management. *J For*, Mar. 1928. 26:315–25. Many references to the Forest Preserve. 4028

Pulpwood cutting experiment begun in Adirondacks. *J For*, Jan. 1931. 29:135–36. Extracted from Bulletin 135 of the Division of Horticulture, Massachusetts Agricultural College, by M. Westveld. Cooperative project by Finch, Pruyn and Company, the Cornell School of Forestry and the Northeastern Forest Experiment Station. 4029

Radford, Harry V. . . .Artificial preservation of timber and History of the Adirondack beaver. Albany, J.B. Lyon, 1908. p.345–418. illus. plates, folded maps. Reprinted from the 10th, 11th and 12th Reports of the New York State Forest, Fish and Game Commission. 4030

Rafter, George W. Stream flow in relation to forests. *Am Forestry Assn Proc*, 1897. 12:139–65. Author's name incorrectly cited as George S. Rafter. Includes the upper Hudson. 4031

Recknagel, Arthur Bernard. Adirondack growth figures confirm prediction table. *J For*, Sept. 1946. 44:680. 4032

Recknagel, Arthur Bernard and others. Experimental cutting of spruce and fir in the Adirondacks. *J For*, Oct. 1933. 31:680–88. tables, map. Experimental plots at New-comb, N.Y. on Finch, Pruyn and Company land. 4033

Recknagel, Arthur Bernard. Five-year remeasurement of sample plots. *J For*, Nov. 1936. 34:994–95. Sample lots located in Essex and Hamilton counties. 4034

Recknagel, Arthur Bernard. Forestry in the Adirondacks. *J For*, Feb. 1918. 16:244. Signed: A.B.R. 4035

Recknagel, Arthur Bernard. Forestry on the Whitney preserve in the Adirondacks. *J For*, Feb. 1936. 34:111–13. 4036

Recknagel, Arthur Bernard. Growth and development of Adirondack stands. *J For*, Apr. 1939. 37:346. Five one-acre plots measured. 4037

Recknagel, Arthur Bernard. Growth of spruce and balsam in the Adirondacks. *Am Pap & Pulp*, 1925. 48:71–72. A report on growth study made in 1923 on lands of Finch, Pruyn and Company. 4038

Recknagel, Arthur Bernard. Growth of spruce and balsam in the Adirondacks. *J For*, Oct. 1922. 20:598–602. table. 4039

Recknagel, Arthur Bernard. Growth of white spruce in the Adirondacks. *J For*, Dec. 1923. 21:794–95. 4040

Recknagel, Arthur Bernard. Inspection, supervision, and control of private forestry measures, methods and cost. *J For*, Jan. 1920. 18:23–25. 4041

Recknagel, Arthur Bernard. A practical application of Pressler's formula. *For Quar*, June 1916. 14:260–67. tables. Data used were obtained in connection with work done in the Catskills and Adirondacks during 1914 and 1915. 4042

Recknagel, Arthur Bernard. Private forestry in the northeastern states with special reference to northern New York. *J For*, Jan. 1939. 37:22–24. 4043

Recknagel, Arthur Bernard. Pulpwood stands and consumption. *Paper*, Apr. 9, 1919. 24: no.5:38. Estimate of privately owned standing timber in thirteen Adirondack counties. 4044

Recknagel, Arthur Bernard and Westveld, M. Results of second remeasurement of Adirondack cutting plots. *J For*, Nov. 1942. 40:837–40. tables. Condensed in *Pulp and Paper of Canada*, Dec. 1942, 43:966–68, under title "How Cutting Affects Forest Growth; Results of Second Measurement of Adirondack Cutting Plots." 4045

Recknagel, Arthur Bernard. Sample working plan for Adirondack softwoods. *Emp St For Prod Assn Bul*, Oct. 1922. 15:2–8. tables. Issued as a reprint with the following item. Ithaca, 1922, 16p. 4046

Recknagel, Arthur Bernard. Second growth hardwoods in the Adirondacks. *J For*, Feb. 1921. 19:129–30.   4047

Recknagel, Arthur Bernard. Some aspects of logging in the Adirondacks. *Pulp & Pa*, June 20, 1918. 16:558–59.   4048

Recknagel, Arthur Bernard. Sustained yield of Adirondack spruce and fir. *J For*, Mar. 1933. 31:343–44. table.   4049

Recknagel, Arthur Bernard. Timber resources of New York state. *Am Lumberman*, Mar. 20, 1920. no.2340:65.   4050

Recknagel, Arthur Bernard. What the private timberland owners are doing and have done in forestry in the Adirondacks. *J For*, Mar. 1931. 29:429–31. Abstract in *Empire State Forest Products Association Bulletin*, Dec. 15, 1930, 35:3–6.   4051

Reed, Frank A. Adirondack lumbering. *NYS Ranger Sch*, 1948. p.5–8, 15. illus.   4052

Reed, Frank A. C.J. Strife Adirondack operation. *Northeast Log*, Nov. 1952. 1:no.4:8–9, 24. illus.   4053

Reed, Frank A. George Colvin's logging operation. *Northeast Log*, Aug.–Sept. 1952. 1: no.2:8, 23. illus. At McKeever.   4054

Reed, Frank A. Gould's old-time logging operations. *Northeast Log*, Feb. 1953. 1:no.7: 8–9, 25. illus. G.H. Gould mill located at junction of Moose and Black rivers.   4055

Reed, Frank A. Hasleton lumber company operations. *Northeast Log*, Apr. 1954. 2:no.8: 8–9. illus. At Wilmington, N.Y.   4056

Reed, Frank A. and Simmons, Louis J. The woodsmen's field day. *Northeast Log*, Oct. 1953. 2:no.2:10–11. See also "Woodsmen's Field Day" in issue for Oct. 1954, 3:no.4:16–17, 26; "Woodsmen's Field Days" in *North Country Life*, Summer 1955, 9:no.3:28–33 (pictures with brief text).   4057

Reed, Frank A. Woodsmen's field day at Tupper. *Northeast Log*, Oct. 1952. 1:no.3:8, 24. illus.   4058

Reforestation begun by a New York lawyer. *Field & S*, Aug. 1915. 20:409. Work of Richard James Donovan in planting 430,000 pine trees at Pine Park between Loon Lake and Lake Placid.   4059

Reid, Kenneth A. For better trout fishing. n.p. 1954. 4p. Leaflet reprinted from *Northeastern Logger*, June 1954. Cutting program at Whitney Park.   4060

Rice veneer company Adirondack operations. *Northeast Log*, July 1952. 1:no.1:6–7. illus.
                                                4061

Rice veneer company buys McKeever. *Lumber Camp News*, Aug. 1949. 11:no.4:4.   4062

Richards, Edward. A study of the growth of spruce and balsam pulpwood on cut-over ridge land in Lewis county, N.Y. *J For*, Jan. 1925. 23:20–29. table.   4063

Roberts, Tony. Adirondack's timber shortage. *Am For*, Nov. 1951. 57:no.11:14–18, 41–42.   4064

Rodgers, Andrew Denny. Bernhard Eduard Fernow: a story of North American forestry. Princeton, Princeton university press, 1951. 623p. ports. Covers first attempt at scientific forestry in the Adirondacks. Progress in forestry education: Cornell, p.251–80.   4065

Roger, Earl Josiah. The growth of red pine in plantation (Pinus resinosa) in the Ranger school forest, Wanakena, New York. 52 leaves. mounted photographs, charts. Master's thesis, State University of New York, College of Forestry, Syracuse, 1938. Typescript.   4066

Rosasco, Edwin M. A preliminary study on the effect of sodium arsenate, used as a chemical debarking agent, upon wildlife and wildlife environment. 100 leaves. mounted photographs, charts, map. Master's thesis, State University of New York, College of Forestry, Syracuse, 1952. Typescript. Abstract in Graduate Theses, p.58. Huntington Forest.
                                                4067

Rutherford, William Jr. Reproduction of Adirondack hardwoods. *NYS Ranger Sch*, 1949. p.12–14. illus.   4068

Safety speaks at Old Forge. *Northeast Log*, July 1954. 2:no.11:20–21. illus. Logging safety conference. See also article by John Stock, "The Adirondacks Start to Creep," in issue for Mar. 1955.   4069

Sage, Dean. Decay of spruce in the Adirondacks. *Nation*, Dec. 20, 1883. 37:506.   4070

Samson, Nelson T. Woods labor in the Adirondacks (Hamilton county, N.Y.). 175 leaves. tables, forms. Doctoral thesis, State University of New York, College of Forestry, Syracuse, 1952. Typescript. Abstract in Graduate Theses, p.37.   4071

Schwartz, G. Victor. Railroad forestry. *Emp For*, 1931. 17:35–39. illus. D & H reforestation program.   4072

Seagears, Clayton B. A woodsmen's field day —or bulging biceps vs gallons of gas. *NYS Con*, Oct.–Nov. 1953. 8:no.2:40. Annual field day at Tupper Lake.   4073

Searles, R.M. Producing trees at the Lake Clear nursery for New York state's reforesting program. *NYS Ranger Sch*, 1933. p.40–42. illus.   4074

Sharp appreciation in Adirondack timber. *NY Lumber*, Feb. 15, 1905. 38:11.   4075

Shirley, Hardy L. Forestry opportunities in the Adirondacks. *Northeast Log*, Aug. 1955. 4:no.2:8–9, 28–31. illus. 4076

Simmons, Louis J. Elliot hardware company buy Barbour tract. *Northeast Log*, Feb. 1953. 1:no.7:18. Around Follensby Pond. 4077

Simmons, Louis J. Emporium forestry mill changes hands. *Lumber Camp News*, May 1949. 11:no.1:1, 4. History of the Adirondack holdings of the company. 4078

Simmons, Louis J. Lumber company fireeaters of 52 years ago. *Lumber Camp News*, Feb. 1952. 13:no.10:7. illus. Hose Company No. 1 of the A. Sherman Lumber Company, Tupper Lake. 4079

Simmons, Louis J. Old reporter recalls peak lumbering era in Tupper Lake sector. *Northeast Log*, Jan. 1953. 1:no.6:35. 4080

Simmons, Louis J. Tupper Lake lumbering industry. *Northeast Log*, Aug. 1953. 1:no.12: 10, 30. See also article "Mr. and Mrs. Albert Brooks. . . ," p.36. 4081

Simonds, Walter Wesley. Natural regeneration on cut-over hardwood lands in the western Adirondacks. 63 leaves. mounted photographs, tables, graphs. Master's thesis, Cornell University, 1922. Typescript. Study made on the property of the Oval Wood Dish Corporation, Tupper Lake. 4082

Sisson, Stanley H. Use of tractors in winter log-hauling. *Emp St For Prod Assn Bul*, Dec. 1921. 12:26–29. Used by Raquette River Paper Company. 4083

Smith, Frank Berkeley. Facts from the north woods. *For & Stream*, Feb. 26, 1891. 36:104. Observations on lumbering after one-hundred-fifty-mile trip through the high peak area. 4084

Snell, Walter Henry. Blister rust in the Adirondacks. *J For*, Apr. 1928. 26:472–86. 4085

Snell, Walter Henry. Dasyscypha agassizii on Pinus strobus. *Mycologia*, Sept.–Oct. 1929. 21: 235–42. plate. Studies of damage caused by white pine blister in the Adirondacks. 4086

Snell, Walter Henry. Forest damage and the white pine blister rust. *J For*, Jan. 1931. 29: 68–78. charts. Observations in the Adirondacks. 4087

Snell, Walter Henry. The relation of cultivated red currants to the white pine blister rust in New York state. *J For*, Oct. 1941. 39: 859–67. Twenty-nine of the seventy-two cases studied were in the Adirondack area. 4088

Snell, Walter Henry. Some observations upon the white pine blister rust in New York. *Phytopathology*, Mar. 1929. 19:269–83. illus. table. 4089

Snell, Walter Henry. Two pine plantings near cultivated red currants in New York. *J For*, June 1941. 39:537–41. One near Lewis, Essex County, the other near Warrensburg. 4090

Society of American foresters. New York section. Sample plots committee. Suggested forest management requirements for the forests of New York state. *In* Empire state forest products association. Annual meeting, Syracuse, Nov. 9, 1922. Compiled by S.N. Spring. Reprinted from *New York Lumber Trade Journal*, Nov. 15, 1922, p.2. 4091

Spaulding, Perley. Notes upon tree diseases in the eastern states. *Mycologia*, May 1912. 4: 148–51. Includes discussion of some diseases in the Adirondacks. 4092

Spears, Raymond Smiley. Adirondack forest problems. *For & Stream*, July 25, 1908. 71: 137. Notes on lumbering. 4093

Spectator, pseud. In an Adirondack lumber camp. *Outlook*, Jan. 4, 1902. 70:18–19. 4094

Spiller, A.R. Forestry pays: a summer's work with the Forest service. *Emp For*, 1929. 15:47–48. illus. Elk Lake. 4095

Spring, Samuel Newton. The development of forestry in New York state. *Emp For*, 1934. 20:7–12. illus. 4096

Spring, Samuel Newton. How the forest comes back after cutting. *Emp St For Prod Assn Bul*, Dec. 1921. no.12:14–19. tables. Investigations made on slope of Mt. Morris near Tupper Lake. 4097

Spring, Samuel Newton. Seeing forestry work in the Adirondacks; story of an informal gathering of foresters to view Dr. Fernow's work. *Lumb World R*, Nov. 10, 1917. 33:47–48. illus. 4098

Spring, Samuel Newton. Studies in reproduction—the Adirondack hardwood type. *J For*, Oct. 1922. 20:571–80. tables. 4099

State foresters study blister rust. *Am For*, Dec. 1921. 27:782, 794. illus. Observations made at Lake George, Horicon, Chestertown, etc. 4100

Sterling, Ernest Albert. Adirondack forest musings. *Am For*, Oct. 1921. 27:620–23. illus. Lumbering. 4101

Sterling, Ernest Albert. Forest management on the Delaware and Hudson Adirondack forest. *J For*, May 1932. 30:569–74. 4102

Stickel, Paul W. and Marco, Herbert F. Relation between fire injury and fungal infection. *J For*, Apr. 1936. 34:420–23. Study made at Tahawus. 4103

Stickel, Paul W. Relation of forests to the evaporating power of the air. *NE Wat Works*, Sept. 1933. 47:229–38. illus. 4104

Stock, Jack. The woodsmen's field day. *Lumber Camp News*, Aug. 1950. 12:no.4:6. Other articles on the woodsmen's field day are in *Lumber Camp News*, Sept. 1949, 11: no.5:1, 6; Sept. 1950, 12:no.5:6; July 1949, 11:no.3:1–2; July 1950, 12:no.3:1, 12, 14; Sept. 1951, 13:no.5:1, 16. In the *Northeastern Logger*, July 1952, 1:no.1:8.   4105

Strong, David E. Determination of the growth of northern hardwoods on the Huntington forest. 128 leaves. mounted photographs, charts. Master's thesis, State University of New York, College of Forestry, Syracuse, 1950. Typescript. Abstract in Graduate Theses, p.38.   4106

Switzer, Harry D. A method of studying growth exemplified by Adirondack spruce and fir. *J For*, Dec. 1932. 30:1008–11. tables.   4107

Ten Eick, C.W. The hardwood brush disposal problem as seen in the Adirondacks— Summer 1920. *Emp St For Prod Assn Bul*, Nov. 1920. no.7:6–7. Extract from report of graduate student in forestry at Cornell University.   4108

Timber estimate for the Adirondacks. *News Pr Ser Bur*, Dec. 19, 1918. no.11:3.   4109

Trafton, George E. Plan of forest management for Whitney park. *NYS Ranger Sch*, 1949. p.23–26. illus.   4110

Tupper Lake as a lumbering center. *Lumber Camp News*, June 1948. 10:no.2:1, 6.   4111

Twombly, Gray M. An economic study of red spruce (Picea rubens Sarg.) in northern New York state. 94 leaves. tables, charts. Master's thesis, State University of New York, College of Forestry, Syracuse, 1954. Typescript. Abstract in Graduate Theses, p.73. Study made at Paul Smiths.   4112

United States bobbin & shuttle co. *Lumber Camp News*, Aug. 1950. 12:no.4:1. illus. Plant built at Tupper Lake in 1948.   4113

Vagnarelli, Adelaide Nora. A history of lumbering in the Ausable valley (1800–1900). A critical essay. 53 leaves. map. Master's thesis, Cornell University, 1944. Typescript.   4114

Vance, Lee J. Busy times in the Adirondacks. *Harper W*, Feb. 27, 1892. 36:214. Lumbering.   4115

Vance, Lee J. Lumbering in the Adirondacks. *Godey*, Mar. 1896. 132:229–34. plates, illus. Illustrations are from photographs by S.R. Stoddard. Condensed in *The Cloud Splitter*, Jan.–Feb. 1955, 18:no.1:4–7.   4116

Wallace, Richard J. An analysis of twenty-three years of air temperature observations on four forest sites in the western Adirondacks. 215 leaves. mounted photographs, charts, maps. Doctoral thesis, State University of New York, College of Forestry, Syracuse, 1953. Typescript. Abstract in Graduate Theses, p.74.   4117

Westveld, M. Experimental cutting area in the Adirondacks. *J For*, May 1933. 31:599.   4118

Westveld, M. Large scale experiment in methods of cutting. *Emp St For Prod Assn Bul*, Dec. 15, 1930. 35:7–8. Experiment on land of Finch, Pruyn and Company near Newcomb, by Northeastern Forest Experiment Station.   4119

Whipple, Gurth Adelbert. Twenty years of New York forestry; importance of protecting the lumber supply has grown rapidly in the public mind since 1900; reforestation hardly known until recent years. *State Service*, May–June 1922. 6,i.e.8:204–7.   4120

Whipple, James Spencer. Future of the forestry movement in New York state. *NYS For Assn Bul*, June 1914. 1:no.1:38–40.   4121

Wilm, H.G. Forests and water. *NYS Ranger Sch*, 1954. p.12–16. illus. Relation of forest cover to water yield, applied to the Adirondacks.   4122

Woodford, A.J. and Mason, C.E. Logging under the Webb covenant. *NYS Con*, Aug.–Sept. 1952. 7:no.1:6–7. illus. Nehasane Park.   4123

Working plans for the Adirondacks. *Forester*, Jan. 1901. 7:6. Editorial. Brief account of plans for Township 40, Hamilton County.   4124

Zimmerman, Jack. The natural restocking of Adirondack old fields. A study of abandoned land in parts of Hamilton and Essex counties. 99 leaves. illus. charts, maps. Master's thesis, State University of New York, College of Forestry, Syracuse, 1936. Typescript.   4125

MINING

Arranged by date
General

Magnus, Harry C. Abrasives of New York state. *In* New York (state). State geologist. Report 23, 1903, p.158–79. Includes discussion of the garnet and diatomaceous earths of the Adirondack area.   4126

Newland, David Hale. The mining and quarry industry of New York state. Report of operations and production, 1904–1936. Albany, 1905–38. 17v. (New York State Museum Bulletins 93, 102, 112, 120, 132, 142, 151, 161, 166, 174, 178, 190, 196, 277, 295, 305, 319.) Reports from 1904– by D.H. Newland and others. Consult index of each number for material on Adirondack mines and mining.   4127

Newland, David Hale. Mineral production of New York. *Eng & Min J*, May 16, 1908. 85:1007-8.   4128

Newland, David Hale. The mineral production of New York in 1908. *Eng & Min J*, June 26, 1909. 87:1273-74.   4129

Newland, David Hale. Mineral output in New York in 1909. *Eng & Min J*, May 28, 1910. 89:1110.   4130

McDonald, P.B. Mining in northern New York. *Eng & Min J*, Apr. 5, 1913. 95:689-92. illus. map.   4131

Clark, C.S. Exploring for Adirondack ores. *Iron Tr R*, Mar. 25, 1915. 56:617-19. illus. map. Description of work near Port Henry.   4132

Hooper, Frank C. Mineral resources of northern and central New York. *Up-Stater*, Mar. 1929. 1:no.2:12-13.   4133

Newland, David Hale. The early history of mining in northern and central New York. *Up-Stater*, May 1929. 1:no.3:9, 15, 18. illus.   4134

Linney, Joseph Robert. A century and a half of development behind the Adirondack iron mining industry. *Min & Met*, Nov. 1943. 24:480-87. port. illus. maps.   4135

Mining in the Adirondacks. *Geog R*, Oct. 1944. 34:663-64.   4136

Otte, Herman Frederick. The expanding mineral industry of the Adirondacks. Albany, New York state department of commerce, 1944. 50p. tables, maps. (New York State. Executive Department. Division of Commerce Publication no.10.) Reprinted Aug. 1944. Iron, titanium, zinc, lead, etc. Originally published in multilith form, 1943. 102p.   4137

Linney, Joseph Robert. Eastern magnetite, shipping product drops 10% owing to lack of experienced miners. *Min & Met*, Feb. 1946. 27:85. illus. Includes discussion of the Adirondack mines at Lyon Mountain, Tahawus, Clifton mines and Jones and Laughlin.   4138

Mining active in the Empire state. *Min & Met*, Oct. 1947. 28:518-19. illus.   4139

Linney, Joseph Robert. Eastern magnetite; review of 1947. *Min & Met*, Feb. 1948. 29:93-94. illus. Includes Adirondack companies.   4140

Adirondack mining. . .is diversified, important, accessible and has a promising outlook. *Eng & Min J*, Nov. 1950. 151:no.11:75-77. illus. Brief text with pictures.   4141

Le Visuer, K.G. Use of magnetic ores from New York state. *Blast Fur*, Feb. 1951. 39:200-2.   4142

New York state towns boom as J. & L. enlarges Benson mines. *Iron Age*, May 10, 1951. 167:119.   4143

Hartnagel, Chris Andrew and Broughton, John Gerard. The mining and quarry industries of New York state, 1937 to 1948. Albany, 1951. 130p. (New York State Museum Bulletin 343.)   4144

Prucha, John James. Mining and mineral resources in the Forest preserve counties. *In* New York (state). Legislature. Joint legislative committee on natural resources. Report, 1953. p.61-64.   4145

Prucha, John James. Mining and prospecting in New York. *NYS Con*, Feb.-Mar. 1955. 9:no.4:12-13. map. Followed by "Mining Laws of New York" by Percy Lieberman, p.13-15. See also letters in Apr.-May issue, 9:no.5:41.   4146

Iron

Cozzens, Issachar. Examination of iron ores from the northern part of the State of New-York. *Ly Nat Hist Annals*, Jan. 1825. 1:378-83. Ores from Moriah, Peru and Westport.   4147

Van Orden, Jacob. . . .In the court for trial of impeachments and the correction of errors. Catskill, N.Y. Printed at office of the "Messenger," 1831. 17p. Brief on behalf of Anthony R. Livingston, appellant, vs. The Peru Iron Company, and others, signed J. Van Orden . . .Abraham Van Vechten. Litigation over ownership of tract containing valuable iron ore.   4148

Emmons, Ebenezer. Papers and documents relative to the iron ore veins, water power and woodland &c. &c. in and around the village of McIntyre, in the town of Newcomb, Essex county, State of New York. . . N.Y. P. Miller, 1840. 54p. map. Copy in Columbia University Library. This report was made for the Adirondack Iron and Steel Company and published in the hope of attracting more capital.   4149

Emmons, Ebenezer. Report of Prof. E. Emmons in answer to a resolution of the Assembly, calling for information in relation to the steel ore at Duane. Albany, 1841. 4p. Assembly document 182, 1841.   4150

Greatest iron mines in the world. *Am Q J Agric & Sci*, July 1845. 2:129-30. Short discussion of mines at Newcomb.   4151

Hodge, James T. Adirondack steelworks. *Am Rail J*, May 19, 1849. 22:307-8.   4152

Hodge, James T. Iron ores and iron manufacture of the U.S. New York. *Am Rail J*,

Sept. 8–Oct. 13, 1849. 22:559–62, 575–77, 591–95, 607–9, 623–24, 639–40. Describes various operations in the Adirondacks.   4153

Adirondack iron and steel company, New York. . . N.Y. W.E. & J. Sibell, 1854. 47p. maps. Quotes Emmons' report "Magnetic Ores of Adirondack" in Natural History of New-York, Pt.4, p.244–63.   4154

Lesley, J.P. The iron manufacturer's guide to the furnaces, forges and rolling mills of the United States. . . N.Y. J. Wiley, 1859. 772p. charts. Another edition, 1866. Includes a list of the furnaces and the location of iron ore bodies in northern New York.   4155

Peru magnetic steel-iron works in Clinton and Essex counties, New York. Prospectus. N.Y. H. Spear, 1865. 14p. map. Copy in the New York Public Library.   4156

Adirondack iron company. Am Iron & Steel Assn Bul, Dec. 11, 1867. 2:107. Notice of the incorporation of the company.   4157

Adirondack iron ore co. The iron ores of Lake Champlain; or, The Adirondack region; their cheapness of production and superiority of the metal made of them, with remark in relation to the magnitude and value of the mines of the Adirondack iron ore co. N.Y. J.F. Trow & co. 1867. 11p. illus. diagrs.   4158

Frost, Orin C. Iron in northern New York. Am Iron & Steel Assn Bul, June 25, 1874. 8: 196. Extensive deposits in Jefferson, Lewis and St. Lawrence counties.   4159

Maynard, George William. The iron mines of Lake Champlain, United States of America. London, 1874. 28p. chart, tables.   4160

Chahoon, George. Iron making in northern New York—Catalan forges. Am Iron & Steel Assn Bul, Aug. 20, 1875. 9:251. Reprinted from New York Iron Age. Description of forges of J. & J. Rogers Iron Company and Peru Steel and Iron Company.   4161

Homes, Henry Augustus. Notice of Peter Hasenclever, an iron manufacturer of 1764–69. Albany. J. Munsell, 1875. 8p. Page 7 discusses his holdings on Lake Champlain.   4162

The Peru steel and iron company. Am Iron & Steel Assn Bul, Mar. 5, 1879. 13:52. Company in receivership.   4163

A consolidation in northern New York. Am Iron & Steel Assn Bul, Apr. 27, 1881. 15:109. Consolidation of Chateaugay Iron Company, the Chateaugay Ore Company and the private manufacturing interest of Hon. Andrew Williams.   4164

Chester, Albert H. The iron region of central New York. An address delivered before the Utica mercantile and manufacturing asso-ciation, Utica, N.Y. Utica, N.Y. Roberts, 1881. 20p. Includes sections on Lake Champlain ores, p.6–7, and ores of northern New York, p.9–11.   4165

Taws & Hartman. Notes on blast furnaces. Am Iron & Steel Assn Bul, Feb. 22, 1882. 16:61. Enlargement of furnaces, Crown Point Iron Company.   4166

Swank, James M. History of the manufacture of iron in all ages and particularly in the United States. . . Philadelphia, Author, 1884. 428p. 2d edition, Philadelphia, American iron and steel association, 1892, 554p. Includes list of early mines in northern New York.   4167

Putnam, Bayard T. Notes on the samples of iron ore collected in New York. In Pumpelly, Raphael. Report on the mining industries of the United States. . . Washington, 1886. p.89–144. (U.S. Tenth Census, v.15.) Washington, Essex, Clinton, Franklin and St. Lawrence counties, p.105–22.   4168

Smock, John Conover. A review of the iron-mining industry of New York for the past decade. Am Inst Mining Eng Tr, Feb. 1889. 17:745–50.   4169

Smock, John Conover. . . .First report on the iron mines and iron-ore districts in the State of New York. Albany, Van Benthuysen, 1889. 70p. folded map. (New York State Museum Bulletin 7.)   4170

Blake, William Phipps. Note on the magnetic separation of iron ore at the Sanford ore bed, Moriah, Essex county, N.Y. in 1852. Am Inst Mining Eng Tr, June 1892. 21:378–79.   4171

Rossi, Auguste J. Titaniferous ores in the blast-furnace. Am Inst Mining Eng Tr, Feb. 1893. 21:832–67. Adirondacks, p.834–45.   4172

Kemp, James Furman. A brief review of the titaniferous magnetites. Sch Min Q, July 1899. 20:323–56. Essex County, p.341–44.   4173

Granbery, J.H. The Northern iron company's blast furnace. Eng & Min J, July 21, 1906. 82:98–102. illus. diagrs.   4174

Newland, David Hale and Hansell, N.V. Magnetite mines at Lyon mountain, N.Y. The geology of an interesting district, nature of the ore, and methods of mining. Eng & Min J, Nov. 10–17, 1906. 82:863–65. illus. diagrs. Corrections, Nov. 24, 1906, 82:981.   4175

Witherbee, Frank Spencer. History of the iron industry of Essex county, New York, prepared for the Essex county republican, 1906. Port Henry, N.Y.? 1906. 39p. Copy in the Witherbee Collection, Sherman Free Library, Port Henry.   4176

Some forgotten iron ore history. *Am Iron & Steel Assn Bul*, Feb. 22, 1907. 41:20. Lake Champlain iron ores in 1872 used for fettling in puddling furnaces as far west as Pittsburgh. Answer by Jacob Reese correcting the date to 1856 (Mar. 9, 1907, 41:29).   4177

A great Adirondack iron ore deposit. *Iron Age*, Oct. 14, 1909. 84:1143, 1148–53. illus. table, map. History of the McIntyre deposit. Based on Henderson-McIntyre correspondence.   4178

Iron ore mining in eastern United States. *Eng & Min J*, Apr. 2, 1910. 89:704. Lake Champlain district.   4179

Bixby, George F. History of the iron ore industry of Lake Champlain... *NY State Hist Assn Proc*, 1910. 10:169–237.   4180

Birkinbine, John. The ABC of iron and steel; beneficiating iron ores. *Iron Tr R*, Feb. 2, 1911. 48:265–72. illus. Includes Mineville.   4181

Kellogg, L.O. Notes on Lake Champlain iron mines. *Eng & Min J*, Dec. 6, 1913. 96: 1065–67.   4182

Stark, C.J. Varied sources of ore for eastern furnaces. *Iron Tr R*, Feb. 12, 1914. 54:315–19, 345b. illus. Includes discussion of large ore dock to be built at Port Henry.   4183

St. Clair, Stuart. Titaniferous iron ore deposits. *Penn St Min Q*, June 1914. 1:112–18.   4184

Witherbee, Frank Spencer. The iron ores of the Adirondack region. *Am Iron & Steel Inst Yrbk*, 1916. 6:328–57. Discussion by Frank E. Bachman and John L.W. Birkinbine. Partially reprinted in *Iron Age*, Nov. 2, 1916, 98:1039–42; and in *Iron Trade Review*, Nov. 2, 1916, 59:891–94, illus.   4185

Spurr, Josiah Edward. Ore injection at Edwards, N.Y. *Eng & Min J*, Apr. 26, 1924. 117:684–89. illus. maps.   4186

Nichol, R.H. Mining Adirondack magnetite. *Eng & Min J*, July 20, 1929. 128:90–92. illus.   4187

Linney, Joseph Robert. A history of the Chateaugay ore and iron company. Albany? Press of the Delaware and Hudson railroad, c1934. 176p. illus. diagrs. Copy in the Witherbee Collection, Sherman Free Library, Port Henry.   4188

Barker, Elmer Eugene. The rise and decline of the iron industry in the eastern Adirondack region. *Ver Hist Soc Proc*, Dec. 1940. n.s.8:374–76. Abstract.   4189

Oliver, Frank Joseph. Titaniferous Adirondack ores being reworked. *Iron Age*, Mar. 5, 1942. 149:no.10:53–54. illus. map.   4190

Barker, Elmer Eugene. The story of Crown Point iron. Cooperstown, N.Y.? 1942. 20p. illus. Reprinted from *New York History*, Oct. 1942, 23:419–36.   4191

New York state's iron ores draw new attention. *Eng & Min J*, May 1943. 144:no.5:67–69. map.   4192

Lake Champlain district grew to important iron center century ago; rich ore deposits, some still producing led to the building of many eastern New York state iron-works. *Steel Facts*, Aug. 1943. no.61:6–7. Short history of mines at Port Henry and Tahawus.   4193

Gillies, Donald B. Economics of the current revival in Adirondack iron ore mining. *Min & Met*, Nov. 1943. 24:478–79. port.   4194

Hunner, Guy B. Development and operation of Clifton mines, Hanna ore company. *Min & Met*, Nov. 1943. 24:517–22. illus. port. diagrs.   4195

Parsons, Arthur Barrette. Mining iron ore in the Adirondacks. *Min & Met*, Nov. 1943. 24: 475–76. Editorial comment.   4196

Robie, Edward H. Jones & Laughlin's development at Benson mines. *Min & Met*, Nov. 1943. 24:523–25. port. illus.   4197

Iron ore mining and processing in New York. *Engineer*, Aug. 18–25, 1944. 178:122–23, 151–52. diagrs. map. Description of large-scale revival of iron mining and processing of iron ore in the Adirondack region.   4198

Oliver, Frank Joseph. Large scale working of Adirondack magnetites. *Iron Age*, Jan. 25–Feb. 1, 1945. 155:no.4:50–55; 155:no.5:52–56. illus. tables, map.   4199

Adirondack renaissance. *Steelways*, Aug. 1945. 1:no.2:28–31. Iron mining activity in the Adirondacks. Reprinted in *North Country Life*, Fall 1946, 1:no.1:28–36, illus.   4200

Anderson, Sven A. and Jones, Augustus. Iron in the Adirondacks. *Econ Geog*, Oct. 1945. 21: 276–85. illus. tables, maps.   4201

Linney, Joseph Robert. Eastern magnetite, 1945–48. *Min & Met*, Feb. 1945, Feb. 1946, Feb. 1947, Feb. 1948. 26:96–97; 27:85; 28:73; 29:93–94. illus. Includes discussion of the various mines in the Adirondacks.   4202

Barker, Elmer Eugene. Crown Point iron, a vanished Adirondack industry. *Cloud Splitter*, Jan.–Feb. 1947. 10:no.1:5–7.   4203

Hawkes, Herbert Edwin Jr. Magnetic exploration for Adirondack iron ore. *Wash Acad Sci J*, Oct. 15, 1947. 37:373–74. Abstract.   4204

Trost, Alfred H. Adirondacks mining; its past and its future. *Can Min J*, May 1948. 69:no.5: 75–80. illus. Short history of iron mining.   4205

J & L pushes development of New York iron ore mines. *Steel*, Aug. 2, 1948. 123:66–67. illus.   4206

Steel industry has new interest in Adirondack iron. *Bsns W*, Aug. 21, 1948. no.990:25. illus.   4207

Adirondack iron ore for Jones & Laughlin; illustrations with text. *Eng & Min J*, Sept· 1948. 149:88–89.   4208

Jones & Laughlin increasing ore output from Benson mines. *Blast Fur*, Sept. 1948. 36:1099–1100. illus.   4209

Peterson, Ronald B. The saga of New York iron; ore resources of Empire state basis of active mining industry during past two hundred years. *NYS Lab Ind Bul*, Feb. 1950. 29: no.2:29–32. illus.   4210

World's largest open-pit magnetite iron ore mine. *NYS Lab Ind Bul*, Feb. 1950. 29:no.2:28. illus. Jones & Laughlin, Star Lake.   4211

Gillies, Donald B. Adirondack iron ore field still offers many challenges. *Eng & Min J*, June 1950. 151:no.6:84–87.   4212

Neu, Irene D. Iron-ore mining in the New York Adirondacks. *Exp Ent Hist*, Oct. 15, 1950. 3:no.1:35–43.   4213

Castaño, John R. and Garrels, Robert Minard. Experiments on the deposition of iron with special reference to the Clinton iron ore deposits. *Econ Geol*, Dec. 1950. 45:755–70. illus.   4214

Iron-ore production expands. *Eng News R*, Feb. 28, 1952. 148:no.9:34–36. illus. plan, diagr. map. Benson mines.   4215

Webb, W.R. and Peterson, M.O. Maintenance and training pay safety dividends for Benson mines. *Min Eng*, Aug. 1952. 4:768–69. illus.   4216

Sanford, Robert S. Truck haulage at an iron mine in the Adirondack mountains, New York. Washington, 1952. 7p. plates, tables. (U.S. Bureau of Mines Information Circular 7629.) Reproduced from typescript.   4217

Ni-hard used in iron ore beneficiation; New York state operations make good use of Plattsburg foundry's abrasion-resistant castings. *Nickel Topics*, 1953. 6:no.3:1, 6–7. illus.   4218

Garnet

Hooper, Frank C. Garnet as an abrasive material. *Sch Min Q*, Jan. 1894. 16:124–27. illus. Adirondack deposits and machines for processing.   4219

Hooper, Frank C. The American garnet industry. *Min Ind*, 1897. 6:20–22. The Adirondack mines of New York, p.20–21.   4220

Garnet mines in the Adirondacks. *Eng & Min J*, Oct. 14, 1899. 68:461. illus. Descrip-

tion taken from Colvin's Report of the State Land Survey. Gore Mountain deposit.   4221

Newland, David Hale. Garnet in New York in 1905. *Eng & Min J*, Jan. 6, 1906. 81:70.   4222

Newland, David Hale. Garnet in New York. *Eng & Min J*, Jan. 4, 1908. 85:92. Reviews the garnet output of the Adirondack mines for the preceding decade.   4223

Newland, David Hale. Garnet in New York. *Eng & Min J*, Jan. 9, 1909. 87:81.   4224

Miller, William John. The garnet deposits of Warren county, New York. *Econ Geol*, Aug. 1912. 7:493–501. diagr. map. Also in New York State Museum Bulletin 164, p.95–102. Describes mines of the northeast corner of Warren County.   4225

New York garnets. *Eng & Min J*, Nov. 29, 1913. 96:1016–17.   4226

Skerrett, Robert G. The world's greatest garnet quarry, mining a high-grade abrasive with which to smooth and to polish manufactured products. *Comp Air M*, Aug. 1923. 28:581–85. illus. North River Garnet Company.   4227

Wormser, Felix Edgar. Mining, concentrating, and marketing garnet. *Eng & Min J*, Oct. 4, 1924. 118:525–31. illus.   4228

Mennie, T.S. Modern garnet mills operated, immense deposit of garnet ore is worked in Warren county, N.Y.; description of methods used in crushing and grading. *Ab Ind*, Feb. 1925. 6:51–54. Barton Company.   4229

Myers, W.M. and Anderson, C.O. Developments in production and use of abrasive garnet. *Cement Mill*, July 5, 1925. 27:36, 38, 40.   4230

Myers, W.M. and Anderson, C.O. Garnet, its mining, milling and utilization. Washington, G.P.O. 1925. 54p. plates, diagrs. tables. (U.S. Bureau of Mines Bulletin 256.) Includes the Adirondack deposits and mining companies.   4231

Myers, W.M. and Anderson, C.O. Abrasive garnet production. *Ab Ind*, Mar.–May 1926. 7:87–89, 112–13, 153–54. The April issue is almost completely on Warren County garnet mines.   4232

Lisle, T. Orchard. Red garnets by the ton, a remarkable quarry near Lake George, N.Y. *Rocks & Min*, Oct. 1945. 20:471.   4233

Shaub, Benjamin Martin. Paragenesis of the garnet and associated minerals of the Barton mine near North Creek, New York. *Am Min*, July–Aug. 1949. 34:573–82. illus. Abstracts in *American Mineralogist*, Mar.–Apr. 1948, 33: 208, and in *Geological Society of America Bulletin*, Dec. 1947, 58:1226–27.   4234

Gore mountain garnet. *Pittsburgh People*, Dec. 1952. 13:no.12:3–7. plates. Picture story of Barton mines. 4235

From hornblende to garnets. . . *Chem & Eng News*, Apr. 25, 1955. 33:1778. illus. Studies made by Robert H. Wentorf Jr. 4236

Other Minerals

Blake, William Phipps. Contribution to the early history of the industry of phosphate of lime in the United States. *Am Inst Mining Eng Tr*, Feb. 1892. 21:157–59. Early attempts to utilize the apatite of the Sanford vein. 4237

Reynolds, Cuyler. Finding gold in New York state. *Sci Am*, Mar. 1898. 78:202. Hadley, N.Y. 4238

Nevius, J. Nelson. The Hadley, N.Y. gold mill and its history. *Eng & Min J*, Sept. 3, 1898. 66:275–76. Reviews the history of Adirondack mining and prospecting for gold from 1889. 4239

Courtis, William Munroe. Adirondack sea-sand gold. *Eng & Min J*, Sept. 24, 1898. 66:363–64. Letter on the Adirondack gold swindle. 4240

New York gold. *Min Coll*, Oct. 1898. 5:128. Note about operations at Hadley, N.Y. 4241

Nevius, J. Nelson. The Sacandaga mining and milling co. and the Sutphen process. *In* New York (state). Museum. 52d annual report, 1898. 1:r82–87. plates. At Hadley, N.Y. 4242

Adirondack gold deposits, N.Y. *Eng & Min J*, Aug. 26, 1899. 68:241. Editorial branding as a fake Boston enterprises claiming to have rich gold-bearing sands in the Adirondacks. 4243

Adirondack gold mines. *Eng & Min J*, May 19, 1900. 69:582. Editorial disclosing several "Adirondack schemes" that "have no basis whatever to stand on." 4244

Indian river gold mining co. Prospectus. Boston, 1900? 8p. Copy in the Engineering Societies Library, New York City. 4245

Mount Tom gold mining co. Prospectus. Boston, 1900. 13p. Copy in the Engineering Societies Library, New York City. Property located near Belford on the Beaver River in Lewis County. 4246

New York gold mines co. Story of gold in the Adirondacks. Philadelphia, 1904. 8p. Copy in the Engineering Societies Library, New York City. 4247

Newland, David Hale. Graphite in New York. *Eng & Min J*, Aug. 2, 1905. 80:241. Workings of Joseph Dixon Crucible Company at Chilson Hill near Ticonderoga and in town of Hague, west of Lake George. 4248

Newland, David Hale. The New York graphite industry in 1905. *Eng & Min J*, Jan. 13, 1906. 81:88. Discusses graphite occurrences in Adirondacks. 4249

Newland, David Hale. Graphite mining in the U.S.—New York. *Min Ind*, 1906. 15:432–34. Production during 1906. 4250

Newland, David Hale. Graphite in New York. *Eng & Min J*, Jan. 4, 1908. 85:36. 4251

Ihne, F.W. Graphite mining. . .New York. *Min Ind*, 1908. 17:493–94. 4252

Newland, David Hale. The Adirondack graphite industry. *Eng & Min J*, Jan. 9, 1909. 87:99. 4253

Gold in the Adirondacks. *Eng & Min J*, Mar. 19, 1910. 89:620–21. Opinions of experts and reports of assayists concerning chances for successful mining of gold in the Adirondacks. 4254

Chance, Henry Martyn. Gold in the Adirondacks. *Eng & Min J*, Apr. 2, 1910. 89:695. Account of tests made on some ore from a St. Lawrence County mine (mercury was loaded when test was made). 4255

Roberts, John T. Jr. Gold in the Adirondacks. *Eng & Min J*, May 14, 1910. 89:1002. Tests made in 1909. 4256

Carpenter, Warwick Stevens. Lure of the Adirondack gold. *Outing*, Feb. 1911. 57:522–32. illus. 4257

Newland, David Hale. Adirondack gold schemes. *Eng & Min J*, Feb. 24, 1912. 93:392. Shows extent of "boom." 4258

The Adirondack gold swindle. *Eng & Min J*, Mar. 2, 1912. 93:437–38. Editorial reviewing various schemes. 4259

Adirondack gold again. *Eng & Min J*, Nov. 21, 1914. 98:928. Editorial telling of another Adirondack gold swindle. 4260

Jones, Robert W. Graphite industry in New York. *Eng & Min J*, Oct. 28, 1916. 102:773–75. illus. 4261

Newland, David Hale. Graphite mining in New York. *Eng & Min J*, Jan. 19, 1918. 105:151. 4262

Taylor, A.S. Feldspar; a mineral having many uses. *Comp Air M*, Sept. 1924. 29:985–88. illus. Description and activities of the Crown Point Spar Company. 4263

Sturla, George Alan. Some Adirondack gold tales of the "brick" variety, and otherwise. *Pine Log*, Mar. 1925. 2:no.2:8–10, 25–27. 4264

Newland, David Hale. The prospects for gold discoveries in New York state. Albany, N.Y. University of the State of New York, 1933. 6p. (New York State Museum Circular 12.)

Gold occurs in some sands at 0.00503/ton equivalent to a trace. Prospects for richer finds slight. Geology of Adirondacks and Canada discussed.   4265

Broughton, John Gerard and Burnham, Koert D. Occurrence and uses of wollastonite from Willsboro, N.Y. N.Y. 1944. 8p. illus. map. (American Institute of Mining and Metallurgical Engineers Technical Publication 1737.) Abstract in *Economic Geology*, Jan.–Feb. 1944, 39:86.   4266

Porter, Mrs. Marjorie (Lansing). Treasure on Willsboro mountain; wollastonite, a mineral recently found to be useful, is being mined in Essex county. *No Country Life*, Spring 1951. 5:no.2:46–47.   4267

Shaub, Benjamin Martin. Moonstone from Olmstedville, New York. *Rocks & Min*, Sept.–Oct. 1953. 28:451–55. illus.   4268

Wollastonite goes modern. *The Flame*, Dec. 1953. 7:no.1:4–9. illus.   4269

Special Locations
MacIntyre Development

Extensive experiments with titaniferous ores will be conducted by McIntyre iron co. *Iron Tr R*, Oct. 30, 1913. 53:797–81.   4270

Kellogg, L.O. Experiment in smelting titaniferous magnetite. *Eng & Min J*, Sept. 27, 1913. 96:604. MacIntyre Iron Company leased furnace at Port Henry for experiments.
4271

Bachman, Frank E. The use of titaniferous ore in the blast furnace. *Am Iron & Steel Inst Yrbk*, 1914. 4:371–419. plates, chart, tables. Test of titaniferous ore in the blast furnace of the Northern Iron Company carried out by the MacIntyre Company.   4272

Cone, Edwin F. Titaniferous ores in the blast furnace; important results of Port Henry experiments. *Iron Age*, Oct. 22, 1914. 94:936–39. illus.   4273

Titaniferous ores in the blast furnace. General conclusions from the Port Henry experiments on Adirondack ores. *Iron Age*, Dec. 24, 1914. 94:1470–73. tables.   4274

Woodbridge, Dwight Edwards. Titaniferous ores in the blast furnace—a recent experiment. *Lake Sup Min Inst Proc*, 1914. p.223–28. Account of experiments carried on at Port Henry.   4275

Hagar, I.D. Titanium and the MacIntyre development. *Paint Ind*, Dec. 1941. 56:410–18. Issued as reprint. Also in *Paint, Oil and Chemical Review*, Dec. 18, 1941, 103:no.26:18, 24–32, port.   4276

MacIntyre development; historic mine reopened. *Min & Con R*, July 15, 1942. 44:

no.13:7, 17. illus. Includes history of mine.
4277

Hagar, I.D. Ilmenite and magnetite produced in quantity at National lead's new MacIntyre development. *Min & Met*, Dec. 1942. 23:594–96. illus. Condensed from paper read before American Institute of Mining Engineers, Oct. 24, 1942.   4278

Hagar, I.D. MacIntyre development—a new source of titanium. *Eng & Min J*, Dec. 1942. 143:no.12:47–49. illus.   4279

Killinger, Paul E. Report on the titanium mine at Tahawus, N.Y. *Rocks & Min*, Dec. 1942. 17:409.   4280

A source of titanium. *Fortune*, Mar. 1943. 27:no.3:46, 50. MacIntyre mine.   4281

Vivian, C.H. Century-old iron workings now yield titanium. *Comp Air M*, Aug. 1943. 48:7100–5. illus.   4282

Herres, Otto and others. MacIntyre development of the National lead company at Tahawus, N.Y. *Min & Met*, Nov. 1943. 24:509–16. port. illus. diagr.   4283

Simmons, Louis J. Tahawus; the symbol of a new era. *No Country Life*, Spring 1947. 1:no.3:19–20. MacIntyre mines.   4284

Adirondack mine yields white pigment. *Lumber Camp News*, Apr. 1948. 9:no.12:3.
4285

Begor, C.R. and Quam, C.A. Drilling and blasting at Tahawus. *Min Cong J*, Aug. 1948. 34:no.8:24–27. illus.   4286

Milliken, Frank R. Metallurgy at National lead co. MacIntyre development. N.Y. 1948. 14p. illus. tables. (American Institute of Mining and Metallurgical Engineers Technical Publication 2355.)   4287

Sanford, R.S. Truck haulage at the National lead company open-cut ilmenite-magnetite mine, Tahawus, N.Y. Washington, U.S. Bureau of mines, 1950. 14p. plates. (U.S. Bureau of Mines Information Circular 7584.)
4288

Tahawus cloudsplitter, Nov. 1951. "Reprint MacIntyre anniversary issue." Tahawus, N.Y. n.d. 9p. ports. illus.   4289

Mining MacIntyre ore. *Tahawus Cloudsplitter*, Apr. 1955. 6:no.4:4–5, 7. illus.   4290

National lead company. MacIntyre development, Titanium division, National lead company, Tahawus, New York. n.p. n.d. 8 leaves. charts. Mimeographed. History and development of mines at Tahawus.   4291

Mineville and Port Henry

Port Henry iron ore company. *Am Iron & Steel Assn Bul*, Feb. 14, 1872. 6:186–87. Description of mine.   4292

Witherbee, T.F. Blowing in the Cedar Point iron company's furnace at Port Henry, Essex county, N.Y. *Am Iron & Steel Assn Bul*, June 7, 1876. 10:163. Abstract of paper read before American Institute of Mining Engineers, Feb. 1876. 4293

The iron mines of Mineville, N.Y. preparing for a great blast. *Leslies Illus*, Apr. 28, 1877. 43:140. illus. 4294

Hoefer von Heimhalt, Hans. Die kohlen- und eisenerz-lagerstatten Nord-Amerikas. Wien, Faesy & Frick, 1878. 259p. double table, diagrs. folded map. Visit to Mineville, N.Y. p.173–79. 4295

Vacation notes from northern New York. On Port Henry. *Eng & Min J*, Aug. 31, 1889. 48:184. Iron industry of region. 4296

Lake Champlain iron region. *US Assn Char Work J*, 1889. 8:no.4:218–27. Port Henry mines. 4297

Birkinbine, John. Crystalline magnetite in the Port Henry, New York mines. *Am Inst Mining Eng Tr*, Feb. 1890. 18:747–62. map. Describes the Lover's Pit at Mineville, with statistics of production, analyses, etc. 4298

Langdon, N.M. The use of magnetic con- centrates in the Port Henry blast-furnaces. *Am Inst Mining Eng Tr*, Oct. 2, 1891. 20:599– 601. Also in *Engineering News*, Oct. 17, 1891, 26:351–52. 4299

Ries, Heinrich. Magnetite deposits at Mine- ville, N.Y. and a description of the new elec- tric concentrating plant. *Mines & Min*, Sept. 1903. 24:49–51. illus. 4300

The Mineville magnetite mines; recent im- provements of the mining and separating plant of Witherbee, Sherman & co. Port Henry, N.Y. *Iron Age*, Dec. 17, 1903. 72:no. 25:10–19. illus. 4301

Granbery, J.H. Magnetite deposits and min- ing at Port Henry, N.Y. *Eng & Min J*, May 12–June 23, 1906. 81:890–93, 986–89, 1035– 38, 1082–84, 1130–32, 1178–79. illus. tables, maps. Reprinted with revisions under title "The Port Henry Iron Mines," N.Y. 1906. 4302

Hodgkins, A.E. Mine accounting at Mine- ville, N.Y. *Eng & Min J*, Sept. 22, 1906. 82: 530–33. illus. 4303

Electrical equipment for Port Henry iron mines. *Eng & Min J*, Mar. 30, 1907. 83:610. 4304

Stephenson, B.S. Magnetite ore deposits at Mineville: recent improvements in mining and concentrating methods in the Port Henry district. *Iron Tr R*, Aug. 26–Sept. 2, 1909. 45: 371–77, 416–20. illus. Part 1. General de- scription of workings—heavy deposits. Part

2. Variety of ores shipped from workings, power furnished by five plants—testing lab- oratory. 4305

A day among the iron ore operations of the Port Henry district. Large delegations of iron and steel manufacturers inspect upper New York state mines. *Iron Tr R*, Aug. 4, 1910. 47:241–44. illus. 4306

The Eastern pig iron association at Port Henry; a visit to Witherbee, Sherman & company's properties in the eastern Adiron- dack district—important new mining and concentrating operations. *Iron Age*, Aug. 4, 1910. 86:266–70. diagr. 4307

Stoltz, Guy C. The Cheever mines, Port Henry, N.Y. *Eng & Min J*, Oct. 21, 1911. 92:809–12. illus. Mines worked before the Revolution now being modernized. 4308

Kellogg, L.O. Magnetite mines near Port Henry, N.Y. *Eng & Min J*, Nov. 8, 1913. 96:863–68. illus. 4309

Improvements at Port Henry iron mines. *Iron Age*, June 24, 1915. 95:1390–92. diagrs. 4310

Blatchly, Charles A. Iron mines at Port Henry, N.Y. *Eng & Min J*, Mar. 20, 1920. 109:702–4. illus. 4311

Henry, Earl C. Mining methods in the Mine- ville (N.Y.) district. *Am Inst Mining Eng Tr*, Sept. 1922. 72:226–32. diagrs. Abstract in *Mining and Metallurgy*, Nov. 1922, 3:no.191: 57–58. 4312

Cummings, A.M. Method and cost of min- ing magnetite in the Mineville district, New York. Washington, U.S. Bureau of mines, 1928. 12p. figs. (U.S. Bureau of Mines In- formation Circular 6092.) Mimeographed. 4313

Cummings, A.M. Mining magnetite in the New York Mineville district. *Eng & Min J*, Feb. 2–9, 1929. 127:190–95, 234–37. diagrs. 4314

Myners, T.F. Magnetic concentration meth- ods and costs of Witherbee, Sherman and company, Mineville, N.Y. Washington, 1932. 27p. (U.S. Bureau of Mines Information Cir- cular 6624.) 4315

Roche, H.M. Eastern magnetite in 1938. *Min & Met*, Jan. 1939. 20:7–8. Mineville, N.Y. 4316

Republic Steel Corporation

Revives interest in eastern mine. *Steel*, Aug. 7, 1939. 104:31. Republic Steel lease. 4317

Adirondack iron. *Du Pont M*, May 1940. 34: no.5:10–11, 24. illus. Republic Steel's devel- opment. 4318

Linney, Robert J. Republic Steel's operations at Port Henry, Mineville and Fisher Hill.

Min & Met, Nov. 1943. 24:488–502. port. illus. diagr.   4319

Linney, William J. Operations of the Chateaugay division of Republic Steel at Lyon mountain. *Min & Met*, Nov. 1943. 24:503–8. port. illus.   4320

Stiefel, Fred W. Inclined mine shaft sunk in the Adirondacks, large iron ore deposits opened up in New York state. *Civ Eng*, Apr. 1944. 14:137–39. illus. diagrs. Republic Steel's Fisher Hill mine near Port Henry.   4321

Vivian, C.H. Old Adirondack mine again producing iron. *Comp Air M*, Oct. 1944. 49:254–59. illus. Republic Steel at Fisher Hill mine near Port Henry.   4322

Paine, R.S. Reclaiming pillars of iron ore. Republic Steel corporation at its Port Henry, N.Y. operations successfully reclaims over ½ million tons of high grade iron ore from pillars left on the "21"–Bonanza-Joker mine. *Exp Eng*, Nov.–Dec. 1944. 22:249–52, 278. illus. diagrs.   4323

How Republic concentrates Adirondack iron ores. *Eng & Min J*, July 1945. 146:no.7:90–93. port. illus. diagrs. History of Adirondack iron mining operations of Republic Steel.   4324

Campbell, Tom. The Adirondacks, Republic's ace in the hole. *Iron Age*, Aug. 19, 1948. 162:119–22. illus.   4325

Ore for tomorrow. *Time*, Aug. 23, 1948. 52:no.6:66. illus.   4326

Gillies, Donald B. Adirondack iron ore mining, its economic and potential value to the steel industry. *Steel*, Aug. 30, 1948. 123:72–77. illus.   4327

Republic Steel is developing a new iron mine in northern N.Y. and exploring near Antwerp. *Eng & Min J*, Sept. 1948. 149:no.9:103. illus. Lyon Mountain—extension of Chateaugay bed.   4328

Republic Steel's old "81." *No Country Life*, Fall 1948. 2:no.4:43–45. illus. Lyon Mountain.   4329

Adirondack awakening. *Republic Repts*, Fall 1948. 10:no.4:4–5, 20–21. illus.   4330

AGRICULTURE

Bender, Ray. Essex county farm bureau organized in 1916. *Top o' the World*, Mar. 1939. 3:no.2:9, 13. illus.   4331

Champlain valley horticultural society. Proceedings of the horticultural convention, held at Burlington, Vt. February 11, 1851 and organization of the Champlain valley horticultural society, with an appendix containing a list of fruits reported by the Standing fruit committee. Keeseville, N.Y. Republican office, 1851. 72p.   4332

Clinton county agricultural society. Proceedings. . .at its annual meeting, held at Plattsburgh, December 26th, 1850, and list of premiums for 1851. Keeseville, N.Y. D. Turner, printer, 1851. 32p. Copy in the Henry E. Huntington Library, San Marino, Cal.   4333

Dean, Amos. Address before the Agricultural society of Essex county, September 18, 1851. Elizabethtown, N.Y. Livingston & Sergeant, 1851. 12p. Cover title. Discusses soil of the county.   4334

Eggleston, R.W. History of the Grange in Essex county, N.Y. Plattsburgh, N.Y. Clinton press, n.d. 24p. illus. Copy at the Headquarters House, New York State Historical Association, Ticonderoga.   4335

Emmons, Ebenezer. Agriculture of New York; comprising an account of the classification, composition and distribution of soils and rocks. . .together with a condensed view of the climate and agricultural productions of the state. Albany, 1846–54. 5v. front. illus. partly col. maps (1 folded). (Natural History of New York pt.5.)   4336

Fippin, Elmer Otterbein. The soils and agricultural development of northern New York. *Cornell Count*, Apr. 1916. 13:570–75.   4337

Fogg, S.H. "Sap's up." *Top o' the World*, Mar. 1939. 3:no.2:9. Maple sugar.   4338

New York (state). Assessors. Report on the agricultural and other resources of New York. *In* New York State Agricultural Society. Transactions, 1864. 23:234–379. folded maps. Also issued as a separate, Albany; Van Benthuysen, 1864, 152p. Report by State Assessor, Theodore C. Peters.   4339

Smith, Clarence C. Agriculture in up-state New York. *Up-Stater*, Jan. 1930. 2:no.1:9, 17. table.   4340

Titus, James H. Address before the Agricultural society of Franklin county, N.Y. delivered at the annual meeting, October 6th, 1853. . . N.Y. William C. Bryant & co. 1853. 38p. Agricultural progress in county.   4341

Van Wagner, Edith, comp. . . .Agricultural manual of New York state arranged by counties. . . Albany, 1922. 857p. incl. front. plates, diagrs. maps (partly folded). (New York State Department of Farms and Markets. Division of Agriculture Bulletin 133.)   4342

Watson, Winslow Cossoul. An address delivered before the Essex county agricultural society, September 21, 1854. Published by request of the Society. Elizabethtown, N.Y. Post print, n.d. 16p. Agriculture in Essex County.   4343

Watson, Winslow Cossoul. A general view and agricultural survey of the county of Essex. Taken under the appointment of the New York State Agricultural Society. Extracted from the New York State Agricultural Society Transactions for 1852. Albany, Van Benthuysen, 1853. p.649–898.   4344

Watson, Winslow Cossoul. Supplement to the report on the survey of Essex county. Extracted from the New York State Agricultural Society Transactions for 1853. Albany, Van Benthuysen, 1854. p.699–741.
4345

RESORTS AND HOTELS

Adirondack cottage sites. *For & Stream*, Feb. 17, 1906. 66:266.   4346

Adirondack summer business. *For & Stream*, Mar. 7, 1903. 60:183. Extract from Report of the New York State Forest Superintendent, 1902–3. Hotels etc.   4347

The Adirondacks. *For & Stream*, Mar. 7, 1903. 60:181. Brief editorial on importance of vast summer and autumn tourist business.
4348

Aesthetic and sanitary vs. commercial values. *Outlook*, June 23, 1906. 83:401. Editorial showing the Adirondacks cannot be a storage reservoir and great summer resort at the same time.   4349

Bahler, Martin. Flume cottage, an Adirondack mountain resort in Keene Valley, Essex county, N.Y. Keene Valley, N.Y.? n.d. 4p. Unpaged leaflet, caption title. Copy in Yale University Library.   4350

Bergstrom, Herman. Board and room, $2.00 a day. *Cloud Splitter*, Sept.–Oct. 1948. 11:no. 5:10–11. 1899 prospectus of an Adirondack hotel.   4351

Bruce, Dwight Hall. The Adirondacks. *For & Stream*, Sept. 8, 1892. 39:202. Signed: D.H.B. Tourist season of 1892.   4352

C., F.S. Some Adirondack resorts. *For & Stream*, July 19, 1883. 20:487. Franklin County.   4353

Calhoun, William. The tourist went that-a-way. *No Country Life*, Winter 1953. 7:no.1: 38–39, 46.   4354

Cranford, T.L. Adirondack extortion. *For & Stream*, Oct. 6, 1887. 29:209. Complaint about Paul Smith.   4355

Delaware & Hudson railroad corporation. The D. & H. season of 1895. Summer hotel and boarding house register. Albany? 1895?

119p. illus. map. Cover title: Mountain, Lake and Meadow.   4356

Flemming, Richard Carl. The Ruisseaumont at Lake Placid. *Gameland*, Jan. 1896. 8:232. illus.   4357

Frazer, Orange. Adirondack extortion. *For & Stream*, Sept. 29, 1887. 29:182. Claimed Paul Smith overcharged him for provisions.
4358

Hagerty, Gilbert. Dreams and dollars. *No Country Life*, Summer 1955. 9:no.3:56–65. illus. Liberty Eatery, a Whitehall restaurant.
4359

A half-way house. *For & Stream*, Aug. 24, 1882. 19:64. Moody's at Tupper Lake.   4360

History of Paul Smith's resort; developments closely woven in life story of honored founder. *For Leaves*, Winter 1926. 20:no.2:18–29. port. From the *Adirondack Enterprise*.   4361

The Hotel Alcadel in the Adirondacks, Hurricane, Essex co. New York. N.Y. 192—? 4p. illus. map. Unpaged leaflet. On East Hill, Keene. Also includes advertisement of Hurricane Mountain Inn.   4362

Hotel Ampersand. The Adirondacks as a winter health resort including a description of the new Hotel Ampersand. . . N.Y. Giles Litho. n.d. 48p. illus. folded map. Copy in Munson Collection, Saranac Lake Free Library.   4363

The Hotel Champlain and its surroundings. n.p. 1890. 7 leaves.   4364

Kelleher, Goodman. Goodman Kelleher, Boniface. . . A cook's story of his own broth. Lake George, N.Y. Adirondack resort press, 1945. 133p. plates, ports. Life of chef and hotelkeeper, Lake Placid and Saranac Lake.
4365

Lake George and Fort William Henry hotel. A descriptive and historical sketch. Philadelphia, Ketterlinus printing house, 1892. 40p. illus.   4366

Lake view house, the only first class hotel at Ausable chasm. N.Y. Terwilliger & Peck, 1880? 3 leaves.   4367

Leonard, S.R. Sr. The Mattesons and their Mountain home. *No Country Life*, Spring 1951. 5:no.2:29–36. ports. illus. Famous hotel at Morehouseville.   4368

Merrill, Fannie B. Life at Paul Smith's. *For & Stream*, June 18, 1891. 36:433–34.   4369

Mills, Borden H. Sr. Adirondack hostelries of the 19th century. II. The Willey house. *Ad-i-ron-dac*, Sept.–Oct. 1950. 14:100–1. illus. On East Hill, Keene.   4370

Mills, Borden H. Sr. Adirondack hostelries of the 19th century. III. The Adirondack house at Keene Valley. *Ad-i-ron-dac*, Jan.–Feb. 1951. 15:4–5, 7. illus. Correction in Mar.–Apr. issue, 15:38.   4371

Mills, Borden H. Sr. Raquette lake house (1856–73). *Ad-i-ron-dac*, Jan.–Feb., Mar.–Apr. 1949. 13:12–14, 34–35.   4372

Murray, William Henry Harrison. The Adirondacks then and now. *Golden Rule*, Aug. 22, 1877. 2:no.48:4. Hotel menu.   4373

The new Columbian park hotel. The sportsman's paradise. Under new management. Located on Cranberry lake, Carthage, N.Y. Brownell, 1905. 6p. illus. Oblong leaflet. 4374

The 1931 outlook hailed with optimism by Adirondack resorts association; two-day conference. . .brings most optimistic forecast for travel this year. *Motordom*, Feb. 1931. 24:no. 8:21.   4375

R., C.H. Adirondack game resorts. *For & Stream*, Sept. 7, 1882. 19:106. Various places to stay.   4376

Rice, Philip E. The vacation hotel, modern inns of the Adirondacks offer complete services for comfort and recreation in a world of famous pleasure ground. *Motordom*, June 1931. 24:no.12:23. illus. port.   4377

The Sagamore, Lake George. Season 1880. Lake George, N.Y. 1880? 32p. illus. Also Season of 1894, issued by Possons, Glens Falls, N.Y. unpaged.   4378

Saranac Lake Guide, pseud. The Saranac lake region. The fable of the frogs. *For & Stream*, June 30, 1881. 16:427. Competition among the hotelkeepers for the sportsman's trade.   4379

Some famous Adirondack hostelries. *Woods & Wat*, Spring 1902. 5:no.1:18.   4380

Stoddard, Seneca Ray. Summer inns of Lake George and Lake Champlain. *St No Mo*, Aug. 1908. 4:99–121. illus.   4381

Stringham, Henry. Stopping over at Mountain view, in the Adirondacks. *NYC Lines Mag*, Nov. 1926. 7:no.8:94.   4382

Tahawus house, in the Adirondacks, Keene Valley. Troy, N.Y. Troy times art press, n.d. illus. Unpaged leaflet.   4383

The Traveler, pseud. Among the summer hotels. *Ang & Hunt*, June 1910. 2:308–10. illus. Includes Nunn's Inn, Cranberry Lake, and The New Heritage, Lake Bonaparte.
                                          4384

Whiteface inn, Lake Placid, N.Y. Adirondacks. Season June 15th to October 1st. n.p. Adirondack co. 1907? 12 leaves. illus. 4385

Wilson, Sloan. Lollapalooza and the Rogers Rock hotel. *New Yorker*, Oct. 10, 1953. 29: no.34:98, 100, 103–7.   4386

COMMUNICATIONS, TRANSPORTATION AND PUBLIC WORKS

Adirondack power and light corporation. Corporate history. Schenectady, N.Y. 1924. 279p. Title page dated July 1, 1924.   4387

Benedict, Farrand Northrop. Report on a survey of the waters of the upper Hudson and Raquette rivers, in the summer of 1874, with reference to increasing the supply of water for the Champlain canal and improving the navigation of the Hudson river, as authorized by the Legislature April, 1874. *In* New York (state). Canal commissioners. Annual report, 1873–74. p.83–160. plate, maps. Assembly document 6, 1875. Includes reports of W.B. Cooper, F.F. Judd and J.F. Potter.   4388

Blakemore analytical reports, inc. Summary of report on the Adirondack power and light corporation. N.Y. 1927. 120 leaves. illus. tables, map.   4389

Brief and argument on the liability of the State of New York, for damages caused by the breaking away of the North lake reservoir, on the Black river canal, on April 21st, 1869. Submitted. . .by the counsel for the claimants, December 1870. Utica, N.Y. White & Floyd, 1870. 58p. Signed: Charles A. Sherman, Francis Kiernan of counsel for claimants.   4390

Cobb, George H. The interest of northern

New York in water power and water transportation. *In* New York state waterways association. 2d annual convention. Proceedings, 1911. p.32–39. 4391

Cone, Gertrude E. Studies in the development of transportation in the Champlain valley to 1876. 150 leaves. tables, folded maps. Master's thesis, University of Vermont, 1945. Typescript. 4392

Dearborn, Henry Alexander Samuel. Letters on the internal improvements and commerce of the west. Boston, Dutton & Wentworth, 1839. 119p. Letter VI, p.63–77, expresses need for a canal or railroad from Ogdensburg to Lake Champlain and discusses the products of northern New York. 4393

Failure of the Dalton concrete core-wall dam, Mineville, N.Y. *Eng News*, May 9, 1912. 67:900–2. illus. diagrs. Dam collapsed Apr. 23, 1912. Description of the dam and its failure. 4394

Fight on Adirondack power. *Elec W*, Sept. 8, 1923. 82:504. 4395

Garrett, Paul Willard. Adirondack power & light's future. *Elec W*, Dec. 20, 1924. 84:1340. chart. 4396

Gow, George B. The story of a great enterprise. The Hudson river water power company. The story of its works at Spier Falls. . . together with some account of its relations to the varied industries. . . Glens Falls, N.Y. Glens Falls publishing co. c1903. 77p. ports. illus. Includes some material on the Adirondacks. 4397

Hill, Henry Wayland. An historical review of the waterways and canal construction in New York state. Buffalo, N.Y. Buffalo historical society, 1908. 549p. port. maps. (Buffalo Historical Society Publications, v.12.) Many scattered references to the Adirondacks. 4398

Lakeman, Curtis E. State control of water power. *R of Rs*, Jan. 1909. 39:57–59. Includes Conklingville dam on the Sacandaga River. 4399

McElroy, Samuel. Analysis of the Black river flood case of April, 1869. Prepared at request of Hon. Charles H. Doolittle and Charles A. Sherman, counsel for claimants. . .and submitted to the Board of state canal appraisers, December, 1869. Utica, N.Y. Roberts, 1870. 71p. Includes examination of the North Lake reservoir and faults in its construction. Bound with the copy in the New York State Library: Appendix 1, Opinion of Beman Brockway and William Wasson; Appendix 2, Extracts from Testimony. 4400

Meyer, Balthasar Henry, ed. History of transportation in the United States before 1860. . .by Caroline E. MacGill and a staff of collaborators. Washington, Carnegie institution, 1917. 678p. tables, maps (part folded). Canals and water routes in New York, Chapter VI. Railroads in New York, Chapter XIII. 4401

New York (state). Canal appraisers. Annual report for 1858. Albany, 1859. 90p. tables. Senate document 100, 1859. Ausable River claims, Appendix, p.65–90. 4402

New York (state). Canal appraisers. Black river claims. Before the Canal appraisers, Samuel North, J. Gay and George C. Greene, in the matter of the claims of William M. Coburn and others vs. State of New York. Points and brief on behalf of the state, Levi H. Brown, Samuel Earl, Charles Rhodes and P.S. Palmer, of counsel for the state. Oswego, N.Y. Palladium printing co. 1871. 313, 78p. p.97–100 omitted in numbering. "In the matter of claims against the State of New York, for damages alleged to have arisen and been caused by the breach of the North Lake reservoir and the water discharged therefrom." 4403

New York (state). Canal appraisers. Testimony in the claims of the citizens in the valley of the Ausable river in the counties of Essex and Clinton. . .for alleged damages to their property occasioned by the breaking away of the dam across the south branch of the Ausable river, in the town of Keene. . .Sept. 30, 1856. Albany, Weed, Parsons & co. 1858. 368p. 4404

New York (state). Canal board. In the Canal board of the State of New York. In the matter of the claims of John S. Bussing. . .and 122 other parties agt. the State of New York. The Ausable claims. n.p. n.d. 23p. Signed: John H. Reynolds, counsel for claimants. 4405

New York (state). Governor (William H. Seward). Documents accompanying the Governor's message. Albany, 1840. 11p. Senate document 2, 1840. Part 4, p.7–9, is a letter from George E. Hoffman on providing means of transportation to the northern part of the state, to attract settlers. 4406

New York (state). Legislature. Assembly. Report of the select committee on petitions for the improvement of Racquette and Moose rivers. Albany, 1850. 32p. Assembly document 68, 1850. 4407

New York (state). Legislature. Assembly. Report of the select committee on the improvement of the St. Regis river. Albany, 1856. 2p. Assembly document 112, 1856. 4408

New York (state). Legislature. Assembly. Report of the select committee on the petitions of the inhabitants of Essex, Franklin and Warren counties. Albany, 1851. 4p. Assembly document 94, 1851. Appropriation for the improvement of the Saranac River and lakes.   4409

New York (state). Legislature. Assembly. Report of the select committee relative to the survey of the Sacondaga, Schroon and the middle branch of the Hudson river. March 7, 1831. Albany, 1831. 3p. Assembly document 248, 1831.   4410

New York (state). Legislature. Assembly. Committee on commerce and navigation. Report. . .relative to the improvement of Beaver river. Albany, 1860. 4p. Assembly document 91, 1860.   4411

New York (state). Legislature. Assembly. Committee on internal affairs of towns and counties. Report on the petition of J.D. Kingsland, and others, for relief to certain towns in Clinton and Essex cos. Albany, 1859. 4p. Assembly document 149, 1859. Damage caused by break in dam at Ausable Forks.   4412

New York (state). Legislature. Senate. Memorial of George A. Simmons and six other gentlemen (a committee for that purpose) stating the results of a survey of a railroad and steamboat route from Lake Champlain to the county of Oneida. Albany, 1846. 58p. folded map. Senate document 73, 1846. Appendix contains report of Farrand N. Benedict on "a line of slack-water navigation through the northern counties of New-York," p.10–33; 2d report, p.34–58.   4413

New York (state). Legislature. Senate. Report of the select committee on the improvement of the navigation of Raquette river. Albany, 1854. 4p. Senate document 24, 1854.   4414

New York-Breakwater, Port Kent. Memorial of inhabitants of the northern section of New York, for a breakwater at Port Kent, N.Y. Nov. 25, 1836. Washington, 1836? 8p. 24th Congress, 2d Session, House of Representatives document 44.   4415

Northern inland lock navigation co. A report of the committee appointed by the directors of the Northern inland lock navigation company, in the State of New York, to examine Hudson's river. N.Y. W. Durell, 1792. 20p. Examination and survey of the country between the Hudson River and Wood Creek to make it navigable. See Sabin, v.8, no. 33523.   4416

Perkins, A.H. The power situation in the State of New York. Eng M, Aug. 1912. 43:

737–46. Includes discussion of Adirondack streams.   4417

Pierce, Wallace E. Lake Champlain, its past, present and future as a water highway. In New York state waterways association. 14th annual convention, 1923. p.19–21.   4418

Porter, Dwight. Reports on the water-power of the Hudson river basin and the Lake George outlet. In U.S. Census. 10th census, 1880, v.16, p.335–411. Also separately paged, 1–69.   4419

Porter, Mrs. Marjorie (Lansing). "Number please!" No Country Life, Summer 1949. 3: no.3:18–21. illus. History of telephone communications in northern New York.   4420

Post office at Gabriels. For Leaves, Autumn 1925. 20:no.1:66–67.   4421

Potter, Frederick A. . . .On the Beaver river dam project. For & Stream, Nov. 1924. 94: 672, 674. Letter on damage resulting from the dam.   4422

Radio station WHDL seeks more power. Up-Stater, Jan. 1930. 2:no.1:19–20. Only radio station located in the Adirondacks, at Tupper Lake.   4423

Sims, C.F. Needed improvements in Lake Champlain. In New York state waterways association. 7th annual convention, 1916. p.43–44. Effect on shipping of lower levels of Lake Champlain.   4424

U.S. War department. Letter from the Secretary of war, transmitting a copy of the report and estimates for the improvement of the harbors of Plattsburg, Port Kent, and Burlington bay on Lake Champlain. Washington, Gales & Seaton, 1834? 8p. 23d Congress, 1st Session, House of Representatives document 131. Report signed: Hartman Bache.   4425

U.S. War department. Letter from the Secretary of war, transmitting a report of the Chief engineer relative to the survey of Plattsburgh harbor, February 14, 1867. Washington, 1867. 4p. 39th Congress, 2d Session, House of Representatives document 89. 4426

Walworth, Hiram. Four eras in the history of travelling between Montreal and New York from 1793 to 1892. Plattsburgh, N.Y. Telegram printing house, 1892. 8p. Brief travel notes from the Plattsburgh Republican.   4427

CANALS

Arranged by date

New York (state). Legislature. Report of the commissioners appointed by joint resolutions of the honorable the Senate and Assembly of the State of New York, of the thirteenth and fifteenth of March, 1810, to explore the route of an inland navigation, from Hudson's river to Lake Ontario and Lake Erie. N.Y. 1811. 38p.   4428

New York (state). Board of commissioners on the northern or Champlain canal. Report, Mar. 18, 1817. Albany, n.d. 91–97, 52p. Brief description of northern New York state; urging construction of a canal needed for lumbering.   4429

New York (state). Canal commissioners. Report. . .on the canals from Lake Erie to the Hudson river and from Lake Champlain to the same. Presented to the Legislature Jan. 31, 1813. Albany, J. Buel, 1818. 45p. folding table.   4430

Haines, Charles G. comp. Public documents, relating to the New-York canals, which are to connect the western and northern lakes, with the Atlantic ocean, with an introduction. Printed under the direction of the New-York corresponding association, for the promotion of internal improvements. N.Y. William A. Mercien, printer, 1821. 484p. folded tables, folded maps. Copies in American Geographical Society and Duke University Library. Important source material on the Champlain canal.   4431

New York (state). Legislature. Assembly. Committee on canals. Report on petition for a survey and estimates for a canal between Lake Ontario and Lake Champlain. *In* New York (state). Assembly journal, 1823. v.46, p.585–86. Also published as Assembly document 126, 1823.   4432

Petition of inhabitants of the northerly part of the state, praying for aid, to make a canal from Lake Ontario near Ogdensburgh to Lake Champlain, near Plattsburg. Albany, 1823. 3p. Assembly document 68, 1823. 4433

Report of the committee on the subject of the Ontario and Champlain canal. Potsdam, N.Y. 1823. 6p. Listed in Sabin, v.14, p.2.   4434

New York (state). Legislature. Assembly. Standing committee on canals and internal improvements. Report. . .on the Memorial of the counties of St. Lawrence, Franklin, and Clinton, praying for an act, authorizing a survey of the route of a canal to connect Lakes Ontario and Champlain. *In* New York (state). Assembly journal, 1824. p.804–8.   4435

Spafford, Horatio Gates. A pocket guide for the tourist and traveller, along the line of the canals, and the interior commerce of the canals of the State of New-York. N.Y. T. & J. Swords, 1824. 72p. Includes route, tolls, points of interest along the Champlain canal. 2d edition with additions and corrections published in 1825.   4436

Hutchinson, Holmes. Papers alluded to in the communication of the Canal commissioners in relation to the survey and examination of the route of the proposed canal from Ogdensburgh to Lake Champlain. Albany, 1825. 34p. Assembly Journal, 1825, Appendix G.   4437

Memorial of the counties of St. Lawrence, Franklin and Clinton to the Legislature of New-York, for an act to authorize a survey of the route of a canal from the river St. Lawrence to Lake Champlain. . .with a memorial from the city of New-York, and an abstract of the debates in the Assembly on the bill brought in. Albany, Packard & Van Benthuysen, 1825. 45p. Sabin cites slightly different title.   4438

New York (state). Canal commissioners. Communication on the survey of a route for a canal from the river St. Lawrence to Lake Champlain. Albany, 1825. 36p. Assembly document 183, 1825.   4439

New York (state). Laws, statutes, etc. Laws of the State of New York in relation to the Erie and Champlain canals, together with the annual reports of the Canal commissioner and other documents requisite for a complete official history of those works. . . Albany, E. & E. Hosford, 1825. 2v. front. folded maps.   4440

A view of the Grand canal, from Lake Erie to the Hudson river. . . Also, a description of the Champlain canal. N.Y. Printed for J. Low, 1825. 28p. incl. front.   4441

New York (state). Canal commissioners. Report. . .pursuant to the act entitled "An act to provide for the survey of certain canal routes therein mentioned," made to the Assembly. Mar. 6, 1826. Albany, 1826. 29p. Assembly Journal, 1826, Appendix F. Black River Canal, p.2–5.   4442

U.S. Congress. House. Committee on roads and canals. Report on memorial of the citizens of New York to construct a canal between lakes Champlain and Ontario, May 22, 1826. Washington, 1826. 3p. 19th Congress, 1st Session, House report 230. 4443

Memorial of the counties of St. Lawrence, Franklin and Clinton, to the Legislature. . . pray for an act authorizing a survey of the route of a canal, to connect lakes Ontario and Champlain. . . n.p. 1829. 29p. Signed: B. Raymond.   4444

New York (state). Legislature. Senate. Committee on canals. Memorial of a committee . . .composed of delegates from Oneida, Lewis, Jefferson and St. Lawrence, on the subject of a canal to connect the navigable waters of the Black river with the Erie canal.

Albany, 1836. 16p. folded map. Senate document 21, 1836.   4445

New York (state). Legislature. Senate. Committee on canals. Report of the majority. . . on the petitions and memorials relative to the construction of the Black river canal. Albany, 1836. 15p. Senate document 36, 1836.   4446

New York (state). Canal commissioners. Communication. . .transmitting the report of the survey in continuation of the Black river canal. February 29, 1840. Albany, 1840. 120p. folded map. Assembly document 233, 1840.   4447

New York (state). Legislature. Senate. Report of the select committee, in relation to the management and expenditures on the northern section of the Champlain canal, and Glens Falls feeder. Albany, 1846. 231p. tables, partly folded. Senate document 144, 1846.   4448

New York (state). Canal board. Communication. . .transmitting the report of D.C. Jenne, resident engineer, in relation to the supply of water for the Black river canal and Black river. Albany, 1850. 6p. Senate document 102, 1850.   4449

New York (state). Canal board. Report. . . on the bill to supply the Black river canal and the Black river with water. Albany, 1850. 3p. Senate document 98, 1850.   4450

American geographical and statistical society. Memorial on canal connection of Champlain valley with St. Lawrence river. Albany, 1857. 8p. Senate document 14, 1857. 4451

Sweet, Sylvanus H. Documentary sketch of New York state canals. . .accompanying State engineer and surveyor's report for 1862. Albany, Van Benthuysen, 1863. 480p. tables. folded maps.   4452

New York (state). State engineer and surveyor. Report. . .relative to the quantity of water diverted from the Black river feeder to supply the Black river & Erie canals. Albany, 1866. 7p. Assembly document 46, 1866. Signed: Daniel C. Jenne, division engineer.   4453

New York (state). Canal board. Reply. . .to a resolution of the Assembly, inquiring as to the effect the structure now being placed across Lake Champlain, at Ticonderoga, will have upon the commerce, etc. of the state. Albany, 1871. 6p. Assembly document 94, 1871.   4454

Weed, Smith M. Ship canal from the Hudson river to Lake Champlain. Speech. . .in Assembly April 15th, 1873. Albany, Argus co. 1873. 31p. folded map. In favor of the canal. 4455

Delaware & Hudson railroad corporation. Report to the stockholders of the Delaware and Hudson canal company. . .May 8th, 1877. N.Y. P. Barnes, 1877. 104p.   4456

Deane, Silas. Canal from Lake Champlain to the St. Lawrence. In Canada. Public archives. Report, 1889. p.80–88. Letters written to promote the canal.   4457

Whitford, Noble Earl. History of the canal system of the State of New York together with brief histories of the canals of the United States and Canada. . . Albany, Brandow printing co. 1906. 2v. plates, tables, partly folded. diagrs. folded maps. Contains extensive bibliography.   4458

Francis, Lewis W. The transportation of iron ore on the Champlain canal. In New York state waterways association. 9th annual convention. Proceedings, 1918. p.51–55. Shipping of iron ore by Witherbee and Sherman.   4459

Loomis, Alfred Fullerton. Inland waterways, Champlain canal and Lake Champlain, from Waterford to Rouses Point. Country Life, Sept. 1921. 40:88. map.   4460

New York (state). State engineer and surveyor. History of the barge canal of New York state, by Noble E. Whitford. . . Albany, J.B. Lyon, 1922. 610p. front. ports. plates. Supplement to the Annual Report, 1920/21.   4461

Potter, Elsie Austin. The influence of the Champlain canal on eastern New York and western Vermont (1823–1860). 108, 9, 7 leaves. Master's thesis, Cornell University, 1939. Typescript.   4462

Copeland, Fred O. Champlain canal days. Vermonter, Aug. 1941. 46:155–60. illus.   4463

Graves, Harold F. Black river canal. No Country Life, Summer 1948. 2:no.3:17–19. illus.   4464

Dunn, James Taylor, ed. A trip on the Northern canal. NY Folk Q, Winter 1950. 6:234–39. Humorous letter written in 1832 about a trip from Troy to Whitehall on the Champlain canal.   4465

O'Hara, John E. Erie's junior partner: the economic and social effects of the Champlain canal upon the Champlain valley. 391 leaves. Doctoral thesis, Columbia University, 1951. Microfilm edition available through University Microfilms.   4466

RAILROADS

An argument showing why the state should aid in the construction of a railroad through the wilderness of northern New York, respectfully submitted for the consideration of the Legislature and the Executive. Albany, Van Benthuysen, 1870. 16p. Cover title: A Plea for the Northern Wilderness. 4467

Electric traction on Adirondack railways as a preventive of forest fires. *Eng News*, Aug. 19, 1909. 62:210. Rejected by Public Service Commission as too costly. 4468

Fire loss remedies. *For & Stream*, Apr. 10, 1909. 72:567. Editorial on the decision of Public Service Commission of 2d district that railroads burn oil from April to November to prevent fires. 4469

Franchot, R. and Peek, A. Mason. Report of a survey for a railroad route from Schenectady to Ogdensburgh. . .January 1, 1868. Albany, 1868. 30p. tables, folded map. Assembly document 61, 1868. 4470

Hale, Matthew. Gov. Fenton and his veto of the Plattsburgh & Whitehall railroad bill; speech of. . .Hale. . .in Senate, April 8, 1868; also a debate between. . .John O'Donnell, H.C. Murphy, A.X. Parker and Matthew Hale. n.p. n.pub. 1868. 16p. Cover title. Effect on the Champlain valley. Copy in the New York State Library. 4471

Hayward, James. Report of the proposed rail-road between Boston and Ogdensburgh. Boston, Carter, Hendee and Babcock, 1831. 46p. One of the proposed routes through the Adirondacks. 4472

Hungerford, Edward. Early railroads of New York. *NY Hist*, Jan. 1932. 18:75–89. Short discussion of some of the early north country railroads. 4473

Radford, Harry V. Benefits of Adirondack railroads. *For Leaves*, Autumn 1904. 1:no. 4:18–19. illus. 4474

Riding swift stagecoaches through Adirondack forests was pastime of summer hotel guests in 1895. *D & H Bul*, Mar. 1, 1938. 18:35–36. Train service from the experience of a retiring crew dispatcher, Ovid S. Benjamin. 4475

Some Adirondack novelties. *Am Angler*, July 21, 1888. 14:37. On building railroad to Jayville. 4476

Williams, C.H. Some north woods reminiscences; old time railroader tells of memories of pioneer days in the Adirondacks. *NYC Lines Mag*, Dec. 1924. 5:no.9:54c–54d. Includes tales of private railroad cars. 4477

The Adirondack Company

Adirondack. *In* Donaldson, A.L. A history of the Adirondacks. N.Y. Century, 1921. v.2, p.280–82. Reprint of an editorial from the *New York Times* of Aug. 9, 1864 based on a pamphlet advertising the building of the Adirondack Company's railroad. 4478

Adirondack company. The Adirondack company: its position, property and resources. N.Y. Adirondack co. 1864. 39p. 4479

Adirondack company. The Adirondack company; its railroad and estate. N.Y. Kennard & May, 1872. 18p. maps. 4480

Adirondack company. The Adirondack company; its railroad and estate containing estimates of the probable costs and business from the road. . .including a report from the consulting engineer, 1870. N.Y. J.O. Seymour, 1870. 55p. map. 4481

Adirondack company. Adirondack company by-laws. n.p. n.pub. 1870? 5p. Copy in the Munson Collection, Saranac Lake Free Library. 4482

Adirondack company. Adirondack company's charter, amendments, and the laws relating thereto. N.Y.? 1871? 10p. Caption title. 4483

Adirondack company. The Adirondack company's railroad and estate. n.p. n.pub. 1870? 49p. Copy in the Munson Collection, Saranac Lake Free Library. 4484

Adirondack company. A brief statement of the leading features and resources of the great northern forest in northern New York, the position of the Adirondack co., with reference thereto, and its estate and franchises. N.Y. W.C. Bryant & co. 1864. 32p. map. 4485

Adirondack company. Closing argument for state aid to the Adirondack company's railroad. Albany, Van Benthuysen, 1870. 7p. Copy in the Engineering Societies Library, New York City. 4486

Adirondack company. The wilderness of northern New York and the Adirondack company's railroad, showing their importance to the city of Albany and the state at large. Albany, Van Benthuysen, 1870. 21p. map. 4487

Adirondack railway co. The Adirondack railway company. Its present condition and future prospects, by Silas Seymour. N.Y. Jones printing co. 1883. 14p. map. 4488

Adirondack railway company. The Adirondack railway company, and its real estate. Being a review of Mr. George Leavitt's report upon the value of the Company's lands in the Adirondack region. By Silas Seymour. N.Y. C.F. Ketcham & co. 1885. 14p. Copy in the Engineering Societies Library, New York City. 4489

Adirondack railway company. Articles of association and by-laws of the Adirondack railway company. N.Y. Jones printing co. 1883. 41p. 4490

Adirondack railway company. Letter from T. Haskins DuPuy. . . n.p. 1883? 4p. Copy in the Engineering Societies Library, New York City. Letter to Silas Seymour approving the route of the railroad.   4491

Butler, Benjamin Clapp. Handbook of the Adirondack railway. Albany, Weed, Parsons & co. 1870. 42p. Advertisements not included in paging. Copy in the Munson Collection, Saranac Lake Free Library.   4492

New York (state). Governor (John T. Hoffman). Veto of the Governor on the bill entitled "An Act to facilitate the construction of the railroad of the Adirondack company, and its extension to the waters of the St. Lawrence river." Albany, 1870. 6p. Assembly document 207, 1870. Lincoln 6:172–76.
                                                    4493

Seymour, Silas. Adirondack company's railroad. Report of Silas Seymour, consulting engineer. N.Y.? 1870. 20p. folded maps. 4494

Seymour, Silas. Observations concerning eastern and western railway transport, with distance tables, from New York and Boston to Chicago. The Adirondack railway and its relations to through traffic. N.Y. C.F. Ketcham, 1885. 16p.   4495

Weatherwax, David S. The Adirondack railway company; passenger traffic. *Rail & Loc*, May 1953. no.88:55–58. plate, map.   4496

Weatherwax, David S. Locomotives of the Adirondack railway company, 1864–1902. *Rail & Loc*, Oct. 1948. 74:36–38. plates. 4497

Northern Railroad

Doherty, Laurence. History of the Northern New York railroad. *Rail & Loc*, Sept. 1938. 47:90–94. illus.   4498

Memorial adopted by a convention of the people of the counties of St. Lawrence, Franklin and Clinton, praying for the construction of the Ogdensburgh and Lake Champlain rail-road as a state work. Albany, 1841. 5p. Assembly document 32, 1841. 4499

Memorial, statistics and correspondence in relation to a rail-road, from Ogdensburgh to Lake Champlain, respectfully submitted to the Legislature of New-York. Ogdensburgh, N.Y. Times office, 1839. 53p. folded map.
                                                    4500

New York (state). Governor (William H. Seward). Message from the Governor transmitting the report of Mr. Casey, in relation to the Ogdensburgh and Lake Champlain railroad. Albany, 1842. 23p. table. Assembly document 70, 1842. William R. Casey.   4501

New York (state). Legislature. Assembly. Report of the commissioners appointed to cause a survey to be made of the several routes for a railroad from Ogdensburgh to Lake Champlain. Albany, 1841. 115p. folded map.

Assembly document 43, 1841. Appendix contains: Report of Edward Broadhead, Chief Engineer; Reports of Division Engineer; Extracts from Report on the Geology and Mineralogy of Franklin and Clinton Counties. . .by B. Roberts.   4502

New York (state). Legislature. Assembly. Committee on railroads. Report. . .on the petition of inhabitants of the counties of St. Lawrence, Franklin, Clinton and Essex, in relation to the Ogdensburgh and Lake Champlain rail-road. Albany, 1839. 15p. Assembly document 233, 1839. Accompanied by statement of Messrs. Hopkins, Platt and Duane on advantages to business etc.   4503

New York (state). Legislature. Senate. Committee on rail-roads. Report. . .on the petitions for the construction of the Ogdensburgh and Champlain rail-road by the state. Albany, 1840. 12p. Senate document 44, 1840.
                                                    4504

New York (state). Secretary of state. Communication. . .transmitting the report of a survey of a rail-road from Ogdensburgh to Lake Champlain. Albany, 1839. 57p. Assembly document 133, 1839. Report of Edwin F. Johnson, Chief Engineer.   4505

The northern railroad in New York. With remarks on the western trade. Boston, Freeman & Bolles, 1845. 36p. Signed: J.G. Hopkins. Arguments in favor of the proposed Ogdensburgh railroad.   4506

Northern railroad company (New York). Report of directors. no.1–8, 10–11, 14–16 (1846–53, 1855–56, 1859–61). Boston, 1846–61. Title of no.2–16 reads: Annual Report. Copies in New York Public Library.   4507

Northern railroad company (New York). Report of the directors of the Northern railroad company, New York, submitted to the stockholders, June 5, 1848. Ogdensburgh, N.Y. Hitchcock & Smith, 1848. 12p. table.
                                                    4508

Northern railroad company (New York). Report of the examining committee on the management and working of the Northern (N.Y.) railroad. Ogdensburgh, N.Y. Smith & Oswell's steam press, 1851. 48p.   4509

Northern railroad company (New York). Report of the trustees of the 2nd mortgage bondholders of the Northern railroad co. (from Ogdensburgh to Rouse's Point) New York, submitted January 17, 1857. Ogdensburgh, N.Y. Tillotson & Stillwell, printers, 1857. 37p.   4510

Ogdensburg, N.Y. Citizens. To the honorable members of the Senate and Assembly. The merits of the Ogdensburgh and Champlain rail-road, with interesting information relative to the business and resources of the northern counties. 1838. n.p. n.pub. 1839? 16p. Thomson 2287.   4511

Ogdensburgh and Champlain rail-road. Resolutions of meeting at Albany, February 18, 1839, and correspondence in regard to the railroad. n.p. 1839? 7p. Thomson 2288.   4512

Ogdensburgh and Lake Champlain railroad company. Copy of the acts under which the Northern railroad company of New York was incorporated, and under which the railroad now owned by the Ogdensburgh and Lake Champlain railroad company was originally built. Ogdensburgh, N.Y. Republican & Journal steam presses, 1866. 96p.   4513

Ogdensburgh and Lake Champlain railroad company. Report of the condition of the Ogdensburgh and Lake Champlain railroad company, 1879. Boston, Wright & Potter, 1879. 20p. Auditor's report.   4514

Ogdensburgh and Lake Champlain railroad company. To the stockholders. Boston, 1880. 2 leaves. Cover title. Plan to reorganize the road. Copy in the New York Public Library.
4515

Parsons, C. and others. Bondholders' agreement and plan for reorganization of the Ogdensburgh and Lake Champlain railroad co. 20 Aug. 1896. n.p. 1896. 2 leaves. Copy in the New York Public Library.   4516

Sacket's Harbor and Saratoga Railroad

Edwards, A.F. Report of the different routes and estimates of the Sacket's Harbor & Saratoga rail-road, October 1853. Saratoga Springs, N.Y. G.M. Davison, 1853. 109p. folded map.   4517

Hamilton, E.C. Sackett's Harbor and Saratoga railroad. The comments of E.C. Hamilton, on the printed circular of Anson Blake. Albany, Weed, Parsons & co. 1854. 15p. 4518

Lake Ontario & Hudson river railroad company. Statement of the general features and prospective advantages of the Lake Ontario & Hudson river railroad (late Sacket's Harbor & Saratoga railroad). N.Y. W.E. Sibell, 1857. 21p. map.   4519

New York (state). Land office. Communication from the commissioners of the Land office relative to land conveyed to Sacketts Harbor and Saratoga railroad company. Albany, 1855. 4p. Assembly document 96, 1855.   4520

New York (state). Legislature. Assembly. Committee on railroads. Report on the memorial of the Sacket's Harbor and Saratoga railroad company, Mar. 6, 1854. Albany, 1854. 32p. Assembly document 88, 1854.   4521

New York (state). Legislature. Assembly. Committee on ways and means. Report. . .on the petition of the Sacketts Harbor and Saratoga railroad co. Albany, 1857. 16p. Assembly document 53, 1857.   4522

New York (state). Legislature. Senate. Committee on railroads. Report. . .on the memorial of the Sacketts Harbor and Saratoga railroad company. Albany, 1855. 4p. Senate document 31, 1855.   4523

New York (state). Legislature. Senate. Committee on railroads. Report. . .on the memorial of the Sacketts Harbor and Saratoga railroad company. Albany, 1855. 24p. Senate document 53, 1855.   4524

Ogdensburg the proper terminus on the St. Lawrence river of the projected Saratoga railroad. With references to trade with Canada, the great Ottawa valley and the west. Ogdensburg, N.Y. J. Hopkins & Foster, 1857. 12p. Resolutions to make Ogdensburg the terminus of the Sackets Harbor and Saratoga Railroad.   4525

Sacket's Harbor and Saratoga railroad co. Board of directors. n.p. 1853. 1 leaf. Letter soliciting donations of land. Copy in the New York Public Library.   4526

Sacket's Harbor & Saratoga railroad. Charter and all laws pertaining to the Sacket's Harbor & Saratoga railroad. Utica, N.Y. Roberts, 1853. 72p.   4527

Sacket's Harbor & Saratoga railroad. Charter & by-laws of the Sacket's Harbor & Saratoga railroad. Boston, J. Wilson & son, 1852. 8p. map.   4528

Sacket's Harbor and Saratoga railroad. Engineer's report of the preliminary surveys of the Sacket's Harbor & Saratoga railroad. 2. ed. Boston, Bazin & Chandler, 1851. 15p. Signed: Bryant P. Tilden Jr. Copy in the Engineering Societies Library, New York City.   4529

Sacket's Harbor & Saratoga railroad co. Evidence in favor of the south route, gathered from the official report of A.F. Edwards. n.p. 1854. 8p.   4530

Sacket's Harbor and Saratoga railroad co. Facts incidental to the question before the Legislature concerning the routes. n.p. n.d. 1 leaf. Copy in the New York Public Library.
4531

Sacket's Harbor and Saratoga railroad co. Lands granted, conveyed or pledged to aid the construction of this road. Capital stock. Comparison of the two routes. n.p. n.d. 1 leaf. Copy in the New York Public Library.   4532

Sacket's Harbor and Saratoga railroad co. Memorial of the Sacket's Harbor and Saratoga railroad co. asking authority to improve the navigation of lakes and rivers in northern New York. Albany, 1855. 18p.   4533

Sacket's Harbor and Saratoga railroad co. Official documents abridged on the subject of the Sacket's Harbor and Saratoga railroad, together with the minority report against changing the route of said railroad. Albany, J. Munsell, 1854. 23p.   4534

Sacket's Harbor and Saratoga railroad co. Report of the committee to investigate the affairs of the company. N.Y. E. & J. Sibell, 1855. 30p.   4535

Van Arnam, Ralph N. and Van Arnam, L.S. The Sackets Harbor and Saratoga railroad. *No Country Life*, Fall 1948. 2:no.4:32–36, 53. illus. map.   4536

Other Railroads

Beaver dams flood abandoned Tekene branch. *D & H Bul*, Jan. 1, 1938. 18:5–7, 12–13. 4537

Black river & Utica railroad company. Report of the chief engineer to the directors, June 1, 1854. Utica, N.Y. Roberts, 1854. 84p. maps.   4538

Bragdon, Henry. The passing of the Grasse river railroad. *High Spots Yrbk*, 1940. p.71–74.   4539

Bruce, Dwight Hall. Syndicating the Adirondacks. *For & Stream*, Apr. 21, 1892. 38: 371. Signed: D.H.B. Route of railroad purchased by Dr. Webb.   4540

Burnett, Charles Howard. Conquering the wilderness: the building of the Adirondack & St. Lawrence railroad by William Seward Webb, 1891–92. Norwood, Mass. Plimpton press, 1932. 86p. front. (port.). Edition limited to 400 copies.   4541

Comfort, Randall. When Lake Placid was three days away. *NYC Lines Mag*, Jan. 1926. 6:no.10:44. Railroader's reminiscences. 4542

Coniff, W.T. The Delaware & Hudson. *Trains*, Jan. 1945. 5:no.3:24–25. illus. 4543

Construction of the Elizabethtown terminal railroad. *Ang & Hunt*, June 1910. 2:302. illus.   4544

Dales, Douglas S. Seven-eighths of a mile. *Rail Mag*, May 1940. 27:74–76. Marion River Carry Railroad.   4545

Delaware & Hudson railroad corporation. A century of progress; history of the Delaware and Hudson company, 1823–1923... Albany, J.B. Lyon, 1925. 755p. front. illus. Chapters on the Adirondack Railroad, Chateaugay & Lake Placid Railway Company, Champlain Transportation Company, Lake George Steamboat Company.   4546

Delaware & Hudson railroad corporation. Official freight shipping guide and industrial

directory. Albany, D. & H. 1922–27. 7v.? Edited by Warwick Stevens Carpenter. 4547

Delaware & Hudson railroad corporation. Memorial of the excursion from New York to Montreal, given...upon the occasion of the opening of the New York and Canada railway, November 16th, 17th and 18th, 1875. N.Y. Baker & Goodwin, printers, 1876. 153p. plates, folded map. Includes reprint from *Plattsburgh Republican:* "Historical Sketch: Early Struggles for Railroad Communication South, and Final Success."   4548

Evans, Albert I. A friendly voice is silenced. *No Country Life*, Winter 1947. 1:no.1:20–22. Saranac Lake Division of D. & H. discontinued.   4549

Frogs croaked sole greeting as first passenger train reached Saranac Lake's tent station. *D & H Bul*, Feb. 1, 1937. 17:19–20. port. Frank Rochette.   4550

Grasse river railroad. Gateway to Cranberry lake via the Grasse river railroad. n.p. n.pub. 1922. 15p. illus. map.   4551

Grasse river railroad corporation. Annual report, v.1– Conifer, N.Y. 1949–date. v.p. illus. Includes descriptive material about Conifer.   4552

Harlow, Alvin Fay. The road of the century; the story of the New York Central. N.Y. Creative age press, 1947. 447p. plates, front. ports. "In the north country," p.401–6. 4553

Hastings, Philip R. Pacifics to Placid; oil-burning K-11's wheel tonnage and tourists over an Adirondack mountain branch which New York Central leases from Delaware & Hudson. *Trains*, Sept. 1950. 10:no.11:23–26. illus. New locomotives.   4554

Haworth, James A. Wilderness railroad. *No Country Life*, Spring 1954. 8:no.2:20–22. illus. New York and Ottawa Railroad.   4555

Hungerford, Edward. The story of the Rome, Watertown & Ogdensburgh railroad. N.Y. McBride, 1922. 269p. plates, ports. 4556

New York (state). Legislature. Assembly. Report of the select committee on the petition of Jeremiah Drake and others for the purchase of certain lands. Albany, 1837. 5p. Assembly document 279, 1837. Extension of the Mohawk and St. Lawrence Railroad.   4557

New York (state). Legislature. Assembly. Committee on railroads. Report...in relation to a survey of the Mohawk and St. Lawrence railroad... Albany, 1839. 17p. Assembly document 262, 1839.   4558

New York (state). Legislature. Assembly. Committee on railroads. Report...on the petitions of the Saratoga and Washington rail-road company, and others. Albany, 1839. 10p. Assembly document 166, 1839.   4559

O'Donnell, Thomas Clay. The sapbush run, an informal history of the Black river & Utica railroad. Boonville, N.Y. Black river books, 1948. 156p. plates, ports. Brown's Tract, p.79–91.   4560

Papers and documents relative to the Mohawk and St. Lawrence rail-road and navigation company... Albany, J. Munsell, 1838. 25p. map.   4561

Proceedings of the meeting of the inhabitants of Saratoga and Warren counties, interested in the project of the Saratoga and Warren rail-road, held at Corinth, Saratoga county, Sept. 25, 1846. Saratoga Springs, N.Y. C.F. Paul, 1846. 30p. Copy in the Sherman Free Library, Port Henry.   4562

The recently constructed Prospect mountain line at Lake George, N.Y. Eng News, Oct. 3, 1895. 34:226–27. illus. diagrs. Completion of railroad up Prospect Mountain.   4563

"Sea-going" railroad at Lake George. D & H Bul, Aug. 1, 1937. 17:117–18.   4564

Seely, S.A. A mountain railroad arms against forest fire; how the New York Central is equipped for forest defense. Am For, July 1928. 34:427–28. illus. On the Adirondack and Ottawa Divisions.   4565

Snow trains; thousands ride winter sports specials running to North Creek, Ticonderoga and Lake George. D & H Bul, Mar. 1, 1938. 18:39–41, 46.   4566

Utica and Black river railroad co. Annual report to stockholders. 1876–85. Utica, N.Y. 1876–85. 10v. tables, maps.   4567

Utica and Black river railroad co. Routes and rates for summer tours. Utica, N.Y. 1884. 99p. illus. maps (part folded). Cover title. Also published in 1882, 91p.   4568

Warren county railroad, N.Y. The annexed remarks and estimates. . .as submitted by the commissioners, to the public. N.Y. J.M. Elliot, 1883. 8p. Sabin 101501.   4569

ROADS AND BRIDGES

Automobile road up Whiteface mountain. Motor Tr, Oct. 1927. 19:no.7:5–6. illus.   4570

Before the Champlain bridge commission. Memorandum for Ticonderoga Chamber of commerce. n.p. n.pub. 1926? 13p. Dated Ticonderoga, Jan. 20, 1926.   4571

Benedict, Darwin. Early Adirondack roads. Cloud Splitter, May–June 1948. 11:no.3:2–4.   4572

Bentley, Harriet A. The old military road from Fort Edward to Lake George, 1755. n.p. n.pub. c1927. 29p.   4573

Brighton roads. For Leaves, Summer 1910. 7:no.2:50–57. illus. Reprinted from the Adirondack Enterprise. Road building in Town of Brighton, Franklin County.   4574

Building a memorial highway. Contract & Eng Mo, Jan. 1934. 28:no.1:17–22. illus. Construction of Whiteface Memorial Highway.   4575

Champlain bridge handles record volume of traffic. Motordom, June 1931. 24:no.12:42.   4576

Completing road along west side of beautiful Lake George; shortens distance between Lake George and Ticonderoga by thirty miles. Motordom, Apr. 1930. 23:no.11:9. illus.   4577

Cone, Gertrude E. Early roads in the Champlain valley. No Country Life, Summer 1949. 3:no.3:44–48.   4578

Cone, Gertrude E. Early stage routes in the Champlain valley. No Country Life, Fall 1949. 3:no.4:37–39.   4579

Conkling, Penelope. Our old covered bridges. Up Mo, Oct. 1941. 2:no.7:14–15. illus. Description of bridges of northern and central New York.   4580

Deep foundations for Lake Champlain bridge built with open coffer dams. . . Eng News R, Nov. 21, 1929. 103:796–800. illus. diagrs.   4581

Doherty, Laurence. The Rouses Point bridge. Rail & Loc, May 1940. 52:58–63. plate.   4582

The great trail of the Adirondacks; International highway cutting through the famous regions of mountains and lakes, a glamorous vacation tour. Motordom, June 1930. 24:no.1:20–21. illus.   4583

Hall, Roy F. Highway maintenance in "Little Siberia." No Country Life, Fall 1948. 2:no.4:9–10, 46.   4584

Jay's covered bridge. No Country Life, Winter 1953. 7:no.1:1–2. illus. Editorial urging preservation of the bridge.   4585

Marvin, Theodore. Whiteface mountain highway; one of America's great scenic roads nears completion. Exp Eng, Oct. 1934. 12:285–92. illus. diagrs. map.   4586

Memorial highway on Whiteface mountain. Scen & Hist Am, Jan. 1937. 4:28.   4587

Mills, Borden H. Sr. Mt. Tahawus road project of 1858. Cloud Splitter, Jan.–Feb. 1949. 12:no.1:4–5.   4588

New roads into the Adirondacks. Up-Stater, May 1929. 1:no.3:18. illus. Highway construction.   4589

New York (state). Legislature. Assembly. Report of the commissioners appointed. . . April 21st, 1828, to lay out and open a road from Cedar Point, westward through the towns of Moriah and Newcomb, in the county of Essex. . .to the Black river opposite the village of Lowville in the county of Lewis. *In* New York (state). Legislature. Assembly. Journal, 1829. p.452–57.   4590

New York (state). Legislature. Assembly. . . . Report of the select committee on the bill for the construction of a bridge over the Hudson river at or near Stony Creek. Albany, 1855. 3p. Assembly document 106, 1855.
                                                4591

New York (state). Legislature. Assembly. Committee on internal affairs of towns and counties. Report. . .on the petition of supervisors and others of Hamilton county. Feb. 24, 1860. Albany, 1860. 17p. Assembly document 94, 1860. Petition asked for wagon roads etc. Description of the area.   4592

New York (state). Legislature. Joint commission on bridge connection between the states of New York and Vermont across Lake Champlain. 5th annual report, 1931. Albany, 1932. 17p. Legislative document 105, 1932. Financial report. Earlier reports, 1927–30, appear to have been issued in typescript or mimeographed form.   4593

New York (state). Legislature. Joint commission on bridge connection between the states of New York and Vermont across Lake Champlain. . . .Final report. . . Albany, J.B. Lyon, 1927. 35p. incl. folded plates, tables, diagrs. maps (part folded). Legislative document 59, 1927. Appendix B, p.25–28: Hartnagel, C.A. "Geology of Territory Between Port Henry and Wright, with Notes on the Five Sites for a Proposed Bridge. . . "   4594

New York (state). Legislature. Joint commission on bridge connection between the states of New York and Vermont across Lake Champlain. . . .Preliminary report. . . Albany, J.B. Lyon, 1926. 39p. incl. folded plates, tables, diagrs. (1 folded) maps (1 folded). Legislative document 93, 1926.   4595

New York (state). Legislature. Joint commission on bridge connection between the states of New York and Vermont across Lake Champlain. Routes to Lake Champlain bridge. The new gateway between Adirondacks and Green mountains. N.Y. 1932. 8p. folder.   4596

New York (state). Legislature. Senate. Committee on railroads. . . .Reports of Mr. Geddes, chairman, and Mr. Dart and Mr. Owen, members of the Committee on railroads, on the subject of bridging Lake Champlain at Rouses Point. Albany, 1851. 114p. plan, maps. Senate document 20, 1851. Includes testimony offered by the Northern Railroad Company in favor of the erection of the

bridge, and testimony of persons opposed to it.   4597

New York (state). Public works, Department of. Report on revised state arterial route plans in the Plattsburgh urban area. Prepared. . .in cooperation with Bureau of public works, U.S. Dept. of commerce. Albany, 1953. 19p. col. maps.   4598

New York (state). Public works, Department of. Report on state arterial route plans in the Plattsburgh urban area. Prepared. . .in cooperation with Bureau of public works, U.S. Dept. of commerce. Albany, 1951 1v. (various paging) illus.   4599

New York (state). Whiteface mountain highway commission. Annual report, no.1–2. Albany, 1940–41. 2v. plates, illus. tables.
                                                4600

New York bridge over Moose river completed. *Constructioneer*, Dec. 10, 1947. p.26. illus. At McKeever.   4601

Plans completed for Champlain bridge, site selected and Legislature expected soon to make necessary appropriation; Vermont to pay 40%. *Motordom*, Jan. 1927. 20:no.8:5. illus. map.   4602

Shorey, Archibald Thompson. Old Carthage road. *Cloud Splitter*, Mar. 1943. 6:no.3:5–6. History of an old Adirondack road.   4603

Shorter route to the north woods. *State Service*, Dec. 1917. 1:no.5:32. illus. Building new road along Lake Champlain.   4604

Spanning Lake Champlain. *Motordom*, June 1934. p.10. Lake Champlain bridge.   4605

Spofford, Charles Milton. Lake Champlain bridge. *Am Soc Civil Eng Proc*, Dec. 1931. 57: 1467–99. plate, tables, charts, diagrs. map. Discussion by Robert W. Abbett, Henry W. Troelsch, Jacob Field and Clarence W. Hudson, Mar. 1932, 58:493–97; reply by Spofford, Oct. 1932, 58:1387–88. Digest in *Proceedings* of American Society of Civil Engineers, Dec. 1929, 55:2535–48. This also contained "Deep Piers" by George Burrows, p.2545–46, and "Methods for Bridge Foundations" by J.W. Rollins, p.2946–47.   4606

Stoddard, Seneca Ray. Adirondack highways. *St No Mo*, July 1908. 4:33–49. illus. Carriage trip from Plattsburgh to Saranac via Chateaugay.   4607

To bridge Lake Champlain in 1927. *Motordom*, Jan. 1926. 19:no.8:21. Ready for legislative action.   4608

U.S. War department. Letter from the Secretary of war, transmitting a report of Major General Jacob Brown upon the subject of the military road leading from Plattsburg to Sackett's Harbor. Washington, Gales &

Seaton, 1823. 6p. U.S. Congress, 17th Congress, 2d Session, House document 33.   4609

Whiteface mountain road to open new grandeur; excavated through hard Adirondack granite, the new memorial highway will give motorists first big chance to gaze upon the top of the state. *Motordom*, Mar. 1934. p.5.   4610

STEAMBOATS AND OTHER CARRIERS

Benedict, Darwin. Tootin' teakettle. *Cloud Splitter*, July–Aug. 1946. 9:no.4:9–10. Early steamboats on Lake Champlain and Lake George.   4611

Burger, William H. Sidewheelers on Lake Champlain. *No Country Life*, Fall 1955. 9: no.4:13–19. illus.   4612

Champlain transportation company. Centenary of the Champlain transportation company: a century of service 1826–1926. Chicago, Poole bros. inc. 1926? unpaged. col. illus. (6p. folder.)   4613

Champlain transportation company. Steamboats of Lake Champlain, 1809–1930. Albany, c1930. 184p. front. illus. ports. facsims. map. Compiled by Ogden J. Ross.   4614

Cone, Gertrude E. Early sailing craft on Lake Champlain. *No Country Life*, Winter 1950. 4:no.1:41–43.   4615

Copeland, Fred O. Farewell, steamer Chateaugay! *Vermonter*, Mar. 1940. 45:51–53. Lake Champlain steamship.   4616

Heard, Augustine A. Carriers of the lake. *NY State Hist Assn Proc*, 1910. 10:67–70. Types of boats used on Lake Champlain.   4617

Hill, Ralph Nading. Saga of the side wheelers. *Am Heritage*, Sept. 1949. n.s.1:36–38. Steamers on Lake Champlain.   4618

Horsford, Marion. Fair Lake Champlain. *Vermonter*, July 1915. 20:134–37. illus. Steamer travel on the lake.   4619

Ichabod, pseud. A steamboat on the Upper Saranac. *For & Stream*, Feb. 15, 1877. 8:19.   4620

Lake George steamboat company. The steamboats of Lake George, 1817 to 1932. Albany, c1932. 174p. front. illus. ports. maps. Prepared by Ogden J. Ross.   4621

Lane, Carl D. American paddle steamboats. N.Y. Coward-McCann, 1944. 250p. plates, col. front. Brief mention of steamers on Lake George and Lake Champlain.   4622

Loomis, D.A. Steamers which have been engaged in regular traffic on Lake Champlain during 124 years. *Vermonter*, Feb. 1933. 38:32.   4623

Pollard, Louise. The Champlain transportation company. *Vermonter*, Feb. 1933. 38:29–31.   4624

Smith, Levi. About Lake Champlain. *Vermonter*, May 1913. 18:95–97. Route of steamer with a few historical notes.   4625

Wilkins, F.H. Lake Champlain. *Vermonter*, May 1915. 20:92–94. Steamer trip on the lake.   4626

Wilkins, F.H. Lake Champlain reminiscences. *Vermonter*, Sept. 1915. 20:186–88. Steamers built for passenger service during last hundred years.   4627

Wilkins, F.H. Lake Champlain steamers. *Vermonter*, Jan. 1916. 21:13–16. Short history of steamboating and list of steamers.   4628

Wilkins, F.H. Reveries. *Vermonter*, July 1915. 20:127–29. History of steamers on Lake Champlain.   4629

LIFE AND MANNERS

Adirondack, pseud. The Hermitage. *Sport Rev*, Sept. 24, 1910. 38:298. Hamilton Busbey camp near Brant Lake.   4630

Adirondack camps. *For & Stream*, May 30, 1908. 70:847. See also article by R.S. Spears in issue for May 30, 70:856–57. Editorial about depredations of camps.   4631

Barber, Arthur William. Clinton county's anti-slavery convention of 1837; Friends of immediate emancipation met with much opposition and were persecuted with scarcely less bitterness than in the south. *Up-Stater*,

May 1930. 2:no.3:9, 18–19. Meeting held in Beekmantown.   4632

Breen, Ann. Hide and seek killer. *Argosy*, Dec. 1955. 341:34–37, 86–88. illus. James Arlon Call.   4633

Burton, Harold B. Forty acres on a mountain. *Ad-i-ron-dac*, May–June 1953. 17:48–49, 59. See also letter in July–Aug. issue, 17:82. Acquiring a lot on Big Slide Mountain.   4634

Conway, Tom. The manhunt 102 days long. *Real Detective*, Apr. 1955. vol.W:no.10:52–53, 67–69. illus. The Call case.   4635

Crowningshield, Gerald. Dialect of north-eastern New York. *Am Speech*, Apr. 1933. 8: no.2:43–45.   4636

Dix, William Frederick. Summer life in luxurious Adirondack camps. *Ind*, July 2, 1903. 55:1556–62. illus. Description of some of the more elaborate summer homes and camps in the Adirondacks.   4637

Ellis, Harvey. An Adirondack camp. *Crafts-man*, July 1903. 4:281–84. illus. Working plans and specifications for an ideal summer home in the Adirondacks.   4639

Essex county garden club. The founders' gardens. Baltimore, Md. Waverly press, 1929. 90p. An account of the founding of the Club with brief histories of the founders' gardens. Blank pages provided for photographs.   4640

Essex county home bureau. Out of Essex county kitchens. n.p. 1954. various paging. illus. map. Cookbook.   4641

Ettman, Seymour J. Murder manhunt and the AWOL major. *True Detective*, Mar. 1955. 6:no.5:14–19, 84–86. illus. The Call case.
                                                4642

He robbed shooting camps. *For & Stream*, Feb. 16, 1901. 56:124. Elmer Johnson con-victed of looting closed hunting camps. 4643

Hungerford, Edward. Old houses of our north country. *Country Life*, Apr. 1924. 45: no.6:60–62. illus.   4644

Kellogg, Alice M. Luxurious Adirondack camps. *New Broad M*, Aug. 1908. 21:207–12. illus. Attractive features of the great north woods with a description of some of the more elaborate summer homes.   4645

Lane, David F. North country mansions. *NY Hist*, July 1943. 24:392–404.   4646

"Lawing" in the north woods. *Harper W*, Nov. 18, 1882. 26:725–26. illus.   4647

McDavid, Raven I. Midland and Canadian words in upstate New York. *Am Speech*, Dec. 1951. 26:248–56.   4648

McLellan, Hugh, ed. A centennial history of Champlain lodge, no.237, Free and accepted masons, 1851–1951; including a sketch of Harmony lodge, no.154, 1807–1833. Edited by Hugh McLellan and Charles W. McLellan. Champlain, N.Y. Moorsfield press, 1951. 57p.   4649

Mann, E.R. The bench and bar of Saratoga county; or, Reminiscences of the judiciary, and scenes in the court room, from the organ-ization of the county to the present time. Ballston, N.Y. Waterbury & Inman, 1876. 391p.   4650

North country house for many children: W.E. Clark house at Lake Placid, New York.

Arch Rec, Feb. 1948. 103:106–11. illus. diagrs. plans. Home of the principal of the North Country School.   4651

Platt, Jonas. An address to the Temperance society of the County of Clinton, delivered 26th February, 1833. Published at the re-quest of the Society. Plattsburgh, N.Y. F.P. Allen, 1833. 23p. Copy in Yale University Library.   4652

Porter, Mrs. Marjorie (Lansing). A log cabin speaks: the story of the Adsit cabin near Willsboro and the pioneer family who built it. *No Country Life*, Fall 1955. 9:no.4:22–26.   4653

Proceedings of the Clinton county anti-slavery convention, to which is appended the call of said convention, the Plattsburgh pro-test, and the reply, directed by the conven-tion. Held at Beekmantown, April 25 and 26. Plattsburgh, N.Y. Platt & Blanchard, print-ers, 1837. 31p. Copy in the Henry E. Hunt-ington Library, San Marino, Cal.   4654

Shepard, Augustus D. Camps in the woods . . .with a foreword by Robert W. Chambers; compiled and edited by R.W. Sexton. Illus-trations from original drawings prepared in the office of Mr. Shepard, and from photo-graphs by John Wallace Gillies, inc. N.Y. Architectural book publishing co. inc. c1931. 96p. front. illus. incl. plans.   4655

Smith, Jeanie Oliver. A faith purchase. *Game-land*, June 1897. 11:9–10. A farm between West Canada Creek and Black Creek used as summer home.   4656

Starbuck, Bob. The greatest manhunt. *True Police Cases*, Apr. 1955. 7:no.74:32–34, 66–68. The Call case.   4657

Stow, Gardner. Address, delivered before the Keeseville Temperance society, on the 25th February, 1834. . . Keeseville, N.Y. A. Emons, 1834. 11p. Copy in Harvard University Library.   4658

Summer home of C.C. Parlin in the Adiron-dacks. *House & Gard*, June 1939. 75:supp.12–13. illus. plans.   4659

Teall, Edna West. Essex county life in the 1880's. Mother was an optimist. *No Country Life*, Spring 1954–Winter 1955. 8:no.2:38–40; 8:no.3:55–58; 8:no.4:24–27; 9:no.1:20–21.
                                                4660

Thomas, C.K. Pronunciation in upstate New York. *Am Speech*, Apr. 1935–Apr. 1937. 10: 107–12, 208–12, 292–97; 11:68–77, 142–44; 307–13; 12:122–27.   4661

Tucker, Philip C. Address delivered at the installation of the Ausable river lodge, no.149, at Keeseville, September 28th, 1849. Keese-ville, N.Y. Jon. F. Morgan, 1849. 24p. Copy in Harvard University Library.   4662

Vacation houses. . .summer home and guest cottage at Silver bay, Lake George, N.Y. *Arch Rec*, July 1941. 90:no.1:66–68. illus. plans. 4663

Wack, Henry Wellington. Kamp Kill Kare, the Adirondack home of Hon. Timothy L. Woodruff. *Field & S*, Feb. 1903. 7:651–61. plate, illus. 4664

Water living at Lake Placid. *House & Gard*, Aug. 1949. 96:no.2:30–33, 92–95. illus. (part col.) plans. Island home of Mr. and Mrs. Robert Rose. 4665

The well designed small house can offer urbane comfort and convenience even in an Adirondack lumber camp. *Arch For*, Dec. 1948. 89:no.6:70–72. illus. plans. Located at Sabattis. 4666

Wicks, William S. . . .Log cabins and cottages; how to build and furnish them. 6th ed. N.Y. Forest & stream publishing co. 1908. 47p. plates. Includes many cabins in the Adirondack region. 4667

Wikoff, Climena M. comp. Placid eating. Saranac Lake, N.Y. Currier press, 1954. 122, 6p. Cookbook. 4668

FOLKLORE AND BALLADS

Adirondack Jim, pseud. Signs of a cold winter. *Recreation*, Jan. 1903. 18:31. 4669

Augar, Pearl Hamelin. French beliefs in Clinton county. *NY Folk Q*, Autumn 1948. 4:161–71. 4670

Bancroft, John Randolph. "Ole Joe." *Ad-i-ron-dac*, Jan.–Feb. 1948. 12:no.1:4. See note on p.8. Joe Bolio and his ballads. 4671

Bartlett, Rinda M. The lore of Warren county, New York. . . 54 leaves. Master's thesis, Cornell University, 1943. Typescript. 4672

Benedict, Darwin. Gas on the stomach. *Cloud Splitter*, Jan.–Feb., Mar.–Apr. 1946. 9:no.1: 4–5; 9:no.2:8–9. Folk tales and story about an Adirondack guide. 4673

Betts, Charles E. One night near Indian pass. *Ad-i-ron-dac*, July–Aug. 1951. 15:71. Ghost on a bicycle. 4674

Bisbee, Ernest E. The Empire state scrap book of stories and legends of old New York. Lancaster, N.H. Bisbee press, c1939. 56p. illus. maps. 4675

Boylan, John P. Putting on the dog. *Fort Tel Eng*, June 1948. 9:no.6:19–20. Humorous telephone tales of the Saranac Lake area. 4676

Brown, Gertrude M. Adirondack guide stories. *High Spots*, Oct. 1934, Jan. 1935. 11: no.4:13–16; 12:no.1:22–24. 4677

Brown, Gertrude M. J.P. Brown's fight with wolves. *High Spots*, Oct. 1935. 12:no.4:28–29. 4678

Brown, Gertrude M. Leonard Brown's forest fire. *High Spots*, July 1935. 12:no.3:26–27. 4679

Brown, Gertrude M. Old guide stories. *High Spots*, July 1934, Jan. 1936, July 1936. 11: no.3:27–28; 13:no.1:11; 13:no.2:18–19. 4680

Brown, Gertrude M. Uncle Henry Brown's hunting stories. *High Spots*, Jan. 1937. 14: no.1:24. 4681

Burnham, John Bird. Echoes of the New York show. *For & Stream*, Apr. 7, 1900. 54: 265. In his column "Game Bag" Burnham tells some Adirondack tales. 4682

Burnham, John Bird. Told at the sportsmen's show. *For & Stream*, Mar. 17, 1900. 54:206–7. Panthers near Mt. Seward and other Adirondack tales. 4683

Burr, C.G. A camp fire yarn. *Field & S*, May 1911. 16:86–87. 4684

Chamberlain, Mary E. Folk-lore from northern New York. *J Am Folk-Lore*, Oct.–Dec. 1892. 5:336–37. Brief note about superstitions. 4685

Clark, Theobald. Treasure roundup. *No Country Life*, Spring, Summer, Fall 1950, Winter 1951. 4:no.2:44–45; 4:no.3:55–56; 4:no.4:34–35; 5:no.1:40–42. First article includes the story of Scott's silver mine as told in Street's "Indian Pass"; second article is on buried treasure at North Canada Creek; third account has title: "Vanishing Treasure of Lake Pleasant"; the fourth article is on legend of silver mines near Pharaoh Mountain. 4686

Corson, R.H. One day in the Adirondacks: A Jud Smith story, by Switch Reel, pseud. *For & Stream*, Feb. 1915. 84:86–87. illus. 4687

Cutting, Edith E. Lore of an Adirondack county. Ithaca, N.Y. Cornell university press, 1944. 86p. (Cornell University Studies in American History, Literature, and Folklore, 1.) Extract in *North Country Life*, Spring 1948, 2:no.2:28–30, with title "Some Tall Tales from the Up-histed Country." 4688

Cutting, Edith E. Peter Parrott and his songs. *NY Folk Q*, Summer 1947. 3:124–33. 4689

Cutting, Edith E. A York state songbag: the Douglas Stevens manuscript. *NY Folk Q*, Autumn 1948. 4:172–81. Describes a manuscript of 89 songs current in northern New York, 1843–56. 4690

Dailey, William Nelson Potter. Fireside legends of the Adirondack. *No Country Life*, Summer 1951. 5:no.3:28–30. 4691

Daring exploits and perilous adventures... Hartford, Conn. Ezra Strong, 1843. 504p. plates. Joe Call, the modern Hercules, p.128–33.   4692

Dorr, Henry Gustavus. Mohawk Peter; legends of the Adirondacks, and Civil war memories; illustrations by Nellie L. Thompson. Boston, Cornhill publishing co. c1921. 275p. front. plates.   4693

Dorson, Richard M. Yorker yarns of yore. *NY Folk Q*, Spring 1947. 3:5–27. "A Marvelous Hunting Story," p.23–27, takes place near Ampersand.   4694

Dunham, Harvey Leslie. French Louie. *NY Folk Q*, Aug. 1946. 2:182–90. Louis Seymour.   4695

Dunn, Adda Ann. Songs, riddles and tales of Saratoga county. *NY Folk Q*, Autumn 1949. 5:211–19. Collected in Hadley and Conklingville.   4696

Eames, Frank. Landon's ould dog and Hogmanay fair. *NY Folk Q*, Autumn 1947. 3:248–51.   4697

Extracts from "Gelyna" ("The Talisman," N.Y. 1830). *Ft Ti Mus Bul*, Winter 1950. 8:179–89. Legend about Gelyna Vandyke and Major Edward Rutledge. Battle of Ticonderoga (Abercrombie expedition).   4698

Flanders, Mrs. Helen (Hartness). "Blue mountain lake" and "Barbara Allen." *NY Folk Q*, Winter 1946. 2:52–58.   4699

Flint, Peter. Madame Liberté's winter buck, a Boreas river legend. *For & Stream*, Nov. 28, 1914. 83:709.   4700

Flint, Peter. Uncle Oliver and the moose; an Adirondack story. *For & Stream*, Mar. 11, 1899. 52:183. A story of the year 1845.   4701

Fowler, Barnett. Adirondack liar. *NYS Con*, Aug.–Sept. 1948. 3:no.1:6. Cyrus Brown, tall tales of Adirondacks.   4702

Franz, Eleanor Waterbury. Folklore trails in Herkimer county. *No Country Life*, Summer 1949. 3:no.3:15–17. Includes Nat Foster and Chester Gillette case.   4703

Gray, R.P. Balladry of New York state. *NY Hist*, Apr. 1936. 34:147–55.   4704

Hudowalski, Mrs. Grace (Leech). Greater love. *Cloud Splitter*, Oct. 1939. 2:no.5:11. Folk tale of early Adirondack settlers.   4705

Hudowalski, Mrs. Grace (Leech). Keep smiling. *Cloud Splitter*, Jan. 1941. 4:no.1:6. Legend concerning sign on Faxon's Pond, Chestertown.   4706

Hudowalski, Mrs. Grace (Leech). Legendary silver. *Cloud Splitter*, Nov. 1939. 2:no.6:7–8. Legend about silver on Nye Mountain.   4707

Hudowalski, Mrs. Grace (Leech). So 'tis said. *Ad-i-ron-dac*, Jan.–Feb. 1950. 9:11. Reprinted in *North Country Life*, Summer 1950, 4:no.3:9, with title "A Legend of Pitch-off Mountain Pass." The tinker drowned in Cascade Lakes.   4708

Hudowalski, Mrs. Grace (Leech). Tinker's cascade. *Cloud Splitter*. Oct. 1940. 3:no.6:4. Legend about the Cascade Lakes.   4709

Judge Brewster's tales of Essex county. Told to Mrs. Barbara Way Hunter. *NY Folk Q*, Winter 1954. 10:298–307. O. Byron Brewster.   4710

Kaiser, Robert A. Lumberman's ballad "Shannel's mill." *NY Folk Q*, Summer 1955. 11:133–35.   4711

Kaplan, Israel. A John Brown ballad. *NY Folk Q*, Spring 1953. 9:37–50.   4712

Karpeles, Maud. Square dance figures from northern New York. *Eng Folk Dance Soc*, 1931. ser.2:no.4:9–13. First five figures noted with assistance of Marjorie Sinclair at Schroon Lake.   4713

Knowles, Archibald Campbell. Balsam boughs, being Adirondack and other stories. Philadelphia, Porter & Coates, 1893. 200p. plates. Includes legend of Heart Lake.   4714

Lavin, Mrs. Barbara Hofheins. Cranberry again. *NY Folk Q*, Summer 1955. 11:128–31. Supplements Manley's "Lore of Cranberry Lake" in Summer 1954 issue.   4715

McDavid, Raven I. Folk vocabulary of New York state. *NY Folk Q*, Autumn 1951. 7:173–92. Includes some material from the north country.   4716

MacDougal, Harry M. 'Ren Dow and the devil. *NY Folk Q*, Autumn 1947. 3:237–42.   4717

Manley, Atwood. Lore of Cranberry lake, Adirondacks. *NY Folk Q*, Summer 1954. 10:111–14.   4718

Mills, Borden H. Sr. Moonshine and deer stalking don't mix. *Cloud Splitter*, Sept.–Oct. 1946. 9:no.5:7.   4719

O'Hora, Edgar B. Si Brown and Big Dick; a couple of boys from New York state. *NY Folk Q*, Aug. 1946. 2:209–12. Indian Lake country.   4720

Porter, Mrs. Marjorie (Lansing). Archives. The Porter north-country collection of lore and ballads. *NY Folk Q*, Spring 1953. 9:56–58. See also "Across the Editor's Desk" in *North Country Life*, Spring 1953. 7:no.2:52–53.   4721

Porter, Mrs. Marjorie (Lansing). Them as can—sings. *Ad-i-ron-dac*, Nov.–Dec. 1947. 11:no.6:15. Folklore and ballads collected by Mrs. Porter.   4722

Porter, Mrs. Marjorie (Lansing). The woods are full of 'em. *Ad-i-ron-dac*, Sept.–Oct. 1947. 11:no.5:6–7. port. Mrs. Lily Delorme's ballads. 4723

The sea serpent up a tree in the "north woods" of New York. *Am Angler*, Aug. 4, 1883. 4:68–69. illus. Humorous tale of Bisby. 4724

Shorey, Archibald Thompson. Adirondackana. *Cloud Splitter*, Feb. 1943. 6:no.2:2–3. Some Adirondack lore and quaint expressions. 4725

Shorey, Archibald Thompson. A grace from the north country. *NY Folk Q*, Spring 1954. 10:47. Keeseville farmer's yearly grace (verse). 4726

Shorey, Archibald Thompson. Mr. Glasbrouck's bears. *Ad-i-ron-dac*, May–June 1950. 14:67. illus. 4727

Skinner, Charles Montgomery. Myths and legends of our own land. Philadelphia, J.B. Lippincott, 1896. 2v. plates. Adirondacks and Lake George, 1:80–92. 4728

Smithling, Genevieve. "A Black river thaw." *NY Folk Q*, May 1945. 1:107–9. A ballad. 4729

T., C. McV. "Old Joe Call." *For & Stream*, Nov. 15, 1883. 21:303. Resident of Jay. 4730

Thompson, Harold William. Body, boots & britches. Philadelphia, J.B. Lippincott, 1940. 530p. Folk songs and tales of many people and places in the Adirondack area. Mountaineers, Ch.12. "Mart Moody and His Adirondack Buck" reprinted in *North Country Life*, Summer 1947, 1:no.3:41–42. 4731

Warner, Anne and Warner, Frank. Songs: "Brave Wolfe." *NY Folk Q*, Summer 1954. 10:151–52. Version sung by "Yankee John" Galusha. 4732

Wheeler, Mrs. Ann (King). Ballads and tales of Blue mt. lake, Adirondacks. *NY Folk Q*, Summer 1954. 10:115–22. 4733

Witthoft, John. A snake tale from northern New York. *NY Folk Q*, Summer 1947. 3:134–37. Setting is near Cranberry Lake. 4734

Younker, Ira M. Another north country tale from Judge Brewster. *NY Folk Q*, Summer 1955. 11:132. O. Byron Brewster. 4735

PRINTING AND PUBLISHING

Hill, William Henry. A brief history of the printing press in Washington, Saratoga and Warren counties, State of New York. With a check list of their publications prior to 1825 and a selection of books relating particularly to this vicinity. Fort Edward, N.Y. Tory press, 1930. 117p. front. 4736

Porter, Mrs. Marjorie (Lansing). Essex and Clinton county newspapers of an earlier day. *No Country Life*, Winter–Summer 1950. 4: no.1:23–24; 4:no.2:35–36; 4:no.3:52–54. 4737

Veritas, pseud. Journalism in Washington county. Salem, N.Y.? 1887–1894. v.p. 5 broadside reprints from the *Salem Review-Press*, probably by James Gibson. The Gibson papers are described in W.H. Hill's "History of Washington County" (no.660). Broadsides in the Crandall Public Library, Glens Falls. 4738

PERIODICALS RELATING TO THE ADIRONDACKS

The Ad-i-ron-dac, *see* no.6507.

The Adirondack enterprise. Special magazine section. Saranac Lake, N.Y. Kenneth W. Goldthwaite, 1910? 32p. illus. Contents: The charm of Adirondack days, p.5–8; Incidents of Adirondack camping, by E.S. Whitaker, p.9–11; Sending messages from Whiteface, p.12–13; Fly casting on an Adirondack stream, by E.F.R., p.13; An open camp in the Adirondacks, by K.S. and F.F., p.14–15; Saranac Lake, p.20–22; Capturing beaver for release in the Adirondacks, by H.S. Hofer, p.22, 31; His first deer, by D.E.P., p.26–28. Copy in the Saranac Lake Free Library. 4739

The Adirondack enterprise. Souvenir edition. Saranac Lake, N.Y. 1889. 11p. illus. Contents: The Pontiac Club carnival, Saranac Lake, N.Y. 1898: a complete history of that most superb winter fete; The fancy dress carnival; Storming of the ice fortress; The carnival from an artistic standpoint; The economic value of the carnival, etc. Description of the first winter carnival at Saranac Lake. Copy in the Saranac Lake Free Library. 4740

The Adirondack mountain club. Bulletin, *see* no.6510.

American forests. v.1–Jan.? 1895– Princeton, N.J. 1895–97; Washington, American forestry association, 1898–date. Monthly (v.1–2 bimonthly). Title varies: Jan.?–Mar.? 1895, New Jersey Forests; Apr.? 1895–Dec. 1901, The Forester; Jan. 1902–Aug. 1908, Forestry and Irrigation. 4741

The Cloud splitter, *see* no. 6541.

The Conservationist. v.1–4. Jan. 1917–Dec. 1921. Albany, 1917–21. 4v. Monthly; published by the New York State Conservation Commission. Suspended Aug. 1917–July 1918.   4742

Cornell forester. v.1–6. June 1920–May 1926. Ithaca, N.Y. Cornell university, 1920–26. 6v. Annual published by undergraduate forestry students at Cornell.   4743

Empire forester; edited by the students of the New York state college of forestry. v.1– Jan. 1915– Syracuse, N.Y. Syracuse university, 1915– Published annually at the College of Forestry, Syracuse.   4744

Forest leaves. v.1–28, no.2. Dec. 1903–Dec. 1934. Gabriels, N.Y. Sanitarium Gabriels, 1903–34? 28v. Quarterly. The early issues contain many articles on the Adirondacks.
4745

The Forest preserve, and supplements, *see* nos.1833, 1850, 1890, 1966.

High spots and High spots yearbook, *see* nos.6546, 6547.

High spots bulletin, *see* no.6513.

Journal of the outdoor life. v.1–32, no.12. Feb. 1904–Dec. 1935. Saranac Lake, N.Y. National tuberculosis association, 1904–35. 32v. Monthly. Title varies: Outdoor Life, 1904–Jan. 1905.   4746

Lake Placid life. N.Y. Clayton E. Brooke, 193—? Issue for Winter 1930–31 (56p.) in Saranac Lake Free Library; issues for Jan., Feb., and Mar. 1931 in Hicks Collection, Lake Placid Club.   4747

The Living wilderness. v.1, no.1– Sept. 1935– Washington, Wilderness society, 1935–date. Quarterly since 1945.   4748

Lumber camp news. v.1–14. May 1939–June 1952. Old Forge, N.Y. 1939–52. 14v. Monthly. Three experimental issues preceded regular publication. Merged into Northeastern Logger, July 1952.   4749

Moorsfield antiquarian. v.1–2. May 1937–Feb. 1939. Champlain, N.Y. Moorsfield press, 1937–39. 2v. illus. facsims. Quarterly. Edited by Hugh McLellan and C.W. McLellan.   4750

New York (state). State university. College of forestry, Syracuse. Bulletin, no.1– 1913– Syracuse, N.Y. 1913–date.   4751

New York (state). State university. College of forestry, Syracuse. Circular, no.1–60. 1912–29. Syracuse, N.Y. 1912–29. Nos. 48–50, 52–59, not published.   4752

New York (state). State university. College of forestry, Syracuse. Technical bulletin, no.1– 1914– Syracuse, N.Y. 1914–date.   4753

New York (state). State university. College of forestry, Syracuse. Roosevelt wildlife forest experiment station. . . .Roosevelt wildlife annals. v.1–4, no.2. Oct. 1926–May 1936. Syracuse, N.Y. 1926–36. 4v. "Papers of a more technical nature or having less widespread interest than the Bulletins."   4754

New York (state). State university. College of forestry, Syracuse. Roosevelt wildlife forest experiment station. Roosevelt wildlife bulletin, v.1, no.1– Dec. 1921– Syracuse, N.Y. 1921–date. "Papers of technical nature dealing with the various phases of forest wildlife, its management and conservation."   4755

New York conservationist. v.1, no.1– 1923– Lockport, N.Y. New York conservation association, 1923–date. V.1, no.1–v.6, no.11, 1923–Apr. 1928, issued as Grouse and New York Conservationist.   4756

The New York forester. v.1, no.1– Apr. 1944– Syracuse, N.Y. 1944–date. Newsletter published by the New York Section of the Society of American Foresters, Syracuse. Bimonthly, v.1–2; quarterly, v.3–date. Processed.   4757

New York forestry. v.1–9, no.3, v.10, no.1–2. June 1914–Oct. 1923, 1925–27, Jan.–June 1930. N.Y. New York state forestry association, 1914–30. 13v.? Title varies: issued in 1914 as the Association's Bulletin; Oct. 1915–Oct. 1916 as its Journal; 1924–27 as its Yearbook. 1928–29 not published. Merged into New York Conservationist.   4758

New York state conservationist. v.1, no.1– Aug.–Sept. 1946– Albany, New York state conservation department, 1946–date. Bimonthly.   4759

North country life. v.1, no.1– Fall 1946– Ogdensburg, N.Y. 1946–date. Quarterly.
4760

Northeastern logger. v.1, no.1– July 1952– Old Forge, N.Y. 1952–date. illus. Monthly. Succeeds Lumber Camp News.   4761

Outing; sport, adventure, travel, fiction. v.1–82, no.1. May 1882–Apr. 1923. Albany, N.Y. 1882–1923. 82v. Monthly. Title varies.
4762

The Pine log. Saranac Lake, N.Y. Harold Van Wert ed. and pub. 1924–? Published monthly. Only two issues located (v.1, no.2, Aug. 1924 and v.2, no.2, Mar. 1925).   4763

The Reveille: Essex county historical society quarterly. v.1, no.1– Mar. 1955–date. Elizabethtown, N.Y. 1955–date.   4764

Saranac Lake rehabilitation guild, inc. Guild news, *see* no.4938.

Stoddard's Northern monthly. v.1–4, no.3. May 1906–Sept. 1908. Glens Falls, N.Y. S.R. Stoddard, 1906–8. 4v. July–Sept. 1908 issues have title Stoddard's Adirondack Monthly. Issue for June 1908 not published. 4765

Tahawus cloudsplitter; published monthly by the MacIntyre development of Titanium division, National lead company. v.1, no.1– Dec. 1949– Tahawus, N.Y. 1949–date. illus. ports. 4766

Ticonderoga, Fort. Museum. Bulletin. v.1, no.1– Jan. 1927– Fort Ticonderoga-on-Lake Champlain, N.Y. 1927–date. illus. ports. facsims. maps. Usually published twice a year. No.1 has title: The Haversack. V.3, no.2 (serial no.14) and v.5, no.2 (serial no.27) incorrectly numbered, no.13 and 26 respectively. 4767

Top o' the world news: the Washington, Essex and Warren counties magazine. v.1, no.1–v.3, no.3. Nov. 1936–Apr. 1939. Lake George, N.Y. and Glens Falls, N.Y. Top o' the world mills, 1936–39. illus. Monthly. Incomplete file at Crandall Library, Glens Falls. 4768

Up-stater: devoted to the welfare of northern and western New York. v.1–3, no.2. Jan. 1929–May 1931. Boonville, N.Y.; Watertown, N.Y. New York development association, 1929–31. 3v. Bimonthly. Subtitle varies. 4769

Upstate monthly. v.1, no.1– Apr. 1940– Utica, N.Y. 1940–date. Title of v.3, no.7, is The Upstate. Suspended publication with Dec. 1942/Jan. 1943 issue, v.3, no.7. 4770

Woods and waters. v.1–8, no.4. 1898–1905/6. N.Y. 1898–1906. Quarterly. Edited by Harry V. Radford. Donaldson (v.2, p.309) says: "The only magazine ever devoted exclusively to the Adirondacks..." V.1 and v.2 not located. "Verplanck Colvin's opinion of Woods and Waters" in issue for Spring 1902, 5:no.1:13. 4771

NEWSPAPER COLUMNS ON THE ADIRONDACKS

ADK corner. In the Saranac Lake *Adirondack Enterprise*, Summer 1953–date. Weekly, on Mondays or Tuesdays. Edited by Peter A. Ward through June 1954, by P. Fay Loope, Feb. 21, 1955–date. Suspended July 1954– Jan. 1955. 4772

The Footpath. In Sunday issues of the Albany *Times-Union*, 1945–48. Published by the Albany chapter of the Adirondack Mountain Club. Editor: 1945, Frances (Boone) Seaman; 1946–48, Darwin Benedict. 4773

The Footpath: a column devoted to the Adirondack Mountain Club; edited by Russell M.L. Carson. In the Glens-Falls *Post-Star*, July 6, 1928–June 4, 1929. Weekly. Also in the Lake Placid *News* and the Plattsburgh *Daily Republican*. Valuable for Adirondack history. 4774

The Long brown path; edited by Raymond H. Torrey. In the New York *Post*, 1920–38. This column, which appeared as a full page every Friday in the 20's and in shorter form on Tuesdays and Fridays in the early 30's, in 1934 became a daily single column. It is an invaluable source for Adirondackana. 4775

Woods & waters. A weekly column by Paul Schaefer. In the Schenectady *Gazette*, Mar. 9, 1934–Apr. 12, 1935. 4776

HEALTH AND MEDICINE

GENERAL

The Adirondack wilderness. The great forest park of the State of New York, in a sanitary point of view. *Sanitarian*, Sept. 1873. 1:241–52. map. 4777

Ash, Robert Henry. A recipe for rest that one doctor prescribes. *NYC Lines Mag*, June 1920. 1:no.3:35. Air, sun and pines in the Adirondacks sure to improve health. 4778

Baldwin, Edward Robinson. Gift of philanthropy to science; the Saranac laboratory for the study of tuberculosis. *Sci Am*, Mar. 6, 1897. 76:152–54. 4779

Baldwin, Edward Robinson. The historical development of tuberculosis prevention in America with special reference to New York state. *NY State Hist Assn Q*, Oct. 1923. 4: 234–40. 4780

Baldwin, Edward Robinson. Review of theoretical considerations and experimental work relative to opsonins with observations at the Saranac laboratory. *NY Med J*, June 27, 1908. 89:1227. 4781

Baldwin, Edward Robinson. Some results of the climatic and sanatorium treatment of tuberculosis in the Adirondacks. *Alb Med Ann*, 1900. 21:213–17. 4782

Bell, John. Note on Adirondack mineral water. *Med Times*, Jan. 16, 1871. 1:144–45. Therapeutic qualities of Whitehall spring. 4783

Bell, John. Observations on the Adirondack mineral spring. *Med Rec*, Mar. 1, 1870. 5:33–34. Discovered in 1868 in the village of Whitehall. 4784

Biggs, Hermann Michael. An Adirondack tent house. *J Outd Life*, Apr. 1905. 2:65–67. illus. Tent for tuberculosis patients. 4785

Bruen, Edward T. The southern Adirondacks. *Am Clin & Climat Assn Tr*, 1886. 3: 202–8. Also in *New York Medical Journal*, July 3, 1886, 44:1–3. Beneficial effects of climate at Blue Mountain Lake. Reprinted in Hochschild, H.K. Township 34, N.Y. 1952, p.525–30. 4786

C., E.H. The Adirondack tooth carpenter, a drawing from nature. *For & Stream*, Apr. 9,

1874. 2:132. Dental extraction by a guide. 4787

Clemens, Samuel Langhorne. Mark Twain on the Adirondacks, an extract from a letter to a personal friend in New York city. *Four Tr News*, Sept. 1902. 3:109. facsim. Therapeutic effect of the Adirondacks. 4788

Cook, Marc. Camp Lou. *Harper*, May 1881. 62:865–76. Life of consumptive in the Adirondacks. 4789

Cook, Marc. The wilderness cure. N.Y. Wood, 1881. 153p. 4790

Corliss, Hiram. Brief notices of the medical topography and diseases of Washington county. *Med Soc SNY Tr*, 1850. p.225–29. 4791

Dayton, Roy. Inauguration of the Edward L. Trudeau foundation and the Trudeau school of tuberculosis. *Am Rev Tub*, July 1950. 62: no.1B:104–19. port. School and Foundation among the accomplishments of Dr. Edward R. Baldwin. Bibliography of the writings of Dr. Baldwin. 4792

Early Essex county medicine. *NY State Hist Assn Bul*, May 1945. 13:6–8. 4793

The great white plague. *St No Mo*, Mar. 1908. 3:142–44. 4794

Hewat, Andrew Fergus. Tuberculosis in United States. A visit to Saranac Lake. *Edin Med J*, Mar. 1927. 34:136–48. 4795

Hospital for Saranac Lake. *Outdoor Life*, Apr. 1904. 1:20. illus. plan. Projected tuberculosis hospital. 4796

Lathrop, John E. Back to life. *Colliers*, May 24, 1913. 51:no.10:5–6, 32–34. illus. Taking the cure at Saranac. 4797

A list of periodical medical literature available in the village of Saranac Lake, N.Y. n.p. n.pub. 1915. 10p. Unpaged leaflet. Probably compiled by Lawrason Brown. Copy in the Saranac Lake Free Library. 4798

Long, Esmond Ray. The concept of resistance to tuberculosis with special reference to the contributions of Edward R. Baldwin. *Am Rev Tub*, July 1950. 62:no.1B:3–12. Includes bibliography. 4799

Loomis, Alfred L. The Adirondack region as a therapeutical agent in the treatment of pulmonary phthisis. *Med Rec*, Apr. 26–May 3, 1879. 15:385–89, 409–12.   4800

Medical society of the county of Clinton. Constitution & by-laws, list of members, officers & brief account of its early history. Plattsburgh, N.Y. J.W. Tuttle, 1904. 22p.   4801

Milne, Rev. A.D. The woman that lives without eating, being an authentic narrative of Mrs. Simeon Hays, of Chester, Warren co. N.Y. Glens Falls, N.Y. Messenger book & job office, 1858. 47p. Copy in Yale University Library.   4802

New York (state). Health, Department of. Division of public health education. Ragweed pollen surveys. Old Forge, N.Y. Central Adirondack association, inc. n.d. 8p. illus. tables. Summary of surveys through 1944. Includes Adirondack areas.   4803

North, Charles Edward. An investigation of recent outbreaks of typhoid fever in an Adirondack camp, and the discovery of a typhoid carrier. *Med Rec*, Mar. 25, 1911. 79:517–23. diagrs. Reprinted in Hochschild, H.K. Township 34, N.Y. 1952, p.549–55.   4804

The outdoor life. *St No Mo*, Mar. 1908. 3: 140–42. Editorial on tuberculosis.   4805

Powell, Horatio. An account of the diseases prevalent in Clinton county, New-York, during 1807. *Med Rep*, Aug.–Oct. 1809. Hexade 2:no.6:347–50. Read before the State Medical Society.   4806

Prescott house; the transfer of Prescott house gives Saranac Lake the opportunity for leadership in the field of rehabilitation. *No Country Life*, Summer 1950. 4:no.3:30–31. illus. Under the auspices of the Saranac Lake Study and Craft Guild.   4807

Reben, Martha, pseud. (Rebentisch, Martha Ruth). The healing woods; with decorations by Fred Collins. N.Y. Crowell, c1952. 250p. illus. map on lining paper. Reviewed by W.H. Burger in *The Ad-i-ron-dac*, Nov.–Dec. 1952, 16:111–12; by Helen Hyden in *North Country Life*, Fall 1952, 6:no.4:55–57; by Rockwell Kent in *Living Wilderness*, Spring 1952, no. 40:20–21. Extract entitled: A "Robinson Crusoe" Experience on Weller Pond, in *North Country Life*, Fall 1952, 6:no.4:12–16.   4808

Reben, Martha, pseud. (Rebentisch, Martha Ruth). The way of the wilderness. N.Y. Crowell, 1955. 276p. illus. Sequel to "The Healing Woods."   4809

Ryan, Edmund. The cure at Saranac. *Bookm*, Aug. 1904. 19:580–82.   4810

Saranac laboratory for the study of tuberculosis. Tuberculosis in industry; report of the symposium held June 9–14, 1941 sponsored by the Trudeau school of tuberculosis. Editor Leroy U. Gardner, M.D. N.Y. National tuberculosis association, c1942. 374p. illus. tables, charts.   4811

Saranac Lake, N.Y. Board of trustees. . . . Regain your health in air conditioned by nature. Saranac Lake in the Adirondacks. n.p. n.pub. n.d. 40p. illus. At head of title: Pioneer health resort.   4812

Saranac Lake medical facilities, inc. The health services of Saranac Lake, New York. Saranac Lake, N.Y. 1952. 4p. Unpaged leaflet. Also an edition in Spanish entitled: Las Facilidades Médicas de Saranac Lake, N.Y.   4813

Saranac Lake medical facilities, inc. Saranac Lake, New York. The health center in the Adirondacks. Saranac Lake, N.Y. 1952. 12p. illus. Unpaged leaflet. Also an edition in Spanish entitled: Saranac Lake, Nueva York, E.U. de A. El Centro de Salud en las Montañas Adirondack.   4814

Saranac Lake medical facilities, inc. Saranac Lake en las montañas Adirondacks. . . renombrado centro curativo. Saranac Lake, N.Y. 1952. 16p. port. illus. Unpaged leaflet. Text in Spanish.   4815

Saranac Lake rehabilitation guild. Rehabilitation routes: the picture story of the Saranac Lake rehabilitation guild. . . Saranac Lake, N.Y. 1952. 24p. illus. Unpaged leaflet.   4816

Saranac Lake society for the control of tuberculosis, incorporated. Annual report, 1– Saranac Lake, N.Y. 1907–date. Reports located for 1909, 1910, 1914–16, 1919–21, 1923–30, 1932–33, 1936–49.   4817

Shoemaker, G.E. The Adirondacks as a health resort. *Med & Surg Rep*, July 31, 1886. 55:129–32.   4818

Simpson, William. Adirondack camp-fire. *For & Stream*, Feb. 8, 1913. 80:165–66, 187. illus. Sojourn at various resorts near Saranac to regain health.   4819

Smith, Isabel. Wish I might. Foreword by Edward Streeter; preface by Dr. Francis B. Trudeau. Decorations by Mercedes Herold. N.Y. Harper, c1955. 234p. illus.   4820

Stearns, William F. Coordinated planning in the community. *Am J Pub Health*, June 1954. 44:747–49. Saranac Lake Rehabilitation Guild, formerly the Saranac Lake Study and Craft Guild.   4821

Stickler, Joseph William. The Adirondacks as a health resort. Showing the benefit to be

derived by a sojourn in the wilderness. . .
N.Y. Putnam, 1886. 198p.　　　　4822

Todd, William S. The Adirondacks; a resort for health and recreation. *Conn Med Soc Proc*, 1887. 3:87–94. Read before the Fairfield County Association. Raquette Lake.　4823

Trudeau, Edward Livingston. The history and work of the Saranac laboratory for the study of tuberculosis. *Johns Hop Hosp Bul*, Sept. 1901. 12:271–75. plates. Contains list of the author's writings. Also issued as a reprint, illustrated.　　　　　　　4824

Trudeau, Edward Livingston. The history of the tuberculosis work at Saranac Lake. *Med News*, Oct. 24, 1903. 83:769–80. illus.
　　　　　　　　　　　　　　　4825

Trudeau school of tuberculosis, Saranac Lake, N.Y. Prospectus of course of study. Saranac Lake, N.Y. 1916. 16p. illus.　　4826

Wardner, LeRoy H. Adirondack medicine. A historical outline. *NY State J Med*, Apr. 15, 1942. 42:794–98. Also issued as reprint. Extracts in *North Country Life*, Fall 1949, 4: no.4:7–8, 59–62.　　　　　　4827

Washington County, N.Y. Health preparedness commission. Health and medical care, Washington county, N.Y. A study of resources and needs for health and medical care in Washington county, N.Y. Albany, New York state health and preparedness commission, 1944. 41p. illus.　　4828

Williams, Helena V. Curing tuberculosis at Saranac; annual sale of Christmas seals soon to begin a reminder of the great work being done at the sanatorium founded by Dr. Trudeau. *State Service*, Sept.–Oct. 1922. 6,i.e.8: 306–8. illus.　　　　　　　4829

HOSPITALS AND SANATORIA

THE ADIRONDACK COTTAGE SANITARIUM
(TRUDEAU)

At work in Dr. Trudeau's memorial. *Survey*, July 8, 1916. 36:393–94. illus.　　4830

Baldwin, Edward Robinson. Dr. Trudeau's visible monument. The Adirondack cottage sanitarium. *J Outd Life*, June 1910. 7:165–69. illus.　　　　　　　　　　4831

Baldwin, Edward Robinson. The Trudeau sanatorium anniversary, forty years of continuous progress. *J Outd Life*, Jan. 1925. 22: 7–10. illus.　　　　　　　　　4832

Brown, Lawrason. An analysis of 1500 cases of tuberculosis discharged from the Adirondack cottage sanitarium from two to eighteen years ago. *Am Med Assn J*, Nov. 21, 1903. 41:1268–72. charts.　　　　　4833

Brown, Lawrason and Allen, A.H. A brief study of a diphtheria epidemic at the Adirondack cottage sanitarium. . . *Am J Med Sci*, Feb. 1907. 133:297–302.　　4834

Brown, Lawrason and Heise, Fred H. The effect of six weeks' bed rest upon patients entering Trudeau sanatorium. Reprinted from *American Review of Tuberculosis*, Dec. 1922, 6:926–28, table.　　　　4835

Brown, Lawrason. A study of the cases of pulmonary tuberculosis treated with tuberculin at the Adirondack cottage sanitarium. Leipzig, Barth, 1904. p.235–334. tables. Reprinted from *Zeitschrift für Tuberkulose und Heilstättenwesen*, 1904, 4:no.4.　　4836

Brown, Lawrason and Heise, Fred H. . . .A study of two hundred and sixty-four cases admitted to the Trudeau sanatorium. . . n.p. n.d. 7p. Reprinted from the *Transactions* of the Association of American Physicians, 1924.
　　　　　　　　　　　　　　　4837

Brown, Lawrason. The ultimate results of sanatorium treatment. Reprinted from the *Transactions* of the Sixth International Congress on Tuberculosis, 1908, p.927–37, charts.
　　　　　　　　　　　　　　　4838

Brown, Lawrason and Pope, E.G. The ultimate test of the sanatorium treatment of pulmonary tuberculosis and its application to the results obtained in the Adirondack cottage sanitarium. *Z Tub*, 1908. 12:no.3:206–15. tables.　　　　　　　　4839

Brown, Lawrason and Heise, Fred H. The value of the Trudeau sanatorium's five diagnostic criteria of pulmonary tuberculosis in negative diagnoses. . . Reprinted from *American Review of Tuberculosis*, July 1924, 9: 398–405, table.　　　　　　　4840

Cole, Elizabeth. Fifty years at Trudeau sanatorium. An historical sketch in honor of its birthday. Trudeau, N.Y. Currier press, 1935. 68p. ports. illus. Cover title.　　4841

Dahme, Johanna A.M. Trudeau sanitarium. *Med J & Rec*, Aug. 17, 1927. 126:250–55. illus. port.　　　　　　　　4842

Deavitt. George's letters home, by George Bumlong, pseud. Saranac Lake, N.Y. 1903. 24p. Author's name supplied by Munson.

Copy in the Munson Collection, Saranac Lake Free Library. Letters written from Trudeau. 4843

DeWitt, Francis. The how to get well book, by a former patient of the Adirondack cottage sanitarium. Saranac Lake, N.Y. Riverside publishing co. 1906. 78p. Copy in the Saranac Lake Free Library. 4844

Dr. Trudeau honored. *Outlook*, Feb. 26, 1910. 94:420–22. Twenty-fifth anniversary of Trudeau Sanatorium. 4845

The founder's aides. *J Outd Life*, Jan. 1925. 22:47–52. illus. Brief descriptions of persons who helped make Trudeau Sanatorium a success. 4846

Heise, Fred H. and Brown, Lawrason. The present condition of patients discharged from the Trudeau sanatorium. London, John Bale, 1925. 7p. Reprinted from *Tubercle*, Feb. 1925. 4847

Heise, Fred H. and Brown, Lawrason. A study of the occurrence of hemoptysis, pleurisy, râles, tubercle bacilli and x-ray findings in 1000 consecutive cases admitted to the Trudeau sanatorium. Reprinted from *American Review of Tuberculosis*, Feb. 1923, 6:1078–83, tables. 4848

Lyman, David Russell. The influence of Dr. Trudeau on the sanatorium movement. *J Outd Life*, Jan. 1925. 22:28–31. illus. 4849

Mabie, Hamilton Wright. Dr. Edward L. Trudeau. *Am Mag*, June 1910. 70:181–82. port. Twenty-fifth anniversary of founding of Adirondack Cottage Sanitarium by Dr. Trudeau. 4850

Miller, Roland B. Trudeau. *NYS Con*, Feb.–Mar. 1955. 9:no.4:33. illus. Closing of the sanitarium. See also "Beginning of the End" in *Time*, Dec. 6, 1954, 64:no.23:66. 4851

O'Hare, Frank A. Trudeau rifle club—how patients of the Adirondack cottage sanitarium pass many pleasant and healthful hours. *J Outd Life*, Sept. 1907. 4:293. 4852

Trudeau, Edward Livingston. The Adirondack cottage sanitarium. *In* New York (state). Fisheries, game and forest commission. 4th annual report, 1898. p.348–53. plates. Preceded by a two-page article: "Sanitary Benefits of the Adirondack Forest." 4853

Trudeau, Edward Livingston. The Adirondack cottage sanitarium for the treatment of incipient pulmonary tuberculosis. *Practitioner*, Feb. 1899. 62:131–46. illus. 4854

Trudeau, Edward Livingston. A brief retrospect. *J Outd Life*, Feb. 1905. 2:12–13. Signed: E.L.T. Short history of the Adirondack Cottage Sanitarium. 4855

Trudeau, Edward Livingston. The first people's sanitarium in America for the treatment of pulmonary tuberculosis. *Z Tub*, 1900. 1:no.3:230–40. 4856

Trudeau sanatorium. Adirondack cottage sanitarium. Twenty-fifth anniversary. 1885 ...1910. .. Troy, N.Y. Troy times art press, 1910? 24p. ports. illus. Unpaged leaflet. 4857

Trudeau sanatorium. Annual report. Saranac Lake, N.Y. 1886–1951. The last annual report was issued Sept. 30, 1951. The "Studies of the Edward L. Trudeau Foundation" were published with the annual report. Original name: Adirondack Cottage Sanitarium. The Sanatorium also issued a Newsletter, the last number in 1950. 4858

Trudeau sanatorium. The house that Trudeau built: an illustrated souvenir... Trudeau, N.Y. 1928. 74p. front. port. illus. 4859

Trudeau sanatorium. Rules and information for patients. Saranac Lake, N.Y. T.A. Wright, 1906. 6 leaves. Another edition, undated. 13p. Copy in the New York Academy of Medicine Library. 4860

Trudeau sanatorium. Trudeau sanatorium, Trudeau, New York. Saranac Lake, N.Y. 1954? 20p. illus. Oblong unpaged leaflet. Last circular issued. 4861

Trudeau sanatorium. The Trudeau sanatorium for the treatment of tuberculosis. n.p. 1946. 25p. illus. Small oblong folder. 4862

Trudeau sanatorium. The twenty-fifth anniversary of the Adirondack cottage sanitarium ...Feb. 15, 1910. Trudeau, N.Y. 1910. 29p. port. illus. Reprinted from the *Adirondack Enterprise*. The name of the sanatorium was changed shortly after Dr. Trudeau's death. 4863

Trudeau workshop. Trudeau workshop catalogue. Saranac Lake, N.Y. n.d. 12p. illus. Brief text. The workshop was established in 1945. 4864

A victim of progress. Sanatorium closes on optimistic note. *Life*, Dec. 27, 1954. 37:no. 26:76–79. illus. Closing of Trudeau. 4865

Walters, J.R. The Adirondacks as a winter health resort. *Harper W*, Feb. 9, 1895. 36: 136–38. port. illus. Followed by brief article: "The Late Dr. Alfred L. Loomis." 4866

OTHER HOSPITALS AND SANATORIA

American legion, New York. Mountain camp at Big Tupper lake, N.Y. Some facts of interest and resume of the history of the American legion mountain camp, Tupper Lake, N.Y. Tupper Lake, N.Y. 1953. 4 leaves. Reproduced from typewritten copy. From 1922 to 1926 a camp for tubercular patients; from 1927 to date, used for recreation and convalescents. 4867

D., M.M. The Edward Smith memorial infirmary. *For Leaves*, Winter 1926. 20:no. 2:8. illus. New infirmary at Sanatorium Gabriels.   4868

History of Sanatorium Gabriels *For Leaves*, Autumn 1908. 5:no.3:32–39. Text in English, French and German.   4869

Mayhew, R.H. The successful sanatorium. *For Leaves*, Autumn 1925. 20:no.1:15–17. Sanatorium Gabriels.   4870

New York (state). State hospital for treatment of incipient pulmonary tuberculosis, Ray Brook. Annual report, no.1– 1900–date. Albany, 19— –date.   4871

Newcomb, Elizabeth W. Stony Wold sanatorium. *J Outd Life*, Oct. 1905. 2:231–32. illus. History of the founding.   4872

Placid memorial hospital fund. Health high in the Adirondacks. Lake Placid, N.Y. c1948. 15p. illus. plans.   4873

A profitable sanatorium. *Outlook*, Feb. 9, 1907. 85:295–96. Stony Wold.   4874

Reception cottage, Saranac Lake, N.Y. Annual report, no.1–49; April 1902–1950. Saranac Lake, N.Y. 1902–50. 49v. Name changed to Prescott House, Inc. in 1944. Closed in 1950.   4875

Sanatorium Gabriels. In the Adirondacks, 1897. *For Leaves*, Winter 1910. 7:no.4:4–11. illus. History.   4876

The Sanatorium Gabriels on Sunrise mount. *For Leaves*, Spring 1907. 4:no.1:32–33. illus. From the *London News*, July 1897.   4877

Saranac Lake's new Reception hospital. *J Outd Life*, Feb. 1905. 2:15. illus.   4878

Stony Wold sanatorium. Annual report of the corporation. N.Y. 1910. The Sanatorium also published a leaflet "Stony Wold in the Adirondacks." Copies located as follows: v.1, no.4, June 1924; v.2, nos.7, 10, 11–12, undated.   4879

Sunmount comes to Tupper Lake. Adirondack mountains, Tupper Lake, New York. N.Y. Rudge, n.d. 14p. ports. illus.   4880

Tupper Lake chamber of commerce and American legion auxiliary, inc. department of New York. The Sunmount story: Veterans administration hospital, Sunmount, New York. N.Y. William E. Rudge's sons, 1954. 11p. ports. illus.   4881

RELIGIOUS HISTORY

Beales, E.J. The shrine at Gabriels, N.Y. in the Adirondack mountains. *For Leaves*, Winter 1926. 20:no.2:12–16. illus. port. 4882

Brown, George Levi, ed. Father Comstock and the First Congregational church of Lewis. Lewis, N.Y. Post & gazette print, 1901. 19p. port. 4883

Bulkley, C.H.A. Twenty years of church life; an anniversary discourse by Rev. C.H.A. Bulkley, pastor of the Presbyterian church. Port Henry, N.Y. Herald book & job printing office, 1880. 26p. Copy in the Sherman Free Library, Port Henry. 4884

Bull, Henry J. A history of the First Methodist Episcopal church of Saranac, Clinton county, New York. n.p. 1912. 54p. plates, front. port. 4885

Champlain, N.Y. Presbytery. The Christian and apostolic abolition of slavery, stated and recommended in a report read before the Presbytery, February 13, 1855. Rouse's Point, N.Y. 1855. 24p. Copy in Yale University Library. 4886

Elizabethtown, N.Y. Congregational church. Manual. Elizabethtown, N.Y. 1874. 20p. 4887

Erwin, James. Reminiscences of early circuit life. Toledo, O. Spear, Johnson & co. 1884. 378p. port. By a minister in the Northern New York Conference of the Methodist Episcopal Church who visited many communities in the Adirondack area. 4888

Essex and Champlain Baptist association. Seventy-fourth anniversary held with the Baptist church of Elizabethtown, Oct. 6, 7 and 8, 1908. n.p. n.pub. n.d. 38p. illus. ports. Cover title differs slightly. Copy in the Sherman Free Library, Port Henry. 4889

Harkness, N.Y. Methodist Episcopal church. Souvenir program. Twenty-fifth anniversary. 1907–1932. . . n.p. n.d. 16p. illus. port. Unpaged leaflet. 4890

Harmon, Willard P. "The history of Congregationalism in Essex county." A paper read. . .September 27, 1928. n.p. Essex county association, n.d. 14 leaves. Mimeographed. Copy in the Sherman Free Library, Port Henry. 4891

Harriman, Rev. Charles C. Sermon. . .delivered at the dedication service of the Lillian Le Roay Kavanaugh memorial, St. John's Episcopal church, Diamond Point, Lake George, N.Y. August 17th, 1930. Cohoes, N.Y. Rickman press, 1930. unpaged. 4892

Hartley, Isaac Smithson. Sundays in the Adirondacks. Utica, N.Y. Wm. T. Smith, 1889. 125p. 4893

Hodges, Graham R. Working together on Main street. *Christian Cent*, May 13, 1953. 70:572–73. Association of churches at Ticonderoga. 4894

Holden, Charles C. and Hanchett, Mrs. Elbert. First Baptist church of Ticonderoga, New York. . . n.p. n.pub. 1954. 16p. Mimeographed. 4895

Hudowalski, Mrs. Grace (Leech). Old Beard. *Cloud Splitter*, Mar. 1941. 4:no.3:9. Story of establishment of a union church in North Elba. 4896

Inscriptions from old graveyards. *Moors Ant*, May 1937–Feb. 1939. 1:68–73, 144–52, 224–31, 300–11; 2:77–83, 161–69, 263–68, 347–59. Includes Adirondack sites. 4897

Jones, Mabel Merryfield. Minerva Baptist church. *No Country Life*, Summer 1948. 2:no.3:41–43. illus. 100th anniversary. 4898

Keeseville, N.Y. First Congregational church. The confession of faith and covenant. . . Keeseville, N.Y. Anson H. Allen, 1835. 12p. Copy in collection of Mrs. Marjorie L. Porter. 4899

Keeseville, N.Y. First Congregational church. One hundredth anniversary of the organization of the First Congregational church, Keeseville, N.Y. Keeseville, N.Y. 1906. 63p. front. ports. Cover title: 1806–1906. 4900

Keeseville, N.Y. Methodist Episcopal church 1827–1902. Souvenir program. 75th anniversary. Keeseville, N.Y. 1902. 7 leaves. illus. 4901

Keeseville, N.Y. Methodist Episcopal church. 1827–1927. Souvenir program. One hundredth anniversary. . .September nineteen hundred twenty-seven. Keeseville, N.Y. 1927. 16p. illus. ports. History of the church. Compiled by Rev. H.J. White. 4902

Kellogg, Rev. Paul A. The first hundred years; a centennial history of the Church of the cross, Ticonderoga, New York. 1839–1939. n.p. 1939? unpaged. Mimeographed. Copy in the New York State Historical Association Headquarters House, Ticonderoga. 4903

Lake George, N.Y. Caldwell Presbyterian church. Report of the treasurer. . .from Oct. 1, 1871 to April 1, 1873. Minutes of the Annual meeting of the congregation, and revised sketch history of the church. Albany, N.Y. Van Benthuysen, 1873. 43p.   4904

Lake George Baptist association. Minutes of the fiftieth anniversary. . .1867. . . Albany, Van Benthuysen, 1868. 16p.   4905

Lake George Baptist association. Minutes of the fifty-second anniversary. . .1869. . . Glens Falls, N.Y. Messenger printing establishment, 1869. 16p.   4906

Laramee, Rev. E.C. Annals of Notre Dame church of the assumption of the B.V.M., Redford, N.Y. Redford, N.Y. 1931. 86p. plates. Bound with this is an 84p. edition in French.   4907

Laramee, Rev. E.C. Historical sketch of Notre Dame church of the assumption, B.V.M., Redford, N.Y. Souvenir of the consecration, October 13th, 1898. Redford, N.Y. 1899. 77, 65p. Second half of the text is in French.   4908

Lauer, Solon. Life and light from above. Boston, Lee & Shepard, 1895. 250p. Also published in San Diego by the Life and Light Publishing Co. 1896. Leaves from an Adirondack journal, p.174–212.   4909

Nye, Charles Freeman. Address. . .at the centenary exercises of the First Presbyterian-Congregational church and society, Champlain, New-York; with a sketch of the past 25 years by the pastor, Rev. D. Elmer Hattie. Champlain, N.Y. Privately printed at the Moorsfield Press, 1928. 27p.   4910

Patten, Marjorie. The country church in colonial times as illustrated by Addison county, Vt. Tompkins county, N.Y. and Warren county, N.Y. N.Y. G.H. Doran, c1922. 106p. front. illus. charts, map. (Committee on Social and Religious Surveys.)   4911

Pettengill, Amos. The doctrine of baptisms, illustrated in two sermons, delivered at Champlain, N.Y. 1811. . . Plattsburgh, N.Y. A.C. Flagg, 1812. 56p.   4912

Pierre Huet de la Velinière, priest on Lake Champlain, 1790–1791. Moors Ant, Feb. 1938. 1:239–55. Includes letters from the Pliny Moore papers. Earliest Catholic church on northern New York shore of Lake Champlain. Located at Chazy, Clinton County, not at Split Rock, Essex County.   4913

Plattsburgh, N.Y. First Presbyterian church. Hand book, 1910. n.p. 1910? unpaged. illus.   4914

Plattsburgh, N.Y. First Presbyterian church. Proceedings at the centennial anniversary of the organization. . .October first and third, 1897. n.p. n.d. 127p. ports. plates. Errata slip tipped in.   4915

Port Henry, N.Y. Presbyterian church. Souvenir book, Port Henry, N.Y. 1902. Published by the Ladies' aid society of the Presbyterian church. Port Henry, N.Y. Essex county publishing co. n.d. unpaged. plates, ports. Contains a short historical sketch.   4916

Porter, Mrs. Marjorie (Lansing). The Mother Cabrini shrine. No Country Life, Winter 1949. 3:no.1:27–28. illus. Outdoor shrine of the Patent Church near Peru.   4917

Post, Henry A. Sermon preached in the Presbyterian church, Warrensburgh, Warren co. N.Y. September 26th, 1861. . . Albany, Weed, Parsons & co. 1861. 27p.   4918

Ryan, Thomas Francis. The Church of the good thief and the padre of the thieves. Plattsburgh, N.Y. Clinton press, 1942. 31p. port. illus. Dannemora.   4919

Saranac Lake, N.Y. Church of St. Luke the beloved physician. Commemoration of the seventy-fifth anniversary of the consecration . . .July 11th, 1954. Saranac Lake, N.Y. 1954. 16p. illus. ports. Unpaged leaflet. 4920

Smith, John Talbot. A history of the diocese of Ogdensburg. N.Y. John W. Lovell co. 1885. 354p. ports. front.   4921

A souvenir of Ticonderoga Methodism compiled in celebration of the 125th anniversary of Methodism in Ticonderoga. . . n.p. n.pub. 1936? 19p. Cover title: Ticonderoga Methodism, 1911–1936. Compiled by Arthur Carr.   4922

Taylor, John. Journal of Rev. John Taylor's missionary tour through the Mohawk and Black river countries in 1802. In Documentary history of the State of New York, Albany, 1850. 3:671–96.   4923

Washington union Baptist association. Minutes of the thirty-second anniversary. . .June 5, 1866. Albany, Weed, Parsons & co. 1866. 27p.   4924

Washington union Baptist association. Minutes of the thirty-fourth anniversary. . .1868. Cambridge, N.Y. Washington county print, 1868. 28p.   4925

Wickes, Sarah J. History of the Congregational church, Willsboro, Essex co. N.Y. Ticonderoga, N.Y. Press of the Sentinel, 1902. 33p.   4926

Wolfe, Paul. The foundation of God standeth sure. A sermon preached in the Keene Valley Congregational church on August 27th, 1950 . . . n.p. n.pub. n.d. 8p. 25th anniversary of Wolfe's coming to Keene Valley.   4927

EDUCATION

GENERAL

Barker, Elmer Eugene. What Crown Pointers were reading one hundred years ago. *NY Hist*, Jan. 1950. 31:31–40. An interesting analysis of lists of magazines and journals passing through the Crown Point post office one hundred years ago. 4928

Drahos, Nicholas. Our camp program. *NYS Con*, Apr.–May 1955. 9:no.5:15. illus. map. Conservation Department program. 4929

Garesche, Claude F. An investment in better living. The National lead company at Tahawus finances a $160,000 YMCA building. *No Country Life*, Summer 1948. 2:no.3:48–50. illus. Text of an address delivered Apr. 11, 1948 when building was turned over to YMCA. 4930

Keenan, Joseph. The development of public education in Warren county. 110 leaves. tables, map. Master's thesis, New York State College for Teachers, Albany, 1940. Typescript. 4931

Lonergan, Carroll Vincent. The country school at the crossroads. *No Country Life*, Fall 1946. 1:no.1:14–15. Reprinted from *New York State Education*, Oct. 1945. Crown Point. 4932

Morgan, Barbara. Summer's children; with forewords by Dr. Mary Fisher Langmuir and Helen Haskell. A photographic cycle of life at camp. Scarsdale, N.Y. Morgan & Morgan publishers, c1951. 159p. illus. Extract in *Living Wilderness*, Summer 1952, no.41:8–12. Reviewed by D.A. Plum in *The Ad-i-ron-dac*, Nov.–Dec. 1952, 16:111. Camp Treetops, near Lake Placid. 4933

Mousaw, Cyrus John. A study of educational need and opportunity in the town of Crown Point, Essex county, N.Y. Prepared at the suggestion of Rural education bureau, State education department. Albany, University of the State of New York, 1928. 29p. port. illus. plates, maps. (University of the State of New York Bulletin no.907.) 4934

Ostrander, Chester Brooks. A history of public education in the county of Essex, New York. 114 leaves. plates, facsim. maps. Master's thesis, New York State College for Teachers, Albany, 1940. Typescript. 4935

Peet, Creighton. What is wilderness camping? n.p. 1955? 2p. Reprinted from *American Forests*, Nov. 1955. Description of Tanager Lodge Camp—Fay Welch, director. 4936

Pinchot, Gifford. The need of forest schools in America. *Gard & For*, July 24, 1895. 8: 298. Refers in part to the problem of forestry in the Adirondacks. 4937

Saranac Lake rehabilitation guild, inc. Guild news, v.1, no.1– May 29, 1936– Saranac Lake, N.Y. 1936– Monthly. The Guild's name was originally the Saranac Lake Study and Craft Guild. 4938

Saranac Lake study and craft guild. Report of activities for the year 1943–1944. Saranac Lake, N.Y. 1944. 28p. illus. "The Guild was founded in 1936 to demonstrate the therapeutic values of adult education." Name later changed to Saranac Lake Rehabilitation Guild, Inc. 4939

Sisson, Al and Burger, William H. Camp Dudley. *No Country Life*, Fall 1953. 7:no.4: 26–30. illus. 4940

Williams, Roscoe L. The history of secondary education in Washington county. 150 leaves. plates, facsim. map. Master's thesis, New York State College for Teachers, Albany, 1937. Typescript. 4941

SCHOOLS AND COLLEGES

NEW YORK STATE COLLEGE
OF FORESTRY, CORNELL

The Adirondack problem. *Ind*, Dec. 24, 1903. 55:3081–83. Editorial condemning private ownership in Adirondacks. Urges support of State College of Forestry. 4942

Bailey, Liberty Hyde. Statement on the forestry situation. To the governors of the

Cornell club of Rochester. n.p. n.pub. n.d. 12p. Statement made at Rochester, Dec. 22, 1913. Advocates forestry courses in the Department of Agriculture at Cornell. 4943

The collapse of the New York state college of forestry. *For Quar*, Nov. 1903. 2:42–44. 4944

Controversy in New York. *For & Irrig*, Feb. 1902. 8:47–48. Cornell Forestry School's experimental plot. 4945

Cornell's Adirondack forestry. *For & Stream*, Dec. 28, 1901. 57:501. Editorial review of Cornell College forestry case. 4946

Cornell's forest reserve. *Am Arch*, Oct. 20, 1900. 70:22. Reprinted from *New York Tribune*. 4947

Fernow, Bernhard Eduard. Axton plantations. *J For*, Dec. 1917. 15:988–90. 4948

Fernow, Bernhard Eduard. Beginnings of professional forestry in the Adirondacks being the 1st and 2nd annual reports of the New York state college of forestry, Cornell university. *In* New York (state). Fisheries, game and forest commission. 5th annual report, 1899. p.401–52. plates, illus. Also published as New York State College of Forestry, Cornell University Bulletin no.2, 1900 (no.4956). 4949

Fernow, Bernhard Eduard. The Cornell college forest. *For & Stream*, May 3, 1902. 58: 346. Located near Saranac Lake. 4950

Fernow, Bernhard Eduard. The New York state college of forestry. *Science*, Oct. 14, 1898. n.s.8:494–501. 4951

Fernow, Bernhard Eduard. What is the New York state college of forestry doing in the Adirondacks? *Recreation*, Jan. 1901. 14:59–60. 4952

Hosmer, Ralph Sheldon. Forestry at Cornell . . .a retrospect of proposals, developments, and accomplishments in the teaching of professional forestry at Cornell university 1898–1948. Ithaca, N.Y. Cornell university, 1950. 64p. port. illus. Includes comment on and references to the forestry experiment at Axton in 1898–1903 and brief comments on the Cornell forest near Newcomb. 4953

Jentsch, Fritz A.L. Professor B.E. Fernow und der Adirondack wald. *Z Forst*, Feb. 1905. 37:108–13. An English translation of part of this article appeared in the *Forestry Quarterly*, Feb. 1905, 3:32–38, with title "An Expert Opinion on the Cornell Forest Experiment," followed by remarks by E.B. Fernow. 4954

New York (state). College of forestry. Annual report, 1–6. 1898–1903. Albany, 1899–1904. v.p. Assembly document 38, 1899; Assembly document 36, 1900; Assembly document 34, 1901; Assembly document 38, 1902; Assembly document 11, 1903; Senate document 7, 1904. 4955

New York (state). College of Forestry. Beginning of professional forestry in the Adirondacks; 1st and 2nd annual report of the director of New York state college of forestry. Ithaca, N.Y. 1900. 56p. (New York State College of Forestry, Cornell University Bulletin no.2.) 4956

The New York state college of forestry. *Am Nat*, Nov. 1898. 32:875. Editorial on the establishment of New York State College of Forestry at Cornell with demonstration forest in the Adirondacks. 4957

The New York state college of forestry. *Forester*, Dec. 1901. 7:304–8. illus. 4958

Recknagel, Arthur Bernard. The story of Axton. *Cor For*, May 1924. 4:9–14. illus. 4959

Shepard, Edward Morse. The public interest involved in the Cornell forestry experiment. N.Y. 1904. 27p. 4960

Spears, Raymond Smiley. Adirondack notes. *Field & S*, Sept. 1906. 11:505–6. Criticism of the management of Cornell College of Forestry tract. 4961

Spears, Raymond Smiley. Prof. Fernow and the Adirondacks. *Outlook*, Apr. 6, 1907. 85: 815–16. Letter on the Adirondack experiments of the Cornell State College of Forestry. 4962

Three state bills. *For Quar*, July 1903. 1:156–57. Comment on the Governor's veto of three bills, one of which was the appropriation for the New York State College of Forestry. 4963

NEW YORK STATE UNIVERSITY COLLEGE OF FORESTRY, SYRACUSE

Baker, Hugh Potter. The State ranger school and its place in forestry education. *NYS Ranger Sch*, 1930. p.7–8. 4964

Baker, Hugh Potter. Teaching scientific forestry; valuable work done by a state institution. *Sci Am*, May 6, 1916. Suppl. 81:296–97. illus. 4965

Bedard, W. Delles. The Warrensburg utopia. *Emp For*, 1930. 16:56–57. State College of Forestry (Syracuse) senior camp at Pack Demonstration Forest. 4966

Bits of summer camp history. *Camp Log*, Dec. 1922, p.46–48. illus. Summer camp at Cranberry Lake. 4967

Bonstead, C.D. Ranger school graduates class, enrolls new students. *Lumber Camp News*, Apr. 1952. 13:no.12:6. illus. 4968

"Breck," pseud. History of the Ranger school. *Camp Log*, 1929. 15:74–76. 4969

Colburn, H.E. The Ranger school twenty-five years ago. *NYS Ranger Sch*, 1937. p.15–18. illus. 4970

Coolidge, P.T. The pioneer days. *NYS Ranger Sch*, 1937. p.12–14, 26. illus. At the Ranger School. 4971

Craig, Robert Jr. New York state ranger school. *Emp For*, 1920. 6:70–72. illus. A similar article describing the School appeared in 1919, 5:64–65. 4972

Dubuar, James Francis. The New York state ranger school. *Bul Schools*, Mar. 1945. 31:224–27. plate. At Wanakena, N.Y. 4973

Dubuar, James Francis. The Ranger school. *Emp For*, 1921. 7:36–37. illus. 4974

Dubuar, James Francis. Reforestation and plantation improvement on the Ranger school forest. *NYS Ranger Sch*, 1935. p.11–16. illus. Aid of C.C.C. 4975

Dubuar, James Francis. The State ranger school. *Camp Log*, Dec. 1922. p.19–21. illus. 4976

Ernst, G.W. The 1915 summer camp. *Emp For*, 1916. 2:22–26. illus. map. 1915 camp at Cranberry Lake. Articles on the summer camp appear in each issue of the annual. 4977

Fenska, Richard Robert. The Pack forest. *Camp Log*, 1929. 15:5–8. History of the forest. 4978

Field, Earle. The New York state college of forestry at Syracuse university: the history, founding and early growth, 1911–1922. 285 leaves. tables. Doctoral thesis, Maxwell Graduate School of Citizenship and Public Affairs, Syracuse University, 1954. Typescript. Includes brief history of the Cornell School of Forestry. 4979

Fivaz, A.E. The Roosevelt wildlife experiment station and its relation to forestry. *Emp For*, 1920. 6:47–50. port. 4980

Forestry college collects data on 2½ million Adirondack acres. *NY Forester*, Nov. 1950. 7:no.4:2. Survey, being made by the College of Forestry, Syracuse, of the Adirondack and Catskill forest land. Under special appropriation at the request of the State Board of Equalization and Assessment. 4981

Forestry in New York state. *Outlook*, Nov. 9, 1912. 102:521. Editorial on the Rich Lumber Company's gift of 1800 acres at Cranberry Lake to New York State College of Forestry at Syracuse. 4982

Foster, Clifford H. and Kirkland, Burt P. The Charles Lathrop Pack demonstration forest, Warrensburg, N.Y. Results of twenty years of intensive forest management. Washington, Charles Lathrop Pack Forestry Foundation, 1949. 36p. illus. figs. map. Description of region, history and objectives of project, management results, economics, lessons for public and private forests. 4983

Gill, Tom. Show windows of forestry. The Charles Lathrop Pack demonstration forests in the Adirondacks. *Up-Stater*, Nov. 1929. 1:no.6:14, 22, 26. illus. Reprinted from *Nature Magazine*, July 1927. 4984

Haddock, P.J. Ranger school alumni hold eighteenth reunion. *Northeast Log*, Oct. 1952. 1:no.3:28. illus. Accounts of 1950 and 1951 reunions are in *Lumber Camp News* for Sept. 1950 and 1951, 12:no.5:16 and 13:no.5:8. 4985

Israels, Josef 2d. Fantastic forest: Huntington forest of the Roosevelt wildlife forest experiment station. *Sat Eve Post*, Aug. 22, 1942. 215:no.8:14–15, 67–68. illus. 4986

Johnson, E.A. The Ranger school. *Emp For*, 1917. 3:50. 4987

King, Ralph Terence, Dence, W.A. and Webb, W.L. History, policy and program of the Huntington wildlife forest station. *Roos Wildlife Bul*, Sept. 1941. 7:393–460. illus. tables, map. 4988

Kovalcik, Jerome G. New York College of forestry summer camp. Pack experimental forest. *Northeast Log*, Nov. 1953. 2:no.3:6–7, 30. illus. 4989

McCarthy, Edwin Florince. The forester goes to the woods. *NYS Ranger Sch*, 1937. p.7–11. illus. 1912 survey of the Ranger School Forest. 4990

McCarthy, Edwin Florince. The New York state ranger school. *Emp For*, 1916. 2:59–61. illus. 4991

Myers, Frank B. Then and now. *Emp For*, 1932. 18:1–2, 4–5. Reminiscences of the founding of the School of Forestry. 4992

New wood products laboratory. *Am For*, June 1954. 60:no.6:36. 4993

New York (state). State university. College of forestry, Syracuse. Annual report, 1936/37–1944/47. Syracuse, 1937–48. The first annual report was issued as Bulletin no.20, with title: Activities of the College. None issued 1940/41. Report for 1944/47 issued in 1948 with title: The New York State College of Forestry Today & Tomorrow. 4994

New York (state). State university. College of forestry, Syracuse. The Charles Lathrop Pack demonstration forest administered by the New York state college of forestry, Syracuse university. Syracuse, N.Y. 1929? 8p. illus. maps. Folded broad.ide. 4995

New York (state). State university. College of forestry, Syracuse. A history of its first twenty-five years, 1911–1936. Edited by Raymond J. Hoyle and Laura D. Cox. Syracuse, N.Y. 1936. 177p. plates, tables. List of publications of the college, p.163–71.　　　4996

New York (state). State university. College of forestry, Syracuse. New York state ranger school, Wanakena, New York. Announcement of courses, 1947–1949. Syracuse, N.Y. 1947. 13p. illus. 1917 and 1922 editions were issued as *Circulars* 14 and 37. The School was founded in 1912.　　　4997

New York (state). State university. College of forestry, Syracuse. Opportunities for graduate work and research at the New York state college of forestry, Syracuse university. Syracuse, N.Y. 1948. 45p. illus. graph. (Bulletin, v.21, no.1-a.)　　　4998

New York (state). State university. College of forestry, Syracuse. Summer forest camp in the Adirondacks. Syracuse, 1913. 8p. illus. (Circular no.3). Also issued in 1917 and 1919 (Circulars 12 and 29).　　　4999

New York (state). State university. College of forestry, Syracuse. Ranger school, Wanakena, N.Y. Alumni news, 1926– Wanakena, N.Y. 1926– illus. Annual.　　　5000

New York state college acquires a wild life station. *For Worker*, Nov. 1932. 8:no.6:5–6. Gift of Huntington Forest.　　　5001

The New York state college of forestry at Syracuse university. *Am For*, July 1912. 18: 453–57. illus. History of the Cornell School and the organization of the new college.　　　5002

The Pack demonstration forest; state college carries on interesting experiments in progressive forestry. *Lumber Camp News*, Mar. 1949. 10:no.11:1, 13, 16.　　　5003

Plumley, L.P. Ranger schools. *NYS Ranger Sch*, 1953. p.22–25. Includes history of Wanakena.　　　5004

Reidy, Genevieve L. comp. Graduate theses 1944–1954. Syracuse, N.Y. New York state university, College of forestry, 1955. 116p. Abstracts. Appendix, p.83–98, contains list of Graduate Theses, 1914–43.　　　5005

Rude, John K. The new Charles Lathrop Pack demonstration forest. *Emp For*, 1928. 14:35–38. illus.　　　5006

Schmoe, Floyd W. The Roosevelt wildlife experiment station. *Emp For*, 1922. 8:66–68. illus.　　　5007

Shirley, Hardy L. The Ranger school tomorrow. *NYS Ranger Sch*, 1952. p.12–14. Discussion of the continuation of the School. 5008

Smith, S.D. The Ranger school. *Emp For*, 1918. 4:45–47. illus.　　　5009

Soper, H.S. The Adirondack trip. *Emp For*, 1916. 2:75-77. illus. Winter trip to see lumbering operations. See also humorous account of same trip, entitled "Adirondacks Ain't Alps" by "Jawn" Banks, p.96–97.　　　5010

Spring, Samuel N. A dean's eye view of the Ranger school. *NYS Ranger Sch*, 1937. p.5–6. illus.　　　5011

T., J.A. Babes in the woods. *Camp Log*, 1927. 13:31–33. illus. Collecting trip in the Five Ponds region.　　　5012

A wild life station in Adirondacks. *Science*, Sept. 16, 1932. n.s.76:248–49. Also in *American Forests*, Oct. 1932, 38:563. Announcement of gift of Huntington Wildlife Station to School of Forestry at Syracuse.　　　5013

A wild life station in the Adirondacks given the New York state college of forestry by Mr. and Mrs. Archer Huntington of New York. *Emp For*, 1933. 19:55–57. illus.　　　5014

OTHER SCHOOLS AND COLLEGES

Apollos' fortune. *Time*, Apr. 5, 1937. 29:no. 14:50–51. port. Paul Smith's fortune left to establish Paul Smith's College of Arts and Sciences.　　　5015

Barnes, Mary Clark. A Sunday at Glenmore. *Service*, May 1907. 6:106–9. illus. Glenmore School for the Culture Sciences.　　　5016

Basile, Richard E. . . .Resort management at Paul Smith's college. *Resort Management*, June 1951. 5:no.1:9–10. illus.　　　5017

Browne, Marion Josephine. A fortnight at Cliff Haven, by M.J. Brunowe, pseud. *Cath World*, Nov. 1900. 72:254–64. Catholic Summer School of America.　　　5018

Catholic summer school of America. Progress of the summer-school at Cliff Haven, N.Y. on Lake Champlain. . . n.p. 1906? 8p. Cover title.　　　5019

Champlain (N.Y.) college is closed. *Sch & Soc*, Aug. 22, 1953. 78:59–60. Brief history.　　　5020

Davidson, Thomas, 1840–1900. The education of the wage-earners. . .edited with an introduction by Charles M. Bakewell. Boston, Ginn, c1904. 247p. Primarily on the Bread-Winners' College but of interest in the history of the Glenmore School for the Culture Sciences; contains many of Davidson's letters written from Hurricane.　　　5021

Engineer forestry co. at Paul Smith's college. *J For*, May 1951. 49:400.　　　5022

Experiment station established at Paul Smiths to explore forest management methods. *Lumber Camp News*, Aug. 1948. 10:no.4:1, 5. illus.　　　5023

Fire at Paul Smith's college. *Lumber Camp News*, June 1952. 14:no.2:22. illus. 5024

Gilbert, Amy M. ACUNY. The Associated colleges of upper New York; a unique response to an emergency in higher education in the State of New York. . . Ithaca, N.Y. Cornell university press, 1950. 524p. front. ports. illus. tables, maps. 5025

Glenmore school for the culture sciences. A summer course of study in the Adirondacks . . .Season 1893. n.p. n.pub. 1893. 8p. Copy in the Loomis Collection, Keene Valley Public Library. Also published in 1892 and 1894. Circulars for the years 1902–9 have title: Glenmore Summer School of the Culture Sciences. The School was established in 1890 by Thomas Davidson. After his death in the fall of 1900 it was carried on until 1910 by Charles Bakewell. File in the Davidson Collection, Yale University Library. 5026

Guise, C.H. Cornell foresters in camp. *Am For*, Nov. 1919. 25:1487–88. illus. Located on Turner Preserve north of Tupper Lake. 5027

Hosmer, Ralph Sheldon. The Pack forestry prizes. *Cor For*, May 1924. 4:30–32. port. 5028

Juckett, Edwin A. An early Adirondack school. *No Country Life*, Winter 1952. 6:no.1: 21–23, 70. Early history of the Keene Valley school; author was principal, 1927–39. 5029

Keeseville academy. Things of the Cabal; its origin, principles, history and a sketch of its members. Keeseville, N.Y. E.R. Follett & co. printers, 1854. 12p. Debating society. Copy in the collection of Mrs. Marjorie L. Porter. 5030

Lathrop, George Parsons. The Catholic summer school of America. President McKinley's visit. *Harper W*, Aug. 21, 1897. 41:838. illus. p.837. At Bluff Point, Lake Champlain. 5031

McCluskey, William A. So you remember. . . A picture history of Lake Placid school, Lake Placid club school, Northwood school, 1905–1955. n.p. n.pub. n.d. 60p. ports. illus. 5032

More than a century of education. *Tahawus Cloudsplitter*, Sept. 1954. 5:no.7:5–7. illus. History of Newcomb School. 5033

Murray, John Clark. A summer school of philosophy. *Scot Rev*, Jan. 1892. 19:98–113. Thomas Davidson's summer school on East Hill (Glenmore School for the Culture Sciences). 5034

The new home of the summer-school at Plattsburgh. *Cath World*, Apr. 1893. 57:67–84. ports. illus. map. Catholic Summer School of America. 5035

O'Shea, John J. The Catholic Champlain, 1893–95. *Cath World*, Sept. 1893, July 1894, July 1895. 57:853–62, 59:563–68, 61:560–63. ports. illus. Catholic Summer School of America. 5036

Paul Smith experimental forest established by action of college board. *NY Forester*, Aug. 1948. 5:no.3:6–7. 5037

Paul Smith's college. Bulletin, v.1, no.1. May 1942. Saranac Lake, N.Y. n.d. 23p. ports. illus. Calendar etc. Owing to the war the College did not open until Sept. 1947. 5038

Paul Smith's college. Catalog. . .1947–1948. . . Paul Smith's, N.Y. 1947. 54p. front. illus. tables, maps. 5039

The Paul Smith's college summer school. Paul Smith's, N.Y. 1944. Unpaged folder. illus. Summer school held prior to the opening of the College. 5040

Reed, Frank A. Paul Smith experimental forest. *Northeast Log*, Aug. 1953. 1:no.12:6–7, 27. illus. 5041

Rutherford, William Jr. Timber management at Paul Smith's. *Lumber Camp News*, Jan. 1952. 13:no.9:3–5, 16. illus. 5042

Saranac Lake, N.Y. Union school. Catalogue. . .1892–93. Union free school district no.1, town of Harrietstown, Franklin county, New York. n.p. 1892? 38p. 5043

School in the Adirondacks. *Arch Rec*, Dec. 1942. 92:no.6:28–35. illus. plans. North Country School near Lake Placid. 5044

Sheepskins passed out at Paul Smith's. *Lumber Camp News*, June 1952. 14:no.2:9. illus. Paul Smith's College. 5045

Walworth, Hiram. History of the Plattsburgh academy, 1811–1871. Plattsburgh, N.Y. Telegram printing house, 1892. 37p. plate. 5046

Walworth, Hiram. Recollections of the old Plattsburgh academy, from 1846–1851. Plattsburgh, N.Y. Telegram printing house, 1891. 22p. plate. 5047

Weston, Stephen F. The Glenmore summer school. *St No Mo*, June 1906. 1:no.2:10–11. illus. Glenmore School for the Culture Sciences. 5048

White, James Addison. The founding of Cliff Haven, early years of the Catholic summer school of America. N.Y. 1950. 105p. (United States Catholic Historical Society Monograph Series, 24.) 5049

Wolcott, O.A. Physical training law in operation—in the Adirondacks. *Bul Schools*, Dec. 15, 1916. 3:1. Steps taken to comply with new law providing for physical training for school children. Clinton County. 5050

LIBRARIES

Adirondack library, Saranac Lake, N.Y. Catalogue of Adirondack library of Saranac Lake, N.Y. N.Y. Press of J.J. Little & co. 1893. 56p. 5051

Hoey, Mary. For the ill and literate. The Reader's information service of the Saranac Lake study and craft guild offered in coopera- tion with the Saranac Lake free library. . . Saranac Lake, N.Y. 1950? Unpaged folder. illus. map. Reprinted from the *Guild News*, Apr. 1950. 5052

Murray, Eleanor S. Manuscripts as resources. Reprinted from the *Vermont Quarterly*, Apr. 1952, p.89–103. Description of the library at Fort Ticonderoga. 5053

New sanitarium library ready. *J Outd Life*, June 1905. 2:113. illus. Opening of Mellon Memorial Library at Trudeau. 5054

New York (state). University. Historical sketch of the Lake Placid public library, Lake Placid, N.Y. Plattsburgh, N.Y. E.J. Marsh, 1902. unpaged. illus. 5055

Plum, Dorothy Alice. Adirondackana. *Ad-i-ron-dac*, Nov.–Dec. 1951. 15:112, 115. The Munson Collection at the Saranac Lake Free Library. See also note of exhibition in issue for Jan.–Feb. 1952, 16:13. 5056

White, William Chapman. 90 feet of Adiron-dackana in the Saranac Lake free library. *NYS Con*, Apr.–May 1952. 6:no.5:12–15. illus. 5057

RECREATION IN THE ADIRONDACKS

GENERAL

Adirondack playground; a vacation playground unsurpassed for every outdoor pleasure. *Up Mo*, July 1941. 2:no.4:14–15. illus. 5058

Adirondacks—answer to a happy vacation; the greatest playground in the east, with 5,000 ft. mountains, myriad lakes, forests of pine contain wonders in profusion. *Motordom*, June 1932. p.5. 5059

Amateur, pseud. First visit to the Raquette. *For & Stream*, Mar. 9, 1876. 6:66. 5060

Amateur, pseud. Long lake, Newcomb, Indian pass. *For & Stream*, May 13, 1875. 4:212. 5061

Amateur, pseud. On to "G" lake. *For & Stream*, Apr. 5, 1877. 8:127. Near Piseco. Lake shaped like G. 5062

Amateur, pseud. Swinging round the circle; or, Fresh from the woods. *For & Stream*, Aug. 26, 1875. 5:33–34. Fishing and exploring from Utica across to Lake George and Lake Champlain. 5063

Bailey, Richard. College week, 1947. *Cloud Splitter*, Nov.–Dec. 1947. 10:no.6:10–12. IOCA in the Adirondacks. 5064

Ball, S.W. A cheap trip to the Adirondacks. *For & Stream*, May 25, 1882. 18:324–25. From Blue Mountain Lake by boat; on foot to Lake Placid. 5065

Bark shanty on T lake—50 years ago. *NYS Con*, Apr.–May 1949. 3:no.5:31. illus. 5066

Bartlett, W.H. "Isola Bella"—an adventure on Schroon lake. *Sharpe's Lond M*, 1853. 3: 243–46. Night spent on an island in Schroon Lake. 5067

Be-Murrayed Adirondacks. *For & Stream*, Oct. 12, 1876. 7:154. Diminishing opportunities for good sport. 5068

Benedict, Mrs. Martha (Nord). My first trip to Adirondak loj. *Cloud Splitter*, Mar.–Apr. 1945. 8:no.2:4–6. 5069

Benjamin, Jack T. The why of it. *Cloud Splitter*, Dec. 1940. 3:no.8:5–10. Weekend at Heart Lake. 5070

Boardman, William H. Lovers of the woods. N.Y. McClure Phillips, 1901. 239p. front. Excerpts in Adirondack League Club Yearbook, 1902, p.39–47, with title "Moose River Fishing." 5071

Brandreth, Paulina. Trails of enchantment; introduction by Roy Chapman Andrews. N.Y. G. Howard Watt, 1930. 318p. front. plates. Signed: Paul Brandreth. Outdoor life, deer hunting. 5072

Bray, Ira L. An analysis of summer recreational use of the Adirondack Forest preserve with special emphasis on campsites and trails. 127 leaves. charts, maps. Master's thesis, State University of New York, College of Forestry, Syracuse, 1952. Typescript. Abstract in Graduate Theses, p.66. 5073

Breck, Edward. The way of the woods; a manual for sportsmen in northeastern United States and Canada... N.Y. Putnam, 1908. 436p. front. illus. "Concise yet thorough and authoritative information on every subject connected with life in the North Woods" (Donaldson). 5074

Bruce, Dwight Hall. Adirondack jottings. *For & Stream*, July 25, 1889. 33:3. Signed: D.H.B. 5075

Burroughs, Julian. A family motor-boat cruise with John Burroughs. *Country Life*, June 1910. 18:197–98. illus. Boat trip from New York City to Lake Champlain. 5076

Carpenter, Warwick Stevens. An Adirondack patteran; the nomadic summer life of the north woods in camps, permanent and transitory. *For & Stream*, Aug. 1915. 84:475–77. 5077

Carpenter, Warwick Stevens. New York's Forest preserve playground. *Conservationist*, July 1920. 3:99–103. illus. Also in *Playground*, Dec. 1920, 14:542–46. 5078

The Cascade lakes. *Ad-i-ron-dac*, July–Aug. 1955. 19:72–73. Part I by Pauline Goldmark; Part II by Abigail C. Dimon. Includes description of the Cascade House. 5079

Cheney, Mrs. Mary A. (Bushnell). Life and letters of Horace Bushnell... N.Y. Harper,

1880. 579p. ports. Vacation in the Adirondacks, p.497–501. Extract, "A Swift Descent," in *The Ad-i-ron-dac*, Jan.–Feb. 1953, 17:8, 19. 5080

Chittenden, Lucius Eugene. Personal reminiscences, 1840–1890. . . N.Y. Richmond, Croscup & co. 1893. 434p. front. (port.). Adirondacks, p.139–69. 5081

College week. *IOCA Bul*, Fall 1928. p.7–10. 5082

Comstock, Louisa M. Adirondacks; all yours! *Bet Hom & Gard*, Apr. 1947. 25:no.8:60–61. illus. map. 5083

Cowles, Frederick H. Recollections of the Adirondacks. *No Country Life*, Fall 1952, Winter 1953, Fall 1953. 6:no.4:42–44; 7:no.1:47–48; 7:no.4:35–39. A boy's introduction to the mountains. 5084

Crow, Charles H. The Adirondacks unveiled. *For & Stream*, Nov. 28, 1878. 11:338. Humorous article about a bear hunt and a climb up Mt. Marcy. 5085

Dailey, Elric J. Keep your head and know what to do when lost in the woods. *Am For*, Oct. 1925. 31:616–19. illus. 5086

Dailey, Elric J. The new Adirondacks. *Fur News*, July 1923. 38:no.1:12–13, 32–33. illus. Improvement in hunting, fishing and trapping. 5087

Dittmar, Adolph G. High peak photography in winter. *Ad-i-ron-dac*, Jan.–Feb. 1953. 17:6, 15. 5088

Dittmar, Adolph G. High peak photography with the Leica. *Ad-i-ron-dac*, July–Aug. 1950. 14:78–80. 5089

Dobson, B.A. "Come again in hunting time"; a novice's first trip to the woods, as told by himself. *Field & S*, July 1907. 12:217–24. illus. 5090

Extending public camp sites in the mountains; Conservation commission making it more convenient and pleasant for motor campers in the Adirondacks and Catskills. 50 new sites just established at Lake George battlefield. *Motordom*, June 1927. 21:no.1: 1–4. illus. 5091

Farrell, Edward D. Adirondack trips. *For Leaves*, Spring 1911–Winter 1911–12. 8:no.1: 3–16; 8:no.2:18–32; 8:no.3:3–17; 8:no.4:35–49. illus. ports. Accounts of trips made over a period of forty years into the section near Morehouseville and the Adirondack League Club's tract. The first part also appeared in the issue for Spring–Summer 1921, 17:no.1: 26–40. 5092

Fitch, W.A. For an Adirondack trip. *Outing*, July 1882. 1:8–9. Routes and rates from New York to various points of entry. 5093

Ford, A.H. 20,000 miles of waterways for the marine vacationist; what the present and future has in store for the cruiser in motor, houseboat or canoe, with a description of the more important routes offered by our continent. *Field & S*, June 1907. 12:134–37. 5094

Fuller, A.R. Midwinter in the Adirondacks. *For & Stream*, Mar. 19, 1885. 24:150. News notes from Meacham Lake. 5095

Fuller, A.R. Winter in the Adirondacks. *For & Stream*, Apr. 26, 1883. 20:248. News and game notes from Meacham Lake. 5096

Gibbs, A.D. Voice of the rapids. *Field & S*, Mar. 1908. 12:972. On fishing trip the sound of water resembles "Cornell." 5097

Gibbs, John T. Vacationing in New York state parks and forests. *NYS For Assn NL*, June 1933. p.7–9. 5098

Glover, Mrs. Helen (Wardwell). From the journal of Helen Wardwell, 1881. *Ad-i-ron-dac*, Mar.–Apr. 1953. 17:26–27. illus. Vacation at Keene Valley. 5099

Golf with a thrill, courses amid mountains and lakes, 2000 feet up, provide golfer with the best fun of vacation season. *Motordom*, June 1931. 24:no.12:28. illus. 5100

Hackett, Frank S. New York woods for boys' summer camps. *Conservationist*, Aug. 1921. 4:115–18. illus. 5101

Hooker, Mrs. Mildred P. (Stokes). Camp chronicles. n.p. Privately printed, 1952. 83p. plates. unpaged. Illustrated with early photographs. Describes camp on an island in Upper St. Regis Lake. 5102

Jeffers, LeRoy. The call of the mountains: rambles among the mountains and canyons of the United States and Canada. N.Y. Dodd, Mead, 1922. 282p. incl. mounted col. front. plates. Scattered references to the Adirondacks; brief note on Mt. Marcy. 5103

Joensson, Daphne. College week. Aftermath. *IOCA Bul*, Fall 1937. p.2–4. 5104

Johnson, Clifton. New England and its neighbors. N.Y. Macmillan, 1902. 335p. plates, illus. In the Adirondacks, p.70–105. 5105

Judson, Edward Z.C. Sport as brain food, by Ned Buntline, pseud. *For & Stream*, Dec. 22–29, 1881. 17:406–7, 427. Sports provide relaxation needed for mental stimulation. 5106

Juvenal, pseud. Adirondack notes. *For & Stream*, Aug. 25, 1906. 65:300. 5107

Keene, Harry P. A delightful outing. *Field & S*, June 1901. 6:224–25. illus. Two-week vacation at Minerva. 5108

Kirschenbaum, Mildred. Life in the woods. *Ang & Hunt*, Feb. 1910. 2:120–22. illus. Winter spent on Fulton Chain. 5109

Knapp, W.H. Adirondack atmosphere. *Ang & Hunt*, Feb. 1910. 2:100–2. Trip to Paul Smiths, St. Regis River and Saranac. 5110

Langdale, H.L. Children, tents and a canoe. *Outing*, Oct. 1919. 75:28–31, 55–56. illus. Family vacation at Lake George. 5111

Lee, Mary. Shooting wild life with the camera at night. *NY Times Mag*, Aug. 26, 1928. p.12–13, 20. illus. Hobart V. Roberts, photographer. 5112

Levick, James J. The Adirondacks. *Phila Med Times*, Sept. 24, 1881. 11:813–17. Places to stay and means of transportation. 5113

Markham, Charles C. Hints for the Adirondacks. *For & Stream*, Aug. 13, 1874. 3:3. Equipment and ways of getting to the Adirondacks. 5114

Mason, C.W. Lost in the woods. *Lumber Camp News*, June 1949. 11:no.2:26. Girl lost near St. Huberts. 5115

Mason, C.W. A strange story of the woods. *Lumber Camp News*, Dec. 1949. 11:no.8:8. Man lost in North Lake country. 5116

Mason, Clifford R. Recreational planning for the state-owned forest lands of New York. 145 leaves. mounted photographs, folded charts and maps (part colored). Master's thesis, State University of New York, College of Forestry, Syracuse, 1938. Typescript. 5117

Mather, Fred. An Adirondack night. *For & Stream*, Feb. 15, 1896. 46:132–33. Camping near head of Fourth Lake in Fulton Chain. Noisy hunters. 5118

Mears, Edw. N. Kirk. The story of my vacation... Worcester, Mass. Press of Charles Hamilton, 1881. 20p. An eleven-year-old's account of his vacation in the Adirondacks. Copy in the Hicks Collection, Lake Placid Club. 5119

Moody, Martin Van Buren. Uncle Mart Moody's Adirondack experiences. *Woods & Wat*, Autumn 1903, Summer, 1904. 6:no.3: 14–15; 7:no.2:10–11. illus. The second article is on bear trapping. 5120

Mulholland, William D. New York's recreation policy in Adirondack park. *High Spots*, Apr. 1932. 9:no.2:21–22. 5121

Murray, William Henry Harrison. Camping out. *Golden Rule*, June 27, 1877. 2:no.40:1. Originally published in the *Christian Union*, June 20, 1877, 15:no.25:552. 5122

Murray, William Henry Harrison. How I sail Champlain. *Outing*, May 1891. 18:96–104. illus. Description of his yacht. Lake Champlain Yacht Club. 5123

New York (state). State council of parks. New York state parks. 1929. Albany, J.B.

Lyon, 1929? 115p. illus. maps. The Adirondack region, p.57–74. 5124

New York (state). State university. College of forestry, Syracuse. Department of forest recreation. Vacation trips in central and western New York. *Am For*, June 1923. 29:341–46. illus. map. Includes "In Your Car Through the Adirondacks" and "By Canoe Through the Adirondacks." 5125

New York central railroad company. Canoeing and fishing in the Adirondack mountains. n.p. 1911. 16p. folded leaflet. illus. maps. Copy in the Hicks Collection, Lake Placid Club. 5126

New York's great forest playground, Adirondacks and Catskills make an alluring vacation resort for the weary and pleasure seeking; mountains oldest on the continent. *State Service*, July–Aug. 1922. 6,i.e.8:225–58. illus. 5127

New York state's great game preserve calls to the hunter, forest, lake and stream soon to beckon sportsmen from near and far. *Motordom*, Oct. 1930. 24:no.5:16–17. illus. 5128

1935 college week in the Adirondacks. *IOCA J*, Nov. 1935. 1:no.1:3, 21. Lake Colden. 5129

The 1933 college week. *IOCA Bul*, Nov. 1933. 2:no.2:2–3. maps. 5130

Nixon, Edgar Burkhardt. The armchair mountaineer. *Ad-i-ron-dac*, Jan.–Feb., July–Aug. 1954. 18:20, 74. These two issues of an occasional column are on trash in the woods and rainy days. 5131

Nott, Charles C. Jr. An Adirondack idyl; a story. *Outing*, Oct. 1893. 23:16–20. illus. Camping and hunting. 5132

Ondack, Adrion, pseud. St. Regis river region. *For & Stream*, Nov. 25, 1880. 15:326. Sporting notes from the middle branch of the St. Regis River. 5133

One Hundred Islands, pseud. Notes from Lake George. *For & Stream*, Sept. 15, 1881. 17:124. 5134

Oppenheim, Nathan. Two trips to Lake George. *Harvard Mo*, Apr. 1887. 4:65–75. Summer romance. 5135

Osborne, Lithgow. Speech...Adirondack mountain club meeting. April 25, 1936. *High Spots*, July 1936. 13:no.2:8–12. Recreation in the Forest Preserve. 5136

Osgood, J. Picknicking in the Adirondacks. *Outing*, July 1889. 14:284–88. 5137

Outing of famous men in the Adirondacks; Edison, Burroughs and Ford spend part of the summer in the mountain wilds near Saranac Lake, discussion of politics part of their recreation. *State Service*, Sept. 1919. 3:no.9: 23–24. illus. 5138

Pach, Alfred. A horseback vacation in the Adirondacks. *Country Life*, June 1910. 18:205–6. illus. Albany to Pyramid Lake. 5139

Palmer, A.D. America's finest vacation lands reached by the New York Central lines. *NYC Lines Mag*, May 1920. 1:no.2:57–58. Adirondacks for summer vacations. 5140

Pammel, Harold Emmel. The recreational resources of the Fulton chain region. 199 leaves. mounted photographs, folded maps. Master's thesis, State University of New York, College of Forestry, Syracuse, 1925. Typescript. 5141

Pratt, George DuPont. The use of the New York state forests for public recreation. *Soc Am For Proc*, July 1916. 11:281–85. Reprinted in *New York State Forestry Association Journal*, Oct. 1916. 3:no.2–4:11–14. 5142

Prescott, Herbert F. What New York offers outdoor folks. *Outd Pic*, Aug. 1925. 2:no.6:9–10. illus. Recreational facilities of the Forest Preserve. 5143

R., J. Jr. The Adirondack region. *Rod & Gun*, July 15, 1876. 8:251. Places to go and equipment needed. 5144

R., J. Jr. Random notes in the Adirondacks. *For & Stream*, Aug. 25, 1881. 17:65–66. Sporting notes from various areas. 5145

Rabinowitz, Sue. College week '44. September 9–17. *IOCA Bul*, Fall 1944. p.15–16. Lake Colden. 5146

Radford, Harry V. Adirondack department, *Field & S*, June 1901–Aug. 1904. Monthly. Not in issues for Sept. and Oct. 1903 and Apr., May and July 1904. 5147

Radford, Harry V. Why New York welcomes sportsmen to the Adirondacks. *For Leaves*, Summer 1904. 1:no.3:25–29. illus. 5148

Recknagel, Arthur Bernard. Proposed recreation reserve. *NY Forestry*, Apr. 1918. 5:no.1: 23–28. map. Proposed reserve near Saranac. 5149

Recreational opportunities in our public forests. *Bul Schools*, Apr. 1922. 8:172, 175. illus. 5150

Rice, Arthur F. Pack-basket, rifle and rod. *For & Stream*, Nov. 6, 1897. 49:362–63. illus. Vacation at Blue Mountain Lake. 5151

Robinson, Alonzo Clark. Going into the "north woods." *Outing*, Nov. 1906. 49:246–47. Description and advice from one with long Adirondack experience. 5152

Rockwell, Joel Edson. Camping out. *Presbyterian*, Sept. 19, 1863. 33:149. Signed: J.E.R. Includes song: "The Saranac Lumbermen." 5153

Rockwell, Joel Edson. Getting into the woods. *Presbyterian*, Sept. 5, 1863. 33:141. Signed: J.E.R. Trip to the Saranacs. 5154

Rockwell, Joel Edson. Homeward bound. *Presbyterian*, Sept. 26, 1863. 33:153. Signed: J.E.R. Recommends camping for ladies. The last of a series of articles describing a clergyman's vacation in the North Woods, camping, hunting and fishing. 5155

Rockwell, Joel Edson. The Saranac lakes. *Presbyterian*, Sept. 12, 1863. 33:145. Signed: J.E.R. To Duck, Floodwood and Rawlins ponds. See also article with similar title in issue for Sept. 24, 1864, 34:no.39:1. To Folingsby's Pond, from Corey's. 5156

Royal sport of the mountains; ashore and afloat amid myriad lakes, forest green and mountain heights, summer goers find most joyous recreation of all. *Motordom*, June 1931. 24:no.12:18–19. illus. 5157

Sage, Dean. Vacations in the woods. *In* Noah Porter, a memorial by friends, ed. by George S. Merriam. . . N.Y. Scribner, 1893. p.153–57. 5158

Schaefer, Paul A. November in the Adirondacks. *Ad-i-ron-dac*, Nov.–Dec. 1948. 12:no.6: 10. illus. 5159

Seaman, Mrs. Frances (Boone). My most memorable winter. *Cloud Splitter*, Mar.–Apr. 1949. 12:no.2:10–11. Spending a winter at Forked Lake. 5160

Sears, George Washington. Rough notes from the woods, by Nessmuk, pseud. *For & Stream*, Aug. 12, Sept. 2, 16, Nov. 18, 25, 1880. 15:26, 84, 125, 304, 325. Reprint of Aug. 12, 1880 article in *Forest and Stream*, Aug. 16, 1913, 81:200. Canoeing and fishing; Fulton Chain and Brown's Tract. 5161

Sears, George Washington. Woodcraft, by "Nessmuk," pseud. N.Y. Forest and Stream publishing co. c1884. 149p. front. (port.) illus. (Forest and Stream Series, v.3.) Numerous other editions. Brief review in *The Cloud Splitter*, May–June 1950, 13:no.3:12–13. 5162

Sharples, Mary. College week—1936. *IOCA Bul*, Fall 1936. p.5–8. 5163

Shorey, Archibald Thompson. Ah spring! *Ad-i-ron-dac*, Mar.–Apr. 1946. 10:no.2:4. 5164

Shorey, Archibald Thompson. Behind the ranges. . . *Ad-i-ron-dac*, May–June 1951. 15: 52–53. 5165

Shorey, Archibald Thompson. Helping the amateur naturalist. *Bul Schools*, Apr. 1, 1937. 23:139–41. plates. Brief description of work of camp naturalist at Fish Creek Pond campsite during two summers. 5166

Shorey, Archibald Thompson. Schussing on the Oswegatchie. *High Spots Yrbk*, 1942. p.15. illus. Canoe and fishing trip.   5167

Smith, Clarence C. Recreation in the Adirondacks. *Up-Stater*, May 1929. 1:no.3:5–6. illus.   5168

Smith, Clarence C. Up-state vacation facilities. *Up-Stater*, May 1930. 2:no.3:3–5, 20. illus. map.   5169

Smith, Clarence C. Up-state vacationing, greatest variety of beautiful scenery in the world within a radius of a few hundred miles in New York state. *Up-Stater*, Apr. 1930. 2: no.2:3–5. illus.   5170

Smith, Harry P. The hosts of the Adirondacks invite you... *Motordom*, June 1932. p.21. port. illus.   5171

Spears, Raymond Smiley. A bicycle in the woods. *For & Stream*, Oct. 3, 1896. 47:274. Bicycle trip in northern Herkimer County.   5172

A Sportsman's Wife, pseud. Reminiscences of the north woods. *For & Stream*, Feb. 12, Mar. 12, 1874. 2:2–3, 66–67. Living in the Adirondacks.   5173

Summer sport fills the Adirondacks; enjoyment of endless variety awaits the Adirondack goer amid the mountains and lakes. *Motordom*, June 1930. 24:no.1:16–17. illus.   5174

Thackray, Emily A. Camps and tramps for women. *Outing*, Aug. 1889. 14:333–42. illus.   5175

Tips to take you to the Adirondacks. *Bet Hom & Gard*, Apr. 1947. 25:no.8:178, 180. Information on campsites, fishing and dress.   5176

Tunxis, pseud. Long lake loiterings. *For & Stream*, Feb. 1, 1883. 20:3.   5177

Tyler, Alanson Ranger. Rambling around; or...observations on a trip to and from the Board of governors meeting held at Johns brook lodge. *Ad-i-ron-dac*, Nov.–Dec. 1953. 17:110–11, 125.   5178

V., F.P. Lost in the woods. *For & Stream*, Jan. 6, 1906. 66:12.   5179

"The wane of the Adirondacks." *For & Stream*, Aug. 27, 1891. 37:101. Editorial on changing conditions.   5180

Ward, Peter A. Canine clamor. *Cloud Splitter*, Sept.–Oct. 1948. 11:no.5:2–4. Story of Chrissie Wendell, a dog who became a 46-er.   5181

Warfield, William. Finding the worth-while in mountain resorts, some places for rest and recreation in the mountains of the eastern states—vacationing in Maine, New Hampshire, New York and southward to North Carolina. *Travel*, May 1915. 25:no.1:44–47, 61–62. illus.   5182

Warner, Charles Dudley. The Adirondacks verified. *Atlan*, Jan.–June 1878. 41:63–67, 218–22, 343–46, 522–29, 636–46, 755–60. Contents: I. How I Killed a Bear; II. Lost in the Woods; III. A Fight with a Trout; IV. A-hunting of the Deer; V. A Character Study; (Orson Phelps); VI. Camping Out.   5183

A week in the Adirondacks. *For & Stream*, June 9, 1887. 28:435. Spring visit to Adirondack Preserve Association clubhouse (Essex County).   5184

Wheeler, Arthur Leslie. Around the Sawtooth range; ten days' tramping and trout fishing in the Adirondacks. *For & Stream*, July 17–24, 1909. 73:97–98, 137–39.   5185

White, Intry. Economy camp. *Outing*, May 1888. 12:168–71. Trip from Plattsburgh to Ausable, then to Keene Valley, on foot.   5186

Wightman, Robert S. Summers in the Adirondacks...a memoir of mother and father, 1902–1911, 1917–1921. n.p. Author, 1921. 203p. plates, ports. Family summer camp on the Grasse River; later on the Oswegatchie.   5187

Wood, Jerome. On and about Lake Champlain. *Amat Sportsman*, Aug. 1904. 31:no.4:14–15. Fishing and sailing possibilities.   5188

Worcester natural history society. Season of 1886. Special twelve days' trip...through the Adirondack mountains... Boston, n.d. 15p.   5189

World famous recreation, spell of the Adirondack wonderland stirs the vacationists' pulse in adventuring to these joyous places. *Motordom*, June 1931. 24:no.12:7–8. illus.   5190

Worthington, Mrs. Ruth (Drake). From Adirondacks to Green mountains. *Ver Horse*, Jan. 1939. 3:no.1:1–6, 26–28. illus. Log of horseback trip from Saranac Lake to Woodstock, Vt. Valerie and her rider won the Green Mountain Horse Association's 100-mile Trail Ride.   5191

Zack, pseud. A cheap trip to the north woods. *For & Stream*, Apr. 21, 1881. 16:230. Canada Lake and West Canada Creek area.   5192

Zoophilus, pseud. The old grey buck, a reminiscence of Folingsby, Jr. *For & Stream*, Nov. 30, 1876. 7:257–58. Camping on St. Regis River near Paul Smiths.   5193

GUIDES AND EQUIPMENT

The Adirondack guide-boat. *NYS Con*, Aug.–Sept. 1955. 10:no.1:10–11. illus. Photographs by Seneca Ray Stoddard, no text.				5194

Adirondack guides. *Am Angler*, Sept. 22, 1883. 4:186. Reprinted from the *Sunday News*. Reminiscences of Capt. Alvin Parker, John Plumbley, Sabattis, Alvah Dunning, etc.				5195

The Adirondack guides. *Sh & Fish*, Feb. 8, 1906. 39:368–70. Reports of meetings of Brown's Tract Guides Association (including summary of address by Harry V. Radford on the Adirondack Park) and the Adirondack Guides Association.				5196

Adirondack guides association. Proceedings of annual meeting. *For & Stream*, 1892–1910. v.38–74. These reports are in early February issues.				5197

Adirondack guides association. Season of 1897... n.p. n.d. 1p. Broadside describing the Association and listing members. Photographic copy in Saranac Lake Free Library.				5198

Adirondack notes. *Sh & Fish*, Jan. 26, 1905. 37:328–29. Report of meetings of the Adirondack Guides Association and of the Brown's Tract Guides Association.				5199

Alexander, J.C. Out of the pack basket. *Ad-i-ron-dac*, July–Aug. 1951, Jan.–Feb. 1952. 15: 72–74, 79; 16:27–28, 39.				5200

Beardslee, Lester A. The Adirondack guide system, by Piseco, pseud. *For & Stream*, May 3, 1883. 20:262–64.				5201

Benedict, Darwin. Saga of the guideboat. *Cloud Splitter*, May–June, 1946. 9:no.3:3–4, 8. History of the Adirondack guide boat.				5202

Bernier, Joseph. Guiding at St. Huberts. *Emp For*, 1924. 10:25–27. illus.				5203

Black river association. Report. *For & Stream*, 1897–1902. v.49–59. The reports usually appeared in second issues in December. Guides association.				5204

Brown's tract guides association. Report of annual meeting. *For & Stream*, 1901–11. v.56–76. Usually in the third issue in January. Signed: W.E. Wolcott.				5205

Colvin, Verplanck. Address at the first annual meeting of the Adirondack guides association held at Saranac Lake, March 2, 1892. n.p. n.pub. n.d. 4p. Unpaged folder. Copy owned by Seaver A. Miller.				5206

Colvin, Verplanck. Portable boats. *Alb Inst Tr*, 1876. 8:254–65. Part printed in *Forest and Stream*, July 8, 1875, 4:347.				5207

Dawson, George. About guides. *For & Stream*, May 19, 1906. 66:795. Signed: G.D. Complaint about guides on the Raquette.				5208

Death of Ernest Coulson. *For & Stream*, Sept. 10, 1898. 51:209. Guide shot during the hunting season.				5209

Ehrhardt, John Bohne. The 10-pound canoe. *NYS Con*, June–July 1950. 4:no.6:31. port. On Nessmuk's complete trail outfit (26 lbs.).				5210

Fosburgh, Peter W. Guides and guiding. *NYS Con*, Oct.–Nov. 1949. 4:no.2:8–9. ports.				5211

Foster, C.S. A narrow escape. *For & Stream*, Nov. 12, 1910. 75:776.				5212

Goldthwaite, Kenneth W. 'Twas not a dog. *For Leaves*, Winter 1906. 3:no.1:28. Henry Prentiss' skunk story, reprinted from the *Adirondack Enterprise*.				5213

Grady, Joseph A. Adirondack guide boats. *Up Mo*, Aug. 1941. 2:no.5:23. illus. History of development; names of makers.				5214

Guiding not what it used to be. *J Outd Life*, Aug. 1906. 3:255–57. illus.				5215

Home of Rushton canoes. *Field & S*, Apr. 1908. 12:1085.				5216

Howard, William Gibbs. Open camps. Albany, Adirondack mountain club, 1922. 12p. illus. Reprinted in 1925.				5217

Juvenal, pseud. Adirondack notes. *For & Stream*, Aug. 2, 1902. 59:89. News notes include the death of Louis Watso, Indian guide.				5218

Keller, Allan. Murder in the Adirondacks. *No Country Life*, Fall 1946. 1:no.1:16–18. Murder of Eula Davis, guide and woodsman.				5219

King, Thomas G. Adirondack guides. *Recreation*, Sept. 1902. 17:183–84. Not as good as in former years.				5220

Lempfert, O.C. A good tent for the north woods. *For & Stream*, Aug. 1927. 97:468–70, 500. illus. charts. Testing a tepee in the Adirondacks.				5221

Miller, Clinton H. Jr. A trail blazing menace. *Ad-i-ron-dac*, May–June 1951. 15:43. Deplores unauthorized blazing.				5222

Miller, John Henry. The Adirondack guides' association. *Recreation*, May 1895. 2:383. Brief history with aims of the Association.				5223

Miller, Roland B. Adirondack guideboat. *NYS Con*, June–July 1948. 2:no.6:6–7. illus. Adaption of this article in *North Country Life*, Fall 1950, 4:no.4:22–23.				5224

Miller, Roland B. The Adirondack pack-basket. *NYS Con*, Aug.–Sept. 1948. 3:no.1:8–9. illus. 5225

Miller, Roland B. The light truck of the Adirondacks. *Am For*, July 1951. 57:no.7:20–21, 30. illus. Directions for building a guide boat. 5226

Miller, Seaver Asbury. The Adirondack guides' association; its organization and chief promoter. *Sport Mag*, Mar. 1898. 2:no.3:129–32. ports. 5227

Mulholland, William D. The Adirondack open camp. *NYS Con*, Aug.–Sept. 1949. 4:no.1:23. 5228

Murray, William H.H. Adirondack outfit. *Rod & Gun*, Aug. 5, 1876. Also in *The Golden Rule*, July 19, 1876, p.6. Clothing. 5229

New York (state). Conservation department. Licensed guides in the New York state Forest preserve. Albany, J.B. Lyon, 1935. 15p. illus. Also issued in 1927 (20p.) and 1931 (16p.). 5230

Ondack, Adrion, pseud. Hints for Adirondack visitors. *For & Stream*, May 6, 1880. 14:264. Suggestions on equipment and guides. 5231

The passing of the Adirondack guide. *For & Stream*, Dec. 22, 1894. 43:529. Due to lack of game. 5232

Portable boats. *For & Stream*, Aug. 26, 1875. 5:40–41. Some of the kinds used exclusively in the Adirondacks. 5233

R., J. Jr. The Adirondack guides. *For & Stream*, July 19, 1883. 20:482. In defense of guides. 5234

R., J. Jr. Outfit for the Adirondacks. *For & Stream*, Aug. 3, 1882. 19:4–5. Necessary equipment. 5235

Radford, Harry V. The sportsman and his guide; an address delivered at the annual banquet of the Brown's tract guides' association, at Old Forge, N.Y. Jan. 8, 1903. *Field & S*, Feb. 1903. 7:691–94. illus. Also in *Woods and Waters*, Spring 1904, 7:no.1:16–19. John Plumbley. 5236

Rolston, Ben. Out of the pack basket. *Cloud Splitter*, Mar.–Apr. 1951. 14:no.2:9–10. List of equipment. 5237

Scribner, Kimball and Fayant, Frank. An open camp in the Adirondacks. *Four Tr News*, June 1904. 6:399–401. illus. 5238

Seaman, Mrs. Frances (Boone). Long lake guides and their descendants. *Cloud Splitter*, Sept.–Oct. 1949. 12:no.5:5–7. Early Adirondack guides. 5239

Sears, George Washington. In defense of the Adirondack guides, by Nessmuk, pseud. *For & Stream*, Aug. 18, 1881. 17:48. 5240

Sears, George Washington. The "Sairy Gamp," by Nessmuk, pseud. *For & Stream*, Oct. 18, 1883. 21:221. Description of guide boat. 5241

A serviceable boat. *Am Angler*, Apr. 21, 1883. 3:244. diagr. Designed by Gen. R.U. Sherman for use in the Adirondacks. 5242

Shorey, Archibald Thompson. The Adirondack leanto, a few days' work and it's yours. *NYS Con*, Aug. 1946. 1:no.1:19. diagr. 5243

Smith, Clarence C. The guide business; an account of an interview with Wellington Kenwell, one of the old-time Adirondack guides. *Up-Stater*, Sept. 1930. 2:no.5:10. 5244

Spaulding, N.E. Brant lake fishing boats. *For & Stream*, Nov. 14, 1908. 71:781. illus. Description of boats. 5245

Spears, John Randolph. A spruce bark camp in the Adirondacks. *Chaut*, Sept. 1890. 11:714–17. Northwood, near Prospect. 5246

State registration of guides. *Conservationist*, June 1919. 2:92–93. The first registration of guides in New York state. 5247

Tasker, S.P.M. Jr. An Adirondack outfit. *For & Stream*, Apr. 3, 1897. 48:267. Cutting down weight for a hunting trip. 5248

Tent in the woods. *NYS Con*, Oct.–Nov. 1948. 3:no.2:16–18. illus. Photographs of a hunting camp in the Forest Preserve. 5249

"Uncle Mart" Moody. *Northeast Log*, July 1952. 1:no.1:27. One of his stories. 5250

Webster, George O. Adirondack pioneer woodsmen. *High Spots*, Apr. 1935. 12:no.2:29–31. (Famous Adirondack Guides, no.10.) 5251

Welch, Fay. The Adirondack lean-to. *Girl Scout*, June–July 1932. 9:65–66, 76. illus. 5252

Wilson, H.G. The Adirondack pack-basket. *Fur News*, Apr. 1921. 33:no.4:22. Origin and use. 5253

CANOEING

Adirondack canoe cruising. *Outing*, June 1920. 76:164–68. maps. Short and long trips in the vicinity of Fulton Chain, Raquette, Long and Saranac lakes.   5254

American canoe association, 16th annual meet, Bluff Point, Lake Champlain. *For & Stream*, Aug. 31, 1895. 45:191–92. illus. map.   5255

Bailey, Richard. Five days and a foldboat. *IOCA Bul*, Spring 1947. 1:no.1:12–17. See also his article entitled "Five Days in a Fold-boat" in *The Cloud Splitter*, July–Aug. 1947, 10:no.4:2–5. Lake George and Lake Champlain.   5256

Bell, James Christy. Three men in a boat. *High Spots Yrbk*, 1940. p.65–70.   5257

Bodin, Arthur Michael. Bibliography of canoeing; compiled, subject indexed, and partially annotated. N.Y.? 1954. 64p. Reproduced from typewritten copy. Includes Adirondacks. Reviewed by D.A. Plum in *The Ad-i-ron-dac*, July–Aug. 1955, 19:80. Brief note in *The Cloud Splitter*, Sept.–Oct. 1954, 17: no.5:12.   5258

Bruce, Dwight Hall. An Adirondack trail. *For & Stream*, July 18, 1889. 32:526–27. Signed: D.H.B. By boat from Paul Smiths to Old Forge.   5259

Bulger, John D. 90 miles down the Indian. *NYS Con*, June–July 1949. 3:no.6:4–7. illus. map. Canoe and fishing trip.   5260

Canoe trips for you—Hudson river, Champlain canal, Lake George, Lake Champlain. *All Outdoors*, May 1915. 2:298–99. illus. map.   5261

Canoeing in the Adirondacks. *Recreation*, Aug. 1905. 23:184–86. Fulton Chain.   5262

Chittenden, Horace H. Canoeing: Lake George, Lake Champlain and the Hudson river. *For & Stream*, Feb. 17, 1900. 54:137. Response to request for information on planning a vacation trip. For criticism see A.G. Whittemore in issue for Mar. 17, 1900, 54: 217, and article signed "Romeo" in issue for Apr. 7, 1900, 54:274.   5263

Christopher, Larry. Nature: $80 F.O.B. *Am For*, Sept. 1948. 54:403, 426–27. illus. Two-week canoe trip on Lake George.   5264

Clark, .H.D. The Oswegatchie canoe trip. *Camp Log*, Dec. 1922. p.38–39. illus.   5265

Dittmar, Adolph G. and Dittmar, Mrs. Mary (Colyer). Let's go canoeing! *Cloud Splitter*, May–June, July–Aug. 1944. 7:no.3:9–10; 7: no.4:7–9. Canoe trips around Old Forge etc.   5266

Dobson, Meade C. Canoe-hike. *High Spots Yrbk*, 1944. p.24. illus. Blue Mountain Lake from Raquette Lake village.   5267

Eastman, Irving W. Canoe trip on Lake Champlain. *Vermonter*, Autumn 1916. 21: 213–16. From Essex, N.Y. to northern part of the lake.   5268

Farnham, Charles Haight. Running the rapids of the upper Hudson. *Scrib Mo*, Apr. 1881. 21:857–70. Author's name given in Poole's Index.   5269

Flip, pseud. The Lake Champlain canoe meet. *Outing*, Dec. 1887. 11:262–64.   5270

Hard, Josephine Wilhelm. An Adirondack carry; from lake to lake in the heart of the great north woods. *Four Tr News*, Jan. 1906. 10:373–75. illus.   5271

Howard, William Gibbs. Adirondack canoe cruising. *Mt Mag*, July 1927. 6:4–7. illus. map.   5272

Howard, William Gibbs. Adirondack canoe routes. Albany, New York state conservation department, 1955. 30p. illus. folded map. (Recreation Circular 7.) Earlier editions, 1920, 1931, 1949, 1953.   5273

Howard, William Gibbs. Beauty of Adirondack canoe routes; directions and information for those who would enjoy this means of travel through the mountain wilderness; pleasure in the many side trips. *State Service*, May 1920. 4:389–401. illus.   5274

Hutchins, L.W. Outboard to Lake George. *Outing*, Sept. 1916. 68:596–607. A trip from New York to Lake George in a canoe with an outboard motor.   5275

Jack, pseud. Through north woods by canoe. *For & Stream*, June 1–8, 1912. 78:687–88, 719–20. illus. Fulton Chain.   5276

Jessup, Elon H. Up the Saranacs. *Outing*, Nov. 1918. 73:65–68, 110–11. illus. Canoeing and fishing trip.   5277

Johnson, Ralph. A canoe trip on the Fulton chain of lakes. *Camp Log*, Dec. 1922. p.31–33. illus.   5278

Kalland, Anna. It can't be done. *Outing*, Mar. 1923. 81:267–72. illus. Two nurses paddle a canoe from New York City to Lake George.   5279

Kelleye, Arthur W. An auto canoe trip to the 'Dacks. *Fur-Fish-Game*, June 1926. 43:no.6: 4–6. illus. Fulton Chain.   5280

Lake George meet. *For & Stream*, Aug. 18, 1881. 17:44. American Canoe Association.   5281

Lemmon, Robert S. Canoeing on river and lake. . . *Travel*, July 1914. 23:no.3:44–46, 65. illus. Includes Fulton Chain and Blue Mountain Lake. 5282

The log of an Adirondack cruise, by two of the crew. *Conservationist*, Feb. 1921. 4:23–26. Canoe trip from Lower St. Regis Lake to Lower Saranac Lake. 5283

Mattison, C.H. Canoeing in the Adirondacks: a practical account of a two weeks vacation spent in the woods on a hundred and fifty mile cruise. *Field & S*, June 1907. 12:107–18. illus. 5284

Miller, Warren Hastings. We discover the Adirondacks. *Field & S*, Oct.–Nov. 1917. 22: 525–27, 591–93. illus. Trip from Old Forge to Saranac. 5285

Mills, Borden H. Sr. By paddle and portage. *Country Life*, June 1909. 16:156, 158, 160. illus. Description of a 150-mile trip through the depths of the Adirondack forest. 5286

Mills, Borden H. Sr. Canoe cruising in the Adirondacks. *Recreation*, June 1908. 27:262–63, 294–95. 5287

Mills, Borden H. Sr. Tupper to Tahawus, 1908. *Ad-i-ron-dac*, May–June 1955. 19:44–47, 53. illus. Diary of canoe trips. 5288

Nash, R.H. An overland canoe trip. *For & Stream*, Oct. 5, 1912. 78:434–35, 443–46. Fulton Chain to Saranac Lake. 5289

Neide, Charles A. The canoe Aurora; a cruise from the Adirondacks to the Gulf. N.Y. Forest & stream publishing co. 1885. 215p. Lake George, p.9–11. 5290

Nichols, Louis L. The north woods by canoe. *Am For*, Sept. 1924. 30:524–25, 542. illus. Adirondack guide boat used from Inlet to Saranac Lake village. 5291

Oliver, Frank Joseph. A trip up the Oswegatchie river. *High Spots*, Apr. 1935. 12:no.2: 24–29. map. 5292

Out of the past, a record trip in a guide-boat. *NYS Con*, Aug.–Sept. 1948. 3:no.1:27. Chester Stanton made a trip between Forked Lake and Old Forge. 5293

Peters, Pete. Top canoe route. *Saga*, Jan. 1955. 9:no.4:7. illus. 5294

Prichard, William. A wilderness canoe trip on the Hudson river near its source. *Cloud Splitter*, May–June 1955. 18:no.3:2–5. Abstract of article in Utica *Observer-Dispatch*, June 6, 1864. 5295

Roseberry, C.R. Canoeing on the Saranacs. *Cloud Splitter*, Sept.–Oct. 1955. 18:no.5:7–9. 5296

Saranac to Old Forge via Tuppers. *For & Stream*, Aug. 30, 1913. 81:287. Itinerary of a canoe trip. 5297

Schenck, Gilbert V. The Lost lake canoe trip in the Adirondacks. *Recreation*, May 1909. 29:249. illus. 5298

Seagears, Clayton B. 2 days or 2 weeks by canoe. *NYS Con*, June–July 1952. 6:no.6:18–19. map. 5299

Seaman, Mrs. Frances (Boone). Cold river valley—by canoe. *No Country Life*, Summer 1947. 1:no.4:43–46, 48. 5300

Seaman, Mrs. Frances (Boone). Exploring the Raquette. *Cloud Splitter*, Mar.–Apr. 1945. 8:no.2:8–9, 18. 5301

Sears, George Washington. Cruise of "The Nipper," by Nessmuk, pseud. *For & Stream*, Dec. 8–15, 29, 1881. 17:365–66, 385–86, 425–26. Canoe trip from Fulton Chain to Tupper Lake and return. 5302

Sears, George Washington. Cruise of the "Sairy Gamp," by Nessmuk, pseud. *For & Stream*, Sept. 13–27, 1883. 21:22, 44, 63, 122, 142–43, 162–63. Moose River, Fulton Chain and Raquette lakes. 5303

Shorey, Archibald Thompson. Canoeing in the Adirondacks. *Cloud Splitter*, June 1940. 3:no.5:17. Suggested trips. 5304

Shorey, Archibald Thompson. Canoes and campsites. *NYS Con*, June–July 1947. 1:no.6: 4–6. map. 5305

Shorey, Archibald Thompson. Easy paddles. *NYS Con*, Aug.–Sept. 1952. 7:no.1:8–9. maps. 5306

Smith, Kenneth R. Through the Adirondacks by canoe, including Fulton chain, Tupper lake, Raquette, Blue mountain and Long lake. *For & Stream*, May 31, 1913. 80:686–87, 695. illus. 5307

Snedeker, Florence Watters. A family canoe trip. N.Y. Harper, 1892. 137p. incl. front. illus. plates. (Harper's Black and White Series.) 5308

Syms, Harriette. Our Adirondack canoe trip. *Conservationist*, Sept. 1921. 4:135–39. illus. Fulton Chain. 5309

Theall, Frederick. A trip thru the Saranacs. *Camp Log*, Dec. 1922. p.36–37. illus. 5310

Vaux, C. Bowyer. Canoeing, the ninth annual American canoe association meet at Lake George. *Outing*, Oct. 1888. 13:73–74. 5311

Vosburgh, Hiram L. The log of two city chaps. *Ang & Hunt*, Sept. 1910. 2:453–58. illus. Fulton Chain. 5312

Warburton, William John. By canoe from Lake George to the Atlantic. *Outing*, Sept. 1893. 22:464–68. 5313

Whipple, Gurth Adelbert. An Adirondack canoe trip. *For & Stream*, July 23–30, 1910.

75:146, 153–55, 185–86, 194–97. illus. From Little Tupper Lake to Old Forge.   5314

Whyte, Herbert. Vacation in a canoe. *Outing*, June 1910. 56:382–84. Fulton Chain trip suggested for beginners.   5315

Woodworth, Benjamin R. Canoe cruise in the Adirondacks. *For & Stream*, Jan. 3, 17, 1884. 21:465, 505. Big Moose Lake and Second Lake.   5316

HIKING, CLIMBING, CAMPING

GUIDEBOOKS

Adirondack mountain club, inc. Guide to Adirondack trails: northeastern section. Albany, N.Y. c1950. 127p. folded maps. 1st edition, 1935; 2d edition, 1941; 3d edition, 1945; 4th edition, 1950. Editions 1–4 contain "Suggestions for Starting an Adirondack Library" by Russell M.L. Carson. Editions 1 and 2 edited by Orra A. Phelps; 3–5, by A.T. Shorey.   5317

Adirondack trail improvement society. ATIS trail guide—abbreviated. St. Huberts, N.Y. 1948. 4p. cover emblem, map. Compiled by Harold Weston.   5318

Baker, Walter. Washington county trails. *Ad-i-ron-dac*, Sept.–Oct. 1952. 16:86–89. illus. Correction in Nov.–Dec. issue, 16:110. Includes Buck and Black mountains.   5319

Denniston, Robert. Adirondack trail times with suggested trips from Keene Valley, Adirondak loj, Johns Brook lodge. Elizabethtown, N.Y. W.D. Denton printing co. 1950. 20p. See also his article on same subject in *The Ad-i-ron-dac*, July–Aug. 1946, 10:no.4:7. Planned as a supplement to the Adirondack Mountain Club *Guidebook*. Useful brief manual.   5320

Hopkins, Arthur S. The trails to Marcy. Albany, New York state conservation department, 1955. 23p. illus. folded map. (Recreation Circular 8.) Earlier editions published in 1922, 1925, 1932, 1935, 1936, 1938, 1949.   5321

Howard, William Gibbs. Northville-Placid trail. Albany, Adirondack mountain club, 1924. 21p. illus. maps. For more recent information see A.T. Shorey's article with same title in *The Ad-i-ron-dac*, July–Aug. 1947, 11:no.4:6–7.   5322

Longstreth, Thomas Morris. The Lake Placid country; a guide to 60 walks and climbs from Lake Placid including the most interesting trails from the Marcy and Ausable lakes region with 20 motor trips possible from Lake Placid. Lake Placid Club, N.Y. Adirondack camp and trail club, 1922. 76p. front. map.   5323

Mulholland, William D. Lake Placid trails Albany, New York state conservation department, 1947. 24p. illus. folded map. (Recreation Circular 10.)   5324

National lead co. Three new Adirondack trails opened to the public on National lead company property. n.p.n.d. 2 leaves.   5325

O'Kane, Walter Collins. . . .Trails and summits of the Adirondacks. Boston & N.Y. Houghton, 1928. 330p. front. plates, folded map. (Riverside Outdoor Handbooks.) Reviewed in *Mountain Magazine*, July 1928, 7:9–10, and in *The Cloud Splitter*, Nov. 1943, 6:no.8:5–6. Extract entitled "The Building of the Adirondacks" in *The Living Wilderness*, Mar. 1946, no.16:10–12, map.   5326

Porter, Lewis Morgan. Nipple top via Bear den and Dial. *Ad-i-ron-dac*, May–June 1955. 19:54, 57.   5327

Porter, Lewis Morgan. Trail notes. *Ad-i-ron-dac*, Nov.–Dec. 1949. 13:132. Corrections and additions to the Adirondack Mountain Club's *Guide*.   5328

Porter, Lewis Morgan. Trail notes. *Ad-i-ron-dac*, Mar.–Apr. 1951. 15:39. East Dix.   5329

Shorey, Archibald Thompson. New areas to explore. *Cloud Splitter*, May–June 1946. 9:no.3:16. New trails for proposed guidebook "Guide to the Southeastern Adirondacks."   5330

Shorey, Archibald Thompson. Trails in the Lake George region. Albany, New York state conservation department, 1954. 7p. illus. First issued in 1950.   5331

Shorey, Archibald Thompson. Trails in the Piseco lake region. Albany, New York state conservation department, 1938. 5 leaves. map. Mimeographed.   5332

Shorey, Archibald Thompson. Trails in the Schroon lake region. Albany, New York state conservation department, n.d. 10 leaves. maps. Mimeographed.   5333

Wickham, Robert Sloane. Friendly Adirondack peaks. Binghamton, N.Y. Privately published, 1924. 192p. front. illus. maps. "Adirondack Mountain Club edition, limited to five hundred copies."   5334

HIKING AND CLIMBING

Adams, Charles Christopher. Delights of the wild forest trail. *State Service*, Feb.–Mar. 1921. 5:100–3. Also issued as a separate. On hiking in general, with some reference to the Adirondacks.   5335

An Adirondack mountain jaunt. *Outdoor Life*, Nov. 1904. 1:121–23. Description of a walk from Saranac Lake to Keene Valley, including climbs of five mountains.   5336

B., C.E. A week in the Marcy country. *Camp Log*, 1928. 14:13–18. Hiking and camping trip.   5337

Bachli, Werner O. On ADK trails. *Ad-i-ron-dac*, May–June 1952. 16:47, 58, 60. Trail maintenance.   5338

Beetle, David Harold. Go climb a tower. *Up Mo*, July 1941. 2:no.4:10, 16. Climbing various fire towers.   5339

Beetle, David Harold. You can climb mountains. *Up Mo*, July 1940. 1:no.4:22–23. illus. Suggested climbs in the Adirondacks.   5340

Betts, Charles E. Snow in summer. *Ad-i-ron-dac*, May–June 1952. 16:55–56. The Range.   5341

Bird, J. Sterling. In the heart of the Adirondacks. *Ad-i-ron-dac*, Sept.–Oct.—Nov.–Dec. 1954. 18:80–83, 85. Lake Sanford, Heart Lake, to Preston Ponds, including Algonquin.   5342

Brooks, C.H. An Adirondack tramp. *For & Stream*, Oct. 24, 1908. 71:658. illus. A short account with itinerary of a 275-mile tramp in sixteen days. Thirteenth Lake, Speculator, Raquette and Indian Pass, Marcy.   5343

Brown, Thomas Kite. On the trail at dusk. n.p. n.pub. 1930. 10p. port. illus. Reprinted in *Appalachia*. The founder of Back Log Camp relates a camping experience. Written in 1917.   5344

Brownell, Baker. A three cornered hike. *Recreation*, Aug. 1910. 32:96–98. illus. From Buffalo to Ticonderoga through the Adirondacks.   5345

Burger, William H. Shambles at Shattuck's. *Ad-i-ron-dac*, May–June 1951. 15:56. Blow-down near Long Lake.   5346

Burton, Harold B. What a way to amuse yourself! *Sat Eve Post*, Dec. 29, 1951. 224: no.26:16–17, 36, 38–39. illus. Color photographs include five Adirondack scenes. On the pleasures of climbing; refers to the Adirondack Mountain Club and the Adirondack 46ers.   5347

Carpenter, Warwick Stevens. Mountain climbing in eastern Appalachia. *Outing*, Dec. 1912. 61:355–69. illus. Appalachian Mountain Club's ascent of several of the great peaks in the Adirondacks.   5348

Carpenter, Warwick Stevens. Sidelights on Adirondack mountain tops. *NYS For Assn J*, Oct. 1915. 2:40–43. Indian Pass.   5349

Chamberlain, Allen. Making the tramper's dream come true. *Conservationist*, Aug. 1920. 3:115–18. illus. Reprinted in *State Service*, May–Oct. 1923, 7,i.e.9:141–44, with title "Lure of the Mountain and Forest Trail." Hiking in the Adirondacks.   5350

Christie, John L. An Adirondack walking trip: 1909. *Ad-i-ron-dac*, Sept.–Oct. 1951. 15: 84–85, 91–92. From Piseco to Blue Mountain Lake.   5351

Craig, Ronald B. Forest trails, with suggestions for the Adirondacks. *Conservationist*, Oct. 1921. 4:147–51. illus. Reprinted in *State Service*, Sept.–Oct. 1922. 6,i.e.8:291–94.   5352

Cram, Mildred. Encounter in the rain. *Woman's Day*, Dec. 1951. 15:no.3:33, 86. illus. Describes meeting Woodrow Wilson on the trail to St. Huberts.   5353

Crandall, Carl H. Adirondack Easter. *Ad-i-ron-dac*, Mar.–Apr. 1952. 16:35. Ausable lakes.   5354

Dittmar, Adolph G. Jr. My most memorable trip. *Cloud Splitter*, July–Aug. 1948. 11:no.4: 9–10. Hiking in the Adirondacks.   5355

Dittmar, Mrs. Mary (Colyer). My most memorable trip. *Cloud Splitter*, Sept.–Oct. 1947. 10:no.5:11–12. Climbing and camping in the high-peak region.   5356

Endicott, William and Schuyler, Margaret. The range from Johns Brook. *Cloud Splitter*, Oct. 1939. 2:no.5:10. illus.   5357

Excursion of the Appalachian mountain club to the Adirondacks. *Appalachia*, June 1888. 5:162–63.   5358

For mountain climbers are the forest secrets. *Motordom*, June 1933. p.30. illus.   5359

Forster, Herman. How do you walk? *Ad-i-ron-dac*, May–June 1947. 11:no.3:4–5. On looking for wild flowers while hiking.   5360

Frederich, Charles. Week-end hikes in northern New York. *Recreation (NY)* Mar. 1917. 56:130. Oswegatchie River country.   5361

Freeborn, Frank W. Some Adirondack paths. *Appalachia*, Dec. 1888, May 1890, July 1891. 5:222–31; 6:51–60, 231–35. The article that appeared in Dec. 1888 was published separately: Boston, Appalachian Mountain Club, 1889, 20p. map, plate.   5362

Gleason, A.W. Notes by an Adirondack tramp. *Field & S*, May 1902. 7:73–76. illus. Reminiscences of thirty summers of hiking.   5363

Goodwin, James A. Climbs in the Adirondacks. *Appalachia*, June 1938. 22:27–32.   5364

Gowie, Orville C. Babes in the woods. *Cloud Splitter*, Sept.–Oct. 1946. 9:no.5:5–6. Trip into Johns Brook Lodge.   5365

Haeusser, Dorothy O. Bewitched, bothered and bewildered. *Cloud Splitter*, July–Aug. 1952. 15:no.4:14–15. What to do when lost.   5366

Haeusser, Dorothy O. Head for the hills. *NYS Ed*, Mar. 1954. 41:448–49. illus. Reprinted in *North Country Life*, Fall 1954, 8: no.4:37–39. Hiking as a hobby for teachers. The "Social Climbers."   5367

Haeusser, Dorothy O. Santanoni and Panther. *Cloud Splitter*, Sept.–Oct. 1952. 15:no.5: 8–9.   5368

Hammond, Henry D. They beat you to it. *Cloud Splitter*, July–Aug.—Nov.–Dec. 1946. 9:no.4:3–5; 9:no.5:2–3, 6; 9:no.6:4–6. Early climbers in the Adirondacks.   5369

Harmes, Edward A. Long lake to Heart lake. *Ad-i-ron-dac*, Sept.–Oct. 1949. illus. Hiking.   5370

Harmes, Edward A. To all and sundry who walk in the rain. *Cloud Splitter*, July–Aug. 1947. 10:no.4:12.   5371

Harmes, Edward A. Why? *Ad-i-ron-dac*, Mar.–Apr. 1948. 12:no.2:10–11, 14. illus. Rewards of climbing.   5372

Hart, Merwin K. Jr. Further ventures into the little great range. *Ad-i-ron-dac*, Jan.–Feb. 1951. 15:15. Climbing nameless peak near Snowy Mountain.   5373

Heathcote. A day of mountain climbing. *For & Stream*, Sept. 25, 1909. 73:491. Trip up Colvin, Marcy, Haystack, Basin, Saddleback and Gothics. Times given.   5374

"Heaven up-h'istedness"; mountain climbing in the Adirondacks is becoming a favorite pastime among vacationists. *No Country Life*, Winter 1948. 2:no.1:36–38, 62. illus.   5375

Hine, Mrs. Marie. Mountain novitiate. *Cloud Splitter*, July–Aug. 1947. 10:no.4:9–11. First trip to the high peaks.   5376

Hopkins, Arthur S. The White trail. *High Spots*, Dec. 1929. 6:no.4:2, 5. port. Named in honor of William A. White.   5377

Howard, William Gibbs. Camps and trails in the Forest preserve. *Conservationist*, Oct. 1920. 3:147–50.   5378

Hudowalski, Edward C. Caribou pass. *Ad-i-ron-dac*, July–Aug. 1946. 10:no.4:15.   5379

Hudowalski, Edward C. Cold river. *Cloud Splitter*, Oct. 1939. 2:no.5:13. Club hike to climb "Couchee," Seymour and the Sewards.   5380

Hudowalski, Edward C. "Random scoots." *Cloud Splitter*, July–Aug. 1952. 15:no.4:4–8. On use of map and compass.   5381

Hudowalski, Mrs. Grace (Leech) and Nash, C. Howard. 21 trailless peaks. *High Spots Yrbk*, 1939. p.13–26. Directions for climbing trailless peaks.   5382

Huntington, Adelaide. A walking trip through the Adirondacks. How plans for a long-cherished vacation were carried out by "two a-foot." Adventures in finding bed and board. *Sub Life*, Aug. 1912. 15:no.2:81–82. illus. From Blue Mountain Lake village to Lake George.   5383

Jessup, Elon H. We hike into the Adirondacks. *Outing*, Oct. 1918. 73:16–18. illus.   5384

Kamphaus, Mary. Adirondack hikes out of Back log camp. *Mt Club Md*, Oct.–Nov.–Dec. 1953. 20:no.2:15–17.   5385

Lofty mountains await traveler on international highway. *Motordom*, June 1932. p.8–9. illus. Hiking.   5386

Macklin, Philip and Macklin, Richard L. Adirondack diary. *Cloud Splitter*, Jan.–Feb., Mar.–Apr. 1944. 7:no.1:2–4; 7:no.2:7–9. Hiking in the high-peak region.   5387

Macklin, Richard L. Adirondack diary. *Cloud Splitter*, Nov.–Dec. 1944. 7:no.6:5–6. Climbing among the trailless peaks.   5388

Marshall, George. Approach to the mountains. *Ad-i-ron-dac*, Mar.–Apr. 1955. 19:24–27, 38. illus. See also letter from William B. Glover in July–Aug. issue, 19:77–78, "Early 20th Century Adirondack Trips."   5389

Marshall, George. Lost pond. *Cloud Splitter*, June 1941. 4:no.6:2–3. Account of trip to Lost Pond, near Scott Pond.   5390

Marshall, George. The 3900 footers. *Cloud Splitter*, June 1942. 5:no.6:2–4.   5391

Marshall, Robert. Adirondack peaks. *High Spots*, Oct. 1932. 9:no.4:13–15. Account of day's ascent of fourteen peaks.   5392

Marshall, Robert. The high peaks of the Adirondacks; a brief account of the climbing of the forty-two Adirondack mountains over 4,000 feet in height. . . Albany, Adirondack mountain club, inc. c1922. 38p. incl. front. illus. folded map.   5393

Martin, Newell. Modern haste on the hilltops. *High Spots*, Jan. 1932. 9:no.1:29–30. (Historical Adirondack Character Series, no.6.) Record climbs.   5394

Martin, Newell. Six summits. *High Spots*, July 1931. 8:no.3:2–7. Marcy and other range peaks from St. Huberts.   5395

Martin, Newell. Six summits: invitation and advice to my granddaughters. Huntington, N.Y. 1927. 14p. 5396

Menz, Mrs. Helen (Colyer). My most memorable trip. *Cloud Splitter*, Nov.–Dec. 1947. 10: no.6:13–14. Hiking in the Elk Lake region. 5397

Miller, Clinton H. Jr. Scott's and Wallface ponds. *Ad-i-ron-dac*, Mar.–Apr. 1951. 15:30–31. illus. 5398

Mills, Borden H. Sr. To J.B.L. from the north. *Cloud Splitter*, May–June 1947. 10: no.3:11–12. Klondike trail. 5399

Mills, Borden H. Sr. Tramping and camping in the Adirondacks. *Recreation*, June 1910. 31: 296–97. illus. 5400

Moore, William. The story of a young man's tramp across three states, cooking his meals and camping along three hundred sixty miles of road in New Hampshire, Vermont and New York. N.Y. Markey press, c1911. 76p. Lake George area, p. 37–42. 5401

Mountain climbing; one of the biggest thrills of the Adirondacks; trails well marked; Mount Marcy the highest peak, a popular climb. *Motordom*, June 1929. 23:no.1:34. 5402

Mountaineering in Scotland and the northeastern U.S. contrasted. *Geog R*, Jan. 1934. 24:148–49. Adirondack and White mountains contrasted with the mountains of Scotland. 5403

Nixon, Edgar Burkhardt. The armchair mountaineer. *Ad-i-ron-dac*, July–Aug. 1955. 19:74–75. The Great Range. 5404

Nixon, Edgar Burkhardt. Explorer scouts discover high peaks. *Ad-i-ron-dac*, Sept.–Oct. 1952. 16:84–85. illus. 5405

Oliver, Frank Joseph. Second thoughts on the 46 peaks. *Ad-i-ron-dac*, Nov.–Dec. 1948. 12:no.6:6–7. 5406

Our tour to Lake George. *Wilkes Spirit*, Oct. 4, 1862. 7:66–67. Walking trip to the lake. 5407

Phelps, Mrs. Orra (Parker). My first trip to Heart lake. *Cloud Splitter*, Mar.–Apr. 1945. 8: no.2:2–3. 5408

Plum, Eleanor Mary. By trail. *Cloud Splitter*, July–Aug. 1952. 15:no.4:16. 5409

Porter, Lewis Morgan. A trip to the Moose river country. *Ad-i-ron-dac*, Mar.–Apr. 1949. 13:36–38. 5410

Price, Fraser P. Five seconds on Phelps trail. *Ad-i-ron-dac*, Sept.–Oct. 1950. 14:103–5. Narrow escape when tree falls at night. 5411

Prince, Ruth. "Every year about this time." *Cloud Splitter*, July–Aug. 1945. 8:no.5:7. Weekend at Johns Brook Lodge. 5412

Prince, Ruth. My most memorable trip. *Cloud Splitter*, July–Aug. 1947. 10:no.4:13–14. Camping and hiking among the high peaks. 5413

Puffer, Louis B. Forty-seveners. *Cloud Splitter*, July–Aug. 1948. 11:no.4:5–6. Camping and hiking among the high peaks. 5414

R., J.K. Trails to Horseshoe. *Camp Log*, 1926. 12:38, 81. map. Various trails from the Syracuse camp to the New York Central station. 5415

Radford, Harry V. Adirondack mountain climbing. *Four Tr News*, Sept. 1902. 3:103–5. illus. Reprinted in *Forest Leaves*, Autumn 1905, 2:no.4:35–37. 5416

Riech, Charles A. Introducing Long lake. *Ad Mt Club Bul*, May–June 1944. 8:no.3:4, 6. 5417

Robe. A tramp and a camp. *For & Stream*, Oct. 8, 1897. 49:285–86. From Chateaugay Lake by way of Ragged Lake, Round Pond and Salmon River to Plumadore Pond. 5418

Shorey, Archibald Thompson. "It's a dandy!" *Ad-i-ron-dac*, Sept.–Oct. 1950. 14:105. Suggested hikes. 5419

Shorey, Archibald Thompson. June snowstorm. *Cloud Splitter*, Jan.–Feb. 1951. 14: no.1:5–6. 5420

Shorey, Archibald Thompson. The range trail. *NYS Con*, June–July 1951. 5:no.6:8. diagr. 5421

Shorey, Archibald Thompson. Tips for a long week-end. *Ad-i-ron-dac*, July–Aug. 1949. 13:91. Suggested hikes in the vicinity of Pharoah Mountain. 5422

Shorey, Archibald Thompson. Trails for trampers. *No Country Life*, Summer 1948. 2: no.3:20–23. Reprinted from *New York State Conservationist*, Aug.–Sept. 1947. 2:no.1:14–15. Hiking in the high-peak area. 5423

Snyder, Roy. More snow at Cold river. *Cloud Splitter*, Mar.–Apr. 1951. 14:no.2:3–5. 5424

Spears, Raymond Smiley. Adirondack trails. *For & Stream*, July 9, 1898. 51:22–23. Old Indian trail, Canachagala Lake; Bisby trail. 5425

Spellbinder, pseud. The five wise men. *Conservationist*, July 1909. 2:106–9. illus. Fifty-mile tramping trip around Speculator and the South Canada Lake region. 5426

Spennrath, Florence G. Hazel the "hex." *Ad-i-ron-dac*, Sept.–Oct.—Nov.–Dec. 1954. 18:92–93. Blowdown near Marcy, Colden. 5427

A sure way to capture the forest secrets. *Motordom*, June 1932. p.14–15. illus. 5428

Taylor, Charles Keene. Eight boys and ninety miles. *St N*, July 1918. 45:833–37.
5429

Thomas, Leland E. Climbing mountain peaks; the chronicle of an interesting trip through that veritable sportsman's paradise, the Ausable valley. *Sport Dig*, Jan. 1923. 2: no.1:37–40, 86. illus.   5430

Trent, George D. The man who wasn't there. *Ad-i-ron-dac*, Jan.–Feb. 1955. 19:7–9, 13. Effect of the "great Adirondack manhunt" on vacation in the high-peak area. Comment in May–June issue, 19:59.   5431

Trowbridge, Mrs. Eleanor (Daboll). The lonely lookouts. *Ad-i-ron-dac*, Jan.–Feb. 1952. 16:6–7. Collecting fire towers. See letter from Herbert McAneny in Mar.–Apr. issue, 16:34.   5432

Van Alstyne, Sally and Strube, Janet. To Flowed lands we must go. *Cloud Splitter*, Sept.–Oct. 1949. 12:no.5:8–9.   5433

Ward, Margaret C. My most memorable trip. *Cloud Splitter*, Nov.–Dec. 1948. 11:no.6: 11–12. Camping and climbing.   5434

Ward, Peter A. Amateurs' random scoot. *Ad-i-ron-dac*, Mar.–Apr. 1947. 11:no.2:6–7. Street and Nye mountains.   5435

Ward, Peter A. How I met the mountains. *Cloud Splitter*, Sept.–Oct. 1950. 13:no.5:9–13. First experience in camping and climbing.
5436

Ward, Peter A. Our days in the Cold river region. *Cloud Splitter*, May–June 1950. 13: no.3:2–4.   5437

Ward, Peter A. Putt-Putt takes me bushwacking. *Cloud Splitter*, July–Aug. 1949. 12: no.4:2–4. Loon Lake.   5438

Warfield, Ben Breckenridge. Some unblazed trails in the Adirondacks. *Appalachia*, Dec. 1931. 18:378–87. illus.   5439

Webb, Janet. Girl scout primitive camp. *Ad-i-ron-dac*, Mar.–Apr. 1950. 14:41. Heart Lake.   5440

Wendell, Roland M. Our goal—the upward call. *No Country Life*, Winter 1949. 3:no.1:8–11. illus.   5441

Williams, Asa S. The lost lake of the Adirondacks. *Field & S*, July 1903. 8:190–91. illus. Lake in the Cold River country.   5442

Wilson, H.G. On foot in the Adirondacks. *Fur-Fish-Game*, May 1929. 49:no.5:24–26.
5443

Woodward, Mrs. Dorothea and Woodward, Walter. The Woodwards' most memorable trip. *Cloud Splitter*, May–June 1948. 11:no.3: 12–15. Temporarily lost in the woods around Keene.   5444

Individual Mountains

B. Mounting Mt. Ampersand. *J Outd Life*, Nov. 1906. 3:395–96. illus.   5445

B., P.A. The magnet. *Camp Log*, 1927. 13:37–40. illus. Climbing Mt. Marcy.   5446

Bernays, David. Inside Pitchoff. *Ad-i-ron-dac*, May–June 1951. 15:50–51, 56. illus. Exploration of Pitchoff caves.   5447

Bullard, Herbert F. The Giant personified. *High Spots*, July 1933. 10:no.3:12–15. illus. Giant Mountain.   5448

Burnham, John Bird. An outing in the snow. *For & Stream*, Apr. 5, 1902. 58:262–63. Climbing Dix at Easter during a bear hunt.   5449

Cline, Albert Collins. The first Marcy trip. *Camp Log*, Dec. 1922. p.34–35. illus. First trip of the season from College of Forestry's summer camp.   5450

Crandall, Carl H. Marcy reconnaissance. . .or where are those Sherpas? *Ad-i-ron-dac*, Mar.–Apr. 1954. 18:30–31.   5451

Dittmar, Adolph G. The back way to Sawteeth. *Ad-i-ron-dac*, Nov.–Dec. 1949. 13:122.
5452

Dodge, James W. Why climb a mountain? *PTM*, Oct. 1927. 2:no.4:16–17. illus. Marcy by way of MacIntyre and Avalanche Pass.
5453

Douglas, H.S. Climbing the "Cloud-cleaver." *Vermonter*, 1923. 28:2–10. illus. Boy Scout trip from Burlington. Interesting details of Marcy climb.   5454

Engels, Vincent. Colden, alt. 4,712. *Commonweal*, Nov. 11, 1938. 29:69–71. Climbing Colden.   5455

Foxie, pseud. and Bren, pseud. A trip to Mount Marcy. *Camp Log*, 1926. 11:21–22.
5456

Goodwin, James A. A new trail to Big slide. *Ad-i-ron-dac*, Sept.–Oct. 1951. 15:83.   5457

Greene, Laura A., Hannay, Betty and Plum, Dorothy Alice. A masterpiece of understatement. . . *Ad-i-ron-dac*, Jan.–Feb. 1952. 16:15. illus. Signed: G-H-P. The Non-46ers attempt Pitchoff.   5458

Haeusser, Dorothy O. My favorite mountain. *Cloud Splitter*, Sept.–Oct. 1953. 16:no.5:9–10. Iroquois.   5459

Hale, Edward Everett. An ascent of Mount Dix from the east. *High Spots*, July 1932. 9: no.3:7–9.   5460

Hammond, Henry D. Assault on Jay ridge. *Ad-i-ron-dac*, Jan.–Feb. 1950. 14:4–7. illus.
5461

Hammond, Henry D. The Hammonds on Basin. *Ad-i-ron-dac*, July–Aug. 1952. 16:68–69. illus.   5462

Hammond, Henry D. With the Rover boys in the Adirondacks; or, Lost on Saddleback. *Ad-i-ron-dac*, Nov.–Dec. 1952. 16:100–1, 115.   5463

Hart, Merwin K. Jr. Climb the Sawtooth range. *Ad-i-ron-dac*, Nov.–Dec. 1947. 11:no.6: 16.   5464

Hart, Merwin K. Jr. "Little great range": Blue ridge mountain. *Ad-i-ron-dac*, Sept.–Oct. 1949. 13:100–1.   5465

Hart, Merwin K. Jr. Sawtooth range revisited. *Ad-i-ron-dac*, May–June 1949. 13:56–57.   5466

Hiscock, L. Harris. DeBar mountain. *Ad-i-ron-dac*, Jan.–Feb. 1953. 17:16–17.   5467

Hosley, Neil. The Mount Marcy trip. *Camp Log*, Dec. 1922. p.57–60. illus. Silviculture trip.   5468

Hudowalski, Edward C. Chimney mt. *Cloud Splitter*, Oct. 1941. 4:no.7:2–3.   5469

Hudowalski, Mrs. Grace (Leech). Arcady. *Cloud Splitter*, Feb. 1941. 4:no.2:2–3. Climbing around Algonquin.   5470

Hudowalski, Mrs. Grace (Leech). Esther. *Cloud Splitter*, Apr. 1939. 2:no.2:4–5. Esther McComb and Mt. Esther. Also in *The Adirondack Mountain Club Bulletin*, Apr.–May 1938. 3:no.2:8, with title "The First Ascent of Mount Esther."   5471

Hudowalski, Mrs. Grace (Leech). My pappy done tole me. *Cloud Splitter*, July–Aug. 1944. 7:no.4:3–4. First climb up Marcy.   5472

Jessup, Elon H. Shinnying up Ampersand. *Outing*, Jan. 1919. 73:184–86, 206. illus.   5473

Knapp, Louis H. Seward range. *Cloud Splitter*, Nov.–Dec. 1947. 10:no.6:19–20. Climbing the Sewards.   5474

Kolenberg, Bernard. Mount Marcy and I. *Ad-i-ron-dac*, Sept.–Oct. 1953. 17:94–99. illus. Ascent by a photographer.   5475

Langdon, Palmer H. Climbing Mount Marcy. *For & Stream*, Aug. 20, 1910. 75: 289–90. Via Ausable lakes.   5476

Loope, P. Fay. Moods of Marcy. *Ad-i-ron-dac*, Jan.–Feb. 1949. 13:4–5, 8–9. illus.   5477

Lowe, John T. Carr. A change of worlds on Marcy. *Ad-i-ron-dac*, July–Aug. 1950. 14:82–84.   5478

McKenzie, J. Daniel and McKenzie, Mrs. Lillian G. Sawtooth safari. *Ad-i-ron-dac*, Mar.–Apr. 1950. 14:36–40, 44. illus.   5479

Marshall, Robert. A day on Gothics. Aug. 11, 1920. *High Spots Yrbk*, 1942. p.10–12. illus. Climbing the Great Range.   5480

Miller, Philip Schuyler. The bear went over the mountain. . . *Ad-i-ron-dac*, Nov.–Dec.

1949. 13:124–27. illus. Climbing East Dix by an unmarked route.   5481

Mills, Borden H. Sr. My first ascent of Marcy. *Cloud Splitter*, Jan.–Feb. 1945. 8:no.1:7–10.   5482

Nash, Duane H. The Sewards—1955. *Ad-i-ron-dac*, Nov.–Dec. 1955. 19:104–5, 118.   5483

Newkirk, Arthur Edward. Have you tried this? . . .Rocky peak ridge. *Ad-i-ron-dac*, Sept.–Oct. 1947. 11:no.5:4.   5484

Parsons, Wales. A trip to Mount Lyon. *Ad-i-ron-dac*, Jan.–Feb. 1955. 19:12–13. Ascent made in 1875.   5485

Phonetic celebration. *Phon M*, Oct. 1847. 2: 33–39. Description of ascent of Whiteface by the "Phonic mountaineers." Written in Dr. Comstock's Phonotypes and reprinted from *Westport Patriot*. Tahawian Association. 5486

Plum, Eleanor Mary and Menz, Mrs. Helen (Colyer). Crane mountain. Illustration by Pauline Menz. *Ad-i-ron-dac*, July–Aug. 1950. 14:81.   5487

R., J. Jr. Up an Adirondack mountain. *For & Stream*, Aug. 9, 1883. 21:22. Black Mountain, near Fulton Chain.   5488

Reich, Charles A. We climbed Pyramid! *Ad-i-ron-dac*, Mar.–Apr. 1945. 9:no.2:5, 7.   5489

Schneider, Elsie. A trip up Whiteface mountain. *For & Stream*, Jan. 25, 1913. 80:106–7. illus.   5490

Schneider, Elsie. A vacation in the Adirondacks. *For & Stream*, Nov. 9, 1912. 79:588, 604–6. illus. Climbing Mt. Marcy.   5491

Shorey, Archibald Thompson. Not Santanoni or Dix, but Skylight. *Cloud Splitter*, Mar.–Apr. 1953. 16:no.2:5–6.   5492

Shorey, Archibald Thompson. The Tongue mountain trail. *Ad-i-ron-dac*, Jan.–Feb. 1950. 14:8.   5493

Stevens, Paul W. Phelps mountain. *Ad-i-ron-dac*, Jan.–Feb. 1955. 9:10. Climbing a trailless peak.   5494

Tyler, Alanson Ranger. Spur-of-the-moment exploration. *Ad-i-ron-dac*, Sept.–Oct. 1951. 15:93. New route down Armstrong. 5495

Weld, Paul. My most memorable trip. *Cloud Splitter*, Sept.–Oct. 1948. 11:no.5:12–13. Climb up Allen.   5496

West, Alton C. The slide on Wright. *High Spots Yrbk*, 1940. p.63–65. illus. p.43. 5497

Rock Climbing

Bailey, Richard. With the rock climbers. New rock climb in Chapel pond pass. *Ad-i-ron-dac*, Sept.–Oct. 1950. 14:109, 111. 5498

Bernays, David. The pinnacles of Chapel pond notch. *Ad-i-ron-dac*, July–Aug. 1950. 14:76–77. illus.   5499

Burton, Harold B. Rock climbing is fun! *Ad-i-ron-dac*, Mar.–Apr. 1947. 11:no.2:5, 7. 5500

Goodwin, James A. Rock climbing, a mountaineering technique. *Ad-i-ron-dac*, July–Aug. 1949. 13:82–83, 91. illus. Includes reference to several Adirondack locations.   5501

Goodwin, James A. Rock climbing: instruction. *Ad-i-ron-dac*, Sept.–Oct. 1949. 13:108–9.
                                              5502

Goodwin, James. A. Rock climbs in the Adirondacks. *Ad Mt Club Bul*, June–July, Aug.–Sept. 1938. 2:no.4:8–9, 15; 2:no.5:6–7. illus.
                                              5503

Goodwin, James A. Some Adirondack rock climbs. *Ad-i-ron-dac*, Jan.–Feb. 1951. 15:12–13, 15.   5504

Harmes, Edward A. Climb on Wallface. *Cloud Splitter*, May 1942. 5:no.5:2–3.   5505

Wiessner, Fritz H. Rock climbing in the northeast. *IOCA Bul*, Winter 1948. 2:no.1: 42–48, 72. illus. Includes Adirondacks. 5506

Wiessner, Fritz H. Wallface: up the cliff. *High Spots Yrbk*, 1939. p.49–50. illus. p.46–47.   5507

CAMPING

Andrews, Mrs. Mary Raymond (Shipman). "A woman in camp." *Outing*, June 1894. 29: 84–87.   5508

Bowker, R.R. A college camp at Lake George. *Scrib Mo*, Mar. 1879. 17:617–31. illus. 5509

Buck, pseud. Our first camping trip. *For & Stream*, Oct. 27–Nov. 3, 1900. 55:323–24, 343–44. Fulton Chain.   5510

Burnham, John Bird. Spring in the Adirondacks. *For & Stream*, Apr. 28, 1900. 54:325. Camping trip to Dix and McComb.   5511

Burroughs, John. Locusts and wild honey. Boston, Houghton, Osgood & co. 1879. 253p. "A Bed of Boughs," p.167–96. First published in *Scribner's Monthly*, Nov. 1877, 15: 68–83. Numerous later editions. On camping.   5512

Camping on state lands in New York. *Amer Angler*, June 1920. 5:83–84.   5513

Campsite data. *NYS Con*, June–July 1955. 9:no.6:12–13. charts, map.   5514

Candee, Mrs. Helen Churchill (Hungerford). An Adirondack campfire. *Illus Am*, Aug. 7, 1897. 22:183. illus. Adirondack camp life.
                                              5515

Catlin, Clay. In camp. *Gameland*, Aug. 1897. 11:87–89. Camping trip.   5516

Clark, Helen S. Camping in the woods. *Outing*, Aug. 1891. 18:415–17.   5517

Corson, R.H. Women in camp, by Switch Reel, pseud. *For & Stream*, May 2, 1914. 82: 575–76. illus.   5518

Crandall, Carl H. "Dear Bill." *Ad-i-ron-dac*, May–June 1954. 18:52–54. Junior campers in the Adirondacks.   5519

Cutting, Estar. Mid-woods. *Outing*, Jan. 1919. 73:192–93. Life in an Adirondack camp home.   5520

Denniston, Robert. Memories of winter camp. *Cloud Splitter*, Sept.–Oct. 1948. 11:no.5:8–9. Winter Camp, near Johns Brook Lodge. 5521

Duryea, Edward Sidney. Around the camp fire. *For & Stream*, Aug. 31, 1895. 45:182. Camping at Long Lake.   5522

Dyer, Walter Alden. Camping in the Adirondacks. *Country Life*, July 1905. 8:344–45. Upper end of Long Lake.   5523

Frazer, Orange. Camping out. *For & Stream*, Sept. 22, 1887. 29:162. St. Regis area. 5524

Goodyear, Sarah. In the wilderness. *For & Stream*, Oct. 15, 1874. 3:145–46. Camping on Little Round Pond, Hamilton County. 5525

Gowie, Orville C. "And the rains came." *Cloud Splitter*, Oct. 1940. 3:no.6:10. Camping trip in Colden region.   5526

Gowie, Orville C. Modern "babes in the woods." *Cloud Splitter*, Oct. 1941. 4:no.7:7–8. Camping trip; climb up Allen Mountain.
                                              5527

Hannon, Thomas Eugene. ADKer hostels in the Adirondacks. *Cloud Splitter*, Nov.–Dec. 1949. 12:no.6:6–9. Camping and climbing in the Adirondacks.   5528

Hannon, Thomas Eugene. Duck hole. *Cloud Splitter*, July–Aug. 1949. 12:no.4:5–7. Camping and hiking.   5529

Jack, pseud. Salt-water campers in the woods. *For & Stream*, Sept. 2, 1911. 77:371–74. illus. Camping trip on the Fulton Chain.   5530

Lewis, Frank M. August camp, 1954. *Appalachia*, Dec. 1954. mag. no.119:268–69. In the Adirondacks. The great man hunt.   5531

Longstreth, Thomas Morris. Camping on state. *Outing*, Jan. 1917. 69:405–16. illus. Summer of 1916 spent on Indian Lake at Camp Fellows across from Back Log Camp. Photographs taken by Thomas K. Brown Jr.   5532

Markham, Charles C. Artist-life in the Adirondacks. *For & Stream*, Sept. 14–21, 1876. 7:82, 98. Camping on Round Pond near Rainbow Pond.   5533

Miller, Warren Hastings. Camping out. N.Y. Doran, c1918. 322p. incl. front. plates. Adirondacks, p.104–30.   5534

Mills, Borden H. Jr. Wild mountain oats. *Cloud Splitter*, May–June 1947. 10:no.3:8–10. Account of camping trip in the Marcy region.   5535

Mulholland, William D. Adirondack campsites. Albany, J.B. Lyon, 1955. 40p. illus. tables. (Recreation Circular 3.) Issued by the New York State Conservation Department. First published, 1931. Earlier editions, by Pettis, with title "Adirondack Highways" (no.5542).   5536

Mulholland, William D. Campsite. *NYS Con*, Oct.–Nov. 1947. 2:no.2:22–23. illus. map. Fish Creek Pond campsite.   5537

Mulholland, William D. Public campsites of the Forest preserve. *NYS For Assn NL*, June 1933. p.13–14.   5538

Northrup, Ansel Judd. Camps and tramps in the Adirondacks, and grayling fishing in northern Michigan. . . Syracuse, N.Y. Davis,

Bardeen & co. 1880. 302p. "A running narrative of camping experiences."   5539

Northrup, M.S. Notes from the north woods. *For & Stream*, June 10, 1886. 26:388. Camping in Hamilton County.   5540

Oliver, Frank Joseph. Planning a menu. *Ad-i-ron-dac*, July–Aug. 1947. 11:no.4:5.   5541

Pettis, Clifford Robert. Adirondack highways. Albany, New York state conservation department, 1927. 35p. illus. map. (Recreation Circular 3.) Later issues by W.D. Mulholland have title: "Adirondack Campsites" (no.5536).   5542

Phelps, Orra A. At home in the woods. *High Spots Yrbk*, 1939, p.51–56.   5543

Radford, Harry V. Camping in the Adirondacks. *Four Tr News*, July 1902. 3:20–22. illus.   5544

Radford, Harry V. A thousand welcomes, brother camper. *For Leaves*, Spring 1904. 1:no.2:22–24. illus. Sales talk for the Adirondacks.   5545

Rice, Arthur F. Camp saints' rest. *For & Stream*, Oct. 10, 1896. 47:282. St. Regis region.   5546

Rice, Arthur F. Camp sixteen. *For & Stream*, Oct. 24, 1896. 47:323.   5547

Ryan, D.E. Outdoor manners. *NYS Con*, June–July 1954. 8:no.6:7–8. illus. Vandalism in the Adirondacks.   5548

Senior, pseud. A reminiscence of 1866. *For & Stream*, June 18, 1891. 36:434. Camping at Beach's Lake near Long Lake.   5549

Sherman, Richard U. A fortnight in the wilderness. *For & Stream*, Jan. 7–14, 1875. 3:338–39, 355. Camping in Brown's Tract.   5550

Shorey, Archibald Thompson. How to forget the war! *Cloud Splitter*, Sept.–Oct. 1944. 7:no.5:2–4. Camping trip in the Oswegatchie country.   5551

Spears, Eldridge A. Afoot in the Adirondacks. *For & Stream*, Nov. 2, 1907. 69:689–90.   5552

Spears, Raymond Smiley. Adirondack camp troubles. *For & Stream*, May 30, 1908. 70:

856–57. See also editorial, "Adirondack Camps," May 30, 1908, 70:847. Depredations by camp thieves.   5553

Swartwout, Janet von. Heads; or, The City of the gods, a narrative of Olombia in the wilderness. N.Y. Olombia publishing co. 1894. 2v. in 1. illus. Also published with subtitle: "or, In the wilderness." Camping at Fulton Chain.   5554

Sycamore, pseud. Camping in the Adirondacks. *Recreation*, Aug. 1904. 21:94–95.   5555

Taylor, Mrs. Percy E. The mountains of New York and New England; a camper's vivid description of the Adirondacks, Green and White mountains, including interesting side-trips to some of the most interesting historical and scenic beauty spots in the eastern states. *Motordom*, Aug. 1926. 20:no.3:3–5. illus.   5556

Thees, Oscar D. Camp Bill Cody: how dad and the girls enjoyed a pleasant camping trip. *Field & S*, July 1907. 12:212–16. illus. Thirteenth Lake House, Hour Brook and Hour Pond.   5557

Tichenor, George. Wilderness campsite. *Sports Illus*, July 18, 1955. 3:no.3:34–35. illus. State campsite at Forked Lake.   5558

Tuttles, George S. A camping trip in the Adirondacks. *Fur News*, Sept. 1915. 22:no. 3:6–7. Trip from Saranac Lake to Ampersand Mountain.   5559

Walker, R.H. Tribulations of a tramp in the Adirondacks. *For & Stream*, Sept. 3, 1874. 3:51. Rainy camping trip in John Brown's Tract.   5560

Ward, Peter A. I hate Philbert! *Cloud Splitter*, May–June 1944. 7:no.3:7–9, 11. Camping at Indian Falls.   5561

Welch, Fay. Good manners out of doors. *Bul Schools*, Mar. 1952. 38:177. figs. Check list of camp etiquette.   5562

HUNTING AND FISHING

GENERAL

Adams, Zab Boylston. The Adirondacks, a story told by Paul Smith. *For & Stream*, Oct. 22, 1891. 37:266. Hunting adventure.   5563

Adirondack big game. *Field & S*, Nov. 1907. 12:598–600.   5564

Adirondack fish and game. *For & Stream*, June 5, 1884. 22:362. Two letters signed Adrion Ondack and W.L. Howard giving sport news from various areas.   5565

Adirondack hunters killed. *For & Stream*, Nov. 12, 1910. 75:776. Discussion of shooting accidents during the 1910 season.   5566

Allen, J.C. Adirondack game notes, by Clericus, pseud. *Arms & Man*, Oct. 10, 1907. 43:8.   5567

Allen, J.C. Incidents of the woods, by Clericus, pseud. *Arms & Man*, Nov. 28, 1907. 43:176. Obstacles met by sportsmen.   5568

Amateur, pseud. Sport near Lake Champlain. *Am Sportsman*, Aug. 1873. 2:171. Fishing and hunting prospects.   5569

B. Adirondack notes. *For & Stream*, July 8, 1893. 41:8–9. Notes on fish and game.   5570

B., F. Sport in the Brown tract. *For & Stream*, Dec. 31, 1874. 3:323.   5571

Bar Lock, pseud. Two weeks in the Adirondacks. *Rod & Gun*, May 8–15, 1875. 6:83, 99–100. Trip to Chazy Lake.   5572

Bass, W.H. Gun licenses. *For & Stream*, Jan. 6, 1907. 68:138.   5573

Beach, Anna. Trip to the north woods. *Cloud Splitter*, July–Aug. 1947. 10:no.6:6. 1861 account of a fishing and hunting trip in the Adirondacks contributed by Orra A. Phelps.   5574

Benham, J.D. An Adirondack game resort. *Field & S*, Nov. 1906. 11:676–77.   5575

Billy, pseud. A typical tourists' trip. *For & Stream*, Aug. 31, 1882. 19:88. Hunting near Old Forge.   5576

Billy the Boy, pseud. Two huntsmen bold. *Ang & Hunt*, Aug. 1910. 2:440.   5577

Bird dogs in the Adirondacks. *For & Stream*, Jan. 21, 1911. 76:98. Favors permitting dogs for hunting birds.   5578

Bruce, Dwight Hall. In the Adirondacks. *For & Stream*, Sept. 20, 1902. 59:223. Signed: D.H.B. News notes, hunting.   5579

Burke, Martin. In the Adirondacks, with rod and rifle. *Cath World*, Oct. 1885. 42:10–20.   5580

Burnham, John Bird. Two days' hunt at North Hudson. *For & Stream*, Dec. 9, 1899. 53:465–66.   5581

Byron. Upper Adirondacks in '56. *For & Stream*, Aug. 27, 1891. 37:106. Trip from Chazy to the Saranacs.   5582

C., A. St. Regis district. *For & Stream*, July 1, 1889. 32:508. Hunting and fishing possibilities. 5583

C., C.H. Adirondack sports. *Am Sportsman*, Feb. 14, 1874. 3:314. Hunting in Lower Saranac region. 5584

C., J. An Adirondack trip. *For & Stream*, Nov. 9, 1895. 45:405–6. Introducing a tenderfoot to hunting and camping near T Lake. 5585

Camping and hunting, by Vernette, John and Henry. *St No Mo*, Feb. 1908. 3:80–84. At Number Four. 5586

Catostomus, pseud. A trip to the Adirondacks. *Am Sportsman*, June 27, 1874. 4:195. Hunting at Otter Lake. 5587

Cheney, Albert Nelson. Adirondack game notes. *For & Stream*, Aug. 29, 1896. 47:165–66. Signed: A.N.C. 5588

Copeland, Fred O. Silken wings and merry whistle; an adventure with dog and shotgun into the historic gateway of Champlain. *For & Stream*, Jan. 1917. 87:17–19. illus. 5589

Covert, Byron V. Two weeks at Big Moose lake. *For & Stream*, Oct. 24, 1896. 47:326–27. 5590

Crow, Charles H. October in the Adirondacks. *For & Stream*, Jan. 1, 1874. 1:325–26. Hunting at Lower Saranac Lake. 5591

Curtis, George William. Editor's easy chair. *Harper*, Oct. 1862. 25:706–7. Brief comments on hunting in the Adirondacks. 5592

D., B.C. Catering for an Adirondack dinner. *For & Stream*, Mar. 25, 1875. 4:99. 5593

D., J.H. The Adirondacks in 1858. *For & Stream*, Aug. 27, 1891. 37:103–4. Hunting and fishing trip to Ragged Lake. 5594

Dailey, Elric J. Hunting conditions in the Adirondacks. *Sport Dig*, July 1925. 4:no.7: 22–23, 61. illus. 5595

Dailey, Elric J. When the leaves turn gold. *Fur News*, Nov. 1922. 36:no.5:12–13. 5596

Dodd, Mark Dixon. Hunting in the Adirondacks. *For & Stream*, Aug. 26, 1905. 65:170. 5597

Don't shoot until you know. *For & Stream*, Aug. 26, 1899. 53:161. Editorial on shooting accident on Eighth Lake, Fulton Chain. 5598

Eaton, George Boardman. Stillwater camp, by Jacobstaff, pseud. *For & Stream*, Jan. 23, 1904. 62:65–66. ports. Week's trip on the De Grasse River. 5599

Eurus, pseud. An Adirondack hunting trip. *For & Stream*, Sept. 8, 1894. 43:206. 5600

Fish and game notes from the Adirondacks. *Sport Rev*, May 29, 1909. 35:593. Short editorial on good season. 5601

Fletcher, J.P. Adirondack notes. *Am Field*, Mar. 17, 1906. 65:239. Notes on deer and moose. 5602

Fletcher, J.P. In the northern Adirondacks. *For & Stream*, July 29, 1905. 65:90–91. Hunting trip north of Loon Lake. 5603

Flint, Peter. Bears and deer in Adirondack. *For & Stream*, Nov. 7, 1914 83:595–96. 5604

Flint, Peter. Foxes and game. *For & Stream*, Mar. 24, 1905. 64:233. Near Ticonderoga. 5605

Flint, Peter. Major's cure. *For & Stream*, Nov. 29, 1902. 59:433–34. Retraining a hunting dog at Eagle Lake, near Ticonderoga. 5606

Flint, Peter. The season at Eagle lake. *For & Stream*, Nov. 7, 1908. 7:736. Notes on fish and game. 5607

Flint, Peter. Shantying out for bears, deer, and grouse in southeastern Adirondacks— the extermination of bucks threatened. *For & Stream*, Dec. 19, 1914. 83:801–2. 5608

Fritz, pseud. A reminiscence of the Racquet in 1873. *For & Stream*, June 29, 1876. 6:335. Hunting trip from the Lower (Adirondack) Works across to the Raquette. 5609

Furnside, J.W. An Adirondack episode. *Recreation*, Mar. 1904. 20:214. 5610

Gerster, Arpad Geyza Charles. Recollections of a New York surgeon. N.Y. Hoeber, 1917. 347p. front. plates, ports. Canoeing and fishing in the Adirondacks, p.275–83. Portrait of Alvah Dunning, p.316 (also in Donaldson, v.2, opp. p.113). Note on Alvah Dunning, p.320–21. 5611

Gibbs, A.D. A trip to the Adirondacks, and a few deductions drawn therefrom. *Field & S*, Mar. 1907. 11:1031–32. 5612

Goodale, Grace. Hunting on the Stillwater. *Recreation*, Feb. 1901. 14:92. 5613

Gus, pseud. Hunting in the Adirondacks. *Am Sportsman*, Nov. 8, 1873. 3:83. Upper Saranac Lake. 5614

Hallock, Charles. The sportsman's gazetteer and general guide... N.Y. Orange Judd, 1883. 692, xiii, 218p. plates, port. The Adirondack Region, pt.2, p.111–18. 5615

Hammond, Samuel H. Hills, lakes and forest streams; or, A tramp in the Chateaugay woods. N.Y. Boston, J.C. Derby; Phillips, Sampson & co. 1854. 340p. plates, front. Later editions have titles: "Hunting Adventures in the Northern Wilds" and "In the Adirondacks."   5616

Hammond, Samuel H. Hunting adventures in the northern wilds; or, A tramp in the Chateaugay woods, over hills, lakes and forest streams. N.Y. Boston, J.C. Derby; Phillips, Sampson & co. 1856. 340p. plates, front. First published with title "Hills, Lakes and Forest Streams," 1854. Later editions have title "In the Adirondacks." Reprinted: N.Y. Derby & Jackson, 1859 and 1860; Philadelphia, J.E. Potter, 1863, 1865, and in an undated edition.   5617

Hammond, Samuel H. In the Adirondacks; or, Sport in the north woods. . . Philadelphia, Columbian printing co. 1890. 340p. (Columbia Library no.9.) Earlier editions appeared under titles "Hills, Lakes and Forest Streams" and "Hunting Adventures in the Northern Wilds."   5618

Hammond, Samuel H. Wild northern scenes; or, Sporting adventures with the rifle and the rod. N.Y. Derby & Jackson, 1857. 341p. front. plates. Reprinted 1859, 1869 (c1863).   5619

Hastings, W.W. Around and about a new Adirondack camp. For & Stream, Nov. 25, 1899. 53:422–23. Hunting near Old Forge.   5620

Hastings, W.W. A few days in the Adirondacks. For & Stream, Jan. 7, 1899. 52:2–3. Hunting on the Fulton Chain.   5621

Hilliker, G.W. The Adirondacks' northern slopes. For & Stream, Nov. 18, 1899. 53:410.   5622

Holberton, Wakeman. A hunt at the Adirondack club. For & Stream, Nov. 8, 1888. 31:306–7.   5623

Hoover, Matthew Henry. Wild ginger, wood sorrel and sweet cicely; stories of many types, new to the printed types. . .by Matt Hoover. N.Y. Broadway publishing co. c1909. 346p. double front. plates. Browsing in the Adirondacks, p.112–38. An Autumn Hunt in the Adirondacks, p.289–313.   5624

Howard, William Gibbs. Forest lands as public hunting ground. NYS Sport, Apr.–May 1936. 2:no.6:5–6; 2:no.7:5–6. illus. 5625

Hudson, Harry. The Fulton chain. For & Stream, Oct. 6, 1892. 39:288.   5626

Hunt, J.H. Three runs in the Adirondacks and one in Canada. N.Y. Putnam, 1892. 94p. front. illus.   5627

Huntington, Henry Smith. Adirondack diary —1853. NYS Con, Aug.–Sept. 1950. 5:no.1:

22–24. illus. Lake George, Adirondac, Indian Pass.   5628

In the Adirondacks with rod and rifle. For Leaves, Summer 1905. 2:no.3:20–27. illus.   5629

Ives, H.L. Reminiscences of the Adirondacks. Potsdam, N.Y. Elliott Fay & son, printers, 1915. 124p. plates, ports. Cover title: Recollections of the Adirondacks. Hunting and fishing sketches.   5630

J. Panthers and deer. For & Stream, Nov. 5, 1885. 25:286.   5631

Jackson, Robert. A trip through the Adirondacks—Canadian sport compared. For & Stream, Sept. 9, 1875. 5:66–67. Comparison of Fourth Lake area with Mushoka District in Ontario.   5632

John Brown's tract. Knick Mag, Feb. 1856. 47:179–82. Hunting twenty years earlier.   5633

Judson, Edward Z.C. How I found a new lake, by Ned Buntline, pseud. For & Stream, Mar. 3, 1881. 16:91. Hunting along Cascade Brook.   5634

Juvenal, pseud. Adirondack notes. For & Stream, June 28, 1902. 58:505. Notes on hunting and fishing.   5635

Juvenal, pseud. Fun in the Adirondacks. For & Stream, Oct. 31, 1896. 47:347. Hunting incidents.   5636

K., E.H. Shooting casualties. For & Stream, Oct. 8, 1898. 51:289.   5637

K., W.S. My Adirondack pipe. Memories of a pleasant month spent in the Adirondacks. Printed for private circulation. N.Y. Jenkins press, 1887. 81p. Copy in Yale University Library. Author may be W.N. Purdy (see Phillips, p.205).   5638

Killed and injured while hunting. 16 fatal accidents and 52 injured in the New York state woods during season of 1924. State Service, Dec. 1924. 8:111–12. Lists of persons involved, with location; many in the Adirondacks.   5639

King, William. Reminiscences of forty years. Loon lake in 1856. For & Stream, Sept. 8, 1881. 17:110.   5640

Kingsley, H.J. Deer and elk in winter woods. Outing, Feb. 1918. 71:317. illus. Hamilton County.   5641

Landon, J.S. Hunting conditions in the Adirondacks. Ang & Hunt, Nov. 1910. 2:568–69. port.   5642

McHarg, John B. Jr. Early summer in the Adirondacks. For & Stream, June 25, 1898. 50:519. News notes from Old Forge.   5643

Mack, G.A. On the dirt floor at Saranac. Recreation, Apr. 1901. 14:277–78.   5644

Marsh, John H. Memoirs of my father's hunting days. Oshkosh, Wis. 1923. 27p. 5645

Mayer, A.M. ed. Sport with gun and rod in American woods and waters. N.Y. Century, c1883. 892p. illus. 5646

Morris, Robert T. Hopkins's pond and other sketches. N.Y. Putnam, 1896. 227p. front. One Deer, p.176–89; Trout in a Thunderstorm, p.199–203. In preface author states that he used the pen name "Mark West" when writing for *Forest and Stream*. "Hopkins's Pond" reprinted in *Forest and Stream*, Dec. 28, 1895, 45:552. "Trout in a Thunderstorm" reprinted in *Forest and Stream*, Aug. 17, 1882, 19:50. 5647

Now & Then, pseud. A trip to Cranberry lake. *For & Stream*, Mar. 2, 1876. 6:50. 5648

Ondack, Adrion, pseud. Deer and partridge. *For & Stream*, Dec. 1, 1881. 17:348. Report on game in the St. Regis area. 5649

Osceola, pseud. Adirondack notes. *For & Stream*, Sept. 12, 1889. 33:147. Hunting along the Stillwater. 5650

Osceola, pseud. Odd incidents. *For & Stream*, Oct. 17, 1889. 33:243. Hunting along the Stillwater. 5651

Overbaugh, D.C. A trip to Lake Champlain. *For & Stream*, May 5, 1887. 28:322–23. 5652

Pastnor, Paul. Three weeks on the Raquette. *For & Stream*, June 18, 1891. 36:430–32. illus. 5653

Purdy, Fred Leslie. Hunting with Uncle Hi. *For & Stream*, Sept. 24–Nov. 5, 1910. 75:493–94, 534–35, 574–76, 615–16, 652–54, 694, 733–34. A series of letters written by a sportsman sojourning on the Grasse River. 5654

R., J.H. An Adirondack outing. *For & Stream*, Jan. 1, 1891. 35:471. Hunting at Star Lake. 5655

Radford, Harry V. Boyhood adventures in the Adirondacks. *For Leaves*, Winter 1908–Spring 1909, Autumn 1909–Winter 1909. 4:no.4:25–32; 5:no.1:25–31; 5:no.3:12–15; 5:no.4:12–16. Contents: My First Adventure with a Bear. Three Foxes. A Trip to the Center of the Earth. A Panther and a Wolf. The first of this series is "An Adirondack Trouting" (no.6133). 5656

Raymond, pseud. Grampus lake—the Adirondacks in August. *Am Angler*, Oct. 28, 1882. 2:273–75. Reprinted from the *Newark Call*. Camping and fishing trip with Sabattis as guide. 5657

Rice, Arthur F. An unsuccessful trip. *For & Stream*, Nov. 16, 1895. 45:421. St. Regis River. 5658

Robinson, John C. From an Adirondack guide. *Am Angler*, Mar. 28, 1885. 7:203. Observations on game and fish at Long Lake. 5659

Russell, Todd. Hunting the Adirondack grouse. *Outing*, Oct. 1909. 55:61–63. Forest Preserve for hunting. 5660

S., F.A. Indian lake country. *For & Stream*, Jan. 5, 1888. 29:465. 5661

Sedge Grass, pseud. An outing at Camp Ananias. *For & Stream*, Sept. 21, 1895. 45:245. Hunting trip to Long Lake. 5662

Shep, pseud. An Adirondack trip. *Amat Sportsman*, Mar. 1905. 32:no.5:11–12. Hunting on headwaters of West Canada Creek. 5663

Shooting in the Adirondacks. *All the Year*, Sept. 29, 1860. 3:585–88. Extracts in *Forest and Stream*, Mar. 5, 1874, 2:57, with title "Pol Smith of St. Regis." Paul Smith guides hunting party. Largely descriptive of area around Paul Smiths. Also Tupper, St. Regis and Upper Saranac lakes. 5664

Smith, Judson Newman. An Adirondack journey. *Argosy*, Sept. 1895. 20:522–27. illus. Plates by Stoddard, Chandler and Baldwin. 5665

Smith, Paul. An experience on the Upper St. Regis. *For Leaves*, Dec. 1903. 1:no.1:9–11. illus. 5666

Spears, Raymond Smiley. Adirondack conditions. *For & Stream*, Sept. 19, 1898. 71:455–56. Hunting prospects and state policy toward the Adirondacks. 5667

Spears, Raymond Smiley. Adirondack game. *For & Stream*, Nov. 7, 1908. 71:734–35. Game notes. 5668

Spears, Raymond Smiley. Adirondack notes. *For & Stream*, Jan. 13, 1894. 42:30. Report on the hunting and fishing season. 5669

Spears, Raymond Smiley. Bird dogs in the north woods. *For & Stream*, Oct. 22, 1910. 75:654. Reprinted in *The Angler and Hunter*, Nov. 1910. 2:586–87. 5670

Spears, Raymond Smiley. A few post-season tears. *For & Stream*, Nov. 11, 1911. 77:713. illus. Reports on the hunting season. 5671

Spears, Raymond Smiley. From Adirondack letters. *For & Stream*, Dec. 10, 1898. 51:466. 5672

Spears, Raymond Smiley. The game season. *For & Stream*, Sept. 24, 1910. 75:495–96. Opening of the hunting season in the Adirondacks. 5673

Spears, Raymond Smiley. The little known of the Adirondacks. *Field & S*, July 1907. 12:204–6. 5674

Spears, Raymond Smiley. The season in the Adirondacks. *For & Stream*, Nov. 16, 1907. 69:776. Review of the hunting season. 5675

Spears, Raymond Smiley. That Adirondack "Kid." *For & Stream*, Sept. 16, 1899. 53: 227. 5676

Sperry, Charles T. The passing of "Old Golden." *Ang & Hunt*, Apr. 1910. 2:192–94. port. illus. North Lake. 5677

Sport in the Adirondacks. *Sport Rev*, Oct. 30, 1909. 36:423. Big Moose Lake, Cranberry Lake and Fulton Chain. 5678

Stone, William Leete, 1835–1908. Fifty years ago. *St No Mo*, Oct. 1907. 2:401–16. Hunting trip near Crane Mountain in 1855. 5679

Streever, Fred L. The American trail hound. N.Y. A.S. Barnes, c1948. 202p. front. illus. Includes the Adirondacks. 5680

Thompson, H.H. Cooking fish and "floating" deer. *Am Angler*, July 7, 1883. 4:5–6. Signed: H.H.T. Guides on Fulton Chain cook fish well. First deer floating experience. 5681

Two months in the forest. *Am Sportsman*, Jan. 24, 1874. 3:263. South Pond. 5682

Van Santvoord, Seymour. Trout and venison. *Outing*, Oct. 1885. 7:74–82. Long Lake. 5683

W., T.G. A day in the Adirondacks. *For & Stream*, Dec. 2, 1894. 43:555. 5684

Waidmannsheil, pseud. A hunt in the Adirondacks. *Amat Sportsman*, July 1907. 37:no. 3:8–9. 5685

Walsh, John. My rubber boots and Saranac. *For Leaves*, Spring 1905. 2:no.2:6–13. Hunting trip in winter with wrong foot covering. 5686

Warning. *For & Stream*, Sept. 24, 1910. 75: 487. Editorial on prevention of shooting accidents. 5687

Warwick, Frank. In the Moose river country. *For & Stream*, Sept. 13, 1883. 21:123–24. 5688

Webber, Charles Wilkins. The hunter naturalist. Romance of sporting; or, Wild scenes and wild hunters. Philadelphia, Lippincott, 1852. 610p. col. front. illus. plates (some col.). Also published under title: Wild Scenes and Wild Hunters. Contents: A Bird's-eye View of the Speculator (Mt. Speculator): Wild Lakes of the Adirondack, Ch. XX. Trolling in June (on Round Lake and Lake Pleasant) Ch. XXI. A Night Hunt up the Cungamunck, Ch. XXII. Trouting on Jessup's River, Ch. XXIII. Anecdotes of Moose and Deer Among Northern Lakes, Ch. XXIV. Chapter XVIII reprinted in *Godey's Lady's Book*, Oct. 1851, 43:204–7. 5689

Webber, Charles Wilkins. Romance of natural history; or, Wild scenes and wild hunters. Philadelphia, Lippincott, 1852. 610p. front. plates, illus. First published as "The Hunter Naturalist." Wild Lakes of the Adirondack, Ch. XVII. Trouting on Jessup's River, Ch. XVIII. Moose and Deer-Hunting Among the Northern Lakes, Ch. XIX. 5690

Webber, Charles Wilkins. Wild scenes and wild hunters; or, The romance of sporting. Philadelphia, Claxton, Remsen & Haffelfinger, 1875. 610p. front. illus. Also published under titles "The Hunter Naturalist"; "Romance of Natural History"; "Wild Scenes and Wild Hunters of the World." Adirondacks, Chs. XX–XXIV, p.472–535. For titles of these chapters see entry under "The Hunter Naturalist" (5689). 5691

Webber, Charles Wilkins. Wild scenes and wild hunters of the world. Philadelphia, J.W. Bradley, 1852. 610p. plates, illus. Same as "The Hunter Naturalist" (1851) and "Wild Scenes and Wild Hunters." 5692

Whish, John D. Big deer and bigger bear rewarded some Adirondack hunters. *For & Stream*, Feb. 1917. 87:82. 5693

Worden, George H. Over Rag wheel mountain. *Outing*, Nov. 1889. 15:153–56. 5694

Deer

A., J.D. A bit of glory. *Recreation*, Mar. 1901. 14:190. 5695

Adirondack June deer slaughter. *For & Stream*, July 10, 1897. 49:26. Two communications signed W.H.B. and Fontinalis. 5696

An Adirondack night experience. *For & Stream*, Sept. 17, 1898. 51:223. Still-hunting. 5697

Alawishus, pseud. A two weeks deer hunt in Cold river country. *Fur-Fish-Game*, June 1927. 45:no.6:21–22. illus. 5698

Allen, J.C. Adirondack deer. *For & Stream*, Jan. 4, 1896. 46:11. 5699

Ampersand, pseud. Deer driving. *For & Stream*, June 12, 1884. 22:384. Unsportsmanlike method of hunting. 5700

Anderson, W.P. On a blazed trail. *For & Stream*, June 18, 1891. 36:434–35. Otter Lake area. 5701

AuSable, pseud. Adirondack deer. *For & Stream*, Oct. 27, 1887. 29:265. Report on the hunting season. 5702

AuSable, pseud. Adirondack deer hunts. *For & Stream*, Nov. 15, 1888. 31:323. North Elba. 5703

An author's adventure. *Sport Rev*, Dec. 4, 1909. 36:543. Stephen Chalmers' encounter with a buck at Saranac Lake. 5704

B. Adirondack deer and public rights. *For & Stream*, Mar. 24, 1906. 66:465. Notes on deer. Opposition to large Rockefeller holdings. 5705

B., G.L. Deer in northern New York. *For &
Stream*, Nov. 1, 1888. 31:286. Résumé of the
hunting season. 5706

Barnes, Almont. Floating for deer. *Field & S*,
Mar. 1900. 5:128–31. illus. 5707

Bishop, Bainbridge. The Adirondack deer.
For & Stream, Feb. 4, 1886. 26:26. Objection
to action by the Board of Supervisors of Essex
County approving deer hounding. 5708

Boardman, William Henry. The ring and
the deer. *Harper*, May 1901. 102:963–65. Tale
of a deer near the old Philosopher's Camp.
5709

Bourlier, W.S. A white-tailed deer hunt in
the Adirondacks. *Field & S*, Aug. 1916. 21:
523–26. illus. Cranberry Lake. 5710

Brandreth, Paulina. Bucks of Cathedral mead-
ow, by Paul Brandreth, pseud. *Field & S*,
Feb. 1938. 42:no.10:30–31, 64–65. illus. Near
Long Lake. 5711

Brandreth, Paulina. Clean kills; still-hunting
the whitetail deer, by Paul Brandreth, pseud.
For & Stream, Nov. 1928. 98:669–71, 708.
illus. 5712

Brandreth, Paulina. The fine art of deer hunting; points on the great game by an old
hunter, by Paul Brandreth, pseud. *Field &
S*, Sept.–Oct. 1914. 19:489–94, 631–34. Includes accounts of deer hunts in the Burnt
Mountain Lake region. 5713

Brandreth, Paulina. The fire on Albany
mountain; hunting deer with Sheriff Cole
and a vivid experience with a destructive
forest fire in the Adirondacks, by Paul Brandreth, pseud. *For & Stream*, Apr. 1923. 93:174–
75, 202–5. illus. 5714

Brandreth, Paulina. Good luck. *For & Stream*,
May 12, 1906. 66:752–53. 5715

Brandreth, Paulina. Hints on deer shooting.
For & Stream, Oct. 1, 1904. 63:281–83. 5716

Brandreth, Paulina. Hunting the whitetail,
long may he live to grace our forests, by Paul
Brandreth, pseud. *For & Stream*, Oct. 1923.
93:547–49, 599–601, 606–8. illus. 5717

Brandreth, Paulina. Still-hunting the white-
tailed deer, by Paul Brandreth, pseud. *Field
& S*, Mar. 1913. 17:1192–95. illus. 5718

Brandreth, Paulina. The sunrise buck; a day
on a stand and an evening beside the camp-
fire with an Adirondack guide, by Paul
Brandreth, pseud. *For & Stream*, Apr. 15,
1911. 76:568–71. 5719

Brandreth, Paulina. The wiles of the whitetail, by Paul Brandreth, pseud. *For & Stream*,
Oct. 1926. 96:590–91, 626–28. illus. 5720

Brooks, Raymond Everett. An Adirondack
deer hunt which was profitable for the am-
munition makers. *Fur News*, Dec. 1920. 32:
no.6:6–7. 5721

Brown, George L. Adirondack deer hunting.
For & Stream, Dec. 23, 1905. 65:515. 5722

Bruce, Dwight Hall. Adirondack deer hounding. *For & Stream*, Mar. 5, 1885. 24:105. 5723

Burnham, John Bird. Adirondack deer hunting conditions. *For & Stream*, Sept. 24, 1898.
51:246. See comment (with same title) by
Juvenal, pseud. in issue for Oct. 1, 1898, 51:
268. 5724

Burroughs, John. A night-hunt in the Adirondacks. *Putnam*, Aug. 1868. n.s.2:149–54.
5725

C., H. Adirondack deer. *For & Stream*, Oct.
9, 1890. 35:228. 5726

Cap Lock, pseud. Deer in the north woods.
For & Stream, Dec. 2, 1886. 27:364. Beaver
River hunting trip. 5727

Cheney, Albert Nelson. Adirondack deer
shooting. *For & Stream*, Oct. 21, 1893. 41:
342. Fulton Chain. 5728

Chrystie, Percival. The Adirondack deer.
For & Stream, Dec. 29, 1894. 43:559. Against
"water-killing." 5729

Clark, W.E. Deer in the Adirondacks. *Recreation*, Sept. 1896. 5:129. illus. 5730

Cleveland, Grover. Fishing and shooting
sketches, illustrated by Henry S. Watson.
N.Y. Outing publishing co. 1907. 209p. port.
plates, illus. 5731

Confessions of a deer slayer. *For & Stream*,
Nov. 7, 1896. 47:369. Reply to Deerslayer,
pseud. Oct. 31, 1896, 47:346. Reprinted from
the *New York Mail & Express*. 5732

Cook, Sam. The Adirondack deer season.
Field & S, Oct. 1904. 9:618–22. illus. 5733

Cool, Byron E. Deer of Canachagala lake.
For & Stream, Oct. 15, 1898. 51:309. Adirondack League Club tract. 5734

Crans, George E. Deer hunting in the olden
days. *Ang & Hunt*, Oct. 1910. 2:511–14. illus.
At Cranberry Inlet. 5735

Curtis, George William. From the easy chair.
N.Y. Harper, c1891–94. 3v. "Killing deer,"
v.3, p.28–36. 5736

Curtis, H.N. My first deer. *Outing*, Jan. 1888.
11:372–75. 5737

D., J.W. A magnificent Adirondack deer.
For & Stream, Sept. 23, 1905. 65:251. 5738

Dailey, Elric J. Beyond the trail's end; a deer
hunting expedition in the farback Adirondacks. *Fur-Fish-Game*, Dec. 1925. 42:no.6:
21–23. illus. South of Ampersand. 5739

Decker, F.L. A deer hunt in the Adirondacks.
For & Stream, Jan. 14, 1899. 52:27. 5740

Deer hunting. *Am Sportsman*, Oct. 11, 1873. 3:22–23. Along the Raquette River.   5741

Deer hunting in New York state. *D & H Bul*, Nov. 1937. 17:165–67, 172–73. illus.   5742

Deer in Adirondack lakes. *For & Stream*, Aug. 7, 1890. 35:48–49. Hamilton County.   5743

Deer in the Adirondacks. *For & Stream*, Dec. 8, 1881. 17:368.   5744

A deer jacking record. *For & Stream*, Apr. 24, 1897. 48:321. Editorial on season of 1893 at Big Moose Lake.   5745

Deer stalking on bicycles. *Sport Rev*, Oct. 13, 1906. 30:398. Party camping near Paul Smiths using bicycles.   5746

Doll, George F. Two Adirondack deer and how the greenhorn of the party chanced to bring them into camp. *Field & S*, Jan. 1909. 13:781–85. illus.   5747

The Dominie, pseud. Driving a buck. *For & Stream*, Feb. 5, 1874. 1:405. Little Tupper Lake.   5748

Donohue, Frank Laurence. Deer hunting and deer laws. *For & Stream*, Dec. 12, 1896. 47:466.   5749

Duryea, Morris Jesup. His first deer. *For & Stream*, July 18, 1903. 61:45.   5750

The economic view of deer hounding. *For & Stream*, Feb. 25, 1886. 26:88–89.   5751

Eurus, pseud. An Adirondack deer hunt. *For & Stream*, Sept. 11, 1897. 49:205. Indian Lake.   5752

Fenton, Charles. Still hunting on Mt. Vanderwacker. *For & Stream*, Apr. 27, 1876. 6:178–79. Hunting trip made in 1857.   5753

Fletcher, J.P. A deer hunt in the Adirondacks. *Amat Sportsman*, Nov. 1905. 34:no.1:9–10.\illus. Lake Pleasant.   5754

Flint, Peter, Adirondack deer hunting. *For & Stream*, Jan. 9, 1904. 62:28.   5755

Flint, Peter, Adirondack deer hunting. *For & Stream*, Dec. 30, 1905. 65:533.   5756

Flint, Peter, Capturing a buck on foot. *For & Stream*, Oct. 21, 1899. 53:329–30. Near Ticonderoga.   5757

Floating for deer. *Knick Mag*, Apr. 1862. 59:337–39.   5758

Floating for deer in the Adirondacks. *Harper W*, Oct. 24, 1868. 12:677, 679. illus.   5759

Foster, Maximilian. Where the big game runs; wildernesses where the sportsman finds noble quarry within striking distance of the great cities. Hunting deer in the Adirondacks, moose and caribou in Maine and Canada, and grizzly, elk and pronghorn in the Rockies. *Munsey*, Dec. 1900. 24:426–40. illus.   5760

Fuller, A.R. Adirondack winter notes. *For & Stream*, Feb. 15, 1883. 20:46–47. Still-hunting at Meacham Lake.   5761

Fuller, A.R. Deer in the Adirondacks. *For & Stream*, Dec. 4, 1884. 23:367.   5762

G., P.B. Deer hunting ethics. *For & Stream*, Sept. 6, 1888. 31:126. Fulton Chain.   5763

Gale, J. Thomson. Adirondack deer and hounds. *For & Stream*, Feb. 25, 1899. 52:150.   5764

Gianini, Charles A. Whitetails, the reveries of an Adirondack deer hunter. *For & Stream*, Jan. 1927. 97:25–26, 55–56. illus.   5765

Grant, H.D. When Adirondack deer were wantonly killed with clubs. *J Outd Life*, Mar. 1906. 3:53–54.   5766

Gray, H.T. A deafened doe. *Recreation*, Oct. 1900. 13:252. St. Regis.   5767

H. Stalking bucks by squash light. *For & Stream*, Oct. 11, 1883. 21:217.   5768

Hammond, Samuel H. and Mansfield, L.W. Country margins and rambles of a journalist. N.Y., Boston, J.C. Derby, Phillips, Sampson & co. 1855. 356p. Adirondacks, p.293–329. First published in the *Albany State Register*.   5769

Hastings, W.W. Deer hunting days in the Adirondacks. *For & Stream*, Apr. 22, 1899. 52:302–3. illus.   5770

Hazard, Caroline. Memoirs of the Rev. J. Lewis Diman, D.D. . . .compiled from his letters, journals, and writings. Boston, Houghton, 1887. 363p. Deer hunt on the Raquette, p.243.   5771

Hector, pseud. Still-hunting on the Oswegatchie *For & Stream*, Oct. 6, 1894. 43:295.   5772

Hermalin, D.M. Big game hunting for poor men; being a treatise on how a salaried man living in New York city may spend a two weeks' vacation, enjoy himself, and secure a deer, all for fifty dollars or less. *For & Stream*, Jan. 10, 1914. 82:37–39. illus. Cranberry Lake region.   5773

Hermalin, D.M. Big-game hunting in New York state. *For & Stream*, Feb. 24, 1912. 78:236–37. illus. Hunting deer near Cranberry Lake.   5774

Hermalin, D.M. The last of the monster; being an episode about old and experienced hunters and a tenderfoot. . . *For & Stream*, Aug. 22, 1914. 83:240–41. illus. A deer hunting story from the Cranberry Lake region.   5775

Hoadley, Edgar R. A night on the Raquette. *Recreation*, Aug. 1896. 5:89–92.   5776

Hoffman, Charles Fenno. Scenes and stories of the Hudson. 2. The deer hunt. *Am Mo*

Mag (*NY*) Apr. 1836. n.s.1:401–6. The first part of this series appeared in the Jan. 1836 issue with title "Mohegan-ana." 5777

Hounding deer in the Adirondacks 25 years ago; some recollections of an old hunter. *J Outd Life*, Sept. 1905. 2:185–88. illus. 5778

Hopper, Raymond G. Primeval Adirondacks. *For & Stream*, June 18, 1891. 36:432–33. Smith's Lake in northwestern Adirondacks. 5779

Hudson, William Lincoln. On the trail of old Mike. *Field & S*, Sept. 1908. 13:405–10. illus. 5780

Irenasus, pseud. Deer shooting in the Adirondacks. *Am Sportsman*, Nov. 1872. 2:27. Near Paul Smiths. 5781

Jack bluff and bluster. *For & Stream*, Aug. 20, 1885. 25:61. Editorial on jacking. 5782

Jack-hunting deer. *For & Stream*, May 28, 1891. 36:369. Editorial on restrictions on hunting on tract of the Adirondack League Club. 5783

Juvenal, pseud. The Adirondack deer season. *For & Stream*, Oct. 20, Dec. 1, 1906. 67:614, 864–65. 5784

Juvenal, pseud. The Adirondack deer season again. *For & Stream*, Dec. 8, 1906. 67:906. 5785

Juvenal, pseud. Mud-sounding in the Adirondacks. *For & Stream*, Nov. 28, 1903. 61: 421. Tenderfoot caught in the mud during a deer hunt. 5786

Juvenal, pseud. A night watch in the Adirondacks. *For & Stream*, Jan. 29, 1898. 50: 87. 5787

Koller, Lawrence R. Shots at whitetails. Drawings by Bob Kuhn. Boston, Little, Brown, c1948. 362p. illus. Includes Adirondacks. 5788

Lawson, Lem. Training Adirondack deer dogs. *For & Stream*, Feb. 13, 1897. 48:128. 5789

Lempfert, O.C. Phantoms of the forest; an Adirondack deer hunt plus a bear that took it and kept on coming. *Field & S*, Oct. 1929. 34:no.6:36–37, 101–2. illus. 5790

Low, James Jr. Floating and driving for deer; or, The adventures of a night and day in the Adirondacks. Geneva, The Continental Herald & Swiss Times, 1873. 62p. 5791

McChesney, Calvin S. Hunting facts from a sportsman's notebook. *Conservationist*, Mar. 1921. 4:42–43. Moose River valley. 5792

Marble, George L. My first buck. *Sh & Fish*, Nov. 17, 1904. 37:109–10. Hunting at Tupper Lake. 5793

Markham, Charles C. An Adirondack deer hunt. *For & Stream*, July 29, 1875. 4:388. At Round Pond and Big Clear Pond. 5794

Markham, Charles C. Among the Adirondacks. Sunrise on Little Tupper's lake—A deer hunt at Rock pond—Chase after a buck. *For & Stream*, Dec. 25, 1873. 1:308. 5795

Martin, John S. The clearing buck. *Field & S*, Oct. 1942. 47:no.6:11–13, 63–64. illus. 5796

Martindale, Paul. A deer-hunt on the Bouquet. *Knick Mag*, June 1855. 45:577–83. Started from Elizabethtown accompanied by Apollos Newell. 5797

Mayo, Earl Williams. A September night in the Adirondacks. *Illus Am*, Sept. 19, 1896. 20:408–9. illus. Reminiscences of a deer hunt at night near Cranberry Lake. 5798

Miller, Seaver Asbury. At Round lake in the Adirondacks. *Recreation*, Feb. 1898. 8:122–23. 5799

Miss Diana in the Adirondacks. *Harper W*, Aug. 25, 1883. 27:529, 535. illus. Full-page illustration and short account of deer hunting experience. 5800

A month at the Racket. *Knick Mag*, Sept.– Nov. 1856. 48:290–94, 356–63, 485–92. Raquette Lake. 5801

Morley, J.D. Favors hounding. *Recreation*, July 1902. 17:40–41. 5802

Motisher, Robert W. Adirondack deer hounding. *For & Stream*, Jan. 23, 1904. 62:67. 5803

Musset, pseud. Adirondack deer. *For & Stream*, Dec. 22, 1894. 43:536. 5804

Musset, pseud. Adirondack deer hounding. *For & Stream*, Oct. 13, 1894. 43:316. 5805

Musset, pseud. Adirondack deer hounding. *For & Stream*, Dec. 7, 1895. 45:493. 5806

Musset, pseud. Adirondack deer hunting. *For & Stream*, Dec. 22, 1892. 39:533. 5807

Musset, pseud. Deer in the Adirondacks. *For & Stream*, Dec. 9, 1886. 27:384. Dissatisfaction with the present law. 5808

Newberry, A. St. J. Water killing deer. *For & Stream*, Nov. 28, 1896. 47:425. 5809

A night hunt. *For & Stream*, Nov. 24, 1881. 17:326–27. Along the Raquette. 5810

Night-hunt in the Adirondacks. *Broadway*, Mar. 1870. ser.2:4:431–35. 5811

North Woods, pseud. Adirondack deer. *For & Stream*, Nov. 20, 1890. 35:351. Deer hounding. 5812

Not dead yet. *Field & S*, Mar. 1906. 10:1155. Hounding deer in Essex County. 5813

Nu Delta, pseud. Adirondack deer hounding. *For & Stream*, May 1, 1890. 34:288. 5814

Ondack, Adrion, pseud. Hounding and still hunting. *For & Stream*, Mar. 10, 1881. 16: 108–9. Near middle branch of the St. Regis River. 5815

"Open season on deer hunters." *Sport Rev*, Nov. 20, 1909. 36:495. Discussion of accidents during hunting season. 5816

Otis, R.C. A deer hunt in the Adirondacks. *Fur News*, Nov. 1923. 38:no.5:37. 5817

P. Adirondack deer. *For & Stream*, July 30, 1885. 25:7. 5818

Portsa, pseud. The Adirondack deer. *For & Stream*, Dec. 10, 1885. 25:385. Summary of the hunting season. 5819

Portsa, pseud. Adirondack deer. *For & Stream*, Oct. 29, 1891. 37:291. Near Wilmurt. 5820

Portsa, pseud. Adirondack deer hunting. *For & Stream*, Dec. 1, 1892. 39:467. Discussion of hunting season. 5821

Potter, Frederick K. Adirondack deer trails of 1908. *For & Stream*, Oct. 1924. 94:594–95, 625–26. illus. 5822

Preston, Emma A. A woman scores on deer. *Field & S*, Oct. 1906. 11:589. Along Fulton Chain. 5823

R., J.H. Adirondack deer killing methods. *For & Stream*, Mar. 12, 1891. 36:149. Discussion of floating and hounding. 5824

Rawson, Edward Sidney. The buck duellist. *For & Stream*, Nov. 8, 1902. 59:363–64. 5825

Redner, D.S. Jr. My first still hunt. *Field & S*, Jan. 1903. 7:613–14. Near Euba Mills. 5826

Rice, Mrs. Arthur F. A woman's telling shot. *Recreation*, Aug. 1896. 5:84–85. illus. On St. Regis River. 5827

Roberts, Georgia. An Adirondack buck. *Outing*, Oct. 1897. 31:22–24. illus. Hunting on the Oswegatchie. 5828

Rodemeyer, J. A day in the Adirondacks. *Recreation*, Oct. 1897. 7:263–65. Near North Creek. 5829

Schenck, M. Adirondack deer. *For & Stream*, Jan. 4, 1896. 46:11. 5830

Schoonmaker, W.J. The white tail buck of Mud pond. *High Spots Yrbk*, 1942. p.7–8. illus. 5831

Seale, Marcus O. Rifle and pack in the Adirondacks. *Field & S*, Sept. 1918. 23:389–91. illus. Cranberry Lake. 5832

Severinghaus, C.W. Adirondack deer. *NYS Con*, Dec. 1950–Jan. 1951. 5:no.3:34. One-column note giving statistics of the take for 1950, 1949 and 1945–48. 5833

Shaw, Joseph T. Our Adirondack deer hunt. *Field & S*, Mar. 1914. 18:1183–89. illus. 5834

Shepard, Frank E. A large Adirondack buck. *For & Stream*, Feb. 2, 1895. 44:88. 5835

Shurter, Joseph W. Deer hunting in the Adirondacks. *For & Stream*, Apr. 12, 1883. 20: 205–7. Trip in 1881 to Indian Clearing on Moose River. 5836

Shurter, Joseph W. Various matters. *For & Stream*, Dec. 6, 1902. 59:449. Notes on deer and hunting in the Adirondacks. 5837

Smith, Ezra G. An Adirondack deer hunt. *For & Stream*, Mar. 30, 1901. 56:244. 5838

Smith, Ezra G. Human hounds dog deer. *For & Stream*, Feb. 16, 1901. 56:129. Too many parties employ human dogging. 5839

Solitude, pseud. An Adirondack deer hunt. *For & Stream*, Jan. 25, 1908. 70:136. Near Old Forge. 5840

Spears, Raymond Smiley. Adirondack deer. *For & Stream*, Dec. 13, 1902. 59:467. 5841

Spears, Raymond Smiley. Adirondack deer. *For & Stream*, Nov. 4, 1905. 65:370–71. On supply of deer. 5842

Spears, Raymond Smiley. Adirondack notes. *For & Stream*, July 27, 1895. 45:72. Moose River. 5843

Spears, Raymond Smiley. Getting a big buck. *For & Stream*, Oct. 2, 1897. 49:266. Moose River country. 5844

Spears, Raymond Smiley. A heavy deer. *For & Stream*, Nov. 13, 1897. 49:387. Heaviest deer of season shot at Fourth Lake. 5845

Spears, Raymond Smiley. In the north woods. *For & Stream*, Oct. 30, 1909. 73:696. Deer hunting notes. 5846

Stafford, E.L. An Adirondack deer hunt. *Amat Sportsman*, Feb. 1907. 36:no.4:3–5. illus. Annual deer hunt of Chestigue Hunting Club in Chestertown. 5847

Still-hunting in the town of Schroon. *For & Stream*, Sept. 19, 1896. 47:227. 5848

Sumner, E.E. The big buck of Spring pond carry. *For & Stream*, Apr. 23, 1898. 50:328. Exceptionally large buck killed in the southern part of Township 2 in St. Lawrence County. 5849

Sylvanus, pseud. Deer stalking in the Adirondacks. *Rod & Gun*, June 12–19, 1875. 6:161, 182. Along the Cedar River. 5850

Tanck, John E. and Passer, Franklin J. Still-hunting. *NYS Con*, Oct.–Nov. 1951. 6:no.2: 6–7. diagr. Stalking whitetails. 5851

Van Dyke, Theodore Strong. The still-hunter. N.Y. Fords, Howard & Hulbert, 1883. 390p. Includes hunting in the Adirondacks. 5852

Visitor, pseud. Real deer hounding in July. *For & Stream*, Aug. 22, 1914. 83:238–39. Notes from Eagle Lake. 5853

W. Adirondack deer. *For & Stream*, Sept. 29, 1894. 43:267.   5854

W., F.H. A deer hunt in the Adirondacks. *For & Stream*, Nov. 26, 1874. 3:242. Betna Ponds.   5855

W., M. My first buck. *Wilkes Spirit*, Sept. 10, 1859. 1:2–3. Hunting in Number Four area.   5856

Warburton, G.A. Can a novice get a deer? *Recreation*, Sept. 1904. 21:165–66.   5857

Warner, Charles Dudley. An Adirondack deer hunt. *For & Stream*, Feb. 4, 1886. 26: 28. Reprinted from his "In the Wilderness." Partially reprinted in Stedman & Hutchinson, v.8, p.449–56.   5858

Webb, Edward L. A three days' deer hunt. *Field & S*, Oct. 1907. 12:489–90.   5859

Whitney, Casper W. The butchery of Adirondack deer. *Harper W*, Jan. 16, 1892. 36: 58–61. illus.   5860

Willitts, Frederick C. On the trail of the white-tail. *Outing*, Dec. 1918. 73:138–40, 167–70. Northern Adirondacks.   5861

Withington, L.A. A deer hunt in the Adirondacks. *Field & S*, Nov. 1903. 8:545–47. illus.   5862

Wolcott, W.E. Adirondack deer. *For & Stream*, Oct. 20, 1900. 55:307.   5863

Wolcott, W.E. "Them big white birds." *For & Stream*, Oct. 24, 1903. 61:320. An Adirondack deer story.   5864

Wood, Richard K. Afoot in deer country. *Fur News*, Nov. 1921. 34:no.5:18–19, 36–38. illus. Near the Duck Hole.   5865

Wood, Richard K. Trap lines and deer trails. *Sport Dig*, Nov. 1924, Jan., Apr. 1925. 3:no. 11:12–14; 4:no.1:15–17; 4:no.4:17–20, 62–64. illus. Deer hunting in the Cold River country.   5866

Wulff, Lee. Adirondack fireball. *Outdoor Life*, Sept. 1953. 112:no.3:42–43, 102–4. illus. Deer hunting near Blue Ridge.   5867

X. An Adirondack deer country. *For & Stream*, Mar. 29, 1883. 20:170. At Paul Smiths. 5868

Other Game

An Adirondack panther. *For & Stream*, Mar. 1, 1902. 58:165. Reprinted from the *Elizabethtown Post*.   5869

An Adirondack wildcat. *For & Stream*, May 17, 1898. 50:365. Reprinted from *Northern Tribune*, Boonville. Hunter's experience along the Fulton Chain.   5870

Adventure with a panther. *For & Stream*, Mar. 9, 1876. 6:66. On road from Corinth to Conklingville.   5871

Ballard, Frank S. Goose shooting on Lake Champlain. *Recreation*, Jan. 1895. 2:143–46. illus.   5872

Ballard, William F. Bruin on the rampage. *For & Stream*, Sept. 21, 1882. 19:145. One of Colvin's guides tells of an encounter with some bears on the South Branch of the Moose River.   5873

Bassler, Anthony. An Adirondack black bear. *Recreation*, Sept. 1901. 15:190–91. Bear hunting near Lake Pleasant.   5874

Blakesley, Fred E. The grouse gunner in the Adirondacks. *Fur News*, Sept. 1921. 34:no. 3:5, 27–28. illus.   5875

Brown, Elliott C. Three days ducking on Lake Champlain. *Outing*, Nov. 1899. 35: 130–34. illus.   5876

Camilla, pseud. Jerry's "Panthy" hunt. *For & Stream*, Jan. 2, 1904. 62:3–4. Cold River area.   5877

Colvin, Verplanck. Narrative of a bear hunt in the Adirondacks. *Alb Inst Tr*, Jan. 18, 1870. 6:227–40. Also issued as a reprint, Albany, J. Munsell, 1870, 16p. An exciting, vivid, scientific account of a two-day chase starting Dec. 31, 1869 in the direction of Jessup and Indian rivers. Colvin describes the pursuit and capture of a black bear. 5878

Dailey, Elric J. Keen nose, a tale of the most elusive fox in the 'Dacks. *Fur-Fish-Game*, Aug. 1926. 44:no.2:20–22. illus. Cold River valley.   5879

Elk killed in the Adirondacks. *Field & S*, Oct. 1903. 8:488.   5880

Flint, Peter. For an Adirondack panther hunt; certainly two big cats still exist in a mountain fastness. *For & Stream*, May 23, 1914. 82:687–88.   5881

Flint, Peter. Partridges near Ticonderoga. *For & Stream*, June 17, 1899. 52:467. 5882

Flint, Peter. The ruffed grouse scarcity. *For & Stream*, Feb. 15, 1908. 70:257. Eagle Lake.   5883

Foster, Thomas. Dat one day on Lake Champlain. *Outing*, Dec. 1919. 75:146–47, 180. Humorous experience of four duck hunters.   5884

Glover. An Adirondack bear capture. *For & Stream*, June 2, 1894. 42:468. Near Lake Pleasant.   5885

A Guide, pseud. A panther story. *Am Sportsman*, Dec. 6, 1873. 3:147. An adventure of John Cheney's.   5886

Knox, M.V.B. How I missed shooting a panther. *Field & S*, Dec. 1903. 8:618–21. illus.   5887

Lambert, W.S. A fox hunt in the Adirondacks. *For & Stream*, Jan. 15, 1898. 50:45.
5888

Lempfert, O.C. The outlaw of the Adirondacks. *For & Stream*, Oct. 1929. 99:720–21, 751–53. illus. Is the black bear game or vermin? 5889

Phelps, Chandley L. The black bear. *For & Stream*, Nov. 6, 1884. 23:286. Hunting bear on the Moose River. 5890

Potter, Frederick K. Adirondack bears. *For & Stream*, Dec. 1923. 93:689, 725–29. illus.
5891

R., J.H. An Adirondack elk. *For & Stream*, Sept. 21, 1901. 57:227. 5892

Senator Chahoon's bear. *For & Stream*, Sept. 23, 1899. 53:249. Reprinted from the *Plattsburg Press*. Bear shot with bird shot. 5893

Simonds, Elijah. Even a girl can kill a trapped bear. *For & Stream*, Sept. 21, 1895. 45:250. At Brainard's Falls. 5894

Smiley, James. A trapper and his bear. *Fur News*, Mar. 1923. 37:no.3:38–39, 50. Near West Canada Lakes. 5895

Smith, Paul Jr. Elk in the Adirondacks. *For Leaves*, Spring 1904. 1:no.2:15–16. illus. 5896

Spears, Raymond Smiley. Two bears. *Fur News*, Dec. 1917. 26:no.6:8–9. illus. Bear hunting north of Wilmurt. 5897

Sportsman, pseud. Fox hunting at Ticonderoga. *For & Stream*, Mar. 30, 1912. 78:400–1.
5898

W., N.B. An Adirondack squirrel hunt. *For & Stream*, Aug. 20, 1891. 37:84–85. Near Lake George. 5899

Warner, Charles Dudley. How I killed a bear. *In* Mayer, Alfred Marshall. Sport with gun and rod in American woods and waters. N.Y. Century, c1883. p.820–26. Condensed in *North Country Life*, Spring 1948, 2:no.2:57–62. From his "In the Wilderness." 5900

Whipple, James Spencer. First wild boar hunt in United States; it took place only a few weeks ago in the wildest part of the Adirondacks, first herd brought from Germany and released in the north woods many years ago. *State Service*, May 1919. 3:no.5:61–64. illus. Originally released in Litchfield Park.
5901

Wilson, H.G. Chance shots at Adirondack foxes. *Fur News*, Jan. 1922. 35:no.1:26, 58–59. illus. 5902

Wilson, H.G. Shooting mink. *Fur News*, Jan. 1923. 37:no.1:22–23, 46–47. illus. 5903

FISHING

General

Adirondack fishing. *For & Stream*, Jan. 1, 1885. 23:448. 5904

Adirondack fishing rights. *For & Stream*, Nov. 12, 1891. 37:333. Law for Fulton Chain and similar areas. 5905

Adirondack fly casts. *For & Stream*, July 9, 1898. 51:21. 5906

The Adirondacs. *Am Sportsman*, Aug. 1873. 2:170. Fishing near Paul Smiths. 5907

An advertising dodge. *For & Stream*, Aug. 23, 1883. 21:62. Misleading fishing advertisements. 5908

Angling in the Adirondack region. *Sport Rev*, June 12, 1909. 35:649. 5909

Arthur, L.W. The fight among the rocks and shallows. *Field & S*, Aug. 1911. 16:399–400.
5910

B. A Chateaugay experience. *For & Stream*, Nov. 19, 1885. 25:323–24. 5911

B., F. Trip to north woods. *For & Stream*, Aug. 6, 1874. 2:403. Fishing on the Stillwater and Albany Lake. 5912

B., W.W. Rainbow lake, Adirondacks. *For & Stream*, Aug. 22, 1896. 47:146. 5913

Bachelor, Ward. "A day in the north woods." *Lippincott*, Oct. 1881. 28:399–404. Fishing yarn. 5914

Bailey, Robeson. Lake fishing in the Adirondacks. *For & Stream*, June 1928. 98:335–37, 359–60. illus. 5915

Beardslee, Lester A. Adirondack experiences —seeking for rest, by Piseco, pseud. *For & Stream*, July 13, 1876. 6:368. Fishing trip near Piseco Lake. 5916

Beardslee, Lester A. The Adirondack fishing at Piseco lake, by Piseco, pseud. *For & Stream*, June 15, 1876. 6:302. 5917

Beardslee, Lester A. Jock's lake, by Piseco, pseud. *For & Stream*, July 5, 1888. 30:476–77. 5918

Beck, C.F. Recent catches in Lake Champlain. *Am Angler*, Oct. 22, 1887. 12:269. 5919

Bender, Ray. Shantytown. *NYS Con*, Dec. 1947–Jan. 1948. 2:no.3:8–9. illus. Reprinted in *North Country Life*, Winter 1949, 3:no.1: 17–19, with title "Ice Fishing on Lake Champlain." 5920

Bisbee, Eugene Shade. Game fishing on the New York Central. *NYC Lines Mag*, Mar. 1928. 8:no.12:13–14. 5921

Bisbee, Eugene Shade. Nervous trout and lurking bass lure many. *NYC Lines Mag*, Aug. 1928. 9:no.5:11–12. illus. 5922

Brandreth, Paulina. Long lake—a sportsman's arcady, by Paul Brandreth, pseud. *For & Stream*, Oct. 4, 1913. 81:421–23, 440–41. illus. 5923

Burham, J.T. In the Adirondacks. *Field & S*, Aug. 1906. 11:388. 5924

Burnham, John Bird. The Boquet river. *For & Stream*, Sept. 10, 1898. 51:213. Signed: J.B.B.Trout and bass fishing. 5925

Burnham, John Bird. Fishing in northern New York. *For & Stream*, June 11, 1898. 50: 468–69. Signed: J.B.B. Lake Champlain. 5926

Burnham, John Bird. Lake Champlain fishing. *For & Stream*, Aug. 27, 1898. 51:170. Signed: J.B.B. 5927

C., H.S. Adirondack waters. *For & Stream*, June 12, 1890. 34:412. Thirteenth Pond. 5928

C., J.G. An Adirondack trip. *For & Stream*, Sept. 9, 1880. 15:109. Boreas River and Long Pond. 5929

Camilla, pseud. The veteran's pool. *For & Stream*, Feb. 7, 1903. 60:112. Adirondack fishing story. 5930

Chahoon, George. The fly in North Elba. *For & Stream*, Sept. 23, 1880. 15:149. 5931

Cheney, Albert Nelson. Angling notes. *For & Stream*, Jan. 1893–Aug. 10, 1901. v.40–57. Column appearing in many issues; includes fishing in the Adirondacks. 5932

Cheney, Albert Nelson. Fishing in Lake George—effects of restocking. *Am Angler*, Feb. 16, 1884. 5:100–1. Signed: A.N.C. 5933

Cheney, Albert Nelson. In the north woods— camping with ladies. *Am Angler*, Dec. 9, 1882. 2:369–71. Signed: A.N.C. Fishing trip to Raquette Lake. 5934

Cheney, Albert Nelson. One rainy day. *Am Angler*, Oct. 13, 1883. 4:228–29. Signed: A.N.C. Brant Lake fishing trip. 5935

Cheney, Albert Nelson. A pond that nobody knows. *For & Stream*, May 24, 1888. 30:346–47. Pond located between Lake George and Lake Champlain. 5936

Cheney, Albert Nelson. Schroon lake—black bass and salmon trout. *Am Angler*, Oct. 7, 1882. 2:229–30. Signed: A.N.C. 5937

Cheney, Albert Nelson. Scores, etc. on Schroon lake (Essex co. N.Y.). *Am Angler*, Aug. 19, 1882. 2:116–17. Signed: A.N.C. 5938

Cheney, Albert Nelson. Then and now—my big score. *Am Angler*, Mar. 25, 1882. 1:196–97. Signed: A.N.C. Fishing in Twelfth Pond. 5939

Chrystie, Percival. Adirondack fishing. *For & Stream*, Oct. 19, 1907. 69:620. Lower Saranac Lake. 5940

Clark, Lewis Gaylord. Fishing excursion to 'John Brown's tract.' *Knick Mag*, Oct. 1857. 50:414–17. Expedition up the Black River accompanying Canal Board surveyors; an account of a trip with the North Woods Walton Club was to follow, but it was not published, although a note in the November issue stated that it would appear in the next issue; in Apr. 1858 (51:434) the editor states: "We shall refer further to the North-Woods Walton Club when we conclude next month our 'Trip to John Browne's Tract.' " 5941

Covert, Byron V. Three weeks in the Adirondacks. *For & Stream*, June 22, 1901 56:487. 5942

Cranberry lake. *For & Stream*, Mar. 17, 1887. 28:151. 5943

Crow, Charles H. A day on the Racquette— Tupper lake and Bog river. *For & Stream*, Apr. 16, 1874. 2:146. 5944

D. The Adirondacks. *For & Stream*, May 26, 1887. 28:395. 5945

D., G.V.W. My first fishing trip. *J Outd Life*, May 1906. 3:143. 5946

Dawson, George. Angling talks; being the winter talks on summer pastimes. Contributed to the "Forest and stream." N.Y. Forest & stream publishing co. 1883. 78p. "Contents chiefly concern angling in the Adirondack lakes and rivers." 5947

Dawson, George. Pleasures of angling with rod and reel for trout and salmon. N.Y. Sheldon, 1876. 264p. front. plates. Trout fishing in the Adirondacks, p.205–64. 5948

Dominick, George F. Jr. Adirondack notes. *For & Stream*, Apr. 18–May 2, 1903. 60:308, 350. 5949

Ewbank, Ernest L. From Hendersonville to the Adirondacks. *Amer Angler*, Sept. 1921. 6:258. 5950

Farrell, John J. Fishing through the ice, a popular sport in the Adirondacks. *NYC Lines Mag*, Feb. 1921. 1:no.11:37–38. illus. 5951

Fernald, Charles D. Saranac lake to Canada by water. *Recreation*, Aug. 1902. 17:111. Fishing trip along Saranac River to Lake Champlain. 5952

Finch, J.C. An Adirondack hunter and fisherman. *NYC Lines Mag*, Oct. 1924. 5:no.7:86. illus. Fishing on the Moose River. 5953

Fishing and fishing grounds—Lake Champlain. *Am Angler*, Apr. 21, 1883. 3:247–48. 5954

Fishing in Bisby waters. *Am Angler*, Mar. 29, 1884. 5:193–94. From the Annual Report of the Bisby Club.   5955

Fishing in New York lakes and streams. *Am Field*, Aug. 23, 1924. 102:230. Fulton Chain.   5956

Fishing laws for Lake Champlain. *For & Stream*, Dec. 18, 1884. 23:410.   5957

Flint, Peter. Lake Champlain's big fish. *For & Stream*, Oct. 18, 1902. 59:313. Review of fishing season.   5958

Fly Rod, pseud. A month in the Adirondacks for $50. *For & Stream*, Mar. 21, 1878. 10:115. Fishing trip on Brown's Tract.   5959

Gill, John M. A trip to the Adirondacks. *For & Stream*, July 10, 1879. 12:449. Lake Pleasant.   5960

Goodspeed, Charles Eliot. Angling in America, its early history and literature. Boston, Houghton, 1939. 381p. front. plates, ports. facsims. Includes the North Woods and Long Island; North Woods Walton Club and Philosophers' Camp.   5961

Green, Charles A. From the Adirondack mountains. *For & Stream*, July 3, 1909. 73:19. Notes on a fishing trip.   5962

Green, Charles A. Hail to the Adirondacks! *For & Stream*, June 11, 1874. 2:275.   5963

Greene, C.W. Survey notes on Indian lake. *NYS Con*, Apr.–May 1948. 2:no.5:20. illus. Fishing notes.   5964

H. The trip to Snag lake. *For & Stream*, June 7, 1883. 20:367–68. Up West Canada Creek.   5965

H., K.J. Fine scores at Cranberry lake inlet. *Am Angler*, Sept. 8, 1888. 14:157.   5966

Hallock, Charles. The fishing tourist; angler's guide and reference book... N.Y. Harper, 1873. 239p. front. illus. Part II, Ch. II, "The Adirondacks," p.67–79. Originally published in *Harper's Magazine*, Aug. 1870, 41:321–38, with title "The Raquette Club."   5967

Held, Ernest. An old fisherman's yarn. *Ang & Hunt*, Sept. 1910. 2:459–61. Fishing trips on the Oswegatchie.   5968

Herbert, Henry William. Frank Forester's Fish and fishing of the United States...third edition, revised and corrected, with an ample supplement by the author. N.Y. Stringer & Townsend, 1855. 359, 86p. fronts. (part col.) plates, illus. Includes comments on the red-fleshed trout of Hamilton County, a letter (on fishing in Louis Lake), supplement p.21–24; and "Of Trolling for Lake Trout in Hamilton County, New-York," supplement p.66–73.   5969

Hill, W.W. The Beaver river country, N.Y. *For & Stream*, Aug. 13, 1874. 3:2–3.   5970

Hiscock, L. Harris. The conversion of George. From brook trout to Lake Meacham pike. *Amer Angler*, Sept. 1921. 6:283–84. illus.   5971

Holberton, Wakeman. An Adirondack evening. *For & Stream*, Sept. 9, 1886. 27:129. East Pond.   5972

Huston, Samuel Craig. The Adirondacks. *For & Stream*, June 30, 1894. 42:557. Upper Saranac Lake.   5973

Hutton, T. Radcliffe. Adirondack's big records. *Amer Angler*, Oct. 1920. 5:274–75. Fish records.   5974

Ibis, pseud. Reminiscences of the Raquette. *For & Stream*, May 23, 1889. 32:354. Fishing trip starting at Blue Mountain Lake.   5975

Ives, Martin Van Buren. The Adirondacks. *For & Stream*, May 28, 1885. 24:346. Fishing in western Adirondacks.   5976

J. Lake Champlain fishing. *For & Stream*, July 17, 1897. 49:49.   5977

Jones' lake. *Am Angler*, Nov. 12, 1887. 12:313. Near Panther Mountain.   5978

Judson, Edward Z.C. Seth Green on the stream. *Am Angler*, Mar. 4, 1882. 1:153–54. Signed: Ned Buntline. Meeting with Seth Green while fishing near Blue Mountain Lake.   5979

June on the West Canada. Mr. X gets 'em when he needs 'em. *NYS Sport*, Jan. 1939. 4:no.3:3. illus.   5980

Juvenal, pseud. Adirondack fishing. *For & Stream*, Sept. 1, 1906. 67:341.   5981

Juvenal, pseud. Adirondack notes. *For & Stream*, June 10, 1909. 72:981. Poor fishing season.   5982

Kansas, pseud. Two weeks at Spruce lake. *For & Stream*, Aug. 27, 1891. 37:105–6. 5983

Korax, pseud. Camp of "The Triad." *For & Stream*, Aug. 7, 1890. 35:51. Fourth Lake.   5984

La Bier, Myra J. The sum and substance of a fishing trip. *For & Stream*, June 8, 1895. 44:465. Boreas River.   5985

Lake Champlain fishing. *For & Stream*, Feb. 25, 1905. 64:159. Copy of petition sent to Hon. Raymond Prefontaine, Canadian Minister of Marine and Fisheries, adopted by the North American Fish and Game Protective Association.   5986

Lake George notes. *For & Stream*, July 24, 1890. 35:9.   5987

Lanman, Charles. Adventures of an angler in Canada, Nova Scotia, and the United States. London, Richard Bentley, 1848. 322p.

front. (port.) illus. Includes chapter on "John Cheney, the Adirondack hunter, and some of his exploits," p.50–114. Phillips states that this is the English edition of Lanman's "Tour to the River Saguenay..." 5988

Lanman, Charles. A tour to the river Saguenay in lower Canada. Philadelphia, Curry & Hart, 1848. 231p. Adirondacks, p.50–92. Published in England with title "Adventures of an Angler in Canada..." 5989

The laws governing fishing in Lake Champlain. *Am Angler*, Dec. 27, 1884. 6:403–4. 5990

Lincoln, Robert Page. On the headwaters of the West Canada. *Sport Dig*, Oct. 1925. 2: no.10:28–31, 75–76. illus. Piseco Lake. 5991

McNulta, John. Fifty years with a fly. Part XXI. *Field & S*, July 1900. 5:341–42. Fishing trip in Brown's Tract. 5992

Mather, Fred. A cast with "Piseco." *For & Stream*, July 29, 1886. 27:7. West Canada Creek and Wilmurt Lake. 5993

Mattison, Mrs. C.H. Breaking in a novice. *Ang & Hunt*, May 1910. 2:272, 274. illus. Fishing in western Adirondacks near Forestport. 5994

Merrill, Charles A. Gossip about noted Adirondack waters. *Am Angler*, July 29, 1882. 2:72. 5995

Michael, Charles Ritter. Mr. Coolidge is learning to play. Fishing takes its place alongside politics at summer White house in Adirondacks... *NY Times Mag*, Aug. 1, 1926. p.1–2, 19. illus. 5996

Millard, E.E. Random casts; or, Odds and ends from an angler's note book, by E.M.E. N.Y. Derby bros. 1878. 175p. Southern Adirondacks, near Morehouseville. 5997

Miller, Ben. In the Adirondacks: experiences and impressions of a southern angler upon his first visit to the north woods. *Field & S*, May 1908. 13:19–22. illus. 5998

Morrell, T.S. The Adirondacks in early spring. *Am Angler*, June 9, 1883. 3:355–57. Fishing trip from Blue Mountain Lake to the Saranacs. 5999

Morrell, T.S. The Adirondacks in May. *Am Angler*, June 17–24, 1882. 1:385–87, 403–5. port. Signed: Old Izaak. Fishing trip to Long Lake with Sabattis as guide. 6000

Morrell, T.S. Camping on Boreas ponds (1868). *Am Angler*, Feb. 4–11, 1882. 1:82–83, 99–100. Signed: Old Izaak. 6001

Morrell, T.S. Early spring fishing in the Adirondacks. *Am Angler*, Aug. 4–11, 1888. 14: 68–70, 83–84. Signed: Old Izaak. Near Blue Mountain Lake. 6002

Morris, C.P. At Cranberry lake, next to catching fish oneself comes the pleasure of watching masterful exponent of the art. *For & Stream*, May 1919. 89:228, 234. 6003

Murdick, I.H. Chazy lake. *For & Stream*, July 6, 1895. 45:11. 6004

Murray, William Henry Harrison. Rod and reel. *Field & R*, Mar. 1878. 1:74–75. Extract from his "Adventures in the Wilderness." 6005

Musquash, pseud. Adirondack notes. *For & Stream*, Oct. 8, 1885. 25:207. Fishing trip to the Saranacs, Raquette and Blue Mountain lakes. 6006

My first Adirondack trip, a boyhood reminiscence. *For & Stream*, Oct. 4, 11, 25–Nov. 8, 1883. 21:188, 208, 248–49, 269–70, 289–90. Fishing trip in 1875 along the Fulton Chain to Long and Saranac lakes. 6007

N. The Beaver river country. *For & Stream*, July 23, 1874. 2:370–71. Fishing trip from Number Four. 6008

N., A.J. Jocks's lake. *For & Stream*, June 15, 1876. 6:298. Fishing trip in 1863. 6009

Natura, pseud. Wane of Adirondack fishing. *For & Stream*, June 23, 1892. 38:593. 6010

Northrup, Ansel Judd. Fishes and fishing in the Adirondacks from the sportsman's point of view. *In* New York (state). Forest, fish and game commission. Annual report, 1902–3. p.275–94. plates. 6011

Novice, pseud. In the Adirondacks. *For & Stream*, July 3, 1897. 49:12. Boreas River. 6012

Old Pilot, pseud. Deep trolling in Lake George. *For & Stream*, Mar. 22, 1877. 8:98. 6013

Ondack, Adrion, pseud. Angling in the Adirondacks. *For & Stream*, May 18, 1882. 18: 310. St. Regis area. 6014

Orlando. An Adirondack vacation. *Sh & Fish*, Aug. 16, 1906. 40:367. 6015

Osceola, pseud. The north woods. *For & Stream*, May 29, 1890. 34:371. 6016

Piscator, pseud. Tenderfeet in the Adirondacks. *For & Stream*, May 14, 1898. 50:383. Fishing up the Saranac River. 6017

Prime, William C. I go a-fishing. N.Y. Harper, c1873. 365p. St. Regis Waters in Old Times, Ch. VII. The St. Regis Waters Now, Ch. VIII. 6018

R., J. Jr. June in the north woods. *For & Stream*, July 13, 1882. 18:466. Fishing trip to Brown's Tract. 6019

R., J. Jr. A trip to Brown's tract. *For & Stream*, Feb. 2, 1882. 18:13–14. 6020

R., P.M. An unsuccessful angler. *For Leaves*, Winter 1909. 5:no.4:32–33. illus. Lake Placid.   6021

Reynolds, Bob. Adirondacks fishing. *Outdoor Life*, Aug. 1937. 80:no.2:8. Brief note on various fishing areas.   6022

Rice, W.C. A trip to Moose pond; or, How I violated the game law. *For Leaves*, Summer 1907. 4:no.2:44–48. illus.   6023

Richmond, W.L. An Adirondack memory. *Field & S*, Apr. 1909. 13:1082–84. illus. Moose River.   6024

S., F.M. A June day on the Black river. *For & Stream*, Jan. 22, 1885. 23:509. Near North Lake reservoir.   6025

S., H.E. Chateaugay and Plumador. *For & Stream*, Jan. 27, 1887. 27:30.   6026

S., W. Adirondack waters. *For & Stream*, June 26, 1890. 34:455.   6027

Schaefer, Paul A. White thunder. *Cloud Splitter*, July–Aug. 1946. 9:no.4:6–8. Fishing trip near Sacandaga.   6028

Seagears, Clayton B. Adirondack fishing notes. *Ad-i-ron-dac*, May–June 1946. 10:no.3:4–5.   6029

Shadow, pseud. My trip to the Adirondacks. *For & Stream*, July 21, 1887. 28:550. Meacham Lake.   6030

Spears, Raymond Smiley. Adirondack fishing. *For & Stream*, May 28, 1910. 74:859–60.   6031

Spears, Raymond Smiley. Adirondack fishing notes. *For & Stream*, June 8, 1895. 44:464.   6032

Spears, Raymond Smiley. Effect of automobile and motor cycle on fishing conditions. *For & Stream*, July 25, 1914. 83:112. illus. Chief cause for the reduction of the supply of fish in Adirondack waters.   6033

Spears, Raymond Smiley. Fishing in the Adirondacks. *For & Stream*, June 5, 1909. 72:898. Review of conditions.   6034

Spears, Raymond Smiley. Light rods and small flies. *For & Stream*, Aug. 5, 1911. 77:212–14. Equipment best suited to Adirondack fishing.   6035

Spears, Raymond Smiley. Some Adirondack gossip. *For & Stream*, June 20, 1908. 70:981. Fishing notes.   6036

Spears, Raymond Smiley. That boy in the Adirondacks. *For & Stream*, Sept. 10, 1898. 51:210–11.   6037

Sperry, Charles T. Hard luck. *Ang & Hunt*, July 1910. 2:382, 384. Fishing on Twin Lakes in western Adirondacks.   6038

Spinner, F.E. A veteran of the craft. *Am Angler*, June 27, 1885. 7:405. Fishing trip

through the Fulton Chain, Raquette and Long Lake.   6039

Spring, George H. comp. Angling guide to Adirondack fishing in the towns of Ticonderoga, Crown Point, North Hudson, Moriah and Schroon, N.Y. Ticonderoga, N.Y. Ticonderoga chamber of commerce, 1945. 7p.   6040

Stanstead. Lake Champlain. *For & Stream*, Nov. 30, 1895. 45:473–74.   6041

Stanstead. Lake Champlain net fishing. *For & Stream*, Dec. 13, 1902. 59:471.   6042

Stanton, Sanford E. Memories—a week's fishing trip in the Adirondack mountains. *Ang & Hunt*, June 1910. 2:303–5. Oswegatchie country.   6043

Sum, Sam, pseud. Wood's bar, Lake Champlain. *Am Angler*, Mar. 3, 1888. 13:134–36.   6044

Swirl, pseud. Angling days on Lake Champlain. *For & Stream*, Mar. 10, 1887. 27:135.   6045

T., C. McV. Adirondack fishing notes. *For & Stream*, May 15, 1897. 48:391.   6046

T., T. In the Adirondacks. *For & Stream*, July 6, 1895. 45:11. Lake Koshaka.   6047

T., W.S. On Lake Champlain. *For & Stream*, Nov. 22, 1902. 59:411. Near Port Kent.   6048

Thompson, H.H. An angling reminiscence. *For & Stream*, June 7, 1913. 80:721. Below foot of Long Lake.   6049

Thompson, H.H. Camp Morse. *Am Angler*, June 20, 1885. 7:385–89. Signed: H.H.T. A trip to Piseco Lake and along the Stillwater with George Morse as guide.   6050

Thompson, H.H. Camping on Jock's lake in 1863. *Am Angler*, July 5, 1884. 6:1–4. map. Signed: H.H.T.   6051

Thompson, H.H. Camping twenty years ago. *Am Angler*, Apr. 12, 1884. 5:225–30. illus. Signed: H.H.T. Raquette Lake, Cold River.   6052

Thompson, H.H. Deep snow in the "northwoods" of New York. *Am Angler*, Mar. 31, 1883. 3:199. Signed: H.H.T. Possibility of late fishing season.   6053

Thompson, H.H. A matter of eels. *Am Angler*, Feb. 10, 1883. 3:88. Signed: H.H.T. Bisby lakes.   6054

Tierney, Jack. Our hibernating fisherman. *Up Mo*, Mar. 1941. 1:no.12:14. illus. Ice fishing on Lake Champlain.   6055

Tom, William. A trip to John's brook and Lake Champlain. *Am Angler*, May 19, 1888. 13:313–14.   6056

The Traveler, pseud. The Traveler goes up the Fulton chain. *Ang & Hunt*, July 1910.

2:386, 388. Ways to get there and fishing possibilities. 6057

Trembley, Charles C. Fishing in the Adirondacks. *J Outd Life*, Aug. 1907. 4:245–47. illus. Signed: C.C.T. 6058

Trudeau, Francis B. Fishing for health; 2d ed. Utica, N.Y. Horrocks-Ibbotson co. 1954. 8p. illus. Reprinted from the *Dupont Magazine*, Apr.–May 1954. 6059

Up de Graff, Thomas G. The state dam—Adirondacks. *Am Angler*, Jan. 26, 1884. 5: 53–54. Fishing trip near Ragged Lake. 6060

Van Cleef, J.S. The great Back bay of Lake Champlain. *For & Stream*, Sept. 1, 1900. 55: 167. 6061

Van Cleef, J.S. Nets in Lake Champlain. *For & Stream*, Oct. 26, 1901. 57:329–30. 6062

Van Nest, A.R. Memoir of Rev. George Washington Bethune. N.Y. Sheldon & co. 1867. 446p. plates, front. ports. "Art of Angling," p.199–225, includes stories from Piseco. 6063

Wa-hoo, pseud. Walton falls and Bluff mountain. *For & Stream*, Apr. 6, 1882. 18:185–86. West Canada Creek area. 6064

Walton, pseud. Adirondack fishing. *For & Stream*, Mar. 7, 1896. 46:199. 6065

Webster. Forked lake and other waters, N.Y. *Am Angler*, Aug. 5, 1882. 2:88. 6066

Wild, Edward W. An Adirondack idyl. *Recreation*, Dec. 1896. 5:311–12. illus. Lincoln Pond. 6067

Winans, Richard Maxwell. An Au Sable champion. *Outing*, Jan. 1911. 57:481–89. illus. 6068

Wolcott, W.E. Adirondack fishing. *For & Stream*, June 7, 1902. 58:447. 6069

Wood, George B. Cranberry lake, Adirondacks. *For & Stream*, Aug. 8, 1896. 47:108. 6070

Wood, A Lance, pseud. A day in Keene Valley. *Am Angler*, July 7, 1888. 14:6–7. 6071

Wood, A Lance, pseud. A trip to the Au-Sable. *Am Angler*, Sept. 3–10, 1887. 12:147–48, 162–63. The Ausable River. 6072

Wooley, Frank M. An angler discourses of his hobby. *NYC Lines Mag*, Apr. 1925. 6:no. 1:47–48. illus. Lake Champlain. 6073

Wooley, Frank M. Lake George—an angler's paradise. *NYC Lines Mag*, June 1924. 5:no.3:36. 6074

Trout

Aiken, Walter. Adirondack large trout record. *For & Stream*, Aug. 9, 1888. 31:48. 6075

Allerton, Reuben G. Brook trout fishing, an account of a trip of the Oquossoc angling association to northern Maine in June, 1869. N.Y. Perris & Browne, 1869. 59p. incl. front. illus. plates, port. Adirondacks, p.30–43. 6076

Angler, pseud. In the Adirondacks. *For & Stream*, July 25, 1896. 47:68. Trout fishing near Mineville. 6077

B., G.T. Lost on a trout stream. *For & Stream*, Sept. 15, 1887. 29:148. Near West Canada Creek. 6078

Bailey, Robeson. Days along the River Meacham; a tale of little-known Adirondack trout stream. *For & Stream*, June 1929. 99: 418–19, 436–37, 463. illus. 6079

Barnard, H.R. An Adirondack laker. *Recreation*, Sept. 1902. 17:177. 6080

Barrell, A.C. An Ausable expedition principally to catch trout, but also to enjoy the pure gold of good-fellowship. *Field & S*, Aug. 1933. 38:no.4:7–9, 46. 6081

Beardslee, Lester A. Piseco's big trout, by Piseco, pseud. *For & Stream*, June 7, 1877. 8:284. 6082

Bergman, Ray. Speckled trout of the Adirondacks. *For & Stream*, Aug.–Sept. 1925. 95:459–61, 496–98, 525–27, 571. 6083

Bergman, Ray. Trout of the AuSable, some interesting theories and incidents. *For & Stream*, Dec. 1927. 97:721–23, 751–52. illus. diagrs. Ausable River. 6084

Bisbee, Eugene Shade. Trout fishing in the Adirondacks. *NYC Lines Mag*, May 1929. 10:no.2:17–18. 6085

Bissell, C.A. The Arbutus lake park trout waters. *For & Stream*, July 8, 1905. 65:33. In Archer M. Huntington preserve. 6086

Boston, pseud. Lake trout fishing on Lake George. *For & Stream*, June 14, 1877. 8:298. 6087

Brandreth, Paulina. In pursuit of the rainbow. *Field & S*, July 1904. 9:258–59. 6088

Brewer, Leighton. Virgin water; thirty-five years in quest of the squaretail trout. N.Y. Coward-McCann, 1941. 223p. plates. Adirondacks, Chs. 1 and 3. 6089

Brimmer, F.E. Adirondack trout streams. *Fur News*, May 1921. 33:no.5:6–7, 23–27. illus. Directions for reaching some good trout streams. 6090

Browne, Stewart R. Lake trout fishing in Lake George, with a few directions as to what to do when you get them. *For & Stream*, Aug. 1915. 84:477. 6091

C., A. Trout in the Adirondacks. *For & Stream*, May 26, 1881. 16:331. 6092

C., A.H. One March day—trouting. *Am Angler*, Apr. 1, 1882. 1:211–12. Fishing Half-way Brook. 6093

Camilla, pseud. Bait and buoys. *For & Stream*, Aug. 22, 1903. 61:147. Fishing for rainbow trout.   6094

Cheney, Albert Nelson. The lake trout. *Am Angler*, June 30, 1883. 3:401–2. illus. Under heading: Game fishes of America. Fresh water series. Includes lake trout in Lake George and other Adirondack lakes.   6095

Cheney, Albert Nelson. A trip after lake trout. *Am Angler*, June 2, 1883. 3:340–42. Signed: A.N.C. Lake George.   6096

Cheney, Albert Nelson. Trout fishing in the Hudson river. *Am Angler*, Nov. 25, 1882. 2:345–46. Headwaters of the Hudson.   6097

Cheney, Albert Nelson. Undoing a trout. *Am Angler*, May 2, 1885. 7:276. Signed: A.N.C. Fishing in Essex County.   6098

Davis, Charles D. Fishing for trout in the Adirondacks. *For & Stream*, Sept. 21, 1912. 79:365. At head of title: An amateur's experience. Cranberry Lake.   6099

Davison, J.L. Big trout in the Adirondacks. *For & Stream*, July 23, 1904. 63:76.   6100

Dodd, Mark Dixon. Adirondack trout. *For & Stream*, Jan. 7, 1911. 76:19–20. Fishing adventures along the Canachagala Creek, a tributary of the Moose River.   6101

Douglas, E.M. The prize "laker" of South pond. *Field & S*, Jan. 1915. 19:961–62. 6102

Dun, Olive. Caring for your trout, after you catch them. *NYC Lines Mag*, Apr. 1921. 2:no.1:35–36. illus. Hints for Adirondack anglers.   6103

Elliott, Frank. Clint Gilbert's trout stream. *Field & S*, July 1904. 9:226–29. illus.   6104

Extracts from the journal of the Lake Piseco trout club. *In* Walton, Izaac. The complete angler... (Bethune edition). N.Y. & London, 1847. p.134–38. Statistics on trout taken 1843–46.   6105

Fly fishing for trout. *Sport Rev*, July 15, 1905. 28:64–65. Description of flies for use in Adirondacks.   6106

Give them a chance...to choose your fly. A short story of Ausable river browns, by one who's been there. *NYS Sport*, Feb. 1938. 3:no.7:3. illus.   6107

Goodridge, S.W. Adirondack trout. *For & Stream*, Oct. 4, 1883. 21:189. Minerva. 6108

H., F.E. A week with the trout. *For & Stream*, July 5, 1888. 30:477. Cranberry Lake. 6109

H., W.W. Cranberry lake; description and trout. *For & Stream*, July 28, 1894. 43:72.   6110

Harris, C.S. My queen of the waters. *Field & S*, Jan. 1916. 20:876–78. illus. Near Northville.   6111

Holland, Raymond Prunty. High spots; incidents in last year's trout fishing that will long linger in memory's storehouse. *Field & S*, Apr. 1930. 34:no.12:22–23, 71–74. illus. East Branch of the Ausable River.   6112

Juvenal, pseud. Adirondack trout. *For & Stream*, June 23, 1906. 66:997.   6113

Kingman, Henry. Big lake trout fights two hours. *For & Stream*, June 1923. 93:309, 314. Upper Saranac Lake.   6114

The largest Adirondack trout. *For & Stream*, July 19, 1888. 30:509. Editorial on record trout from Cranberry Lake.   6115

Lincoln, Robert Page. Adirondack trout beyond the beaten paths and gay vacation crowds. *Field & S*, Feb. 1930. 34:no.10:24–25, 97–98. illus.   6116

Lockwood, Kenneth F. Brook trout in the Boreas country. *Amer Angler*, Aug. 1919. 4:193.   6117

Lost and found. *For & Stream*, Aug. 21, 1909. 73:300. Trout fishing experience on Cascade lakes.   6118

McHarg, John B. Jr. An Adirondack trout record. *For & Stream*, June 17, 1899. 52:468–69. illus.   6119

Martin H. Glynn's first trout; for a few delightful days in the Adirondacks the Governor forgot the cares of state and became a confirmed disciple of Izaak Walton. *For & Stream*, Sept. 12, 1914. 83:331–32. illus.
                                     6120

Mather, Fred. Trouting on Wilmurt lake. *For & Stream*, June 11, 1885. 24:391.   6121

May, George B. Large Adirondack trout. *For & Stream*, July 6, 1901. 57:9. Big catch in Piseco Lake.   6122

Moorehead, W.K. A few words on the trout. *J Outd Life*, Apr. 1905. 2:56–57. illus.   6123

Morrell, T.S. Adirondack camping in 1868. *Am Angler*, Mar. 1892. 21:266–72. illus. Signed: Old Izaak.   6124

Murray, William Henry Harrison. Trouting in the Adirondacks. *Golden Rule*, July 12, 1876. 1:no.41:6. From his "Adventures in the Wilderness."   6125

Norris, Thaddeus. The American angler's book: embracing the natural history of sporting fish, and the art of taking them...to which is added, Dies piscatoriae: Describing noted fishing places. Philadelphia, Porter & Coates, ᶜ1865. 701p. front. (port.) plates, illus. (Memorial edition.) Trout fishing in the Adirondacks, p.545–64, 668–69; in Hamilton County, p.503–10.   6126

Norton, Mortimer. Adirondack trout beauties. *Fur-Fish-Game*, Aug.–Sept. 1929. 50:no.

3:8–9, 14; 50:no.4:11–12. illus. Contents: A Mishap on Panther Mountain Stream. Fishing the Turbulent West Canada Creek. 6127

Old Pilot, pseud. Brook trout fishing at Lake George. *For & Stream*, Apr. 19, 1877. 8:168. 6128

P., C.M. An Adirondack trout string. *For & Stream*, May 11, 1901. 56:371. 6129

Purdy, Fred Leslie. Trout in northern New York. *For & Stream*, June 26, 1909. 72:1018. Grass River area. 6130

R., C.M. A big Adirondack lake trout. *For & Stream*, June 11, 1898. 50:469. 6131

Radford, Harry V. Adirondack trout fishing. *Sh & Fish*, Sept. 20, 1906. 40:468. North Creek. 6132

Radford, Harry V. An Adirondack trouting. *Woods & Wat*, Autumn 1900. 3:no.3:5–6. Also in *Field and Stream*, July 1902, 7:216–17, and in *Forest Leaves*, Summer 1905, 2:no.3: 34–36. The first of a series of boyhood sketches. For others in the series see no.5656. 6133

Radford, Harry V. Trout fishing in the Adirondacks. *Four Tr News*, Apr. 1902. 2:228–29. illus. 6134

Raven, pseud. My first trouting. *Wilkes Spirit*, Dec. 10, 1859. 1:2C9–10. Washington County. 6135

Rhead, Louis, ed. The speckled brook trout (Salvelinus fontinalis) by various experts with rod and reel; ed. and illus. by Louis Rhead, with an introduction by Charles Hallock. N.Y. R.H. Russell, c1902. 15p. numbered A–O, 184p. col. front. illus. plates. Adirondacks, p.67–101. 6136

Ryther, Mrs. George D. A record catch of trout. *Ang & Hunt*, Apr. 1910. 2:224–25. illus. Cranberry Lake. 6137

Scott, Genio C. Fishing in American waters: a new ed. . . N.Y. Harper, 1875. 539p. front. illus. Red trout of Long Lake, p.261–63. 6138

Scott, H.B. Big trout of the Oswegatchie. *Field & S*, Nov. 1915. 20:706–9. illus. 6139

Smiley, James. Trout fishing. *Fur News*, July–Aug. 1923. 38:no.1:30–31, 45–47; 38:no.2: 32–34. At Wilmurt, Morehouse, North Lake. 6140

Spaulding, Edward. Adirondack lake trout. *For & Stream*, Dec. 15, 1900. 55:462. 6141

Spears, Raymond Smiley. A heretic in trout flies. *Outing*, July 1913. 62:466–70. Jock's Lake outlet. 6142

Stanton, Sanford E. Luring salmon trout. *Am Angler*, Oct. 27, 1888. 14:269. At Star Lake. 6143

Stoddart, Alexander. Hooray! Fishing time is here and the splendid trout of the Adiron-

dacks call to every angler. *NYC Lines Mag*, Apr. 1920. 1:no.1:29–32. illus. 6144

Stone, Livingston. On the passing of the brook trout. *Field & S*, Nov. 1905. 10:720. 6145

Sumner, E.E. Adirondack trout. *For & Stream*, Apr. 30, 1898. 50:352. Notable catches at Saranac Lake. 6146

Tamarack, pseud. Trouting in the Adirondacks. *Amer Angler*, Apr. 1919. 3:696–700. 6147

Trout, S. Almond, pseud. Trout fishing in the Salmon river. *Recreation*, Feb. 1900. 12: 126–27. 6148

Trouting season in the Adirondacks. *Sport Rev*, May 8, 1909. 35:509. Opening of fishing season. 6149

Uncle Jack, pseud. Some remarkable catches. *For & Stream*, Apr. 30, 1885. 24:271. 6150

W., A.L. Brown trout. *For & Stream*, July 6, 1907. 69:21. Saranac River. 6151

Warner, Charles Dudley. A fight with a trout. *In* Mayer, Alfred Marshall. Sport with gun and rod in American woods and waters. N.Y. Century, c1883. p.827–32. Also in *American Angler*, May 1919, 4:52-56. From his "In the Wilderness." 6152

Wells, Henry P. Weighing trout in the woods. *Harper W*, May 24, 1890. 34:403–5. illus. 6153

Where trout cry to be caught; an account of a trip to Indian lake in the Adirondacks. *NYC Lines Mag*, May 1923. 4:no.2:30H. 6154

Willard, Francis A. Brown trout in the Adirondacks. *For & Stream*, Aug. 10, 1901. 57: 109. Mill Creek. 6155

Wilson, H.G. A summer of trout fishing. *Fur-Fish-Game*, May–June 1926. 43:no.5:33–35; 43:no.6:33–35. illus. 6156

Witherbee, Walter C. A brown trout record. *For & Stream*, June 2, 1894. 42:472. Near Port Henry. 6157

Wolcott, W.E. Adirondack trout. *For & Stream*, July 5, 1902. 59:10. 6158

Wolcott, W.E. Adirondack trout. *For & Stream*, Apr. 16, 1904. 62:317. 6159

Wolcott, W.E. The Adirondack trout season. *For & Stream*, Sept. 5, 1903. 61:182. 6160

Wolcott, W.E. Luck. *For & Stream*, Aug. 6, 1898. 51:111–12. 6161

Wood, Richard K. Trout—"two at a crack." *Fur News*, Aug. 1920. 32:no.2:24–25. illus. Boreas River. 6162

Worden, George H. Trouting in the north woods. *Outing*, Apr. 1891. 18:77–79. illus. Many lakes in Herkimer and Hamilton counties. 6163

Other Fish

Adirondack black bass. *For & Stream*, Sept. 8, 1894. 43:208.   6164

B. Lake George pickerel. *For & Stream*, Nov. 21, 1896. 47:411.   6165

B., J.H. Whitefish of the Oswegatchie. *For & Stream*, Mar. 29, 1877. 8:113. Near Cranberry Lake.   6166

Backus, M.M. Lake Champlain. Its back bays, and its black bass. *Am Angler*, Feb.2, Feb. 16–23, 1884. 5:66–68, 98–100, 114–16. map.   6167

Backus, M.M. Lake Champlain. Pickerel on the fly—weight and measure of black bass. *Am Angler*, July 19, 1884. 6:38–39.   6168

Bisbee, Eugene Shade. Fighting for "sassy" bass in northern and southern waters. *NYC Lines Mag*, May 1928. 9:no.2:20–22. Lake Champlain.   6169

Bishop, Bainbridge. Bass fishing in Lake Champlain. *For & Stream*, Mar. 26, 1885. 24:168.   6170

Browne, Stewart R. Bass fishing in Lake George. *For & Stream*, Sept. 12, 1914. 83: 356.   6171

Cheney, Albert Nelson. Black bass in Lake Champlain. *For & Stream*, May 14, 1885. 24:309–10.   6172

Cheney, Albert Nelson. Decrease of black bass in Lake George—the Texas club. *Am Angler*, Aug. 25, 1883. 4:114–15. Signed: A.N.C. Fishing trip in the Adirondacks with the Texans.   6173

Cheney, Albert Nelson. Schroon lake—big black bass—taking a back seat. *Am Angler*, Nov. 10, 1882. 2:150–51. Signed: A.N.C.   6174

Cheney, Albert Nelson. The Texas club opens the bass season. *Am Angler*, Aug. 11, 1883. 4: 85–86. Signed: A.N.C. Lake George.   6175

Closson, J.F. Ned Buntline's Raquette river bass. *Recreation*, Mar. 1903. 18:186.   6176

Ferris, L. Champlain smelt. *For & Stream*, Apr. 18, 1896. 46:320.   6177

Glens Falls, pseud. Hints on bass fishing. *For & Stream*, Jan. 17, 1878. 9:453. Long and Round ponds, Warren County.   6178

Harmsworth, Alfred C. Salmon in Lake George. *For & Stream*, June 8, 1895. 44:464.   6179

Harris, William Charles. Black bass fishing at West Port. *For & Stream*, July 23, 1874. 2: 378.   6180

Harris, William Charles. Striped bass in summer—Adirondack fishing. *Outing*, Aug. 1902. 40:640–42.   6181

Hastings, W.W. Lake George bass experience. *For & Stream*, Dec. 10, 1898. 51:473.   6182

Heathcote. Smelt fishing in Lake Champlain. *For & Stream*, Apr. 6, 1895. 44:269.   6183

Landon, Jud. In the Adirondacks. *Recreation (NY)*, June, Aug. 1916. 54:264; 55:79. Old Forge, bass fishing.   6184

Mahony, John. Some Adirondack bass fishing. *For & Stream*, Aug. 1925. 95:478–79, 504–6. illus.   6185

Mandell, D.W. Pickerel in Adirondack waters. *For & Stream*, May 4, 1876. 6:198. 6186

Morse, C.H. Smelt in Lake Champlain. *For & Stream*, Apr. 6, 1895. 44:269.   6187

Nash, Spencer M. Bass in the Adirondacks. *For & Stream*, Nov. 12, 1891. 27:333.   6188

Old Pilot, pseud. Bass fishing in Lake George. *For & Stream*, May 31, 1877. 8:269.   6189

Pettit, James S. The gamy bass of the Saranac region. *Amer Angler*, May 1920. 5:12–13. illus.   6190

Sangemo, pseud. The north woods pike, he is on the job twelve months a year and is waiting for you now. *For & Stream*, Feb. 1917. 87:76–77. Taking game fish through the ice.   6191

Tahawus, pseud. Pickerel in Adirondack waters. *For & Stream*, Apr. 6, 1876. 6:133–34. Lake Sanford.   6192

Tamarack, pseud. The northern pike of Lewey lake once famed for its brook and lake trout, this Adirondack sheet of water becomes the home of ravenous pike of huge proportions. *For & Stream*, Oct. 1919. 89: 534–35, 552.   6193

Van Cleef, J.S. Pop-squash. *For & Stream*, Nov. 24, 1900. 55:410. Small-mouthed black bass in Lake Champlain.   6194

Wager, A.L. The black bass of the Back bay, Lake Champlain. *Am Angler*, Oct. 4, 1884. 6:215.   6195

Whiffen, Edwin T. Angling for Adirondack frostfish, the delicate frostfish of northern waters may be successfully taken with hook and line if methods are adapted to its peculiar characteristics. *For & Stream*, Oct. 1918. 88:592, 614. illus.   6196

Wilson, E.K. Second rate fish in Adirondack waters. *For & Stream*, Apr. 13, 1876. 6:149. Spread of pickerel to Raquette.   6197

Wolcott, W.E. Black bass fishing. *For & Stream*, June 14, 1902. 58:469.   6198

TRAPPING

Ballard, M.E. A trip to the Adirondacks. *Fur News*, Oct. 1913. 18:318–21. South of Cranberry Lake. 6199

Dailey, Elric J. Adirondack beaver trapping. *Fur-Fish-Game*, Apr. 1928. 47:no.4:67–68. illus. 6200

Dailey, Elric J. Beaver, fox and otter plentiful in Adirondacks. *Fur News*, Jan. 1922. 35:no.1:9. 6201

Dailey, Elric J. Beaver trapping prospects in the Adirondacks. *Fur News*, Nov. 1923. 38:no.5:5, 45. illus. 6202

Dailey, Elric J. Big woods trapping. *Fur News*, Feb. 1923. 37:no.2:16–17, 59–60. Near the Grass River. 6203

Dailey, Elric J. The Bog ponds trapline. *Fur-Fish-Game*, Sept. 1925. 42:no.3:38–40. illus. 6204

Dailey, Elric J. Haunts and habits of Adirondack's wild life in which a New York state registered guide and trapper tells of fur and game conditions in this well-stocked region. *Sport Dig*, Oct. 1924. 1:no.10:14–16, 72–76. illus. 6205

Dailey, Elric J. In the fur and game country. *Fur-Fish-Game*, Dec. 1926. 44:no.6:20–22. illus. Near Upper Raquette Lake. 6206

Dailey, Elric J. In the land of spruces. *Sport Dig*, Oct. 1925. 2:no.10:25–27, 87. illus. 6207

Dailey, Elric J. The January trapline. In the land of snow. *Fur-Fish-Game*, Jan. 1927. 45:no.1:60–63. illus. 6208

Dailey, Elric J. Life in the fur country. An account of a day on the trapline in the Adirondacks. *Sport Dig*, Nov. 1927. 6:20–24. 6209

Dailey, Elric J. Life in the trapper's country. *Fur-Fish-Game*, Oct. 1928. 48:no.4:11–12. illus. Sawtooth Range. 6210

Dailey, Elric J. The Moose mountain trap line. *Fur News*, Jan. 1924. 39:no.1:20–21, 40–41. illus. 6211

Dailey, Elric J. North woods trapping. *Fur News*, May 1922. 35:no.5:12–13, 43. illus. Roaring Brook. 6212

Dailey, Elric J. On a far back trapline. *Furology*, Dec. 1923. 3:no.1:7–9. 6213

Dailey, Elric J. On the trail of sly reynard; an account of a fox trapping trip in the foothills of the Adirondacks. *Fur News*, Oct. 1922. 36:no.4:13–14. illus. 6214

Dailey, Elric J. The otter country. *Fur News*, Oct. 1923. 38:no.4:12–13. illus. 6215

Dailey, Elric J. Out for fur and fun; an account of one month's auto trapping in St. Lawrence county and the Adirondack foothills. *Fur News*, Feb. 1922. 35:no.2:20–21, 44–45. illus. 6216

Dailey, Elric J. The rival trappers of Lost chasm. *Fur News*, Sept. 1923. 38:no.3:20–21. illus. Near the Sawtooth Mountains. 6217

Dailey, Elric J. "Spot trapper" Dailey's auto trapline. *Sport Dig*, Mar. 1924. 3:no.3:22–24, 88–90. illus. 6218

Dailey, Elric J. Traplines and trails; a book of master trapping methods. Columbus, O. Hunter-trader-trapper co. c1925. 242p. illus. Adirondack trapping, p.52–59; many other references to trapping in the Adirondacks. 6219

Dailey, Elric J. Trapped out country. *Fur News*, Jan. 1923. 37:no.1:16–17. illus. Northern New York. 6220

Dailey, Elric J. "Trapping"—the sport of most thrills. *Sport Dig*, Dec. 1925. 4:no.12:17–18, 50–51, 53–55. illus. 6221

Dailey, Elric J. Trapping the Grass river flow; the life of a trapper, though filled with hardship, contains as many joys as that of his city brother. *Sport Dig*, Jan. 1926. 5:no.1:8–9. illus. 6222

Dailey, Elric J. The wilderness trap-line. *Fur News*, July 1922. 36:no.1:19, 34. illus. Catamount Mountain. 6223

Drahos, Nicholas and Maunton, Ed. Catching coyotes: the scent post set. *NYS Con*, Dec. 1954–Jan. 1955. 9:no.3:22–23. illus. Trapping at Newcomb. 6224

Helmes, C.A. Fox trapping in the Adirondacks; how man stakes his wits against the most cunning and resourceful of all wild animals; Reynard's wonderful scent often saves him. *State Service*, July–Aug. 1920. 4:581–83. illus. 6225

Keith, E.F. The Adirondack trapper. *Fur-Fish-Game*, Nov. 1929. 50:no.5:24–26. Campfire tales. 6226

Keith, E.F. Around the loop. *Fur News*, Dec. 1923. 38:no.6:55. illus. Fox trapping in high-peak area. 6227

Keith, E.F. Bear trapping in the Adirondack mountains. *Fur-Fish-Game*, Nov. 1926. 44:no.5:11. illus. 6228

Keith, E.F. The crafty mink. *Fur News*, May 1924. 39:no.5:45–47. illus. 6229

Keith, E.F. My trapping trip on the North branch. *Fur News*, Jan. 1921. 33:no.1:26–27. Bouquet River. 6230

Keith, E.F. Recollections of an Adirondack trapper. *Fur-Fish-Game*, June 1925. 41:no.6: 16, 24.   6231

Keith, E.F. Trapping in the Adirondacks. *Fur News*, Apr. 1920. 31:no.4:5.   6232

Keith, E.F. Trapping the far-back country. *Fur-Fish-Game*, Oct. 1925. 42:no.4:34–35. Mount Dix.   6233

MacDougall, Clint. Slim pond beaver. *Fur-Fish-Game*, Jan. 1952. 47:no.1:42–43. Trapping beaver in Whitney Park.   6234

Newhouse, Sewell. The trapper's guide. A manual of instructions for capturing all kinds of fur-bearing animals, and curing their skins: with observations on the fur trade, hints on life in the woods, and narratives of trapping and hunting excursions; by S. Newhouse and other trappers and sportsmen. . .ed. by J.H. Noyes. Wallingford, Conn. Oneida community, 1865. 118p. front. (port.) illus. 2d edition, Wallingford, Conn. 1867. 3d edition, edited by the Oneida Community, N.Y. Oakley, Mason & co. 1867. 3d edition also published in N.Y. by Mason, Baker & Pratt, 1872. 8th edition, rev. Ed. by John Humphrey Noyes, Community, N.Y. Oneida Community, 1887. 9th edition, rev. N.Y. 1894. Also published by Forest & Stream, N.Y. 1894. Pocket edition, Kenwood, N.Y. 1895. Newhouse trapper's guide. Published by the Oneida Community, Oneida, N.Y. 1905. A Young Trapper's Experience, by John P. Hutchins, p.138–42. An Amateur in the North Woods, by Charles S. Joslyn, p.159–74. Camping and trapping in Brown's Tract.   6235

Perils of the trail, a trip over a mountain trap line. *Fur-Fish-Game*, Jan. 1926. 43:no.1: 14–16. illus.   6236

Potter, Frederick K. The last Adirondack wolf, how Reuben Cary followed its trail through winter woods and finally succeeded in trapping the wary animal. *For & Stream*, Feb. 1923. 93:60, 89–91. illus.   6237

Smiley, James. Baits. *Fur News*, Nov. 1919–Jan. 1920. 30:no.5:4–5; 30:no.6:4–5; 31:no. 1:4–5.   6238

Smiley, James. Home again—spot trapping in the Adirondacks. *Fur News*, Feb. 1923. 37:no.2:40–42. West Canada Creek near Wilmurt.   6239

Smiley, James. Two-month trapping season ideas. *Fur News*, Apr. 1923. 37:no.4:38–39. Suggested changes for trapping season.   6240

Spears, Raymond Smiley. Game and trapping. *For & Stream*, Apr. 23, 1910. 74:656.   6241

Spears, Raymond Smiley. On an Adirondack trap line. *For & Stream*, Apr. 6, 1907. 68:528–30. illus.   6242

Wilson, H.G. The Adirondack country. *Fur News*, Sept. 1923. 38:no.3:5, 46–47. illus.   6243

Wilson, H.G. Prosperous mink trapping. *Fur News*, Jan. 1925. 40:no.1:42–43, 45. illus.   6244

Wilson, H.G. Weasel trapping. . . The white weasel is the mid-winter standby of many Adirondack trappers. *Fur News*, Feb. 1922. 35:no.2:24. illus.   6245

Winter in the wild wood. *Harper W*, Mar. 26, 1887. 31:227–28. illus.   6246

Wood, Richard K. The Big Moose trap line; the story of a spring trapping trip in the Adirondacks. *Fur News*, Dec. 1920. 32:no.6:4–5, 52. illus.   6247

Wood, Richard K. Cabin life, how Dick Wood and two friends spent a month in the Adirondacks. *Fur News*, Jan. 1921. 33:no.1: 6–7. illus. Near Cold River Flow.   6248

Wood, Richard K. Cold river trail. *Fur News*, Feb. 1921. 33:no.2:8–9, 35. Cold River country.   6249

Wood, Richard K. The February trap line. *Fur News*, Feb. 1920. 31:no.2:3, 51–52. illus.   6250

Wood, Richard K. Otter's trail. *Fur News*, Mar. 1921. 33:no.3:8–9, 55. illus.   6251

Wood, Richard K. The winter trapline. *Fur-Fish-Game*, Jan. 1926. 43:no.1:20–22. illus.   6252

Wood, Richard K. With Randall on the Boreas. *Fur News*, Feb.–Mar. 1918. 27:no. 2:8–9, 61; 27:no.3:8–9. illus. port.   6253

WINTER SPORTS

Alexander, Clifford. Some notes on winter camping. *Ad-i-ron-dac*, Jan.–Feb. 1950. 14: 16–18.   6254

Apperson, John S. Adirondacks are ideal for winter sports. Article VII, section 7 of state constitution has safeguarded for this area the principal attraction of winter sports.

n.p. Ski committee of New York state trails conference, inc. 1937. 4p.   6255

Battling for icy honors at Lake Placid. *Lit Digest*, Feb. 6, 1932. 112:no.6:30, 32. illus.   6256

Big carnival days delight Saranac lake winter merry makers, new snowshoe and ski trails, curling, ski-joring and picnics in the mountains feature season's diversion. *Motordom*, Dec. 1930. 24:no.6:12. illus. 6257

Brilliant season expected at Lake Placid in Adirondacks. *NYC Lines Mag*, Dec. 1928. 9:no.9:37. illus. 6258

Brimmer, F.E. Winter pleasure and profit. *Fur News*, Feb. 1923. 37:no.2:20–21. illus. Snow shoeing; types of snowshoes. 6259

Burnham, John Bird. A winter camp on Wadleigh brook. *For & Stream*, Jan. 30, 1897. 48:86. 6260

Dewey, Godfrey. Bob sleighing—America's youngest winter sport. *In* United States eastern amateur ski association. Year book, 1929. p.48–50. illus. Building bob-sled run at Lake Placid. 6261

The discovery of winter; the north country awakens to its many opportunities for fun and health. *No Country Life*, Winter 1948. 2: no.1:4–5. 6262

Ely, Catherine Beach. Winter sports in New York and New England. *Motordom*, Dec. 1932. p.6–7. illus. 6263

Empire state greatest winter playground. . . from all over the country thousands of motorists learn the real lure of winter vacations. *Motordom*, Dec. 1929. 23:no.7:4–5. illus. 6264

Flickinger, Katherine and Hart, Merwin K. Jr. Skis, snowshoes and crampons. *Ad-i-ron-dac*, Nov.–Dec. 1949. 13:128–29. Adirondack Mountain Club Winter Activities Committee trophies. 6265

Fowler, Barnett. Winter sports right here in New York. *NYS Con*, Dec. 1948–Jan. 1949. 3:no.3:2–3. illus. 6266

Gardner, Paul. Who said Placid bob run! *Holiday*, Feb. 1947. 2:no.2:25, 114–15. 6267

Garren, H.L. Figure skating—the artsport. *Up Mo*, Feb. 1941. 1:no.11:16–17. illus. At Lake Placid. 6268

Going to Speculator means real enjoyment; all attractions of winter fun are "on tap" at this genial center on shores of Lake Pleasant . . . *Motordom*, Dec. 1930. 24:no.6:13. illus. 6269

Halliday, E.M. Winter sports in the country. *Argosy*, Dec. 1894. 19:227–32. illus. 6270

Hamilton county centers extend a welcome; Speculator, Inlet and Long lake, in the central and lower Adirondacks; offer splendid facilities for winter-time enjoyment, new slides and carnival programs in store for holiday vacationists. *Motordom*, Dec. 1931. 25: no.6:14–15. illus. 6271

Hart, Merwin K. Jr. Skis, snowshoes and crampons. *Ad-i-ron-dac*, Jan.–Feb., May–June

1950. 14:14, 66. Report from Adirondack Mountain Club Winter Activities Committee. 6272

Hicks, Harry Wade. Lake Placid club winter sports. *Intercollegiate Athletics*, Jan. 1924. 1: no.3:11, 18. illus. Author's name given as W.H. Hicks. 6273

Hicks, Harry Wade. Winter sports at Lake Placid club, Essex co. N.Y. *Skisport*, 1923–24. 18:27–29. illus. 6274

Hicks, Harry Wade. Winter sports in the Adirondacks. *Am For*, Jan. 1927. 33:9–13. illus. 6275

Howard, William Gibbs. Winter trip to Johns brook. *Mt Mag*, Oct. 1928. 7:37–38. illus. 6276

Howland, Harold Jacobs. A winter tramp in the north woods. *Outlook*, June 3, 1905. 80:283–96. illus. Snowshoe journey through Indian and Avalanche passes. 6277

Hudowalski, Edward C. Notes on winter camping. *Ad-i-ron-dac*, Jan.–Feb. 1947. 11: no.1:7. 6278

Kiernan, John. Sports the frozen northland gave us... *NY Times Mag*, Jan. 5, 1930. p.4–5. illus. 6279

Kimball, Francis P. The great white playground, the Empire state, with its beautiful mountains, lakes and forests, offers the gayest winter centers—all manner of fun at hand to drive dull care away. *Motordom*, Dec. 1931. 25:no.6:45. illus. 6280

Kimball, Francis P. Winter sport days are here, January brings winter vacations in the great outdoor playgrounds of the Adirondacks, Canada and New England. *Motordom*, Jan. 1930. 23:no.8:6–7. illus. 6281

King winter, the big "whoopee" maker. *Motordom*, Dec. 1930. 24:no.6:3. illus. 6282

Lake Placid enthusiasts celebrate 25th year of winter sports. *NYC Lines Mag*, Jan. 1930. 10:no.10:48. illus. 6283

Lake Placid opens big season of winter sports. *NYC Lines Mag*, Jan. 1923. 3:no.10:39. 6284

Life goes to Lake Placid. *Life*, Mar. 20, 1944. 16:no.12:126–29. illus. 6285

Longstreth, Thomas Morris. Lake Placid, the winter capital of America, attracts throngs of sport lovers. *NYC Lines Mag*, Feb. 1920. 2:no.1:45–46. illus. 6286

Longstreth, Thomas Morris. Sports in the zero zone. *Harper*, Feb. 1919. 138:374–83. illus. Winter sports at Lake Placid. 6287

Maedonald, R.H. The Saranac lake ice carnival. *Four Tr News*, Dec. 1902. 3:265–67. 6288

Martin, George W. Sno birds of Lake Placid club. *In* United States eastern amateur ski association. Year book, 1930. p.83–84. illus. on p.82.   **6289**

Morgan, Donald Fair. Down the run on a streaking bobsled. . . *NY Times Mag*, Feb. 28, 1928. p.10, 21. illus.   **6290**

Morgan, Donald Fair. On snow and ice. *College Humor*, Jan. 1929. 16:no.2:60–61, 105–6. illus. College week at Lake Placid.   **6291**

Motor sledding at Saranac lake. *Sci Am*, Mar. 9, 1912. 106:217. illus.   **6292**

Mount Van Hoevenberg run. *Pic*, Mar. 21, 1939. 5:no.6:32–35. illus. ports.   **6293**

Mountain-sides echo shouts and laughter of sport lovers in snowy Adirondacks. *NYC Lines Mag*, Jan. 1928. 8:no.10:31–32. illus.   **6294**

The new sport of bobsledding. . . *Wint Sports*, Apr. 1931. 1:no.7:2, 21. illus.   **6295**

New York (state). Conservation department. The Mt. Van Hoevenberg Olympic bobsled run at Lake Placid, N.Y. n.p. n.pub. 1936. 6p. Dated Oct. 1936.   **6296**

New York Central railroad company. The Adirondacks: land of winter sport. n.p. 1916? 16p. illus. Unpaged leaflet.   **6297**

New winter sports program in the central Adirondacks. *Up-Stater*, Jan. 1931. 3:no.1: 10. A bond issue authorized by Hamilton County to develop parks at Indian Lake, Lake Pleasant and Speculator.   **6298**

Norman, Andre. Courting winter in the Adirondacks; the exhilarating season of winter sports in northern New York, outdoor life at Lake George, Lake Placid and some other all-year resorts. *Travel*, Jan. 1915. 24:no.3: 46–48. illus.   **6299**

Now winter sport hits 'on high.' *Motordom*, Jan. 1931. 24:no.7:10. illus.   **6300**

Paxton, Harry T. Bobsledders don't use brakes. *Sat Eve Post*, Jan. 29, 1949. 221:no. 31:32–33, 87, 89–90. col. illus. Bob-sled run on Mt. Van Hoevenberg.   **6301**

Pope, Katherine. Snow-shoeing. *Four Tr News*, Dec. 1904. 7:386–88. illus.   **6302**

Porter, Lawrence and Steiger, W.A. Illuminated ice at Lake Placid club, N.Y. *Gen Elec R*, Sept. 1930. 33:514–18. illus. Special lighting for winter sports.   **6303**

Rockwell, George L. A winter camp on the St. Regis: pen pictures of wood life in the Adirondacks in the season of frost and snow. *Field & S*, Feb.–Mar. 1908. 12:818–22, 916–20. illus.   **6304**

Shea, Jack. Jack Shea's story. *Wint Sports*, Oct. 1931. 1:no.1:5, 28. port. Ice skating.   **6305**

Shorey, Archibald Thompson. Thirty below on Cedar lake. *Ad-i-ron-dac*, Jan.–Feb. 1952. 16:8, 14. Winter camping.   **6306**

Shorey, Archibald Thompson. Winter camping. *Ad-i-ron-dac*, Jan.–Feb. 1953. 17:9. Reprinted from *The Cloud Splitter*, Nov. 1941.   **6307**

Skating, skiing and snowshoeing attract winter sports lovers to Lake Placid. *NYC Lines Mag*, Feb. 1926. 6:no.11:38–39. illus.   **6308**

Smith, Clarence C. Winter sports in the Adirondacks; America's premier winter playground arranges a variety of entertainment this season. *Up-Stater*, Nov. 1929. 1:no.6:5–7, 28, 30. illus.   **6309**

Spears, Raymond Smiley. Winter camping in the Adirondacks. *Country Life*, Jan. 1909. 15:272–73, 294–96. illus. Describes conditions a camper must count on meeting. **6310**

Speculator—new winter sports center, all winter delights and plenty of gayety await you at the famous new colony on the shore of Lake Pleasant. *Motordom*, Dec. 1929. 23: no.7:8–9. illus.   **6311**

Summer ice skating. *Up Mo*, Aug. 1941. 2: no.5:22. illus. History of the rink at Lake Placid.   **6312**

Take a cue from winter—it's a joy; gay places of the north provide a stirring contrast with winter life in the cities. *Motordom*, Jan. 1933. p.4. illus.   **6313**

Taylor, Frank H. Charms of a snow-bound camp. *Four Tr News*, Feb. 1904. 6:71–74. illus. Blue Mountain Lake area.   **6314**

Thrilling sports and colorful pageant mark annual mid-winter carnival at Saranac Lake. *NYC Lines Mag*, Mar. 1920. 2:no.2:41–42. illus.   **6315**

Townsend, Reginald T. Lake Placid days. *Country Life*, Jan. 1925. 47:no.3:60–62. illus.   **6316**

Townsend, Reginald T. Our winter wonderland. *Country Life*, Dec. 1920. 39:no.2:34–42. illus. (partly col.). Lake Placid.   **6317**

Trainer, J.N. A vacation on snowshoes. *Recreation*, Jan. 1909. 29:34. illus. Winter camping trip near Big Moose Lake.   **6318**

Trevor, George. The champagne of winter sports. . . *Sportsman*, Jan. 1930. 7:no.1:38–40, 108. illus. Construction of the bob-sled run at Lake Placid. Notes on Swiss runs. **6319**

Trevor, George. Down the ice-sheathed corkscrew. *Liberty*, Feb. 6, 1932. 9:no.6:30–34. illus. Bob-sledding.   **6320**

Trevor, George. Racing bobs. *Outlook*, Feb. 25, 1931. 157:303–4, 317–18. illus. Mount Van Hoevenberg run.   **6321**

Upstate attracts winter tourists. *Up-Stater*, Jan. 1929. 1:no.1:8–9. illus. 6322

Van Dyke, Paul A. High peak camping in winter. *Ad-i-ron-dac*, Jan.–Feb. 1952. 16:4–5. 6323

Welch, Fay. Footprints in the snow. *Ad-i-ron-dac*, Jan.–Feb. 1948. 12:no.1:10–11. illus. Animal tracks and winter hiking. 6324

Wharton, Hazel K. Bob sledding in the Adirondacks. *Am For*, Feb. 1938. 44:58–60, 78. illus. 6325

When the snow flies. *Up Mo*, Dec. 1941. 2: no.9:3. 6326

Will omit Adirondack ice carnival this winter. *J Outd Life*, Dec. 1905. 2:283–84. illus. Carnival at Saranac Lake. 6327

Winter centers gay as sport season opens; January–February are big months of diversion in the north with the Olympics at Lake Placid bringing world famous stars to this region... *Motordom*, Jan. 1932. p.6–7. illus. 6328

A winter empire awaits you; New York state with its noted winter places, beckons all to merry making in royal fashion. *Motordom*, Dec. 1930. 24:no.6:4–5. illus. 6329

Winter sport high spots for thrills and pleasure. *Up Mo*, Jan. 1941. 1:no.10:14–15. illus. 6330

Winter sport in the Adirondacks. *J Outd Life*, Jan. 1906. 2:315–18. illus. 6331

Winter sports. *Lake Pl Life*, Jan.–Feb. 1931. p.21, 23, 25, 27–29; p.16–17, 21, 23, 27–29, 37, 41–42. See also Winter program events, Jan. 1931, p.34–35, and Winter sports at Lake Placid Club, Jan. 1931, p.41–42. 6332

Winter sports at Saranac Lake. *Motordom*, Jan. 1930. 23:no.8:26. illus. 6333

Winter sports at Saranac Lake. *Playground*, Jan. 1921. 14:no.8:627–29. 6334

Winter sports in the Adirondacks. *Sport Rev*, Jan. 7, 1905. 27:8. * 6335

Winter sports open at Lake Placid in "American Switzerland." *NYC Lines Mag*, Jan. 1926. 6:no.10:55. illus. 6336

Winter sports season at Lake Placid now in full swing. *NYC Lines Mag*, Jan. 1921. 1:no. 10:25–27. illus. 6337

Wright, Mary Isabel. All's merry at Lake Placid; bob sleighing is a new sport on the program this winter, preparatory to 1932 winter Olympic games at Placid. *Motordom*, Dec. 1929. 23:no.7:6–7. illus. 6338

Wright, Mary Isabel. King Winter plays his favorites. 4p. illus. Reprinted from *Motordom*, Jan. 1929, 22:no.8:2–5, 24. 6339

Wright, Mary Isabel. Winter sports season at Lake Placid is begun. *NYC Lines Mag*, Dec. 1927. 9:no.9:45. illus. 6340

OLYMPIC GAMES

American Olympic committee. Report... games of the Xth Olympiad... III Olympic winter games, Lake Placid, New York, Feb. 4–13, 1932. Edited by Frederick W. Rubien... N.Y. 1932. 347p. ports. illus. diagrs. 6341

At America's playland. *Recreation* (*Nat*) Jan. 1932. 25:564–65. illus. 6342

Dewey, Godfrey. The Olympic winter games. *In* United States eastern amateur ski association. Year book, 1928. p.25–30. illus. 6343

Dewey, Godfrey. The third Olympic winter games. *Kiwan Mag*, July 1932. 17:307. 6344

Dewey, Godfrey. Third Olympic winter games—Lake Placid 1932. *In* United States eastern amateur ski association. Year book, 1929. p.14–16. diagr. illus. 6345

Gage, Earle W. The Olympic winter games. *AAA Travel*, Jan. 1932. 2:no.4:6–7, 15. illus. 6346

The great Olympics come to Lake Placid; approach of the world's most brilliant winter sports show makes this the premier goal of American sport lovers—stars of 25 nations competing in the greatest winter event of this generation—everyone welcome and all may enjoy thrills. *Motordom*, Dec. 1931. 25:no. 6:7–9. illus. 6347

Lake Placid prepares for 1932 Olympic winter sports. *NYC Lines Mag*, July 1929. 10:no. 4:51. 6348

Lattimer, George M. The Olympics in retrospect. *Wint Sports*, Nov. 1932. 3:no.2:14–15. illus. 6349

Morgan, Donald Fair. The III Olympic winter games. *Bridle & G*, Jan. 1932. 11:no.1: 8–9, 26–27. illus. 6350

1932 winter Olympics at Lake Placid; New York state enthusiastic over selection of Lake Placid which is already preparing for 1932. *Motordom*, Dec. 1929. 23:no.7:20. port. 6351

Olympic games (winter) Lake Placid, 1932. Official report, III Olympic winter games, Lake Placid 1932. . .compiled by George M. Lattimer. n.p. n.pub. c1932. 291p. incl. illus. plates, ports. figs. maps. 6352

Olympic games (winter) Lake Placid, 1932. III Olympic winter games, Lake Placid, Essex county, New York, Feb. 4–13, 1932. Albany, J.B. Lyon, n.d. 24p. incl. cover. illus. map. Schedule of games and advertisement for Essex County. 6353

Olympic games (winter) Lake Placid, 1932. III Olympic winter games, Lake Placid, USA, February 4–13, 1932. n.p. n.pub. n.d. 16p. illus.   6354

Olympic news. Issued by the American Olympic association. . .N.Y. Vol. 5, nos. 9–10, 11–12, Sept.–Oct., Nov.–Dec. 1931, and Vol. 6, nos. 1 & 2, Jan. and Feb. 1932, are on the III Olympic winter games at Lake Placid.   6355

Rice, Grantland. Winter knights; Olympic winter sports, Lake Placid. *Colliers*, Feb. 13, 1932. 89:no.7:22. illus.   6356

Smith-Kieland, Ingv. Olympic ski handling censured. . . *Wint Sports*, Jan. 1933. 3:no.5: 4–6, 22.   6357

Swift, Otis Peabody. Lake Placid ready for Olympics, offers regal sport program. Lake Placid club and village arrange noted events with world stars coming to entertain winter goers. *Motordom*, Dec. 1930. 24:no.7:6–7. illus.   6358

IIIrd Olympic winter games. . . *Wint Sports*, Feb. 1932. 2:no.5:5–8. port.   6359

III Olympic winter games, event of worldwide importance to be held at Lake Placid in 1932. *Up-Stater*, Jan. 1931. 3:no.1:3–4. illus.   6360

White, Elwyn Brooks. . . .Midwinter madness. *New Yorker*, Feb. 20, 1932. 8:no.1:38–44. illus.   6361

Winter Olympic games to have 20 nations participating, at Lake Placid. *NYC Lines Mag*, Oct. 1931. 12:no.2:19.   6362

Winter Olympics at Placid. World's most colorful ice pageant. *Gas Logic*, Feb. 1932. 51:no.2:3–4. illus.   6363

WINTER MOUNTAIN CLIMBING

Adirondack mountain club, inc. Winter mountaineering and ski touring competitions. Information and rules. n.p. 1949. 6p. illus. 6364

Adirondack mountain club, inc. Winter activities committee. Adirondack mountain club Winter activities committee announces the first annual winter mountaineering school at Adirondak loj, Lake Placid, New York, December 28–31, 1954. Albany, 1954. 2p. illus. Broadside.   6365

Adirondack mountain club, inc. Winter activities committee. The advanced winter badge. n.p. 1953. 4p. Unpaged leaflet.   6366

Adirondack mountain club, inc. Winter activities committee. The winter mountaineering guide, by Kim Hart. Utica, N.Y. 1953. 13p. illus.   6367

Allis, J. Ashton. A winter climb of Mount Marcy. *Mt Mag*, Jan. 1928. 6:55–56. illus.   6368

Bailey, Richard. First winter ascents of two Adirondack peaks. *Ad-i-ron-dac*, Jan.–Feb. 1949. 13:10. Cliff Mountain and Herbert (Marshall) Mountain.   6369

Bailey, Richard. My favorite Adirondack winter climb. *Cloud Splitter*, Jan.–Feb. 1955. 18:no.1:8–13. illus. Mt. Colden.   6370

Barker, E. Gilbert and Van Dyke, Paul A. The advanced winter badge. *Ad-i-ron-dac*, Jan.–Feb. 1953. 17:7, 15. Report of the Winter Activities Committee, Adirondack Mountain Club.   6371

Barker, E. Gilbert. Winter travel in the blowdown. *Ad-i-ron-dac*, Nov.–Dec. 1951. 15:106–9. Winter ascent of Seward and an unsuccessful attempt to climb Santanoni.   6372

Dirlan, Peter B. C.C.C. winter ascents of Panther, Couchsachraga. *Ad-i-ron-dac*, Jan.–Feb. 1954. 18:8–9, 11.   6373

Distin, William G. New Years day on Whiteface. *For Leaves*, Spring 1910. 6:no.1:3–8. illus.   6374

Flurscheim, C.H. Mt. Marcy. *Cloud Splitter*, Mar.–Apr. 1947. 10:no.2:4–5. Early ski climb of Marcy.   6375

Goodwin, James A. Winter mountaineering. *Ad-i-ron-dac*, Nov.–Dec. 1949. 13:121–22.   6376

Hammond, Henry D. How we climbed Sentinel. *Ad-i-ron-dac*, July–Aug. 1951. 15:64–66. illus. Climb through blowdown.   6377

Harris, F.H. Up a mountain on skis. *Country Life*, Feb. 1921. 39:48–50. illus.   6378

Harris, Martin S. Princeton outing club winter range trip. *Ad-i-ron-dac*, Jan.–Feb. 1953. 17:4–5. illus.   6379

Hart, David C. Cornell on Dix. *Ad-i-ron-dac*, Mar.–Apr. 1950. 14:30–32. illus. First recorded winter ascent of the entire Dix range.   6380

Hart, David C. First recorded winter ascents of Dial and Dix. *Ad-i-ron-dac*, Mar.–Apr. 1949. 13:39.   6381

Hart, Merwin K. Jr. First winter mountaineering school held at Adirondak loj. *Ad-i-ron-dac*, Jan.–Feb. 1955. 19:17. See also account by William Endicott in *The Cloud Splitter*, Mar.–Apr. 1955, 18:no.2:10–13. 6382

Hart, Merwin K. Jr. Iroquois conquered on skis! *Ad-i-ron-dac*, Mar.–Apr. 1948. 12:no.2: 8–9.   6383

Hine, Charles. Nippletop—on snowshoes! *Cloud Splitter*, Mar. 1942. 5:no.3:9–11.   6384

La Farge, Christopher Grant. A winter ascent of Tahawus. *Outing*, Apr. 1900. 36:69–75. illus.   6385

Lange, Willem Maurits III. Heffalump tracks! *Ad-i-ron-dac*, May–June 1955. 19:56–57. Santanoni peaks.   6386

LeBeau, Donald J. First winter ascent of Wallface. *Ad-i-ron-dac*, Nov.–Dec. 1951. 15:104–5. illus.   6387

Longstreth, Thomas Morris. Chinning up Whiteface in winter. *Outing*, Dec. 1920. 77:115–18. illus.   6388

Loope, P. Fay. Winter sunrise on Marcy. *Ad Mt Club Bul*, Mar. 1944. 8:no.2:4, 6. Ski trip.   6389

A midwinter sleep on Marcy's summit. *Cloud Splitter*, Mar.–Apr. 1953. 16:no.2:3. Review of an article from the Plattsburgh *Daily Republican*, Feb. 28, 1929, in The Footpath, edited by R.M.L. Carson.   6390

Ormsbee, Alexander F. Another winter ascent of Mount Marcy. *Appalachia*, July 1910. 12:135–38. Trip from Westport, by sleigh and snowshoes, in Feb. 1910.   6391

Pond, W.H. First winter ascent of Mt. Marcy. *Ad-i-ron-dac*, Mar.–Apr. 1950. 14:28–29. illus.   6392

Price, Fraser P. and Bachli, Werner. Gothics in winter. *Ad-i-ron-dac*, May–June 1949. 13:62–63.   6393

Puffer, Louis B. Good old web feet. *High Spots Yrbk*, 1942. p.20–21. illus. Snowshoe trip up Allen, via Ausable lakes.   6394

Snow climbing in the Adirondacks. *High Spots*, Jan. 1932. 9:no.1:2–5, 25. Account of climbing Marcy in winter by Benjamin S. Pond and C. Grant LaFarge. Arranged by R.M.L. Carson. Reprinted in Mt. Marcy anthology (*High Spots*, July 1937) p.39–42, illus.   6395

Thompson, Ethel. Up Noonmark! *Cloud Splitter*, Apr. 1942. 5:no.4:12–13. Ski trip.   6396

Van Dyke, Paul A. After the storm. *Ad-i-ron-dac*, Mar.–Apr. 1951. 15:29, 33. December trip to Duck Hole, in blowdown area. 6397

Van Dyke, Paul A. 1950–51 Winter mountaineering conference. *Ad-i-ron-dac*, July–Aug. 1951. 15:75.   6398

Van Dyke, Paul A. Virgin snow. *Ad-i-ron-dac*, Jan.–Feb. 1951. 15:10–11, 16. illus.   6399

Wells, Lewis A. A January ascent of Mount Marcy. *Appalachia*, June 1908. 11:340–43.   6400

Why bother about the Alps? Mountain climbing in New York state has become the prime diversion of thousands of winter vacationists. *Motordom*, Dec. 1929. 23:no.7:14. illus. 6401

Winter ascent. *Cloud Splitter*, Mar.–Apr. 1950. 13:no.2:6–7. Dix range.   6402

Winter ascent of Mount McIntyre. *Mt Mag*, July 1928. 7:13–14. illus.   6403

SKIING

Baldwin, Henry Ives. The relative antiquity of skiing in the Adirondacks. *Am Ski Ann*, 1937–38. p.58–63. illus.   6404

Burton, Harold B. Mountaineering on skis. *Am Ski Ann*, 1936–37. p.29–33. plates. Cross-country skiing.   6405

Burton, Harold B. Ski touring. *NYS Con*, Feb.–Mar. 1948. 2:no.4:10. illus. Skiing in the high-peak region.   6406

C., D. —And the Continental congress. *Ski Bul*, Feb. 4, 1938. 8:no.8:4, 6. Skiing at Ticonderoga.   6407

C., P. Ticonderoga, a story of community cooperation. *Ski Bul*, Feb. 4, 1938. 8:no.8:6–8. port. map.   6408

Carpenter, Delphine. Five and dime ski center. *Ski Bul*, Dec. 5, 1941. 12:no.5:5–6. Whiteface development.   6409

Casselman, W.A. The north gate. *Ski Bul*, Feb. 8, 1941. 11:no.15:5–6. Ski trails from Adirondak Loj.   6410

Dewey, Godfrey. Olympic ski hill at Lake Placid. *In* United States eastern amateur ski association. Year book, 1929. p.31–32. illus.   6411

Draper, Arthur G. On Gore mountain. *Ski Bul*, Jan. 30, 1941. 12:no.11:12–13. Skiing news from North Creek area.   6412

Draper, Arthur G. Whiteface ski development. *Am Ski Ann*, 1947. p.274.   6413

Eastern interscholastic championship. Lake Placid. . .1949. *Am Ski Ann*, 1950. p.197–98.   6414

Elkins, Frank. North Creek champions. *Am Ski Ann*, 1944–45. p.159–60.   6415

Garrison, John L. Sun, snow and skis: a modern guide to eastern skiing. N.Y. McGraw-Hill, c1946. 318p. illus. Lake Placid, p.187–97.   6416

Grout, H. McIntire Jr. Christies or eggbeaters? *Ad-i-ron-dac*, Jan.–Feb. 1946. 10:no.1:4–5. Controlled skiing.   6417

Heidrick, Arthur G. When thaw-time plagues the skier. *Ad-i-ron-dac*, May–June 1949. 13:60–61.   6418

Hicks, Harry Wade. Lake Placid club, N.Y. *Ski Bul*, Dec. 29, 1933. 4:no.2:4.   6419

Hicks, Harry Wade. Lake Placid ski council. *Am Ski Ann*, 1944–45. p.162–63.   6420

Hicks, Harry Wade. Skiing at Lake Placid. *Skisport*, 1922–23. 17:52–53.   6421

Hicks, Harry Wade. Skiing in New York state. *Am Ski Ann*, 1935–36. p.103–10. plates. Includes skiing at Adirondak Loj and Old Forge. 6422

Howard, William Gibbs. The ski trail program. *High Spots Yrbk*, 1939. p.57–63. Conservation Department plans. 6423

Kehoe, Robert P. Cross-country skiing. *High Spots Yrbk*, 1939. p.35–37. 6424

Korn, Bennet H. GI skiing at Lake Placid. *Am Ski Ann*, 1945–46. p.211–13. illus. 6425

Lake Placid. *Ski Bul*, Jan. 11, 1935. 5:no.4:3. 6426

Lake Placid again. Kate Smith trophy. *Am Ski Ann*, 1944–45. p.148–51. 6427

Lake Placid ski council. Lake Placid ski guide. Lake Placid, N.Y. c1947. 31p. illus. 1 folded map. 6428

Lake Placid tournament. *Am Ski Ann*, 1945–46. p.195–96. 6429

Langley, Roger. Lake Placid—Aspen, scenes of the world championship. *Am Ski Ann*, 1950. p.47–48. illus. 6430

Langley, Roger. The world ski championship at Lake Placid—Nordic events. *Am Ski Ann*, Feb. 1950. 34:no.3:13–18. illus. 6431

Leggett, Edward H. My most memorable trip. *Cloud Splitter*, Jan.–Feb. 1948. 11:no. 1:13–15. 6432

Loope, P. Fay. Marcy trail much improved. *Ski Bul*, Jan. 29, 1937. 7:no.7:13. 6433

MacKenzie, Ronald M. Search mission. *Am Ski Ann*, 1944–45. p.97–99. port. illus. Rescue by the Lake Placid Ski Patrol. 6434

MacKenzie, Ronald M. Summer jumping at Lake Placid. *Am Ski Ann*, 1949. p.221–22. 6435

Morgan, Donald Fair. Flying on skis. Broadside preprint of article for *Every Week Magazine*, Jan. 24, 1932. illus. Copy in Hicks Collection, Lake Placid Club. 6436

Mulholland, William D. Ski trails. *NYS Ranger Sch*, 1933. p.27–28, 66. 6437

Nash, Leslie C. Lake Placid and the new era. *Ski News*, Mar. 8, 1940. 10:no.16:5–6. 6438

Nash, Leslie C. Whiteface trail. *Ski Bul*, Jan. 6, 1939. 9:no.7:6. Work on ski trail. 6439

New York (state). Bureau of state publicity. Ski trails of New York state. Albany, J.B. Lyon, n.d. 23p. maps. Includes Adirondacks. 6440

New York (state). Bureau of state publicity. Ski trails of New York state prepared. . .with the cooperation of H.W. Hicks. . .and E.H.

Hull. . . Albany, J.B. Lyon, 1939? 8p. Folded broadside. Copy in the Hicks Collection, Lake Placid Club. 6441

New York (state). Whiteface mountain authority. The story of Whiteface mountain ski center. n.p. 1949. 10p. illus. Mimeographed. 6442

The 1947 National cross-country and the Classic combined championship. Lake Placid club. . .1947. *Am Ski Ann*, 1948. p.211–12. 6443

Norris, R. Hosmer. De luxe ski trail at North Creek. *Ski Bul*, Mar. 31, 1933. 3:no.15:7. Brief note with map. 6444

Off to the mountains (by Gore mountain ski club). *Top o' the World*, Dec. 1937. 2:no. 1:8, 13. illus. 6445

Osborne, Lithgow. New York state's ski trails. *Ski Bul*, Dec. 16, 1938. 9:no.5:5–7. Adirondacks and Catskills. 6446

Owners' liability in ski accidents discussed by Charles H. Tuttle. *Top o' the World*, Feb. 1939. 3:no.1:1, 10. 6447

Resurrection of Whiteface lodge. *NYS Con*, Dec. 1951–Jan. 1952. 6:no.3:22–23. illus. Pictures with brief text; rebuilding after the fire. 6448

Schenectady winter sports club. Ski trails of the Adirondacks, Catskills, Berkshires. 1934–5. n.p. n.d. 24p. maps. Published by Trails Committee of the Adirondack Mountain Club, Committee on Skiing and the Schenectady Winter Sports Club. Also published for 1935–36 season, 36p. 6449

Shorey, Archibald Thompson. Herringboners jubilee. *Cloud Splitter*, Jan. 1940. 2:no.8:4–5. 6450

Shorey, Archibald Thompson. Skiing cross-country. *NYS Con*, Dec. 1949–Jan. 1950. 4: no.3:34. Trip to Lake Colden through Avalanche Pass. 6451

Summer ski jumping in the east. *Am Ski Ann*, 1950. p.199–200. Contains Ronald MacKenzie's "Lake Placid Summer Jump." Followed by report "The Eastern Convention at Lake Placid." 6452

Swayze, George. Ski trails. *Hud Riv Mag*, 1941. 4:7–8. 6453

Thousands of skiers enjoyed vacations on Gore mountain ski trails at North creek. *Top o' the World*, Mar. 1939. 3:no.2:12–13. illus. 6454

$250,000. *New Yorker*, Nov. 15, 1941. 17:no. 47:18. Cost of ski trail on Whiteface. 6455

U.S. Works progress administration. New

York city. Skiing in the east; ski trails and how to get there. N.Y. Barrows, 1939. 334p. map. (American Guide Series.) Taken from the Warren County Guide. 6456

Upstate—the skiers' paradise. *Up Mo*, Jan. 1941. 1:no.10:6. illus. 6457

White, John A. Whiteface mountain ski center. *Am Ski Ann*, 1944–45. p.163–64. illus. 6458

Wilderness ski trails at Adirondak loj, Lake Placid club, N.Y. n.p. n.d. map. Folded broadside. Description of trails. 6459

CLUBS AND PRIVATE PRESERVES

GENERAL

Adams, Samuel Hopkins. William Rockefeller, maker of wilderness. *Colliers*, Apr. 22, 1905. 35:no.4:15, 18. On the obliteration of Brandon, Township 16, Franklin County. 6460

An Adirondack preserve. *For & Stream*, Jan. 26, 1882. 17:511. Purchase of 13,000 acres in Township 40, Hamilton County (most of Raquette Lake) by George W. Cotterill and Joel B. Erhardt, to prevent lumbering. 6461

Adirondack preserves. *For & Stream*, Apr. 4, 1889. 32:209. Editorial opposing private parks. 6462

Adirondack preserves. *For & Stream*, July 15, 1899. 53:47. Describes the Rockefeller preserves. 6463

Adirondack preserves. *For & Stream*, Feb. 28, 1903. 60:161. Brief editorial commending care taken of private preserves. 6464

Adirondack preserves and hotels. *For & Stream*, July 27, 1895. 45:67. 6465

American game parks. *For & Stream*, May 18, 1895. 44:390. Reports on many of the parks in the Adirondack area. 6466

Another forest preserve. *For & Stream*, Sept. 10, 1891. 37:145. Purchase of 1,000 acres of the Long Pond tract by the Long Pond Fish and Game Association. 6467

Another large Adirondack park, a movement which is likely to be beneficial. *For & Stream*, Apr. 11, 1878. 10:182. Editorial on large holding of W.W. Durant. 6468

Evolution of the Adirondacks. *Sport Rev*, Aug. 27, 1904. 26:229. Sale of large tract on Blue Mountain Lake to a syndicate of New Yorkers. 6469

Fences in the Adirondacks. *For & Stream*, July 4, 1903. 61:7. Contributions, one signed "Didymus" and the other by Raymond S. Spears, on the private preserve question. See answer by Charles L. Paige in issue for July 25, 1903, 61:64–65. 6470

Flint, Peter. Private parks do not protect game. *For & Stream*, Dec. 13, 1913. 81:757–58. 6471

Foster, Maximilian. American game preserves. The threatened extinction of our native game animals, and the effort to save them by establishing great private parks in which they are preserved and bred. *Munsey*, June 1901. 25:376–86. illus. Nehasane Preserve, p.384–85. Litchfield, p.385–86. 6472

Hallock, Charles. The Adirondack close. *For & Stream*, Oct. 10, 1903. 61:280. On the preserve question. 6473

Hallock, Charles. Club preserves. *For & Stream*, Oct. 3, 1889. 33:205. 6474

Ives, H.L. Some Adirondack preserves. *For & Stream*, May 21, 1898. 50:406. Short history of Vanderbilt Preserve, Vilas Preserve, Cutting Tract, Granshu Preserve, Hollywood Preserve, Massawepie Club, and others. Includes account of a bear hunt. 6475

Kelly, Allen. An Adirondack park. *Harper W*, July 19, 1890. 34:563. plans. Outlines history of despoiling and problems posed by reserves of sportsmen's clubs. Gives purpose of the Adirondack Park Association. Kildare Club and Adirondack Club included. 6476

Miller, Seaver Asbury. Sporting clubs in the Adirondacks. *Outing*, Aug. 1898. 32:475–82. illus. Describes some of the larger clubs and their preserves. 6477

New York (state). Forest commission. Private preserves in the Adirondack forest. *In* its Annual report for the year 1893. 1:151–201. plates. Illustrations are by S.R. Stoddard. 6478

New York (state). Forest, fish and game commission. Private preserves. *In* its Report, 1902–3. p.36–44. Includes list of preserves. 6479

Palmer, T.S. Private game preserves and their future in the United States. Washington. G.P.O. 1910. 16 leaves. plate. (U.S. Department of Agriculture Circular 72.) States objection to the sixty preserves in the Adirondack area. Résumé in *Sportsman's Review*, June 4, 1910, 37:537. 6480

Preserves in the Adirondack park. *For & Stream*, Dec. 29, 1894. 43:552. 6481

Shurter, Joseph W. Game preserves and Adirondack ruin. *For & Stream*, July 18, 1903. 61:46. 6482

Shurter, Joseph W. The preserve question. *For & Stream*, Sept. 26, 1903. 61:241. Advantages and disadvantages of the large preserves. 6483

Spears, Raymond Smiley. From a woodsman's view-point—against sportsmans clubs. *For & Stream*, May 11, 1895. 44:368. 6484

Two Adirondack preserves. *Sport Rev*, May 12, 1906. 29:509. Editorial on the observation of game laws on two types of reserves. 6485

W., S.M. A woman on a game preserve. A superintendent's wife who tried but failed to become reconciled to a life in the forest. *For & Stream*, Oct. 2, 1909. 73:528–29. One of the large private preserves. 6486

Walsh, George Ethelbert. American game preserves. *Outing*, Feb. 1901. 37:539–44. illus. 6487

Whiton, L.C. The St. Regis camps. *For & Stream*, June 18, 1891. 36:435. Various sporting clubs in area. 6488

INDIVIDUAL CLUBS

THE ADIRONDACK LEAGUE CLUB

Adirondack league club. Annual report (financial). N.Y. Copies located for 1924, 1931, 1932. The Annual Report of the treasurer issued 1931–date. Copy located for 1940. 6489

Adirondack league club. Bulletin, v.1, no.1– April 1922– N.Y. 1922–? Copies located for Apr., July and Oct. 1922, v.1, nos.1–3. 6490

Adirondack league club. Club manual. Various places. 1926–48. Issued annually. Copies located for 1926–27, 1934, 1938–48. 6491

Adirondack league club. Code of regulations. N.Y. 1920. 26p. 6492

Adirondack league club. Handbook. N.Y. 1892– front. tables, maps. Copies located for 1892–97. 6493

Adirondack league club. Prospectus. N.Y. P.F. McBreen, printer, 1890. 12p. folded maps. An eight-page edition also issued with title: Prospectus, 1890. 6494

Adirondack league club. To the members of the Union league club. N.Y. 1895. 12p. 6495

Adirondack league club. Yearbook. N.Y. 1891–date. plates, maps. Title varies: Adirondack League Club, Incorporated June 18, 1890; Constitution, By-laws. . . Not published in 1933, 1935–38, 1940. 6496

The Adirondack league club. *For & Stream*, Mar. 30, 1893. 40:275. 6497

Adirondack league club. *Recreation*, Aug. 1900. 13:125. Aims and accomplishments. 6498

The Adirondack league club opening. *For & Stream*, Apr. 27, 1893. 40:366. 6499

Adirondack league's hunt. *For & Stream*, Aug. 19, 1893. 41:143. 6500

An experiment in forestry. *Gard & For*, Feb. 18, 1891. 41:73–74. Editorial on the Adirondack League Club's forestry experiment. 6501

Fernow, Bernhard Eduard. Report. . .to the Executive committee of the Adirondack League club. *In* Adirondack league club. Yearbook, 1891. p.43–59. Report on salable timber. 6502

Great Adirondack game preserve. *Sport Rev*, Oct. 28, 1905. 28:483. Description of tract and list of officers and camp owners. 6503

The preserve system. *For & Stream*, June 26, 1890. 34:449. Editorial on the purchase of a large tract by the Adirondack League Club. 6504

Smyth, Charles Henry Jr. Sketch of the physiographic development of the Adirondack league club preserve. n.p. 1899. 9p. 6505

THE ADIRONDACK MOUNTAIN CLUB

ADK presidents. *Ad-i-ron-dac*, Nov.–Dec. 1947. 11:no.6:6–11. Greetings and reminiscences of former ADK presidents Macalpine, Ayres, Lowe, Kelsey, Andrews, Carson, Knauth, Myers, Hackett and Pratt, on the 25th anniversary of the Club. 6506

The Ad-i-ron-dac (formerly the Bulletin). v.9, no.1– Jan.–Feb. 1945– Albany, Adirondack mountain club, inc. 1945–date. Bimonthly. Numbering of volumes continued from *The Bulletin*. Preceded by *High Spots, High Spots Bulletin* and *The Adirondack Mountain Club Bulletin*. 6507

Adirondack mountain club, inc. The Adirondack mountain club: what it is, what it does. N.Y. 1936? 4p. Unpaged leaflet issued on both salmon and white paper. 6508

Adirondack mountain club, inc. The Adirondack mountain club incorporated: purpose and scope. Organized Apr. 3, 1922. Albany, 1922. 12p. illus. 6509

Adirondack mountain club, inc. Bulletin. v.1, no.1—v.8, no.6. May 1937—Nov.–Dec. 1944. Albany, 1937–44. Bimonthly. Name changed to *The Ad-i-ron-dac* in 1945. Preceded by *High Spots* and *High Spots Bulletin.* Not published July, Oct., Dec. 1937, Feb. 1938.   6510

Adirondack mountain club, inc. Charter members of the Adirondack mountain club. n.p. n.d. 4p. Oblong leaflet.   6511

Adirondack mountain club, inc. Constitution and by-laws. . .adopted. . .Apr. 3, 1922. n.p. n.d. 8p. Constitution also issued in 1930, 1938, 1947 and 1949. Included in 1942 Roster.   6512

Adirondack mountain club, inc. High spots bulletin. v.1, no.1–v.2, no.2. Oct. 1936–Feb. 1937. Albany, 1936–37. 2v. Only three issues appear to have been published: v.1, Oct. 1936, v.2, nos.1–2, Jan. and Feb. 1937. 6513

Adirondack mountain club, inc. Johns brook lodge. Albany, 1924. 4p. leaflet. illus. plans. Proposed lodge.   6514

Adirondack mountain club, inc. Johns brook lodge. Albany, Peters print, 1925? 4p. illus. Unpaged leaflet. Appeal for funds.   6515

Adirondack mountain club, inc. Johns brook lodge. . . Glens Falls, N.Y. Glens Falls Post co. n.d. 12p. illus. map. Green cover; map is dated 1928. Another edition, 1929? 15p. 6516

Adirondack mountain club, inc. Johns brook lodge. . . Albany? 1929? 16p. illus. map. The Johns Brook Lodge folder was issued yearly when the Lodge was in operation. Title varies. 1946–date, usually a reprint from *The Ad-i-ron-dac.*   6517

Adirondack mountain club, inc. Milestones 1922–1926. Albany, 1926. 6p. Unpaged oblong folder outlining achievements of the Club.   6518

Adirondack mountain club, inc. Officers, governors, committee and chapter chairmen and roster of members, 1954. n.p. 1954. 33p. Other editions of the Roster appeared in 1931, 1935, 1936, 1939, 1940, 1942, 1947, 1948, 1949, 1950, 1951. The 1938 "Constitution and By-Laws" included the Roster. 6519

Adirondack mountain club, inc. Report of the Conservation committee. . .1936. 3 folios. Main report signed by Peter Cantline, chairman. Two-page dissenting minority report signed by George Marshall.   6520

Adirondack mountain club, inc. Spend your mountain vacation at Johns brook lodge. . . Albany, Peters print, 1941? 8p. map. Lists four chapters of the Club.   6521

Adirondack mountain club, inc. This is the Adirondack mountain club. Folded broadside. illus. Published every three or four years. Latest edition, 1955.   6522

Adirondack mountain club, inc. To the Board of governors. . . n.p. 1929? 4p. Letter signed by Arnold W. Knauth, president, dated March 15, 1929. On Homer Brown's offer to sell land and buildings to the Club.
                                          6523

Adirondack mountain club, inc. What have we done? Albany, 1926. unpaged. Oblong folder. Brief statement of the accomplishments of the Club.   6524

Adirondack mountain club, inc. Adirondak loj chapter. Bulletin, no. 1– May 7, 1936–. n.p. 1936–date. Title varies. Usually published twice a year. Early issues mimeographed. Publicity for Adirondak Loj. 6525

Adirondack mountain club, inc. Adirondak loj chapter. Welcome! An invitation to Adirondak loj. . . n.p. 1953. 4p. illus. 6526

Adirondack mountain club, inc. Conservation committee. Report. . .January 26, 1935. *NYS For Assn NL,* May 1935. p.21–24. 6527

Adirondack mountain club, inc. New York chapter, inc. Handbook of information, 1939. N.Y. 1939. 36p. Includes history of the New York Chapter. Also published in 1949. 6528

Adirondack mountain club, inc. New York chapter, inc. Year book, 1926. Albany, Boyd printing co. 1926? 26p. First yearbook. Contains a little material about the main club. Also issued in 1927 and 1931.   6529

Adirondack mountain club, inc. Organization committee. List of qualified charter members February 1922. n.p. 1922. 2p. 6530

An Adirondack mountain club. *Conservationist,* May 1921. 4:78–79. Editorial approving the proposed club.   6531

Albany chapter—ADK—the first notice. *Cloud Splitter,* Mar.–Apr. 1952. 15:no.2:2–3.
                                          6532

Albany chapter—an early record. *Cloud Splitter,* May–June 1952. 15:no.3:2–3. 6533

Albany chapter, incorporated. *Cloud Splitter,* Nov.–Dec. 1954. 17:no.6:2–3.   6534

An Albany chapter project. *Cloud Splitter,* Mar.–Apr. 1954. 17:no.2:1–5. History of *The Cloud Splitter* and reprint of first issue. 6535

Baldwin, Henry I. Early days of the ADK. *Ad-i-ron-dac,* Nov.–Dec. 1955. 19:103. 6536

Bergstrom, Mrs. Alice (Nord). Now. *Cloud Splitter,* Nov.–Dec. 1947. 10:no.6:7–9. Appraisal of the Albany Chapter.   6537

Bingham, Nellie. Thirty years with the New York chapter. *Ad-i-ron-dac,* Sept.–Oct. 1955. 19:84–85.   6538

Carson, Russell Mack Little. Charter member looks at twenty-five years. *Cloud Splitter,* Nov.–Dec. 1947. 10:no.6:2–3. Brief history.
                                          6539

Carson, Russell Mack Little. So the Adirondack mountain club is twenty years old. *High Spots Yrbk*, 1942. p.4–6. illus.   6540

The Cloud Splitter. Albany, Albany chapter of the Adirondack mountain club, 1938–date. illus. Published bimonthly. Mimeographed.   6541

Denniston, Robert. Johns brook lodge—1949. *Ad-i-ron-dac*, Sept.–Oct. 1949. 8:102–3. illus.   6542

Dobson, Meade C. Recollections of the formation of the Adirondack mountain club. *Ad-i-ron-dac*, Nov.–Dec. 1947. 11:no 6:3. 6543

Draper, John C. Adirondack mountain club. *Mt Mag*, Feb. 1929. 7:62–63.   6544

Goldthwaite, George Edgar. Early days of the Adirondack mountain club—I. *Ad-i-ron-dac*, May–June 1950. 14:58, 63.   6545

High spots, v.1, no.1–v.14, no.4. Nov. 1922–Dec. 1937. Albany, Adirondack mountain club, inc. 1922–37. Monthly Nov. 1922 through Mar. 1924; irregular Apr.–Dec. 1924; quarterly Jan.–Mar. 1925—Jan.–Mar. 1927 and Apr. 1929–Dec. 1937. Issues for July and Oct. 1927 and Jan., May and July 1928 appeared in *The Mountain Magazine*, v.6, no.1–4—v.7, no.1. Duplicate numbering: v.5, no.1, Jan.–Mar. 1927 and July 1928 (v.5, no.2 dated Dec. 1928). Succeeded by *The Adirondack Mountain Club Bulletin*.   6546

High spots; the yearbook of the Adirondack mountain club. N.Y. & Albany, Adirondack mountain club, inc., 1939–44. 4v. illus. plates. Issued for 1939, 1940, 1942 and 1944.   6547

Howard, William Gibbs. Proposed Adirondack mountain club. *Ad-i-ron-dac*, Nov.–Dec. 1947. 11:no.6:4–5. Speech given at the organization meeting, Dec. 5, 1921.   6548

Howard, William Gibbs. Some early history of the Adirondack mountain club. *Cloud Splitter*, May 1939. 2:no.3:2–3.   6549

Kelsey, Frederick T. The Adirondack mountain club. *Ski News*, Mar. 8, 1940. 10:no.16: 6–7. Work of Club in promoting skiing. 6550

Leggett, Edward H. Jr. Harking back to the early days of the chapter. *Cloud Splitter*, Sept.–Oct. 1952. 15:no.5:4–7. Albany Chapter. 6551

Menz, Pauline. A new chapter is formed. *Ad-i-ron-dac*, Jan.–Feb. 1950. 14:12–13. illus. The Non-46ers.   6552

Metcalf, Thomas R. Life at JBL; or, Reminiscences of a former hutmaster. *Ad-i-ron-dac*, May–June 1953. 17:50–51.   6553

Mullarkey, Rosine M. Johns brook lodge. *Mt Mag*, July 1927. 6:29–30. illus.   6554

Myers, John Platt. An address. *Mt Mag*, May 1928. 6:97–98. port. At the 6th annual meeting of the Club.   6555

Newkirk, Arthur Edward. What are we for? *Cloud Splitter*, Sept.–Oct. 1954. 17:no.5:2–3.   6556

Nixon, Edgar Burkhardt. The Adirondack mountain club. *IOCA Bul*, Winter 1948. 2:no.1:50–51.   6557

Plum, Dorothy Alice. *The Ad-i-ron-dac's* ancestors. *Ad-i-ron-dac*, Jan.–Feb. 1952. 16:13–14. Periodicals published by the Club. 6558

Plum, Dorothy Alice. To be or not to be? *Ad-i-ron-dac*, July–Aug. 1954. 18:73. Non-46er nonsense. See also "Non-Forty-sixers Meet" in issue for Nov.–Dec. 1952, 16:102.   6559

Plum, Eleanor Mary. Memories of an ADKer. *Cloud Splitter*, Sept.–Oct. 1952. 15:no.5:11–12. Albany Chapter.   6560

Strube, Janet. The Adirondack mountain club. *Cloud Splitter*, July–Aug. 1954. 17:no.4: 1–2. Aims of the Club.   6561

Strube, Janet. Then. *Cloud Splitter*, Nov.–Dec. 1947. 10:no.6:4–6. History of the Albany Chapter.   6562

Stürcke, Albert. Hikes. N.Y. 1926. 148p. Description of outings of Adirondack Mountain Club and Green Mountain Club (not in the Adirondacks).   6563

Wessels, William L. Speech. . .at 1 p.m. from the top of Marcy. *High Spots*, Dec. 1937. 14:no.4:7–9. illus.   6564

THE ASSOCIATION FOR THE PROTECTION OF THE ADIRONDACKS

"Adirondack," pseud. The Association for the protection of the Adirondacks. *Woods & Wat*, Autumn 1902. 5:no.3:12–14. illus. 6565

Adirondack forest preservation. *For & Stream*, Feb. 2, 1907. 68:176. Report on the Association.   6566

Adirondack preservation. *For & Stream*, Feb. 3, 1906. 66:177. Description of a dinner given by the Association.   6567

Association for the protection of the Adirondacks. Annual report, no.3–1902/3–date. N.Y. 1903–date. 1st and 2d reports not published. The Reports of this Association are valuable source material for the history of the Forest Preserve.   6568

Association for the protection of the Adirondacks. Constitution. n.p. n.pub. n.d. 4p. By-laws, p.3–4. The Association was incorporated June 20, 1902.   6569

Association for the protection of the Adirondacks. List of officers and members. January

1, 1903. N.Y. Gilliss press, 1903? 47p. See also its List of Members, Jan. 1, 1925.   6570

Association for the protection of the Adirondacks. *For & Stream*, June 28, 1902. 58:508. Notice of incorporation. See also short article in *Engineering and Mining Journal*, May 17, 1902.   6571

Depew, Chauncey M. National Appalachian forest reserve. Speech. . .in Senate of the United States, June 7, 1902. Washington, 1902. 8p. (Association for the protection of the Adirondacks. Publication no. 1.) The first A.P.A. publication. Donaldson, v.2, p.310–13, lists Publications 1–30.   6572

Higley, Warren. The Association for the protection of the Adirondacks: what it has accomplished in one year. *Woods & Wat*, Summer 1903. 6:no.2:18–19. illus.   6573

LAKE PLACID CLUB

Adirondak loj club, Essex co NY. . . Lake Placid club, N.Y. Forest press, n.d. 8p. illus. Unpaged leaflet.   6574

Dewey, Godfrey. Address of welcome. *J Home Econ*, Mar. 1915. 7:107–8. Address on aims of the Club, given before the Institution Section of the American Home Economics Association.   6575

Dewey, Melvil. Lake Placid club, N.Y. *NY State Hist Assn Q*, Apr. 1924. 5:158–62.   6576

Howland, Harold Jacobs. Old winter in his home. *Ind*, Feb. 14, 1916. 85:232–33. illus.   6577

Lake Placid club. Circular. Morningside, N.Y. 1904. 7 leaves. illus.   6578

Lake Placid club. Club notes, no.1–232. Mar. 1905–June 1935. Lake Placid club, N.Y. 1905–35. Published irregularly. Issued for members.   6579

Lake Placid club. Handbook. Lake Placid club, N.Y. 1894? 80p. illus. Also issued in 1901 (224p.) and in 1914 (709p.). Reprinted in 1920.   6580

Lake Placid club. Lake Placid club. Fulton, N.Y. Morrill press, 192— 50p. Cover title. Also published in 1924 and 1930 by the Forest Press.   6581

Lake Placid club. Lake Placid club education foundation. n.p. 1923. unpaged.   6582

Lake Placid club. Lake Placid club; fall. n.p. 1928? 24p. Cover title.   6583

Lake Placid club. Lake Placid club in Adirondaks. Outline. Lake Placid club, N.Y. Forest press, 1924. 16p. illus. Text in simplified spelling.   6584

Lake Placid club. Lake Placid in winter on Adirondack lakes, Placid, Mirror and Heart. n.p. 1907? illus. A prospectus.   6585

Lake Placid club. Lake Placid club news. August 12, 1917–September 12, 1930. Lake Placid club, N.Y. 1917–30. 4v. Weekly July–Sept., mid-Dec.–Feb. Issued for members.   6586

Lake Placid club. Lake Placid club on Adirondack lakes Placid, Mirror and Heart, Essex co. N.Y. Lake Placid club, N.Y. c1902. 32p. illus.   6587

Lake Placid club. Lake Placid club organ. Lake Placid club, N.Y. Forest press, 1925. 16p.   6588

Lake Placid club. Outline. Morningside, N.Y. 1904. 9 leaves. illus. 10th season.   6589

Lake Placid club. Placid peeks: Lake Placid club notes, December 1954. 50th anniversary of winter sports. Lake Placid club, N.Y. 1954. 16p. illus. Issued for members.   6590

Lake Placid club. Sno birds of Lake Placid club. . . Winter sports program 1924–1925. Lake Placid club, N.Y. 1924–25. unpaged.   6591

Lake Placid club. Yearbook, 1928–1930. Lake Placid club, N.Y. Forest press, 1928–30. 3v. plates.   6592

Lake Placid club. Winter house. n.p. 1904. 5 leaves.   6593

Lake Placid club educational foundation. The work of the Foundation and its relation to the Club and the Company. . .report of a special committee of the Board of trustees, March 1947. n.p. n.d. 31p. illus.   6594

Lake Placid club, one man's dream. *Wardman PV*, Nov. 1, 1926. Copy in the Saranac Lake Free Library.   6595

Longstreth, Thomas Morris. Lake Placid and an experiment in intelligence. Reprinted from The Adirondacks. . .by T. Morris Longstreth. N.Y. Century, 1917? p.231–57. Brief foreword by Melvil Dewey.   6596

Placid park club. n.p. 1897. 22p. illus. Placid Park Club was the original name of Lake Placid Club. Change made in 1900.   6597

Townsend, Reginald T. A university club in the wilderness. *Country Life*, June 1920. 38:no.2:50–53. illus. Also issued as a reprint, Lake Placid Club, Forest Press, 1923.   6598

Willy, John. Impressions of Lake Placid club. . . *Hotel Mo*, Oct. 1923. 31:44–56. Also issued as a reprint.   6599

OTHER CLUBS AND PRESERVES

The Adirondack association. *NYS Con*. Aug.– Sept. 1954. 9:no.1:30. Founding of the Adirondack Park Association.   6600

Adirondack camp and trail club. Constitution and by-laws. . .adopted 1912. n.p. n.d. 12p. For note on founding of the Club see

Donaldson, v.2, p.24. In May 1923 the name was changed to the Camp and Trail Club of the Lake Placid Club. 6601

Adirondak civic leag. Bulletin. Reprinted from Lake Placid news. n.p. 1924? 16p. The Leag was organized August 1924. This bulletin includes the by-laws and the opening address by Melvil Dewey. Copy in the Hicks Collection, Lake Placid Club. 6602

The Adirondack club of Lake Placid, N.Y. *Lake Pl Life*, Jan.–Mar. 1931. p.30–32; p.30–31, 33; p.30–31, 33. plan. 6603

Adirondack 46ers meet at Heart lake. *Ad-i-ron-dac*, July–Aug. 1949. 13:85, 87. illus. 6604

Adirondack preservation association. *For & Stream*, May 5, 1887. 28:325. Annual meeting. The Adirondack Preserve Association is described in the New York State Forest Commission Report for 1893, p.163–64. 6605

Adirondack trail improvement society. n.p. n.d. 4p. Describes organization of the Society, Sept. 14, 1897. Another four-page pamphlet with similar title reports work done the first year. Signed: S. Burns Weston, Secretary. 6606

Amateur, pseud. The North woods Walton club. *For & Stream*, Jan. 28, 1875. 3:387. Description of the 1859 excursion. Written by one of the members. Ned Buntline was on this trip. 6607

American legion, New York. Mountain camp at Big Tupper lake, N.Y. Report of the superintendent. Tupper Lake, N.Y. 1933–date. charts. Reproduced from typewritten copy. 6608

Another Adirondack tragedy. *For & Stream*, Sept. 29, 1900. 55:241. Editorial on the accidental shooting of Mrs. Kerr and Dr. Bailey on the Tahawus Club preserve. 6609

Another phonetic celebration. *Phon M*, Nov. 1847. 2:49–51. Part of the article is written in Comstock's phonotypes. Reprinted from the *Westport Patriot*. Description of the "Tahawus Celebration" held at the Adirondack Iron Works and on the summit of Mt. Marcy, by the Tahawian Association. See also the issue for June 1847, p.221–28, for poem written to celebrate the engraving of "Dr. Comstock's new alphabet" on top of Mt. Marcy (no.6628). The issue for Dec. 1847, p.88–89, has a note on the Tahawian Association. 6610

Attempts to destroy great game preserve. *Sport Rev*, July 23, 1910. 38:79. Fires set on the Rockefeller Preserve in retaliation for closing old game trails. 6611

Ausable club, St. Huberts, N.Y. Year book, 1908. St. Huberts, N.Y. 1908. 63p. 6612

Auskerada club. Aughstagradi. A tale of the Auskeradas. N.Y. 1897. 24p. plates, maps (1 folded). unpaged. Legend of the Huron chief who won possession of the Auskerada lakes; followed by description of Auskerada Park and plan for development. About twelve miles northeast of Dolgeville. Copy in the Saranac Lake Free Library. 6613

Back log camp. Back log camp, 1896–1946. On Indian lake,—Sabael, N.Y. Philadelphia, Lyon & Armour, 1946. 12p. port. illus. Brief history of the camp. 6614

Back log camp. Back log camp in the Adirondacks. On Indian lake, Sabael, N.Y. General information and rates for 1955. n.p. 1955. 16p. illus. Unpaged folder. Annual announcement. See also its "A Greeting to Old Campers. . . ," 1955, 4p. illustrated folder. 6615

Back log camp. The Back log idea. Back log camp, Indian lake. Philadelphia, 1911–30. illus. map. Oblong leaflet. Ten undated editions, 1911–30. Also issued in slightly larger format, 1931–41, four undated editions. 6616

Back log camp. The Back log idea. Back log camp, Raquette lake, Adirondacks, N.Y. n.p. 1906? 12p. illus. map. Description of camp at head of North Bay. Back Log was at Raquette from 1900 to 1910. In 1911 it was moved to Indian Lake. 6617

Back log camp. Information about fishing at Back log camp, Indian lake, N.Y. Philadelphia, J.C. Winston, 1927? 4p. port. 6618

Bisby club. Trustees' annual report. v.p. 1881–92. The Bisby Club was made part of the Adirondack League Club in May 1893. 6619

Blance, Cabla. Game preserves. *For & Stream*, Jan. 23, 1904. 62:66. Opening of the Webb Preserve. 6620

A brief resume of the season at Camp Undercliff, Lake Placid. *NYC Lines Mag*, Oct. 1925. 6:no.7:40–41, 104. illus. 6621

Camp Undercliff to open early. *NYC Lines Mag*, Dec. 1924. 5:no.9:54a. illus. N.Y. Central camp on Lake Placid. 6622

Cascade lakes club. Adirondacks. The Cascade lakes club. . . Troy, Troy times art press, n.d. illus. Folded broadside in cover. Probably issued about 1910. Copy in the Hicks Collection, Lake Placid Club. 6623

Cheney, Albert Nelson. Schroon lake—the Texas club. *Am Angler*, Aug. 5, 1882. 2:88. Signed: A.N.C. The Texas Club was a group of Texans who fished in the Adirondacks every year. 6624

Cheney, Albert Nelson. Schroon lake fish-culture association. *Am Angler*, Sept. 9, 1882.

2:165. Signed: A.N.C. Organization and list of officers. 6625

Cheney, Albert Nelson. The Schroon lake fish culture association. *Am Angler*, May 5, 1883. 3:277. The Association is restocking Schroon and Paradox lakes with lake trout. 6626

Coffin, Henry S. Adirondack mountain reserve, 1887–1937. n.p. n.pub. 1937. 4p. Address at the 50th anniversary, Aug. 26, 1937. The Ausable Lake and Mountain Club, controlling the Adirondack Mountain Reserve. 6627

Comstock phonetic alphabet. *Phon M*, June 1847. 1:221–28. Written in phonotypes. The following heading appears at the beginning of this long epic poem: "Written at the request of David P. Holton, Esq. to celebrate the event of engraving the Alphabet on Tahawus, a mountain in northern New York, that is 6,000 feet high, being the loftiest in the Adirondack range." Verses apparently written by Dr. Andrew Comstock. Tahawian Association. 6628

Didymus, pseud. The Webb preserve. *For & Stream*, Jan. 16, 1904. 62:48. 6629

Dr. Webb's preserve open. *For & Stream*, Jan. 2, 1904. 62:10. 6630

Doings at Bisby. *Am Angler*, Oct. 27, 1883. 4:259. The Bisby Club. 6631

Durant, William West. The Brandreth preserve. *For & Stream*, Sept. 18, 1897. 49:226. 6632

Dyer, William H. A summer in Ga-wan-ka. *Emp For*, 1921. 7:75-76. Short description of tract to be opened for development. 6633

Emerson, Edward Waldo. The early years of the Saturday club, 1855–1870. Boston, Houghton, 1918. 515p. front. plates, ports. Contains sketches of the members of the Philosophers' Camp. 6634

Emerson, Ralph Waldo. Journals of Ralph Waldo Emerson, with annotations; ed. by Edward Waldo Emerson and Waldo Emerson Forbes. Boston, Houghton, 1909–14. 10v. fronts. plates, ports. facsims. Notes on Adirondack trip, v.9. p.158–61. Philosophers' Camp. 6635

Fenton, Charles. Then and now. *Recreation* Oct. 1905. 23:363–64. Early days on Number Four. Fenton Game Preserve Association. 6636

Finley, Harry. My vacation at Camp Undercliff. *NYC Lines Mag*, May 1929. 10:no.2:67. illus. Includes climb of Whiteface. 6637

Flickinger, Katherine. Adirondack 46ers. *Ad-i-ron-dac*, July–Aug. 1948. 12:no.4:11. 6638

Forest home club of Saranac Lake, N.Y. Constitution, rules, members. Saranac Lake, N.Y. Adirondack Enterprise press, 1899? 7 leaves. 6639

French, J. Clement. Rod, rifle & rapids in the Adirondacks & Life in the woods. Two lectures. New Haven, Tuttle, Morehouse & Taylor press, 1912. 39p. Hollywood Club, near the Raquette River. 6640

Ga-wan-ka, inc. Okara, a section in Ga-wan-ka, the Adirondack playground. n.p. c1920. 32p. incl. illus. col. plate, folded map. Area in Fulton Chain section with mountain lodges of Japanese architectural design. 6641

Hallock, Charles. The Raquette club. *Harper*, Aug. 1870. 41:321–38. illus. Reprinted in his "The Fishing Tourist." 6642

Howell, Edwin I.H. Ausable lake and mountain club. *St No Mo*, June 1906. 1:no.2:8–9. illus. 6643

Hudowalski, Mrs. Grace (Leech). They of the high hills. *Ad-i-ron-dac*, Nov.–Dec. 1946. 10:no.6:6–7. Adirondack 46ers. 6644

Interest growing in Camp Undercliff. *NYC Lines Mag*, Jan. 1926. 6:no.10:63. illus. Located at Lake Placid. 6645

Jeems, pseud. The Adirondack preserve association. *Am Angler*, July 2, 1887. 12:6. Brief history. 6646

L., W.J. At the sign of the Lone pine. *Ang & Hunt*, June 1910. 2:289–92. illus. The Lone Pine Club on Cranberry Lake. 6647

Lake Champlain yacht club. *For & Stream*, June 23, 1887. 28:469. Editorial on organization. 6648

Lake George association. Annual, 1914–15. n.p. n.d. 26p. 6649

Lake George association. Officers of the Association Aug. 25, 1945. n.p. n.d. 4p. 6650

Lake George association. Report of treasurer 1941–42. n.p. n.d. 3p. Also Report for 1944–45, 3p. 6651

Litchfield, Edward H. Litchfield park. *For & Stream*, Apr. 22, 1899. 52:309. Report on animals in the Park. 6652

McIver, Elizabeth Putnam. Early days at Putnam camp. Reprint of a paper read at the annual meeting of the Keene Valley historical society, September 1941. n.p. n.d. 29p. illus. An account of the beginning and growth of Putnam Camp, with details of life there with the group of famous people visiting it. 6653

Marshall, George. Phelps, Holton and the phonic mountaineers. *Ad-i-ron-dac*, Jan.–Feb. 1954. 18:4–7. Tahawian Association. 6654

Marshall, George. Trailless peaks. *Ad-i-ron-dac*, Sept.–Oct. 1955. 19:96–97. Letter by

Eleanor M. Plum on p.95; comment by the Adirondack Forty-sixers.   6655

Masten, Arthur Haynsworth. Tahawus club, 1898–1933. Burlington, Vt. Free press interstate corp. c1935. 90p. front. plates, port. History of Tahawus Club and its predecessors.   6656

Mather, Frederic Gregory. The Lake Champlain yacht club. *Outing*, Jan. 1889. 13:340–49. illus.   6657

Murray, William M. Camp Manhattan: a retrospect upon some of its early years. N.Y. De Vinne press, 1911. 135p. Privately printed. Copy in the Keene Valley Public Library (Loomis Collection). The camp was located on Lake George.   6658

Nelson, F.G. Summer home of Grasse river outing club. *Recreation*, Jan. 1896. 4:17. illus. History of the Club and list of members. 6659

A new Adirondack preserve. *For & Stream*, June 15, 1901. 56:466. Fenton Game Preserve Association, Inc.   6660

N.Y. Central veterans' association takes over biggest Lake Placid camp. *NYC Lines Mag*, July 1924. 5:no.4:20–23. illus. Camp Undercliff.   6661

North woods Walton club. Utica, N.Y. Curtis & White, 1858. 16p. See comment by L.G. Clark in *The Knickerbocker*, July 1858, 52:89–90, including letter from Cassius M. Clay to C.M. Scholefield. Also note in Jan. 1858 issue, 51:110. Copy owned by Ward Edwards.   6662

North woods Walton club. Programme for 1859. . . Utica, N.Y. Roberts printer, 1859. 27p. Copy in the New York State Library.   6663

Osborn, Minott Auger, ed. Camp Dudley; the story of the first fifty years. N.Y. Huntington press, 1934. 230p. illus. maps on lining papers. YMCA camp—oldest organized camp for boys—located near Westport. 6664

Phelps, Mrs. Orra (Parker). An early Adirondack club. *Cloud Splitter*, May–June 1948. 11:no.3:7–9. Philosophers' Camp.   6665

The Philosophers' camp. *For Leaves*, Summer 1905. 2:no.3:4–8. ports.   6666

Pitcher, Charlotte A. With some famous American authors in the Adirondacks. *NY State Hist Assn Q*, Jan. 1924. 5:40–47. Philosophers' Camp. Stillman, Emerson, Lowell.   6667

Plum, Dorothy Alice. Adirondack rarities. *Ad-i-ron-dac*, July–Aug. 1951. 15:77. The North Woods Walton Club.   6668

Porter, Lewis Morgan. Forty-six plus or minus. *Ad-i-ron-dac*, Sept.–Oct.—Nov.–Dec.

1954. 18:90. Followed by "Report of Resolutions Committee, Adirondack Forty-sixers."   6669

The Ragged lake club. *For & Stream*, Feb. 12, 1885. 24:48. Organization of the Club.   6670

Rockefeller's fight with the woodsmen. *Ang & Hunt*, Oct. 1910. 2:514. Attempt to keep trespassers out of the preserve.   6671

S., C.G. An ideal game preserve. *Recreation*, Apr. 1901. 14:263–65. illus. Litchfield Preserve.   6672

St. Regis yacht club. Club book. . .1898. . . N.Y. Arthur Mountain & co. 1898? 42p. tables. Also published in 1904 and 1907. Copies in the Saranac Lake Free library. 6673

St. Regis yacht club. St. Regis yacht club, fiftieth anniversary, 1897–1947. Upper St. Regis, N.Y. 1947. 95p. plates.   6674

Speare, E. Ray. Hollywood club memoirs. n.p. Privately printed, 1952. 69p. plates. Illustrated with twenty-four photographs.   6675

Spears, Eldridge A. Organization in the Adirondacks. *For & Stream*, Apr. 3, 1909. 72:534. Herkimer Game Protective Association.   6676

Stillman, William James. Autobiography of a journalist. Boston, Houghton, 1901. 2v. fronts. ports. Sections on The Philosophers' Camp and Life in the Wilderness appeared in *The Atlantic*, May and June 1900, 85:463–79, 619–28. Adirondacks: Chs. 10, 12, 13, 15. Philosophers' Camp.   6677

Stillman, William James. The Philosophers' camp: Emerson, Agassiz, Lowell and others in the Adirondacks. *Century*, Aug. 1893. 46:598–606.   6678

Strube, Janet. Back log saga. *Cloud Splitter*, Sept.–Oct. 1944. 7:no.5:12–13. Vacation at Back Log Camp, Indian Lake.   6679

Tahawian association. Minutes of a meeting, Oct. 18, 1847. *In* Carson, R.M.L. Peaks and people of the Adirondacks. Garden City, N.Y. Doubleday, Page, 1927. p.267–69. In addition to planning distribution of phonotypes, the club proposes a road from Keene Flats to the summit of Tahawus (Mt. Marcy).   6680

Thompson, H.H. The Bisby club. *Am Angler*, May 9, 1885. 7:295–96. Signed: H.H.T. 7th Annual Report.   6681

To save the Adirondacks. *Eng & Min J*, May 17, 1890. 49:566. Organization of the Adirondack Preserve Association.   6682

Trout, pseud. Ragged lake club. *For & Stream*, May 21, 1885. 24:331. Description of the lake and the Club.   6683

Undercliff, Veterans' camp, delights guests. *NYC Lines Mag*, Sept. 1924. 5:no.6:30. On Lake Placid.   6684

Ward, Peter A. Hail 46er! *Ad-i-ron-dac*, Mar.–Apr. 1946. 10:no.2:6. The Wendell's dog, Chrissie, aspires to be an Adirondack 46er.   6685

Waterhouse, Alice. Adirondacking. *Cloud Splitter*, Nov. 1940. 3:no.7:5–6. History of the Adirondack 46ers.   6686

The way leads up. *Ad-i-ron-dac*. July–Aug. 1946. 10:no.4:8–9. Adirondack 46ers.   6687

Wendell, Chrissie. As I see them. "A dog's eye view of the 46." *Ad-i-ron-dac*, Nov.–Dec. 1948. 12:no.6:8–9. illus. Chrissie, a spaniel-terrier-spitz was the first canine member of the Adirondack 46ers.   6688

When philosophers camped in wilds; story of how Emerson, Agassiz, Lowell, Stillman and other noted men spent their summers in the Adirondacks—why Longfellow refused to go. *State Service*, Aug. 1919. 3:no.8:43–44. Philosophers' Camp. Includes poem by James S. Owen of Yonkers.   6689

The Wilderness club, inc. The Wilderness club. n.p. n.pub. 1921. 16p. loose plates in pocket, map. On Lake Brantingham, Lewis County.   6690

Wilmurt Lake, Hamilton county, N.Y. *Am Angler*, June 13, 1885. 7:376. On the formation of the Mountain Home Club.   6691

Wilson, Margaret L. The Adirondack park association. *Ad-i-ron-dac*, Sept.–Oct. 1955. 19:89. Statement by the Secretary. The Association was organized May 1954.   6692

Wolcott, W.E. The Walton club. *For & Stream*, May 22, 1897. 48:402–3. North Woods Walton Club. Name originally Brown's Tract Association.   6693

Ziegenfuss, H.L. Piseco and T-lake falls. *For & Stream*, Feb. 16, 1882. 18:44–45. Founding of the Piseco Club in 1842.   6694

BIOGRAPHY

COLLECTIVE

Adirondack old timer. *Northeast Log*, Sept. 1954. 3:no.3:10–11. illus. 6695

Biographical review. This volume contains biographical sketches of the leading citizens of Clinton and Essex counties, New York. . . Boston, Biographical review publishing co. 1896. 543p. ports. 6696

Burger, William H. The Hands of Elizabethtown: two outstanding jurists belonging to the north country. *No Country Life*, Fall 1951. 5:no.4:46–49. ports. Augustus N. Hand and Learned Hand. 6697

Burger, William H. Some conservation men. *No Country Life*, Summer 1950. 4:no.3:4–9. ports. Biographical sketches of several men in the Conservation Department stationed in the Adirondack area. Clinton West, Walter Rice, William E. Petty, Lucius Russell. 6698

Cutter, William Richard, ed. Genealogical and family history of northern New York, a record of the achievements of her people in the making of a commonwealth and the founding of a nation. N.Y. Lewis historical publishing co. 1910. 3v. fronts. illus. ports. 6699

Dowling, Victor James. Heroes of America's origins: Isaac Jogues, Rene Goupil, Joseph Lalande. *Ill Cath Hist Rev*, July 1926. 9:no.1:39–55. 6700

Essex county republican annual, 1889, 1891–1894. Port Henry, N.Y. & Keeseville, N.Y. W. Lansing & son, 1889, 1891–94. 5v. Published also as the "Plattsburgh N.Y. Sentinel Annual," 1891–95. The sketches were written by Hannah Lansing (pen name, Nell Clifford). Sketches and portraits of noted men and women of the Champlain Valley and Adirondacks. 6701

Gerster, Arpad Geyza Charles. Etching as a diversion. *Med Pick*, Oct. 1916. 2:363–68. ports. illus. Includes portrait and sketch of Alvah Dunning. Also comments on Hank Bradley, Wesley Bates and Bill Dart (guides). 6702

Hosmer, Ralph Sheldon. Some Adirondack pioneers. *Bul Schools*, Mar. 1944. 30:255–58. ports. DeWitt Clinton, Ebenezer Emmons,

Franklin B. Hough, Verplanck Colvin. Story of steps leading to formation of the Forest Preserve. 6703

Lattimer, Grace C. and Clark, Lucy. Two number one men of the Adirondacks. *Up Mo*, July 1941. 2:no.4:16–17. ports. Biographical sketches of Jack Garren and Maurice Callahan. 6704

Martin, Newell. Two great Adirondack guides. *High Spots*, Jan. 1936. 13:no.1:29–31. Reminiscences of Willard Gibbs and William James. 6705

Mather, Fred. Men I have fished with; sketches of characters and incidents with rod and gun. . . N.Y. Forest & stream publishing co. 1897. 371p. front. ports. 6706

Mather, Fred. My angling friends: being a second series of sketches of men I have fished with. . . N.Y. Forest & stream publishing co. 1901. 369p. front. port. Includes Alvah Dunning, Ned Buntline, Charles Hallock. 6707

Other Adirondack matters. *Woods & Wat*, Winter 1901–2. 4:no.4:12–14. illus. Alvah Dunning and Orson Phelps. 6708

Porter, Mrs. Marjorie (Lansing). The Slaters carry on. *No Country Life*, Spring 1948. 2:no.2:42–43. From the *Essex County Republican*. Family of blacksmiths in Ausable Forks. Napoleon Slater. 6709

Robie, Edward H. A mining family. *Min & Met*, Dec. 1944. The Linneys. 6710

S. Incidents of Adirondack history. *For & Stream*, Apr. 24, 1897. 48:323–24. Notes on Alvah Dunning, Nick Stoner and Nat Foster. 6711

Simms, Jeptha Root. Trappers of New York; or, A biography of Nicholas Stoner and Nathaniel Foster together with anecdotes of other celebrated hunters. . . Albany, J. Munsell, 1850. 280p. plates, ports. 2d edition, 1851; 3d edition, 1857. Reprinted in 1860, 1871 and 1935. The 1935 edition published in St. Johnsville, N.Y. includes "new supplementary matter by Lou D. MacWethy." 6712

Some interesting stories of noblemen who came to live in the United States. *For Leaves*,

Spring 1909. 6:no.1:15–21. illus. James LeRay de Chaumont and Joseph Bonaparte.   6713

Spencer, Alfred. Spencer's roster of native sons (and daughters). For each locality upstate New York, a roster of its eminent sons and daughters from earliest settlement to the present time. Bath, N.Y. Courier press, c1941. 287p.   6714

Titus, John H. Adirondack pioneers: biographical sketches and anecdotes of men that made the Adirondacks famous. Troy, N.Y. Troy times art press, 1899. 47p. ports.   6715

INDIVIDUAL BIOGRAPHY

*

Arranged by biographee

Alexander, Edward Johnston. The man and the legend. *High Spots Yrbk*, 1939. p.39–44. Anson H. Allen of bear fight fame.   6716

Brown, Charles Walter. Ethan Allen, of Green mountain fame, a hero of the Revolution. Chicago, W.A. Donohue & co. c1902. 261p. "The Capture of Ticonderoga," p.83–100.   6717

Chipman, Daniel. Memoir of Col. Seth Warner. To which is added the life of Col. Ethan Allen, by Jared Sparks. Middlebury, Vt. L.W. Clark, 1848. 226p. Life of Ethan Allen, p.87–226.   6718

Moore, Hugh. Memoir of Col. Ethan Allen. . . Plattsburg, N.Y. O.R. Cook, 1834. 252p.   6719

Pell, John. Ethan Allen. Boston, Houghton, 1929. 331p. front. plates, ports. map, plan, facsims. Attack on Ticonderoga, Chs. 10 and 11.   6720

Spargo, John. Ethan Allen at Ticonderoga. Rutland, Vt. Tuttle co. 1926. 34p.   6721

Wing, Leonard F. Ethan Allen, the soldier; an address. *Ver Hist Soc Proc*, Mar. 1937. n.s.5:5–21.   6722

Mount Allen's namesake lives in Massachusetts. *High Spots*, Mar. 1923. 1:no.5:3–4. ports. Biographical sketch of Rev. Frederick B. Allen. Reproduction of pencil sketch of "Old Mountain Phelps" by Mr. Allen's daughter, Mrs. B. Reston Clark. See also Frederick Lewis Allen's "Frederick Baylies Allen: a Memoir," privately printed, 1929. Pages 28–29 are on the naming of Mount Allen and include quotations from Carson's "Peaks and People."   6723

My neighbour. A monthly journal of the Episcopal city mission. Boston, 1892– The issue for Oct. 1923 (v.32, no.10) contains articles by and about Frederick B. Allen, with portraits.   6724

Steele, Vern. Benedict Arnold. *No Country Life*, Spring 1953. 7:no.2:40–41. Battle of Valcour Island.   6725

Dr. E.M. Austin dies in Tupper Lake. *Lumber Camp News*, Aug. 1948. 10:no.4:5. Brief biography of Eugene M. Austin, doctor at Tupper Lake since 1891.   6726

Conners, Frank P. Irving Bacheller and his "writing" school. *No Country Life*, Fall 1946. 1:no.1:20–22. illus. Condensed from the *North Countryman*.   6727

Packard, Edward Newman. Edward R. Baldwin. *Am Rev Tub*, July 1950. 62:1B:1–2.   6728

Houghton, Harris A. Dr. William Beaumont: his life and associations in Plattsburgh, N.Y. *NY Acad Med Bul*, Apr. 1931. ser.2:no.7:287–301. illus. See also Jesse Shire Myers' "Life and Letters of Dr. William Beaumont. . ." St. Louis, Mo. 1912.   6729

Steiner, William R. Dr. William Beaumont, an appreciation. *In* Plattsburgh, N.Y. Physicians hospital. Medical and surgical year book, 1930. p.191–97. plate. The plate is a facsimile of the title page of Beaumont's famous book, "Experiments and Observations on the Gastric Juice. . . ," published in Plattsburgh in 1833.   6730

Martin, Newell. Charlie Beede. *High Spots*, July 1933. 10:no.3:9–10. port. (Great Adirondack Guides, no.3.)   6731

Cummings, William A.E. "Verde Beede." *High Spots*, Apr. 1932. 9:no.2:14–15. (Historical Adirondack Character Series, no.7.)   6732

Byrne, Mrs. Margaret H. (Myers). The Walter Biesemeyer memorial leanto. *Ad-i-ron-dac*, July–Aug. 1955. 19:77. Dedication. Photograph in Sept.–Oct. issue, 19:91.   6733

Byrne, Wayne H. In memoriam—a lean-to. *NYS Con*, Aug.–Sept. 1955. 10:no.1:35. Memorial to Walter Biesemeyer.   6734

Walter Biesemeyer, beloved ADKer, dies. *Ad-i-ron-dac*, Sept.–Oct. 1953. 17:99.   6735

Brown, George L. Bainbridge Bishop. *For & Stream*, Apr. 29, 1905. 64:332. Death of angler well known in Lake Champlain area.   6736

Mather, Fred. Men I have fished with. LXII: Wallace Eugene Blackford. *For & Stream*, Mar. 5, 1898. 50:188–89.   6737

Marshall, Robert. Mills Blake. *High Spots*, Mar. 1930. 7:no.1:13.   6738

Marshall, Robert. Mills Blake, Adirondack explorer. *Ad-i-ron-dac*, May–June 1951. 15: 46–48. port.   6739

Bertin, Georges. . . .Joseph Bonaparte en Amérique. . . Paris, Librairie de la Nouvelle revue, 1893. 422p. port. folded tables. Adirondacks, Ch.2.   6740

Malcolm, James. Former king lived in northern New York. *State Service*, Jan. 1931. p.41–44. port. Joseph Bonaparte.   6741

Ralph, Alta M. Count of "Little France"; a Bonaparte in northern New York. *Americana*, Apr. 1924. 18:151–65. Joseph Bonaparte's sojourn in the Adirondacks.   6742

Tomlinson, Everett Titsworth. When the king of Spain was an exile in northern New York. *Ind*, Feb. 20, 1902. 54:449–52. Joseph Bonaparte.   6743

Brace, Charles Loring. The life of Charles Loring Brace, chiefly told in his own letters; ed. by his daughter. . . N.Y. Scribner, 1894. 503p. front. port. Preface signed: Emma Brace. Adirondack letters, p.205, 223, 344, 464.   6744

Press comment on the death of Byron Brewster. *No Country Life*, Winter 1954. 8:no.1:43–44. Justice of the State Supreme Court and native of Essex County.   6745

Burnham, John Bird. Gens des bois. I: Guy Brittell. *For & Stream*, Jan. 7, 1899. 52:3–4. Adirondack trapper.   6746

Adams, Charles Francis, 1835–1915. Richard Henry Dana, a biography. Boston, Houghton, 1890–91. 2v. fronts. (ports.). "Adirondacks and John Brown," v.1, p.145–64.   6747

Atkinson, Eleanor. The soul of John Brown; recollections of the great abolitionist by his son. *Am Mag*, Oct. 1909. 68:633–43. illus. ports. Includes life at North Elba.   6748

Barton, William Eleazer. John Brown and Abraham Lincoln. Response to the John Brown memorial association in its presentation of a picture to Lake Placid club, delivered by Rev. William E. Barton, D.D., at the Club on May 9, 1928. Lake Placid Club, N.Y. 1928. 4p. Reprint from *Lake Placid News*, May 18, 1928. 100 copies printed. Copy in the John Carter Brown Library, Brown University.   6749

Bowditch, Henry Ingersoll. Letter to a lady patient to whom was promised an account of a visit to John Brown's grave. *In* Von Holst, Hermann. John Brown; edited by Frank Preston Stearns. Boston, Cupples & Hurd, 1889. p.197–203. plate. Written from Saranac Lake, July 27, 1865. Addressed to Mrs. H-.   6750

Brewster, O. Byron. John Brown of North Elba. *NY Hist*, Oct. 1952. 33:406–12.   6751

Brewster, W.H. and Brewster, B.B. John Brown. A brief biography, with letters by the liberator. . . n.p. n.pub. n.d. 24p. Pamphlet sold at the John Brown farm in 1929.   6752

The burial of John Brown. *NY Illus News*, Dec. 24, 1859. 1:81, 84–85. ports. illus. Other illustrations on pages 92–93. Sketches made at North Elba by reporter who attended the funeral.   6753

Carmer, Carl Lamson. John Brown and his legend. *Yankee*, Apr. 1953. 17:no.4:41–46. ports. illus. *Yankee* visits the scene, p.47–52.   6754

Clemens, Will M. John Brown, the American reformer. II. *Pet Mag*, Feb. 1898. n.s.8: 107–16. At North Elba.   6755

Collins, John O. "John Brown's body." *Four Tr News*, May 1903. 4:241–43. illus.   6756

Dailey, William Nelson Potter. Incidents at John Brown's funeral. *State ·Service*, Jan.–Mar. 1924. 10:30–33. illus. Author's name is misspelled in article (Bailey).   6757

Dana, Richard Henry Jr. How we met John Brown: a letter. *Atlan*, July 1871. 28:1–9. Entertained by John Brown at North Elba, on trip from Westport to Indian Pass, etc.   6758

Featherstonehough, Thomas. The final burial of the followers of John Brown. *New Eng M*, Apr. 1901. n.s.24:128–34. Burial at North Elba.   6759

Flick, Alexander Clarence. John Brown memorial statue. *NY Hist*, July 1935. 16: 329–32.   6760

Gould, Elizabeth Porter. John Brown at North Elba. *Outlook*, Nov. 21, 1896. 54: 909–11.   6761

Higginson, Thomas Wentworth. A visit to John Brown's household in 1859. *In* his Contemporaries. Boston,. Houghton, 1900. p.219–43. Reprinted from James Redpath's "Life of Captain John Brown," 1859.   6762

Hughes, Beatrice. The John Brown farm and homestead. *Conservationist*, Aug. 1921. 4:122–24. illus. Reprinted in *State Service*, Sept. 1922, 6,i.e.8:303–5, with title "Thousands Visit John Brown's Grave."   6763

John Brown. *Macmil*, Oct. 1888. 58:443–52.   6764

The John Brown farm. *In* New York (state). Fisheries, game and forest commission. Annual report, 1896. p.470–83. Quotes Higginson and other sources. Account of the official dedication of the farm as state property. 6765

John Brown memorial association. John Brown in bronze, 1850–1859, containing program and addresses of the dedicatory ceremony and unveiling of the monument of John Brown, May 9, 1935. . . Lake Placid Club, N.Y. 1935. 41p. plates, illus. ports. 6766

John Brown memorial association. . . .35th annual pilgrimage to the grave of John Brown. . . Lake Placid, N.Y. 1955. unpaged. ports. illus. 6767

John Brown's grave in Adirondacks; home of noted abolitionist before he was hanged in Virginia; old farm now maintained by the state. Property given to Brown to help in escape of slaves. *State Service*, Dec. 1917. 1:no.5:33–36. illus. port. 6768

Lee, Francis W. John Brown's grave. *Gard & For*, Mar. 11, 1896. 9:108–9. Letter to the editor quoting Kate Field on the inscription on John Brown's boulder. 6769

Lee, Mary. John Brown rests amid the mountains. . . *NY Times Mag*, Oct. 20, 1929. p.7, 23. illus. port. Describes home at North Elba. 6770

Life of John Brown; a sketch. n.p. n.pub. 19—? 16p. 6771

Lyman, Henry Harrison. Oration at North Elba, N.Y. . .July 21, 1896. *In* New York (state). Fisheries, game and forest commission. Annual report, 1896. p.483–94. Author's second initial given erroneously as *L*. 6772

McClellan, Katherine Elizabeth. A hero's grave in the Adirondacks. Saranac Lake, N.Y. c1896. 20p. illus. port. John Brown's life in the Adirondacks. 6773

Mather, Frederic Gregory. Cottage and grave of old John Brown. *Fr Leslies Pop Mo*, Nov. 1891. 32:621–24. illus. 6774

Nichols, May Ellis. An Adirondack pilgrimage. *Nat Mag*, July 1903. 18:476–79. illus. John Brown. 6775

Orcutt, Samuel. History of Torrington, Connecticut, from its first settlement in 1737, with biographies and genealogies. Albany, J. Munsell, 1878. 817p. front. illus. plates, ports. John Brown at North Elba, p.335–39. Poem by W.E. Channing, "Burial of John Brown," p.413–19. 6776

Phillips, Wendell. Burial of John Brown. *In* his Speeches, lectures and letters. Boston, Redpath, 1863. v.1, p.289–93. Delivered at

John Brown's grave, North Elba, Dec. 8, 1859. 6777

A pilgrimage to John Brown's mountain. *Knick Mag*, Mar. 1862. 59:232–37. 6778

Redpath, James. Public life of John Brown, with an autobiography of his childhood and youth. Boston, Thayer & Eldridge, 1860. 407p. port. plates. 6779

Rex, Millicent B. John Brown at Lake Placid. *Americana*, Apr. 1931. 25:141–49. 6780

Sanborn, Franklin Benjamin. The life and letters of John Brown. . . Boston, Roberts, 1885. 645p. ports. facsims. 2d edition, 1891. Adirondacks, p.90–115. 6781

Sanborn, Franklin Benjamin. Memoirs of John Brown, written for Rev. Samuel Orcutt's History of Torrington, Ct. with Memorial verses by William Ellery Channing. Concord, Mass. 1878. 107p. ports. illus. Channing's poem "The Burial of John Brown," p.101–7. 6782

Sanborn, Franklin Benjamin. Recollections of seventy years. Boston, Badger, 1909. 2v. fronts. plates. port. facsim. Concord and North Elba (John Brown), v.1, ch.4. 6783

Santway, Alfred W. A brief sketch of the life of John Brown. . . Watertown, N.Y. Alfred W. Santway, c1934. 20p. port. illus. 6784

Shaw, Albert. John Brown in the Adirondacks. *R of Rs*, Sept. 1896. 14:311–17. illus. port. 6785

A sketch of the life of John Brown. n.p. n.pub. n.d. 12p. Published before the appearance of Sanborn's "Life and Letters of John Brown" (1885). 6786

Thompson, Mrs. Ruth (Brown). Ruth Thompson's last letter to her father, written at North Elba, November 27, 1859. *Mass Hist Soc Proc*, Jan.–Mar. 1908. 41:330. 6787

Van Rensselaer, Mrs. Marianna (Griswold). John Brown's grave. *Gard & For*, Jan. 29, 1896. 9:47. Letter to the editor. 6788

Villard, Oswald Garrison. John Brown, 1800–1859; a biography fifty years after. Boston, Houghton, 1911. 738p. plates, front. facsims. ports. map. Extensive bibliography, p.689–709. 6789

Young, Joshua. The funeral of John Brown. *New Eng Mag*, Apr. 1904. n.s.30:229–43. illus. ports. 6790

F., M.H. A brave life. *Overland*, Oct. 1885. ser.2:6:360–67. Life of wife of Capt. John Brown, Mary Anne (Day) Brown. 6791

Lyman, David Russell. Lawrason Brown, 1871–1937. Reprinted from the *American Review of Tuberculosis*, Mar. 1938, 37:361–66. Signed: D.R.L. 6792

Porter, Mrs. Ma. jorie (Lansing). Lewis Stacy Brown, artist. *No Country Life*, Winter 1952. 6:no.1:48–49. port. Native of Chazy. 6793

Carson, Russell Mack Little. W. Scott Brown. *High Spots*, Jan. 1935. 12:no.1:26. port. Obituary. 6794

Banks, Robert Lenox. Protector William H. Burnett. *For & Stream*, Dec. 12, 1896. 47:472. 6795

Derieux, James C. John Burnham—conservationist and hunter. *Field & S*, May 1929. 34:no.1:20–22, 71–73. illus. Chief Game Protector of New York state. 6796

Derieux, James C. There'll never be a time when everybody is broke. *Am Mag*, May 1932. 113:no.5:67, 88, 90. illus. Life of John Bird Burnham. 6797

Spears, Raymond Smiley. The New York chief protector. *For & Stream*, Nov. 25, 1905. 65:437. On appointment of John B. Burnham. 6798

Harmes, Edward A. John Burroughs in the Adirondacks. *Ad-i-ron-dac*, Nov.–Dec. 1953. 17:112, 127. 6799

Riley, Ruth V. John Burroughs. *High Spots*, July 1931. 8:no.3:17–18. (Historical Adirondack Character Series, no.5.) 6800

Hall, C. Eleanor. Joe Call, the Lewis giant. *NY Folk Q*, Spring 1953. 9:5–27. 6801

Hopkins, Arthur S. Russ Carson. *Cloud Splitter*, Apr. 1940. 3:no.3:2–3. 6802

Brandreth, Paulina. Old Leviathan of Burnt mountain lake. *For & Stream*, Jan. 4, 1913. 80:5–6, 31. Signed: Paul Brandreth. Day spent with Reuben Cary. 6803

Brandreth, Paulina. Reuben Cary: forest patriarch. *High Spots*, July 1934. 11:no.3: 29–32. (Great Adirondack Guides, no.7.) Signed: Paul Brandreth. 6804

Brandreth, Paulina. Reuben Cary—forest patriarch; a biographical sketch of a well known Adirondack guide. *For & Stream*, June 20–27, 1914. 82:821–22, 854–55. Signed: Paul Brandreth. 6805

Bishop, Morris. Champlain, the life of fortitude. N.Y. Knopf, 1948. 364p. illus. map. 6806

Constantin-Weyer, Maurice. Samuel de Champlain. *Rev Heb*, Dec. 27, 1930, Jan. 3–10, 1931. 39:387–418; 40:36–52, 196–227. 6807

Hill, Henry Wayland. Samuel Champlain and the Lake Champlain tercentenary: an address by Senator W.H. Hill. . .secretary of the New York tercentenary commission. Delivered before the Vermont historical society on November 10, 1908. *Ver Hist Soc Proc*, 1908–9 i.e. 1907–8. p.39–61. 6808

Paltsits, Victor Hugo. Samuel Champlain. *Travel*, July 1909. 14:452–56. illus. 6809

A.N. Cheney. *For & Stream*, Aug. 24, 1901. 57:141. His accomplishments. 6810

Hill, William H. A.N. Cheney and his gun. *NYS Con*, Aug.–Sept. 1955. 10:no.1:8. illus. See letter from Dan Brenan in issue for Oct.–Nov. 1955, 10:no.2:41. 6811

Hudowalski, Mrs. Grace (Leech). He works with angels. *No Country Life*, Winter 1951. 5:no.1:12–14. port. Biographical sketch of craftsman who manufactures Christmas tree ornaments—James Cheney, descendant of John Cheney. 6812

Riley, Ruth V. John Cheney, "the mighty hunter." *High Spots*, June 1930. 7:no.2:12–13. port. (Historical Adirondack Character Series, no.1.) 6813

Tahawus, pseud. John Cheney and the bear. *For & Stream*, Aug. 5, 1875. 4:413. Description of a battle between Cheney and a bear; includes a letter from Cheney's wife on his condition. 6814

Marshall, Robert. Herbert Clark. *High Spots*, Oct. 1933. 10:no.4:8–11. (Great Adirondack Guides, no.4.) 6815

Allen, George P. A history and genealogical record of the Alling-Allens of New Haven, Conn. the descendants of Roger Alling, first. . .from 1639 to the present time. New Haven, Conn. Price, Lee & Adkins, 1899. 317p. incl. plates, ports. front. Biographical sketch of Verplanck Colvin, p.71–79. Separately published as a ten-page pamphlet with title "Biographical Sketch of Verplanck Colvin of Albany, N.Y. . ." New Haven, 1899. 6816

Bayle, Francis L. An appreciation of Verplanck Colvin. *High Spots*, Oct. 1934. 11: no.4:29–31. 6817

Boos, John E. Verplanck Colvin. *Cloud Splitter*, Jan. 1943. 6:no.1:2. Personal recollections. 6818

Colvin. *In* Reynolds, Cuyler. Hudson-Mohawk genealogical and family memoirs. . . N.Y. 1911. v.1, p.457–62. Verplanck Colvin. 6819

Miller, Roland B. Verplanck Colvin. *NYS Con*, Feb.–Mar. 1954. 8:no.4:20–23. port. illus. Supplementary note in Dec. 1954–Jan. 1955 issue, p. 32. 6820

Lewis, Tayler. My old schoolmaster. A paper read at the University convocation of the State of New York, July 8, 1874. . .With a biographical sketch of the Rev. Cyrus Comstock. Albany, Weed, Parsons & co.

1875. 23p. Cyrus Comstock was first Congregational minister in Essex County; church at Lewis, N.Y.   6821

Smith, George H. Cyrus Comstock, father of Congregational churches in Essex county. *No Country Life*, Winter 1948. 2:no.1:42–43. illus.   6822

Hahn, Joe. Poet and prophet. *Up Mo*, Oct. 1941. 2:no.7:16–17. port. Life of Marc Cook.   6823

Thomas Creighton. Oval wood dish vice-president dies at Tupper Lake. *Lumber Camp News*, Apr. 1952. 13:no.12:20. port.   6824

Mather, Fred. Men I have fished with. LX: Amos J. Cummings. *For & Stream*, Dec. 11, 1897. 49:472–73.   6825

Fosburgh, Peter W. Pat Cunningham. *NYS Con*, Sept.–Oct. 1952. 7:no.1:17. port. Brief obituary.   6826

Henry Platt Cushing. *Science*, June 3, 1921. n.s.53:510–12. Eulogies by J.M. Clarke, C.H. Smyth and R. Ruedemann.   6827

Clark, John Murray. A modern wandering scholar. *Spectator*, Oct. 6, 1900. 85:453–54. Unsigned. Thomas Davidson.   6828

Dublin, Louis I. Thomas Davidson: educator for democracy. *Am Scholar*, Spring 1948. 17:201–11.   6829

James, William. A knight-errant of the intellectual life: Thomas Davidson: who tried to "be on earth what good people hope to be in heaven." *McClure*, May 1905. 25:3–11. illus. Founder of the Summer School of the Culture Sciences, Glenmore. (Keene, N.Y.)   6830

Knight, William Angus. Memorials of Thomas Davidson, the wandering scholar. Boston & London, Ginn, 1907. 241p. front. (port.). Glenmore, p.55–79, 107–19.   6831

A modern Socrates—minus Zantippe. *Cur Lit*, July 1905. 39:90–91. port. Thomas Davidson.   6832

Thomas Davidson. *In* Knight, William Angus. Some nineteenth century Scotsmen. . . Edinburgh, Oliphant, Anderson & Ferrier, 1903. p.351–63. Bibliography of Davidson's works, p.448–56. Partially reprinted in Knight's "Memorials of Thomas Davidson."   6833

George Dawson. *For & Stream*, Feb. 22, 1883. 20:61. Obituary.   6834

Simmons, Louis J. Mrs. Ida DeLancett, 83, of old Tupper Lake family dies. . . *Lumber Camp News*, May 1940. 12:no.1:4. She and her husband operated early hotel in Tupper Lake.   6835

Burger, William H. Melvil Dewey. *No Country Life*, Spring 1951. 5:no.2:26–28, 43. 6836

Dawe, George Grosvenor. Melvil Dewey: inspirer: doer—1851–1931; biographic compilation. Lake Placid Club, N.Y. 1932. 391p. plates, ports. facsims. map. Lake Placid Club, p.230–50.   6837

Gray, Allison. That darned literary fellow across the lake; interview with Melvil Dewey. *Am Mag*, Apr. 1927. 103:no.4:56–59, 128–32. illus.   6838

Jast, L. Stanley. Recollections of Melvil Dewey. *Lib Rev*, Autumn 1934. no.31:285–90.   6839

Kudlaker, J.S. Melvil Dewey; the sage of Lake Placid. *Lib Misc*, Nov. 1913. 2:68–70. ports.   6840

Rider, Fremont. Melvil Dewey. Chicago, American library association, 1944. 151p. front. illus. ports. (American Library Pioneers no.6.)   6841

Longstreth, Thomas Morris. Alfred Lee Donaldson. 1866–1923. In memoriam. Nov. 6, 1923. n.p. n.pub. n.d. 4p. Unpaged leaflet.   6842

O'Neill, J.F. Alfred Lee Donaldson, historian of the Adirondacks. *J Outd Life*, Nov. 1924. 21:670–71, 673. port.   6843

Illick, Joseph S. A quarter of a century of service. *NYS Ranger Sch*, 1944. p.15–16. Tribute to James Francis Dubuar.   6844

White, William Chapman. The last of the Dukettes. *No Country Life*, Fall 1952. 6:no.4: 45–46. Reprinted from the New York *Herald Tribune*.   6845

Mather, Fred. Alvah Dunning. *For & Stream*, Mar. 22, 1902. 58:239–41. port. 6846

Mather, Fred. Men I have fished with. XXXVIII: Alvah Dunning. *For & Stream*, Apr. 10, 1897. 48:288–89.   6847

Norris, Isaac T. A meeting with Alvah Dunning. *For & Stream*, Mar. 22, 1902. 58:231.   6848

Marshall, George. Dr. Ely and his Adirondack map. *NY Hist*, Jan. 1954. 35:32–48. port. Also issued as a separate without portrait. Reprinted in *The Ad-i-ron-dac*, May–June 1954, 18:44–49, 53. Extracts in *Living Wilderness*, Autumn 1954, no.50:36. Reviewed in *Appalachia*, June 15, 1954, mag. no.118:113. William Watson Ely.   6849

Hopkins, Albert. Sketch of Dr. Emmons. *Wms Q*, June 1864. 11:260–69. Author's name supplied by the Williams College Library. Ebenezer Emmons.   6850

Marcou, Jules. Biographical notice of Ebenezer Emmons. *Am Geol*, Jan. 1891. 7:1–23. port.   6851

Charles Fenton. *Field & S*, Nov. 1905. 10:718. Notice of the death of the proprietor of Fenton House.   6852

Charles Fenton. *For & Stream*, Oct. 14, 1905. 65:309. Obituary.   6853

Burnham, John Bird. Gens des bois. II: Guy Ferguson. *For & Stream*, Mar. 11, 1899. 52:182–83.   6854

Porter, Mrs. Marjorie (Lansing). The garden on a sand dune. *No Country Life*, Spring 1947. 1:no.3:44–45. port. Mrs. Olive Fifield's summer home on Cumberland Bay.   6855

Haviland. In the Adirondacks—Folingsby's pond. *For & Stream*, Jan. 8, 1874. 1:340. Story of Moses Folingsby, the Englishman for whom the pond was named.   6856

Headley, Joel Tyler. Folingsby's pond. *Hours at Home*, Aug.–Sept. 1869. 9:352–59, 427–35. Life of man for whom the pond was named.   6857

Hudowalski, Mrs. Grace (Leech). Folingsby's. *Cloud Splitter*, June 1940. 3:no.5:12, 14.   6858

Curtiss, Arthur Leslie Byron-. The life and adventures of Nat Foster, trapper and hunter of the Adirondacks. Utica, N.Y. Thos. J. Griffiths, 1897. 286p. plates. A new edition with second preface was published in Boonville, N.Y. Willard press, 1912, 217p. port.   6859

Colonel William F. Fox. *In* New York (state). Forest, fish and game commission. Annual report, 1907–8–9. p.72–77. port.   6860

Carmer, Carl Lamson. Come all ye gallant shanty-boys. *In* his The Hudson. N.Y. Farrar & Rinehart, ᶜ1939. p.366–77. Sketch of "Yankee John" Galusha.   6861

John Galusha dies at Minerva, N.Y. *Lumber Camp News*, Oct. 1950. 12:no.6:17.   6862

An Adirondack memorial. *For & Stream*, Apr. 20, 1907. 68:613. Memorial of Eva Gardiner, wife of "Ned Buntline."   6863

Baldwin, Edward Robinson. Tributes to Dr. Leroy Upson Gardner. *Occup Med*, July 1947. 4:no.1:1–16. port. Includes list of Dr. Gardner's writings.   6864

Adirondack guide dies. *Lumber Camp News*, Dec. 1950. 12:no.8:10. John Garland.   6865

Pell, John. The saga of Will Gilliland, *NY Hist*, Oct. 1932. 13:390–403.   6866

Walworth, Hiram. William Gilliland. *Am Hist Register*, Aug. 1895. 2:1438–44. port.   6867

Wardenburg, Martha Bigelow. Will Gilliland, pioneer of the valley of Lake Champlain. *Ver Hist Soc Proc*, Sept. 1941. n.s.9: 186–97.   6868

Trudell, Theresa. Joe Gokey of Tupper Lake. *NY Folk Q*, Autumn 1954. 10:208–11.   6869

Brown, J. Hypkin. A chapter in the life of Daniel Gorman, M.D. *For Leaves*, Autumn 1905. 2:no.4:4–25. illus.   6870

Jogues, Isaac. Notice sur René Goupil. *In* Jesuits. Letters from Missions (North America). Jesuit relations. Cleveland, 1896. v.28, p.116–35. Text in French and English. 6871

Juvenal, pseud. One of the veterans. *For & Stream*, Oct. 17, 1906. 61:295. illus. port. Life of Nathaniel S. Graves.   6872

Seth Green. *Am Angler*, Aug. 25, 1888. 14:121. Obituary of superintendent of the Fulton Chain hatchery; editorial comment, p.113.   6873

Death of Frank Grey, well known guide. *Sport Rev*, Feb. 20, 1909. 35:201.   6874

Clarke, John Mason. James Hall of Albany— geologist and palaeontologist, 1811–1898. Albany, 1921. 565p. 2d printing, 1932. Includes Hall's work in the Adirondack counties of the New York State Geological Survey, beginning in 1836, and his part in the great controversies with Emmons.   6875

A memoir of Charles Hallock. *Wild Mag*, Apr. 1889. 2:223–24. port.   6876

Dubuar, James Francis. J. Otto Hamele (the man and his work). *NYS Ranger Sch*, 1949. p.5–8, 14. port. Hamele was responsible for the Rich Lumber Company's gift of land for the Ranger School of the College of Forestry.   6877

Reed, Frank A. J. Otto Hamele. *NYS Ranger Sch*, 1949. p.41–42. illus. Address, August 5, 1949, at the dedication of bronze plaque at the Ranger School.   6878

In memoriam—John Hammond. Chicago, P.F. Pettibone & co. 1890. 90p. port. Prominent citizen of northern New York.   6879

Mr. S.H. Hammond as sportsman and author. *Sport Rev*, Jan. 13, 1906. 29:36. Samuel H. Hammond.   6880

Dobson, Meade C. Mel Hathaway's clearing. *Cloud Splitter*, Oct. 13, 1942. 5:no.7:4–5. Reprinted in *The Ad-i-ron-dac*, May–June 1945, 9:no.3:5.   6881

Plum, Eleanor Mary. Mel Hathaway and the early days of Johns brook lodge. *Ad-i-ron-dac*, May–June 1952. 16:53, 58.   6882

Riley, Ruth V. Reverend Joel T. Headley. *High Spots*, Dec. 1930–Jan. 1931. 7:no.4—8: no.1:19–20. illus. (Historical Adirondack Character Series, no.3.)   6883

Hudowalski, Mrs. Grace (Leech). Adirondac tragedy. *Cloud Splitter*, Jan. 1940. 2:no.8:2–3.

Sequel to *Iron Dam;* continues story of David Henderson.   6884

Hudowalski, Mrs. Grace (Leech). Iron dam. *Cloud Splitter*, Dec. 1939. 2:no.7:8–9. Discovery of iron ore by David Henderson.   6885

Johnstone, John. A sermon preached in the Presbyterian church, Jersey city, September 14, 1845, on occasion of the death of David Henderson. Jersey City, N.J. 1845. 39p. 6886

Schaefer, Paul A. Adirondack pilgrimage. *Cloud Splitter*, Sept.–Oct. 1945. 8:no.5:2–5. Account of Henderson Memorial trip.   6887

Hill, John Henry. John William Hill. An artist's memorial. N.Y. 1888. 15p. plates, front. port. Short life of artist who accompanied Ebenezer Emmons on the New York State Geological Survey.   6888

Storey, Moorfield and Emerson, Edward W. Ebenezer Rockwood Hoar: a memoir. Boston, Houghton, 1911. 335p. front. port. Philosophers' Camp, p.144–48.   6889

Barnes, Homer F. Charles Fenno Hoffman. N.Y. Columbia university press, 1930. 361p. Doctoral dissertation, Columbia University.   6890

Charles Fenno Hoffman. *Wild Mag*, Sept. 1888. 1:232–33.   6891

Hoffman, Charles Fenno. The vigil of faith and other poems. Campe's edition. Nurnberg & New York, F. Campe & co. 1846. 68p. Memoir, by Rufus Willmot Griswold, p.v–viii. Copy in the British Museum, London.   6892

Riley, Ruth V. Charles Fenno Hoffman. *High Spots*, Sept. 1930. 7:no.3:6–8. illus. (Historical Adirondack Character Series, no.2.)   6893

Carson, Russell Mack Little. Harvey Holt. *High Spots*, Jan. 1934. 11:no.1:18–22. port. (Great Adirondack Guides, no.5.) Partially reprinted as "Dawn of Adirondack Mountain History" and "Possibility of Earlier Unrecorded Ascents of Emmons" in Mt. Marcy Anthology (*High Spots*, July 1937, 14:no.3:6–8, 12–13, port. and map).   6894

Alexander, Edward Johnston. David P. Holton: phonic mountaineer. *High Spots*, Jan. 1936. 13:no.1:8–11.   6895

Holton, David Parsons. Reminiscences. N.Y. 1874. 32p. Includes material on Holton's Adirondack activities.   6896

Tenney, W.E. Hop. *NYS Con*, Dec. 1952– Jan. 1953. 7:no.3:34. port. Arthur S. Hopkins.   6897

Benedict, Darwin. A north country genius. *Cloud Splitter*, Mar.–Apr. 1954. 17:no.2:8–9. Franklin B. Hough.   6898

Franklin B. Hough—a tribute. *Am For*, July 1922. 28:431–32. port.   6899

Hickcox, John H. A bibliography of the writings of Franklin Benjamin Hough, PhD. M.D. *In* New York (state). University. 99th annual report of the regents, 1886. p.321–47.   6900

Hosmer, Ralph Sheldon. Franklin B. Hough, pioneer in forestry. *Bul Schools*, Mar. 1940. 26:227–30, 262–63. illus. Condensed in *North Country Life*, Summer 1952, 6:no.3:16–20.   6901

Hudowalski, Mrs. Grace (Leech). A major peak gets a new name. *High Spots Yrbk*, 1942. p.26–28. illus. Hough Peak, named for Franklin B. Hough.   6902

Jacobsen, Edna L. Franklin B. Hough, a pioneer in scientific forestry in America. *NY Hist*, July 1934. 15:311–25. port. A well-documented account of Hough's activities with particular reference to the Adirondack Park.   6903

Murray, David. Franklin B. Hough, M.D. PhD. *In* New York (state). University. 99th annual report of the regents, 1886. p.300–19.   6904

For Bill Howard. *NYS Con*, Dec. 1951–Jan. 1952. 6:no.3:30. illus. Brief note on William G. Howard memorial plaque at Lake George.   6905

Howard becomes New York Superintendent of forests. *Am For*, May 1927. 33:300. port. William Gibbs Howard.   6906

Littlefield, Edward Winchester. Bill Howard —an appreciation. *J For*, Apr. 1949. 47: 303–4. William Gibbs Howard.   6907

The William G. Howard memorial leanto. *Ad-i-ron-dac*, Jan.–Feb. 1951. 15:14. illus. See also photograph of plaque and account of dedication in issue for Sept.–Oct. 15:87.   6908

Fowler, Albert V. Tales from the drowned land. *High Spots Yrbk*, 1939. p.27–34. Near Cranberry Lake. Reminiscences of Willard Howland, a guide.   6909

"Developing" a forest investment. *Conservationist*, Mar. 1920. 3:46–47. illus. Story of John Hurd.   6910

Goldmark, Josephine. An Adirondack friendship: letters of William James. *Atlan*, Sept.– Oct. 1934. 154:265–72, 440–47. Many quotations from letters of James. First part mainly on Adirondacks.   6911

James, William. Memories and studies. N.Y. Longmans, 1911. 411p. Thomas Davidson and Keene Valley, p.73.   6912

Lusk, Graham. Theodore Caldwell Janeway, A.M., M.D. n.p. 1918? 4p. port. Reprinted from the *American Journal of the Medical Sciences*, Feb. 1918. 6913

Herman M. Janssen is new sky pilot in Adirondacks. *Northeast Log*, Oct. 1952. 1:no.3:26. port. 6914

H., H.F. The fiddler of Cat mountain. *Camp Log*, 1926. 12:56–57, 83. illus. Biographical sketch of John Jenack, fire observer on Cat Mountain. 6915

Jesup, Henry Griswold. Edward Jessup of West Farms, Westchester co. New York, and his descendants... Cambridge, Privately printed by John Wilson & son, 1887. 442p. Totten and Crossfield Purchase, p.211ff. 6916

Birch, J.J. The saint of the wilderness; St. Isaac Jogues. N.Y. Benziger bros. 1936. 236p. plates, front. 6917

Campbell, Thomas Joseph. Isaac Jogues, S.J. discoverer of Lake George. N.Y. America press, 1911. 55p. front. plates, ports. Monograph, "Pioneer Priests of North America," reprinted with some emendations and additions. 6918

Clarke, Richard Henry. Father Isaac Jogues, S.J. *Cath World*, Oct. 1872. 16:105–21. 6919

Dolan, John W. Father Jogues. *NY State Hist Assn Proc*, 1903. 5:30–52. 6920

Dolan, John W. The life of Father Jogues. A lecture delivered before the Johnstown historical society. Nov. 19, 1903. Johnstown, N.Y. 1903. 16p. 6921

Early, Joseph J. The Lake George Saint Isaac Jogues memorial. *US Cath Hist Soc*, 1939. 30:30–46. 6922

Gerard, J. The first apostle of the Iroquois. *Month*, Mar. 1874. 20:306–24. Isaac Jogues. 6923

Jogues, Isaac. Narrative of a captivity among the Mohawk Indians, and a description of New Netherlands, in 1642–3; with a memoir of the holy missionary by John Gilmary Shea. N.Y. Press of the Historical society, 1856. 69p. See also The Jogues Papers... in the New York Historical Society *Collections*, 2d ser. 3:pt.1:161–229 (1857). 6924

Malloy, J.L. Tercentenary of Lake George. *Cath World*, Sept. 1946. 163:563. On Isaac Jogues. 6925

Martin, Félix. The life of Father Isaac Jogues, missionary priest of the Society of Jesus, slain by the Mohawk Iroquois, in the present state of New York Oct. 18, 1646... with Father Jogues' account of the captivity and death of his companion, René Goupil, slain Sept. 29, 1642. Translated from the French by J.G. Shea. 3d edition. N.Y. Benziger bros. 1885. 263p. front. (port.) map. 6926

Moran, Peter. Father Hecker's chapel. *Commonweal*, Sept. 25, 1936. 24:501–2. New windows telling the story of Isaac Jogues. 6927

New York (state). Father Isaac Jogues memorial commission. Interim report of the Father Isaac Jogues memorial commission to erect a memorial... Submitted Mar. 16, 1938. Albany, J.B. Lyon, 1938. 8p. Legislative document 81, 1938. 6928

New York (state). Father Isaac Jogues memorial commission. Report of the temporary state commission created to select a site to erect a memorial to Father Isaac Jogues, discoverer of Lake George in the year sixteen hundred and forty six and to make recommendations. Submitted Mar. 15, 1937. Albany, J.B. Lyon, 1937. 9p. Legislative document 80, 1937. 6929

Rouvier, Frédéric. Le P. Isaac Jogues de la Compagnie de Jésus, premier apôtre des Iroquois. Lille, France, Soc. Saint-Augustin, 1890. 48p. 6930

Scott, Martin J. Isaac Jogues, missioner and martyr; an adaptation of the original biography of Martin Shea. Rev. ed. N.Y. P.J. Kenedy & sons, c1927. 233p. plates, front. port. 6931

Stephenson, T. Bowman. A Methodist tribute to a Jesuit. *R of Rs*, Aug. 1893. 8:192. Excerpts from article in the *Sunday Magazine*. Isaac Jogues. 6932

Talbot, Francis Xavier. Blessed Isaac Jogues. *US Cath Hist Soc*, Sept. 1929. 19:21–32. 6933

Talbot, Francis Xavier. Jogues' torture on Crown Point. *America*, Oct. 7, 1933. 50:8–10. 6934

Talbot, Francis Xavier. Saint among savages; the life of Isaac Jogues. N.Y. Harper, 1935. 466p. front. facsim. map. 6935

Talbot, Francis Xavier. The torture trail of St. Isaac Jogues. *US Cath Hist Soc*, 1933. 23:7–86. 6936

Pound, Arthur. Johnson of the Mohawks... N.Y. Macmillan, 1930. 556p. front. plates, ports. facsims. maps (1 double). 6937

Burnham, John Bird. Gens des bois. III: Ben Jourdon. *For & Stream*, May 6, 1899. 52: 342–43. port. 6938

Beardslee, Lester A. Stories of Ned Buntline, by Piseco, pseud. *For & Stream*, July 29, 1886. 27:3. Edward Zane Carroll Judson. 6939

Death of Ned Buntline. *For & Stream*, July 23, 1886. 26:506–7. Edward Zane Carroll Judson. 6940

L. Edward Zane Carroll Judson (Ned Buntline). *For & Stream*, July 24, 1897. 49:69–70. port. 6941

Mather, Fred. Men I have fished with. L: Edward Zane Carroll Judson (Ned Buntline). *For & Stream*, July 24, 1897. illus. 6942

Monaghan, Jay. The great rascal: the life and adventures of Ned Buntline. Boston, Little, Brown, 1952. 353p. ports. illus. Edward Zane Carroll Judson. 6943

Pond, Frederick Eugene. Life and adventures of Ned Buntline, by Will Wildwood, pseud. *Wild Mag*, May–Oct. 1888. 1:24–28, 72–78, 128–31, 147–53, 220–25, 278–81. illus. p.147–53, Aug. 1888, is on Judson's life in the Adirondacks. 6944

Pond, Frederick Eugene. The life and adventures of "Ned Buntline." With Ned Buntline's anecdote of "Frank Forester" and chapter of angling sketches by Fred E. Pond ("Will Wildwood"). N.Y. Cadmus bookshop, 1919. 139p. ports. Author's pen name: "Will Wildwood." Published in an edition of 250 copies. Edward Zane Carroll Judson. 6945

H.A. Kelly, veteran Tupper photographer dies at Saranac Lake. *Lumber Camp News*, Mar. 1951. 12:no.11:13. Hugh Kelly, known as "Adirondack photographer." 6946

Adams, Frank Dawson. James Furman Kemp. *In* National academy of sciences. Biographical memoirs. Washington, 1935. 16:1–21. port. 6947

James Furman Kemp. *Eng & Min J*, Nov. 27, 1926. 122:872–73. port. Memorials by Robert Peele and Charles P. Berkey. 6948

James Furman Kemp. *Min & Met*, Dec. 1926. 7:546. port. 6949

Lindgren, Waldemar. James Furman Kemp, to his memory. *Am Geol*, Jan.–Feb. 1927. 22:84–90. Short account of his study of geology in the Adirondacks. 6950

Hourwich, Rebecca. An artist builds a house. *Country Life*, July 1929. 56:35–38. illus. Rockwell Kent's home. 6951

House of Rockwell Kent, Ausable Forks, N.Y. *Arch*, May 1930. 61:285–88. illus. 6952

Kent, Rockwell. This is my own. N.Y. Duell, Sloan & Pearce, c1940. 393p. illus. Story of his home near Ausable Forks. 6953

Pamares, Claude. Homespun heroics. *For Leaves*, Spring 1907. 4:no.1:13–16. illus. Story of Abe Langford of Skinnersville. 6954

Roy Lavoy dies in Tupper Lake. *Northeast Log*, June 1953. 1:no.10:30. port. Woods superintendent of the Oval Wood Dish Corporation. 6955

Smith, Donnal V. "Pants" Lawrence of the Adirondacks. *NY Folk Q*, Summer 1953.

9:85–93. Abridged in *North Country Life*, Fall 1953. 7:no.4:16–19. Frank Lawrence. 6956

C., C.W. James D. LeRay. *For Leaves*, Spring 1907. 4:no.1:3–9. illus. port. 6957

Joseph Robert Linney, a biography. *Exp Eng*, Nov.–Dec. 1944. 22:246–47. port. 6958

Porter, Mrs. Marjorie (Lansing). By his own bootstraps: a tribute to the late Joseph R. Linney. *No Country Life*, Spring 1952. 6:no.2: 9–10. port. 6959

Riley, Ruth V. Benson J. Lossing. *High Spots*, Apr. 1931. 8:no.2:10–13. illus. (Historical Adirondack Character Series, no.4.) Many quotations from Lossing's "The Hudson." The illustration shows Lossing's departure for Tahawus. 6960

Conkling, Howard. Le Chevalier de la Luzerne. Short biography. N.Y. 1908. 62p. ports. 6961

Lyman, Henry Harrison. Memories of the old homestead. Oswego, N.Y. R.J. Oliphant, 1900. 181p. Autobiography of a member of the first Fisheries, Game and Forest Commission, orator at the dedication of the John Brown monument. 6962

Lane, Eastwood. Portrait of a pioneer. *No Country Life*, Spring 1949. 3:no.2:42–46, 62. port. Biographical sketch of Bill McAleese of Cranberry Lake. 6963

Burnham, John Bird. Gens des bois. IV: George McBride. *For & Stream*, Mar. 24, 1900. 54:224–25. Old settler living at Tupper Lake. 6964

Death claims Tupper pioneer. *Lumber Camp News*, Aug. 1951. 13:no.4:16. James D. McBride, civil engineer. 6965

Burger, William H. Father Mac. *No Country Life*, Summer 1952. 6:no.3:6–10. port. Obituary of Father Edwin H. McCarthy. 6966

Commissioner Macdonald bids the forests 'Adieu.' *Motordom*, Feb. 1931. 24:no.8:12–13. port. illus. 6967

Steele, Vern. Thomas Macdonough. *No Country Life*, Fall 1953. 7:no.4:40–41. 6968

Burnham, John Bird. Gens des bois. X: Joseph McGuire. *For & Stream*, May 4, 1901. 56:324–43. In Poke-o-Moonshine country. 6969

Gothamite, pseud. "Uncle Bill" McLaughlin, Adirondack guide. *Sport Rev*, Sept. 23, 1905. 28:344. Obituary. 6970

Quaife, Milo Milton. Detroit biographies: Alexander Macomb, 1782–1841. *Burt Hist Coll*, Nov. 1931. 10:2–16. 6971

Richards, George H. Memoir of Alexander Macomb, the major general commanding the Army of the United States. N.Y. M'Elrath, Bangs & co. 1833. 130p. ports. A brief biographical notice is in the U.S. Army, Corps of Engineers, Professional Memoirs, Oct.–Dec. 1910, 2:242–43.   6972

Hudowalski, Mrs. Grace (Leech). Bob Marshall. *Cloud Splitter*, Dec. 1939. 2:no.7:11. An appreciation of Robert Marshall.   6973

Marshall, George. Adirondacks to Alaska: a biographical sketch of Robert Marshall. *Ad-i-ron-dac*, May–June 1951. 15:44–45, 59. port   6974

Marshall, George, comp. Bibliography of Robert Marshall, 1901–1939, with reviews of his published works and biographical appreciations. *Liv Wild*, Autumn 1951. no.38: 20–23. Supplement, with portrait and illustration, in issue for Summer 1954, no.49: 31–35.   6975

Marshall, George. Robert Marshall as a writer. *Liv Wild*, Autumn 1951. no.38:14–20. ports.   6976

Welch, Fay. Bob Marshall. *High Spots Yrbk*, 1940. p.54–55. Robert Marshall.   6977

Fred Mather. *For & Stream*, Feb. 24, 1900. 54:141. port. p.151. Editorial on death of author of "Men I Have Fished With."   6978

Fisher, Albert Kenrick. Clinton Hart Merriam (1855–1942). *Linn Soc NY Proc*, 1941–45. no.54–57:58–60.   6979

Porter, Mrs. Marjorie (Lansing). Lem Merrill (surveyor-conservationist). Plattsburgh, N.Y. Clinton press, 1944. 45p. ports. Elmer Marcellus Merrill.   6980

"A hiker in outer space." *Cloud Splitter*, Sept.–Oct. 1953. 16:no.5:11. Philip Schuyler Miller.   6981

Bailey, Liberty Hyde. Lucy Millington. *Torreya*, Nov.–Dec. 1939. 39:159–63. illus. port.   6982

Sickels, Mrs. Dorothy (Judd). Keene Valley's pastor—Fredericka Mitchell. *Advance*, Nov. 1945. 137:no.11:10–11. port.   6983

Adirondack, pseud. Death of Martin Moody, Adirondack guide. *Ang & Hunt*, July 1910. 2:363–64. Also in *Sportsmen's Review*, June 18, 1910, 37:584.   6984

Burnham, John Bird. Gens des bois. VI: Martin Van Buren Moody. *For & Stream*, June 2, 1900. 54:423–24. Guide at Tupper Lake.   6985

Goldthwaite, Kenneth W. A few moments with "Uncle Mart" Moody. *For Leaves*, Autumn 1904. 1:no.4:24–25. port.   6986

Goldthwaite, Kenneth W. "Uncle Mart" Moody. *NY Times Mag*, May 10, 1903. p.6. illus.   6987

Burnham, John Bird. Gens des bois. VII: Simeon J. Moody. *For & Stream*, Sept. 8, 1900. 55:183–84. Tupper Lake hunter.   6988

Judge Pliny Moore (1759–1822) obituary notice from the Plattsburgh Republican September 7, 1822, with selections from his papers and historical notes by Hugh McLellan. Champlain, N.Y. Moorsfield press, 1929. 27p. (Pliny Moore Papers, no.2.)   6989

McLellan, Hugh. The Pliny Moore collection—abstract of address... *Ver Hist Soc Proc*, Sept. 1939. n.s.7:189–94. Life of Pliny Moore as shown in a collection of his letters and papers.   6990

Schaefer, Paul A. Back o' yonder. *Cloud Splitter*, July–Aug. 1945. 8:no.5.5–6. Reminiscences of John Morehouse, Adirondack guide.   6991

Burger, William H. George Morgan of Raquette Falls. *No Country Life*, Spring 1952. 6:no.2:24–28. port. illus.   6992

Adirondack Murray. *St No Mo*, Sept. 1907. 2:337–43. port. William Henry Harrison Murray.   6993

Adirondack Murray. *Woods & Wat*, Spring 1904. 7:no.1:20. port. Editorial.   6994

"Adirondack" Murray dead. *For & Irrig*, Apr. 1904. 10:150. Short obituary.   6995

The book that made the Adirondacks. *Outing*, July 1922. 80:140–42. Adirondack Murray.   6996

Carson, Russell Mack Little. Adirondack Murray. *Cloud Splitter*, Mar. 1940. 3:no.2:2–4.   6997

Cook, William H. Letters of a Ticonderoga farmer; selections from the correspondence of William H. Cook and his wife with their son, Joseph Cook, 1851–1885, as edited by Frederick G. Bascom. Ithaca, N.Y. Cornell university press, 1946. 134p. Includes a chapter on Adirondack Murray, p.82–108.   6998

Gothamite, pseud. Adirondack Murray memorial association. *Sport Rev*, July 7, 1906. 30:7. Short biography of W.H.H. Murray with list of members of the committee for the memorial.   6999

A memorial to Adirondack Murray. *Sh & Fish*, July 5, 1906. 40:245. Proposal to form national society to perpetuate Murray's memory. See report of organization of the society in issue for Aug. 30, 1906, 40:407, with title "Adirondack Murray Memorial."   7000

Mr. Murray at home. *Golden Rule*, Sept. 12, 1877. 2:no.51:8.   7001

Mr. Murray's mistakes. *Am Sportsman*, Oct. 25, 1873. 3:57. Editorial on report that Murray shot thirty deer out of season. 7002

Murray, William Henry Harrison. Introduction. *In* his Mamelons and Ungava: a legend of the Saguenay. Boston, De Wolfe, Fiske & co. 1890. p.v–xx. Brief statement about his literary work, with special reference to the Adirondack Tales and the character John Norton. 7003

Murray, William Henry Harrison. One of W.H.H. Murray's reasons for visiting the Adirondacks. Written in 1869. *For Leaves*, Summer 1904. 1:no.3:35–37. illus. 7004

Murray, William Henry Harrison. Reminiscences of my literary and outdoor life. *Ind*, July 28–Aug. 4, 1904. 57:194–200, 277–80. port. 7005

A Murray memorial. *For & Stream*, July 7, 1906. 67:20–21. See also "Murray Memorial Proposed," *Field and Stream*, Sept. 1906, 11:502. Proposed memorial for W.H.H. Murray. 7006

Phantom Falls, pseud. Phantom Falls. *For & Stream*, July 8, 1875. 4:340. Search for W.H.H. Murray's Phantom Falls. 7007

Plankers, pseud. Summer shooting. *For & Stream*, Mar. 29, 1883. 20:168. Complaint about Adirondack Murray shooting woodcock in July. 7008

Radford, Harry V. Adirondack Murray: a biographical appreciation. N.Y. Broadway publishing co. 1905. 84p. front. plates, ports. First printed in *Woods and Waters*, Autumn 1904, 7:no.3:7–18. Reviewed in *Forest Leaves*, Winter 1906, 3:no.1:25, with title "The Interpreter of the Adirondacks," and in *Sportsmen's Review*, Jan. 20, 1906, 29:no.3:65. Reviews also in: *Journal of the Outdoor Life*, June 1906; *Shooting and Fishing*, Nov. 9, 1905; *Outdoors*, May 1906. See also letter about Murray, from Henry Van Dyke to Radford, in *Shooting and Fishing*, Dec. 21, 1905. 7009

Radford, Harry V. Adirondack Murray in Boston. *Sh & Fish*, Feb. 22, 1906. 39:408–9. Letter to Alden Chester with brief introductory note. 7010

Radford, Harry V. The Adirondack Murray memorial association. *Am Field*, July 7, 1906. 66:3. Appeal for funds for memorial. 7011

Radford, Harry V. The Adirondack Murray memorial association. What it aims to accomplish. *Sport Rev*, Feb. 8, 1908. 33:146–47. illus. port. 7012

Radford, Harry V. "Adirondack" Murray's home. *Four Tr News*, Jan. 1905. 8:19. port. illus. 7013

Radford, Harry V. The "Murray rush." *For Leaves*, Winter 1906. 3:no.1:30–34. port.

illus. Interest in the Adirondacks aroused by W.H.H. Murray. 7014

Radford, Harry V. The Murray rush to the Adirondacks. *Sh & Fish*, Oct. 19, 1905. 39:29. port. 7015

Radford, Harry V. W.H.H. Murray in the Adirondack. *Sh & Fish*, Oct. 26, 1906. 39:48. port. illus. Portrait of John Plumley. 7016

Rev. W.H.H. Murray. *Ev Sat*, Nov. 25, 1871. n.s.3:521. port. 7017

Stewart, George, born 1848. Adirondack Murray (Belford's monthly, New York, March, 1891). *In* his Essays from reviews. 2d series. Quebec, 1893. p.93–122. On Murray as author. 7018

Van Dyke, Henry. "On Adirondack Murray." *For & Stream*, Dec. 23, 1905. 65:518. 7019

Birkinbine, John. Biographical notice of William George Neilson. *Am Inst Mining Eng Tr*, 1907. 38:402–5. President of the Adirondack Mountain Reserve for many years. 7020

Leonard, S.R. Sewell Newhouse and the Oneida trap business. *No Country Life*, Winter 1952. 6:no.1:16–18, 70. illus. Newhouse wrote a manual on trapping based on his Adirondack experience. 7021

Hartnagel, Chris Andrew. David Hale Newland, 1872–1943. *Econ Geol*, May 1944. 39:248. 7022

Ruedemann, Rudolf and Goldring, Winifred. Memorial to David Hale Newland. *Geol Soc Am Proc*, 1943. 56:209–16. plate, port. 7023

Sportsmen lose a good friend. *Ang & Hunt*, July 1910. 2:355. port. Obituary of George R. Nunn. 7024

Kraeling, Emil G. Old man of the mountain. *No Country Life*, Spring 1955. 9:no.2:14–20. port. Walt O'Connor, Olmstedville guide. Includes reminiscences of Verplanck Colvin. 7025

O'Donnell, Thomas F. Thomas O'Donnell: an informal history of an informal historian. *No Country Life*, Fall 1954. 8:no.4:5–12. port. Biography of Thomas Clay O'Donnell, author of "The Sapbush Run." 7026

Burton, Harold B. The commissioner. *High Spots Yrbk*, 1940. p.56–62. Lithgow Osborne. 7027

Conservationists in action. . .Lithgow Osborne. *Forest Preserve*, Mar. 1954. 10:14–15. port. 7028

Our new conservation commissioner. *NYS For Assn NL*, June 1933. p.5–6. Short biography of Lithgow Osborne. 7029

Burger, William H. Tom Peacock, Adirondack guide. *No Country Life*, Winter 1953. 7:no.1:23–26. 7030

Atkinson, George Francis. Charles Horton Peck. *Bot Gaz*, Jan. 1918. 65:103–8. ports. 7031

Bessey, Charles Edwin. A notable botanical career. *Science*, July 10, 1914. n.s.40:48. Charles Horton Peck. 7032

Burnham, Stewart Henry. Charles Horton Peck. *Mycologia*, Jan. 1919. 11:33–39. 7033

In memoriam. Stephen Hyatt Pelham Pell, 1874–1950. *Ft Ti Mus Bul*, 1950. 8:no.6. port. illus. The entire issue is devoted to an appreciation of Mr. Pell and history of Fort Ticonderoga. 7034

Old black Joe. *NYS Con*, June–July 1952. 6:no.6:14. Brief biographical data about Joseph Perrin, supplied by C.A. Wardner. 7035

Clifford Robert Pettis. *Am For*, Mar. 1927. 33:149. port. Obituary. 7036

Hosmer, Ralph Sheldon. Clifford R. Pettis, forest builder. *Bul Schools*, Mar. 1942. 28:238–41, 254. port. illus. 7037

Carson, Russell Mack Little. Edmund Forest Phelps. *High Spots*, July 1934. 11:no.3:26–27. Obituary. 7038

Beetle, David Harold. Trail expert. *Up Mo*, Dec. 1941. 2:no.9:13, 24. port. Biographical sketch of Orra A. Phelps. 7039

Robinson, Lucena K. Orra Parker Phelps, 1867–1950. *Ad-i-ron-dac*, Sept.–Oct. 1950. 14:115. 7040

B., G.L. Death of Old Mountain Phelps. *For & Stream*, May 6, 1905. 64:355. Orson Schofield Phelps. 7041

Knox, Martin Van Buren. "Old Mountain" Phelps. *Field & S*, Sept. 1905. 10:492–93. port. 7042

McAneny, Herbert. Old Mountain Phelps. *High Spots*, Apr. 1933. 10:no.2:13–15. port. (Great Adirondack Guides, no.2.) 7043

Mitchell, Rev. Frederica. Old Mountain Phelps. This tribute to Old Mountair Phelps was delivered on the occasion of the Haystack centennial, August 20, 1949... *Ad-i-ron-dac*, Sept.–Oct. 1950. 14:106–7. port. 7044

"Old Mountain" Phelps. *Sport Rev*, May 20, 1905. 27:537. Editorial on his death. 7045

Strube, Janet. Orson Schofield Phelps. *Cloud Splitter*, Jan.–Feb. 1944. 7:no.1:13–14. 7046

Warner, Charles Dudley. Old Mountain Phelps, Marcy guide. *High Spots*, July 1937. 14:no.3:34–37. port. From his "In the Wilderness." 7047

Burnham, John Bird. Gens des bois. VIII: Plumadore. *For & Stream*, Oct. 6, 1900. 55:264–65. Indian guide. 7048

Murray, William Henry Harrison. In memoriam. W.H.H. Murray to John Plumley. *Woods & Wat*, Summer 1901. 4:no.2:7–8. ports. 7049

Merriam, George Spring, 1843–1914, ed. Noah Porter, a memorial by friends. N.Y. Scribner, 1893. 306p. ports. "Vacation in the Woods," by Dean Sage, p.153–57; "In the Adirondacks," by J.H. Twichell, p.157–65. 7050

Howard, William Gibbs. George Du Pont Pratt, Conservation commissioner, 1915–1921. *Bul Schools*, Mar. 1945. 31:228–30. port. 7051

Pratt—hunter and conservationist. *Outing*, Feb. 1916. 67:452–53. port. George Du Pont Pratt. 7052

Brown, Levant Frederick. The honest anglers convention. *Sport Rev*, Nov. 23, 1907. 32:566. Includes a tribute to Harry V. Radford. 7053

Hallock, Charles. Harry V. Radford, sportsman and writer. *Sport Rev*, July 20, 1907. 32:63. port. 7054

Harry V. Radford, the "Adirondack Murray" of today. *Field & S*, June 1901. 6:238–39. port. An abridgment of this article appeared in *Catholic Youth*, June 1902. Announcement of new Adirondack department by Radford. 7055

Little biography no.11—Harry V. Radford. *Four Tr News*, Apr. 1904. 6:253. port. 7056

Walsh, James Joseph. A young Catholic explorer. *Am Cath Hist Soc*, June 1915. 26:111–30. Reprinted in *Forest Leaves*, Autumn 1915, 12:no.1:5–22. Harry V. Radford. 7057

Famous trappers I have known. Bill Randall. *Fur-Fish-Game*, Feb. 1926. 43:no.2:26–27. port. William Randall. 7058

Carson, Russell Mack Little. Mount Redfield was named for William C. Redfield. *Cloud Splitter*, Oct.–Nov. 1940. 3:no.6:2–3, 12–14; 3:no.7:2–9. Redfield's activities in the Adirondacks. 7059

Redfield, John Howard. Recollections. Printed for private circulation. Philadelphia, Morris press, c1900. 360p. Errata leaf tipped in. William C. Redfield's visits to the high mountains of Essex are described in Ch. 28. 7060

Benjamin, Jack T. "In my meditation—" *Cloud Splitter*, Oct. 1940. 3:no.6:6–7. Account of visit to Noah John Rondeau. 7061

Blackburn, John Hall. Back of beyond. *Cloud Splitter*, June 1939. 2:no.4:2–6. Description

of trip to Noah John Rondeau's hermitage.
7062

Hudowalski, Mrs. Grace (Leech). The hermit of Cold river. *High Spots Yrbk*, 1939. p.80–84. port. p.87. Noah John Rondeau.
7063

Hudowalski, Mrs. Grace (Leech). Noah John Rondeau. *IOCA Bul*, Winter 1948. 2:no.1: 40–41, 55.
7064

Rondeau to be on job at Tahawus show. *Lumber Camp News*, Apr. 1951. 12:no.12:7. Tahawus sportsmen's show to have replica of Cold River "town hall."
7065

Seagears, Clayton B. The hermit of Cold river flow. *NYS Con*, Oct.–Nov. 1946. 1:no.2: 8–9. Reprinted in *North Country Life*, Spring 1947, 1:no.3:13–15, illus. port. Noah John Rondeau.
7066

Donaldson, Alfred Lee. Theodore Roosevelt's portentious day on Marcy. *High Spots*, July 1937. 14:no.3:42–43. From his "History of the Adirondacks."
7067

Radford, Harry V. Guide La Casse's story of President Roosevelt's ascent of Mt. Marcy. *Field & S*, Jan. 1902. 6:647–49. port. A full account of events preceding and immediately following the receipt of the news that President McKinley was at the point of death.
7068

Radford, Harry V. President Roosevelt's ascent of Mt. Marcy. *For Leaves*, Winter 1904. 2:no.1:4–8. port.
7069

Roosevelt, Theodore. Theodore Roosevelt: an autobiography... N.Y. Macmillan, 1913. 647p. front. (port.) illus. folded tables. For receipt of news of McKinley, etc. see p.379ff. First printed in *The Outlook*.
7070

Where Roosevelt became president; a thrilling chapter in New York state history, before paved highways opened the Adirondacks. *Motordom*, Feb. 1931. 24:no.8:7, 22. illus.
7071

Williams, Richmond B. TR receives his summons to the presidency. *Bell Tel Mag*, Autumn 1951. 30:197–204. illus. map.   7072

Hicks, Harry Wade. Jed Rossman. *High Spots*, Jan. 1933. 10:no.1:15–17. port. (Great Adirondack Guides, no.1.)
7073

The hunter home from the hill. *High Spots*, Apr. 1937. 14:no.2:15–17. port. Obituary of Jed Rossman.
7074

"Nate" Russel. *Ang & Hunt*, May 1910. 2:249. port. Obituary of guide of Mountainville and Indian Pond.
7075

Carson, Russell Mack Little. Old Sabael. *High Spots*, July 1931. 8:no.3:22–23.   7076

Clay, Cecil. A vindication. *For & Stream*, July 5, 1877. 8:368. Vindication of Mitchell Sabattis.
7077

Juvenal, pseud. Mitchell Sabattis. *For & Stream*, May 26, 1906. 66:832. port.   7078

Kellogg, Henry D. Mitchell Sabattis. *St No Mo*, June 1906. 1:no.2:14–16. port.   7079

Manahan, Mary G. Sebatos and the panther. *For Leaves*, Autumn 1904. 1:no.4:33–36. illus. port. Mitchell Sabattis.
7080

Radford, Harry V. Mitchel Sabattis. *Sh & Fish*, Apr. 26, 1906. 40:45–46. port. Brief biography and tribute.
7081

Riley, Ruth V. Mitchell Sabattis. *High Spots*, Oct. 1934. 11:no.4:11–12. (Great Adirondack Guides, no.8.)
7082

A well known Adirondack figure. *For & Stream*, May 12, 1906. 66:743. Editorial on the death of Mitchell Sabattis.
7083

Woodward, J.H. Mitchell Sabattis. *For & Stream*, May 19, 1906. 66:788.   7084

Bixby, George Stephenson. Peter Sailly (1754–1826) a pioneer of the Champlain valley, with extracts from his diary and letters. Albany, University of the State of New York, 1919. 94p. facsim. (New York State Library History Bulletin 12; University of the State of New York Bulletin 680.) In 1785 Peter Sailly with his family came from France and settled at Plattsburgh. He held numerous offices and took an important part in the War of 1812.
7085

Flood 'n Field, pseud. In the great north woods with rifle and camera. *Sport Rev*, June 13, 1908. 33:654. illus. port. Short biographical sketch of Thomas Salmon.   7086

Fowler, Albert V. The hermit of Big Deer. *High Spots Yrbk*, 1940. p.25–32. Fide Scott.
7087

Brenan, Dan. Nessmuk: he changed a lot of ideas about living in the woods. *NYS Con*, Dec. 1950–Jan. 1951. 5:no.3:10–11. port. illus. Entertaining biographical sketch of George Washington Sears, with particular reference to his summers in the Adirondacks.
7088

The death of "Nessmuk." *For & Stream*, May 8, 1890. 34:305–6. George Washington Sears.
7089

Johnson, Justina. Nessmuk. *For & Stream*, Apr. 22, 1905. 64:310. George Washington Sears.
7090

Mather, Fred. Men I have fished with. LVI: George W. Sears. (Nessmuk.) *For & Stream*, Sept. 25, 1897. 49:249–50.   7091

Shearer, William Lincoln. Nessmuk. Pennsylvania state geographic board honors

George W. Sears. *For & Stream*, Aug. 1907. 97:479, 510–11. 7092

Dunham, Harvey Leslie. Adirondack French Louie: early life in the north woods. . . Utica, N.Y. 1952. 200p. illus. maps. 2d edition, enlarged, published in Utica, 1953, 212p. Reviewed by A. Ettinger in *The Ad-i-ron-dac*, Jan.–Feb. 1953, 17:20, and by Michael J. Kernan Jr. in *North Country Life*, Winter 1953, 7:no.1:55–56, 59, reprinted from the Watertown *Daily Times*. Louis Seymour. 7093

Kenwell, Gerald. French Lewie. *NYS Con*, Aug.–Sept. 1952. 7:no.1:26–27. port. Louis Seymour. 7094

North, Mary Remsen. French Louie—hermit trapper. *High Spots*, Apr. 1933. 10:no.2:20–21. Louis Seymour. 7095

Adams, Joseph. The one-man chamber of commerce. *No Country Life*, Winter 1947. 1:no.2:27–28. Arthur Sharron, postmaster at Plattsburgh. 7096

Shepard, Henry P. I once knew an Adirondack guide. *No Country Life*, Fall 1951. 5:no.4:6–8. Nat Shepard, a guide for the Adirondack League Club. 7097

H. Adirondack hospitality of the olden time. *For & Stream*, Aug. 27, 1891. 37:106. Jack Sheppard, a guide, offers extra food. 7098

Mather, Fred. Men I have fished with. XLVI: Sergt. E.L. (Jack) Sheppard. *For & Stream*, June 26, 1897. 48:506–7. 7099

A.T. Shorey—winter mountaineer. *Ad-i-ron-dac*, May–June 1955. 19:57. Archibald Thompson Shorey. 7100

Mattocks, John. Hon. George A. Simmons, among the "fifties" and his friends, in northern New York. Chicago? 1885. 57p. plates, front. Prominent lawyer of Keeseville. 7101

An Adirondack trapper. *For & Stream*, Feb. 1, 1896. 46:96. Life of Elijah Simonds. 7102

Burnham, John Bird. Gens des bois. V: Elijah Simonds. *For & Stream*, May 12, 1900. 54:362–63. Elizabethtown hunter. See comment by George B. Wood in issue for May 26, 1900, 54:404. 7103

Keith, E.F. The old time stories. *Fur-Fish-Game*, Nov. 1926. 44:no.5:15. Elijah Simonds. 7104

Webster, George O. Elijah Simonds. *High Spots*, Jan. 1935. 12:no.1:12–15. (Great Adirondack Guides, no.9.) 7105

Mather, Fred. Men I have fished with. VII: George W. Simpkins. *For & Stream*, Aug. 15, 1896. 47:126–27. 7106

Pell, John. Philip Skene of Skenesborough. *NY State Hist Assn Q*, Jan. 1928. 9:27–44. port. illus. map. 7107

Frothingham, O.B. Gerrit Smith, a biography. N.Y. Putnam, 1878. 381p. plates, ports. 2d edition published in 1878. 1st edition withdrawn from circulation. See Dictionary of American Biography (Smith). 7108

Gerrit Smith. *Potter Am Mo*, Feb. 1875. 4:160. Obituary. 7109

Harlow, Ralph Volney. Gerrit Smith, philanthropist and reformer. N.Y. Holt, ᶜ1939. 501p. 7110

Ray, Frederick A. Gerrit Smith, the friend of John Brown. *Herk Co Hist Soc*, Sept. 1902 to May 1914. 4:52–59. 7111

Corson, R.H. Jud Smith—an appreciation, by Switch Reel, pseud. *For & Stream*, Dec. 5, 1908. 71:902. 7112

Lent, Ella M. In retrospect—Paul Smith. *J Outd Life*, Jan. 1924. 21:29–30. port. 7113

Long, E. Funny sayings of the late Paul Smith. Brooklyn, N.Y. Language printing, 1913. 48p. port. illus. 7114

Porter, Mrs. Marjorie (Lansing). The famous resort proprietor of a century ago—Paul Smith. *No Country Life*, Fall 1951. 5:no.4: 24–27. 7115

Radford, Harry V. Paul Smith. *Sh & Fish*, Sept. 14, 1905. 38:446. Paul Smith's 80th birthday. Brief biography. 7116

Lusk, William B. Phelps Smith. . . Paul Smiths, N.Y. 1937. 8p. Unpaged leaflet. Funeral address for the son of Paul Smith. 7117

Smith, Stephen K. Historical sketch of events in the life of Stephen K. Smith of Peru, N.Y. Peru, N.Y.? Published by the author, 189—? 64p. Copy in the collection of Mrs. Marjorie L. Porter. 7118

Nichols, Leon Nelson. . . .Nick Spencer, mighty hunter. St. Johnsville, N.Y. Enterprise & News, 1932. 24p. illus. (Tales of the Early Mohawk Region, no.1.) Stories of Nick Spencer including references to Jock's Lake (Honnedaga) and Jonathan Wright. 7119

Balfour, Sir Graham. The life of Robert Louis Stevenson. N.Y. Scribner, 1901. 2v. ports. Stevenson at Saranac, v.2, p.35–44. 7120

Benedict, Darwin. Robert Louis Stevenson at Saranac. *Cloud Splitter*, Sept.–Oct. 1947. 10:no.5:8–10. Account of Stevenson's activities at Baker cottage. 7121

Brown, Lawrason. Stevenson and Saranac. n.p. n.pub. 1915. 15p. Pamphlet reprint from a catalog of an exhibition of Stevenson first editions at the Grolier Club, Nov. 1914. 7122

C., C.W. Stevenson in the Adirondacks, with quotations from his letters. *For Leaves*, Dec. 1903. 1:no.1:13–16. illus.   7123

Chalmers, Stephen. Enchanted cigarettes; or, Stevenson stories that might have been. Boston, Houghton, 1917. 43p. "Read before the Stevenson Society. . .Saranac Lake, New York, October 28, 1916."   7124

Chalmers, Stephen. The penny piper of Saranac; an episode in Stevenson's life; with a preface by Lord Guthrie. Boston, Houghton, 1916. 62p. front. plates, ports. Reviewed in *The Outlook*, Oct. 4, 1916, 114:252–53. Brief sketch of Stevenson's life at Saranac Lake during the winter of 1887–88, done in collaboration with Dr. Edward Livingston Trudeau. First published in *The Outlook*, Oct. 12, 1912, 102:314–20.   7125

Chalmers, Stephen. The singer in the snows. *Med Pick*, Jan. 1915. 1:4–8. illus. Stevenson's stay at Saranac.   7126

Davis, Richard Harding. People, people everywhere. Footprints of a wanderer. N.Y. Stokes, 1936. 355p. illus. Contains a chapter on Stevenson at Saranac.   7127

Duncan, William Henry Jr. Stevenson's second visit to America. *Bookm*, Jan. 1900. 10:455–64. ports. illus.   7128

Field, Isobel. Robert Louis Stevenson. Saranac Lake, N.Y. Stevenson society of America, 1920. 87p. plates, front. port. 7129

Hamilton, Clayton Meeker. On the trail of Stevenson. . . The pictures from drawings by Walter Hale. . . Garden City, N.Y. Doubleday, Page, 1915. 151p. front. plates. Also in *The Bookman*, Mar. 1915, 41:29–44. Life at Saranac Lake, Oct. 3, 1887–Apr. 16, 1888. Characterized as "the most productive period of Stevenson's career in the United States."   7130

Low, Will Hicok. A chronicle of friendships, 1873–1900; with illustrations by the author and from his collections. . . N.Y. Scribner, 1908. 507p. front. illus. port. facsims. A Halt Before Saranac, p.376–86; The Return from Saranac, p.396–406; Stevenson's winter in the Adirondacks.   7131

McClure, Samuel Sidney. My autobiography. VI. *McClure*, Mar. 1914. 42:no.5:95–108. illus. R.L. Stevenson in the Adirondacks, p.102–4.   7132

Osbourne, Lloyd. An intimate portrait of R.L.S., by his stepson. *Scrib M*, Nov. 1923–Feb. 1924. 74:515–24, 673–83; 75:66–73, 163–71. The second installment is on Stevenson at Saranac.   7133

Sanchez, Mrs. Nellie (Van de Grift). Life of Mrs. Robert Louis Stevenson. N.Y. Scribner,

1922. 337p. front. plates, port. Saranac Lake, p.125–33.   7134

Stevenson, Mrs. Margaret Isabella (Balfour). From Saranac to the Marquesas and beyond; being letters written by Mrs. M.I. Stevenson during 1887–1888. . . N.Y. Scribner, 1903. 313p. plates, ports. Life at Saranac, p.1–43.   7135

Stevenson, Robert Louis. The letters. . .to his family and friends; selected and edited, with notes and introduction, by Sidney Colvin. . . N.Y. Scribner, 1900. 2v. ports. plates. (Stevenson's Works, Thistle edition, v.23–24.) Saranac Lake, v.2, p.63–127. 7136

Stevenson and Saranac. Reminiscences of the celebrated author's stay in the Adirondacks. *J Outd Life*, Feb. 1905. 2:8–10. illus.   7137

Stevenson society of America, inc. President's report, 1916–1917. Catalogue of relics. List of members. . . Saranac Lake, N.Y. n.d. 34p. plates, ports. Cover title: The Stevenson Society 1916–1917. Supplements issued under title "General Report. Supplement to Yearbook of 1917." Supplements 1–2, 4–12, located; supplement 3 probably not printed. File in the Saranac Lake Free Library. See Donaldson, v.1, p.288–89.   7138

Stevenson's cottage in Adirondacks, where the great author wrote some of his world-famous books; building at Saranac Lake now a memorial to the distinguished writer. *State Service*, Aug. 1919. 3:no.8:21–23. illus. "A Bookman's Memories," from the *Christian Science Monitor*.   7139

Sullivan, Thomas Russell. Robert Louis Stevenson at Saranac. *Scrib M*, Aug. 1917. 62:242–46.   7140

When Robert L. Stevenson lived in Adirondacks. *State Service*, Jan. 1935. p.48–49. 7141

Williams, Helena Lorenz. Stevenson and Trudeau. *J Outd Life*, Jan. 1925. 22:54–55. illus. ports.   7142

Carson, Russell Mack Little. Alfred Billings Street. *High Spots*, July 1932. 9:no.3:10. (Historical Adirondack Character Series, no.8.)   7143

Catalogue of the library and correspondence of the late Mr. Alfred B. Street of Albany, N.Y. . .to be sold at auction, Monday, May 28th 1906. . . Albany, Argus co. n.d. 44p. port. Contains a brief biographical sketch by F.W. Hoyt.   7144

Memoir of Alfred B. Street, with a portrait. *Bentley*, 1849. 25:563–66. port.   7145

Clarence J. Strife dies in Old Forge. *Northeast Log*, July 1953. 1:no.11:15. port.   7146

Clinton county, N.Y. Bar. Proceedings of the bar of the county of Clinton, New York, with other memorials commemorative of the life and character of William Swetland. Albany, J. Munsell, 1865. 53p. Lawyer in Plattsburgh. 7147

Cooke, Rollin H. Rev. John Todd, D.D. *Berk Hist & Sci Soc*, 1899. 3:73–88. 7148

Eggleston, George Cary. Passages from the life of Dr. John Todd. *Harper*, Feb. 1876. 52:372–82. illus. Includes his life in Long Lake. 7149

Todd, John E. John Todd, the story of his life, told mainly by himself. Compiled and edited by John E. Todd... N.Y. Harper, 1876. 529p. front. (port.) plates, illus. Long Lake etc. p.473–80. 7150

Place, Frank. Raymond H. Torrey. *High Spots Yrbk*, 1939. p.64–71. port. 7151

Ashworth, Robert A. "More than conqueror" ...An address in memory of Dr. Edward Livingston Trudeau. Delivered at the Baker memorial chapel, Trudeau, New York, November 16, 1926. n.p. n.d. 4p. Reprinted from the *Adirondack Enterprise*, Nov. 20, 1926. 7152

Biggs, Hermann Michael. Dr. Trudeau as a pioneer in the anti-tuberculosis movement. *J Outd Life*, June 1910. 7:163–65. 7153

Bowditch, Vincent Yardley. A page of memories. *J Outd Life*, Jan. 1925. 22:35–37. illus. E.L. Trudeau. 7154

Brown, Lawrason. Personal recollections. *J Outd Life*, Jan. 1925. 22:22–23. illus. port. E.L. Trudeau. 7155

Cabot, Richard Clarke. Edward Livingston Trudeau, M.D. *Am J Med Sci*, Nov. 1915. 150:780. port. 7156

Chalmers, Stephen. The beloved physician... n.p. Privately printed, c1915. 43p. port. illus. facsim. Copy inscribed to Dr. Lawrason Brown in Saranac Lake Free Library. Rare first edition of the tribute to Edward Livingston Trudeau. 7157

Chalmers, Stephen. The beloved physician; an appreciation of Edward Livingston Trudeau. *Atlan*, Jan. 1916. 117:87–97. 7158

Chalmers, Stephen. Beloved physician, Edward Livingston Trudeau, 1848–1915. Boston, Houghton, 1916. 73p. plates, ports. facsims. (Trudeau Foundation Studies.) 7159

Chalmers, Stephen. Glory of the white gods. *Outing*, Jan. 1913. 61:456–66. E.L. Trudeau. 7160

Dr. Edward L. Trudeau. *Outlook*, Nov. 24, 1915. 111:699. Brief obituary. 7161

Donaldson, Alfred Lee. Trudeau's life a rare romance in medicine. *NY Times Mag*, Nov. 21, 1915. p.4–6. port. illus. 7162

Edward L. Trudeau: a devoted public servant. *Outlook*, Apr. 28, 1906. 82:975–79. port. 7163

Edward L. Trudeau, M.D. *Johns Hop Hosp Bul*, Mar. 1909. 20:85–87. Honoring him on his 60th birthday. 7164

Edward Livingston Trudeau. *Survey*, Dec. 11, 1915. 35:289–90. port. Brief biography and account of his work. 7165

Edward Livingston Trudeau, a biographical sketch. *J Outd Life*, June 1910. 7:157–61. illus. port. 7166

Edward Livingston Trudeau: a symposium. Lawrason Brown, Allen K. Krause, Charles C. Trembley, Harry A. Pattison. Livingston, N.Y. Livingston press, 1935. 112p. plates, ports. 7167

Father of fresh air. *Lit Dig*, Dec. 11, 1915. 51:1384. E.L. Trudeau. 7168

Flexner, Simon. Edward L. Trudeau, physician, investigator and optimist. *J Outd Life*, June 1910. 7:169–72. illus. port. 7169

Halleck, Fitz Greene. Early hunting days with Dr. Trudeau. *J Outd Life*, June 1910. 7:177–78. illus. 7170

Hallock, Grace Taber. ...Edward Livingston Trudeau, by Grace T. Hallock and C.E. Turner. Boston, D.C. Heath & co. c1929. 168p. illus. ports. (Health Hero Series.) Earlier edition published in New York by Metropolitan Life Insurance Company, c1926, 24p. Excerpt in *North Country Life*, Fall 1948, 2:no.4:16–17, 57–59. 7171

Jacobs, Philip P. Edward Livingston Trudeau. *J Outd Life*, Jan. 1925. 22:6. 7172

Knopf, S. Adolphus. Edward Livingston Trudeau, in memoriam. *Am Med Assn J*, June 22, 1916. 66:244–46. Also published as a separate, Chicago, 1916, 6p. port. 7173

Krause, Allen Kramer. Edward L. Trudeau: a study. *Med Pick*, Mar. 1916. 2:82–85. port. Also issued as a reprint. 7174

Krause, Allen Kramer. Reflections on Doctor Trudeau. *J Outd Life*, Jan. 1925. 22:11–21. illus. ports. Also issued as a reprint. 7175

Letulle, Maurice. Une page de l'histoire de la tuberculose. Le docteur E.-L. Trudeau. *Rev d'Hygiene*, Nov. 1916. 38:929–50. 7176

Luck, William B. Edward Livingston Trudeau. The physician beloved. *Churchman*, Dec. 18, 1915. 12:818–19. port. 7177

Memorial meeting to Dr. E.L. Trudeau. Reprinted from the *Johns Hopkins Hospital Bulletin*, Apr. 1916, v.27, no.302, 34p. 7178

Miller, James Alexander. Some vignettes from tuberculosis history. *Hygeia*, Nov. 1936. 14:985. port. E.L. Trudeau. 7179

Miller, James Alexander. The Trudeau influence. *J Outd Life*, Jan. 1925. 22:33–34. illus. 7180

Muller, James Arthur. The religion of Dr. Trudeau. n.p. n.pub. n.d. 28p. Copy in the Saranac Lake Free Library. 7181

Murphy, Charles John Vincent. Conqueror of the white plague; beloved physician of Saranac. *Read Digest*, Apr. 1940. 36:97–101. Condensed from *The Christian Herald*, Feb. 1940, 3:19. E.L. Trudeau. 7182

Myers, J.A. Tuberculous physicians and their contributions. Edward L. Trudeau. *Hygeia*, June 1929. 7:609–10. illus. port. 7183

Osler, William. Edward L. Trudeau—an appreciation. *J Outd Life*, June 1910. 7:162–63. 7184

Parkman, Mary Rosetta. Heroes of today. ...Edward Trudeau... N.Y. Century, 1917. 326p. plates, ports. facsims. 7185

Smith, Paul. Dr. Trudeau's first winter in the Adirondacks. *J Outd Life*, June 1910. 7:175–76. 7186

Trembley, Charles C. Dr. Trudeau as a woodsman. *J Outd Life*, June 1910. 7:173–75. port. 7187

Trudeau, Edward Livingston. An autobiography. Philadelphia, Lea & Febiger, 1916. 322p. front. plates, ports. An edition was published for the National Tuberculosis Association in Garden City, N.Y. Doubleday, Doran, 1928. Extracts in *Bookman*, Feb. 1916, 42:632–35, under title "Stevenson's Trudeau." A review by Percy F. Bicknell, "Genius of Saranac," in *Dial*, Feb. 3, 1916, 60:110–12. 7188

Ureles, S. A memorial to Dr. Trudeau. *Outlook*, Feb. 12, 1919. 121:264–65. illus. 7189

Walsh, James Joseph. The inventor of fresh air. *Ind*, Dec. 6, 1915. 84:404–5. E.L. Trudeau. 7190

War on one of mankind's arch foes. *Scholastic*, Dec. 15, 1934. 25:no.12:14. port. E.L. Trudeau. 7191

Demcourier, Autumn 1939. v.9. Madison, Wis. Demco library supplies, 1939. 32p. illus. This issue is dedicated to Louis Untermeyer and contains several biographical articles with descriptions of Stony Water, his home near Elizabethtown. 7192

Hicks, Harry Wade. Early days of Adirondak loj. *Ad-i-ron-dac*, July–Aug. 1953. 17:68–69, 81. Henry Van Hoevenberg. 7193

Hicks, Harry Wade. Henry Van Hoevenberg. *High Spots Yrbk*, 1940. p.73–81. 7194

Steele, Vern. An upstate character of colonial times, Frederick William Von Steuben. *No Country Life*, Spring 1951. 5:no.2:41–43. illus. 7195

Edwin R. Wallace. *For & Stream*, Aug. 24, 1901. 57:148–49. Obituary. 7196

Tucker, Willis G. A biographical sketch of the late Prof. Samuel Baldwin Ward, M.D. Ph.D. of Albany, N.Y. Albany, 1915. 23p. front. (port.). One of founders of the Upper Saranac Lake Association. 7197

An Adirondack pioneer. *For Leaves*, Summer 1905. 2:no.3:29–31. port. Life of James M. Wardner. 7198

Burnham, John Bird. Gens des bois. IX: James M. Wardner. *For & Stream*, Nov. 10, 1900. 55:363–64. 7199

Flick, Hugh M. Elkanah Watson and the north country. An address. *Ver Hist Soc Proc*, Sept. 1940. n.s.8:289–96. 7200

Burger, William H. George Webster—an Adirondack minister. *No Country Life*, Summer 1954. 8:no.3:59–62. 7201

Fosburgh, Peter W. Clint West. *NYS Con*, Feb.–Mar. 1954. 8:no.4:inside front cover. port. Brief obituary of Forest Ranger at Lake Colden. 7202

Hosmer, Ralph Sheldon. James S. Whipple, Forest administrator. *Bul Schools*, Mar. 1943. 29:252–54. port. Whipple was Commissioner of the Forest, Fish and Game Commission, 1905–10. 7203

Society of American foresters. New York section dedicates Whipple memorial. *J For*, Nov. 1941. 39:949. Tablet set on the summit of Whiteface Mountain. 7204

Marshall, Mrs. Margaret (White). Afterglow. n.p. n.pub. n.d. 16p. port. Copy in the Loomis Collection, Keene Valley Public Library. Paper on William Augustus White, read by his daughter, Aug. 3, 1940. 7205

Frank S. Witherbee. *Iron Age*, Apr. 19, 1917. 99:969. port. Obituary. 7206

Frank Spencer Witherbee. *Iron Tr R*, Apr. 19, 1917. 60:893. Obituary. 7207

Frank Spencer Witherbee. His life, his family, memorial tributes. N.Y. De Vinne press, n.d. 38p. port. Copy in the Witherbee Collection, Sherman Free Library, Port Henry. 7208

In memoriam. Jonathan G. Witherbee. Port Henry, N.Y.? 1875. 32p. port. Copy in the Witherbee Collection, Sherman Free Library, Port Henry. 7209

Woolsey, Melancthon Lloyd, ed. ...Melancthon Lloyd Woolsey...a memoir, compiled for his descendants by his great-grandson... Champlain, N.Y. Moorsfield press, 1929.

33p. port. plates. (Woolsey Paper, no.3.) 130 copies printed by Hugh McLellan.   7210

The useful life of Ed Worthington. *Red Book*, Mar. 1950. 94:no.5:25. port. Active in the Study and Craft Guild, Saranac Lake.   7211

Crawford, Mary Caroline. The romance of old New England churches. . . Boston, L.C. Page & co. ᶜ1903. 379p. front. port. plates. (Little Pilgrimages.) The ostracism of an abolitionist, p.323–46. Rev. Joshua Young.   7212

THE ADIRONDACKS
IN ART AND LITERATURE

GENERAL

Bacheller, Irving. American backgrounds for fiction; V. The north country of New York. *Bookm*, Feb. 1914. 38:624–28. illus. port. 7213

Champney, Mrs. Elizabeth (Williams). Summer haunts of American artists. *Century*, Oct. 1885. 30:845–60. illus. Includes illustration of the interior of R.M. Shurtliff's studio at Keene Valley. 7214

Clinton county eleventh annual May music festival, Plattsburgh, New York. April 28–May 3, 1930. n.p. n.d. 40p. Program. 7215

Cowdrey, Bartlett. Arthur Fitzwilliam Tait, master of the American sporting scene. *Am Collector*, Jan. 1945. 13:5. illus. Made paintings of many Adirondack scenes that were published by Currier & Ives. 7216

Deerwood—Adirondack music center, Saranac Inn, New York. n.p. 1954. 10p. illus. 7217

Fosburgh, James W. Winslow Homer, artist; a great painter who left an inspiring record of the Adirondacks he knew and loved. *NYS Con*, Aug.–Sept. 1948. 3:no.1:16–18. illus. 7218

Garland, Hamlin. Irving Bacheller; interpreter of the old America to the new. *Red Cross M*, Mar. 1920. 15:no.3:11–14, 79. Reprinted in *State Service*, July–Aug. 1920, 4,i.e.6:566–68, with title "Visit to the Homeland of Eben Holden, Northern New York..." 7219

The home book of the picturesque; or, American scenery, art, and literature. Comprising a series of essays by Washington Irving, W.C. Bryant, Fenimore Cooper...etc. with thirteen engravings on steel, from pictures by eminent artists. N.Y. Putnam, 1852. 188p. 13 plates (incl. front.). Published in 1868 with changes and additions under title "A Landscape Book" (no.7224). Adirondack Mountains, by A.B. Street, p.161. Schroon Lake, p.165. 7220

Howard, John Tasker. Studies of contemporary American composers. Eastwood Lane. N.Y. J. Fischer, 1925. 27p. Evaluation and explanation of Lane's Adirondack sketches. 7221

Jordan, Philip D. A possible source for "A tight fix." *Antiques*, Jan. 1939. 35:no.1:28–29. illus. Possible source of inspiration for the Currier & Ives lithograph that is supposed to have an Adirondack locale. 7222

Keyes, Homer Eaton. A.F. Tait in painting and lithograph, a gallery note. *Antiques*, July 1933. 24:no.1:24–25. Discussion of some of his paintings and lithographs of Adirondack scenes. 7223

A landscape book by American artists and American authors; sixteen engravings on steel, from paintings by Cole, Church, Cropsey, Durand, Gignoux, Kensett, Miller, Richards, Smillie, Talbot, Weir. N.Y. Putnam, 1868. 108p. front. plates. Chapter on the Adirondack mountains, by Street, p.35–37; Schroon Lake, p.44; Lake George, p.96. The essays were written for the volume in its original shape: "The Book of the Picturesque" (no.7220). 7224

Larom, Walter H. Mark Twain in the Adirondacks. *Bookm*, Jan. 1924. 58:536–38. Lower Saranac Lake. 7225

Literary landmarks of the Adirondacks. *Outlook*, Sept. 19, 1908. 90:105–7. The "Spectator" talks of the Adirondack life of Stevenson, Aldrich, Emerson, Lowell, Warner and others. 7226

Marcy attracts men of letters: 1846–1859–1865. *High Spots*, July 1937. 14:no.3:17–27. illus. Extracts from: I. Letters from the Backwoods, by J.T. Headley; II. The Hudson from the Wilderness to the Sea, by B.J. Lossing; III. The Indian Pass, by A.B. Street. 7227

Mather, Frank Jewett. Homer Martin, poet in landscape. N.Y. Privately printed, 1912. 76p. col. front. plates. Two hundred and fifty copies printed by Frederic Fairchild Sherman. Adirondacks, p.29–30, 70–71. Includes reproductions of the following paintings: Lake Sanford, Lake Champlain, Adirondack Scenery. 7228

Peters, Harry T. Currier and Ives, printmakers to the American people. Garden

City, N.Y. Doubleday, Doran, 1929–31. 2v. plates. Arthur Fitzwilliam Tait, v.1, p.99–110.
7229

Reade, R.C. Painter of the Adirondacks. *Int Studio*, Sept. 1923. 77:495–97. illus. port. Archibald Brown.
7230

Richards, Thomas Addison. American scenery, illustrated. . .with 32 engravings on steel. N.Y. G.A. Leavitt, c1854. 310p. front. illus. plates. Lake George and the Adirondacks, p.211–55.
7231

Salmon, Del B. Haunts of "Eben Holden." *Four Tr News*, Jan. 1903. 4:10–12. illus.
7232

Sanborn, Ashton. Winslow Homer's "Adirondack guide." *Boston Mus Bul*, June 1948.

46:48–51. port. illus. The identification of the original of the painting as Harvey Holt (1808–93).
7233

Smith, Martha Voley. A story of two portraits. *DAR Mag*, Feb. 1927. 61:116–22. ports. Copley portraits of Mrs. Crean Brush and her daughter Frances in the Ticonderoga Museum.
7234

Wyant, Alexander H. Sixty paintings. . . described by Eliot Clark. N.Y. Privately printed, 1920. 144p. plates. Copy in the New York Public Library. One of 150 copies printed by F.F. Sherman. Includes reproductions of many of his Adirondack paintings.
7235

ESSAYS

Abbott, Henry. The anxious seat. N.Y. 1914. 25p. illus. partly mounted. The first of the privately printed "birch-bark" books, issued as Christmas greetings, 1914–32. All of them are illustrated, many with mounted reproductions of photographs and maps. Other titles in the series are: Lost Pond, 1915; Camping Out at Cherry Pond, 1916; Old Bare-back and Other Stories, 1917; Camps and Trails, 1918; Fish Stories, 1919; The Chief Engineer, 1920; Cold River, 1921; Muskrat City, 1922; On the Bridge, 1923; Anthony Ponds, 1924; Fishing Brook, 1925; Wild Cat Mountain, 1926; Pioneering at Rowan-wood, 1927; Tirrell Pond, 1928; North Bay Brook, 1929; Psychology of the Lost, 1930; Raquette River, 1931; Pine Brook, 1932. See article by D.A. Plum "Henry Abbott's 'Birch Bark Books' " in *The Ad-i-ron-dac*, July–Aug. 1952, 16:71, 73, port.
7236

An Adirondack evening. *For & Stream*, May 31, 1883. 20:344. An appreciation of nature.
7237

Chalmers, Stephen. Watching the hour glass. Saranac Lake, N.Y. Adirondack enterprise press, 1913. 47p. "Narrative essay about local conditions."
7238

Hepworth, George Hughes. Brown studies, or camp fires and morals. N.Y. Dutton, 1897, c1895. 332p. front. plates. p.14. "My little parcel of wilderness was at the western end of the Adirondacks." Religio-philosophical.
7239

Kirkham, Stanton Davis. East and west; comparative studies of nature in eastern and western states. N.Y. Putnam, 1911. 280p. front. plates. The Wilderness, p.42–57. Still-paddling, p.58–70.
7240

Penrose, Charles. . . .Retrospect of mountain pilgrimage. . . A Newcomen address, 1941. Princeton, N.J. Printed at the Princeton university press, 1941. 24p. illus.
7241

"Topics of the Times" considers the Adirondacks. *Ad-i-ron-dac*, July–Aug. 1951. 15:80. Column by William Chapman White reprinted from the *New York Times* of Aug. 9, 1950.
7242

Warner, Charles Dudley. . . .A-hunting of the deer, and other essays. Boston, Houghton, 1888. 85p. (Riverside Literature Series.) Contents: A-hunting of the Deer; How I Killed a Bear; Lost in the Woods; Camping Out; A Wilderness Romance; What Some People Call Pleasure. (Describes climbing Nipple Top with Old Mountain Phelps as guide.) His "In the Wilderness" also contains some of these essays.
7243

Warner, Charles Dudley. In the wilderness. Boston, Houghton, 1876. 176p. Numerous other editions.
7244

White, William Chapman. North country lilacs. *No Country Life*, Spring 1953. 7:no.2: 5–6. Reprinted from the New York *Herald Tribune*.
7245

FICTION

Abel, Hilde (Mrs. David Albert Davidson). Guests of summer. Indianapolis, Bobbs-

Merrill, 1951. 271p. Scene laid in summer hotel.
7246

Adirondack Bill, pseud. Reddy gets a wampus; a tale of the Adirondacks. *Fur News*, Feb. 1922. 35:no.2:34.   7247

Atherton, Mrs. Gertrude Franklin (Horn). The aristocrats: being the impressions of the Lady Helen Pole, during her sojourn in the great north woods as spontaneously recorded in her letters to her friend in North Britain, the Countess of Edge and Ross; 3d ed. London, N.Y. John Lane, 1901. 309p. Published anonymously.   7248

Aylesworth, Barton O. "Thirteen" and twelve others, from the Adirondacks and elsewhere. St. Louis, Mo. Christian publishing co. 1892. 259p.   7249

Bacheller, Irving. Eben Holden: a tale of the north country. Boston, Lothrop publishing co. 1900. 432p.   7250

Bacheller, Irving. Eben Holden's last day a-fishing. N.Y. Harper, 1907. 60p. front. 7251

Bacheller, Irving. The light in the clearing: a tale of the north country in the time of Silas Wright. . .illustrated by Arthur I. Keller. . . Indianapolis, Bobbs-Merrill, c1917. 414p. front. plates.   7252

Bacheller, Irving. The lonesome man of Huckleberry lake. *Am Mag*, Mar. 1911. 71:649–54. illus. Subject is a guide.   7253

Bacheller, Irving. Silas Strong, emperor of the woods. N.Y. Harper, 1906. 340p. front. map.   7254

Bacheller, Irving. The soloist of Center pond. *Hampton*, Aug. 1911. 27:206–10. illus. Reprinted in *Current Literature*, Dec. 1911, 51:697–99. About an eccentric Adirondack guide.   7255

Bacheller, Irving. A son of heaven. Being the solution of a mystery about a strange personality that once moved among the hills and vales of northern New York. *Rotarian*, Feb. 1936. 48:13–15. illus.   7256

Bacheller, Irving. Tale of two burdens. *Century*, Aug. 1908. 54:548–52. illus.   7257

Bacheller, Irving. Uncle Eb's last day a-fishing. *Century*, Dec. 1906. n.s.51:232–38. plate.   7258

Baldwin, Faith. Juniper tree. N.Y. Rinehart, 1952. 303p.   7259

Best, Herbert. Whistle, daughter, whistle. N.Y. Macmillan, 1947. 300p. Early life in the Champlain valley.   7260

Best, Herbert. Young 'un. N.Y. Macmillan, 1944. 271p. Early fur trading days on Lake Champlain.   7261

Bethune, George Washington. Piseco, a sketch. *In* Knickerbocker gallery. . . N.Y. S. Hueston, 1855. p.117–29.   7262

Blankman, Edgar B. Deacon Babbitt: a tale of fact and fiction. Philadelphia, Winston, 1906. 334p. plates, ports.   7263

Boardman, William Henry. A kind of hero. *McClure*, Mar. 1904. 22:460–65.   7264

Brandreth, Paulina. The silver horn, a forest idyl. *For & Stream*, Nov. 21, 1908. 71:808–10.   7265

Carlstrom, John A. The hermit's secret. *St No Mo*, Aug. 1906. 1:no.4:7–15.   7266

Carlstrom, John A. The phantom bell. *St No Mo*, July 1908. 4:17–32.   7267

Catherwood, Mrs. Mary (Hartwell). Lazarre; with illustrations by André Castaigne. Indianapolis, Bowen, Merrill co. c1901. 436p. front. plates. The lost Dauphin.   7268

Chalmers, Stephen. An ex-tenderfoot and a buck. *Outing*, Sept. 1910. 56:697–708. illus.   7269

Clark, Charles Dunning, d. 1892. The lake rangers. A tale of Ticonderoga, by W.J. Hamilton, pseud. N.Y. Beadle & co. 1868. 98p. (Beadle Dime Novels, no.161.) Copy in the Library of Congress.   7270

Colvin, Addison Beacher. Lumberman "Lew"; a story of fact, fantasy and fiction by Harvester Hiram, pseud. Glens Falls, N.Y. Glens Falls publishing co. 1918. 117p. Scene is Warrensburg, N.Y.   7271

Colvin, Addison Beacher. "Stray steps," by Harvester Hiram, pseud. Glens Falls, N.Y. Glens Falls publishing co. c1920. 200p. Location, The Glen.   7272

Curtis, May Belle. "Kathi" of Skenesborough. Glens Falls, N.Y. Champlain publishing co. c1914. 255p.   7273

Curtis, Newton Mallory. The bride of the northern wilds. A tale of 1743 . . .rev. enl. and cor. N.Y. Burgess, Stringer & co. c1843. 120p. French and Indian wars.   7274

Curtis, Newton Mallory. . . .Giant Jack, the patrol of the mountains. A tale of the Champlain hills. N.Y. Beadle & Adams, 1883. 24p. illus. (Beadle's Dime Library, v.20, no.254.) Previously published under title: The Patrol of the Mountains; a Tale of the Revolution. Copy in the New York State Library.   7275

Curtis, Newton Mallory. The maid of the Saranac; a tale of the War of 1812. N.Y. Williams bros. 1848. 79p.   7276

Deming, Philander. An Adirondack home. *Lippincott*, Aug. 1882. 30:142–51. See George Newell Lovejoy's article, "Mr. Philander Deming," in *The Book Buyer*, Aug. 1902, ser.3:25:15–16.   7277

Deming, Philander. Adirondack stories. Boston, Houghton, 1880. 192p. Other printings: 1886, 1902 and 1907.   7278

Deming, Philander. Benjamin Jacques. *Atlan*, June 1875. 35:699–704.   7279

Deming, Philander. John's trial. *Atlan*, Mar. 1874. 33:276–81. Reprinted in *Forest Leaves*, Winter 1908, 4:no.4:3–14, illus.   7280

Deming, Philander. Lida Ann: an Adirondack sketch. *Atlan*, Jan. 1874. 33:28–35. 7281

Deming, Philander. Lost. *Atlan*, Feb. 1873. 31:218–22. The first of Deming's series of short stories on the Adirondacks.   7282

Deming, Philander. Tompkins and other folks. Stories of the Hudson and the Adirondacks. Boston, Houghton, 1885. 223p. An Adirondack Home, p.186–223.   7283

Deming, Philander. Willie. *Atlan*, July 1874. 34:51–54.   7284

Dreiser, Theodore. An American tragedy. N.Y. Liveright, 1929. 409p. Murder at Big Moose Lake. See article by Eleanor Waterbury Franz: "The Tragedy of the 'North Woods,' " *New York Folklore Quarterly*, Summer 1948, 4:85–97.   7285

Early, Eleanor. Adirondack tales; decorations by Virginia Grilley. Boston, Little, Brown, 1939. 247p. illus. "Campbell's Ghost" reprinted in *North Country Life*, Spring 1947, 1:no.3:53–59.   7286

Evans, Florence (Wilkinson). Strength of the hills. N.Y. Harper, 1901. 395p.   7287

The farmer's daughter, of Essex. Written by herself. N.Y. Printed by Lewis Nichols for Evart Duykinck, 1802. 108p.   7288

Fosburgh, Hugh. The sound of white water. N.Y. Scribner, 1955. 192p. Background near Minerva. Canoe trip.   7289

Foster, David Skaats. Elinor Fenton, an Adirondack story. Philadelphia, Lippincott, 1893. 300p.   7290

Foster, Maximilian. In the forest. N.Y. Doubleday, Page, 1901. 318p. plate. Story of a deer (Adirondack locale), p.26–52. 7291

Francis, John M. Catching a sucker; another "Jud" Smith yarn. *Amer Angler*, Apr. 1921. 5:633–35.   7292

Francis, John M. "Jud's" revenge. *Amer Angler*, June 1920. 5:88–90. Horicon area.   7293

Francis, John M. Like David and Goliath. *Amer Angler*, Oct. 1920. 5:268–69. "Uncle Jud" story—scene Brant Lake.   7294

Francis, John M. The lure of the human hand. (Another "Jud" Smith story.) *Amer Angler*, Aug. 1921. 6:228–29.   7295

Francis, John M. Pulling a bone, another "Uncle Jud" story. *Amer Angler*, Feb. 1921. 5:501–2. Brant Lake locale.   7296

Gilbert, Nelson Rust. The affair at Pine court, a tale of the Adirondacks; with illustrations in color by Frank H. Desch. Philadelphia, Lippincott, 1907. 391p. incl. col. front. col. plates.   7297

Gordon, Julien (Mrs. Van Rensselaer Cruger). Underbrush. *Smart Set*, Sept. 1901. 5:no.1:95–99. Romance based on the life of Henry Van Hoevenberg.   7298

Gould, Mrs. Jennie W. Truth is stranger than fiction. [A Port Henry vs. California story by Zelma Hope.] n.p. W. Lansing & son, 1891. 86p. Copy in the Library of Congress. Author lived in Port Henry.   7299

Hamilton, Francis E. In the north woods. *Munsey*, Nov. 1892. 8:178–82.   7300

Harbaugh, Thomas Chalmers. ...The hidden lodge; or, The little hunter of the Adirondacks... N.Y. Beadle & Adams, c1878. 15p. illus. (Beadle's Half-Dime Library, no.37.) Caption title.   7301

Harbaugh, Thomas Chalmers. ...Piney Paul, the mountain boy. N.Y. Beadle & Adams, c1886. 31p. illus. (Beadle's Pocket Library, no.114.) Cover title. Caption has subtitle: The Little Arrow of the Adirondacks.   7302

Harmes, Edward A. The orphan. *Cloud Splitter*, Sept.–Oct. 1947. 10:no.5:2–4.   7303

Her highness, an Adirondack romance. Boston, Badger, 1910. 309p.   7304

Hicks, Clifton. The little lion. N.Y. Island press, 1946. 256p. Reviewed in the Spring 1950 issue of *North Country Life*. Setting of the novel is St. Regis Falls region.   7305

Hotchkiss, Chauncey Crafts. The strength of the weak. N.Y. Appleton, 1902. 371p. Trip to Lake George and Lake Champlain during French and Indian War.   7306

Huntington, Jedidiah Vincent. The forest. N.Y. Redfield, 1852. 384p. Munson considered this the earliest Adirondack romance. Sequel to "Alban."   7307

Jackson, Mrs. Helen Maria (Fiske) Hunt. Between whiles. Boston, Roberts bros. 1887. 304p. Dandy Steve, p.269–91.   7308

James, George Payne Rainsford. Ticonderoga; or, The black eagle. A romance of days not far distant. N.Y. Harper, 1854. 138p.   7309

Johnson, S. Paige. Zebadiah Sartwell, the miller of Whallonsburgh; illustrated by Wm. L. Hudson; foreword by Stephen G. Clow. N.Y. Broadway publishing co. 1903. 318p. front. (port.) plates.   7310

Laforet, Lucille. Philosophy in the Adirondacks. *Pet Mag*, Oct. 1883. 84:283–88. illus.   7311

Linney, Joseph Robert. The touch of human hands: a novel. Philadelphia, Dorrance & co. c1947. 478p. Life in an Adirondack mining community in the 1920's.   7312

Longstreth, Thomas Morris. Mac of Placid. N.Y. Century, 1920. 339p. front.   7313

Lothrop, Mrs. Harriet Mulford (Stone). An Adirondack cabin: a family story, telling the journeyings by lake and mountain, and idyllic days in the heart of the wilderness, by Margaret Sidney, pseud. Boston, Lothrop, c1890. 432p. illus.   7314

Ludlum, Jean Kate. At Brown's; an Adirondack story. N.Y. Hunt & Eaton, 1890. 341p. front. plates.   7315

Ludlum, Jean Kate. Under oath, an Adirondack story. With illustrations by Warren B. Davis. N.Y. R. Bonner's sons, 1890. 337p. plates.   7316

Lundy, John Patterson. The Saranac exiles: a winter's tale of the Adirondacks. Not by W. Shakespeare. Philadelphia, Author, 1880. 329p. See Raymond's "Story of Saranac" (no.733). Manuscript revision in the New York State Library. Another manuscript copy in the Donaldson Collection, Saranac Lake Free Library. This collection also includes eight other Lundy manuscripts (poems).   7317

McClintock, Marshall. We take to bed. N.Y. Jonathan Cape & Harrison Smith, c1931. 321p. Saranac Lake.   7318

McDermott, William A. Adirondack sketches; stories, by Walter Lecky, pseud. *Cath World*, Jan., Mar., Apr.–July 1894. 58:554–67, 773–82; 59:14–24, 164–73, 322–37, 492–501. illus.   7319

McDermott, William A. Mr. Billy Buttons. A novel. By Walter Lecky, pseud. N.Y. Benziger bros. 1896. 274p. (American Author Series of Catholic Novels.)   7320

Manvill, Mrs. P.D. Lucinda; or, The mountain mourner. Being recent facts, in a series of letters from Mrs. Manvill, in the State of New-York, to her sister in Pennsylvania. Johnstown, N.Y. W. & A. Child, 1807. 150p. For other editions see Wright. Fiction. The locale is the Kayaderisseras Mountains. 7321

Murray, William Henry Harrison. Adirondack letters... *Golden Rule*, Aug. 9–Sept. 6, 1876. 1:no.45–49. On page one of each issue. No. I, En Route, republished in the London and Golden Rule Publishing Co. editions of "Adirondack Tales." No. II, not republished. No. III, republished as "Crossing a Carry in the Dark." No. IV, Climbing White Face, republished in the London and Golden Rule Publishing Co. editions of

"Adirondack Tales." No. V, Sleeping in the Woods, not republished.   7322

Murray, William Henry Harrison. Adirondack tales. Burlington, Vt. Murray lyceum bureau, c1886. 295p. plates. Also published in Springfield, Mass. in 5v. set, c1897–98. Contents of the different editions of "Adirondack Tales" vary. This one contains: John Norton's Christmas; Henry Herbert's Thanksgiving; A Strange Visitor; Lost in the Woods (A Fragment); A Jolly Camp; Was It Suicide? The Gambler's Death; The Old Beggar's Dog; The Ball; Who Was He? "Was It Suicide" appeared in *The Golden Rule*, Aug. 21, 1878. An expanded version of "Who Was He?" in *Golden Rule*, Jan.–May 1879.   7323

Murray, William Henry Harrison. Adirondack tales. London, Richard D. Dickinson, 1878. 338p. Contents: The Story of the Man Who Didn't Know Much; The Story That the Keg Told Me; Sketches (En Route, Crossing a Carry in the Dark, Climbing White-Face).   7324

Murray, William Henry Harrison. The Adirondack tales. Springfield, Mass. Press of Springfield printing & binding co. c1897–98. 5v. fronts. Contents: Vol. 1: The Story of the Man Who Didn't Know Much; Vol. 2: The Story of the Man Who Missed It; The Story That the Keg Told Me, and Who Were They? Vol. 3: Mamelons and Ungava; Vol. 4: Stories of Description and Humor (including How Deacon Tubman and Parson Whitney Celebrated New Year's, Henry Herbert's Thanksgiving, A Ride with a Mad Horse in a Freight Car, Phantom Falls, Jack Shooting in a Foggy Night); Vol. 5: Sermons, lectures and addresses. 7325

Murray, William Henry Harrison. Adirondack tales, with full-page illustrations designed by Darley and Merrill. Engraved by James S. Conant. Boston, Golden Rule publishing co. 1877. 459p. front. illus. Contents: The Story the Keg Told Me; The Man Who Didn't Know Much; Sketches: Adirondack Letters (En Route, Crossing a Carry in the Dark, Climbing White Face).   7326

Murray, William Henry Harrison. Adventures in the wilderness; or, Camp-life in the Adirondacks. Boston, Fields, Osgood, 1869. 236p. front. plates. The volume that started the "Murray Rush." See Donaldson, v.1, p.190–201. Sherrill states that this was also published with titles "Vacation Adventures in the Wilderness" and "Adirondack Adventures in the Wilderness." "Crossing the Carry" reprinted in *Field and Stream*, June 1902, 7:147–50; "Rod and Reel in the Adirondacks" reprinted in *Field and Stream*, July 1902, 7:202–6; "The Wilderness" reprinted in *American Angler*, Oct. 1917, 2:303–8. Reviewed by Darwin Benedict in *The Cloud Splitter*, Apr. 1943, 6:no.4:3–4. "Several of the chapters...were originally published in the Meriden Literary Recorder, during the fall and winter of 1867." Advertisements for this volume appeared in the *Atlantic Monthly*, Apr.–Aug. 1869. The 9th edition was listed in the July issue and the Tourist's Edition in August.   7327

Murray, William Henry Harrison. Cones for the camp fire. Boston, DeWolfe, Fiske & co. c1891. 189p. Excerpts from his books, many from "Adirondack Tales."   7328

Murray, William Henry Harrison. Holiday tales, Christmas in the Adirondacks. Springfield, Mass. Springfield printing & binding co. c1897. 113p. incl. plates, front. (port.) illus. Contents: How John Norton the Trapper Kept His Christmas; John Norton's Vagabond. A story taken from this volume and adapted by Grace Hudowalski appeared in *The Cloud Splitter*, Dec. 1942, 5:no.9:7, with title: Any That Be in Want.   7329

Murray, William Henry Harrison. How Deacon Tubman and Parson Whitney kept New Year's and other stories. St. Johnsbury, Vt. Caledonia county publishing co. 1887. 196p. plates, illus. Contents: How Deacon Tubman and Parson Whitney Kept New Year's; The Old Beggar's Dog; The Ball; Who Was He?   7330

Murray, William Henry Harrison. How John Norton, the trapper, kept his Christmas. Boston, DeWolfe, Fiske & co. 1890. 109p. Also issued in New York by Platt & Peck, 1890, front. plates; reprinted in 1911 by the same firm.   7331

Murray, William Henry Harrison. How the old trapper solved it. *Golden Rule*, Mar. 6–Apr. 17, May 1–June 5, Oct. 9–Dec. 11, 1878. 3:no.23–29, 31–36; 4:no.2–11. Usually on pages 1 and 8. Reprinted as "The Mystery of the Woods."   7332

Murray, William Henry Harrison. John Norton's Thanksgiving party and other stories. Boston, DeWolfe, Fiske & co. c1886. 231p. front. (port.). Contents: John Norton's Thanksgiving Party; Henry Herbert's Thanksgiving; A Strange Visitor; The Shadow on the Wall; Was It Suicide? The Old Beggar's Dog; Who Was He? The first story appeared in *The Golden Rule*, Nov. 28, 1877.   7333

Murray, William Henry Harrison. The mystery of the woods and the man who missed it. Boston, DeWolfe, Fiske & co. 1891. 460p. port. Binder's title: Murray's Adirondack Tales.   7334

Murray, William Henry Harrison. An old timer's adventures in the Adirondacks. *Fur*

News, July 1916–Feb. 1917. 24:no.1:12–13; 24:no.2:4–5; 24:no.3:4–5; 24:no.4:28–30; 24:no.5:6–7, 65–66; 24:no.6:38–39, 49–52; 25:no.1:26–33, 41; 25:no.2:18–19. Contents: The Nameless Creek; Running the Rapids; Loon-shooting in a Thunderstorm; Rod and Reel; Phantom Falls; Jack-shooting in a Foggy Night; A Ride with a Mad Horse in a Freight Car; Sabbath in the Woods.   7335

Murray, William Henry Harrison. Phantom falls. A tale of the Adirondacks. Alpine-on-Hudson, N.J. 1954. unpaged. Printed at the Harbor Press, N.Y. Christmas book issued by George A. Zabriskie. Copy in the Loomis Collection, Keene Valley Public Library.
                    7336

Murray, William Henry Harrison. Phantom falls; a tale of the Adirondacks. N.Y. Harbor press, 1927. 22p. plate. Signed: W.H.H.M.
                    7337

Murray, William Henry Harrison. A ride with a mad horse in a freight-car. *Atlan*, Apr. 1869. 23:503–13. Reprinted in *The Golden Rule*, Sept. 4, 1878.   7338

Murray, William Henry Harrison. Sabbath night in the Adirondacks. *Golden Rule*, July 26, 1876. 1:no.43:1. From his "Adventures."
                    7339

Murray, William Henry Harrison. The story of the man who missed it. *Golden Rule*, Dec. 5, 1877–Feb. 6, 1878. 3:nos.11–12, 14–19. Usually on pages 1 and 8.   7340

Murray, William Henry Harrison. The story the keg told me; and The story of the man who did not know much. Boston, Cupples & Hurd, c1889. 454p. port. Half title: The Adirondack Tales, v.1. Published in Boston by DeWolfe, Fiske & co. 1887. Originally published in *The Golden Rule*, Sept. 27, 1876–May 23, 1877.   7341

Murray, William Henry Harrison. Summer letter from Mr. Murray. *Golden Rule*, July 31, 1878. 3:no.44:1. At Bartlett's.   7342

North, Nelson. Ask and receive, including stories and folklore of the Adirondack and Lake Champlain region. Chicago, Scroll publishing co. 1901. 83p.   7343

Paine, Albert Bigelow. The lucky piece; a tale of the north woods. N.Y. Outing publishing co. 1906. 250p. front.   7344

Peck, Theodora Agnes. White dawn; a legend of Ticonderoga. N.Y. F.H. Revell, c1914. 306p. plates, front.   7345

Phillips, Ephraim. Lucretia; or, Lost in the Adirondacks. A tale of love at Piseco. Schenectady, N.Y. Charles Burrows, 1890. 60p.   7346

Prime, William C. The Owl creek letters, and other correspondence, by W. N.Y.

Baker & Scribner, 1848. 203p. The letters were originally published in the *Journal of Commerce.*   7347

Rockwood, Caroline Washburn. An Adirondack romance. N.Y. New Amsterdam book co. c1897. 181p. front. illus.   7348

Rouse, William Merriam. Bildad road. N.Y. Orlin Tremaine co. c1940. 204p.   7349

Sand, Bergoth. Spring on Mount Pisgah. *J Outd Life*, Feb. 1924. 21:85–86.   7350

Scott, George. Tamarack farm; the story of Rube Wolcott and his Gettysburg girl. N.Y. Grafton, 1903. 236p. front. port.   7351

Sellingham, Ella J.H. The hero of Carillon; or, Fort Ticonderoga in 1777. . . Ticonderoga, N.Y. W.T. Bryan, 1897. 171p.   7352

Sherwin, Grayson N. The romance of St. Sacrement. A story of New France and the Iroquois. Burlington, Vt. Free press printing co. 1912. 197p. plates, illus. Based on Lake George legend.   7353

Smith, Frank Berkeley. The lady of Big Shanty. N.Y. Doubleday, Page, 1909. 323p. illus.   7354

Smith, John Talbot. Saranac; a story of Lake Champlain. N.Y. B. Benziger & co. 1922. 280p. Earlier editions: N.Y. 1892; N.Y. Catholic Publishing Co. 1893; N.Y. W.H. Young & Co. 1897 (3d ed.).   7355

Spears, Raymond Smiley. The kid. *For & Stream*, Nov. 6, 1897. 49:363. Picture of a woods boy.   7356

Stone, William Leete, 1792–1844. Tales and sketches, such as they are. N.Y. Harper, 1834. 2v. "Lake St. Sacrement," v.1, p.121–65.   7357

Stone, William Leete, 1792–1844. Ups and downs in the life of a distressed gentleman. N.Y. Leavitt, Lord & co. 1836. 225p. Ch. IX, p.96–110, takes place on Lake George.   7358

Tibbitts, George Franklin. The mystery of Kun-ja-muck cave. A strange mystery trailing through the beautiful mountain and lake country of the Adirondacks. N.Y. Brieger press, c1924. 319p. col. front. Also published in Cornwall, N.Y. Cornwall Press, c1928, 319p. col. front. plates.   7359

Tippetts, Mrs. Katharine (Bell). Prince Arengzeba, a romance of Lake George (by Jerome Cable, pseud.) and Beautiful Lake George. Glens Falls, N.Y. W.H. Tippetts, 1892. 154p. illus. "Beautiful Lake George," by W.H. Tippetts, p.124–54. Published in the *Lake George Mirror* during the season of 1892.   7360

Tomlinson, Everett Titsworth. The fort in the forest; a story of the fall of Fort William Henry in 1757. N.Y. Grosset & Dunlap, c1904. 341p. plates, front. (Colonial Series.)   7361

Vanamee, Mrs. Lida (Ostrom). An Adirondack idyl. N.Y. C.T. Dillingham & co. c1893. 152p.   7362

Vanderpoel, Lew. A Saranac romance. *For & Stream*, Sept. 4, 1884. 23:103.   7363

Van Dyke, Henry. A lover of music. *In* his The ruling passion. . . N.Y. Scribner, 1906. p.1–48.   7364

Van Hoevenberg, Henry. The devil fungus. *St No Mo*, May 1907. 2:33–48.   7365

Van Hoevenberg, Henry. The forsaken village. *St No Mo*, June 1906. 1:no.2:81–86. 7366

Van Hoevenberg, Henry. An horological revenge. *St No Mo*. Sept. 1908. 4:189–93. illus.   7367

Van Hoevenberg, Henry. The mystery of the great pine. *St No Mo*, May 1908. 3:257–73. port.   7368

Van Hoevenberg, Henry. The phantom clock. *St No Mo*, Aug. 1907. 2:259–73.   7369

Van Hoevenberg, Henry. The silver star. *St No Mo*, Jan. 1908. 3:18–30. Lost silver mine.   7370

Vrooman, Mildred. Tea leaves, a local color story with a Lewis county setting. *No Country Life*, Spring 1952. 6:no.2:6–8, 48–50.   7371

Widdemer, Margaret. Prince in buckskin; a story of Joseph Brant at Lake George. Philadelphia, Winston, 1952. 184p. illus. Battle of Lake George.   7372

Wilkins, W.A. The Cleverdale mystery; or, The machine and its wheels. . . N.Y. Fords, Howard & Hulbert, 1882. 287p. Lake George. Author was editor of the *Whitehall Times.*   7373

Willis, Nathaniel Parker. Inklings of adventure. . . N.Y. Saunders & Otley, 1836. 2v. "Edith Lindsey," v.2, p.105–96. Includes a trip to Trenton Falls.   7374

Wood, Richard K. Land of Christmas trees, a tale of the Adirondacks. *Fur News*, Dec. 1920. 32:no.6:38–40.   7375

Young, Albert A. Stories from the Adirondacks. . .by "Adirondack Al." N.Y. London, F. Tennyson Neely, c1899. 126p.   7376

POETRY

Allen, Alice E. To Mount Marcy. *No Country Life*, Summer 1947. 1:no.4:50–51. illus.
7377

Allen's bear fight up in Keene. *High Spots Yrbk*, 1939, p.38.   7378

Arabella, pseud. Ivy isle; Lake of Luzerne, August 9th, 1871. Paradise found by Arabella. n.p. 1871? 4p. Copy in the New York Public Library.   7379

Auringer, Obadiah Cyrus. The book of the hills: new poems and ballads. Troy, N.Y. Stowell & son, 1896. 84p.   7380

Bacheller, Irving. Him an' me. . . *Harper W*, Dec. 10, 1904. 48:no.2503:18–19. col. illus. Poem about Philo Scott, guide.   7381

Bachmann, P.H. William. Adirondacks. *Ad-i-ron-dac*, Mar.–Apr. 1949. 13:26.   7382

Bachmann, P.H. William. Autumn hills. *Ad-i-ron-dac*, Sept.–Oct. 1949. 13:94.   7383

Bachmann, P.H. William. On Saddleback mountain. *Ad-i-ron-dac*, May–June 1949. 13:61.   7384

A ballad concerning the fight between the English and French at Lake George. Boston, 1755. 1 leaf. Broadside. Copy at the Library Company, Philadelphia. Photostat in the New York Public Library.   7385

Barker, Mrs. Edna L. (Snyder). Song for the ADK. *Cloud Splitter*, May–June 1949. 12:no.3:1.   7386

Barnes, Almont. Adirondacks, poem. *Field & S*, Nov. 1899. 4:288–89. The Au Sable.   7387

Baxter, James Phinney. Isaac Jogues, A.D. 1636. *Mag Am Hist*, Jan. 1861. 25:77–84.   7388

Beane, Carson Henry. In the valley o' Champlain. *Vermonter*, June 1908. 13:171.   7389

Bickers, Quarrier. Early winter in the Adirondacks. *NYC Lines Mag*, Jan. 1928. 8:no.10:45.   7390

Bronaugh, Grace B. Champlain. *Vermonter*, Nov. 1901. 7:375. illus. Discovery of Lake Champlain.   7391

Brown, Cornelia W. The north country. *St No Mo*, Sept. 1906. 1:no.5:10–11. illus.   7392

Brown, W. Scott. Sebille. A pioneer commercial salesman in Essex county. *NYS For Assn J*, Oct. 1915. 2:46–48.   7393

Bruce, Wallace. The Hudson; illustrated by Alfred Fredericks. Boston, Houghton, c1881. 37p. illus. The second poem is on the Adirondacks.   7394

Bugbee, Willis N. The lure of the north. *No Country Life*, Summer 1955. 9:no.3:7.   7395

Bushnell, Frances Louisa. Poems. n.p. De Vinne press, 1900. 81p. Privately printed. Copy in the Loomis Collection, Keene Valley Public Library.   7396

Byrne, Mrs. Margaret H. (Myers). Adirondack summer song. *Ad-i-ron-dac*, July–Aug. 1954. 18:73.   7397

Byrne, Mrs. Margaret H. (Myers). Minutes of the meeting of the Board of governors. . . April 18, 1953. *Ad-i-ron-dac*, May–June 1953. 17:61. Verse by Peggy. See also her "In Absentia" in issue for Sept.–Oct. 1953, 17:104; "Annual meeting. . ." in issue for Jan.–Feb. 1954, 18:19. A. Ranger Tyler's tribute in issue for Mar.–Apr. 1954, 18:31: "Lines to the Poetess Laureate of the Adirondacks."
7398

Cady, Daniel Leavens. Champlain and Lake Champlain; a poem from the programme of the Champlain tercentenary celebration of 1909. Albany, J.B. Lyon, 1926. 29p. plates. illus. map.   7399

Carman, Bliss. "An open letter" from Bliss Carman. Boston, Small, Maynard & co. c1920. 17p. Poem written at Saranac Lake.
7400

Carter, Cornelius. Poems, n.p. n.pub. c.1900. 28p. port. plates. See "The Poet of the Adirondacks" by David Lane in *The Ad-i-ron-dac*, Nov.–Dec. 1950. 14:120–23.   7401

Chalmers, Stephen. The Adirondack girl. *Field & S*, Aug. 1915. 20:408. Reprinted from the *Saranac Lake News*.   7402

Chalmers, Stephen. The gilding-star and other poems. Saranac Lake, N.Y. Saranac Lake news print, c1916. 20 leaves. Some of the poems are about the Adirondacks; most of them appeared originally in the *Saranac Lake News*.   7403

Collins, Alma Twiss. Hills—my hills. Elizabethtown, N.Y. Elizabethtown printing co. c1941. Unpaged.   7404

Cook, Joseph. Lake George poems. N.Y. Knickerbocker press, 1903? 27p. plates. These poems also appear in his "Observations," N.Y. Knickerbocker Press, 1903.   7405

Cook, Joseph. Ticonderoga and Montcalm. *Harper*, Aug. 1875. 51:365–71. illus.   7406

Copeland, Margaret Scott. Snowfall in Champlain valley. *Vermonter*, Feb. 1934. 39:33.   7407

Creamer, Edward Sherwood. Adirondack readings; author's edition. Buffalo, N.Y. Charles Wells Moulton, 1893. 116p.   7408

Cummings, William A.E. Verde. *St No Mo*, Sept. 1907. 2:361–65. George Ferd Beede.
7409

Cutting, Sewall S. Lake Champlain: a poem. Burlington, Vt. 1877. 24p. Copy in Yale University Library.   7410

DeNike, Douglas. Gothics for sunrise. *Cloud Splitter*, Sept.–Oct. 1953. 16:no.5:1.   7411

Dewey, Herbert H. Ramblings of a convalescent—homespun philosophy and dialect tales in prose and verse, reflecting fifty years as farmer, salesman and country storekeeping. Champlain, N.Y. Moorsfield press, 1950. 102p.   7412

Donaldson, Alfred Lee. "The good luck arrow." *J Outd Life*, June 1910. 7:179. On Indian superstition, Saranac.   7413

Donaldson, Alfred Lee. Song of Tahawus. *Country Life*, June 1920. 38:no.2:53. illus. 7414

Donaldson, Alfred Lee. Songs of my violin. N.Y. Putnam, 1901. 66p. illus. Reviewed in *Dial*, Jan. 16, 1902. 32:49. Includes music.   7415

Emerson, Ralph Waldo. May-day and other poems. Boston, Ticknor & Fields, 1867. 205p. The Adirondacs, p.41–62. "A journal dedicated to my fellow travellers in August, 1858." (The Philosophers' Camp.) This poem is reprinted in Donaldson, v.2, p.271–80.   7416

Emerson, Ralph Waldo. Poems. Boston, Houghton, 1904. 531p. front. (port.) plates. (Centenary Edition.) The Adirondacks, p.182–94.   7417

Ferdon, Edwin N. Bring back the moose. *Field & S*, Aug. 1901. 6:352.   7418

Fisher, Ella Warner. Idylls from Champlain. Boston, LeRoy Phillips, c1918. 70p.   7419

Flagg, Edward Octavus. Poems. N.Y. T. Whittaker, 1890. 161p. 2d edition published in 1895; revised and enlarged edition, 1910. Adirondack poems. p.81–91.   7420

Forbes, John A. Ticonderoga. *Vermonter*, Apr. 1924. 29:no.4:57.   7421

Forest scenes. By William Cullen Bryant, Henry Wadsworth Longfellow, Fitz-Greene Halleck, Alfred B. Street. N.Y. Hurd & Houghton, c1864. 95 leaves. incl. illus. plates. Contents: A Forest Hymn, by William Cullen Bryant; The Death of the Flowers, by William Cullen Bryant; When Woods Were Green, by Henry W. Longfellow; Wyoming, a Fragment, by Fitz-Greene Halleck; Forest Pictures in the Adirondacks, by Alfred B. Street.   7422

Foster, Mrs. Jeanne Robert (Oliver). Neighbors of yesterday. Boston, Sherman, French & co. 1916. 125p. plates. North Woods characters.   7423

Goldmark, Josephine. Camp on the island. *Ad-i-ron-dac*, May–June 1955. 19:55. Biographical note, p.42.   7424

Hansen, Mildred A. The Adirondacks. *Up-Stater*, Nov. 1929. 4:no.6:4. illus.   7425

Harmes, Edward A. Bushwhacking. *Cloud Splitter*, Nov. 1940. 3:no.7:13.   7426

Heyer, H. Emerson. Ticonderoga. *Vermonter*, May 1913. 18:93.   7427

Hoffman, Charles Fenno. Vigil of faith and other poems; 4th ed. N.Y. Harper, 1845. 164p. First published by S. Colman. N.Y. in 1842 (64p.). Notes on origins of names in the Adirondacks, p.37–40. An Indian legend with an Adirondack locale.   7428

Horn, Dorothy Ryder. Mountain memories. *Cloud Splitter*, Apr. 1939. 2:no.2:6.   7429

Houghton, Alfred Swift. Ticonderoga. A tribute to the revolutionary and heroic efforts of Ethan Allen and his Green mountain boys. St. Albans, Vt. St. Albans messenger co. print, 1897. 24p. illus. Preface by G.F. Houghton.   7430

Hudowalski, Mrs. Grace (Leech). Adirondack climb. *Cloud Splitter*, May 1939. 2:no. 3:8.   7431

Hudowalski, Mrs. Grace (Leech). My mountains! *Cloud Splitter*, Apr. 1939. 2:no.2:8. 7432

Irving, Minna. The Adirondacks. *NYC Lines Mag*, Feb. 1920. 2:no.1:71.   7433

Irving, Minna. Lake Placid by moonlight. *Four Tr News*, Aug. 1905. 9:95. Reprinted in the *Journal of the Outdoor Life*, Sept. 1905, 2: 196.   7434

Kane, H.A. Twilight on Ragged lake. *Woods & Wat*, Autumn 1905. 8:no.3:16.   7435

Knox, Martin Van Buren. Schroon lake. The Indian legend of its name. A poem. . .with illustrations from paintings by Frances Luella Way. . . Wahpeton, N.D. Author, 1901. 36p. illus. Copy in the Munson Collection, Saranac Lake Free Library.   7436

Lake of Luzerne: wayside musings, after the style of bold Robin Hood. Dedicated to the Sisters three. n.p. 1873. 7p.   7437

Lamberton, John Vinton. Wan trip on Lac Champlain. *Vermonter*, Nov. 1906. 11:319.   7438

Lathers, Helen Q. . . .1841–53, Old Nick Stoner. *No Country Life*, Spring 1955. 9: no.2:21.   7439

Leggett, Benjamin Franklin. An idyl of Lake George and other poems. . . Boston, T.O. Metcalf & co. 1895. 217p.   7440

Leonard-Stuart, Charles. In the Adirondacks—an autumnal automobile spin. *For Leaves*, Autumn 1904. 1:no.4:26–27.   7441

Lindsay, Clarence M. In the Adirondacks. *NYC Lines Mag*, Sept. 1925. 6:no.6:58. 7442

Ludlow, Margery N. From Sawteeth. *Cloud Splitter*, June 1939. 2:no.4:6.   7443

Lyman, O.L. Adirondack maid. *Field & S,* Apr. 1900. 5:196.   7444

Lyman, O.L. Adirondacks. *Field & S,* Mar. 1899. 4:263.   7445

Lyon, Mabel. A poem of Lake George. n.p. n.pub. c1932. 4p. Ballad of Rogers' Slide. Copy in the Headquarters House, New York State Historical Association, Ticonderoga.
7446

McCann, Ray N. The sleeping giant. *No Country Life,* Summer 1948. 2:no.3:40. illus.
7447

McLellan, Isaac. Haunts of the deer. *Wild Mag,* Sept. 1888. 1:212–13.   7448

McLellan, Isaac. Haunts of wild game, or poems of woods, wilds and waters. . . ed. by Charles Barker Bradford. N.Y. Charles Barker Bradford, c1896. 207p. front. illus. ports. Contains memoirs of the author.   7449

Malam, Charles F. Ticonderoga. *Vermonter,* 1927. 32:no.2:17.   7450

Marsh, George T. Call of the great north woods. *For Leaves,* Spring 1908. 5:no.1:17.
7451

Mills, Borden H. Sr. The old Marcy trail. *Ad-i-ron-dac,* May–June 1950. 14:61.   7452

Mills, Borden H. Sr. Plateau lean-to—Labor day, 1942. *Cloud Splitter,* Dec. 1942. 5:no.9:6.
7453

Mills, Borden H. Sr. comp. Psalter for ADKers. *Cloud Splitter,* July–Aug. 1947. 10: no.4:1. Excerpts from the Psalms.   7454

Moore, Roger L. Hitch-up-Matilda. *Ad-i-ron-dac,* Jan.–Feb. 1949. 13:16.   7455

North country poets. Regular feature of *North Country Life,* Winter 1948–date.   7456

Norton, Jennie. Gabriels. *For Leaves,* Winter 1906. 3:no.1:16–18. illus. Sanatorium Gabriels.
7457

Nye, James H. Cloud Splitter in winter. *Cloud Splitter,* Mar.–Apr. 1948. 11:no.2:4. Mt. Marcy.   7458

Palmer, E. Dorcas. Lake Champlain. *Vermonter,* Jan., Apr.–May, Aug.–Sept. 1929. 34:11, 62, 73, 113, 133. Sonnet-lyrics.   7459

Palmer, Francis Sterne. In an Adirondack bay. *Outlook,* June 3, 1905. 80:282. An Adirondack nature lyric.   7460

Pardee, Benjamin D. Two orations, and poetry on different subjects. . . Plattsburgh, N.Y. Samuel Lowell, 1810. 79p. Includes "Lines Written on One of the Mountains in Pleasant Valley," p.57–60; "Lines, Written on Carter's Mountain," p.61–63. Copy

in the Henry E. Huntington Library, San Marino, Cal.   7461

Phelps, Orra A. Tahawus. *High Spots,* Dec. 1937. 14:no.4:15.   7462

Phelps, Mrs. Orra (Parker). ADKers. *Ad-i-ron-dac,* Jan.–Feb. 1948. 12:no.1:3.   7463

Phelps, Mrs. Orra (Parker). A garden. *Cloud Splitter,* July–Aug. 1948. 11:no.4:2.   7464

Phelps, Mrs. Orra (Parker). Mountain carol. *Cloud Splitter,* Nov.–Dec. 1947. 10:no.6:1.
7465

Piatt, Dona. Lake George. *Am Angler,* Feb. 2, 1884. 5:72.   7466

Prince, Mrs. Winifred (Notman). Night on the Giant in the gay nineties. *Ad-i-ron-dac,* Nov.–Dec. 1947. 11:no.6:12.   7467

Rawson, Edward Sidney. An Adirondack elegy. *For & Stream,* Feb. 8, 1896. 46:116. Includes a poem on the death of a buck deer, written by Patrick Sheehy of Schroon Lake.
7468

Rexford, Eben Eugene. In the great north woods. *NYC Lines Mag,* June 1929. 1:no.3: 34.   7469

Rich, Mrs. Helen (Hinsdale). A dream of the Adirondacks, and other poems. N.Y. Putnam, 1884. 171p. "A Dream of the Adirondacks" also appeared in *Forest Leaves,* Winter 1909, 6:no.4:27–30.   7470

The Saranac nightingale's song. *Am Sportsman,* Jan. 1873. 2:49.   7471

Scollard, Clinton. Song for the ter-centenary of Lake Champlain. July 1909. Clinton, N.Y. G.W. Browning, 1909. 11 leaves.   7472

Seaman, William O. Tahawus. *Am For,* Oct. 1927. 33:578. illus.   7473

Smith, Arthur E. Rural legends and lyrics. N.Y. John B. Alden, 1892. 128p.   7474

Smith, Cynthia. Adirondack reverie. *No Country Life,* Spring 1952. 6:no.2:22.   7475

Snyder, Mrs. Maude Alexander. Near to nature in the north country. Watertown, N.Y. c1928. 55p. front. (port.).   7476

Stansbury, Mary Anna Phinney. The surprise of Ticonderoga. *In* Scollard, Clinton. Ballads of American bravery. N.Y. Silver, Burdett & co. c1900. p.13–17. Reprinted from *Youth's Companion.* Battle of Ticonderoga, 1758.   7477

Stevenson, Robert Louis. Ticonderoga. *Scrib M,* Dec. 1887. 2:643–50. illus. Legend of Duncan Campbell.   7478

Stevenson, Robert Louis. Ticonderoga. . . Edinburgh, R. & R. Clark, 1887. 27p. Fifty copies printed. Copy in the Cleveland Public Library.   7479

Stevenson, Robert Louis. Ticonderoga, a legend of the west highlands. N.Y. Printed for Ft. Ticonderoga museum, 1923. 28p. front. illus. map.   7480

Street, Alfred Billings. Forest pictures in the Adirondacks, by John A. Hows. With original poems by Alfred B. Street. Boston, Houghton, c1864. 68p. plates. Also published in New York by James G. Gregory, 1865.   7481

Street, Alfred Billings. The hermit thrush. For Leaves, Autumn 1907. 4:no.3:25.   7482

Strong, Latham Cornell. Poke o' moonshine. N.Y. Putnam, 1878. 117p.   7483

Sumner, Diana Estes. Gems from memory. n.p. n.pub. n.d. 92p. Copy in the Loomis Collection, Keene Valley Public Library.   7484

Sweet, Guy V. Birth of a nation on Lake George. No Country Life, Summer 1947. 1: no.4:8.   7485

Sweet, Homer De Lois. Twilight hours in the Adirondacks. Syracuse, N.Y. Wynkoops & Leonard, 1870. 349p. illus. Blank verse.   7486

Tallmadge, Ruth. I belong to the mountains. Cloud Splitter, Sept.–Oct. 1945. 8:no. 5:10.   7487

Taylor, Belle Gray. In camp on Raquette lake. Recreation, Oct. 1896. 5:191.   7488

Thadams, Narra. The Adirondack trail. NYC Lines Mag, Oct. 1920. 1:no.7:50.   7489

Thurston, Charlotte W. The Adirondacks in October. St No Mo, Apr. 1908. 3:218.   7490

Tilden, Stephen. Tilden's miscellaneous poems, on divers occasions; chiefly to animate & rouse the soldiers. New London, Conn? Timothy Green? 1756. 30p. "The Christian Hero," p.15–19, is on the victory at Lake

George. This poem was reprinted in the Historical Magazine, Nov. 1859–Jan. 1860, 3: 328–30, 359–62; 4:7–9. Copy in the Massachusetts Historical Society Library.   7491

Tobin, Abraham I. Prayer of a mountaineer. Cloud Splitter, Sept.–Oct. 1947. 10:no.5:1.   7492

Untermeyer, Mrs. Jean (Starr). Stony water. Poetry, June 1929. 34:127–30.   7493

Untermeyer, Louis. Adirondack cycle. N.Y. Random house, 1929. 12p. (The Poetry Quartos.)   7494

Van Hoevenberg, Henry. The Indian pass, an Adirondack legend. N.Y. E. Scott, 1888. 10p.   7495

Van Hoevenberg, Henry. The legend of Indian pass. St No Mo, Aug. 1906. 1:no.4: 1–5. illus.   7496

Weld, Paul. Feldspar brook. Cloud Splitter, Feb. 1943. 6:no.2:4.   7497

Whiton, L.C. My Adirondack lodge. Recreation, Apr. 1898. 8:465. illus.   7498

Willey, Eli B. The soldiers' companion: being six poems. . . Plattsburgh, N.Y. Printed for the author, 1814? 24p. Cover title. Includes "Victory at Plattsburgh" and "The Plattsburgh Patriot."   7499

Wilson, Bingham Thoburn. The Adirondacks. Woods & Wat, Spring 1903. 6:no.1:8. Also in Forest Leaves, Dec. 1903, 1:no.1:17.   7500

Wilson, Bingham Thoburn. Ye mountaineer: illustrated by J. Arthur Day. N.Y. F. Tennyson Neely co. c1901. 233p. front. (port.) plates. Long narrative poem about Lake Champlain and Lake George.   7501

Woods, Thomas Francis. Adirondack sergeants. High Spots Yrbk, 1942. p.24. illus.   7502

JUVENILE WORKS

The Adirondack hermit. *Yorker*, Mar. 1947. 5:108. port. Prepared by the Newcomb Chapter (Junior Historians) Newcomb Central School. Noah John Rondeau. 7503

Allen, Alice E. Little Aunt Emmie, with illustrations by Frances Brundage. Philadelphia & London, Lippincott, c1925. 286p. col. front. plates. Fiction. 7504

Allen, Merritt P. In the Knob mountain tower. *In* St. Nicholas magazine. The second St. Nicholas anthology. N.Y. Random house, c1950. p.345–49. Fiction. 7505

Altsheler, Joseph Alexander. The hunters of the hills; a story of the great French and Indian war. . .illustrated by D.C. Hutchinson. N.Y. Appleton, 1916. 359p. col. front. col. plates. The first in his series on the French and Indian wars; the other titles in the series are: Shadows of the North; Rulers of the Lakes; Masters of the Peaks; Lords of the Wild; Sun of Quebec. Fiction. 7506

Altsheler, Joseph Alexander. A soldier of Manhattan, and his adventures at Ticonderoga and Quebec. N.Y. Appleton, 1899. 316p. (Appleton's Library of Historical Fiction.) 7507

Averill, Henry K. A new and concise geographical and historical description of Clinton county accompanying Averill & Hagar's New map of the county, compiled from regional manuscripts and other valuable sources by Averill & Hagar. Plattsburgh, N.Y. Averill & Hagar, 1879. 16p. map. 7508

Bascom, Frederick G. Ticonderoga in history. *Yorker*, Jan.–Feb. 1944. 2:no.5:8–11; 2:no.6:6–9. illus. folded col. map. 7509

Best, Mrs. Allena (Champlin). Hearthstone in the wilderness, by Erick Berry, pseud. illustrated by the author. N.Y. Macmillan, 1944. 244p. illus. Fiction. 7510

Best, Herbert. The Long portage: a story of Ticonderoga and Lord Howe; illustrated by Erick Berry. N.Y. Viking press, 1948. 250p. illus. Fiction. 7511

Blankman, Edgar G. Geography of St. Lawrence county, with map prepared for use in public schools. Canton, N.Y. Plaindealer press, 1898. 126p. illus. plates, ports. map. 7512

Bowers, Bernice. Port Henry in the early days. *Yorker*, May 1943. 1:no.10:3–5. Author was 7th-grade student at the Port Henry School. 7513

Carr, William Henry. The stir of nature: a book for young American naturalists. N.Y. Oxford university press, 1930. 208p. illus. Firsthand accounts of youthful wildlife experiences in New York's Adirondacks, Bear Mt. State Park and on Long Island. 7514

Carter, Susan N. A deer-hunt in the Adirondacks. *Our Young F*, Sept. 1867. 3:536–46. illus. 7515

Chalmers, Stephen. Timothy. *St N*, Apr. 1915. 42:483–94. illus. Bear story; locale: Indian Carry between Raquette River and Upper Saranac Lake. 7516

Curtis, Mrs. Alice (Turner). A little maid of Ticonderoga. . .illustrated by Wuanita Smith. Philadelphia, Penn publishing co. 1917. 216p. front. plates. Fiction. 7517

Dean, Leon W. Guns over Champlain. N.Y. Rinehart, c1946. 245p. War of 1812. Fiction. 7518

Foster, Walter Bertram. With Ethan Allen at Ticonderoga. Philadelphia, Penn publishing co. 1910. 363p. plates, front. Fiction. 7519

Geary, Clifford N. Ticonderoga, a picture story. N.Y. David McKay co. inc. c1953. unpaged. illus. (part col.). 7520

Guernsey, Clara Floreda. The silver rifle: a story of the Saranac lakes. Philadelphia, American Sunday school union, 1871. 256p. Fiction. 7521

Hall, Gertrude Calvert. The Nowadays girls in the Adirondacks; or, The deserted bungalow on Saranac lake. . .illustrated by E.E. Caswell. N.Y. Dodd, Mead, c1915. 302p. plates. Fiction. 7522

Hess, Fjevil. Shanty brook lodge. Illustrations by Ruth King. . . N.Y. Macmillan, 1946. 292p. front. illus. Girl Scouts in the Adirondacks. 7523

Lavery, Adelbert A. Geography of Saratoga county, State of New York. Ballston Spa, N.Y. Journal print, 1905. 36p. folded map. 7524

Longstreth, Thomas Morris. A-wing around Wildyrie. *St N*, Apr. 1921. 48:506–13. illus. 7525

Longstreth, Thomas Morris. Ade of the Marcy mounted, illustrated by William C.

Blood. N.Y. & London, Century, c1926. 254p. front. plates. Lake Placid region.　7526

Longstreth, Thomas Morris. Field of adventure. *St N*, Nov. 1923. 51:56–58. Avalanche Pass in winter.　7527

Longstreth, Thomas Morris. True story of the haunted swamp. *St N*, Aug. 1921. 48: 878–83. Fiction.　7528

Longstreth, Thomas Morris. Winter at Wildyrie. *St N*, Feb. 1922. 49:392–99. illus. Winter sports.　7529

Meek, Sterner St. Paul. Rip, a game protector. N.Y. Knopf, c1952. 266p.　7530

Millington, Mrs. Lucy A. (Bishop). Summer days at Lake George. *St N*, Aug. 1882. 9: 794–803. illus.　7531

Morris, Frederick K. The making of a valley; a billion years along the Hudson. N.Y. T. Nelson & sons, 1936. 75p. illus. diagrs. (Our Changing World.) Textbook on the geology of the Hudson valley.　7532

Neilson, Frances Fullerton. Giant mountain; illustrated by Mary Reardon. N.Y. E.P. Dutton, 1946. 120p. illus. Fiction.　7533

Parkman, Mary Rosetta. Edward Livingston Trudeau; a pioneer of the open. *St N*, Sept. 1917. 44:1020–25. illus. port.　7534

Ralph, Frank. The king's messenger; or, The fall of Ticonderoga. Philadelphia, McKay, c1904. 220p. front. Fiction.　7535

Roy, Mrs. Lillian Elizabeth (Becker). Girl scouts in the Adirondacks. N.Y. George Sully & co. c1921. 224p. plates.　7536

Seton, Ernest Thompson. Rolf in the woods ... Garden City, N.Y. Doubleday, Page, 1926. 436p. illus. front. plates. "Best Adirondack juvenile"—P. Schaefer.　7537

Smith, Laurence Dwight. Adirondack adventure; illus. by Gwen B. Johnson. N.Y. S. Curl, inc. 1945. 286p. front. illus. Fiction.　7538

Walden, Treadwell. My deer-hunts in the Adirondacks. *St N*, Sept. 1889. 16:806–12. illus.　7539

APPENDIX: UNLOCATED TITLES

Adirondack mountain reserve. President's report. Missing from the New York Public Library.

Adirondack stories. N.Y. William Wood. 6v. Listed under title in the *American Catalog*, 1876.

Association for the protection of the Adirondacks. Report of the Committee to investigate truck trails. N.Y. 1936.

———. A sane forest policy for New York state.

The bucaneer of Lake Champlain. . . by Uncle Ben of Rouse's Point. Rouses Point, N.Y. D. Turner, 1854. In Imprint Catalogue, New York Public Library.

The Cardinal: yearbook of the Plattsburgh (N.Y.) Normal school. 1894? Issue containing: Baker, Bertha. Robert Louis Stevenson. Reference from Stevenson House, Saranac Lake.

Channing, William Ellery. Burial of John Brown. Boston, 1860. 8p. Cited in Donaldson, v.2, p.316, as title from Villard.

Colden, Cadwallader David. Memoir containing the history and the description of the State of New-York. N.Y. Davis, 1825. 408p. Cited in Ludewig, Hermann Ernst. The literature of the local history of New York.

Cole, Hiram. Washington county business directory. Albany, J. Munsell, 1859. Listed in Munsell catalogue.

Delaware and Hudson railroad company. Canoe cruising in a summer paradise. Listed in advertisement in its The Adirondacks (1915). Author probably Borden H. Mills Sr.

Goodenow, Sterling. A brief topographical and statistical manual of the State of New York; 3d ed. 1825. Cited in Ludewig. Literature of the local history of New York.

Gordinier, Herman Camp, comp. List of plants collected on Mount Marcy, August 17 and 18, 1855. Troy, N.Y. 1885. 1p.

Cited in House (N.Y.S. Museum Bulletin 328–29). Copy missing from New York State Museum.

Holden, Austin Wells. Early voyages of discovery. First attempts to establish a colony in Canada. Albany, J. Munsell, 1851. Listed in Munsell catalogue.

Jane Arlington. . . by Uncle Ben of Rouse's Point. Rouses Point, N.Y. 1853. In Imprint Catalogue, New York Public Library.

New York (state). Laws, statutes, etc. Game laws of the State of New York. N.Y. Association for the protection of game, 1875. Listed in Phillips, John C. American game mammals and birds. A catalogue. . .

New York. Board of trade and transportation. A proposed bill to remodel the Forest, fish and game commission. . . .Jan. 1901. Listed in Donaldson, p.313.

New York central and Hudson river railroad. America's winter resorts. (Four Track Series.) Missing from the New York Public Library.

New York Saturday journal. Dec. 3, 1881. No. 612 containing: Whittaker, Frederick. Milo Romer, the animal king.

Synchronizer, Sept. 1927. Containing: White, Byron E. Trenton Falls yesterday and today. Listed in Thomas, Howard. Trenton Falls yesterday and today.

Tahawus club. Yearbook.

Warren county teacher's association. Catalogue of the officers and members. . .for 1861/62. . . Albany, J. Munsell, 1862? Listed in Munsell catalogue.

Webber, Charles Wilkins. Romance of natural history; or, Wild scenes and wild hunters. London, Nelson, 1852. Cited in Donaldson, v.2, p.338, as title from Westwood & Satchell.

Wild wood notes, by Scope. Cited in Grady, Joseph F. The Adirondacks: Fulton chain —Big Moose region.

SERIALS AND SOURCES CITED

This list is arranged alphabetically by the citations used in the Bibliography. Periodicals included in the *Union List of Serials* or *New Serial Titles* are listed by title only.

AAA Travel. AAA travel.

Ab Ind. Abrasive industry. Changed to Abrasives.

Acad N Sci Ph J. Academy of natural sciences of Philadelphia. Journal.

Acad Sci St L Tr. Academy of science of St. Louis. Transactions.

Ad-i-ron-dac. Ad-i-ron-dac(Adirondack mountain club, inc.).

Ad Mt Club Bul. Adirondack mountain club, inc. Bulletin.

Adirondack motordom, see *Motordom*.

Advance. Advance (Boston).

Alb Inst Proc. Albany institute, Albany, N.Y. Proceedings.

Alb Inst Tr. Albany institute, Albany, N.Y. Transactions.

Alb Law J. Albany law journal.

Alb Med Ann. Albany medical annals.

All Outdoors. All outdoors.

All the Year. All the year round.

Am Angler. American angler. N.Y. 1881–1900.

Am Arch. American architect and building news. Changed to American architect and architecture.

Am Assn Adv Sci Proc. American association for the advancement of science. Proceedings.

Am Assn Pet Geol Bul. American association of petroleum geologists. Bulletin.

Am Bot. American botanist: devoted to economic and ecological botany.

Am City. American city.

Am Clin & Climat AssnTr. American clinical and climatological association. Transactions.

Am Collector. American collector. N.Y.

Am Fern J. American fern journal.

Am Field. American field. Changed to Field and stream (1874/75), Field (1875/76) and Chicago field (1878/81).

Am For. American forests.

Am Forestry. American forestry. Changed to American forests.

Am Forestry Assn Proc. American forestry association. Proceedings.

Am Game Prot Assn Bul. American game protective association. Bulletin. Changed to American wildlife institute.

Am Geog Soc Bul. American geographical society of New York. Bulletin.

Am Geol. American geologist.

Am Geophys Union Tr. American geophysical union. Transactions.

Am Heritage. American heritage.

Am Hist Rec. American historical record. Changed to Potter's American monthly.

Am Hist Register. American historical register.

Am Inst Mining Eng Tr. American institute of mining engineers. Transactions. Changed to American institute of mining and metallurgical engineers. Transactions.

Am Iron & Steel Assn Bul. American iron and steel association. Bulletin.

Am Iron & Steel Inst Yrbk. American iron and steel institute. Year book.

Am J Med Sci. American journal of the medical sciences.

Am J Sci. American journal of science.

Am Lumberman. American lumberman.

Am Mag. American magazine (N.Y.).

Am Med Assn J. American medical association. Journal.

Am Met Soc Bul. American meteorological society. Bulletin.

Am Min. American mineralogist.

Am Mo Mag (NY). American monthly magazine. N.Y.

Am Mus J. American museum journal. Changed to American museum of natural history, New York. Natural history.

Am Mus Nat Hist Bul. American museum of natural history, New York. Bulletin.

Am Nat. American naturalist.

Am Pap & Pulp. American paper and pulp association. Proceedings.

Am Q J Agric & Sci. American quarterly journal of agriculture and science. Changed to American journal of agriculture and science.

Am Rail J. American railroad journal. Changed to Railway mechanical engineer.

Am Rev. American review, a Whig journal. Changed to American Whig review.

Am Rev Tub. American review of tuberculosis.

Am Scenic & Hist Pres Soc. American scenic and historic preservation society. Annual report.

Am Scholar. American scholar.

Am Ski Ann. American ski annual and skiing journal.

Am Soc Civil Eng Proc. American society of civil engineers. Proceedings.

Am Speech. American speech.

Am Sportsman. American sportsman. Changed to Rod and gun and American sportsman.

Amat Nat. Amateur naturalist: a monthly magazine for all nature students.

Amat Sportsman. Amateur sportsman. Changed to Recreation.

Amer Angler. American angler. N.Y. 1916–21.

Amer Mag. American magazine: a monthly miscellany.

America. America: a Catholic review of the week.

American catalogue. American catalogue... July 1, 1876–Dec. 31, 1910. N.Y. 1880–1911.

Americana. Americana (American historical society, inc. N.Y.).

An King. Animal kingdom: bulletin of the New York zoological society.

Ang & Hunt. Angler and hunter. A magazine for true sportsmen.

Ann Am Acad. American academy of political and social sciences, Philadelphia. Annals.

Antiques. Antiques magazine. Changed to Antiques.

Appalachia. Appalachia.

Appleton. Appleton's journal.

Arch. Architecture. N.Y.

Arch For. Architectural forum.

Arch Rec. Architectural record.

Argonaut. The argonaut, published by the Atlantic chapter of the Sierra club.

Argosy. Argosy. N.Y.

Arms & Man. Arms and the man. Changed to American rifleman.

Around the W. Around the world, N.Y. 1894–.

Assn Eng Soc J. Association of engineering societies. Journal.

Atlan. Atlantic monthly.

Audubon Mag. Audubon magazine.

Auk. Auk.

Belgravia. Belgravia.

Bell Tel Mag. Bell telephone magazine.

Bentley. Bentley's miscellany.

Berk Hist & Sci Soc. Berkshire historical and scientific society, Pittsfield, Mass. Collections.

Bet Hom & Gard. Better homes and gardens.

Bibliography of Franklin Benjamin Hough. Hickcox, John H. A bibliography of the writings of Franklin Benjamin Hough... *In* New York (state). University. 99th annual report of the regents. Albany, 1886. p.321–47.

Biol Soc Wash Proc. Biological society of Washington. Proceedings.

Bird Lore. Bird-lore. Changed to Audubon magazine.

Bk Buyer. Book buyer.

Blast Fur. Blast furnace and steel plant.

Bookm. Bookman. N.Y.

Bost Soc Nat Hist Proc. Boston society of natural history. Proceedings.

Boston Mus Bul. Boston. Museum of fine arts. Bulletin.

Bot Gaz. Botanical gazette.

Brick Ch Life. Brick church life. (Brick Presbyterian church, Rochester, N.Y.)

Bridle & G. Bridle and golfer. Detroit, Mich.

Broad Mag. Broadway magazine. Changed to Hampton's magazine.

Broadway. Broadway.

Bryologist. Bryologist.

Bsns W. Business week.

Bul Schools. New York (state). University. Bulletin to the schools.

Burt Hist Coll. Burton historical collections, Detroit. Leaflet.

Camp Log. New York (state). State university. College of forestry, Syracuse. Camp log.

Can For J. Canadian forestry journal. Changed to Forest and outdoors.

Can Min J. Canadian mining journal.

Can Nat. Canadian naturalist and geologist. Changed to Canadian naturalist and quarterly journal of science.

Carneg Mus Ann. Pittsburgh. Carnegie institute. Museum. Carnegie museum annals.

Cath World. Catholic world.

Cement Age. Cement age.

Cement Mill. Cement mill and quarry.

Century. Century magazine: a popular quarterly.

Char. Charities. Changed to Survey.

Chaut. Chautauquan.

Chem & Eng News. Chemical and engineering news. (American chemical journal. News edition.)

Christian Cent. Christian century.

Churchman. Churchman; an illustrated weekly news magazine.

Civ Eng. Civil engineering.

Cloud Splitter. Cloud splitter; published by the Albany chapter of the Adirondack mountain club.

Col Un Ser Mag. Colburn's united service magazine. Changed to United service magazine.

College Humor. College humor.

Colliers. Collier's weekly.

Commonweal. Commonweal: a weekly review.

Comp Air M. Compressed air magazine.

Conn Hist Soc Coll. Connecticut historical society, Hartford. Collections.

Conn Med Soc Proc. Connecticut medical society. Proceedings. (Connecticut state medical society.)

Conservation. Conservation; forests, waters, soils, minerals. Changed to American forests.

Conservationist. Conservationist.

Constructioneer. Constructioneer.

Contin Mo. Continental monthly.

Contract & Eng Mo. Contractors and engineers monthly. N.Y.

Copeia. Copeia.

Cor For. Cornell forester.

Cornell Count. Cornell countryman.

Cornell Ext Bul. Cornell extension bulletin.

Country Life. Country life. N.Y.

Craftsman. Craftsman: an illustrated monthly magazine.

Cur Lit. Current literature. Changed to Current opinion.

Cushing. Cushing, William. Anonyms: a dictionary of revealed authorship. Cambridge, Mass. 1890.

DAR Mag. Daughters of the American revolution magazine. Changed to National historical magazine.

D & H Bul. Delaware and Hudson railroad company. Bulletin. Albany, N.Y. 1921–.

Denison Univ Sci Lab J. Denison university. Scientific laboratories. Journal.

Donaldson. Donaldson, Alfred Lee. History of the Adirondacks. N.Y. Century, 1921.

Du Pont M. Du Pont magazine.

Dun's R. Dun's review.

Ecology. Ecology.

Econ Geog. Economic geography.

Econ Geol. Economic geology.

Ed & Pub. Editor and publisher.

Edin Med J. Edinburgh medical journal.

Elec W. Electrical world.

Ellis. Ellis, Mary. Index to publications of the New York state natural history survey and New York state museum 1837–1902... Albany, 1903.

Emp For. Empire forester.

Emp St For Prod Assn Bul. Empire state forest products association. Bulletin.

Emp St For Prod Assn Proc. Empire state forest products association. Proceedings.

Emp Statesman. Empire statesman: an independent, privately-owned publication. Albany, N.Y. 1944?–.

Eng & Min J. Engineering and mining journal.

Eng Folk Dance Soc. English folk dance society, London. Journal.

Eng M. Engineering magazine. Changed to Factory and industrial management.

Eng News. Engineering news.

Eng News R. Engineering news-record.

Engineer. Engineer. London.

Essex Inst Bul. Essex institute, Salem, Mass. Bulletin.

Essex Inst Proc. Essex institute, Salem, Mass. Proceedings.

Ev Sat. Every Saturday.

Exp Eng. Explosives engineer.

Exp Ent Hist. Explorations in entrepreneurial history. (Harvard university. Research center in entrepreneurial history.)

Fam Mag. Family magazine.

Federal reporter. Federal reporter. Cases argued and determined in the United States courts of appeals... St. Paul, West publishing co.

Fern Bul. Fern bulletin.

Field & R. Field and river.

Field & S. Field and stream.

Flame. The flame. Boston, Cabot industries, 1947–.

Flower Grower. Flower grower.

For & Irrig. Forestry and irrigation. Changed to American forests.

For & Stream. Forest and stream.

For Leaves. Forest leaves. Sanatorium Gabriels, Gabriels, N.Y.

For Quar. Forestry quarterly. Changed to Journal of forestry.

For Worker. Forest worker.

Forest Preserve. The Forest preserve. Friends of the Forest preserve, Schenectady, N.Y. 1947–.

Forester. Forester. Changed to American forests.

Fort Tel Eng. Fortnightly telephone engineer.

Fortune. Fortune.

Four Tr News. Four track news. Changed to Travel.

Fr Leslies Pop Mo. Frank Leslie's popular monthly. Changed to American magazine.

Frasers M. Fraser's magazine.

Ft Ti Mus Bul. Fort Ticonderoga museum. Bulletin.

Fur-Fish-Game. Fur-fish-game.

Fur News. Fur news and outdoor world. Changed to Fur-fish-game.

Furology. Furology magazine.

Galaxy. Galaxy.

Gameland. Gameland.

Gard & For. Garden and forest.

Gard J. Garden journal of the New York botanical garden. 1951–.

Gas Logic. Gas logic.

Gen Elec R. General electric review.

Gen Q Mag. Genealogical quarterly magazine.

Geog R. Geographical review.

Geol Soc Am Bul. Geological society of America. Bulletin.

Geol Soc Am Mem. Geological society of America. Memoirs.

Geol Soc Am Proc. Geological society of America. Proceedings.

Girl Scout. Girl scout leader.

Godey. Godey's magazine.

Golden Rule. Golden rule: an independent religious family journal.

Gr & NYS Con. The grouse and New York state conservationist. Changed to New York state conservationist.

Gr Rep Mo. Great republic monthly.

Graduate theses. Reidy, Genevieve L. comp. Graduate theses, 1944–1954. Syracuse, N.Y. State university of New York, College of forestry, 1955.

Griffin. Griffin, Appleton Prentiss Clark. Bibliography of American historical societies. . .2d ed. . . Washington, American historical society, 1907.

Guide to nature. Guide to nature.

Hampton. Hampton's magazine.

Harper. Harper's magazine.

Harper Baz. Harper's bazaar.

Harper W. Harper's weekly.

Harvard Mag. Harvard magazine.

Harvard Mo. Harvard monthly.

Hasse. Hasse, Adelaide Rosalie. Index of economic material in documents of the states of the United States: New York. . . Washington, Carnegie institution, 1907.

Health Digest. Health digest. Changed to Health is wealth.

Herk Co Hist Soc. Herkimer county historical society. Papers.

High spots. High spots.

High Spots Yrbk. High spots yearbook.

Hill. Brief history. Hill, William Henry. Brief history of the printing press in Washington, Saratoga and Warren counties. . . Fort Edward, N.Y. 1930.

Hist Mag. Historical magazine and Notes and queries.

Hist Teach Mag. History teachers magazine. Changed to Social studies for teachers and administrators.

Hobbies. Hobbies. Chicago.

Holiday. Holiday.

Hotel Mo. Hotel monthly.

Hours at Home. Hours at home.

House & Gard. House and garden.

Hud Riv Mag. Hudson river magazine.

Hunt Lib Q. Huntington library quarterly. (Henry E. Huntington library and art gallery, San Marino, Cal.)

Hygeia. Hygeia. Chicago.

IOCA Bul. IOCA bulletin. Intercollegiate outing club association.

IOCA J. Intercollegiate outing club association. Journal.

Ill Cath Hist Rev. Illinois Catholic historical review. Changed to Mid-America.

Illus Am. Illustrated American.

Ind. Independent. N.Y.

Int Studio. International studio.

Intercollegiate Athletics. Intercollegiate athletics. Changed to National athlete.

Internat Mag. International magazine of literature, art and science. Changed to International monthly magazine. . .

Iron Age. Iron age.

Iron & Steel. Iron and steel institute, London. Journal.

Iron Tr R. Iron trade review. Changed to Steel.

J Am Folk-Lore. Journal of American folk-lore.

J Econ Ent. Journal of economic entomology.

J For. Journal of forestry.

J Geol. Journal of geology.

J Home Econ. Journal of home economics.

J Mam. Journal of mammalogy.

J Outd Life. Journal of the outdoor life.

J Wildlife Man. Journal of wildlife management.

Johns Hop Hosp Bul. Johns Hopkins hospital, Baltimore. Bulletin.

Kingbird. The kingbird, published by the New York state federation of bird clubs.

Kiwan Mag. Kiwanis magazine.

Knick Mag. Knickerbocker magazine. Changed to Foederal American monthly.

Lady's Realm. Lady's realm.

Lake Pl Life. Lake Placid life. N.Y. Clayton E. Brooke, 193—? Incomplete file in Saranac Lake Free Library.

Lake Sup Min Inst Proc. Lake Superior mining institute. Proceedings.

Land. The land (Friends of the land).

Land & Wat. Land and water.

Leslies Illus. Leslie's illustrated weekly newspaper.

Lib Misc. Library miscellany.

Lib Rev. Library review: a magazine on libraries and literature.

Liberty. Liberty: a weekly for everybody.

Life. Life.

Lincoln. Ford motor company. Lincoln motor company. The Lincoln.

Lincoln. New York (state). Governor. State of New York. Messages·from the governors . . .from. . .1683 to and including the year 1906, with notes. Edited by Charles Z. Lincoln. . . Albany, 1909.

Linn Soc NY Proc. Linnaean society of New York. Proceedings.

Linn Soc NY Tr. Linnaean society of New York. Transactions.

Lippincott. Lippincott's magazine. Changed to McBride's magazine.

Lit Digest. Literary digest.

Liv Wild. Living wilderness.

Lloydia. Lloydia.

Lond Mag. London magazine; or, Gentleman's monthly intelligencer.

Lumb World R. Lumber world review. Changed to Chicago lumberman.

Lumber Camp News. Lumber camp news. Old Forge, N.Y. Changed to Northeastern logger.

Ly Nat Hist Annals. Lyceum of natural history, N.Y. Annals. Changed to New York academy of sciences.

Ly Nat Hist Proc. Lyceum of natural history, N.Y. Proceedings. Changed to New York academy of sciences.

McClure. McClure's magazine. Changed to New McClure's magazine.

Macmil. Macmillan's magazine.

Mag Am Hist. Magazine of American history with Notes and queries.

Mag Hist. Magazine of history with Notes and queries.

Mas Rev. Masonic review.

Mass Hist Soc Coll. Massachusetts historical society. Collections.

Mass Hist Soc Proc. Massachusetts historical society. Proceedings.

Mast Detect Mag. Master detective magazine.

Med & Surg Rep. Medical and surgical reporter. Changed to Cancer digest of America.

Med J & Rec. Medical journal and record. Changed to Medical record (N.Y. 1865–).

Med News. Medical news. Philadelphia.

Med Pick. Medical Pickwick.

Med Rec. Medical record. N.Y. (1865–).

Med Rep. Medical repository.

Med Soc SNY Tr. Medical society of the State of New York. Transactions.

Med Times. Medical times. Philadelphia. Changed to Medical times and register.

Mil Eng. Military engineer.

Min & Con R. Mining and contracting review.

Min & Met. Mining and metallurgy.

Min & Pet Mitt. Mineralogische und petrologische mitteilungen.

Min Coll. Mineral collector, devoted to the interests of the collector, student, dealer.

Min Cong J. Mining congress journal.

Min Eng. Mining engineering.

Min Ind. Mineral industry.

Mines & Min. Mines and minerals. Changed to Colliery engineer.

Miscellaneous reports. New York (state). Courts. The miscellaneous reports. Cases decided in the courts of record. . .other than the Court of appeals and the Appellate division of the Supreme court. Albany, 1893–date.

Mo Weath Rev. U.S. Weather bureau. Monthly weather review.

Month. The month. London.

Moors Ant. Moorsfield antiquarian: a magazine of American history.

Motor Tr. Motor travel.

Motordom. Motordom.

Mt Club Md. Mountain club of Maryland. Bulletin.

Mt Mag. Mountain magazine.

Munsey. Munsey's magazine.

Munson. William C. Munson of Saranac Lake, book collector. His Adirondack library is in the Saranac Lake Free Library.

Mycologia. Mycologia.

NE Wat Works. New England water works association. Journal.

NSS News. National speleological society, Washington. News.

NY Acad Med Bul. New York academy of medicine. Bulletin.

NY Acad Sci Ann. New York academy of science. Annals.

NY Acad Sci Tr. New York academy of science. Transactions.

NY Bot Gar J. New York botanical garden. Journal.

NYC Lines Mag. New York central lines magazine.

NY Fish & Game J. New York fish and game journal. New York state conservation department. 1954–.

NY Folk Q. New York folklore quarterly.

NY Forester. New York forester.

NY Forestry. New York forestry: yearbook of the New York state forestry association.

NY Gen & Biog Rec. New York genealogical and biographical record.

NY Hist. New York history (New York state historical association).

NY Hist Soc Proc. New York historical society. Proceedings.

NY Illus News. New York illustrated news.

NY Lumber. New York lumber trade journal.

NY Med J. New York medical journal. Changed to Medical record.

NY Mirror. New York mirror: a weekly gazette of literature and the fine arts.

NYS Assn St Bul. New York state association. State bulletin.

NYS Bus Prof W. New York state business and professional woman.

NYS Con. New York state conservationist.

NYS Con Council. New York state conservation council, inc. Bulletin.

NYS Ed. New York state education.

NYS For Assn Bul. New York state forestry association. Bulletin. Changed to New York forestry.

NYS For Assn J. New York state forestry association. Journal. Changed to New York forestry.

NYS For Assn NL. New York state forestry association. News letter. Syracuse, N.Y. 1931–40.

NYS Lab Ind Bul. New York (state). Labor department. Industrial bulletin.

NYS Mus Bul. New York (state). State museum. Bulletin.

NYS Ranger Sch. New York (state). State university. College of forestry, Syracuse. Ranger school. Alumni news. Wanakena, N.Y. 1930–.

NYS Sport. New York state sportsman: official organ, New York state conservation council, inc. Syracuse, 1934–.

NY State Hist Assn Bul. New York state historical association. Bulletin.

NY State Hist Assn Proc. New York state historical association. Proceedings.

NY State Hist Assn Q. New York state historical association. Quarterly journal. Changed to New York history.

NY State J Med. New York state journal of medicine.

NY Times Mag. New York times magazine. Supplement to Sunday issues of the New York times.

NY Zoo Soc Bul. New York zoological society. Bulletin.

Nat Geog M. National geographic magazine.

Nat Hist. Natural history.

Nat Mag. National magazine. Boston.

Nat Parks. National parks bulletin (also National parks magazine).

Nat Rev. National review incorporating the English review.

Nation. Nation. N.Y.

Nature M. Nature magazine.

New Broad M. New Broadway magazine. Changed to Hampton's magazine.

New Eng Hist & Gen Reg. New England historical and genealogical register.

New Eng M. New England magazine: an illustrated monthly.

New Mo Mag. New monthly magazine. London.

New Mus Rev. New music review.

New Statesm. New statesman and Nation.

New York reports. New York (state). Court of appeals. Reports of cases decided in the Court of appeals of the State of New York. . .

New Yorker. New Yorker.

News Pr Ser Bul. News print service bureau. Monthly bulletin.

Nickel Topics. Nickel topics. International nickel company.

No Am. North American review.

No Country Life. North country life.

Northeast Log. Northeastern logger. Old Forge, N.Y. 1952–.

Nutt Orn C Bul. Nuttall ornithological club. Bulletin. Changed to The auk.

Occup Med. Occupational medicine.

Ohio J Sci. Ohio journal of science.

Oil Pow. Oil-power.

Old & New. Old and new.

Oneida Hist Soc Proc. Oneida historical society. Proceedings.

Orn & Bot. Ornithologist and botanist.

Orn & Ool. Ornithologist and oologist.

Our Young F. Our young folks.

Outd Pic. Outdoor pictorial.

Outdoor Life. Outdoor life: outdoor recreation.

Outing. Outing; sport, adventure, travel, fiction.

Outlook. Outlook. Changed to New outlook, N.Y.

Overland. Overland monthly.

PTM. P.T.M. (General electric test men alumni association, Schenectady, N.Y.)

Pa Acad Sci Proc. Pennsylvania academy of science. Proceedings.

Paint Ind M. Paint industry magazine.

Pap Ind. Paper industry and paper world.

Paper. Paper.

Penn St Min Q. Penn state mining quarterly.

Personality. Personality.

Pet Mag. Peterson's magazine (Peterson magazine).

Phila Med Times. Philadelphia medical times. Changed to Medical times and register.

Phillips. Bibliography. Phillips, John C. American game mammals and birds. A catalogue of books 1582 to 1925. . . Boston, Houghton, 1930.

Phon M. Phonetic magazine. Changed to Type of the times.

Photo-Era. Photo-era magazine.

Phytopathology. Phytopathology.

Pic. "Pic."

Pine Log. Pine log. Saranac Lake, N.Y. 1924.

Pittsburgh People. Pittsburgh people, published monthly by the Department of public relations, Pittsburgh glass company.

Plant World. Plant world.

Playground. Playground. Changed to Recreation.

Poetry. Poetry.

Poole. Poole's Index to periodical literature. . .rev. ed. 1802–81.

Pop Mech. Popular mechanics magazine.

Pop Sci. Popular science monthly.

Potter Am Mo. Potter's American monthly.

Practitioner. Practitioner. London.

Presbyterian. The Presbyterian. Philadelphia.

Prog Fish Culturist. Progressive fish-culturist. U.S. Fish and wild life service.

Pulp & Pa. Pulp and paper magazine of Canada.

Putnam. Putnam's magazine.

R of Rs. Review of reviews and World's work.

Rail & Loc. Railway and locomotive historical society. Bulletin.

Rail Mag. Railroad magazine.

Rand Notes. Random notes on natural history.

Read Digest. Reader's digest.

Real Detective. Real detective, N.Y. 1954–.

Recorder. Recorder.

Recreation. Recreation.

Recreation (NY). Recreation, N.Y. (1888–Nov. 1917).

Recreation (Nat). Recreation. (National recreation association.)

Red Book. Red book magazine.

Red Cross M. Red cross magazine.

Reports of cases. New York (state). Supreme court. Reports of cases heard and determined in the Appellate division of the Supreme court of the State of New York.

Republic Repts. Republic reports; a magazine for the men and women of Republic steel.

Resort Management. Resort management.

Rev Can. Revue Canadienne.

Rev d'Hygiene. Revue d'hygiène et de police sanitaire. Changed to Revue d'hygiène et de prophylaxie sociales.

Rev Heb. Revue hebdomadaire.

Rhodora. Rhodora.

Rocks & Min. Rocks and minerals.

Rod & Gun. Rod and gun and American sportsman.

Roos Wildlife Ann. Roosevelt wildlife annals (College of forestry, Syracuse).

Roos Wildlife Bul. Roosevelt wildlife bulletin (College of forestry, Syracuse).

Rotarian. Rotarian.

Roy Soc Canada Mem. Société royale du Canada. Mémoires. (Royal society of Canada. Memoirs.)

Roy Unit Ser Inst J. Royal united service institution, London. Journal.

Rural NY. Rural New Yorker.

Sabin. Sabin, Joseph. Bibliotheca Americana. A dictionary of books relating to America... N.Y. 1868–1936.

Saga. Saga: the magazine of true adventure.

Sanitarian. Sanitarian.

Sat Eve Post. Saturday evening post.

Scen & Hist Am. Scenic and historic America.

Sch Min Q. School of mines quarterly. Columbia university.

Scholastic. Scholastic.

Sci Am. Scientific American.

Sci Mo. Scientific monthly.

Sci NL. Science news letter.

Sci Prog. Science progress.

Science. Science.

Scot Geog Mag. Scottish geographical magazine.

Scot Rev. Scottish review.

Scrib M. Scribner's magazine.

Scrib Mo. Scribner's monthly. Changed to Century, a popular quarterly.

Service. Service: a magazine of methods. Chicago, Baptist young peoples union of America. 1904–17.

Sh & Fish. Shooting and fishing. Changed to American rifleman.

Sharpe's Lond M. Sharpe's London magazine of entertainment and instruction.

Sherrill. Sherrill, Cecelia Adelaide. Bibliography of the Adirondacks. *In* New York (state). Fisheries, game and forest commission. Annual report, 1898. p.423–41.

Ski Bul. Ski bulletin.

Ski News. Ski news.

Skinner, John. Book dealer, Lake George, N.Y. Specialist in Adirondackana.

Skisport. The Skisport. (American ski annual and skiing journal.)

Smart Set. Smart set.

Soc Am For Proc. Society of American foresters. Proceedings.

Soc Army Hist Res J. Society for army historical research. Journal.

Soc Hist Mont. Société historique de Montréal. Mémoires.

Soil Sci Soc Proc. Soil science society of America. Proceedings.

Spectator. Spectator. London.

Sport Dig. Sportsman's digest.

Sport Mag. Sportsman's magazine.

Sport Rev. Sportsmen's review.

Sports Illus. Sports illustrated. N.Y. 1954–.

Sportsman. Sportsman. Concord, N.H.

St N. St. Nicholas.

St No Mo. Stoddard's northern monthly.

State Service. State service; the New York state magazine.

Stedman & Hutchinson. Stedman, Edmund Clarence. A library of American literature compiled and edited by Edmund Clarence Stedman and Ellen Mackay Hutchinson. New ed... N.Y. 1894.

Steel. Steel.

Steel Facts. Steel facts.

Steelways. Steelways; published bimonthly by the American iron and steel institute.

Sub Life. Suburban life. Changed to Countryside magazine and suburban life.

Survey. Survey.

Tahawus Cloudsplitter. Tahawus cloudsplitter. (National lead company, Tahawus, N.Y.)

Thomson. Thomson, Thomas Richard. Check list of publications on American railroads before 1841... N.Y. New York public library, 1942.

Time. Time: the weekly newsmagazine.

Top o' the World. Top o' the world news. Top o' the world mills, Lake George, N.Y. 1936–39.

Torrey Bot C Bul. Torrey botanical club. Bulletin.

Torreya. Torreya.

Tour du Monde. Tour du monde.

Town Topics. Town topics.

Trains. Trains.

Travel. Travel. N.Y.

Trillia. Trillia.

True Police Cases. True police cases. N.Y. 1929–. (Fawcett men's group.)

US Assn Char Work J. United States association of charcoal iron workers. Journal.

US Cath Hist Soc. United States Catholic historical society. Historical records and studies.

US Fish Com Bul. U.S. Fish commission. Bulletin.

USGS Bul. U.S. Geological survey. Bulletin.

US N Inst Proc. United States naval institute, Annapolis. Proceedings.

U.S. reports. U.S. Supreme court. United States reports... 1754–.

Unit Rev. Unitarian review.

Univ Roch Lib Bul. Rochester. University. Library. Bulletin.

Up Mo. Upstate monthly.

Up-Stater. Up-stater; devoted to the welfare of northern and central New York. (New York development association, inc.)

Ver Ant. Vermont antiquarian.

Ver Bot C Bul. Vermont botanical club, Burlington. Bulletin.

Ver Hist Soc Proc. Vermont historical society. Proceedings.

Ver Horse. Vermont horse and bridle trail bulletin.

Ver Quar. Vermont quarterly.

Vermonter. Vermonter.

Vicks. Vick's family magazine.

Waddell's Northern New York. Waddell, William Coventry Henry. A paper read before the American geographical and statistical society, November 2, 1854. N.Y. Putnam, 1855.

Wallace's Descriptive guide. Wallace, Edwin R. Descriptive guide to the Adirondacks... N.Y. 1875–97.

Warbler. Warbler.

Wardman PV. Wardman park vista. (Wardman hotels, Washington, D.C.)

Wash Acad Sci J. Washington academy of sciences. Journal.

Wash Acad Sci Proc. Washington academy of sciences. Proceedings.

Wild Mag. Wildwood's magazine.

Wilkes Spirit. Wilkes' Spirit of the times. Changed to Spirit of the times and the New York sportsman.

Wilson Bul. Wilson bulletin.

Wint Sports. Winter sports.

Wms Q. Williams quarterly. (Published by the students of Williams College.)

Woman's Day. Woman's day. N.Y. 1937–. (A & P stores.)

Wood. Wood.

Woods & Wat. Woods and waters.

World's Work. World's work.

Wright. Fiction. Wright, Lyle H. American fiction 1774–1850... rev. ed. San Marino, Cal. 1948.

Yankee. Yankee: a monthly magazine for Yankees everywhere.

Yorker. The Yorker. (Junior historians of the New York state historical society.)

Z Forst. Zeitschrift für forst- und jagdwesen.

Z Kristall. Zeitschrift für kristallographie, mineralogie und petrographie.

Z Prak Geol. Zeitschrift für praktische geologie.

Z Tub. Zeitschrift für tuberkulose.

INDEX

Numbers refer to entries, not pages.

158